Behavioral, Social, and Emotional Assessment of Children and Adolescents

Generally recognized as the standard work in its field, *Behavioral, Social, and Emotional Assessment of Children and Adolescents* is a comprehensive guide for conducting conceptually sound, culturally responsive, and ecologically oriented assessments of students' social and emotional behavior. Written for graduate students, practitioners, and researchers in the fields of school psychology, child clinical psychology, and special education, it will also be of interest to those in related disciplines.

Retaining the fifth edition's structure and content coverage, incorporation of *DSM-5* and federal standards, and integrated approach to culturally responsive assessment, this lightly refreshed 2023 version offers readers a select batch of further updates. The book now includes new references to NASP's 2020 Professional Standards and APA's amended Ethical Principles of Psychologists and Code of Conduct as well as modernized research, data, and terminology pertaining to racial, ethnic, and other identity-based contexts.

In Part I, Foundations and Methods of Assessment, the author provides a general foundation for assessment practice and outlines basic professional and ethical issues, cultural considerations, and classification and diagnostic problems. Part II, Assessment of Specific Problems, Competencies, and Populations, features material on assessing specific social–emotional behavior domains, including externalizing problems, internalizing problems, social skills and social–emotional strengths, and the unique needs of young children. A chapter on school-wide screening methods was also added to the fifth edition.

By weaving together the most recent research evidence and common application issues in a scholarly yet practical manner, *Behavioral, Social, and Emotional Assessment of Children and Adolescents* continues to be the pre-eminent foundation for assessment courses.

Sara A. Whitcomb is Associate Professor in the College of Education at the University of Massachusetts, Amherst, USA.

Behavioral, Social, and Emotional Assessment of Children and Adolescents

Updated Fifth Edition

Sara A. Whitcomb

Routledge
Taylor & Francis Group

NEW YORK AND LONDON

Cover image: Alamy Stock Photo

Fifth Edition published 2018
Updated Fifth Edition published 2023
by Routledge
605 Third Avenue, New York, NY 10158

and by Routledge
4 Park Square, Milton Park, Abingdon, Oxon, OX14 4RN

Routledge is an imprint of the Taylor & Francis Group, an informa business

© 2023 Taylor & Francis

First edition published by Lawrence Erlbaum 1998
Fifth edition published by Routledge 2018

Library of Congress Cataloging-in-Publication Data
Names: Whitcomb, Sara A., author. | Merrell, Kenneth W. Behavioral, social, and emotional assessment of children and adolescents.
Title: Behavioral, social, and emotional assessment of children and adolescents / Sara A. Whitcomb.
Description: Fifth Edition. | New York, NY : Routledge, 2022. | Revised edition of Behavioral, social, and emotional assessment of children and adolescents, 2013. | Includes bibliographical references and index.
Identifiers: LCCN 2022018323 (print) | LCCN 2022018324 (ebook) | ISBN 9781032244587 (hardback) | ISBN 9781032244594 (paperback) | ISBN 9781315747521 (ebook)
Subjects: LCSH: Psychological tests for children. | Child development—Testing. | Behavioral assessment of children. | Teenagers—Psychological testing. | Behavioral assessment of teenagers.
Classification: LCC BF722 .M45 2022 (print) | LCC BF722 (ebook) | DDC 155.4028/7—dc23/eng/20220414
LC record available at https://lccn.loc.gov/2022018323
LC ebook record available at https://lccn.loc.gov/2022018324

ISBN: 978-1-032-24458-7 (hbk)
ISBN: 978-1-032-24459-4 (pbk)
ISBN: 978-1-315-74752-1 (ebk)

DOI: 10.4324/9781315747521

Typeset in Minion
by codeMantra

I continue to dedicate this book to my mentor, Kenneth W. Merrell, who was the original author of this work and a pioneer in the field of behavioral, social, and emotional assessment. I am honored to continue this work, and I wish that I could share with him all of the exciting developments in this area.

CONTENTS

FIGURES

TABLES

PREFACE

The science and practice of psychological and educational assessment of children and adolescents continue to evolve and have experienced some major recent advancements. New innovations and developments continue to emerge, sometimes at a rapid rate that surpasses the ability of the field to keep pace with them. At the same time, psychological and educational assessment practices with youth have continued to be mired in some of the same traps, impasses, and controversies that have existed for years. For some, understanding social–emotional and behavioral assessment as a process aimed at targeting children's instructional needs versus diagnosing pathology is still somewhat of a foreign concept. One only needs to consider briefly the reliance some place on assessment methods and techniques that are substantially lacking in empirical support, a lack of sensitivity of many current assessment practices to important group and individual differences, and the gross misuse of assessment technology for inappropriate purposes to understand that the field still has a continuous journey ahead.

That said, this book is my effort to continue to understand current innovation in social–emotional and behavioral assessment, so that I can continue the work that Ken Merrell began to help elevate the practice of psychological and educational assessment of children and adolescents, to increasingly higher professional standards and a solid evidence-based foundation. This book was developed to provide a comprehensive foundation and guide for conducting comprehensive assessments of child and adolescent social–emotional behavior in a practical, defensible, empirically sound, and culturally appropriate manner. It was written as a graduate-level training textbook and as a professional reference book. It is specifically relevant to the fields of school psychology, clinical child psychology, and special education. Professionals in related fields, who work with children and adolescents with behavioral, social, and emotional problems (e.g., counseling, social work, and child psychiatry), may also find it useful.

While the fifth edition continues to share similar theoretical grounding and the chapter structure of the previous editions, this book represents a major revision that is my attempt to share some of the rapid advances in the field, while also maintaining the comprehensive review of fundamental assessment features. Relevant chapters have been aligned to the *DSM-5* diagnostic categories, which was a significant undertaking. Aligning with the *DSM-5* was particularly challenging, given that many assessment measures and interview tools have yet to be updated. Several measures, however, have been updated, and I did my best to include them. For example, in Chapters 5, 8, and 15, I have provided an extensive review of the recently released BASC-3 assessment and intervention system. In Chapter 13, *Assessing Social Skills and Social–Emotional Strengths,* I have included more strength-oriented measures, as this is an area that seems to be expanding. As much as possible, I have provided information on the integration of technology into the assessment process. So many structured behavioral observation tools are now available for cellphones and computers, for example, that I have incorporated a review of just a few that are fairly inexpensive and easy to use. Additionally, administration and analysis of behavioral assessment data have become so much more efficient with management systems like Pearson's Q-Global, that I referenced how to find such systems as much as possible.

Finally, in my preparation of this book and my current applied work in schools, I get perhaps most excited about the role that social–emotional and behavioral assessment has begun to play within multi-tiered systems of support (MTSS) and Responsiveness-to-Intervention models (RtI). MTSS, a prevention-focused approach to instruction and assessment, is finally gaining traction in schools. I work with many schools as they develop their tiered systems of support related to social–emotional behavior. I'm always thrilled when schools are placing as much importance on teaching behavior as they do on academics. In addition to building the understanding that behavior and social–emotional skills can and should be taught, school professionals have also grasped onto the idea of universal screening methods. Screening a school of children for social–emotional risk enables school professionals to work together to identify appropriate, preventative instructional targets as well as "catch" students, who may benefit from more support, before they spiral into crisis. That said, I decided to add a chapter to this edition focused entirely on universal screening in schools. This chapter provides a review of several screening tools from the perspective of behaviors targeted, technical adequacy information provided, and feasibility or usability. In addition, I have included content related to how a school might attempt to successfully "roll out" a new universal screening method over time.

The chapters are divided into two major sections. Part I, Foundations and Methods of Assessment, includes nine chapters that provide a general foundation for assessment practice. These chapters include coverage of basic professional and ethical issues, cultural considerations, classification and diagnostic problems, and comprehensive introductions to six primary assessment methods: behavioral observation, behavior rating scales, clinical interviewing, sociometric techniques, self-report instruments, and projective–expressive techniques. Part II, Assessment of Specific Problems, Competencies, and Populations, includes five chapters or applications for assessing specific social–emotional behavior domains, including externalizing problems, internalizing problems, other problems, social skills and social–emotional strengths, and the unique needs of young children. The book finishes with the new chapter on universal screening. Together, these two parts provide a framework for a model of assessment that is practical, flexible, sensitive to specific needs, and empirically sound. To the greatest extent possible, this book weaves together the most recent research evidence and common application issues in a scholarly yet practical manner. It is intended to complement professional training and not to act as a substitute for it.

ACKNOWLEDGMENTS

First, I would like to thank Ken Merrell for mentoring me, sharing his knowledge with me, and giving me this opportunity. As I continue authorship on this book, I often find myself wondering, "What would Ken have thought about this?" I miss not being able to share this process with him, but I am forever grateful for this learning experience. Additionally, I would like to acknowledge Daniel Schwartz and Rebecca Novack, editors at Routledge Publishers, for their patience, support, and continued enthusiasm for Ken's work and for their confidence in my ability to write this new edition on my own. I would also like to acknowledge the Routledge production staff, particularly Matthew Friberg, for their careful work and help throughout the process. I look forward to working with Routledge on a sixth edition of this book in the future.

I am very fortunate to have been trained in the University of Oregon's College of Education and School Psychology Program. It was there that I truly realized my professional aspirations with the support of the esteemed faculty. I would like to acknowledge those who have supported this work at my current academic home, the University of Massachusetts in Amherst. I would not have been able to get this done without Kayla Gordon, who co-authored Chapter 15 with me and helped to keep me on track. I would like to recognize all of my graduate students that read chapters and gave feedback. I am lucky to be part of a supportive community.

My understanding of behavioral, social, and emotional assessment has also been shaped by my practical experiences with children in school and home environments. As much as possible, I try to get into schools so that I can informally and formally observe, rate, and hypothesize about behavior. I am so appreciative for the many experiences with the children I have had the chance to meet.

Most importantly, I want to thank my family for their support. Stuart, who always brings me coffee; Jack, who always has an encouraging word; Caeli, who always has a smile and a hug; and Buster and Rona, who remind me to get outside and take a break.

Sara A. Whitcomb

Part I
FOUNDATIONS AND
METHODS OF ASSESSMENT

1

FOUNDATIONS OF ASSESSMENT

This chapter introduces important issues in social–emotional assessment, provides a foundation for understanding the design and flow of subsequent chapters, and overview of the current state of the art in best assessment practices. The chapter begins with an exploration of how theory guides practice, using social cognitive theory and ecological systems theories as preferred models, and then describes some of the philosophical foundations on which present-day assessment practices are built. A discussion of the referral process is then provided, with specific emphasis on how referral processes are tied to spheres within human ecological systems, and how referrals should shape the approach to assessment. Assessment is conceptualized and proposed as a comprehensive problem-solving process. The preferred way for conducting assessments of behavioral, social, and emotional problems is through the use of an aggregated multimethod, multi-source, multisetting design, which is ideally implemented through an approach involving services for all individuals within a population. The "triangle of support" model from the field of public health is seen as an ideal way to consider allocating screening and assessment services to produce the maximum impact within limited resources. A discussion of pertinent legal and ethical issues in assessment follows, and specific recommendations for legal and ethical assessment practices are provided. The chapter ends with a brief discussion of what criteria were used for including specific assessment techniques and instruments within the book. Essentially, this chapter serves as an introduction and guide for understanding the overall goals and the larger picture of the entire book.

THEORETICAL FOUNDATIONS OF SOCIAL AND EMOTIONAL BEHAVIOR

Is theory essential for practice? More specifically, can one conduct reliable and valid assessments of youngsters with behavioral, social, and emotional problems without being firmly grounded in a theoretical orientation to how these problems develop, progress, and change? Well, one might administer some tests and interpret the results under this scenario. But is this type of approach the most desirable? Probably, it is not. Without a solid theoretical background and orientation, the assessor is relegated to the somewhat paraprofessional role of a technician or tester. No matter how skilled, he or she may never fully integrate the assessment findings to the youngster's past, and future, with an adequate degree of continuity or unity. Additionally, developing a solid theoretical understanding of the origins of behavioral, social, and emotional problems may have important implications when it is time to link assessment results to a useful intervention plan.

DOI: 10.4324/9781315747521-2

This book was designed with a specific theoretical foundation of human behavior in mind: social learning or social cognitive theory. In addition, this book includes a strong emphasis on ecological or environmental aspects of behavior, and thus also has a strong emphasis on social-ecological theory. Before delving into an exploration of these two theoretical models, this section first provides a brief discussion of some other approaches to conceptualizing human behavior and how theory shapes practice. Then, in more detail, we explore social cognitive theory and its related aspects, and introduce the notion of social ecological theory.

To say that there is a traditional theory of human behavior, or even a small handful of these theories, in modern psychology, is misleading. Although psychodynamic and behavioral theories were strong and distinct unitary forces in the early days of psychology, neither one of these schools of thought, similar to most other ways of conceptualizing human behavior, is currently considered a unitary force, as they have matured, and to some extent, have split into divergent schools of thought, if not factions, that have a common lineage.

Let us take behaviorism as an example in more detail. In the modern world of behaviorism, there are divergent schools of thought that take significantly different approaches and yet still fall under the umbrella of behaviorism. The "true believers" in behaviorism are probably those who claim the strongest legacy to Skinner, Watson and Raynor, and Thorndike. This contingent of behaviorism is perhaps best exemplified by those who are active practitioners of experimental and applied behavior analysis, which can be traced directly to B. F. Skinner and his brilliant and voluminous work that spanned a 60-year period from 1930 to 1990, making him unquestionably the most influential American psychologist. To summarize applied behavior analysis or the work of Skinner in a few short sentences is presumptuous to say the least. With this caveat in place, however, behavior analysis is grounded in the notion that behavior is shaped by the antecedents that precede it and the consequences that follow. This notion is key to understanding, predicting, and changing behavior. A more recent school of thought within the behavioral world is a diverse group of ideas for understanding and changing behavior that center around the term *cognitive behavior therapy*. This loose-knit faction does claim some legacy to Skinner's work, considering that overt emitted behaviors, consequences, and the environment are important. The emphasis on internal cognitive processes and mediating events that links most theories in cognitive behavioral therapy is a clear departure, however, from the framework advocated by Skinner and his colleagues. In fact, throughout his career, Skinner repeatedly criticized "mentalistic" approaches to learning and behavior. In his later years, Skinner became particularly vocal in this regard. His mid-1980s article titled "The Shame of American Education" (B. F. Skinner, 1984) included an angry and disappointed indictment of the American educational system for failing to adopt scientifically based learning and management procedures and focusing instead on mentalistic or cognitive constructs that could not be easily defined or measured. In his last public address, shortly before his death in 1990, after receiving an award for his lifetime of scientific contributions, Skinner presented a keynote address at a meeting of the American Psychological Association (APA), in which he thoroughly lambasted "cognitive science," portraying it as a misguided attempt to explain human behavior through studying underlying mental processes, which is a throwback to mentalism and turn-of-the-century introspectionism. In addition to receiving four standing ovations during his sometimes dramatic address, Skinner also shocked many in his audience by referring derisively to cognitive science as "the creationism of psychology" (APA, 1990).

The point to be made by this brief discussion of the evolution of modern behaviorism is that the traditional theoretical schools of thought that are discussed in general psychology textbooks have evolved tremendously over the years, often branching into smaller groups that share common backgrounds. This same process is true for other traditional theoretical schools of thought, such as psychodynamic theory, the neurobiological model, and the humanistic movement. The philosophical basis of each of these areas has evolved tremendously over the years, and there is no longer just a small and powerful handful of theoretical schools with which a practitioner may be aligned. Clinicians and researchers today are much more likely to consider themselves "eclectic" in their theoretical approach to human behavior than to align themselves with one school of thought. These present circumstances have had a dual effect: on one hand, the decreasing amount of dogmatism has paved the way for acceptance of new and influential theories, but on the other hand, the current generation of clinicians is perhaps less likely to place a great deal of thought to their theoretical orientation, which could lead to an unanchored approach to assessment and treatment.

Social Cognitive Theory: An Integrated Orientation

Social cognitive theory, a primary underlying orientation in this book, is a sophisticated and complex theory that takes into account not only the multiple causes of behavioral, social, and emotional problems, but also the reciprocal nature of the relationship between causes and effects. This theory is not overviewed in order to proselytize the nonbeliever— it is not a philosophy of life and does not have to carry any metaphysical implications. Although you should understand that it is the framework embedded within this book, social cognitive theory is proposed as a solid foundation for assessment of children and adolescents because it takes into account many potential factors contributing to the assessment problems; it is flexible; and in its fullest form, it has strong implications for linking assessment data to intervention planning.

Components of Social Cognitive Theory Social cognitive theory and the related concepts of *triadic reciprocality* and *observational learning* are based on the work of Albert Bandura (e.g., 1977, 1978, 1986). Most people who have studied psychology and related fields at the graduate level are familiar with Bandura's famous work on social learning processes in aggression. These processes were demonstrated in the famous "Bobo Doll" experiments wherein the effects of models and perceived consequences were found to have a tremendous impact on aggressive and prosocial behavior in school-age and preschool-age children. These particular demonstrations of social cognitive theory do not tell the full story and do not account for the entire complexity of the process. Although it is impossible to detail social cognitive theory completely in a portion of one book chapter (for a comprehensive account, see Bandura's 1986 book, *Social Foundations of Thought and Action*), it is useful to review its major components. As stated by Bandura (1986), social cognitive theory holds that:

> [People] are neither driven by inner forces nor automatically shaped and controlled by external stimuli. Rather, human functioning is explained in terms of a model of triadic reciprocality in which behavior, cognitive and other personal factors, and environmental events all operate as determinants of each other.
>
> (p. 18)

The nature of people is explained in terms of five basic human capabilities: symbolizing capability, forethought capability, vicarious capability, self-regulatory capability, and self-reflective capability.

Symbolizing capability involves the use of various symbols, including language, as a means of altering and adapting to different environments. The use of symbols allows communication with others, even at distant times or places. Forethought capability consists of the anticipation of likely consequences of behavior and is demonstrated by intentional and purposive actions that are future oriented. Vicarious capability is entailed by the fact that not all learning must result from direct experience, but can occur through the observation of other people's behaviors and the consequences that follow them. Self-regulatory capability affects the development of our own internal standards and self-evaluative reactions to our behavior—discrepancies between our internal standards and our actual behaviors govern our future behavior. Self-reflective capability involves self-consciousness, or the uniquely human ability that enables us to think about and evaluate our own thought processes. Together, these five fundamental human capabilities form the basis for our vast human potential and help explain the inner workings that result in our behavioral output.

Triadic Reciprocality: Understanding the Determinants of Behavior The social cognitive viewpoint supports a conception of the causes of human behavior being due to reciprocal determinism. The idea behind reciprocal determinism is that the causes behind one's behavior become influenced and shaped by the behavior itself. Specifically, the type of reciprocal determinism favored by social cognitive theory is known as triadic reciprocality (Bandura, 1977, 1978). This view contends that behavior, environmental influences, and various personal factors (e.g., cognition, temperament, biology) all work together in an interactive manner and have the effect of acting as determinants of each other. Bandura's theory of triadic reciprocality is illustrated in Figure 1.1.

Triadic reciprocality in social cognitive theory can be exemplified in practical terms through an example of the interaction process between parents and a newborn child. Take a scenario where the infant happens to have an irritable or difficult temperament, which is present from birth and is probably biological in nature. The infant's irritable temperament is an example of a personal factor. Because this particular infant tends to cry frequently and in a most distressing tone, is highly demanding, and sleeps for only short periods of time (behavioral factors), an environment is created in which constant

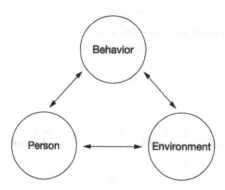

Figure 1.1 An outline of Bandura's (1986) theory of triadic reciprocality

demands, noise, and limited opportunities for sleep interact with the personal factors of the parents to help shape their own behavior and characteristics in the direction of their being constantly tired, more irritable than normal, anxious, frustrated, and perhaps over time, somewhat depressed. The behavior of the parents continues to shape the environment of the infant, and the infant's behavior continues to shape the environment of the parents, which in turn affects their personal characteristics. If the infant persists in being highly irritable and demanding, and the parents tend to reinforce these demands with immediate attention in an attempt to terminate their child's difficult behavior, the child's irritable and demanding personal characteristics will probably become strengthened and persist over time. If the parents learn to deal with their child in a quiet and relaxed manner, the child's demanding irritability may be reduced, and the behavioral demands in the environment may change.

Bandura's early view of the social cognitive and triadic reciprocality models is quite consistent with the most sophisticated contemporary models in the field of developmental psychopathology, namely the *interactional* and the *transformational* models of development of maladaptive behavior in children (M. Lewis, 2000). Although triadic reciprocality and the interactional and transformational models are much too complex to do justice to within a section of a book chapter, they can be reduced into two points on family influences relative to child behavior problems that are highly salient for conducting assessments of behavioral, social, and emotional problems: "(1) children have effects on adults that are equal to adults' effects on children, and (2) family interactions are understandable only when reciprocal influences of parent and children on each other are taken into account" (Kauffman, 1989, p. 165). Kauffman's work on this topic predated the most recent models by nearly a decade and was described as a transactional–interactional model of the development of child behavior disorders. Likewise, some of the seminal research and writing on this topic was developed by Patterson and his associates at the Oregon Social Learning Center (e.g., Patterson, 1982; Patterson, Reid, & Dishion, 1992), who wrote extensively on the phenomena of reciprocal influences in developmental psychopathology, particularly antisocial behavior. Their numerous investigations into the topic for nearly three decades have linked the development and maintenance of child behavioral and emotional problems to coercive, reciprocal interactions within families. It takes only a small leap from these examples of parent–child interactions to understand that human behavior is shaped through complex, mutually influential interactions, whether it is in the home, school, workplace, or community.

In completing our discussion of triadic reciprocality, it is useful to understand that the three parts of the triad (personal, behavioral, and environmental factors) are thought to make differing contributions at various points in time. As Bandura (1986) noted, "Reciprocality does not mean symmetry in the strength of the bidirectional influences . . . [and] the triadic factors do not operate in the manner of a simultaneous holistic interaction" (pp. 24–25). In other words, there are times when an environmental factor may become the strongest influence in the reciprocal interaction, and at other times, personal factors of behavior may become pre-eminent. The important thing to consider is that each factor may influence and shape the other two in some way.

Observational Learning: A Multiprocess Analysis To conclude this excursion into social cognitive theory, it is worthwhile to take a brief look at the process of observational learning. As outlined by Bandura (1977, 1986), observational learning is a model for understanding the learning process in a social context, which is fully compatible with social cognitive theory and triadic reciprocality. Individuals who have only a superficial knowledge of observational learning might consider it to be equivalent to simple modeling or mimicking of behavior, but it is far more comprehensive than such comparisons would suggest. As Bandura (1986) stated, "Most human behavior is learned by observation through modeling . . . [but] in skill acquisition, modeling is more accurately represented as rule learning rather than mimicry" (pp. 47–48).

What are the elements that guide the process of rule learning? Bandura (1986) outlined five different types of effects that are said to guide the process of modeling. Observational learning effects include new behaviors, cognitive skills, and standards of judgment that are acquired through directly observing others. These effects are thought to be stronger when the behavior observed is novel or unique. Inhibitory and disinhibitory effects determine how likely it is that a newly learned behavior will be demonstrated. It is more likely that a newly learned behavior will be performed if a person believes that a positive outcome will result, and less likely if it is perceived that a negative outcome will result. Our perception of what is likely or not likely to happen following our behaviors either inhibits or disinhibits us from performing those behaviors. Response facilitation effects involve the actions of others as social prompts for us to engage in behaviors we have learned. Peer pressure, or encouragement, is an example of how a child is prompted to engage in certain social behaviors. Environmental enhancement effects encompass the physical circumstances of the environment we have observed in that it will result in our performing a behavior in a certain way. For example, a child who has observed two other children fighting on the playground where one child "wins" the fight by throwing a handful of dirt and gravel into the face of the other might engage in the same behavior if confronted with a similar conflict situation, primarily because this child observed that the behavior was successful in the short term. Finally, arousal effects involve the level of emotional intensity, or arousal, that is elicited in observers. When emotional arousal is heightened, the form or intensity of ongoing behaviors can be altered; interactions that might normally result in an argument might result in a physical altercation in an environment of intense emotional arousal. In sum, these five modeling effects can serve to instruct, inhibit or disinhibit, facilitate, and enhance the behaviors we engage in, whether they are prosocial, neutral, or antisocial in nature.

Observational learning also involves four related cognitive processes that help determine how effectively we are able to learn through observation. According to Bandura (1986), these four processes work as follows:

1. *Attentional processes.* Learning will occur through the observational process only if adequate attention is focused on the event. Humans do not give their attention equally to all stimuli—we are more focused and attentive if the behavior is novel or if we consider the model to have high status.
2. *Retention processes.* Retention processes involve the encoding of the event or behavior we have observed into our memory. Two major memory systems are likely to be involved in retention processes: imaginal and verbal.
3. *Production processes.* This subprocess pertains to our ability to perform the behaviors we have observed and retained. In this sense, our motor abilities are often involved and may limit our ability to enact the behavior we have learned. Although virtually all basketball aficionados would pay careful attention to, and be able to retain, a

memory representation of one of basketball phenom LeBron James's patented moves to the hoop, few could actually produce the behavior.

4. *Motivational processes.* In social cognitive theory, there is a differentiation between learning and performance, as we tend not to enact everything we learn. Whether we are motivated to enact a newly learned behavior depends mainly on the incentives we believe are involved. Incentives can be either internal or external and can be direct, vicarious, or self-produced.

The Importance of Context: Ecological Systems Theory

Social cognitive theory provides a sophisticated model for understanding the development of human behavior, particularly the development of behavioral, emotional, and social problems. Like any other theory, social cognitive theory provides a way of considering and understanding a phenomenon, but it is not and should not be considered all-encompassing. No single theory can account for all scientific truth. For these reasons, and because I view the importance of social contexts or environments as extremely critical in children's developmental and learning processes, I advocate within this book an additional theory for framing children's behavioral, social, and emotional problems: the late psychologist Uri Bronfenbrenner's (1977, 1979, 1989) *ecological systems theory.*

Bronfenbrenner's ecological systems theory is not a general theory of human behavior in the same way that behavioral and psychodynamic theories are. Rather, this theory provides a detailed framework for viewing and understanding the importance of social systems and contexts in which humans develop and behaviors are learned and exhibited. Social cognitive theory also includes a strong emphasis on the environment in shaping the behavior and the person, but does not detail specific aspects of social environment in a way that may be generalized across settings. For this reason, ecological systems theory is a highly useful adjunct to social cognitive theory in providing a foundation on which to understand the development of children's social–emotional behavior, and to frame referrals for assessment and intervention.

Originally conceptualized as an ecological theory of child development, Bronfenbrenner's model quickly became influential in psychology and human development, and its influence then spread to the fields of education, family studies, and even business, as it became adapted and increasingly known as ecological systems theory. The premise underlying this theory and model is that every child exists within multiple social ecologies or systems, and that each of these systems may play a key role in the child's development. Figure 1.2 provides an illustration of major components of the model, which consists of a series of four embedded circles, each representing a sphere of influence or social ecology.

At the center of the model is the *microsystem,* which includes the individual child, as well as his or her immediate environments. The home environment, school environment, and the immediate neighborhood in which the child resides are usually considered the most immediate or proximal systems in the child's life. Moving out from the child's immediate environments into broader ecological systems, the *mesosystem* aspect of Bronfenbrenner's model accounts for reciprocal interactions among components of the microsystem. For example, when a child's teacher contacts his or her parent regarding concern over a behavioral or emotional problem and the parent then responds back to the teacher or school team, a mesosystem interaction has taken place. Similarly, the home environment and immediate neighborhood in which the child lives may often interact in a mesosystem manner as the child attempts to make friends, as other children in the

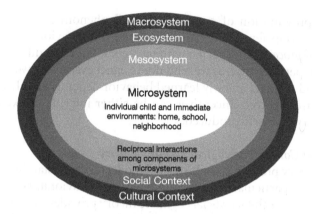

Figure 1.2 Components of Bronfenbrenner's (1977, 1989) ecological systems theory

neighborhood seek out interactions with the child, and as a parent takes steps to promote desirable interactions and to protect the child from negative or potentially dangerous interactions. The *exosystem* aspect of ecological systems theory makes up the third level of the model and moves out from interactions within aspects of the child's immediate environment to include the social context in which these immediate environments operate. For example, the broader school system outside of the child's own classroom, the type of community in which the child's family lives, a parent's workplace, and the extended family system of relatives who do not live with the child's immediate family all could be considered to be part of the exosystem. These exosystem components shape the more immediate aspects of the child's environment in many direct and subtle ways. For example, a child whose family lives in a highly religious community will be exposed to certain norms, values, and behavioral expectations that will differ somewhat from those of a family living in a highly secularized community. Likewise, a child raised in a general community culture where violence and gang activity is normative will be impacted at an exosystem level in a much different way than a child who is raised in a safe and peaceful environment.

Finally, the fourth level of the model is referred to as the *macrosystem*. The outermost layer of the circle reflects the broad cultural context in which the exosystem, mesosystem, and microsystem operate. The general values, beliefs, customs, laws, and resources of the society or nation in which the child lives influence the child's development indirectly. This process occurs by shaping the ways that the more inner systems function, as well as the priorities and values that are promoted within these systems. For example, a child living within the United States not only will receive some basic training in traditional aspects of American citizenship and democracy in school and in the community, but also will likely be exposed to the normative values of individualism, consumerism, pursuit of self-interests, justice, and perhaps even hedonism through exposure to popular culture, media, and the other broad influences that stem from the macrosystem.

Because all children exist within multiple social contexts and because requests for assessment and intervention for children with behavioral, social, and emotional concerns all stem from one or more of these contexts, ecological systems theory is an invaluable contribution. When considered in conjunction with social cognitive theory, this ecological systems theory adds to the foundation for understanding child and adolescent behavior, and it is considered throughout this volume as the process of assessment of behavioral, social, and emotional problems.

Finding Your Own Theoretical Foundation

In sum, although there are many competing theories on the development of human behavioral, social, and emotional problems, social cognitive theory, ecological systems theory, and related contemporary models of developmental psychopathology have many advantages for conceptualizing and assessing child and adolescent behavioral and emotional problems. These theories are especially emphasized in this book. Social cognitive theory and ecological systems theory offer sophisticated and relevant frameworks for conceptualizing the referral problems and treatment issues in assessing children and adolescents. Although it is not necessary to adopt these theories (or any other theoretical approach) wholesale in order to conduct technically adequate assessments, using the approaches that are a foundation for this book will provide a basis for understanding and will allow for better conceptualization of referral problems and for dealing with the assessment-intervention process in a cohesive manner.

The intent of this section has been to illustrate the importance of having a solid theoretical foundation for assessment. It has been my experience that the integrated development of theory and philosophy as a foundation for assessing and treating human behavior is increasingly being ignored or minimized in graduate training programs in professional psychology and related mental health fields. The generic umbrella of "eclecticism" in selecting treatment techniques has some merit but is often used as a substitute for putting any serious thought into the development of a personal and professional framework for conceptualizing child and adolescent social and emotional behavior. What many graduate students and professionals do not fully comprehend is that the move toward pragmatic eclecticism in selecting appropriate treatment modalities—which may be appropriate in many instances—does not replace having a solid theoretical foundation for conceptualizing how problems begin in the first place. Without an underpinning theoretical framework for conceptualizing behavior, the professional who conducts the assessment moves out of the scientist–practitioner mode and relegates his or her conduct to the role of technician.

Social cognitive theory, ecological systems theory, and the compatible interactional and transformational models of developmental psychopathology constitute my personal choice of theoretical foundations and are emphasized throughout this book. Despite the value and appeal of these theories for professionals conducting child and adolescent assessments, it is understood that they will not fit equally as well with all professionals. Readers are strongly encouraged to think seriously about their own views on human behavior and to adopt and develop an appropriate and congruent underlying theoretical framework to guide their practice. The benefits of taking such a step are many.

PHILOSOPHICAL FOUNDATIONS OF ASSESSMENT

Not only is it desirable to approach the assessment process firmly grounded in theory, but it is also important to understand the philosophical foundations on which assessment practices are conducted. One philosophical issue that is important to understand, to become truly educated in psychological and educational assessment, is the difference between *nomothetic* and *idiographic* approaches to scientific inquiry, how these constructs have been adopted into assessment, and how the convergence of the two approaches in assessment is increasingly being viewed as desirable. Many professionals who specialize in assessment have heard these terms, but few have gone beyond a cursory discussion to acquire an understanding of how they came to be and have influenced assessment. This section provides a brief excursion into the meaning of this issue and ends with a discussion of the empirical approach to assessment, a more modern conceptualization of inquiry in this area.

Nomothetic and Idiographic: Definitions and Historical Development

The issue and controversy regarding nomothetic and idiographic approaches to inquiry were examined in detail in two key articles in a special issue on this topic of *Theory and Psychology Journal* (Lamiell, 1998; Mos, 1998). The two seemingly dichotomous terms were first introduced by the German philosopher of science Wilhelm Windelband in 1894, as an attempt to define the differences between two seemingly opposite methods of scientific inquiry, during an era when the use of statistical methods and data aggregation was increasingly supplanting traditional methods of inquiry. According to Windelband, the nomothetic approach to inquiry (sometimes referred to as *nomological*) involved the development of *general scientific laws* through finding *similarities among phenomena:* the abstract, the universal, and the general. The idiographic approach to inquiry was viewed as the opposite of the nomothetic approach. Windelband's view of idiographic inquiry was that it was concerned with identifying *the uniqueness of a phenomenon:* the concrete, the individual, and the unique.

Beginning in the early twentieth century, Windelband's nomothetic–idiographic dichotomy was extremely influential in shaping and articulating methods of epistemology or inquiry in numerous scientific fields. Psychology was no exception. In practice, the use of statistical aggregation, psychometrics, population means, and prediction through general trend analysis became associated with the nomothetic approach to psychology, whereas the use of single case design, ecological analysis, qualitative and informal description, and case studies became associated with the idiographic approach to psychology. The issue was popularized and became the point of much discussion in psychology with the publication of Paul Meehl's (1954) book, *Clinical versus Statistical Prediction*. In this book, Meehl argued that clinical judgment (which he viewed as idiographic) was a poor substitute for quantitative or actuarial prediction based on objective data (which he viewed as nomothetic). According to Barnett and Zucker (1990), nomothetic approaches to assessment focus on actuarial and quantitative data, objective tests, and statistical prediction. Idiographic assessment in the social–emotional behavior domain focuses more on individual and qualitative data, projective tests, and clinical judgment. In the behavioral assessment domain, the use of single-subject data collection and research designs is often considered to be idiographic in nature.

Nomothetic and Idiographic Approaches in Practice

The conflicting opinions that have fomented controversy over the years regarding nomothetic versus idiographic approaches to assessment are unfortunate because they tend to mask two important issues. First, when Windelband introduced the terms in 1894, he was positing them as diverging ways to approach scientific inquiry in general and was not superimposing them on the fields of psychological and educational assessment, which for all intents and purposes did not yet exist in its present form. It was many years later that these terms were connected to assessment. Much of the flack regarding nomothetic versus idiographic assessment is a product of the two terms being adapted beyond their original scope and intent (Lamiell, 1998; Mos, 1998). It might be argued that pitting the two approaches against each other in terms of which is "right" is an arbitrary act that fails to grasp the rich historical context in the philosophy of science and epistemology from which these notions originated.

In reality, most clinicians who practice assessment of children in educational and psychological service settings comingle the nomothetic and idiographic approaches to inquiry on a routine basis, without giving the matter a second thought. Consider a child who is referred to a child study team in a school setting because of concerns regarding his or her behavioral and emotional adjustment. In the comprehensive social–emotional assessment that is ultimately conducted, the team uses a combination of direct behavioral observation, behavior rating scales, interviews, and self-report instruments to gather information. Because the focus is on the unique individual needs of the child, it could be viewed as idiographic. In conducting the observation, the specific and unique behaviors of the child within particular environmental contexts are recorded, which might be viewed as idiographic, but the child's behavior is contrasted with that of social comparison peers, seeking some normative generalizations in a nomothetic manner. The behavior rating scales and self-report instruments involve normative comparisons of the child's obtained scores with those of standardization samples, and T scores and percentile ranks are calculated, which is a nomothetic procedure. The team also carefully looks at the specific items from these instruments, inspecting them qualitatively to seek further understanding of the child, without respect to the normative aspects of such consideration. This approach is certainly idiographic in nature. Skilled and theoretically astute assessment professionals routinely seek to understand children's behavioral and emotional functioning using both means of inquiry to satisfy unique questions. There is typically no need to break into opposing camps on this issue, which in my view reflects a short-sighted lack of understanding of the philosophy of science and the maturation of psychological and educational assessment.

The Empirical Approach to Assessment

A construct that has been articulated in recent years within the area of psychological evaluation and measurement is the "empirical approach" to assessment, sometimes referred to as *empirically based assessment*. Similar to our discussion on nomothetic and idiographic approaches to assessment, it is useful to consider this term further because of its increasing influence. It might be argued that the empirical approach to assessment is most consistent with nomothetic rather than idiographic inquiry, but from a historical perspective this single alignment is questionable, and empirically based assessment is compatible with the idiographic approach.

The term *empirical* originates from the Greek word *empeiria*, which refers to *experience* (Achenbach, McConaughy, & Howell, 1987). Empirical data are based on experience or observations and can be proved or disproved through direct experimentation or observation. In Achenbach, McConaughy, and Howell's conceptualization of empirical assessment, this approach "follows psychometric principles, including the use of standardized procedures, multiple aggregated items, normative-developmental reference groups, and the establishment of reliability and validity" (p. 16). In this book, empirically based assessment is a major focus because it is defensible, replicable, and, when used correctly, holds to high standards of scientific inquiry. Although the scope of this book is broad, particular emphasis is placed on using assessment methods and procedures that are more direct and objective in nature, and compatible with the notion of empirically based assessment.

UNDERSTANDING AND CLARIFYING ASSESSMENT REFERRALS

Any professional with experience in assessing children would agree that referrals for assessment come in a wide variety of dimensions. Sometimes the pervasive nature of the problems leading to the referral make one contemplate why the referral did not happen earlier. At other times, the character of the stated referral issue seems so benign as to make one consider if there was truly a need for it in the first place. What these disparate examples illustrate is that in order to conduct a sound assessment, the reasons for referral and circumstances leading up to the point of referral first must be carefully analyzed and explored.

Almost every child, at some time, will exhibit behavioral, social, or emotional problems that are serious enough to cause some concern for their parents or teachers, but only a few of these problems will ultimately result in a referral for assessment or treatment. What are the factors that result in behavioral, social, or emotional problems being taken to the point of referral?

In contrast to adult mental health clients, who are typically self-referred, children and adolescents are usually referred for assessment by someone else, such as a parent or teacher. It is common for referred children and adolescents not to recognize or admit that their perceived problems exist and not to understand fully why the assessment is happening in the first place. Knoff (1986) suggested that referrals for social, emotional, or behavioral assessment are often "the result of a perceived discrepancy between the referred child's behaviors, attitudes, or interpersonal interactions . . . and some more optimal level desired and defined by the referral source" (p. 4). The basis of these discrepancies is thought to stem from differing perspectives that define the referral source's idea of what constitutes acceptable and unacceptable social–emotional behavior. As we see herein, this notion is very consistent with the notion of ecological systems.

Knoff (1986) postulated three specific perspectives that influence referral decisions and that have direct parallels within ecological systems theory. They include the *sociocultural perspective*, the *community subgroup perspective*, and the *setting-specific perspective*. These three perspectives are as relevant today as when they were first proposed. The sociocultural perspective involves the broad environment within a community: generalized precepts regarding what constitutes acceptable and unacceptable ways of behaving that are pervasive at most levels within a given community or society. This notion is akin to the ecological systems concept of a *macrosystem*. A child or adolescent who is referred because of a discrepancy related to this perspective would likely be exhibiting behaviors that are in opposition to overall societal standards. Community subgroup perspectives are shaped by smaller groups within a community—religious organizations, neighborhoods, and specific cultural or ethnic groups. This notion is akin to the ecological systems concept of an *exosystem*. Referrals that are related to discrepancies from this perspective may involve behaviors or attitudes that are unacceptable within one subgroup but may be acceptable within another. For example, adolescents who listen to musical forms of expression that are lyrically violent in content—such as some forms of rap, heavy metal, or punk—may adopt attitudes based on these forms of expression that may cause considerable concern within some community subgroups but go almost unnoticed within others. The setting-specific perspective involves social behavioral norms that are distinctive to individual settings, such as specific families and classrooms; what is tolerated as normal, by some parents or teachers, may be totally unacceptable to others. The setting-specific perspective is closely akin to the ecological systems notion of a *microsystem*.

The essential point to consider in analyzing referrals from these various perspectives or ecological systems is that all three are interdependent. One cannot focus singly on a given perspective without taking into account the others. A child who comes from a family background in which there is open disrespect or contempt for a general societal standard, such as law and order, may reject typically accepted standards of behavior in the school or community, while maintaining solidarity with the standards set within his or her family. In contrast, a child whose family has recently immigrated from a distant part of the world might adopt typical values of his or her new host culture that create dissension within the family but are hardly cause for notice within the school or larger community. It becomes the job of the clinician to examine the reasons for referral carefully and how these reasons relate to the three basic perspectives. In some cases, referrals may need to be refused as being improper, or at least carefully considered and discussed before proceeding. In other cases, the referral may need to result in a complete assessment to determine to what extent behavioral, social, or emotional problems are present.

ASSESSMENT AS A PROBLEM-SOLVING PROCESS

Given that assessment is one of the primary activities of many psychologists and other education/mental health practitioners, it is surprising that until recently so little attention has been paid to identifying and clarifying the purposes of assessment. There are many specific potential purposes, such as problem clarification, diagnosis, classification, intervention planning, and intervention evaluation. Despite the wide array of complex purposes associated with assessment, some practitioners and administrators continue to view assessment as being synonymous with testing. In reality, these two activities are related but are not necessarily the same. Testing is the process of administering and scoring tests, whether simple or complex. Within the most narrow interpretation of the process, testing can become a means and an end, a nearly self-contained activity. Assessment is clearly superordinate to testing. Assessment, in the broad view, is a process whereby information is gathered regarding a specific problem or issue. This information-gathering process may also involve testing, but not out of necessity. A crucial aspect of the broad view of assessment is that it is a means to an end, rather than an end itself. Ideally the end result of assessment is to gather information that may be used to help solve specific problems.

A few attempts have been made to develop models of assessment as a problem-solving process. Sloves, Docherty, and Schneider (1979) proposed a scientific problem-solving model of psychological assessment that consisted of three basic elements: a six-step problem-solving process, levels of organizational action, and methods. The purpose of this model was to help differentiate the practice of psychological assessment, as a *process* of problem solving, from testing, as one set of methods for problem solving. In a similar vein, Nezu (1993) delineated a conceptual model of assessment based on a problem-solving framework, whereby the clinician is considered the problem solver, and the problem to be solved is the discrepancy between the client's current state and desired state. Both of these model-building attempts are laudable, as are other attempts to promote assessment as a broad problem-solving process. Yet the reality of the situation is that none of these models fully integrates the assessment of social and emotional behavior of children and adolescents into a comprehensive problem-solving process.

A Model for Assessment as a Problem-Solving Process

It is my view that school psychologists, clinical child and adolescent psychologists, and professionals in related disciplines, should approach their respective roles as *data-oriented problem solvers.* For an important historical perspective of this concept of data-oriented problem solving, see Gray (1963), and for more current perspectives, see Deno (1995), Merrell, Ervin, and Gimpel (2006), Walser (2009), Sugai and Horner (2009), and Horner et al. (2015). Given the importance of viewing assessment as part of a broad problem-solving process and the lack of an adequate theoretical model for viewing social–emotional assessment in this regard, I have proposed a four-phase model of assessment as a problem-solving process. Rather than composing a general problem-solving model, Merrell developed this model (which is illustrated in Table 1.1) to be specifically relevant to the problems inherent in assessing social and emotional behavior of children and adolescents.

This model is broad enough in its scope, however, that it can easily accommodate other applications of assessment. This model is based on the premise that within four basic

Table 1.1 A model for assessment as a problem-solving process

---

Phase I: Identification and clarification
    Who is the client (or who are the clients)?
    From the client's perspective, what is the problem?
    What is the intended purpose of the assessment?

Phase II: Data collection
    What information is needed?
    What assessment methods, procedures, and tests will best provide this information?
    Which of the potential means of gathering information are most appropriate for this specific client, problem, and situation?

Phase III: Analysis
    Does the assessment information confirm the problem?
    What other information do the assessment data provide regarding the problem?
    How can the assessment information be used to answer specific referral questions?
    What are the factors that appear to contribute to the problem?
    Is there any missing assessment information that is needed to help analyze this problem?
    If so, how can it be obtained?

Phase IV: Solution and evaluation
    Based on all the available information, what should be the target for intervention? What behaviors should be increased/decreased?
    What appear to be the most appropriate types of intervention?
    What resources are available to implement the intervention?
    Which means of assessment can be used to collect data continuously during intervention?
    Which means of assessment can be used to evaluate the effectiveness of the solution?

---

phases of assessment, a series of essential questions can guide assessment practice into appropriate actions so that assessment truly becomes an integral part of an overall process of data-oriented problem solving. It is congruent with Deno's position that assessment practices have an important role to play in a comprehensive problem-solving orientation to service delivery, which includes three basic elements: formulating the problem, generating and selecting potential solutions, and testing the selected alternatives.

Phase I: Identification and Clarification The first phase is identification and clarification. In this phase, it is crucial to answer some basic questions that will lead to articulating clearly the purpose of assessment. First, it is essential to identify who the client is. In reality, this identification is often complex. We all would agree that the referred child or adolescent is the client, but it also is likely the referral agent, such as a parent or teacher, is the client as well, given that the person has a specific interest in the outcome of the assessment. Determining who is the client is sometimes a challenging task, given that there may be multiple interests involved, and that the specific source and setting of the referral may dictate who is the primary client. Second, it is crucial to delineate clearly what the problem is from the client's perspective. Sometimes the perceived problem is anything but straightforward, and there may be multiple problems from the client's perspective. Third, the clinician must identify what is the intended purpose or purposes of the assessment. It is possible that there will be more than one purpose, such as diagnosing the problem, determining eligibility for specific services, and helping to develop a plan of intervention.

Phase II: Data Collection The second phase of the model is where the assessment data are gathered. Rather than mindlessly gathering information through administration of a standard battery of procedures that is the same for everyone, the data-oriented problem solver will let the purposes of the assessment and the characteristics of the client and problem guide the selection of assessment procedures. First, it is essential to identify clearly what information is needed. Second, one should determine which assessment methods, procedures, and tests will best provide the needed information. Third, after some basic decisions have been made regarding what information is needed, the clinician should analyze carefully the specific nature of the client, problem, and situation, to determine whether some means of information gathering may be more appropriate than others. For example, if the main referral issue is inattentive and hyperactive behavior problems, it would make sense to select a behavior rating scale for completion by parents or teachers specifically designed to evaluate the characteristics of attention deficit hyperactivity disorder (ADHD). In some cases, there also may be evidence of co-occurring conduct problems, such as aggressive and antisocial behavior. In the latter situation, a broad-band externalizing behavior problem rating scale would be a better choice than a scale designed solely to evaluate ADHD characteristics.

Phase III: Analysis In the third phase of the process, the obtained assessment data are analyzed in detail. Some of the questions that may be most useful in guiding this process involve whether the data confirm the problem or what other information the data provide regarding the problem, how the data can be used to answer specific referral questions, what other factors seem to be contributing to the problem, and what, if any, assessment data are missing. If there is necessary assessment information that is missing, the clinician also must ask if this information can be obtained and, if so, how.

Phase IV: Solution and Evaluation The final phase of assessment as a problem-solving process is perhaps the most difficult—using the obtained assessment information to develop a solution to the problem and, ultimately, to evaluate the effectiveness of the solution. First, the main targets for intervention should be selected, based on all the available information that has been obtained. Second, the most appropriate types of intervention for these targets should be identified, as should the potential resources for implementing such intervention. These second and third questions in the phase should guide the development of a specific intervention plan. The fourth and fifth questions in the phase are often overlooked but should be considered essential if assessment will truly result in problem solving. When an intervention plan has been developed, it is also essential to consider how data can be collected continuously during the intervention to help determine whether the desired effect is occurring. This type of continuous data collection is closely linked to the process of formative evaluation, or making decisions that will guide instruction or treatment practices on an ongoing basis. Finally, it is often appropriate to use assessment procedures to assist in summative evaluation, to determine whether or not the intervention has produced the desired changes after it has been implemented.

This proposed model represents a practical, common-sense approach to assessment as a broad process for solving problems. Other models, including models developed individually by clinicians to serve their own purposes, may have the same effect. Regardless of which specific questions are asked or what specific theoretical approach is used to guide the assessment, readers of this book are urged to approach assessment from a broad perspective that is a means to an end, rather than a simple testing perspective where the means becomes an end, or where the end purpose is never clearly defined.

DESIGNING A MULTIMETHOD, MULTISOURCE, MULTISETTING ASSESSMENT

Since about 1980, there have been significant advances in the research and technology base for conducting assessments with children and adolescents. One of the major developments has been the articulation of a model for a broad-based assessment design. The essential feature of this model is that by using various assessment methods with different informants or sources and in several settings, the amount of error variance in the assessment is reduced, and the result becomes a comprehensive representation of the referred child or adolescent's behavioral, social, and emotional functioning. This type of broad-based assessment design has been referred to by various names, including multisetting–multisource–multi-instrument assessment (R. P. Martin, 1988; R. P. Martin, Hooper, & Snow, 1986) and multiaxial empirically based assessment (Achenbach et al., 1987). Although there are some differences between the way these different models have been articulated, the crucial feature of obtaining assessment data on an individual by using many different instruments, methods, sources, informants, and settings remains the same.

To represent the type of broad-based assessment that was just described, I prefer the term *multimethod, multisource, multisetting assessment,* particularly when considering the domain of behavioral, social, and emotional assessment of children and adolescents. Figure 1.3 is a graphic representation of the model.

As an example of how a multimethod, multisource, multisetting assessment might be conducted in actual practice, let's look at the hypothetical case of a child who is referred to a clinic setting because of a variety of behavioral and emotional problems. In terms of

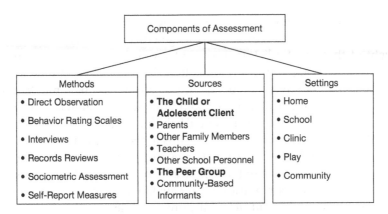

Figure 1.3 A model for multimethod, multisource, multisetting assessment practice

method, it probably would be desirable to include behavioral observation, interviews, rating scales, and self-report instruments as part of the assessment. Within each method, a variety of instruments or specific techniques should be used when possible. In the event that the child was experiencing social adjustment problems and there was easy access to a social group (i.e., school or playground) for assessment, it also might be desirable under some circumstances to gather sociometric assessment data. In terms of source, it would be necessary to gather assessment data from the client and his or her parents at a minimum, and if possible, it would be desirable to include other relevant sources who know the child, well as informants. These other sources might include school personnel, other family members, and community-based individuals such as clergy and youth group leaders. In terms of setting, clinic, home, and school, would be included in an optimal assessment and, when feasible, community-based and play settings.

In reality, it is often difficult to include all of the possible relevant sources and settings, and it is sometimes a problem even to include more than a couple of methods. The main point to consider in this regard is that as the assessment becomes more diverse and broad-based, an *aggregated* picture of the child's behavioral, social, and emotional functioning is obtained. Such an assessment design is considered to be a best practice that has the possibility of reducing error variance and providing a more comprehensive picture of the child.

Some caution is warranted in considering the possibilities and advantages of an aggregated multimethod, multisource, multisetting assessment. Although the vast majority of current professional thinking purports that such a design is a best practice and the most sophisticated way of implementing the assessment, there has historically been some divergence of opinion here, primarily stemming from research that was conducted in the 1980s, among experts in the field of child and adolescent psychopathology (e.g., Arkes, 1981; Loeber, Dishion, & Patterson, 1984; Reid, Baldwin, Patterson, & Dishion, 1988; Wiggins, 1981). Some of these researchers presented persuasive arguments that in specific cases, aggregated multiple assessment data may increase error variance because of covariation among different assessment sources and the inability of clinicians to aggregate effectively assessment data that are contradictory. This argument is compelling and interesting and is, at least partially, the impetus behind efforts that advocate sequential or multiple gating approaches to assessment, which are reviewed in Chapters 3 and 14.

Even some experts who advocate the aggregated multiple assessment model (e.g., Achenbach & Edelbrock, 1984) have acknowledged this possibility.

So, in light of these contradictory arguments, what is the best clinical practice? The position advocated throughout this book is that the informed and judicious use of an aggregated multiple assessment model is almost always the best practice for general social–emotional assessment of children and adolescents. Clinicians and researchers need to be informed, however, of the potential liabilities of their assessment design. In the meantime, additional empirical evidence on this assessment issue would be helpful in assisting those in the child and adolescent assessment field articulate a state-of-the-art assessment model. Because most of these contradictory arguments on assessment design are theory based, but not yet empirically validated, being aware of positions and their possibilities seems to be a prudent step at the present time.

RESPONSE TO INTERVENTION (RtI): A PUBLIC HEALTH APPROACH TO ASSESSMENT AND INTERVENTION

During the past decade there has been much interest in adapting models that were originally developed within the field of public health into the realm of education and mental health services for children and adolescents. The general idea behind the public health approach is that the delivery of services should be carefully planned so that *all* individuals within a population receive some benefit, not just those who have intense needs (Costello & Angold, 2000; Merrell & Buchanan, 2006). Such an approach presumes that there will always be a need to deliver intensive, individualized services to those individuals with intense needs, but by planning for prevention and early intervention services to those individuals with lower levels of current need, latent and emerging problems may be prevented or diminished, thus reducing the percentage of individuals who develop intense or serious problems. This approach is well worth considering in planning for social–emotional assessment and intervention services.

The best known adaptation of the public health approach into educational and children's mental health services is the "triangle of support" model (e.g., T. J. Lewis & Sugai, 1999; Walker et al., 1996), which is presented in Figure 1.4 with adaptations to illustrate how a comprehensive service system might work when focused on school-based services for children and youth with behavioral and emotional problems.

This figure is well-aligned with Response to Intervention (RtI) models that professionals are currently using to address school-based academic assessment and support (Fuchs & Fuchs, 1986). At the bottom of the triangle is the *Universal* level of support, which includes universal screening, prevention efforts, well-articulated schoolwide discipline practices, and a system of effective behavioral support that extends to all students within a school. Assessment at this level consists of brief screening practices that are designed to narrow a population into "good suspects" rather than provide an in-depth evaluation of individual characteristics. The roughly 80% of students in a typical school who do not exhibit significant behavioral or emotional problems will benefit from basic instruction and management strategies, as will those who exhibit more significant challenges. Effective services at the Universal level will have the result of decreasing the number of students at the more intense support levels, and will provide a basis for healthy behavioral, social, and emotional adjustment among all students. The bottom of the triangle is associated with

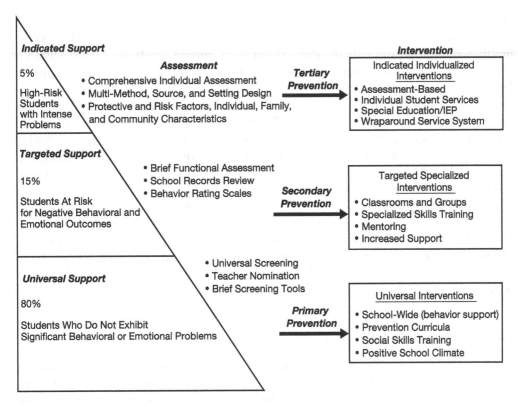

Figure 1.4 A public health approach, "triangle of support" model for students with behavioral and emotional problems

the public health notion of *Primary Prevention,* or maintaining health and preventing the development of problem symptoms.

The middle of the triangle details *Targeted* support, which is aimed at the approximately 15% of students in a typical school who are considered to be "at risk" for negative behavioral or emotional outcomes, and who will likely benefit from being identified using more specific assessment procedures, which would enable them to be the focus of prevention and early intervention strategies delivered in groups or classrooms. Assessment at the Targeted level might consist of brief functional assessments, school records reviews, and behavior rating scales—relatively low-intensity procedures that can yield some useful information about individual students who are considered to be at risk for developing intensive problems. Assessments at this level are also used to monitor the progress of students receiving *targeted* intervention support. The middle of the triangle reflects the public health notion of *Secondary Prevention,* where the goal is to prevent developing problems from worsening into intense needs or disorders.

The top of the triangle focuses on *Indicated* support and reflects the estimated 5% of students within a typical school who are at very high risk in terms of behavioral and emotional functioning. These students should be carefully identified through compre-hensive individual assessment and provided with intensive, individualized interventions. For some of these high-risk students, special education services under the emotionally disturbed, autism, or Other Health Impaired classification categories of Individuals with Disabilities Education Act (IDEA) will be appropriate. Students at the "top of the triangle" should be provided with a range of services and progress monitoring well beyond that which students at the lower levels of support require. Within public health terminology, individuals who exhibit such intense needs are served within a *Tertiary Prevention* framework, where the goal is rehabilitation or reduction of current levels of problems.

Figure 1.4 indicates the basic notions of the triangle model and also illustrates how screening and assessment activities might be tied to each level of the triangle, and how primary, secondary, and tertiary prevention activities and progress-monitoring activities might be put into place following initial screening and assessment. Education and mental health professionals are urged to consider this public health approach as a viable way of planning for assessment and intervention services so that the percentage of a population with intense problems is kept to a minimum, and so that systems of service are put into place to prevent most children and youth from developing notable behavioral and emotional problems in the first place. In an era when the percentage of children and youth who are considered to be at risk is increasing, and where availability of specialized mental health and educational services is remaining static or shrinking, using the public health approach makes sense on many levels.

LEGAL AND ETHICAL ISSUES IN ASSESSMENT

Although a truly comprehensive overview of the legal and ethical issues in assessment is beyond the scope of this book (for more complete discussions of the topic, see DeMers, 1986; Jacob, Decker, & Hartshorne, 2011; Messick, 1988), it is useful to take a brief look at some of these issues that are particularly relevant for assessment of behavioral, social, and emotional problems. By definition, legal issues involve aspects of assessment that are affected by either constitutional or statutory constraints. Ethical issues do not always involve legal constraints, but rather what is considered to be "right" professional practice, as dictated by the codes for ethical conduct developed by professional organizations, such as the American Psychological Association (APA), National Association of School Psychologists (NASP), and American Counseling Association (ACA). Although it is sometimes possible to separate law from ethics, in reality, the two areas are intertwined. Legal constraints affecting assessment practices often have been developed from the basis of professional practice codes, and these codes of ethics for professionals typically take into account important legal constraints that affect the profession.

The Basis for Legal Constraints on Assessment

According to DeMers (1986), there are two basic ways that testing and assessment practices can be affected by the law. The first means of jurisdiction involves constitutional protections to citizens. In this regard, the *equal protection* and *due process* clauses from the 14th Amendment to the U.S. Constitution are the areas most likely to constrain assessment practices, particularly if the individual conducting the assessment is employed by the "state" (e.g., public school districts, corrections agencies, hospitals, clinics). The 14th Amendment "was created to prevent state governments from trespassing on the rights of individual citizens" (Jacob et al., 2011, p. 29). The equal protection clause of this amendment forbids the state to treat, in a different manner, the persons who are similarly situated, unless there is a justifiable reason. Examples of assessment practices that would violate the equal protection clause are those that result in members of a specific gender or racial/ethnic group receiving inferior assessment, classification, or treatment services (i.e., the use of an assessment procedure that was systematically biased against a particular group). The due process clause of the 14th Amendment was designed to prevent "the government from denying life, liberty, or property without (1) a legitimate reason, and (2) providing some meaningful and impartial forum to prevent arbitrary deprivations of those protected interests" (DeMers, 1986, p. 37). Property and liberty interests have been defined broadly through many U.S. Supreme Court decisions—the concept of liberty is now thought to encompass rights to privacy, personal security, and reputation. In the assessment process, many activities potentially could infringe on liberty rights, including the actual conducting of the assessment and the writing and maintaining of confidential assessment reports.

The second way that assessment practices can be affected by law involves various statutory provisions that may be invoked at the state and federal levels. These types of legal constraints typically do not directly involve constitutional provisions but consist of the passage of specific laws by legislative bodies that are considered to be useful in governing professional practices. At the state level, laws for licensing of professional psychologists and other service providers usually contain specific regulations pertaining to who can provide services, how privileged information and confidentiality must be handled, and to what extent clients must be informed of the procedures they might become involved in. Another example of state-level law that affects assessment practices would be school law, in which specific procedures and safeguards governing consent for assessment and release of assessment records are often included. At the federal level, assessment practices in school settings may be affected by the IDEA, the Family Educational Rights and Privacy Act (FERPA), and the Every Student Succeeds Act (ESSA). The IDEA and FERPA both contain provisions relating to parental access to student records and release of records to third parties. The IDEA also contains provisions for selection of appropriate assessment instruments and procedures. ESSA does not include extensive provisions governing the specifics of social–emotional assessment practices, but does require that school districts employ "school-based mental health services providers" and "specialized instructional support personnel" who are involved in assessment. Further, ESSA requires that states report data on the status of school climate and bullying in annual reports, and that in addition to academic performance indicators, states include another indicator of school quality (e.g., school climate, student engagement) as part of its accountability plan (NASP, 2016).

Specific Assessment Practices Affected by Ethics and Law

To be more specific about how social–emotional assessment practices can be affected by legal and ethical constraints, we can identify three distinctive areas that have been addressed in this realm: *informed consent, validity of assessment procedures,* and *right to privacy/confidentiality.* These areas are discussed in this section, with specific comments regarding assessment practices with children and adolescents.

Informed Consent The area of informed consent is broadly construed to mean that before any assessment services are conducted, the client (and/or parent or guardian, in the case of a minor) must receive a sufficient explanation of the purpose and nature of the procedures that will be done and the risks involved, if any, and must give their express consent for participation. Informed-consent regulations are a major feature of the due-process stipulations in the IDEA. Within the regulations of IDEA, there are three components: *knowledge* (parents are to be given a complete explanation of the purposes and procedures of the assessment), *voluntariness* (consent is willfully granted and not obtained through coercion or misrepresentation), and *competence* (parents must be legally competent to give consent, which is usually assumed by school officials). Even when psychologists or other professionals are engaging in assessment activities outside the scope of the IDEA, there are similar ethical expectations for using informed-consent procedures, as indicated by the APA's *Ethical Principles of Psychologists and Code of Conduct* (APA, 2017) and the NASP's *Principles for Professional Ethics* (NASP, 2010).

For many years, the concept of informed consent, as applied to children and adolescents in the United States, was relatively straightforward and uncomplicated; it traditionally has been assumed that parents or guardians were the ultimate holders of the informed-consent right and that the child or adolescent played a secondary role in this process, if any at all. In recent years, evolving ethics and values in society and some new legal and philosophical concepts have begun to put a new spin on how informed-consent issues should be handled with minors. Legally speaking, the right of informed consent still belongs to parents or guardians of minors, especially when considering service delivery under specific systems and laws, such as the IDEA. In legal circles, however, the static nature of informed consent for children and adolescents has been increasingly challenged by a gradually evolving concept that is sometimes referred to as the *mature-minor* doctrine. The basis of this doctrine is that decisions regarding competence and consent should be made on the basis of cognitive capacity (and perhaps emotional maturity) and not age (Hesson, Bakal, & Dobson, 1993; Shields & Johnson, 1992). An adolescent who is intellectually advanced and possesses reasonable emotional maturity might be allowed in some circumstances to provide his or her own informed consent, even without prior parent notification. The most likely situations in which adolescents may give informed consent are when they voluntarily seek mental health treatment, which does not necessarily fall within the realm of IDEA and parental rights to informed consent. This concept is still evolving, however, and is certainly at odds with several sectors of society that are seeking to increase parental empowerment in decisions regarding their children. Until the mature-minor concept becomes widely recognized and better defined, practitioners should be cautious in thinking about using it, but should at least be aware of it and should attempt to stay abreast of informed-consent laws in their own state and with federal laws.

An additional evolving legal–ethical concept involving children and adolescents in mental health research and services is the *assent doctrine.* Simply stated, this concept embodies the idea that researchers and practitioners should, in addition to obtaining appropriate parental consent, allow the child or adolescent to have a voice in whether or not he or she will be involved as a research participant or as the recipient of professional services (Levine, 1995; Powell & Vacha-Haase, 1994; Range & Cotton, 1995). For example, if this concept were implemented fully, the child or adolescent for whom research or services are targeted would have the opportunity to agree to or decline such participation, whether or not he or she has been legally emancipated. This concept is complicated and potentially thorny. Although most persons probably would agree that a mature minor should be able to voluntarily decline or agree to participate in a research study, the point at which one is considered mature enough for self-determination is unclear. Additionally, there are serious potential problems involved when moving assent from the realm of research to the realm of service delivery. If a child or adolescent provides his or her assent for treatment, he or she will likely feel more empowered and positive about the process. But what about refusal of assent? Should a 14-year-old with severe mental health problems—who has been referred by his or her parents for assessment and possible diagnosis and treatment—be allowed to refuse the assessment? According to the NASP *Principles for Professional Ethics* (2010), school psychologists should make every effort to inform students of his/her treatment, but they may continue with service delivery without student assent if treatment is deemed to be beneficial or required by law. These are difficult but important issues. As the concept of assent continues to evolve, practitioners and researchers should strive to stay current with laws in their own state or province and stay aware of the current Zeitgeist involving this issue.

Given that many schools are beginning to embrace the idea of prevention and institute tiered systems of assessment and intervention, further questions regarding when it is necessary to obtain parent consent have surfaced. According to NASP's ethical principles (NASP, 2010), school psychologists do not need to obtain consent when they are conducting observations or consulting with a teacher or an instructional support team on a child's behavior, as long as proposed strategies and interventions fall within the purview of the classroom teacher's role. Furthermore, the principles state that as schools move toward using systematic, universal mental health screening to identify children at risk, it is important, and ethically sound, to ensure that parents are informed of the process and that they have the right to exclude their children from this process at any time. Again, this is an evolving concept in the field and staying current with ethical codes and laws is critical.

The Validity of Assessment Procedures Regarding the legal and ethical aspects of the validity of assessment procedures, there is substantial agreement and an overlap between the provisions of the IDEA and the ethical/conduct codes of APA and NASP. Some of the conditions stated in the public law and in the professional codes include:

1. Tests must be validated for the specific purposes for which they are being used.
2. Tests must have adequate technical (psychometric) properties.
3. Obsolete assessment results should not be used.
4. Assessment procedures must be administered only by persons with specific and adequate training.

Although there have been many criticisms of the technical aspects of many social–emotional assessment instruments (particularly those in the personality and projective–expressive technique realm) (Gregory, 2000; Salvia & Ysseldyke, 2004), in contrast to their counterpart instruments in the domain of cognitive assessment, there have been few legal complaints stemming from the use of inadequate measures in the social–emotional domain (DeMers, 1986). Education and mental health professions, and society at large, generally have been much less vocally critical of social–emotional assessment procedures compared with intellectual and academic achievement tests, despite the fact that the latter category of tests tends to be better researched and possess higher levels of reliability and validity. Whatever the reason for this relative lack of controversy, the potential for future litigation regarding social–emotional assessment procedures appears to be great, and practitioners and researchers are advised to stay current on changing laws and ethics codes regarding validity of assessment procedures.

The Right to Privacy/Confidentiality The third area involves the broad domain of what is most commonly referred to as the right to privacy, but also includes the concept of confidentiality. In this area, procedures and principles have been outlined not only by the IDEA, APA, and NASP standards, but also by FERPA, numerous state statutes, and court decisions related to the right to privacy inferred from, or carved out of, the 14th Amendment to the U.S. Constitution. Within the general area of right to privacy, some key components relating to assessment practices include:

1. Clients (and the parents of minor clients) are provided access to their records and assessment results.
2. Assessment results are not released to third parties without the express consent of the client (or parents of a minor client).
3. Communications between the professional and client are regarded as confidential unless the client has voluntarily waived his or her right to confidentiality or the information obtained in the professional relationship reveals a clear and imminent danger to the client or to other persons (the "duty to warn" principle). Additionally, each U.S. state and Canadian province has laws mandating that reasonable evidence or suspicions of child abuse be reported to the proper legal authority. Within the context of information obtained during a social–emotional assessment, such information would constitute an instance where confidentiality must be breached.

Given the various provisions and exceptions to the laws and ethical codes, clinicians must be careful about the way that promises of confidentiality are stated to their child and adolescent clients. It has been argued that mental health professionals have a primary obligation to respect the wishes expressed by a mature minor in relation to the provision of counseling services, including confidentiality. Given the uncertainties and evolving nature of the mature-minor doctrine, however, and given the legal status of children and adolescents, confidentiality of communication does not exist in a strict sense because parents have a right to be informed of what information is obtained in most situations (DeMers, 1986; Jacob et al., 2011), and there are certain legal exceptions to the rule. This statement is particularly true when service provision is under the blanket of specific federal and state laws that mandate parents' ultimate right to information. Clinicians should avoid making unrealistic promises to their child or adolescent clients that what they say will be kept in strict confidence and instead should help them understand the limits of confidentiality, giving them the power to participate in the process as fully informed as possible.

An additional area to consider regarding privacy and confidentiality is that there has been a long-standing concern among psychologists that using personality assessment instruments, and presumably other social–emotional measures, may result in unjustifiable encroachment of privacy rights (Jacob et al., 2011; Messick, 1965). Within this line of reasoning, the argument is that because they are designed to obtain highly private, personal information, some personality or social–emotional assessment methods may routinely violate privacy rights. This concern, although important, is difficult to define and articulate clearly and would obviously lead to difficult distinctions among various assessment instruments (i.e., which are justifiable and which are not). In practice, adhering to the three component areas outlined in this section and always acting to "do no harm" will reduce the likelihood of invading privacy rights within the context of assessing social and emotional behavior.

Some Concluding Comments on Legal and Ethical Issues

As was stated earlier, the type of assessment instruments that have most often been the targets of legal action are intellectual ability and academic achievement tests rather than social–emotional behavior measures. There is a peculiar irony to this imbalance of legal action. Tests of intellectual ability, as a whole, tend to have better psychometric properties and a more extensive research base than do most behavioral–emotional assessment instruments. When projective personality measures are included, the difference in psychometric quality becomes even more pronounced (Gregory, 2000; Salvia & Ysseldyke, 2004). A possible reason for behavioral–emotional or personality measures not being legally targeted as extensively as intellectual tests was articulated by DeMers (1986), who suggested that there is a limited legal basis for complaints against these types of measures. They have seldom been found to discriminate systematically against particular groups and are most often administered in the context of voluntary work by private citizens, rather than as an action of the state. Although the potential legal entanglements of social–emotional assessment remain high—particularly when assessing students for the purpose of determining if they qualify for special education services as "emotionally disturbed"—these measures are probably not likely to be targeted for action until their use is found systematically to bias opportunities for specific groups of people.

A final interesting point to think about in regard to legal and ethical issues is that they can and do change over time. The codes of ethical practice adopted by professional organizations tend to be influenced by changes in social thought, and statutory regulation at the state level tends to be influenced by changes in the ethical codes of professional organizations. An example of such changing social thought is the mature-minor and assent concepts discussed previously in this section, which for all practical purposes did not exist until only a few years ago. These concepts have begun to evolve as society has begun to consider seriously the notion of self-determination for children and adolescents. Another example of changing legal and ethical standards is that until the mid-1970s, both the American Psychiatric Association and the American Psychological Association officially viewed homosexuality as a form of mental illness. Today, neither organization views homosexuality in this manner, and there is considerable controversy regarding whether it is even ethical for therapists to work with clients who desire to change their sexual orientation (i.e., reparative therapy). This shift in direction over a 40-year period has mirrored changing social trends that have become more accepting of LGBTQ identities (Corey, Corey, & Callanan, 1997). A similar shift regarding social and organization attitudes toward individuals who are considered to have Gender Dysphoria (a current psychiatric diagnostic term) also appears to be a future possibility. In terms of social–emotional assessment practices, it is difficult to predict how legal and ethical constraints will change over time, but it is likely, if not given, that such changes will occur.

CRITERIA FOR INCLUSION OF ASSESSMENT METHODS AND INSTRUMENTS

Throughout this book, six general assessment methods are emphasized: direct behavioral observation, interviewing techniques, behavior rating scales, sociometric approaches, self-report procedures, and projective-assessment techniques (with a special emphasis on cautions and psychometric problems that are usually inherent in this method). With this fifth edition, I have incorporated a new chapter on school-wide screening efforts (Chapter 15). Given that there are many more specific procedures and instruments within each of the several general methods of interest than can be included in any book, the guidelines for including them within this text reflect the following principles:

1. Any procedure or instrument that is advocated or discussed at length must have met at least minimal standards for technical adequacy (i.e., must have sufficient research behind it showing psychometric properties and clinical utility).
2. Any procedure or instrument included must have a high degree of "usability" for the clinician. In other words, any techniques or tests requiring an extensive amount of specialized equipment or training to the point that it is overly burdensome for clinicians to use day-to-day were not included, regardless of the technical properties.
3. In the case of standardized, norm-referenced instruments (such as behavior rating scales and self-report tests) to be included in this text, these instruments must (1) include reasonably large and representative normative populations, and (2) be easily available (i.e., commercially published or easily accessible within the public domain). This third criterion is in addition to the first two being met.

In some cases, the number of possible instruments or techniques that meet the inclusion criteria are well in excess of the capacity for all to be included within one book. Some assessment methods, such as using norm-referenced behavior rating scales and self-report instruments, have experienced a proliferation of new and technically sound tools in recent years, making it virtually impossible to catalog fully and describe the various tools available within a book of this type. Instruments or specific approaches that are representative of each general domain were included as examples of what is available and are not held out as being the only tools available or the absolute best of what are available.

CONCLUSIONS

Assessment (or at least testing) may be conducted with minimal thought regarding a theoretical foundation for social and emotional behavior, but such practice is discouraged because it relegates the assessment professional to the role of a technician. Numerous theories regarding human behavior and personality have influenced psychology, education, and related fields, ranging from behaviorism to psychodynamic theory to humanistic theory. Social cognitive theory, stemming from the work of Bandura, is proposed as a foundation for much of this book and is briefly overviewed. Bronfenbrenner's ecological systems theory is also reviewed and promoted as a way of taking human environments into consideration when conducting assessments. Professionals are urged to integrate theory into their assessment practices, regardless of whether they adopt the orientation of this book or select a competing theory to guide their work.

Theoretical foundations of social and emotional assessment often have emphasized the differences between nomothetic and idiographic approaches to scientific inquiry. Applying these two approaches to the field of social and emotional assessment as a dichotomous and mutually exclusive paradigm ignores the philosophical and scientific bases of these terms, however, as well as the way that assessment is conducted in the real world. Empirically defensible and scientifically sound approaches to child assessment are emphasized throughout this book, without regard to their placement along the idiographic–nomothetic continuum.

Referrals for assessment of child and adolescent social–emotional behavior often occur because of a discrepancy between the child's or adolescent's current level of functioning and an optimal level of functioning desired by the referral source. Such discrepancies may be from standards desired by society in general, by community subgroups, or by specific families or teachers. These perspectives represent distinct spheres within the ecological systems model. It is crucial to recognize these perspectives of the referral source when proceeding with assessment referrals.

Although previous attempts have been made to integrate assessment into an overall process of problem solving, surprisingly little attention has been paid to this area. All too often, assessment practitioners tend to view assessment as a means *and* an end, rather than as one part of an overall process, and administrative practices in many school districts and mental health agencies tend to reinforce this limited view. A four-phase model of assessment as a problem-solving process is proposed. This model includes various practical questions within the phases of identification and clarification, data collection, analysis, and solution and evaluation.

A multimethod, multisource, multisetting model of assessment design is emphasized as best practice throughout this book. This type of assessment design is aimed to overcome error variance associated with specific types of assessment practices by building an aggregated assessment design to the greatest extent that is feasible. By including multiple methods of assessment and various sources of data, and by basing the assessment on more than one setting, the limitations of any one type of assessment may be overcome, and a broad-based picture of the social–emotional behavior of the referred child or adolescent is likely to be obtained.

Given that the percentage of children and youth who are considered to be at risk for developing behavioral and emotional problems continues to increase, while the availability of specialized educational and mental health services to support these youth has remained constant or shrunk, new ways of thinking about assessment and intervention services are needed. The public health approach and well-known triangle of support model is recommended as a way of planning for services for *all* children and adolescents within a given school or community population. Using such an approach will help to identify procedures and goals for screening and assessment, and will help link screening and assessment to appropriate intervention services at the primary, secondary, and tertiary levels of prevention.

There are numerous legal and ethical constraints on assessing children, based on specific statutes or administrative laws of individual states, federal laws affecting educational practice, certain provisions of the U.S. Constitution, and the ethics code of various professional organizations. Specifically the areas of informed consent, validity of assessment procedures, and right to privacy/confidentiality are involved with legal and ethical constraints when assessing social and emotional behavior of children and adolescents.

Legal and ethical constraints regarding assessment and related professional practices are constantly in a state of change, based on the changing values of society. Professionals are advised to keep current on changes that may affect their assessment practices.

REVIEW AND APPLICATION QUESTIONS

1. Compare and contrast social cognitive theory with any other prevailing theory of social–emotional behavior (e.g., behavioral, psychodynamic, humanistic). When it comes to using either theory as a foundation for conducting and reporting an assessment, what are the limitations and advantages of each?

2. After considering the limitations and advantages of a variety of theoretical orientations to social–emotional behavior, reflect upon your experiences with assessment thus far (e.g., textbook readings, lecture information, observing supervisors, direct assessment), consider the theory you find most compelling and most likely to apply to assessment, and argue your perspective regarding why this orientation is a valid approach to childhood assessment.

3. What are the three components of triadic reciprocity within social cognitive theory, and how do they affect each other?

4. What are some ways that assessing social and emotional behavior of children and adolescents can be done as part of a comprehensive process of problem solving?

5. Identify the three major components of informed consent. How might they need to be addressed before conducting a child or adolescent assessment?

6. With respect to the legal and ethical mandates for using assessment procedures that have adequate validity, what types of instruments or procedures commonly used for social–emotional assessment might be problematic?

7. Regarding confidentiality between the clinician and child or adolescent clients, what are some reasonable statements that could be made to help a child or adolescent understand the limits and ramifications of confidentiality when an assessment is being conducted?

8. Define the terms *nomothetic* and *idiographic* as they relate to scientific inquiry in general and social–emotional assessment of children and adolescents in particular.

9. For social–emotional assessment of children and adolescents, what are some potential components within a broad-based multimethod, multisource, multisetting assessment design?

10. A 14-year-old student who has been receiving special education services as "emotionally disturbed" since grade 2 enters the records office of the school and, in a highly emotional and agitated state, demands to see her permanent behavioral file. This file includes several psychological, social work, and psychiatric reports, all of which contain some sensitive information about the student and her family. What is an appropriate way to deal with this situation, maintaining a balance between what is legal and what is in the best interests of the student?

11. A 16-year-old boy is participating in a diagnostic interview with a psychologist in a community mental health center. He was referred to the center by his parents because of their concerns regarding serious depression. During the interview, the boy talks about being jealous and angry with a former girlfriend who broke up with him, and he seems almost obsessed with his anger toward her. At one point in the interview, he angrily states that "if she makes me look like a fool one more time, I'll kill her!" Based on ethical and legal best practices, what is an appropriate way to handle this situation?

2

SOCIAL–EMOTIONAL ASSESSMENT AND CULTURAL DIVERSITY

The topic of psychological and educational assessment and cultural diversity has received a great deal of professional and public attention. Some well-known court cases in the 1970s and 1980s, most notably *Larry P. v. Riles* and *Diana v. State Board of Education* (both in California) and *Guadalupe v. Tempe Elementary School District* (Arizona), placed the issue of cultural validity of standardized assessment instruments in the forefront of professional practice. These cases resulted in calls for change (and, in some cases, legal mandates for change) in special education assessment practices with racial/ethnic-minority youth. During the 1990s, a widespread flurry of professional and public attention accompanied Hernstein and Murray's (1994) book *The Bell Curve: Intelligence and Class Structure in American Life*, which addressed the issue of racial/ethnic differences and possible bias on IQ and achievement tests. These few examples, among many, provide some evidence that the issue of cultural diversity in assessment is complex and has become a serious concern. This concern has stimulated the field to take action in research and practice, as evidenced by numerous books and chapters on the topic (e.g., Castillo, Quintana, & Zamarripa, 2000a, 2000b; Dana, 2000a, 2000b, 2005; Hambleton & Kang Lee, 2013; Kohn, Scorcia, & Esquivel, 2012; Martines, 2008; Rhodes, Ochoa, & Ortiz, 2005; Suzuki, Ponterotto, & Meller, 2001).

Professional, public, and legal attention on this topic has been focused almost exclusively within the domain of cognitive assessment, as is stated in Chapter 1. By comparison, far less attention has been paid to the issue of cultural diversity and behavioral, social, and emotional assessment, and most of this attention has been on assessment with adults rather than children. For whatever reason, the assessment establishment and the public have accepted much of the reasoning on behavioral, social, and emotional assessment across cultures rather uncritically. This statement should not be inferred to mean that there are no critics of these practices. On the contrary, a handful of writers have decried the ongoing state of affairs regarding assessment and cultural diversity, including the social–emotional domain. About 25 years ago, Dana (1996), a scholar in the area of multicultural applications of psychological assessment, stated:

> With few exceptions the psychological tests used in the United States have been designed by Europeans or North Americans and embody a Eurocentric worldview and derivative psychometric technology. Comparisons among ranked individuals or groups expose human differences within a format of psychological judgment using Anglo American normative standards. Standard tests of intelligence, personality, and psychopathology are often assumed to be genuine *etics*, or culture-general in

DOI: 10.4324/9781315747521-3

application. In fact, most of these tests are culture-specific or *emic* measures designed for Anglo Americans, but have been construed as imposed etic measures, or pseudo etics, because the equivalence with different cultural groups has not been demonstrated.

(p. 477, italics added for emphasis)

More recently, Carjuzaa and Ruff (2010) reflected on the increased diversification of U.S. schools and urged educators to question the cultural responsiveness of their overall pedagogical practices, including assessment:

Recognition of the relevance of non-Western knowledge calls into question the tacit assumptions contained within Western standards. These assumptions need to be identified and questioned to facilitate culturally competent instructional assessment. Questioning academic practices is tantamount to acknowledging the lack of neutrality in academic rationality and from this recognition assessment standards can be renegotiated to facilitate cultural equity.

(p. 75)

These strong statements raise many concerns regarding assessment practices with children and youth of diverse cultural backgrounds. Statements such as these also raise many questions, such as:

- Should we assume that standardized norm-referenced tests that are based on representative normative samples that approximate the general U.S. population are not appropriate for use with individuals from racial/ethnic-minority groups?
- Is the use of local norms more appropriate than the use of national representative norms for the assessment of minority children and adolescents who live in areas where their own racial/ethnic group is the majority?
- Are standardized norm-referenced assessment procedures more or less biased than qualitative or unstructured assessment procedures, such as projective techniques and unstructured interviews, for members of racial/ethnic-minority groups?
- Are the assumptions regarding test bias that are based on intellectual and academic achievement measures appropriately inferred for measures of behavioral, social, and emotional functioning?

These are difficult questions, and as shown throughout this chapter, the answers are equally difficult. In many cases, the questions are equivocal or even impossible to answer fully given the relative paucity of empirical evidence in this area. Even the most ardent voices in the area of multicultural assessment acknowledge that the scientific basis of best practice in this area is lacking and that developing best practice is more art than science (Dana, 1998, 2005).

This chapter explores issues of cultural diversity within the framework of behavioral, social, and emotional assessment of children and adolescents. At present, this topic involves questions and issues that simply have not been addressed and answered sufficiently in most cases. This chapter raises awareness regarding some thorny assessment issues that may take several more years of empirical study to be addressed adequately. In comparison with the voluminous evidence and opinion that has accumulated regarding cultural diversity within the framework of intellectual/academic assessment, much less is known in this area regarding personality or behavior assessment (Dana, 1998, 2000a, 2000b, 2005; Hood & Johnson, 1997). Added to this problem is a widely held assumption that, in general, knowledge regarding assessment of children tends to lag behind in comparison with the empirical evidence regarding adult-focused assessment practices.

This chapter begins with a discussion of test and assessment bias in professional practice and the role that organizational standards play in shaping multicultural assessment practices. Next, some concepts related to acculturation, and racial and cultural identity development are presented, including theorized stages of identity development. With some cautions in place regarding potential problems that result from overemphasizing between-group differences (e.g., stereotyping and divisiveness between groups), some general demographic information, and psychosocial characteristics of the major racial and ethnic groups in the United States are presented. Special considerations for culturally responsive assessment of social–emotional behavior within each of the major assess-ment methods are reviewed, with an emphasis on the known problems and solutions regarding each method. The chapter ends with the presentation of 11 recommendations for culturally responsive assessment practice.

TEST AND ASSESSMENT BIAS IN PROFESSIONAL PRACTICE

This section focuses on some specific aspects of assessment theory and practice that are highly related to the area of cultural diversity, including theory of test and assessment bias, examination of current professional standards related to culturally appropriate assessment practices, and an overview of current practices and future directions in this area among professionals.

Test and Assessment Bias

The terms *test bias* and *assessment bias* have been used in various ways in the professional literature. Some discussions of these concepts refer to them in terms of inappropriate uses of assessment instruments, whereas other discussions couch definitions of bias in terms of the properties of the instrument or procedure. In reality, both situations may cause bias. Although there is no universal definition of test or assessment bias, we can consider a psychological or educational assessment instrument or procedure to be biased if it "differentiates between members of various groups on basis other than the characteristic being measured" (Brown, 1983, p. 224). In operational terms, such bias is said to exist if "its content, procedures or use result in a systematic advantage or disadvantage to members of certain groups over other groups and if the basis of this differentiation is irrelevant to the test purpose" (Brown, 1983, p. 224). Behavioral, social, or emotional assessment instruments or procedures would be considered biased if their use resulted in systematic and improper diagnosis, classification, or service provision for a specific group of children or adolescents (i.e., based on race or ethnicity).

Because most discussions of test or assessment bias are usually in relation to cognitive tests (i.e., IQ and academic achievement or aptitude tests), many of the traditional methods of showing that a test is acceptably unbiased may be problematic when assessment of social–emotional behavior is considered. There are some major differences between cognitive and social–emotional tests that make across-the-board methodological comparisons difficult. Virtually all cognitive tests have a correct or "right" answer, are scored in a dichotomous manner (yes/no, correct/incorrect), and result in distributions of scores that closely approximate a normal bell-shaped curve. Conversely, standardized instruments designed to assess social–emotional behavior almost never have a "right" answer and often are scored along a gradient, such as a 4-point scale. In contrast to cognitive tests, distributions of scores of social–emotional instruments are seldom (if ever) normal, but tend to be skewed toward a lack of symptoms or problems in the normal population.

Viewing assessment bias as a yes/no or all-or-nothing proposition is faulty reasoning. Because assessment bias may include the properties of an instrument and the manner in which it is used, it would be incorrect to state unequivocally that a specific assessment tool was absolutely free of any biasing characteristics. Even if the internal properties of an instrument, such as the items, score norms, and sub-scale structure, were shown to be equivalent for various racial and ethnic groups, the instrument still could be used in a manner that may be inappropriate for individuals with particular types of background characteristics. The goal for valid assessment of children's social–emotional behavior should be to implement it in a culturally appropriate manner and to reduce threats of assessment bias.

Professional Ethics and Culturally Appropriate Assessment

Since about the 1980s, there has been increased emphasis within the ethical codes and standards of professional organizations regarding cultural diversity, cultural differences, and cultural appropriateness of assessment materials and intervention techniques. These various ethical standards tend to serve as minimal guidelines. That is, they provide some general statements regarding expectations for appropriate professional practice, but they usually do not go beyond that level of specificity. The most influential professional organizations, that represent individuals who are involved with psychological and educational assessment, have shown an interest in advocating for culturally appropriate assessment practices but in most cases have not prescribed specific models or best practices.

The most recent revision of the *Ethical Principles of Psychologists and Code of Conduct* of the American Psychological Association (APA, 2017) is an extension of the prior revisions of the code (which took place in 1993, 2002, 2010), placing increased emphasis and importance on culturally sensitive practice. For example, in general *Principle D: Justice* and *Principle E: Respect for People's Rights and Dignity* include statements regarding valuing sensitivity to human diversity and cultural differences, and ensuring that biases do not negatively impact practice. Ethical Standard 2.01, *Boundaries of Competence*, establishes that psychologists are expected to become culturally competent:

> Where scientific or professional knowledge in the discipline of psychology establishes that an understanding of factors associated with age, gender, gender identity, race, ethnicity, culture, national origin, religion, sexual orientation, disability, language, or socioeconomic status is essential for effective implementation of their services or research, psychologists have or obtain the training, experience,

consultation, or supervision necessary to ensure the competence of their services, or they make appropriate referrals.

In addition, Standard 9.06, *Interpreting Assessment Results,* focuses on taking into account cultural and linguistic factors when interpreting assessment data:

> When interpreting assessment results, including automated interpretations, psychologists take into account the purpose of the assessment as well as the various test factors, test-taking abilities, and other characteristics of the person being assessed, such as situational, personal, linguistic, and cultural differences, that might affect psychologists' judgments or reduce the accuracy of their interpretations. They indicate any significant limitations of their interpretations.

The National Association of School Psychologists' (NASP) *Principles for Professional Ethics* were most recently approved in 2020. This document includes several global guidelines and specific standards related to culturally appropriate assessment practice. For example, *Principle 1.3*, related to *Fairness, Equity, and Justice*, states:

> In their words and actions, school psychologists promote fairness and social justice. They use their expertise to cultivate school climates that are safe, equitable, and welcoming to all persons regardless of actual or perceived characteristics including race, ethnicity, color, religion, ancestry, national origin, immigration status, socioeconomic status, primary language, gender, sexual orientation, gender identity, gender expression, disability, or any other distinguishing characteristics.
>
> (NASP, 2020, p. 44)

A final example, in regards to *Responsible Assessment and Intervention Practices,*

> *Standard II.3.8*: School psychologists conduct valid and fair assessments. They actively pursue knowledge of the student's disabilities and developmental, cultural, linguistic, and experiential background and then select, administer, and interpret assessment instruments and procedures in light of those characteristics.
>
> (NASP, 2020, p. 47)

The jointly produced *Standards for Educational and Psychological Testing,* a combined effort in 2014 of the American Educational Research Association (AERA), American Psychological Association (APA), and National Council on Measurement in Education (NCME), is a highly influential document among educational and psychological testing experts. Similar to the ethical codes of APA and NASP, the Standards include specific statements regarding culturally appropriate methods of administering and interpreting standardized assessment instruments. In contrast to the two ethical codes, the Standards also include specific details regarding instrument development, and many of these are specific to cultural diversity. Section 3 of the Standards includes four clusters that organize specific Standards 3.1 through 3.20, titled *Fairness in Testing*, and deals specifically with varying views on fairness in assessment bias, and fairness in selection and prediction. These clusters include:

1. Test Design, Development, Administration, and Scoring Procedures That Minimize Barriers to Valid Score Interpretations for the Widest Possible Range of Individuals and Relevant Subgroups.
2. Validity of Test Score Interpretations for Intended Uses for the Intended Examinee Population.
3. Accommodations to Remove Construct-Irrelevant Barriers and Support Valid Interpretations of Scores for Their Intended Uses.
4. Safeguards Against Inappropriate Score Interpretations for Intended Uses.
   (Standards for Educational and Psychological Testing, p. 63)

One example of the Standards that is most relevant for the topic of assessment and cultural diversity includes:

> When credible evidence indicates that test scores may differ in meaning for relevant subgroups in the intended examinee population, test developers and/or users are responsible for examining the evidence for validity of score interpretations for intended uses for individuals from those subgroups. What constitutes a significant difference in subgroup scores and what actions are taken in response to such differences may be defined by applicable laws.
> (Standard 3.6, p. 65)

Regarding Standard 3.6, it is important to consider that significant group-based differences in test scores are not the problem here. It is bias, or differences in group scores that are not meaningfully related to the test construct, that should be eliminated. Consider that with social–emotional assessment instruments, some forms of group differences are expected and contribute to the validity of the assessment tool. For example, given that the research literature is clear regarding gender differences in attention deficit hyperactivity disorder (ADHD) (with boys outnumbering girls by a ratio from 3:1 to 9:1), elimination of all items that show evidence of significant gender differences would render the test useless. Likewise, there are many other psychological and educational constructs in which there might be expected differences based on actual differences in functioning related to gender, culture, or race/ethnicity.

Another sample standard that pertains to fairness in testing, particularly as it applies to sharing data about diverse subgroups is Standard 3.17.

> When aggregate scores are publicly reported for relevant subgroups—for example, males and females, individuals of differing socioeconomic status, individuals differing by race/ethnicity, individuals with different sexual orientations, individuals with diverse linguistic and cultural backgrounds, individuals with disabilities, young children or older adults—test users are responsible for providing evidence of comparability and for including cautionary statements whenever credible

research or theory indicates that test scores may not have comparable meaning across subgroups.

(Standard 3.17, p. 71)

This standard is becoming more relevant in the social–emotional and behavioral assessment domain, as school professionals are being asked to screen large samples of students for risk, and share results of screening efforts "publicly" with other professionals and families as a part of a school-wide effort to identify risk for problems early. Further, many schools are beginning to use these types of data to examine how their practices may reflect explicit or implicit bias against particular groups of individuals. For example, in many schools I currently work with, teachers are being asked to rate the social–emotional behaviors of all students in their classes, using a brief screening method. These data are then analyzed and often aggregated in different ways (i.e., by subgroup) to best understand how teachers perceive student behavior and to identify relevant intervention targets.

In sum, various professional organizations and associations, that have interests in psychological and educational assessment, have made cultural aspects of assessment specific targets of their standards to varying degrees of specificity. Additionally, over the years, these documents have shifted to expand definitions of "diversity" to be more inclusive of the multiple ways in which individuals are diverse (e.g., gender, learning differences) rather than focus on cultural and linguistic diversity exclusively. Although some of the changes that have been evidenced in the various revisions of these codes in recent years have focused attention on cultural-sensitivity issues, some writers (e.g., Dana, 1994, 2005) have argued that the changes have not gone far enough and that the standards still avoid areas that remain controversial. In reality, these guidelines provide only a framework for professionals and do not detail highly specific suggestions for professional practice. It is anticipated that future revisions to these and similar standards will continue to include an increased focus on all forms of diversity, including applications in assessment.

Professional Practice

According to Dana (1995, 2005), there are three major deficiencies in standard psychological assessment practice that result in culturally inappropriate assessment. These deficiencies include test construction, test administration, and interpretation. In Dana's view, test construction may lead to cultural bias because the development of traditional assessment instruments has been based on a psychometric paradigm that may result in culture-specific tests that are appropriate only for individuals within a European American cultural context. Essentially, these types of development practices may create a "one size fits all" assessment instrument that simply is not appropriate for many individuals. In addition, traditional methods of standardized test administration tend to be impersonal and may cause individuals, who are not comfortable with the examiner or situation, to respond in ways that do not reflect their true characteristics. Traditional methods of test interpretation that are rigid and based on culturocentric views of human behavior may result in "overpathologization" of individuals who are not part of the dominant culture or, in other words, characterize them as being "more disturbed than in fact they are" (Dana, 1995, p. 63). It is obvious that to the extent these problems may exist, they violate the spirit and letter of the various professional standards that have been established regarding culturally appropriate assessment. It also is clear that although change in this area has been slow to emerge, it will continue, perhaps with increased speed.

The future of culturally appropriate assessment, according to Dana, will be development, administration, and interpretation procedures that expand the concept of individual differences to include gender and culture, and require increased competence of assessment professionals. "Multicultural assessment adheres to an ethical mandate for moving beyond cultural sensitivity toward cultural competence" (2005, p. 7). He maintains that this future will be in the direction of social constructivism, or constructing specific methods of assessment and interpretation that are flexible and appropriate within a given context for a given individual and where meaning or interpretation is derived in an individualized and unique context. The relationship between examiner and subject will take on a new importance in such an assessment model. Although from an objective or empirical perspective, it is highly arguable that social constructivist approaches will solve the challenges related to assessment across cultural groups, this notion is interesting. However, Dana's position does not reduce the responsibility of assessment professionals to become well trained in psychometric procedures, as he contends that "multicultural assessment is dependent to an even greater extent than standard assessment on adequate psychometric knowledge for selection of relevant tests and methods" (2005, p. 9).

Some fairly recent models for conceptualizing and implementing assessment in a culturally appropriate manner consistent with Dana's recommendations have been articulated. One example is *responsive assessment* (Henning-Stout, 1994; Kea, Campbell-Whatley, & Bratton, 2003; Lezak, 2002; Sullivan, 2010). Responsive assessment is perhaps best characterized as a way of implementing assessment rather than a type of assessment. The traditional mystique surrounding formal psychological testing and the authority position of the professional conducting the assessment are supplanted by a broader view of assessment as a process. In this process, the examiner works with the client and other individuals who have an interest in the outcome of the assessment (i.e., parents, teachers) to design and implement an assessment that is authentic, culturally acceptable, and appropriately focused on the issues of concern. The participants in this process are referred to as stakeholders, reflecting the more egalitarian nature of the relationships of those involved and emphasizing accountability of the examiner. It is certain that other models for implementing psychological and educational assessment in a culturally appropriate manner will continue to emerge during the next decade and that the sociocultural aspects of assessment will play a role of increasing importance.

ACCULTURATION AND IDENTITY DEVELOPMENT

When dealing with the issue of cultural diversity and educational/mental health service delivery, it is crucial to understand that among individuals of all racial and ethnic-minority groups, there is a wide variation in terms of their orientation toward the traditional characteristics of their racial/ethnic group, assimilation into the majority or dominant culture, and their own racial/ethnic identity. Acculturation is defined as "the process of cultural change that occurs in individuals when their own culture and another culture meet; it leads individuals to adopt elements of another culture, such as values and social behaviors" (Sattler, 2008, p. 138). Furthermore, Rhodes et al. (2005) discussed this construct with respect to how standardized assessment measures are developed, stating:

Acquisition of the cultural content of the dominant society is known as acculturation. The process of acquiring culture (i.e., acculturation) is developmentally invariant, predictable, and easily measured. As with other developmental patterns, the simpler, commoner elements of culture are learned first, and the more complex elements are learned later. Standardized tests are based directly on this principle, known as the "assumption of comparability.

(p. 155)

When an individual who is a member of a minority group begins to examine and understand the differences between their group and the majority group, the process of acculturation is inevitable to some extent. The outcome of this process varies widely, however. The actual process of acculturation may include what Sattler (2008) terms as traditionalism, transitional period, marginality, assimilation, and biculturalism. Although acculturation is most often associated with racial and ethnic group identity, it is not limited to this domain. For example, individuals who are members of an obscure religious group that is viewed with disdain by the dominant secular culture because of their separateness and unique practices may go through a similar process, as may individuals who identify as transgender or those who do not have a heterosexual orientation. According to Dana (2005), one of the aspects of acculturation that is often ignored is cultural differences in belief systems, which may include an overall worldview, as well as specific beliefs regarding mind–body relationships, values, spirituality/religion, health and illness, locus of control and responsibility, and notions of individualism versus collectivism.

Factors That Influence Acculturation
In 1985, Kumabe, Nishida, and Hepworth identified several factors that may influence whether individuals from racial and ethnic-minority groups maintain or depart from the traditional cultural practices of their group or allow these traditional practices to coexist with new practices adopted from the majority group. The six primary factors within this model include:

- history of migration experience (i.e., whether it was freely chosen or coerced);
- distance (physical and psychological) from the country of origin and indigenous culture;
- place of residence and socioeconomic status;
- type of neighborhood in the resettlement country (i.e., whether there are others close by who share the same racial/ethnic ties);
- closeness of ties with immediate and extended family; and
- uniqueness of language and customs from the homeland.

Since the time of this Kumabe et al.'s (1985) publication, many other researchers and scholars have taken interest in the topic of acculturation and have identified other key variables that play a role in one's experience. For example, Tartakovsky (2012) noted that an individual's perceived control over life matters could affect acculturation. For example, individuals with an ability to master a new language, with social support, with financial support, and limited experiences with discrimination may be able to acculturate easier than those without these supports. Further, individuals' plans for returning to their home after a period in another country may reduce the levels acculturation.

Whether an individual from a racial/ethnic-minority group maintains strong cultural ties to that group may depend on several important variables, and clinicians cannot presume to understand the degree of acculturation or cultural assimilation without first attempting to investigate it.

Determining Acculturation and Cultural Orientation

In conducting psychoeducational assessments with children, youth, and their families, there may be times when it is essential to determine, as accurately as possible, their level of acculturation and cultural orientation. In some cases, such information may have a direct bearing on how valid the assessment results may be considered. In other cases, acculturation information will be essential for translating assessment data into culturally appropriate intervention plans. There is no universal method of determining acculturation or cultural orientation. Dana (2005) has reviewed several instruments or research tools that have been developed for determining acculturation or cultural orientation of individuals from specific racial/ethnic-minority groups. These instruments often provide information on the traditional culture and the level of acquisition of values of the dominant society. Most tools focus on a particular target group and address behavioral outcomes of respondents, rather than psychological outcomes (Celenk & Van de Vijver, 2011). These tools have been developed primarily for use with adults and older adolescents, however. In most cases, it is unclear how effectively they might be used with children and adolescents, although it is reasonable to assume that they at least could be adapted to provide a general framework.

In the absence of common child-oriented standardized tools for determining acculturation and cultural orientation of youths from various racial/ethnic-minority groups, there are other practices that should be considered. Simple information gathering before the assessment is one possibility. The examiner could review existing records carefully and consult with teachers, parents, and other referral sources regarding such issues as language proficiency and preference, typical social behavior, involvement and participation in customs of the traditional culture, and apparent comfort with adults from other racial/ethnic groups. Another possibility is to attempt to ascertain this information directly from the child or adolescent client during the process of assessment. Admittedly, this latter possibility is difficult in some cases. A racial/ethnic-minority youth who is primarily oriented toward his or her traditional culture may not be comfortable with an examiner who is a member of the majority group, and in the absence of a strong relationship of trust that has been formed between the professional and the client, the obtained data are clearly suspect (Dana, 2008). Special care and perhaps extra time should be devoted to the process of building trust, forming rapport, and generally establishing familiarity between the persons who are of strongly differing cultural backgrounds if useful assessment data are to be gathered. Readers are referred to the previous references by Dana for more information regarding the process of determining acculturation and obtaining valid assessment data with diverse groups of clients.

Development of Racial and Cultural Identity

As has been stated previously in this section, an individual's level of acculturation in his or her traditional culture is likely to depend on many factors, and the general level of acculturation is likely to have an important bearing on how effective traditional methods

Table 2.1 Stages of minority racial and cultural development

Stage	Characteristics
1. Conformity	Depreciating attitude toward self and others of same minority group; discriminatory attitude toward other minority groups; appreciating attitude toward dominant group
2. Dissonance	Conflict between depreciating and appreciating attitudes toward self, others of same minority group, other minority groups, and dominant group
3. Resistance/ immersion	Appreciating attitude toward self and others of same minority group; conflict between empathetic and culturocentric feelings toward other minority groups; depreciating attitude toward dominant group
4. Introspection	Concern with basis of self-appreciation and unequivocal nature of appreciation toward others of same minority group; concern with culturocentric views toward members of other minority groups; concern with basis of depreciation of dominant group
5. Integrative awareness	Appreciating attitude toward self, others of same minority group, and other minority groups; selective appreciation for dominant group

Source: Based on previous work by Atkinson, Morten, & Sue (1989), and Sue & Sue (1990, 1999, 2008).

of assessment will be with the individual. Related to these concepts is the idea of racial or cultural identity development.

In this sense, identity is defined as a sense of belonging to one's racial and ethnic group and how this sense of belonging influences behavior, thought, and affect. Sue and Sue (1990, 1999, 2008) have articulated the emerging evidence and thought regarding racial and cultural identity development among minority group members. Based on a wide variety of research and writing in this area, a general consensus has emerged that such identity development tends to follow a distinct set of stages. These include conformity (Stage 1), dissonance and appreciating (Stage 2), resistance and immersion (Stage 3), introspection (Stage 4), and integrative awareness (Stage 5). These stages are discussed briefly in this section and presented in summary form in Table 2.1.

Stage 1: Conformity During Stage 1, individuals accept and value the characteristics of the dominant culture as being the norm and prefer these values over the traditional values espoused by their own group. Individuals at this stage of development take on a self-depreciating attitude, often viewing their own group with disdain. According to Sue and Sue (2008), the conformity stage "represents, perhaps, the most damning indictment of White racism" (p. 244). Individuals at this stage may be immersed in self-hatred, suffer from low self-esteem, and uncritically adopt the values and views of the dominant culture.

Stage 2: Dissonance and Appreciating During Stage 2, an individual begins to feel discomfort or dissonance regarding some of the beliefs he or she has adopted. For example, "A Latino individual who may feel ashamed of his cultural upbringing may encounter another Latino who seems proud of his/her cultural heritage" (Sue & Sue, 2008, p. 246). This tends to be a gradual process. Conflict begins to emerge between self-depreciation and group depreciation and appreciation. The individual also may begin to have doubts regarding his or her uncritical valuation and acceptance of the dominant culture.

Stage 3: Resistance and Immersion In Stage 3, the individual rejects the values and views of the dominant culture and begins to immerse him or herself in the minority views of his or her own culture. At this point, the attitude toward the majority group becomes negative and depreciating, whereas attitudes toward those of other minority groups begin to become conflicted between feelings of culturocentrism and shared empathy for their differing minority experience. According to Sue and Sue (2008), the three most common feelings that characterize this stage are guilt, shame, and anger. The anger may be directed outwardly with great force to combat racism and oppression.

Stage 4: Introspection As an individual moves into Stage 4, he or she may begin to question the basis and nature of their unequivocal appreciation and acceptance of his or her own group values and the basis for the unanimous rejection of the majority group. Attitudes toward other minorities may reflect concern with ethnocentrism as a basis for forming judgments. As Sue and Sue (2008) stated, "The resistance and immersion stage tends to be a reaction against the dominant culture and is not proactive in allowing the individual to use all energies to discover who or what he or she is" (p. 250). The need for more realistic self-definition and discovery emerges.

Stage 5: Integrative Awareness Individuals who move into Stage 5 have resolved many of their previous conflicts. They now have adopted an attitude that focuses on self-appreciation, group appreciation, appreciation of other minority groups, and selective appreciation of the dominant culture. Their own culture no longer is viewed as being in conflict with the dominant culture. Summed up by Sue and Sue (2008):

> There is now the belief that there are acceptable and unacceptable aspects in all cultures, and that it is very important for the person to be able to examine and accept or reject those aspects of a culture that are not seen as desirable.
>
> (p. 251)

This stage theory of racial and cultural identity, as discussed by Sue and Sue (2008) and others (e.g., Atkinson, Morten, & Sue, 1989), has highly relevant implications for working with children and adolescents. First, like most social–emotional stage theories of development, not all individuals progress neatly through the various stages, and some individuals never proceed past a given stage. Second, it seems to be linked to some extent to cognitive and social–emotional development. It would be highly unlikely or impossible for children or adolescents to have moved through all of the stages because of their limited life experiences and their developing capabilities. Individuals from majority or dominant cultures also may develop racial and cultural attitudes through a similar process, although the characteristics of each stage differ from those presented herein. Essentially, a person in this situation who moves through these stages of identity development progresses from a highly ethnocentric worldview to the development of a nonracist identity. An example of a poignant personal account of how an individual may move through the various stages of racial and cultural identity development is found in *The Autobiography of Malcolm X* (A. Haley, 1996), which vividly tells the story of how a historically prominent African American man moved from an attitude of self-hatred to militant anger to eventual acceptance of the limitations of his previous views shortly before his untimely death.

PROBLEMS WITH CATEGORIES AND GROUP EMPHASIS

One of the major issues in regard to understanding appropriate assessment practices for individuals from specific cultural backgrounds (i.e., similar race/ethnicity) is the development and use of appropriate language and schemas (categories) to describe groups of people. Regarding race and ethnicity, there is no single definition of these terms that is generally agreed on, and it is common for researchers and practitioners to refer to ethnicity, culture, and race in an interchangeable manner when identifying and categorizing individuals by these background characteristics (Watt & Norton, 2004). The term *race* usually is used to imply some observable physical characteristic that is common to a group, such as skin and eye color, hair type, and facial features. *Ethnicity* is the term commonly used to describe characteristics that may be less externally observable, such as a common group cultural history, language, country of origin, or religion.

The terms *race* and *ethnicity* have been under fire in recent years, as has the practice of emphasizing separateness of uniqueness or individuals from specific groups. There are times when these terms and practices can be politically charged. For example, regional allotment of federal government funds is affected by changes in racial category distribution, and district realignment for voting purposes may be affected (Okazaki & Sue, 1995). Many Americans do not fit neatly into simple categories, making categorical models problematic. For example, monoracial categorization excludes biracial and multi-racial groups (Robinson-Wood, 2016). During preliminary planning for the national census for 2000, the U.S. Bureau of the Census briefly considered the possibility of creating a new multiracial category to add to the existing traditional categories, an idea that created tremendous controversy (Eddings, 1997) and that ultimately was rejected (although it later was determined that individuals could check more than one racial category to describe themselves and that the category of "Asian or Pacific Islander" would be separated into two distinct categories). For the 2010 U.S. Census, the Census Bureau also included the category of "Some Other Race" for those who did not identify with any of the listed categories.

In this chapter, the terms *race* and *ethnicity* are used to describe our major focus on cultural diversity. These terms, like all the other categories and labels used to describe groups of people, is imperfect and potentially problematic. For example, take the case of two American children, one who traces his ancestry to Vietnam (his family emigrated to the United States in the 1980s) and the other who traces her ancestry to China (her ancestors emigrated to the United States in the late 1800s). The U.S. Bureau of the Census currently would classify both of these children as "Asian," and a professional research study in which they participated might refer to them in the written report both as Asian American participants. The cultural characteristics they share in common may be truly minimal, however, and in some respects, they might each share more background characteristics with individuals from other groups than with each other.

A related problem in this area is that emphasizing specific group membership tends to place a strong emphasis on differences among persons from various racial and ethnic groups and may in some cases unduly overemphasize such differences. There is an understandable rationale for the practice of describing or trying to understand individuals based on their racial and ethnic background characteristics because this practice is based on the assumption that "such shared cultural-psychological characteristics are related to personality or psychopathology" (Okazaki & Sue, 1995, p. 368). It is easy for this type of grouping emphasis ultimately to distort a simple truth regarding human behavior. With few exceptions, variation within groups is always greater than variation between groups. Let us assume that a norm-referenced self-report test of personality and behavior problems for adolescents, when scrutinized statistically, shows evidence that racial and ethnic Group X tends to have higher scores than racial and ethnic Group Y on a subscale measuring emotional distress. Let us also assume that these differences are small but still significantly different from a statistical standpoint. A focus on the score differences between the two groups might lead to the assumption that members of Group X tend to be in continual emotional turmoil and that perhaps this is a defining characteristic of Group X. Conversely, a critic of norm-referenced testing might argue that the self-report instrument is not appropriate for (or even biased against) members of Group X. Both of these assumptions could mask the truth of the matter: that there is substantially more variation in self-reported emotional distress among persons within each group than there is between the two groups. This issue has been analyzed from a legal context by Richard Thompson Ford, an African American law professor at Stanford University, whose book *Racial Culture: A Critique* (2005) makes an argument against the common presumption that social categories such as race, ethnicity, gender, and sexuality are defined by distinctive cultural practices. Ford argues against law reform proposals that would attempt to apply civil rights protections to "cultural difference," and focuses on the adverse effects of multicultural rhetoric and multicultural rights on individuals who are supposed to benefit from them. Such practices, Ford argues, result in a "difference discourse" that forces minority groups to accept the very stereotypes they may be trying to oppose. In sum, it seems that although emphasis on, and sensitivity to, differences in racial and ethnic groups is necessary and important, too much emphasis may result in distortion of fairly small differences among groups and ultimately lead to stereotyping based on group membership (Sue & Sue, 2008).

CULTURAL DIVERSITY IN THE UNITED STATES: DESCRIPTION OF MAJOR RACIAL AND ETHNIC GROUPS

With the cautions in place regarding the impact of acculturation and moderator variables on racial and ethnic identity, and the potential problems and controversies regarding emphasis on shared group identity and characteristics, this section provides some basic information regarding the major racial and ethnic groups in the United States as they typically are defined. This information includes a focus on population characteristics, including specific issues that may be highly relevant to behavioral, social, and emotional assessment of children and youth.

When considering this information, it is important to recognize that the population distribution statistics for children differ from the statistics for adults or the general population. For example, the 2020 U.S. Census reported that for the general U.S. population, approximately 61% were White, and the remaining 38% were members of racial-minority groups (12.4% Black or African American, 6% Asian, 1.1% American Indian/Alaska Native, 0.2% Native Hawaiian/Pacific Islander, 8.4% Some Other Race alone, and Multi-Racial 10.2%). 18.7% identified as being from Hispanic or Latino origin. When individuals younger than age 18 are considered, however, it is clear that there is a larger percentage of individuals who are members of racial and ethnic groups that are historically thought of as minorities. The population estimates by age group and race indicate that 49.9% of children and adolescents younger than age 15 are non-Hispanic White (Frey, 2019). These estimates also indicate that the child and adolescent population in the United States is more racially and ethnically diverse than the adult population, reflecting such factors as a younger mean age for several racial and ethnic groups and higher birth rates and age-related immigration patterns in some instances.

Another fact to consider in the interpretation of basic information presented on ethnic groups is that the U.S. demographic makeup is changing rapidly. Population estimates for the near future predict increasing ethnic diversity and a gradual but continuous diminishment of the percentage of Americans who are in the current racial and ethnic-majority group White/non-Hispanic. Although the most recent population estimates show that about 61% of all Americans are in the White/non-Hispanic group, this percentage is expected to shrink to a slight majority (barely over half) by the year 2050 (Rosenblatt, 1996). Embedded in this estimate is the projection that Hispanics, who recently became the largest ethnic minority group in the United States, will compose nearly one fourth of the entire U.S. population by the year 2050. It is important to consider the dynamic nature of the American population. In every region of the nation, the population will reflect increasing racial and ethnic diversity in the next few decades. In border states such as California, Arizona, Texas, and Florida, these changes have already made a dramatic impact in education and youth services, and such changes are rapidly spreading to other states.

A final note before discussing each specific racial and ethnic group. First, this is a limited overview that necessarily focuses on only a few key characteristics and at the same time ignores other important characteristics. Readers desiring a more in-depth description of specific racial or ethnic group characteristics should refer to other sources. Second, although it has been stated explicitly and implied previously in this chapter, it is worth repeating: Psychological characteristics associated with specific groups are generalities based on group research. They do not apply to all members, or even most members, of particular groups.

African Americans

African Americans (or Blacks, as the U.S. Census Bureau describes this category) include individuals in the United States who trace their ancestry to the continent of Africa, specifically to native African groups of dark skin color (e.g., as opposed to White South Africans, who trace their African ancestry to European colonists). The 2020 U.S. Census reported that about 13% of the general population was African American, which was the largest racial minority group. Most African Americans live in the District of Columbia (41.4%), followed by Mississippi (36.%) and Louisiana (31.4%) (U.S. Bureau of the Census, 2021).

Although African Americans may include recent immigrants from the African continent who have left their native nations by choice for various personal, political, or economic reasons (or the descendants of individuals who did likewise), this situation is not the most typical. By far, this category includes most individuals whose ancestors were removed from their African homelands through coercive and violent means, primarily by Europeans, through what has been referred to as the *African Diaspora*: the slave trade that flourished in the colonies and states (and other parts of the Western hemisphere) from the 1600s through the mid-1800s. The collective identity and experience of most African Americans is intertwined with the most divisive issue in the nation's history, which was arguably the major factor in the bloody Civil War in the 1860s. For many Americans, the continuing problem of race relations is primarily viewed as a White/Black issue, owing to the tremendous and continuing ramifications from our nation's past, including the history of institutionalized racism.

Some of the major behavioral, social, and emotional considerations regarding African American youth has been discussed by Robinson-Wood (2016). One important characteristic is the emphasis and prestige placed on strong verbal and language skills, especially assertive and emotionally expressive communication. Many Black children and adolescents (particularly those who live in urban poverty areas) may speak a variation of standard English that has been referred to as Black English or Ebonics, which may be used to varying degrees and in various situations, depending on the acculturation of the individual and their connection to the majority culture. Some basic examples of Black English include the use of "do" instead of the standard English use of "does"; omitting "is" and "are" from sentences; and reversing the /s/ and /k/ sounds that appear in that order in Standard English usage, such as pronouncing the word *ask* as "aks." Although the uninitiated interviewer from another culture may mistakenly view the use of Black English as an indication of poor language development, in reality, it is a complex linguistic system that has its roots in the oral language traditions of West African languages. In terms of affect, "black [youth] typically are described as expressive, lively, and extroverted" (Sattler, 1998, p. 283). African American youth have been shown to have similar levels of positive self-concept as White youth but may value such attributes as verbal skills, assertion, and athletic ability at a higher level. Regarding family life, African American families are more likely than White families to be headed by a woman, but typical family structures are likely to be similar among the groups. Many Black youth, particularly those who live in urban poverty centers, may feel alienated from the educational system and believe that it is futile for them to try to succeed in it, particularly since these youth are twice as likely than White youth to experience suspension, expulsion, and corporal punishment in school settings (Murray & Zvoch, 2011). Interpersonally, Black adolescents are known for often forming close associations with same-sex peers. Such close associations may provide a stronger sense of social identity, but also can result in pressure to participate in antisocial activities (i.e., through gang membership) in areas where such groups are common. Although the history of institutionalized racism, cultural appropriation, and lack of opportunities many African Americans have experienced has produced a strong resiliency in some, it has resulted in numerous problems for many African American adolescents, including pressure for participation in gang activities; feelings of rage, futility, and hopelessness; and, particularly among Black adolescent boys, heightened probabilities for death through homicide, and a dramatic overrepresentation in the criminal justice system.

Given some of these unique characteristics and significant challenges common to many African American adolescents, it is crucial to note the faulty thinking that may result from placing too much emphasis on between-group differences and within-group commonality. Although it is important to note the unique characteristics, shared history, and specific challenges faced by many African Americans, it also is important to recognize that there is a growing percentage of African Americans who are middle class, who are highly educated, and who face a different set of circumstances. Pattillo-McCoy (1999a, 1999b, 2000), a sociologist who has researched the topic of the growing middle class in the Black community, has noted that this group is often ignored or overlooked in favor of focusing on stereotypes. She has shown that the research on African Americans is dominated by the study of concentrated urban poverty, even though most African Americans are not poor, even fewer live in extremely poor neighborhoods, and there is a rising percentage of upwardly mobile individuals and families. In addition, in writings such as her critically acclaimed book *Black Picket Fences* (1999a), she argued that a monolithic focus on African Americans is counterproductive. Assessment professionals who work with African American children and adolescents, regardless of their own racial and ethnic background, should take into consideration the within-group diversity among African Americans and understand that Black youth from middle class and highly educated families may have their own unique strengths and challenges.

Asian Americans

Asian Americans comprise a rapidly growing racial and ethnic-minority population in the United States. In the 1990 census, 3.0% of the U.S. population was listed as Asian, and that percentage grew to 3.8% in the 2000 Census. The 2010 Census data indicate that the Asian population was the fastest growing racial minority in the last ten years (U.S. Census Bureau, 2011a), and the 2020 Census indicates that this population has grown to 6%. The absolute numbers and relative percentages of Asian Americans are expected to grow during the next several decades, and this group is expected to comprise 10.7% of the general U.S. population by the year 2050 (Aponte & Crouch, 1995), primarily because of continual immigration to the United States from Asian and Pacific Rim nations. The largest concentrations of Asian Americans are in the West and Pacific Northwest regions of the United States.

Asian Americans constitute an extremely diverse group. Most individuals within this general category trace their ancestral heritage to such varied places as China, Japan, Korea, the Philippines, and several Southeast Asian nations, such as Laos, Cambodia, and Vietnam. Sue and Sue (2008) noted that there are at least 40 distinct subgroups of Asian Americans, each with differing languages, customs, religions, levels of acculturation, and historical reasons for immigration to the United States. Some of these subgroups are recent arrivals to the United States, whereas others have been in the nation for several generations. Many Asian Americans are faced with special challenges, such as English-language competency issues. There is a bimodal distribution of wealth among Asian Americans, with some having achieved great economic success and a large proportion (primarily those of recent Southeast Asian descent) living below the economic poverty level (Sue & Sue, 2008). This notion is attested to by the fact that in the 1990 census, Asian Americans had the highest median family income of any racial and ethnic group, including Whites, but had a higher percentage of families and individuals living at or below the poverty level than Whites. As a group, Asian Americans tend to do well on standardized educational achievement tests, particularly in mathematics and the physical sciences, and they tend to be proportionately overrepresented at prestigious institutions of higher education, such as the University of California at Berkeley and the Massachusetts Institute of Technology. High-profile indicators such as these mask the fact that there is also a substantial percentage of Asian Americans who do not enjoy such notable educational success, because of poverty, discrimination, and significant language barriers (Sue & Sue, 2008).

Although Asian Americans constitute a truly diverse group, there are certain psychosocial characteristics that tend to be associated with the larger group, perhaps because of some common experiences and the heritage of an "Eastern" worldview. One notable characteristic among Asian Americans is respect for the customs and traditions of their forebears and extended family. Asian Americans tend to be more socially and politically conservative than members of other racial and ethnic-minority groups, often resisting change, stressing a high achievement orientation, and avoiding offending others. They may be perceived by some members of other racial and ethnic groups as emotionally restrained because they may not show emotion in overt ways. Asian cultures tend to encourage interdependency and a group orientation and to discourage individualism and an autonomous orientation. Asian American adolescents may experience conflicts regarding opposing pressures of assimilation into mainstream American culture and maintaining traditional family and cultural expectations. Many of these adolescents feel pressure to conform to stereotypes of being a "model minority," high educational achievers, and focused on mathematics and the physical sciences. Asian Americans tend to underuse mental health services (Sue & Sue, 1990, 1999, 2008) and may be uncomfortable with mental health service systems that are based on a Eurocentric tradition.

Hispanic and Latino Americans

The U.S. Bureau of the Census does not include Hispanic or Latino as a racial category. It is considered to be a category of ethnicity that primarily reflects descent from Spanish-speaking countries and culture regions in South and Central America and the Caribbean, Mexico, and the southwestern United States (Aponte & Crouch, 1995) (or Latinx, an increasingly preferred term). In some cases, Hispanic or Latinos may speak French or Portuguese. Obviously, this is a diverse racial and ethnic group. Most people of Hispanic or Latino descent define themselves as White in the census racial category, but 42.2% define themselves as "Some Other Race." Hispanic and Latino individuals now constitute 18.7% of the U.S. population according to the 2020 Census. Hispanics and Latinos constituted 9% of the general U.S. population in the 1990 census and 11.9% of the population in the 2000 census, and now constitute 16% of the adult population and 25.7% of children under 18. Hispanics and Latinos became the largest ethnic minority group in the United States shortly after the 2000 census. Aponte and Crouch (1995) reviewed data projections that Hispanics and Latinos would compose about 20% of the U.S. population by 2050, but in view of the recent rapid growth of this group that has surpassed previous projections, it is feasible that the 2050 percentage could be at least 25%, if not higher. Although population patterns are constantly shifting, in the 1990s and early 2000s, the largest percentage of Hispanic and Latino Americans lived in the West (41%), followed by the South (36%), Northeast (14%), and Midwest (9%) (U.S. Bureau of the Census, 2011b). Currently, the greatest numbers of Hispanic and Latino individuals are in three states: New Mexico, California, and Texas.

Although Hispanics and Latinos constitute an eclectic and diverse ethnic group, most of this group (60%) are of Mexican ancestry, and perhaps the most significant unifying background characteristic among all Hispanics and Latinos is the historical (or present) connection to the Spanish language and ultimately Spanish (and Portuguese) exploration and colonization in the Western hemisphere. Another significant historical commonality among Hispanic and Latino people is the influence of the Roman Catholic religion. Lee and Richardson (cited in Sattler, 1998, p. 291) stated, "Hispanic culture developed as a result of the fusion of Spanish culture (brought to the Americas by missionaries and conquistadors) with American Indian and African (the result of the slave trade) cultures." The culture reflected in this ethnic heritage is eclectic. Historically, the nuclear and extended family and the dominance of fathers and other men, along with a family-centered and home-centered role for women, has played an important role in shaping Hispanic cultural characteristics (Rivers & Morrow, 1995). Group identity seems to be more important to most Hispanics than to most non-Hispanic Whites, with the extended family taking priority over the individual in many cases. According to Sattler (1998), most Hispanic and Latino individuals tend to place a high value on human relationships, identify strongly with their families, and feel comfortable with open displays of affection and emotion.

Because Hispanic and Latino youth are a heterogeneous group, the characteristics that should be especially considered in forming a behavioral, social, or emotional perspective are varied. One characteristic that will be important for a sizable number of Hispanic American youth is language. Youth whose families have emigrated recently to the United States may speak only or primarily Spanish. Non-Spanish-speaking educators and clinicians who work with them are faced with a significant challenge, even if an interpreter is available. Children with this language background who are placed in schools where there is little support for their primary language (i.e., where there are no bilingual or English language learner programs) will feel frustrated and likely will suffer academic problems as they struggle to immerse themselves in a new culture and acquire a new language, particularly if English is not spoken in their homes. Many children in this situation naturally would want to withdraw from an environment that is perceived as being unsupportive of their individual communication needs. A related issue for some Hispanic and Latino youth may be acculturative stress, or difficulties that emerge when trying to assimilate into the dominant culture while still trying to honor the traditions and expectations of their families. Such difficulties, however, may include increased conflict within the family, which may typically be a source of support (Lorenzo-Blanco, Unger, Baezconde-Garbanati, Ritt-Olson, & Soto, 2012). There is the possibility of resistance to treatment recommendations that emanate from an Anglo perspective. Also according to Sattler, more traditional Hispanic and Latino families may have a mistrust for special education programs because they may feel such programs are inappropriate for their child, who may receive special treatment or sympathy for a disability. Instead, parents in this situation may want practical answers to their questions, such as wanting to know how long it will take for the child to overcome the disability. On the other hand, Kuperminc, Darnell, and Alvarez-Jimenez (2008), found that parental involvement in schools increased Hispanic and Latino student academic achievement and improved teachers' expectations for students. People with a traditional Hispanic or Latino orientation may underuse mental health services, but when involved with such services may feel more comfortable with a practical, solution-focused approach to service delivery.

American Indians and Alaskan Natives

Indigenous Americans include individuals who trace their ancestry to the aboriginal inhabitants of the North American continent (i.e., those who lived in North America before European migration). Indigenous Americans comprise a broad category of people, including hundreds of federally recognized tribal groups and several tribal nations. This is the smallest ethnic group within the United States, composing approximately 1% of the general population. Although there are many federally recognized tribes (600), only a few have substantial populations. The largest 10 tribal groupings with more than 80,000 members include: Cherokee, Navajo, Choctaw, Mexican American Indian, Chippewa, Sioux, Apache, Blackfeet, Creek, and Iroquois. (U.S. Census Bureau, 2010). Although population predictions for the next 50 years project that Indigenous Americans will still be the smallest racial and ethnic-minority group in the United States by 2050, the absolute numbers are projected to increase, as will the relative percentage of the population.

Although Indigenous Americans are a diverse people in many respects, certain similar hallmark characteristics have been associated with the various tribal groups. The common ethnic background that ties Indigenous Americans together is considered to be a product of shared historical experiences, political ideologies, and worldviews, rather than cultural similarities (Aponte & Crouch, 1995) because there are many differing tribal languages and cultural customs. A major defining shared historical experience among Indigenous Americans is oppression by the U.S. government (as an instrument of the broader American citizenry) through genocide, appropriation of their ancestral home-lands, forced relocation of their ancestors to reservation areas, and continual violation of treaties. Beginning with the first permanent European settlements on the East Coast and ending with the Atlantic to Pacific borders produced through the "manifest destiny" of the dominant culture, the percentage of Indigenous Americans as a proportion of the general population steadily declined for many years. A shared experience of many Indigenous Americans is poverty, which has resulted from previous generations of genocide and is further enabled by ongoing oppression. Family structures of Indigenous Americans often include a broad extended family rather than a primary emphasis on the nuclear family. Similar to Asian Americans, traditional Indigenous Americans place a stronger respect for older individuals, some of whom may hold particularly venerated positions of respect as tribal Elders. In contrast to the traditions of most European cultures, traditional Indigenous Americans foster a belief in harmony with, rather than mastery over, nature. For many Indigenous Americans, cultural religious beliefs (as opposed to formally theocratic reli-gions) are a highly important aspect of their worldview, with traditional religions empha-sizing a reverence for the forces of nature, mysticism, spirituality, and mythology.

Almost half of all Indigenous Americans live in the West, with another third living in the South. The remaining population is spread throughout the Midwest and Northeast. About 35% of Indigenous Americans live on reservations or tribal lands or villages.

Certain psychosocial characteristics have been associated with Indigenous Americans and may be especially true of those who are more traditional as opposed to assimilated within the majority culture. Understanding some of these characteristics may be essential for conducting effective assessments of Indigenous American children and adolescents. Traditional Indigenous American parents are much more likely than Anglos to use non-coercive and noninterfering methods of parenting (i.e., letting children develop freely), which may be interpreted wrongly by professionals who are not familiar with the culture. Although individuality is respected among traditional Indigenous Americans, there is clearly more of a group orientation as opposed to an individualistic orientation, and modesty and humility are valued characteristics. Many traditional Indigenous American children may be uncomfortable being recognized for individual achievements. Traditional

Indigenous Americans tend to have a less rigid, more flexible view of time than most other racial and ethnic groups, viewing it in terms of natural processes and internal feelings rather than a mechanical clock time. Indigenous American adolescents tend to engage in more alcohol use and start earlier than other U.S. adolescents (Whitesell et al., 2012). Indigenous American adolescents have the highest suicide rate of any racial and ethnic group, which is almost twice as high as that of Whites, the second most suicide-prone group, and alcoholism and drug abuse account for about 50% of Indigenous American deaths (Sattler, 2008). Clinicians who work with Indigenous American adolescents should consider these possible issues carefully and should become educated regarding the specific cultural practices and expectations associated with the specific tribal groups whom they serve. It also is important to recognize that there are tremendously varying degrees of acculturation among Indigenous Americans, and the traditional patterns expressed in this section do not reflect the characteristics of a substantial number of Indigenous Americans.

Some General Characteristics of the Majority Culture

Many discussions of cultural diversity in the education and mental health fields do not address cultural characteristics of the White/Caucasian majority group and instead focus only on characteristics of racial and ethnic-minority groups. The implied assumptions regarding this type of approach are that readers are already familiar with the essential facts and characteristics of the majority group, or that such information is not pertinent to becoming a culturally responsive practitioner. In our view, such an approach simply leads to further perpetuation of incorrect notions regarding cultural diversity. One problem with not including the majority White group in discussions of professional practice and cultural diversity is that it perpetuates a notion that the current Caucasian/White majority culture within the United States is the normative or typical standard rather than a cultural variant. The reality here is that whereas Whites currently constitute more than two thirds of the population in the United States, they do not constitute a majority of the world's overall population, and even within the United States, the proportion of non-Hispanic Whites is now expected to diminish steadily to become a minority (less than 50%) of the U.S. population by about 2050. Another problem with majority-omitting discussions on diversity is that it may foster a belief among members of the current majority culture that they are not ethnic, that they do not have a culture, and that only groups who are variant from this normative perspective should be discussed in examinations of diversity. I contend that such conscious omissions only foster further ethnocentrism by members of the majority group and that this issue is important for a brief discussion in this section.

One of the problems in defining and discussing the White racial majority in the United States is that so many terms are applied to it, and the terminology is at times misleading. For example, the U.S. Bureau of the Census uses the category White, non-Hispanic to classify the current majority group, but other terms that are commonly applied include Caucasian (a racial classification used by anthropologists and ethno-biologists), European American, Anglo, and a host of lesser known terms. Most discussions of the White racial group within the United States are focused on individuals who trace their ancestry to European nations. There is substantial variation in culture and ethnicity among a group so broadly defined. A descendant of the first permanent European settlers to North America several hundred years ago may feel that they have little in common with a modern-day immigrant from Russia or Lithuania, other than the color of their skin. Added to this problem is the fact that there are many individuals in the United States who technically are considered to be White by the census bureau but whose cultural background varies dramatically from that of a stereotypical White Anglo-Saxon Protestant, such as individuals who trace their ancestral heritage to the Arabic and primarily Muslim nations of the Middle East.

Although the people of various European/Caucasian ethnic and cultural groups generally are referred to as comprising a monolithic majority group, not all groups who fit within this constellation historically have been treated this way. Irish immigrants to the United States in the mid-1800s were the objects of substantial discrimination and hostility, as were later immigrants from eastern and southern Europe. Immigrants to the United States from almost all parts of the world and at almost all points in time have faced hostility from the dominant culture. In reality, White or European American immigrants to the United States, although they may face substantial challenges, have had an easier time fitting in within the dominant culture than have Asian Americans, African Americans, Hispanics, and Indigenous Americans because of such issues as skin color and historically shared cultural heritage.

With all the caveats in place, there are certain psychosocial or cultural characteristics that tend to be considered uniquely European in nature and have been used to describe the White majority group in the United States. Individuals in this group, although they may be diverse, tend to share a Western worldview and value system (Corey et al., 1997). Some major characteristics of this worldview include an emphasis on individualism and fulfillment of individual needs, a nuclear family structure, competitiveness, an orientation toward the future, assertiveness, independence, emphasis on youth, nonconformity and individual freedom, mastery over the environment, and individual responsibility. People who hold this value system often go to great lengths to try to gain control over their circumstances and destiny and may not be able to relate well to persons whose worldview and value system emphasize fate or who believe that individual efforts will have little influence on the outcome of a situation. Whites of European ancestry are less likely than Asian Americans and Indigenous Americans to defer personal decisions to the views and needs of the extended family group or elders and instead tend to focus on self-fulfillment as a means of achieving satisfaction or happiness. As is true in the case of all racial and ethnic groups discussed in this chapter, these characteristics may differentiate the group from other groups, but there is likely to be more substantial variation in these areas among individuals within the dominant culture. White readers of this book who question whether the characteristics presented in this section are representative of them should consider carefully how essential it is to not stereotype individuals from other racial and ethnic groups but to use the available information on cultural generalities as a basis for understanding rather than labeling the individual.

ASSESSMENT METHODS AND CULTURAL DIVERSITY: SPECIAL CONSIDERATIONS

This section includes separate discussions of the six methods of assessment that are presented in this book, with an emphasis on what is known regarding the multicultural applications of each method. Each method is associated with certain problems for culturally competent assessment, although substantial progress has been made with some of these methods.

Behavioral Observation

Because there is such a wide variation in potential techniques for direct behavioral observation, the cultural validity of these techniques presumably also may vary widely. The primary advantages of behavioral observation as an assessment method, as detailed in Chapter 3, include the potential of strong experimental validation and replicability, the wide flexibility, and the strong potential ecological validity of assessing behavior within the context of behavior–environment relationships. If the assessor appropriately takes into account the cultural background characteristics of an individual child in designing the observational coding system and interpreting the obtained data, direct behavioral observation may be an excellent choice for culturally appropriate assessment of social–emotional behavior.

There are some potential threats to the validity of direct behavioral observation that may have a significant impact on the cultural appropriateness of this method. Of the potential threats to validity of behavioral observations that are discussed in Chapter 3, the following threats have specific ramifications for culturally appropriate assessment: *lack of social comparison data, observer reactivity,* and *situational specificity of behavior.* Regarding the social comparison problem, failure to compare the observed behavior of a target child appropriately with that of their peers may result in interpretations that are not based on a normative perspective, and deviancy of behavior may be underestimated or overestimated. When observing a child or adolescent who is a member of a racial or ethnic-minority group within a given environment, social comparisons of behavior should be made with other children of their group and children who are in the majority group if possible. Such inclusiveness in defining the social comparison targets may help to differentiate between maladaptive behavior and behavior that simply differs from the norm. In regard to observer reactivity, if the person conducting the observation stands out in some obvious way from the students in the classroom, it is more likely that the students will react behaviorally to the presence of the observer and that the observational data that are obtained may be distorted. If an African American observer went into a classroom in a tribal school on a remote and rural reservation area in the West to collect data, he or she most likely would stand out significantly to the children, simply because of the lack of experience of most of these children with African Americans. Likewise, a White observer entering a school that is composed primarily of African American students and teachers in a similar situation may be likely to create reactivity. To minimize the effects of such reactivity, observers who are in a situation where they stand out as unique should take extra time for settling in and having an adjustment period before beginning the formal observation. With regard to the situational specificity of behavior phenomena, observers should consider carefully that children who are in a substantial racial or ethnic minority situation in classroom or clinic observation settings may behave differently in those environments than they would in environments with which they were more familiar and comfortable. The culturally valid behavioral assessment will include observational data from a variety of normal environments to the greatest extent possible.

Although these cautions and recommendations are based on sound theory and make good sense, it is important to recognize that there is little empirical evidence regarding the effects of race/ethnicity or other cultural variables on the validity of direct behavioral observation. The few studies that have been conducted in this area (e.g., Harvey et al., 2009; Lethermon et al., 1984; Lethermon, Williamson, Moody, & Wozniak, 1986; Turner, Beidel, Hersen, & Bellack, 1984) have indicated that in certain situations, there may be an interaction between the race/ethnicity condition of the observer and the target subjects, and in some circumstances, this interaction may result in biased observational data. It also has been stated, however, that appropriate training of observers may reduce such bias (Lethermon et al., 1986). The recommendations regarding appropriate training and support of observers that are provided in Chapter 3 seem to have special relevance to the topic of culturally valid assessment practices.

Behavior Rating Scales

Because behavior rating scales typically are standardized norm-referenced assessment tools, their validity for use with diverse cultural groups for which they are intended may be ascertained to some extent through the information available in the test manual. In other words, the developers of such instruments should follow specific procedures for item development and accumulation of validity evidence if they desire to make a claim that the instrument is valid for use across groups with differing characteristics along some major demographic domain. For example, the *Standards for Educational and Psychological Testing* (AERA, APA, & NCME, 2014) recommends that test developers should carefully examine the appropriateness of the item content for intended target groups, that groups for which the test is intended should be represented adequately in normative samples, and in certain cases, that research regarding similarity or differences among specific groups should be shown. It is recommended that potential users of behavior rating scales and other standardized norm-referenced social–emotional behavior instruments should scrutinize carefully the contents of the technical manual before deciding to use the instrument with racial/ethnic-minority youth.

One of the ongoing debates (for which there is little empirical evidence) regarding culturally appropriate uses of standardized norm-referenced instruments, such as behavior rating scales, is in regard to the desirable proportion of representativeness of various racial and ethnic groups within the norm group and whether local norms are better than national norms. In other words, does the *assumption of comparability* discussed by Rhodes et al. (2005), and mentioned earlier in this chapter, hold true in specific situations, or does it fail? The standard practice in educational and psychological test development in more recent years has been to ensure that the norm sample of the instrument parallels the characteristics of the general population for which it is intended, to the greatest extent possible. In other words, a test developer who intends the completed instrument to be used generally with children and adolescents in the United States should attempt to develop a norm sample that closely parallels the racial/ethnic, gender, and socioeconomic status characteristics of the general population from the most recent census. In reality, this practice, although laudable and challenging, does not provide evidence of cultural validity a priori, and some experts have criticized the practice because minority groups still comprise a minority within the norm sample against which their scores are to be compared. For illustration purposes, based on the 2020 census, approximately 1% of the population in the United States are Indigenous Americans. Using the standard practice of instrument development, representation of Indigenous Americans in about 1% of the norm sample for the test should satisfy the general standard of equivalency. However, 1% is still a very small proportion, even when it represents the general percentage of a specific subgroup within a general group. In this example, assuming there is a total norming sample of 1,000 for a specific measure—a respectable figure—it would require only ten Indigenous American youth to make the sample of Indigenous Americans in the norming population proportional to the actual percentage in the U.S. population. Such a simplistic application of proportionality raises many questions. For example, if our ten Indigenous American youth in the norming sample are all members of the Yakima tribe in the Pacific Northwest, should we assume that Indigenous American youth in general have been sampled, or is there some concern regarding generalizing the statistical representation to other subgroups, such as the Ojibwa tribe in the northern Midwest? Along this same line of reasoning, it has been proposed that a small representation, even if it is in proportion to the percentage of the group within the total population, might be presumed to result in test bias (e.g., Harrington, 1988).

What can be made of the opposing arguments regarding proportionality in norming? The scant evidence that is available on normative representation within standardized tests may indicate that proportional representation, or even minority overrepresentation within the norm group, may have little impact on the ability of the test to predict behavior or performance in a valid manner, as long as adequate sampling procedures are used in the construction of the norm group, *and the content of the test items is relatively free of cultural bias to begin with* (Fan, Wilson, & Kapes, 1996). The Fan et al. study used varying proportions (0%, 5%, 10%, 30%, and 60%) of differing ethnic groups (White, African American, Hispanic, Asian American) in a tightly controlled standardization experiment and found that there was no systematic bias against any of the groups when they were in the not represented or underrepresented conditions. Fan et al. referred to the notion of proportional representation or overrepresentation of racial and ethnic-minority groups as a best practice as the "standardization fallacy." This interesting study did not target specifically assessment of social–emotional behavior, and a replication using this performance domain would be useful. It is one of the few tightly controlled studies, however, to address the issue of representation of specific racial and ethnic groups within standardization groups, and racial/ethnic differences on scores of standardized social–emotional behavioral measures tend to be less than differences on cognitive measures. Based on the results of this study, it seems that the most important aspects of developing assessment instruments that have wide cultural applicability and validity are the actual content development procedures (to eliminate biasing items) and the use of good sampling methods for construction of the norm group. Other instrument development procedures may also be useful for showing appropriateness with differing racial and ethnic groups, such as conducting specific comparisons with subsamples of various racial and ethnic groups regarding such characteristics as mean score equivalency, internal-consistency properties, and factor structure.

Relatively few studies have been conducted regarding culturally appropriate development and use of behavior rating scales across diverse racial and ethnic groups. In reporting research on a national normative sample for the original Child Behavior Checklist (CBCL), Achenbach and Edelbrock (1979, 1981) noted that the effects of race and ethnicity were minimal if socioeconomic status was used as a controlling covariant. The most recent CBCL (Achenbach, 2001a), however, has been studied with children from 30 or more societies and data suggest that the proposed factor structure fits these international samples well (Rescorla et al., 2007; Rescorla et al., 2011). Other studies using socioeconomic status as a covariant with the normative samples included the School

Social Behavior Scales (SSBS) (Merrell, 1993a, 1993b, 2002b) and the Preschool and Kindergarten Behavior Scales (PKBS) (Merrell, 1994, 1996a, 2002a). Differences in levels of problem behavior scores across racial and ethnic groups may be associated more strongly with variables such as family income and education level than with race and ethnicity. Developers of behavior rating scales and other standardized assessment instruments should ensure appropriate stratification based not only on race and ethnicity, but also on geographical representation and socioeconomic status. Although the actual effects of proportional underrepresentation or overrepresentation of various racial and ethnic groups within general norm samples are still unclear, test developers also would be wise to ensure that the various groups receive adequate representation in the standardization sample.

Interviewing

The area of clinical interviewing is especially important when considering cultural diversity and social–emotional assessment. Interviewing may involve some of the strongest potential barriers to effective cross-cultural assessment, but also is perhaps the most modifiable and flexible social–emotional assessment method, offering great promise in this regard for clinicians who acquire the skills for culturally sensitive interviewing (Hughes & Baker, 1990; Sattler, 2008).

Little attention has been given to the topic of making clinical interviews with children more culturally appropriate. Nevertheless, it is clear that attention to this area is needed. In commenting on culturally responsive assessment practices in the United States, Dana (1996) noted that the traditional information-gathering styles of many assessment professionals of the White majority may pose substantial obstacles for effective assessment. He stated:

> Anglo American assessors have been influenced by medical model service-delivery requirements for compliance with a matter-of-fact, somewhat impersonal style that puts business first and discourages a more personal relationship during the service delivery or later. As a result, many Anglo American assessors expect clients to have an immediate task orientation including cooperation and responsiveness to the test materials. . . . However, most traditional persons cannot respond comfortably to assessment tasks if the assessor uses a social etiquette that is uncomfortable, intrusive, frustrating, or alienating.
>
> (p. 475)

Certainly, conducting clinical interviews in this manner with children in general would be a problem, but it may be substantially more problematic if the child is a member of a racial or ethnic-minority group and has a traditional orientation. So, given what is known regarding traditional clinical interviewing practices and cultural differences among the U.S. population, what should be done to approach this problem? A detailed approach for conducting culturally sensitive interviews, including interviews with parents, was proposed by Rhodes et al. (2005), in a separate chapter on interviewing in their excellent book *Assessing Culturally and Linguistically Diverse Students*. Although too detailed to justly summarize in this section, the recommendations by Rhodes and colleagues for successful interviewing in cross-cultural situations include a strong emphasis on prior preparation for the interview with respect to linguistic and acculturation issues and can be summarized by the following steps in their recommended process:

- preparing for the interview;
- issues to consider before conducting the interview;
- selecting an interview format;
- determining the relevancy of questions;
- asking difficult questions;
- determining who should be involved in the interview;
- what to do if the parent isn't available for a face-to-face interview;
- limitations of conducting the interview by telephone;
- necessary conditions for a successful interview;
- consideration of cultural factors;
- what to do after the interview.

In a similar vein, a cohesive and detailed set of suggestions for culturally competent interviewing of ethnic-minority children (particularly children who are traditional rather than bicultural or marginal in their acculturation) has been offered by Sattler (1998), who made nine recommendations, which are detailed in Table 2.2.

Table 2.2 Nine recommendations by Sattler (1998) for effective interviewing of racial/ethnic minority children and their families

Recommendation	Comments
Learn about the interviewee's culture	Active efforts to learn about cultural issues such as ethnic identification, traditional practices and customs, attitudes toward childrearing and education
Learn about the interviewee's language	Should occur before the interview; if the child/family is not comfortable speaking the language of the interviewer, arrangements should be made for a different interviewer or an interpreter
Establish rapport	Encouragement of the child/family's participation, interest, and cooperation; use diplomacy and tact, and avoid being disrespectful
Identify stereotypes	Inward examination by interviewer regarding their own beliefs, prejudices, and stereotypes regarding the racial/ethnic group of the child/family; consider that these expectations may not be accurate
Clear communication	Avoid use of jargon, slang, technical language, and statements with double meanings; use courtesy and respect in communications; if needed, modify the interview format
Identify family needs	Determine material, physical, and psychosocial needs of child and family, and consider community resources to meet these needs; may be especially important for recent immigrants or families living in poverty
Identify attitudes toward health and illness	What are beliefs regarding illness, healing, traditional rituals, and religious customs? What drugs and folk remedies is child using?
Recognize the extent of acculturation	Determine level of acculturation within traditional group and assimilation into dominant group; for recent immigrants, determine level of functioning before leaving homeland and level of acculturation stress
Accept the interviewee's perspectives	Active efforts by interviewer to accept beliefs and attitudes they may not share, coupled with recognition that problems may not be due to minority status

Learn About the Interviewees' Culture This recommendation would include efforts by the interviewer directed at learning about such factors as family ethnic identification, cultural patterns related to parenting practices, specific family attitudes regarding childrearing, the education and the occupational background of the parents, and the ethnic community with which they may identify themselves. Attempts to learn about the culture should be tempered with the realization that your information may be only partially correct. "Recognize your ignorance about some details of the family's culture . . . if you are not a member of the ethnic group, you may be viewed as a stranger" (Sattler, 1998, p. 313). It also is recommended that the interviewer be frank with the family regarding the lack of knowledge he or she may have regarding their cultural background.

Learn About the Interviewees' Language Attempts to learn about the language of the interviewee and family would include a determination of their preferred language (before the interview) and familiarity with English. This background information is essential in determining if an interpreter is needed for the interview, assuming that there is not another potential interviewer who speaks the language of the family.

Establish Rapport The larger the cultural background differences between the interviewer and the client (and their family), the more time may be needed to establish adequate rapport. Sattler (1998) recommended that the interviewer should "make every effort to encourage the child's and family's motivation and interest" and "take the time to enlist the child's and family's cooperation" (p. 315). Diplomacy, tact, and respect are crucial characteristics of attempts to establish good rapport.

Identify Stereotypes This process is focused on an inward examination by the interviewer regarding his or her own preconceived notions, prejudices, and stereotypes regarding the racial/ethnic group of the child and their family. Assumptions should not be made immediately that the family is traditionally acculturated into the known cultural characteristics of their racial/ethnic group. "Ask them about these matters as needed" (Sattler, 1998, p. 315).

Promote Clear Communication If the child and the family are not bicultural or well assimilated into the culture of the interviewer, specific attempts should be made to ensure that communication is enhanced. Avoidance of technical jargon, slang expressions, unusual idioms, or statements with dual meanings may be necessary. If these ethnic-group differences begin to hamper the interview, the interviewer should try actively to monitor his or her behavior and use other approaches. "Be flexible, and use innovative interviewing strategies tailored to the needs of the family's ethnic group" (Sattler, 1998, p. 316).

Identify Family Needs Particularly if the child and the family are recent immigrants to the United States or if they live in poverty, the interviewer should attempt to ascertain whether they have obvious material, physical, or psychosocial needs and what can be done to connect them with appropriate community resources.

Identify Attitudes toward Health and Illness If the child and the family are traditionally oriented to their ethnic culture, they may have concepts of illness, healing, rituals, and religious beliefs that are unfamiliar to the interviewer and most people within the public school system. In making active attempts to learn about their attitudes and beliefs in this area, the interviewer should try to understand the child's and family's expectations regarding professional treatment and ascertain what prescription drugs, over-the-counter drugs, folk remedies, and illicit drugs the child may be taking.

Recognize the Extent of Acculturation As has been stated many times throughout this chapter, there is tremendous variation among individuals and families regarding how acculturated they are within their racial/ethnic culture and their knowledge and orientation to the dominant culture. If the child and family are recent immigrants to the United States, it is recommended that the interviewer attempt to assess their level of functioning before leaving their homeland and to determine how they are coping with the stresses associated with the process of acculturation.

Accept the Interviewee's Perspectives The interviewer should make a substantial effort to accept the cultural perspectives of the interviewee and his or her family. This is an ideal rather than a technique and in some cases may be difficult to achieve. This process may be the most difficult aspect of culturally responsive assessment and intervention. It involves the willingness of the interviewer to accept perspectives he or she may not share or with which he or she may feel uncomfortable. At the same time, efforts need to be made to achieve a balance between understanding any behavioral, social, and emotional problems within the cultural context and avoiding attributing all individual and family problems to the cultural background and minority group status.

Any competent assessment professional who thoughtfully attempts to implement these suggestions will find that his or her cultural sensitivity in clinical interviewing is enhanced. In some cases, these efforts will not be enough to achieve the desired goal, however. Willingness to conduct more than one interview also may be necessary, and honesty and reliability in communication likely will enhance the trust between the interviewer and the client. "Improved intercultural communication will ultimately depend on changes in the socio political system. Until our society eliminates racism and discrimination, there will always be vestiges of suspicion and mistrust between people of different ethnicities" (Sattler, 1998, p. 317).

Sociometric Techniques

Although sociometric techniques are most likely to be used as assessment tools for research purposes rather than for everyday clinical practice, there is a small but coherent body of evidence indicating that they may be associated with strong racial/ethnic effects. Any professional contemplating the use of sociometrics with a diverse group of children should consider this issue carefully and be aware of potential bias. The primary consistent finding in this area is that *similarity provides a strong basis for positive peer nominations and ratings.* This issue is discussed in Chapter 7 with respect to gender similarity, which has been shown in scores of studies to influence sociometric results of friendship patterns. In other words, boys are more likely to rate or nominate other boys using positive criteria, and girls are more likely to select other girls in this manner. A smaller but also compelling collection of research in this area also has emerged regarding race/ethnicity as a sociometric prediction variable.

A study by Singleton and Asher (1977) explored social interaction patterns among Black and White third-grade students in integrated schools. In this study, race (and sex) was found to be a significant determinant of positive sociometric ratings for play and work. Black children were substantially more likely to select other Black children as the people with whom they would most like to play or work, and White children were equally likely to select White children in this regard. This study, which was conducted shortly after the initiation of court-mandated school integration in many areas of the United States, was timely but did not explore the issue in more detail. The generalities of Singleton and Asher's study were replicated in a later study by Clark and Dewry (1985), who found the same type of racial/ethnic preferences using a more controlled methodology.

More recent sociometric investigations have verified the notion that similarity, whether it be in gender, race, ethnicity, socioeconomic status, or social behavior patterns, provides a strong basis for friendships (Graham & Cohen, 1997; Kupersmidt, DeRosier, & Patterson, 1995). Some of these studies have pushed the issue further, however, and have provided some more specific answers to the question of racial and ethnic similarity in sociometric assessment. Kistner, Metzler, Gatlin, and Risi (1993) examined peer preferences and perceptions among African American and White children in classrooms where there were clear majority patterns (i.e., classrooms where there was a dominance of African American children and classrooms where there was a dominance of White children). Their findings put a different twist on the issue of similarity in sociometric assessment, showing that being in a minority situation, regardless of your racial/ethnic group, was associated with higher rates of peer rejection for girls but not for boys. Another finding from this study was that peer preferences may be influenced by cultural dominance. In other words, a child who is in the racial or ethnic minority in a given classroom (regardless of what race he or she is) is likely to rate children of the dominant group more positively than he or she would if he or she were in the majority and the members of the other group were in the minority. Another study that found an interesting race/ethnicity and gender interaction effect in sociometric assessment was conducted by Kistner and Gatlin (1989). These researchers studied positive and negative nominations of White and Black children, some of whom had learning disabilities, but most of whom did not have disabilities. Predictably, there was a racial/ethnic (and gender) effect for positive nominations, where children were more likely to identify as friends those children with whom they felt they had the most similarity. Effects for negative nominations also were identified, however. Children of both racial and ethnic groups were more likely to reject children of the opposite gender and racial and ethnic group. Similar results can even be found in preschool settings, suggesting that these patterns of behavior begin early (Park, 2011).

These studies all have a common theme, showing that race and ethnicity are likely to be significant factors not only in friendship patterns, but also in patterns of peer rejection. The racial and ethnic make up of the class also seems to be an added factor to consider in sociometric data collection (Jackson, Barth, Powell, & Lochman, 2006). For researchers or clinicians using sociometric techniques, there is an obvious practical implication. Children whose racial and/or ethnic group comprises a small percentage of the overall classroom may be overidentified as socially neglected or rejected, and faulty interpretations might be reached if these cultural variables are not considered fully. It would be advisable to include sociometrics of racial and ethnic-minority youth only within the context of a comprehensive assessment design that overcomes the limitations of reliance on one method.

Self-Report Instruments

In comparison with most areas of behavioral, social, and emotional assessment, a relatively larger body of evidence has accumulated regarding the use of self-report instruments with ethnic-minority populations. Because there has been little research and development work with child populations and self-report assessment until the past decade, most of what is known regarding multicultural applications in this area has come from research with adults. We can use the accumulated knowledge and thinking from the adult population, however, as a basis for developing some general guidelines for assessment practices with children and youth. In general, self-report assessment is an area in which caution should be used for the selection, administration, and interpretation of assessment instruments with members of racial/ethnic-minority groups, particularly those who have a traditional cultural identity and are not highly acculturated within the mainstream majority culture.

The most widely used self-report instrument in existence is clearly the Minnesota Multiphasic Personality Inventory (MMPI) and its recent successors the MMPI-2 and MMPI-A. Several reviews of the use of the MMPI with members of racial and ethnic-minority groups (e.g., Dana, 1993, 1995, 2005; Greene, 1987; Hoffman, Dana, & Bolton, 1987) have indicated that there are clear patterns of profile differences with these groups compared with the general instrument norms. Specifically, research has shown that members of racial and/or ethnic-minority groups, regardless of their clinical status, are more likely than members of the dominant culture in the United States to respond to MMPI items in ways that may result in elevated scores on some of the validity and clinical scales. In Dana's 1995 review, he noted that African Americans are likely to receive high scores on scales F, 6, and 8 as a process of becoming Afro-centric; Hispanic and Latino Americans tend to exhibit similar patterns of score elevations on these scales as a result of traditional cultural orientation; and Indigenous Americans are more likely than majority group members to show elevations on scales F, 4, and 8, regardless of their diagnostic status. Less is known regarding the use of the MMPI with Asian Americans, although some studies have shown that they are likely to receive elevated clinical profiles in comparison with the majority-dominated standardization group. Dana's more recent (2005) review of the MMPI instruments contends that this system can be used effectively with culturally diverse individuals so long as appropriate adaptations are implemented but provides many cautions.

Given that there is no a priori reason to believe that members of racial and ethnic-minority groups should respond to a broad-band self-report measure such as the MMPI measures in ways that show more psychopathology than exists among the majority culture, the history of such differences raises serious questions and concerns. Because the large majority of the cross-cultural MMPI research has been with populations who responded to the MMPI or MMPI-2 rather than the MMPI-A, there is additional reason for caution when using this test with racial and/or ethnic-minority youth. Dana (1995) suggested that the MMPI "should be used only when the assessee has been demonstrated to be comparable to the standardization population on demographic variables, including world view as measured by moderator variables, and speaks English as a first language" (p. 66). In other words, use of the MMPI (and presumably the MMPI-A) with racial and ethnic-minority clients who are traditional in their orientation is not recommended. Although the MMPI-A norms are more racially and ethnically diverse than the norms for the original MMPI, the body of evidence regarding response profiles among racial and ethnic-minority youth is still in the formative stage, and it is prudent to assume that caution is warranted.

The MMPI is a relatively unique type of self-report measure, using empirical criterion keying in the construction of the subscales, using items that are not particularly specific to behavioral, social, or emotional problems (e.g., "I believe in law enforcement," "I like collecting flowers and growing houseplants," or "I would like to be a nurse"), and employing a forced-choice true/false response format. It may be possible that there are some peculiarities associated with the format and structure of the MMPI that make it particularly prone to the racial/ethnic bias in terms of the profile patterns that are produced.

Aside from the implications of research on the MMPI, relatively little is known regarding cross-cultural applications of self-report assessment, but some evidence with the newer generation self-report instruments for children and adolescents is beginning to emerge. Two studies using the Internalizing Symptoms Scale for Children (ISSC) showed that this instrument produces levels of total and subscale scores with African American children (Sanders, 1996) and Indigenous American youth (M. S. Williams, 1997) that are comparable to those of the general normative sample, even with minority children who are from low-socioeconomic-status homes. Information in the technical manual for the Personality Inventory for Youth (PIY) indicates that the overall score levels and profile patterns of racial and ethnic-minority subsamples tend to be similar to those of the general norm population. Some of the research on narrow-band self-report instruments such as the Children's Depression Inventory, Second Edition and Revised Children's Manifest Anxiety Scale, Second Edition (both of which are discussed in Chapter 11) has included large samples of racial and ethnic-minority youth and not shown any substantial biasing effects for race/ethnicity. These studies and a few similar studies with other self-report measures are more encouraging from a cultural-validity perspective than the cross-cultural research with the MMPI and provide some hope that future efforts might show definitively that the new generation of child and adolescent self-report measures is appropriate for use with children from varying racial/ethnic backgrounds.

Projective–Expressive Techniques

The general category of projective–expressive assessment techniques, including thematic approaches, drawing techniques, and sentence completion tasks, continues to be used widely for social–emotional assessment of children adolescents. Although the use of these techniques for diagnostic purposes remains a hotbed of controversy, and the associated limitations and problems have been convincingly documented, they are used widely for cross-cultural applications. A comprehensive review of the professional journal articles available on CD-ROM databases such as PSYCH LIT using the key words *projective testing* quickly reveals that projective–expressive techniques are used widely in research and clinical applications of child assessment throughout the world.

Despite their worldwide popularity, less is known regarding appropriate cross-cultural applications of projective techniques among members of racial and ethnic-minority groups in the United States, particularly where children are concerned. There are also differing perspectives and arguments regarding the appropriateness of traditional projective–expressive techniques in American cross-cultural applications. Hood and Johnson (1997) argued that "projective techniques are personality instruments that undoubtedly have less value as assessment tools for minority clients" (p. 309) because they are based on upper-middle-class majority-group perspectives. Dana (1993, 1995, 2005) has taken the stance that drawing, thematic, sentence completion, storytelling, and other projective–expressive techniques have considerable promise as assessment tools with members of racial and ethnic-minority groups and has provided numerous references for culture-specific applications of such techniques. Dana's generally supportive statements regarding cross-cultural applications of projectives are tempered, however, with his numerous other comments criticizing the Eurocentric theoretical bases on which most of the interpretation systems are built, particularly psychodynamic theory, as not being relevant for interpretation of the products produced in projective–expressive assessments by members of cultural-minority groups, particularly those who are traditional in their acculturation. Instead, Dana has suggested that such techniques be adapted specifically for use with particular racial and ethnic groups through using a constructivist approach to understanding their own cultural norms and values. For example, rather than using the traditional Thematic Apperception Test with Indigenous Americans, he suggests it might be more appropriate to use "tribe-specific picture stimulus cards," and for appropriate interpretation of the responses, "assessors should be familiar with the history, customs, ethnography, fiction, and published life histories of individuals for any tribe whose members are assessed using picture story techniques" (Dana, 1995, p. 67). Similar suggestions are made for adaptations of other projective–expressive techniques for use with racial and ethnic-minority group members, such as using human figure drawings in a general manner, but avoiding existing scoring systems, and using sentence completion tasks developed in the native language of the client.

It is my opinion that projective–expressive techniques have some merit for cross-cultural assessment of children and adolescents because they are nonthreatening, because they may offer a glimpse of the worldview of the client, and because they may provide a basis for relationship and trust enhancement between the evaluator and the child, something that may be especially challenging when strong cultural differences are present. The primary use of projectives for this purpose should be focused on observing and building a relationship with the child and not on making diagnostic inferences using the traditional interpretation techniques. For example, some traditional psychodynamic-based interpretations of drawing techniques often postulate that drawings of trees devoid of leaves may indicate emotional barrenness and that smoke rising out of chimneys of houses may indicate turmoil or conflict within the home. As questionable (if not naive) as such interpretation paradigms are in general, they may be particularly offensive when applied cross-culturally. Would it be unusual for a traditional Navajo youth whose family lives in a hogan, and whose primary heat source is wood fuel, to draw smoke arising from the dwelling? It may be reasonable to assert that projective–expressive techniques have some potentially useful cross-cultural applications, but that extra precautions should be in place for such use, to avoid inappropriate and culturally offensive interpretation and overpathologization. And of course, any cross-cultural application of projective–expressive techniques, in my view, should be tempered further by the overwhelming evidence that such measures tend to have poor stability, and appear to be highly dependent on the context, situation, or recent past of the examinee.

RECOMMENDATIONS FOR CULTURALLY RESPONSIVE ASSESSMENT

This chapter on assessment and cultural diversity has included a wide variety of topic areas, discussions of problems in current assessment practices, and suggestions for specific types of culturally responsive social–emotional assessment practices. Emphasis on cultural diversity within educational and psychological assessment is a relatively recent major focus, and this important topic has been neglected to a great extent in the past. It should be understood that much of our current empirical knowledge and practical applications

Table 2.3 General recommendations for culturally responsive practice in behavioral, social, and emotional assessment of children and youth

- Obtain sufficient background information before planning and conducting assessment
- Cultural background information should include estimates of acculturation and comfort with the majority language and dominant culture
- Use a comprehensive assessment design (multimethod, multisource, multisetting) to overcome the culturally limiting factors of any one method
- Examine new standardized instruments for evidence of multicultural applications
- Remain flexible in the design and implementation of the assessment, making innovations and modifications as needed
- "When in doubt, consult"
- Strive for honesty and open communication regarding cultural issues with the client and his or her family
- Present feedback on assessment results within a culturally acceptable framework
- Strive for sensitization to, and awareness of, within-group and between-group cultural differences
- Research and development work in assessment should emphasize general multicultural applications and specialized techniques for specific populations
- Educators and mental health professionals should introspectively examine their own cultural background, values, beliefs, and ethnocultural assumptions

of this knowledge is provisional. Much of what we currently know and do regarding multicultural applications of assessment is not well documented, and this area seems to be undergoing constant change. It seems likely that there will be important developments in this area in the near future, including substantial experimental innovation.

To conclude this chapter, the yield of information regarding best practices or practical applications for culturally competent behavioral social and emotional assessment of children and youth can be summarized in the following 11 points, which are listed for additional reference in Table 2.3:

1. Assessment professionals should obtain as much information as possible regarding the cultural background characteristics and orientation of the child or adolescent to be assessed, before conducting the assessment, and use this information in developing a tentative plan for the assessment. This issue is particularly important when the examiner is part of the majority culture and the client is not.

2. Cultural background information regarding children and adolescents to be assessed (and their families) always should include some appropriate estimation of their approximate level of acculturation and their comfort with the majority language and dominant culture.

3. Use of a comprehensive assessment design, such as the multimethod, multisource, multisetting model presented in Chapter 1, will help to create an ecologically valid and culturally appropriate social–emotional assessment. The cultural limitations of any one method, instrument, or technique can be curbed through the use of such a broad-based design.

4. In their selection of standardized assessment instruments (i.e., behavior rating scales, structured interviews, and self-report instruments), culturally responsive professionals should carefully examine the technical manuals for evidence of appropriate multicultural applications, in addition to the general characteristics (e.g., reliability and validity) that are traditionally valued.

5. Flexibility should be a key component of culturally appropriate assessment practice. If a given instrument or technique that was administered as part of the original assessment design proves to be obviously inappropriate for a given client, it should be abandoned or discarded. If assessment methods or techniques that were not part of the original design are seen to be valuable in a given situation, they should be adopted.

6. The professional adage "when in doubt, consult" should be particularly adhered to when moving into the realm of cross-cultural or multicultural assessment and intervention services. If one does not know the right answer or direction in a given situation, one should not be afraid to consult with someone one trusts.

7. Honesty and open communication with clients (and their families) who are from different ethnocultural backgrounds is especially important. If an examiner is unsure about a particular custom, belief, or issue that he or she thinks may be part of his or her client's worldview, he or she should respectfully and appropriately ask about it.

8. Assessment results feedback should be presented within a culturally acceptable framework (i.e., aimed toward the specific beliefs of the child's family regarding health, illness, and treatment) so that the results will be more likely to be used to develop appropriate intervention plans.

9. Sensitization to, and awareness of, multicultural within-group and between-group differences can help to create a greater awareness of cultural differences and ultimately may lead to more culturally appropriate assessments.

10. Researchers and other developers of assessment instruments should attempt to the greatest extent possible to make new methods, techniques, and instruments as culturally general as possible and to develop and validate specialized techniques that are designed to meet the needs of unusually specific cultural situations.

11. If they have not previously or recently done so, psychologists and educators of all backgrounds are urged to examine their own values, beliefs, ethnocultural background and assumptions, and general worldview, on a continual basis. This type of introspective self-examination is likely to lead to greater awareness of the strengths and barriers that one's background brings to assessment and treatment situations.

CONCLUSIONS

The topic of cultural diversity within psychological and educational assessment has received increasing professional and public attention. This increased emphasis has been spurred on primarily by legal decisions and well-known public controversies regarding IQ and educational aptitude testing, but also by a changing consciousness within American culture regarding the importance of culture and race/ethnicity in public and private life. There is an increasing consensus among assessment experts and policymakers that our current assessment practices have not gone far enough in promoting equity and utility across various ethnocultural groups.

Test bias and assessment bias are terms that reflect the properties and the uses of assessment instruments and methods. An instrument or technique is considered to have an unacceptable level of bias when it results in one group being systematically disadvantaged or shows group differences based on characteristics other than what are purported to be measured. Although the area of behavioral, social, and emotional assessment has not been scrutinized or criticized in this regard as much as cognitive-ability testing, bias in assessment is still a major concern. Organizations that represent professionals who are concerned with psychological and educational assessment have developed various codes and standards for appropriate practice and ethical behavior. Some of these standards have been revised to include a greater emphasis on the cultural validity of practices, although some have argued that these changes have not gone far enough. There seem to be several problems with the current state of affairs regarding multicultural applications or assessing social–emotional behavior, and efforts have been directed at developing new models and paradigms for culturally appropriate assessment practice.

Acculturation is defined as a process of individual change that occurs when two cultures meet. This process varies widely among individuals and groups and includes such factors as retention of traditions and customs of the native culture and adoption of new customs and values that are part of the new culture. The process of acculturation can be stressful for members of racial and ethnic-minority groups, and the actual types of stresses and outcomes vary as a function of the particular circumstances. Although specific instruments have been developed for determining the level of acculturation of members of particular minority groups, most of these instruments have been aimed at adults rather than youth. The process of determining the level of acculturation may involve such factors as language preferences, adherence to traditional customs, and level of comfort with the new culture. It has been proposed that members of various racial and ethnic groups, including members of the dominant group, may go through various stages of racial/cultural development. Understanding these stages and the process of movement between stages can help professionals understand better the unique characteristics of their clients.

Although increased emphasis on the characteristics of various and ethnic groups has many potential benefits, there are some possible problems that also must be considered. One negative outcome may be the stereotyping of individuals from specific groups based on a few facts known regarding general characteristics of that group. It is crucial to recognize that within-group differences almost always are greater than between-group differences and that each racial/ethnocultural group contains individuals of widely varying characteristics. In addition to inaccurate stereotyping, another possible ramification of not considering this fact is polarization and divisiveness among various groups.

The 2020 U.S. Census indicated that slightly more than two thirds of the general population are members of the White/Caucasian majority group, with the other major racial and ethnic groups, in order of current size, including African Americans, Hispanic and Latin Americans, Asian Americans, and Indigenous Americans. The population of children and adolescents is more diverse than the general population in the United States because of group differences in immigration patterns and birth rates. All demographic projections indicate that the White/Caucasian majority group will continue to shrink in its current proportion of the population and may comprise a slight minority (slightly less than 50%) of the general population by 2050 if present trends continue. All racial and ethnic-minority groups are projected to increase in terms of their absolute numbers of percentages within the general population during this time frame, however. Each of the five major racial and ethnic groups is diverse in its own right but has been associated with specific psychosocial characteristics that may hold true for many group members. Clinicians should become aware of these general characteristics but at the same time recognize that there is a wide variation among individuals within groups.

Each of the six assessment methods emphasized in this book has specific difficulties regarding multicultural applications, but there have been some encouraging developments for culturally competent assessments with each of these methods. Clinicians and researchers should become aware of the problems and limitations associated with multicultural applications of each method and develop assessment plans accordingly.

Certain recommended best practices for assessing social–emotional behavior within a culturally competent framework have been provided to form the basis of clinical and research practices. These recommendations include obtaining sufficient cultural background information on clients before the assessment, using a comprehensive assessment model, selecting instruments and procedures based on their demonstrated multicultural applications, remaining flexible and innovative in the implementation of the assessment, consulting with colleagues as needed, striving for honest communication with clients and their families, presenting assessment results feedback within a culturally acceptable framework, striving for sensitivity to within-group and between-group differences, developing new techniques that will be effective cross-culturally and for specific cultural applications, and introspectively examining one's own belief and value system.

REVIEW AND APPLICATION QUESTIONS

1. Operationally define the term *test bias* (or *assessment bias*) as it relates to behavioral, social, and emotional assessment.
2. Characterize the current status of professional standards and ethical codes for culturally competent assessment. In your view, are the current standards adequate?
3. What have been the major criticisms of current professional practices in educational and psychological assessment, with regard to cultural diversity?
4. Focusing on cultural diversity and assessment practices inevitably leads to a focus on some of the notable characteristics of specific racial/ethnic groups and subgroups within the larger groups. What are some of the potential problems that may occur from making generalizations regarding specific groups?
5. Characterize the projected demographic trends in racial/ethnic diversity in the United States between the present time and the year 2050.
6. For each of the six general methods of assessment that are covered in this chapter, what are some of the major advantages and possible problems for multicultural applications?
7. Operationally define the term *acculturation*.
8. Regarding the proposed stages of racial and cultural identity development, what are some of the similarities and differences in the progression through stages for members of racial and ethnic-minority groups as opposed to members of the majority culture?
9. A 10-year-old Hispanic female is referred to you by the school referral team. The student emigrated from Honduras two years ago and lives with her parents and younger brother. The team is concerned about . . . Using the recommendations for culturally responsive practice (see Table 2.3), discuss and outline how you will go about an assessment.

3

ASSESSMENT AND CLASSIFICATION

One of the traditional purposes of assessing social and emotional behavior is to determine an appropriate diagnosis or classification. The term *diagnosis* historically is linked with the medical model of psychological disorders, whereas the term *classification* is used more in education and by behaviorally oriented researchers. Both terms imply a common element of categorizing and codifying an observable phenomenon based on an existing taxonomy or scheme. Without arguing over conceptual or definitional differences between the two terms, both are subsumed under the more generic term, *classification*, in this chapter. Both terms are related to the notion of *taxonomy*, which comes from the Greek verb *tassein*, meaning "to classify," and *nomos*, meaning "law, science." In the sciences, taxonomic structures are often hierarchical in nature, meaning they classify phenomena from the most important to the least important feature. Taxonomies may also include *network relationships*, which are nonhierarchical. Most people who have completed a middle-school- or high-school-level biology course are familiar with the taxonomic system used to classify living things according to their *domain, kingdom, phylum, class, order, family, genus,* and *species.*

There has been extensive debate within the behavioral sciences regarding the usefulness and current validity of the processes of classification and taxonomy. The traditional view of classification is that the behavioral sciences, like the natural sciences, should develop and use classification taxonomies to create order, to provide a common ground for clinicians and researchers to use in describing problems or strengths, to help predict the future course of behavior, and ideally, to recommend an intervention plan. However, the state of the behavioral sciences is still far from being at the point where these goals for classification are being met, or where there are universally accepted taxonomic classification systems that hold up under tough scrutiny (Gresham & Gansle, 1992; McBurnett, 1996). The problems with traditional classification systems have led to great dissatisfaction by many behaviorally oriented practitioners and researchers. It is important to recognize, however, that during the past decade or two, there have been encouraging improvements in the reliability and usefulness of traditional systems of classification (Kauffman, 2000; Power & DuPaul, 1996).

This chapter discusses several important issues regarding the role of classification in assessment. First, a rationale for conducting classification activities is proposed, which is followed by a discussion of differential diagnosis and classification error. Most of the chapter is devoted to descriptions of current classification systems. Three major classification systems are overviewed, including the *Diagnostic and Statistical Manual for Mental Disorders* (*DSM*) system, the special education classification system from federal

DOI: 10.4324/9781315747521-4

law, and the emerging behavioral dimensions approach. Following the presentation of current classification systems, the chapter includes a brief overview of multiple-gating approaches, which represent relatively new developments in systematic assessment and selection for classification and treatment. The chapter concludes with a brief discussion of some additional issues relating to the assessment–classification process.

WHY CLASSIFY?

There is no doubt that current classification systems in psychology, psychiatry, and education are imperfect. Yet, despite their present flawed state, there is wisdom in the notion that disregarding or abandoning our current systems because of their imperfections may be throwing out the proverbial baby with the bath water. There are some solid pragmatic reasons why classification is often necessary and useful as part of the assessment process. The following four examples are reasons why doing a formal classification as part of an evaluation is often important:

1. Classification can provide some common ground of understanding for different professionals working with the same client.
2. Classification can provide access to needed services for clients.
3. Educational and health service institutions often require classification to remunerate the client or service providers for services.
4. In the absence of an entirely reliable and valid classification taxonomy for behavioral and emotional problems, continuing to work with and refine present systems is a step in the right direction toward developing improved systems.

Although it is true that there are many problems with current classification systems and that they are often used and implemented cynically, I propose that abandoning the use of classification simply because the state of the art is currently marginal is short-sighted. "Giving up all uses of classification is tantamount to abandoning the scientific study of social and behavioral difficulties. Indeed, we need labels for problems to communicate about them" (Kauffman, 1997, p. 158). Thus, the primary purposes of this chapter are to orient the reader to the more common classification systems that are used as part of the assessment process, and to provide a rational argument for how current classification systems can be best used in assessment.

DIFFERENTIAL DIAGNOSIS AND CLASSIFICATION ERROR

The term *differential diagnosis* is often used in psychiatric and psychological literature, but it is often misunderstood and misused. The process of differentially diagnosing or classifying a behavioral, social, or emotional problem essentially involves two steps: (1) making a *binary decision* as to whether the problem is considered normal or abnormal in nature; and (2) reaching a decision regarding *how to classify* the problem specifically (e.g., conduct disorder versus oppositional defiant disorder (ODD); specific learning disability versus emotional disturbance). This differential process is often difficult because it is considered to be one of the most technically demanding aspects of the assessment process. It is also critical for understanding the topography and functionality of symptoms (First, 2013).

Given the imperfect nature of current classification systems, it is inevitable that some errors will be found in many differential diagnostic and classification decisions. Two types of errors are of particular interest for clinicians making classification decisions. A *false-positive error* (also called a *Type I error*) occurs when an individual is classified as having a particular disorder, but in fact does not. A *false-negative error* (also called a *Type II error*) occurs when an individual is classified as being "normal" or not having a specific disability or disorder, when he or she in fact does.

Which type of error is worse? The answer to this question depends on what type of classification decision one is making and what the potential consequences are for making such errors. When conducting initial screening (e.g., to identify children who are in the early stages of developing behavioral, social, or emotional problems), the primary goal is to narrow down from a large group of individuals who may be good suspects, then to look at the narrowed population in more detail. For a screening process, it would be preferable to make a false-positive error rather than a false-negative error because the problem of overselection can be corrected at a later point, but underselection may result in a child, who is in need of help, going for an additional long period of time without receiving it. If you are making a decision as to whether or not an individual has a psychotic disorder, making a false-positive error sets up a potentially high-stakes situation in which the client is improperly labeled, has a good chance of being stigmatized for a long period of time, and may even end up being the recipient of a treatment that is not needed and may have negative side effects, such as the prescription of antipsychotic medications that have significant side effects.

In general, it is recommended that the higher the risks and consequences are in a differential diagnosis and classification decision, the more conservative the approach to making the decision should be. In cases in which a great deal of adverse consequences is a potential, a clinician should even go so far as to take a disconfirmatory approach, which involves approaching the classification decision with the hypothesis that the disorder or disability under question is not present and rejecting that premise only when the evidence to the contrary clearly overwhelms the initial working hypothesis.

CURRENT CLASSIFICATION SYSTEMS

Three different classification systems for arranging behavioral, social, and emotional problems of childhood and adolescence are described in this section. First, the psychiatric-based *DSM* system, which is widely used by mental health professionals, is overviewed. Then the classification categories and definitions based on special education law are discussed. Finally, a relatively recent and promising approach to classification of behavioral, social, and emotional problems, the behavioral dimensions method, is introduced.

The DSM System

Assumptions and Structure of the DSM   Without question, the most widely used system for classification of behavioral, social, and emotional problems in North America—and possibly in the world—is the psychiatric-based *DSM*. The most recent revision of the *DSM* was released in 2013. This fifth revision is referred to as the *DSM-5* (American Psychiatric Association, 2013) and represents over ten years of research and development that included an overhaul of the text-revised version of the fourth edition (*DSM-IV-TR*) (American Psychiatric Association, 2000).

The first edition of the *DSM* was published in 1952 and, like subsequent editions, was based on a medical model of behavioral and emotional problems, which views such disturbances as *mental disease*. The most traditional underlying assumption of this model is that behavioral and emotional problems reside *within the individual,* although this assumption has been tempered to a great extent in more recent years by the influence of behavioral psychology, which provides an alternative framework for viewing problems as a product of eliciting and reinforcing stimuli within a person's environment.

Prior versions of the *DSM* used a *multiaxial* approach to classification. That is, individuals were classified according to five different dimensions or axes, rather than as simply experiencing a given problem. The first axis referred to clinical disorders, and the second referred to personality disorders and intellectual disabilities. The other three axes referred to general medical conditions, psychosocial and environmental problems, and level of adaptive functioning. Within Axes I (clinical disorders) and II (personality disorders and mental retardation), several of the disorders within the classification system were not relevant to children and adolescents, whereas other disorders were specific to the developmental years or are at least considered to be first evident during childhood or adolescence.

Table 3.1 provides a brief overview of the clusters of current chapters of the *DSM-5*, which is a significantly different organization from other versions. Documentation of disorders in the *DSM-5* is no longer organized by the multiaxial structure seen in other versions; instead symptoms of disorders are described with required documentation for severity and client functioning. Table 3.2 specifies the specific chapters within one cluster as an example. The *DSM-5* no longer has a separate chapter on disorders that are first

Table 3.1 Overview of the *DSM-5*

Neurodevelopmental disorders
Schizophrenia spectrum and other psychotic disorders
Bipolar and related disorders
Depressive disorders
Anxiety disorders
Obsessive–compulsive and related disorders
Trauma- and stressor-related disorders
Dissociative disorders
Somatic symptom and related disorders
Feeding and eating disorders
Elimination disorders
Sleep–wake disorders
Sexual dysfunctions
Gender dysphoria
Disruptive, impulse control, and conduct disorders
Substance related and addictive disorders
Neurocognitive disorders
Personality disorders
Paraphilic disorders
Other mental disorders
Medication-induced movement disorders and other adverse effects of medication
Other conditions that may be a focus of clinical attention

Table 3.2 *DSM-5* sample chapter: Neurodevelopmental disorders

---

Neurodevelopmental disorders

Intellectual Disabilities: Mild, Moderate, Severe, Profound, Global Developmental Delay, Unspecified Intellectual Disability

Communication Disorders: Language Disorder, Speech Sound Disorder, Child–Onset Fluency Disorder (Stuttering), Social (Pragmatic) Communication Disorder, Unspecified Communication Disorder

Autism Spectrum Disorder: Autism Spectrum Disorder
Attention Deficit/Hyperactivity Disorder: Attention Deficit/Hyperactivity Disorder (Combined presentation, Predominantly inattentive presentation, Predominantly hyperactive/presentation), Other Specified Attention Deficit/Hyperactivity Disorder, Unspecified Attention Deficit/Hyperactivity Disorder

Specific Learning Disorder
Motor Disorders: Developmental Coordination Disorder, Stereotypic Movement Disorder, Tic Disorders, Other Specified Tic Disorder, Unspecified Tic Disorder

Other Neurodevelopmental Disorders: Other Specified Neurodevelopmental Disorder, Unspecified Neurodevelopmental Disorder

---

diagnosed in childhood or adolescence; rather, particular disorders may include notes or specifiers pertinent to presentation of symptoms in children. This was a purposeful change to create more of a lifespan approach to the description of clinical problems. Further, additional notes are included that encourage professionals to recognize cultural manifestations of certain symptomology.

In the mid-1980s, many professionals within the early childhood field began to vocalize concern that the *DSM* system did not adequately attend to developmental manifestations of clinically concerning behaviors. This spurred the development of the *Diagnostic Classification of Mental Health Disorders of Infancy and Early Childhood (DC: 0–3)* by a task force convened by ZERO TO THREE (1994). The DC: 0–3R (ZERO TO THREE, 2005) was the next version of the manual, which follows a multi-axial format similar to the *DSM-IV* system, and is often used in conjunction with the *DSM-IV* to comprehensively classify childhood disorders. The DC: 0–5 is in development and was available in 2021.

Using the DSM *System in Assessment* Virtually any type of moderate to severe behavioral or emotional problems that might be experienced by a child or adolescent is potentially *DSM-5* diagnosable under one of the many categories available. The all-inclusive nature of this system is both an advantage and a problem. The advantage lies in a clinician being able to use the system to classify a broad range of problems, to provide a common framework of understanding with other professionals, and to have possible implications for treatment (although this third point is arguable).

A problem with the all-inclusive nature of the system is that clinicians using it may end up making classification decisions (and, potentially, intervention recommendations) that are outside of their areas of professional expertise. For example, how many psychiatrists have sufficient training and experience with reading, writing, and arithmetic problems? How many psychologists or clinical social workers have any special training or expertise in diagnosing and treating speech and language problems? The broad, all-inclusive nature of the *DSM* system, along with potential problems of unreliability between different raters, does present some potential difficulties when using the system in assessment.

Another quandary that the *DSM* system poses is that the specific criteria for each category of disorder are not tied to specific assessment techniques, and the classification categories are not clearly linked to common intervention techniques. The responsibility for selecting and using specific assessment techniques or instruments, and eventually developing an appropriate intervention plan, is fully on the shoulders of the clinician or team conducting the assessment. The *DSM* does provide, however, relatively objective criteria for clinicians to follow in making a classification decision, and one of the major improvements of the *DSM-5* was to make these criteria even more objective and thus more reliable.

Consider the diagnostic criteria for *DSM-5* code 313.81 (F91.3), Oppositional Defiant Disorder, a type of problem classification that is not uncommon in children and adolescents who have been referred for psychological or other mental health services. The diagnostic criteria specify a clear time element (the condition must have lasted at least six months) and a list of behavioral conditions (in which at least four of nine specified conditions must be present). The criteria also list severity conditions that include consideration of the number of times per week symptoms are observed and the number of settings in which symptoms are observed. The classification criteria do have, at a minimum, face value of objectivity. Nevertheless, when viewing the complete criteria for Oppositional Defiant Disorder shown in Table 3.3, it becomes clear that classification decision-making also involves a fair amount of subjectivity. For example, what does the "often" in "often loses temper" mean—once a week, once a day, or several times a day? How easy is it in certain cases to determine if the "deliberately" in "often deliberately annoys people" is indeed deliberate?

Obviously the *DSM* system of classification, although it is the most widely used system, has inherent in it many potential pitfalls that clinicians need to be aware of, but if used judiciously, it can help the clinician achieve many of the goals and necessities of assessment.

Improvements to and Changes in the DSM Each subsequent edition of the *DSM* has contained various, sometimes substantial, changes in content and format. Presumably, these changes involve improvements to the system. One of the primary purposes of the change to the last few editions of the *DSM* was to develop more consistency with the World Health Organization's ICD-10 health classification system, which was published in 1992. Presumably, this type of change would make the *DSM* system more useful outside of North America. During the development of the *DSM-IV,* it was reported that the threshold for adding new categories under this revision was higher than in previous revisions of the *DSM* (Spitzer, 1991), an attempt to produce a relatively conservative document that would integrate changes from the *DSM-III-R* only when it was necessary to ensure consistency with the ICD-10 or to integrate new findings. The classification codes in the *DSM-5* include codes from previous versions of the *DSM* as well as codes from the ICD system. In 2014, all clinicians were expected to begin using the ICD codes for diagnosis and billing. This represents a major step in terms of aligning North America with the rest of the world.

Earlier in this section, some of the problems of the *DSM* system relating to assessment and classification were discussed, and to be sure, there has been no shortage of criticisms of the use of the *DSM* system, particularly when used with children and in school settings (Gresham & Gansle, 1992; McBurnett, 1996). There has been optimism, however, that the changes in the *DSM* system over the years have resulted in a more reliable and valid classification system and have been a significant step toward reducing or eliminating

Table 3.3 Example of criteria for a *DSM-5* diagnostic category: Oppositional Defiant Disorder 313.81 (F91.3)

A. A pattern of angry/irritable mood, argumentative/defiant behavior, or vindictiveness lasting at least six months as evidenced by at least four symptoms from any of the following categories, and exhibited during interaction with at least one individual who is not a sibling.

Angry/Irritable Mood
1. Often loses temper
2. Is often touchy or easily annoyed
3. Is often angry and resentful

Argumentative/Defiant Behavior
4. Often argues with authority figures, or for children and adolescents, with adults
5. Often actively defies or refuses to comply with requests from authority figures or with rules
6. Often deliberately annoys others
7. Often blames others for his or her mistakes or misbehavior

Vindictiveness
8. Has been spiteful or vindictive at least twice within the last six months
9. Often argues with adults
10. Often actively defies or refuses to comply with adult requests or rules

Note: The persistence and frequency of these behaviors should be used to distinguish a behavior that is within normal limits from a behavior that is symptomatic. For children younger than five years, the behavior should occur on most days for a period of at least six months unless otherwise noted (Criterion A8). For individuals five years or older, the behavior should occur at least once per week for at least six months, unless otherwise noted (Criterion A8). While these frequency criteria provide guidance on a minimum level of frequency to define symptoms, other factors should also be considered, such as whether the frequency and intensity of the behaviors are outside a range that is normative for the individual's developmental level, gender, and culture.

B. The disturbance in behavior is associated with distress in the individual or others in his or her immediate social context (e.g., family, peer group, work colleagues), or it impacts negatively on the social, educational, occupational, or other impairment areas of functioning.

C. The behaviors do not occur exclusively during the course of a psychotic, substance use, depressive, or bipolar disorder. Also, the criteria are not met for disruptive mood dysregulation disorder.

Specify current severity:
Mild: Symptoms are confined to only one setting
Moderate: Some symptoms are present in at least two settings
Severe: Some symptoms are present in three or more settings

Note: Reprinted with permission from the *Diagnostic and Statistical Manual of Mental Disorders, Fifth Edition* (Copyright © 2013) American Psychiatric Association.

some of the problems associated with earlier versions of the manual. The continuing refinements in the *DSM* system appear to be positive steps in improving the empirical integrity of this influential system (Waldman & Lilienfeld, 1995). The *DSM-5*, released in 2013, had been in development since about 2000 and is a result of continued commitment to empirically supported diagnostic criteria. In fact, the National Institute of Mental Health (NIMH), the National Institute on Drug Abuse (NIDA), and the National Institute on Alcoholism and Alcohol Abuse (NIAAA) granted 1.1 million dollars to support implementation of research planning conferences that aimed to share current research and build research agendas that would support changes in diagnostic criteria published in the *DSM*. Particular areas that this edition aims to address are diagnostic categories that are sensitive to the developmental progression of particular disorders across different ages and genders and a better system to acknowledge the dimensionality of particular disorders (Regier, Narrow, Kuhl, & Kupfer, 2009). Given some of the encouraging developments in the *DSM* system during the last 20 or more years, the possibilities for the long-term refinement of a scientifically sound taxonomy of human behavioral and emotional disorders appears to be improving, and the ultimate goal of a scientifically precise and reliable classification system appears to be within closer reach.

Classification under Special Education Law

Although the *DSM* system is the most commonly used classification structure for behavioral, social, and emotional problems within the mental health professions, professional practice in these areas is governed by an additional definition and classification structure within the public educational systems of the United States. In 1975, the U.S. Congress passed the Education for All Handicapped Children Act (also referred to as P. L. 94–142) as a result of "constitutionally based challenges to the exclusion of handicapped children" (Rothstein, 1990, p. xxiii). Now after four decades of existence, the federal law has had a profound impact on assessment and classification practices within school settings. This law, which since 2004 has been referred to as the Individuals with Disabilities Education Improvement Act (IDEA) also known as IDEA, is designed to ensure the provision of a *free and appropriate public education* and related educational services to all children and adolescents with disabilities. As part of the IDEA, specific classification criteria for disability conditions have been adopted, and specific guidelines for assessment have been enacted. It is beyond the scope of this book to provide a comprehensive understanding of the IDEA, but it is important for school-based and community-based practitioners to have a basic understanding of how the IDEA affects assessment and classification. This section provides a basic outline of the assessment and classification procedures of the IDEA that are pertinent to assessing behavioral, social, and emotional problems. A specific emphasis is placed on the classification category "emotionally disturbed" because it is the area most pertinent to this topic.

General Assessment Guidelines in the IDEA

Before a student with a disability can receive special education services under the auspices of the IDEA, he or she first must be identified as having a disability, and this process typically involves the use of formal assessment practices. Within the IDEA itself and through many court decisions that have been reached over the years, certain assessment requirements and safeguards have been put into place. Nine of these requirements and procedures that are most pertinent to our general topic are briefly listed as follows:

1. Parent consent must be obtained before the assessment is conducted.
2. When the school district requests that an evaluation be done, it is paid for at public expense.
3. Tests must be valid for the purpose for which they are being used.
4. No single assessment procedure may be used as the sole criterion for classification or program eligibility.
5. The assessment procedures must be culturally and racially appropriate; the child must be tested in his or her native language or mode of communication unless it is infeasible.
6. The evaluation is conducted by a multidisciplinary team (MDT) or group of individuals, including at least one team member who is knowledgeable about the child's specific area of disability.

7. The student is assessed in all areas pertinent to the suspected disability.
8. To be eligible for special education, students must meet criteria for a particular disability and demonstrate a need for specialized instruction.
9. The identified student's program must be reviewed annually, and the child must be reevaluated at least once every three years (although this reevaluation does not have to involve formal assessment, unless it is suspected that the child's disability condition has changed).

These nine examples from the IDEA are deceptively simple and straightforward. It is easy to understand what the intent of the law is, but often difficult to implement. As an example, let's look at guideline number 5. It is common for clinicians who are from the majority Anglo culture to conduct an assessment with ethnic minorities who have been raised in cultural conditions much different from those of the majority culture and for whom English is not their primary language. Given that few, if any, clinicians have a proficient command of all the potential languages that might be needed to meet this requirement, their first inclination when approached with cases like these may be not to take on the case. Yet, there is a competing pressure that makes it difficult to refer a problematic case. Particularly in isolated rural areas, the assessment professional in question may be the only person available at the time with technical training in educational and psychological assessment, and there may be no prospect of a qualified professional who is also bilingual. In a situation like this, the examiner is faced with a variety of ethical, technical, and legal dilemmas, of which the solution is often complex (for good discussions of best practices in considering cultural and linguistic factors, see Burr, Haas, & Ferriere, 2015; Nuttall, DeLeon, & Valle, 1990; Rhodes et al., 2005).

Another good example of how these nine guidelines are easy to understand, but complex to implement, can be demonstrated by considering guideline number 3, that test procedures must be valid for the purpose for which they are being used. How many of the assessment instruments used by an examiner in attempting to determine whether or not a child is emotionally disturbed have been validated for that *specific* purpose? Many procedures typically used for this purpose may have good psychometric properties and general evidence of validity, but may not have been adequately validated for that specific use. Given the questionable level of reliability and validity evidence of most projective techniques, it is doubtful that most, if any, would hold up under the scrutiny of a due process hearing or court decision, particularly if they were used as the primary basis for decision making.

Guideline number 6 should be of special interest to clinicians working in nonschool mental health settings. The law is clear in stating that the school MDT has the ultimate responsibility for conducting the evaluation and determining program eligibility; it is not appropriate for one person to make a unilateral decision, even though one person may have conducted most of the evaluation. Some professionals working in medical clinics, community mental health centers, or private practices may be unaware of this requirement, much to the consternation of school personnel when they receive a psychological report that states a child is eligible for special education services as emotionally disturbed, before the child has even been made a focus of concern by the school MDT.

The IDEA Definition of "Emotionally Disturbed" In looking at all of the IDEA's potential special education service categories, the category "emotional disturbance"

(ED, as it is commonly described) is most relevant to the practice of clinical assessment of social and emotional behavior. It is true that such problems often occur concomitantly with other disability conditions, but it is the ED category that most specifically addresses disturbances of behavior, social adjustment, and emotion.

Students who are classified as ED receive the same federal protections as students with other disability conditions (right to a free and appropriate public education and related services) and are potentially provided with a "cascade" of placement and service, ranging from regular classroom placement with the assistance of a behavioral consultant to full-time placement in a residential treatment center. The specific type of placement and service a student with ED is entitled to receive varies depending on the nature and severity of the disability and what the student requires to benefit educationally.

In developing the rules and regulations for implementing the original Education of the Handicapped Act (P.L. 94–142), the U.S. Congress adopted the following definition (which has since been revised to remove the terms "seriously" and "autistic"). This definition was an adaptation of an earlier proposed definition developed by Eli Bower (1981), based on his widely influential research with youth engaging in delinquent and disturbing behaviors in California in the 1950s and 1960s, under the auspices of the California Youth Authority. The adaptation of Bower's definition that was originally embraced in the federal law is as follows:

> *(Seriously) emotionally disturbed* is defined as follows:
> (i) the term means a condition exhibiting one or more of the following characteristics over a long period of time and to a marked degree, which adversely affects educational performance:
>   (A) An inability to learn which cannot be explained by intellectual, sensory, or health factors;
>   (B) An inability to build or maintain satisfactory interpersonal relationships with peers and teachers;
>   (C) Inappropriate types of behavior or feelings under normal circumstances;
>   (D) A general, pervasive mood of unhappiness or depression, or,
>   (E) A tendency to develop physical symptoms or fears associated with personal or school problems.
> (ii) The term includes children who are schizophrenic (or autistic). The term does not include children who are socially maladjusted, unless it is determined that they are also (seriously) emotionally disturbed.

Note that the term *seriously* appears in parentheses before "emotionally disturbed." The law originally passed by Congress and the resulting regulations that integrated Bower's definition referred to this category as "seriously emotionally disturbed." The 1997 reauthorization of the IDEA resulted in the word *seriously* being dropped from the title (Dwyer & Stanhope, 1997). Additionally, autism was removed from ED and given its own classification category with the 1990 reauthorization of IDEA. Otherwise, the same essential definition of the term has been in use for over 30 years.

A careful reading of the federal ED definition shows that using these criteria to make a classification decision is a process, similar to using the *DSM* criteria, that is at least superficially objective, but also involves a great deal of subjectivity. For example, what is a "long period of time" over which the problems must have occurred? Is six weeks too little time to be considered "a long period"? Is one year too much time? How about the phrase "to a marked degree"? What kind of objective criteria can a clinician use to determine how marked the degree of a problem is? The definition of ED from the federal law, like many of the *DSM* diagnostic criteria, carries with it some problems of interpretation and implementation and requires the clinician and members of the MDT to use a fair amount of professional judgment.

The "Emotionally Disturbed" versus "Socially Maladjusted" Issue One of the continuing controversies surrounding the federal definition of ED stems from a brief statement in part ii of the definition: that the term does not include children who are *socially maladjusted* unless it is determined that they are also *emotionally disturbed*. What exactly does this statement mean, and what are its ramifications? Although the IDEA does include the term *socially maladjusted* (SM) within the definition of ED, no operational definition of SM is provided in the law. Traditionally, the term *social maladjustment* has been used to indicate a pattern of behavioral problems that are thought to be willful, goal oriented, and possibly reinforced as part of one's immediate social reference group—a gang member being encouraged by his or her peers to attack a member of a rival gang, for example. The volitional nature of the antisocial behavior engaged in is often linked with social maladjustment, as characterized by Kelly's (1989) statement: "The term socially maladjusted encompasses . . . most individuals described as 'conduct disordered' who demonstrate knowledge of appropriate family, social, and/or school rules and *choose* not to conform to them" (p. 3, italics added for emphasis). Another traditional feature of the way social maladjustment has been conceptualized is that it is antisocial in nature, as typified by the type of behaviors exhibited in the *DSM-5* diagnostic categories Conduct Disorder (CD) and Antisocial Personality Disorder (APD).

Because students identified as ED cannot be expelled easily from school, and because considering a student with severe behavioral problems as SM provides a "loophole" for not providing special education services to them, there has been a great deal of professional interest in this topic since the federal law was enacted. Although earlier studies of state special education regulations indicated that more than half of all states had ignored, or chosen not to deal with, the social maladjustment issue in their state definitions of ED (Mack, 1985), later surveys have shown that a majority of state definitions include the social maladjustment exclusionary clause or some other form of exclusion (Skiba, Grizzle, & Minke, 1994), and there is no evidence from the past two decades that this trend has reversed. In fact, more recent treatments of this topic, such as a special issue of *Psychology in the Schools* (Vol. 41, Issue 8, 2004), and further articles by Cloth et al. (2013), and Sullivan and Sadeh (2014), devoted to the SM versus ED issue, provide ample evidence that the controversy still rages.

Although the federal ED definition provides no guidelines on how to identify social maladjustment, many professionals in education, psychology, and law have developed suggested classification procedures. A common approach, stemming from a legalistic interpretation of the *DSM* system, is characterized by the opinions of attorney Jane Slenkovitch during the 1980s and 1990s (1983, 1992a, 1992b), who contended that a *DSM* diagnosis of Conduct Disorder should be equated with social maladjustment and could legitimately serve to disqualify students from being identified as ED. There also have been continuing attempts to develop psychometric instruments that are purported to be able to distinguish ED from social maladjustment.

In view of the great interest in this particular aspect of the ED definition, it is interesting to note that the term socially maladjusted was never a part of Bower's original definition and that he is on record as being opposed to the inclusion of the term into the federal definition as he considers it unworkable (Bower, 1982). There have been other compelling arguments made for eliminating the social maladjustment clause from the federal ED definition (Council for Children with Behavioral Disorders (CCBD), 1991; C. M. Nelson, Rutherford, Center, & Walker, 1991; Skiba, 1992). In one article, Merrell and Walker (2004) argued that the current ED definition, including the SM exclusionary clause, is untenable and advocated for a general *emotional or behavioral disorders* approach to definition in which the empirically supported internalizing and externalizing behavioral dimensions system serves as the basis for classification and eligibility determination. There is no evidence, however, that this change, or any similar changes, will occur any time soon, given that the 1997 reauthorization of the IDEA retained the social maladjustment exclusion, despite extensive efforts by professional groups such as the CCBD and a national education and mental health coalition of practitioners to urge Congress to adopt a different definition (CCBD, 1991; Forness & Kavale, 2002; Forness & Knitzer, 1992), and that there were no extensive lobbying efforts in this vein prior to the 2004 reauthorization of the law. In fact, it appears that energy from previous years that was aimed at developing a more defensible definition of ED has dissolved, and that the ED/BD field is failing to achieve its promise (Walker, Zeller, Close, Webber, & Gresham, 1999). It will be interesting to see if there is movement on this issue with the anticipated reauthorization of IDEA in the next few years.

For now, professionals conducting school-related assessments of children and adolescents with behavioral, social, and emotional problems should be aware that there are no psychometrically valid and defensible assessment procedures that can be used to make the ED versus SM distinction. Clinicians and program administrators who are forced to deal with this issue must walk a perpetual fine line between empirically validated professional practices and the necessity of making pragmatic decisions based on policies and resource constraints. The final addendum in the current federal definition does allow students who are considered to be socially maladjusted to receive special education services if it is determined that they are also emotionally disturbed, but the interpretation of this particular statement has been problematic, and the statement itself may be construed as using circular logic. In commenting on this and related statements years ago in federal definition discussion of social maladjustment, Kauffman (1997) remarked that "the final addendum regarding social maladjustment is incomprehensible" (p. 28).

State Adaptations of the Federal Definition In practice, the IDEA is carried out by each of the states, who are given a fair amount of leeway in adapting and implementing specific aspects of the rules and regulations. Not all states have adopted this classification category by the *emotionally disturbed* title or its predecessor *seriously emotionally disturbed*. Given that these terms tend to elicit images of psychiatric hospitals and highly disturbing behaviors, many individuals believe the term is pejorative at best, and some states have adopted this part of the IDEA by using other terms, such as *seriously behaviorally disabled, behavior disordered,* or *emotionally impaired.* There is also some variation among states in terms of specific assessment procedures that are to be used in making a classification of ED. Several states require documentation of appropriate intervention plans being implemented with a student before ED classification. Other states require specific assessment procedures, such as direct behavioral observation or rating scales, and some states require an evaluation from a psychiatrist or other medical doctor before allowing classification.

Regarding the differences among labels used to describe and implement ED from state to state, it has long been argued that terms such as *behaviorally disordered* are less stigmatizing and more accurate as a definitional term than *emotionally disturbed* (Feldman, Kinnison, Jay, & Harth, 1983; Merrell & Walker, 2004; Walker, 1982). Also, there seems to be a preference among professionals in the field of special education for the term *emotionally or behaviorally disordered*, which is seen as being less stigmatizing and more inclusive (Kauffman, 2000). Nevertheless, widely varying terms and practices continue to be the norm.

New Directions There is widespread agreement among leaders in the field that the education of children with emotional and behavioral disorders under the IDEA has failed to achieve its promise (Merrell & Walker, 2004; Walker, Nishioka, Zeller, Severson, & Feil, 2000; Walker et al., 1999). Despite more than three decades of intensive effort, less than 1% of children nationally are provided with special education services under the federal law in this area, whereas the evidence overwhelmingly indicates that we should be identifying and serving in the range of 3% to 5% of students who are in need of intensive, individualized services for behavioral and mental health problems. In addition, students with emotional and behavioral disorders have the highest rate of school dropout of any special education group and tend to fare poorly in general after the conclusion of their school experience.

Although there are numerous reasons for this sad state of affairs, one of them is clearly the problem of definition and classification and how it relates to assessment and identification. To this end, Hill Walker, a longtime leader and pioneer in this field, has for several years been advocating a change in the special education definition and classification systems for students with emotional and behavioral disorders:

> I think that the bipolar externalizing–internalizing classification scheme . . . is the best system for use in accounting for school-related disorders. Externalizing refers to acting-out problems that involve excess behavior that is problematic. Disorders such as aggression, disruption, oppositional behavior, noncompliance, and negativism are illustrative of "externalizing" disorders. In contrast, internalizing refers to insufficient amounts of behavior that often involve skill deficits. Examples of internalizing disorders are depression, social isolation and neglect, phobias, anxiety, and immaturity. . . . I believe educators would be well served in adopting this type of bipolar classification scheme in dealing with school-related emotional or behavioral disorders.
>
> (Walker, cited in Kauffman, 1997, p. 163)

More information on the dimensional externalizing–internalizing approach to classification is presented in the next section of this chapter and in subsequent chapters. We enthusiastically endorse the notion of shifting the current special education definition and classification system for students with emotional and behavioral disorders toward an externalizing–internalizing disorder framework (Merrell & Walker, 2004). Such a definition and classification system is empirically sound, easily understood, has a common sense appeal, and is likely to be less stigmatizing than the current system. In addition, it is important to consider that the current system, which has systemic problems of underidentification and underservice in general, is particularly problematic when it comes to identifying students with internalizing disorders (e.g., depression, anxiety, social withdrawal), who tend to be overlooked altogether (Merrell, 2001). One result of a move toward the dimensional system of special education classification may be to increase the visibility of and focus on students with internalizing problems.

Behavioral Dimensions: An Alternative Approach to Classification

In addition to the *DSM* and special education classification systems, a third type of classification system shows considerable promise as an empirically sound way of classifying behavioral, social, and emotional problems that are exhibited by children and adolescents. This method has been referred to by various terms but is specifically referred to as the *behavioral dimensions approach* in this book. The paradigm used in the behavioral dimensions approach is rooted in empirical methods of measuring behavior and complex statistical procedures that allow for the identification of behavioral clusters, which refer to clusters of highly intercorrelated behaviors. The statistical techniques that are most important in identifying intercorrelated behavioral syndromes are factor analysis, cluster analysis, and structural equation modeling. The use of these techniques in the behavioral dimensions approach to classification became prominent between the late 1960s and early 1980s, mainly through the pioneering work of Thomas Achenbach and his colleagues (Achenbach, 1982a, 1982b; Achenbach & Edelbrock, 1981, 1983, 1984), Herbert Quay and his colleagues (Quay, 1975, 1977, 1986a; Quay & Peterson, 1967, 1987), and other behavioral scientists (e.g., Brown & Barlow, 2009). These researchers have developed and refined behavioral dimensions approaches to classify behavioral problems through the use of sophisticated rating scales with empirically derived factor structures, and with the goal of understanding the dimensionality and co-occurrence of clinical disorders, which often gets lost when using categorical, diagnostic tools, such as the *DSM*.

Behavioral Dimensions and the Achenbach System of Empirically Based Assessment (ASEBA) System

Through the development of parent and teacher rating forms of the Child Behavior Checklist (CBCL) (Achenbach & Edelbrock, 1981, 1984, 1991; Achenbach & Rescorla, 2001), Achenbach and his colleagues originally used factor analytic studies to identify two general classification areas within the behavior dimensions approach. The first general classification scheme is referred to as *broad-band syndromes*, which indicates the existence of large general behavioral clusters accounting for many types of related behavioral problems. The two primary broad-band syndromes include *internalizing problems*, which relate to *overcontrolled behavior*, and *externalizing problems*, which relate to *undercontrolled behavior*. Examples of internalizing problems include anxiety, depression, somatic or physical complaints, and social withdrawal. Examples of externalizing problems include delinquent behavior, aggressive behavior, and hyperactivity.

The second general classification scheme in Achenbach's system is referred to as *narrow-band syndromes*, which are smaller behavioral clusters indicating more specific types of behavior, social, or emotional problems. The narrow-band syndromes used in the most recent version of Achenbach's system, which is referred to now as the *Achenbach System of Empirically Based Assessment* (ASEBA), include *Withdrawn, Somatic Complaints,*

Anxious/Depressed, Social Problems, Thought Problems, Attention Problems, Delinquent Behavior, and *Aggressive Behavior*

The ASEBA system includes a variety of different rating and report forms, and these are discussed more specifically in subsequent chapters. Earlier versions of the instruments in this system used different narrow-band syndromes for different age and gender breakdowns, which were based on separate factor analytic studies, but the most current versions use the same "cross-informant" syndromes for each youth assessment instrument for ages six to 18, regardless of gender and age range. The ASEBA is arguably the most sophisticated system of child behavior assessment tools currently available, and it is certainly the most extensively researched. These tools have become widely used by practitioners in school and clinical settings and by researchers. Table 3.4 shows the division of broad-band and narrow-band problem "cross-informant" syndromes used in the ASEBA system of instruments for school-age children and youth.

Example of Behavioral Dimensions Approaches to Specific Classes of Behavior The behavioral dimensions systems advocated by Achenbach and Quay conceptualize dimensions of behavior problems in a global sense, by attempting to define and validate overall classes of behavioral, social, and emotional problems. Some additional work by these researchers has shown, however, that a behavioral dimensions approach to smaller and more discrete classes of behavior is also possible. Using the specific class of delinquent behavior as an example, both researchers (Achenbach, 1982a, 1982b; Quay, 1975, 1986a) identified subtypes of delinquent behavior, using the same general behavioral dimensions methodology that has been overviewed.

Achenbach (1982a) identified three dimensions of subtypes of delinquent activity: (1) socialized–subcultural (low IQ and socioeconomic status, bad companions, gang activities, maintaining social status through illegal behavior); (2) unsocialized–psychopathic (aggressive, assaultive, irritable, defiant, insensitive, feeling persecuted); and (3) neurotic–disturbed (overly sensitive, shy, worried, unhappy). Likewise, Quay's (1975) dimensional findings on delinquent behavior are similar to those of Achenbach's, often using the same labels and terminology. One minor difference between the two-dimensional approaches is that Quay suggested the existence of a fourth category—inadequate–immature (passivity, dependence, tendency toward daydreaming). Because these dimensional classification

Table 3.4 Cross-informant syndrome categories used in the Achenbach System of Empirically Based Assessment

Broad-band syndromes	Narrow-band syndromes	*DSM-5* oriented scales	Narrow-band syndromes
Internalizing problems	Aggressive behavior	Depressive problems	Aggressive behavior
Externalizing problems	Anxious/depressed	Anxiety problems	Anxious/depressed
Total problems	Attention problems	Somatic problems	Attention problems
	Rule-breaking behavior	Attention Deficit/ Hyperactivity	Rule-breaking behavior
	Social problems	Oppositional defiant problems	Social problems
	Somatic complaints	Conduct problems	Somatic complaints
	Thought problems	Thought problems	
	Withdrawn/depressed	Withdrawn/depressed	

Table 3.5 Overview of dimensional subtypes of delinquent behavior merging the findings of Achenbach (1982a) and Quay (1975)

Dimensional subtype	Behavioral description
Socialized–Subcultural	Peer-oriented, group or gang activities, delinquent value orientation, lower in IQ and socioeconomic status, and experiencing less parental rejection than other subtypes
Unsocialized–Psychopathic	Unbridled aggression, assaultive, hostile, defiant, explosive, insensitive to feelings of others, impulsive, thrill-seeking, responding poorly to praise or punishment, feel persecuted
Neurotic–Disturbed	Anxiety, guilt, overly sensitive, social withdrawal, worrying, unhappy
Inadequate–Immature	Highly dependent, passive, tendency toward daydreaming

systems for delinquency subtypes are so similar, they are presented in an integrated manner by four major categories in Table 3.5.

The purpose of presenting this overview of dimensional approaches to subtypes of delinquent behavior is to illustrate not only how the behavioral dimensions approach to classification extends to not just the overall conceptualization of behavior into several broad classes, but also how it can be used within each dimensional class of behavior. One can assume that other general classes of behavioral, emotional, or social problems also can be developed further into dimensional subtypes.

These empirically derived findings are intriguing and suggest that the behavioral dimensions approach to classification may also be useful in developing classification systems at a less global and more micro level. In this specific case, we should note that there have been more recent efforts to create subtypes within the narrow band of delinquent–aggressive behavior or conduct disorders, such as the work of Frick and colleagues (e.g., Frick, 1998; Frick & Ellis, 1999), but it was the work of Achenbach, Quay, and their colleagues who pioneered this approach.

Additional Comments on the Behavioral Dimensions Approach Something to consider when looking at the examples of behavioral dimensions clusters is that the names or titles of the specific dimensions are developed subjectively by the researchers involved which can be misleading if one takes them too literally. When a researcher, through factor analytic or confirmatory studies, identifies the existence of specific behavioral clusters, the researcher develops a name for the factor based on the types of specific behaviors in the cluster. Sometimes the cluster can be labeled in a way that directly indicates what the specific behaviors involved are. For example, one might label a cluster of behaviors that includes "threatens others," "physically fights," "argues," and related behaviors as "aggressiveness," which seems to make good clinical sense. Some clusters of behaviors may fit together well in a statistical sense, but coming up with an equally descriptive label for the cluster can be problematic. For example, one of the narrow-band clusters in the ASEBA system is *Thought Problems*. Intuitively, one might think at first glance that high scores on this cluster may indicate the presence of schizophrenia or other types of psychoses, but this is seldom the case. Some of the actual behaviors found in this cluster include "can't get his/her mind off certain thoughts," "strange ideas," and "stares blankly." Although these characteristics might be commonly seen in severely thought-disordered or psychotic individuals, they also may occur with frequency in individuals with lesser problems. Likewise, researchers sometimes change the names of identified narrow-band clusters because of this concern and because of unease regarding stigmatizing children. For example, the *Rule-Breaking Behavior* narrow-band cluster of the ASEBA system was previously labeled as *Delinquent Behavior*. In a strict sense, the more recent label is more accurate and less stigmatizing because not all rule-breaking behaviors indicated by the items in the cluster involve illegal activity. Clinicians and researchers using assessment and classification systems based on behavioral dimensions always need to look at the specific endorsed behaviors or items in a cluster to make decisions, rather than strictly going by the label or name a behavioral cluster has been given.

MULTIPLE GATING APPROACHES TO ASSESSMENT AND CLASSIFICATION

In Chapter 1, a model for using multiple sources of assessment data obtained from multiple sources and in multiple settings was introduced as a "best practice" in assessing behavioral, social, and emotional problems. The advantages of this multiaxial model were presented, and there is little doubt that its use is preferable from a clinical and a research standpoint to using single-source assessments. Yet, despite the obvious advantages it presents, there are also some potential obstacles. One of the problems in conducting assessments using many sources and instruments is the problem of *behavioral covariation*. If many different sources of information are used in an assessment, a diverse, if not contradictory, portrait of a child's behavioral, social, and emotional status may be obtained. This picture may present a serious problem for data interpretation because it has been posited that many clinicians, perhaps most of them, are not efficient or skilled at effectively aggregating the multiple data sources and detecting covariation across the instruments (Achenbach & Edelbrock, 1984; Reid et al., 1988). Another problem that may become amplified with a multisource, multisetting, and multi-instrument assessment design is that the detection of a class of target behavior or a specific syndrome that has a low base rate is difficult. If multiple data sources are not used in a sequential and methodical fashion, the amount of error in classification may possibly be increased because of the behavioral covariation problem. These are thorny problems for which there are no simple solutions.

New developments in assessment technology are showing some promise in reducing the types of assessment problems that have just been described. One of the most innovative developments in assessment and classification has been the development and refinement of a model for sequentially obtaining multiple sources of behavioral, social, and emotional assessment data, then systematically using this information to make screening and classification decisions. This assessment model has come to be known as *multiple gating*. It is based on the sequential assessment strategy first introduced by Cronbach and Gleser (1965) for applications in personnel selection. Multiple gating in the assessment and classification of child and adolescent psychopathology was first formally articulated and presented by research scientists at the Oregon Social Learning Center (Loeber et al., 1984; Reid et al., 1988).

The basis of multiple gating is that through a series of assessment and decision steps (gates), a large population is sequentially narrowed down to a small population of individuals who are very likely to exhibit the behavioral syndromes in question across settings and over time. The first step (or gate) generally consists of screening a large population of interest using time-effective and cost-effective measures such as rating scales or teacher ranking procedures for the behavioral syndrome of interest (e.g., antisocial behavior, aggression, hyperactivity, internalizing problems). These screening data are then used to narrow down the larger population to a more reasonable number, by allowing only those whose scores or rankings are at a specified level (e.g., over the 50th percentile) to pass through the first gate and on to the second. The initial criteria are established in a fairly liberal fashion, so as to result in many false-positive errors (identification of individuals who do not exhibit in a serious manner the behavioral syndrome in question), but few or no false-negative errors (failure to identify individuals who should be identified). The next gate in the sequence might be additional low-cost data that are obtained across different situations, for example, using lengthier rating scales completed by persons who know the identified persons in different settings. A cutoff criterion is established to determine which individuals will pass through the second gate. Those who pass through the second gate (their numbers should be fairly small at this point) are then assessed using more time-intensive procedures, such as structured interviews with parents and behavioral observations at home and/or school. The final gates also contain established decision rules for passing through, and individuals who do pass through the final points are considered almost certainly to exhibit the behavioral syndrome of interest to a serious degree. These individuals are then referred for additional assessment, final classification, and, potentially, a program of intervention or treatment. The final classification does not have to be a *DSM* or special education category but could consist of any formal operational definition of specific problem areas of interest.

Two examples of published multiple-gating procedures are presented to illustrate the potential uses and steps involved. The first example is a community-based or clinic-based multiple-gating procedure first developed at the Oregon Social Learning Center to identify youths at risk for antisocial and delinquent behavior. The second example is a school-based multiple-gating procedure to identify students with severe behavioral problems.

Community- and Clinic-Based Multiple-Gating Procedure
Many risk factors and behavioral variables have been found to correlate with the specific antisocial behaviors associated with delinquent status among youths. Loeber and Dishion (1983) ranked these etiological variables in terms of their predictive power and noted that the composite measures of parental family management techniques, early childhood conduct problems, poor academic performance, and parental criminality or antisocial behavior were the most powerful predictors. They attempted to apply this predictive information to a sequential multiple-gating procedure using data from 102 boys aged 12 to 16 years (Loeber et al., 1984). The result was a three-stage screening procedure that showed evidence of a high correct classification rate and was significantly less expensive than traditional methods of screening and assessment. The steps of this multiple-gating procedure are illustrated in Figure 3.1.

Gate 1 in the procedure consisted of teacher ratings obtained for each boy in the study. These ratings were conducted using a brief 11-item scale that required the teachers to rate the boys on academic competency and social–behavioral characteristics at school. Boys whose ratings were at the 47th percentile or higher ($N = 55$) were selected to be screened at Gate 2. The second gate consisted of telephone interviews with the parents of the remaining 55 boys. There were at least five interviews with each family, wherein questions

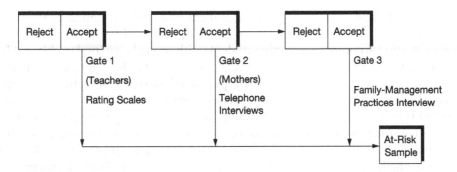

Figure 3.1 Diagram of a clinic-based multiple-gating procedure used to identify youths at risk for delinquency

Source: Adapted from Loeber, Dishion, and Patterson (1984). Copied with permission from SAGE Publications.

regarding family organization, the whereabouts of the target child, and the occurrence of problem behaviors within a 24-hour period were asked. A risk score for this procedure was established, and boys scoring above the 47th percentile ($N = 30$) were moved on to the final gate. This final step, Gate 3, involved structured interviews with the parents and the target children. The content of the interviews was focused on family management procedures, such as the parental monitoring of child activities, parental discipline practices, and perceived disobedience of the target boys. A risk score for the procedure was developed, and boys whose scores were at the 47th percentile or higher ($N = 16$) were passed through this final gate. These boys were found to have an extremely low false-positive error rate when follow-up data on involvement by all participants in delinquent activities were pursued. The researchers concluded that this study provided strong initial evidence for the use of multiple gating in classification, both from empirical and from cost-effectiveness standpoints. Since the publication of the Loeber et al. (1984) study, researchers at the Oregon Social Learning Center have continued to refine the use of multiple-gating assessment procedures in additional investigations. A revised multiple-gating model has been articulated by Reid et al. (1988), and this general model has been adopted in several research studies by other researchers and has influenced the assessment and service delivery models in some settings.

SSBD: A School-Based Multiple-Gating Procedure

Beginning in the mid-1980s, attempts were made to use multiple gating in the development of reliable and cost-effective screening procedures to identify students with serious behavioral disorders in school settings. The initial development of these procedures was based on methodology modeled after the findings of researchers at the Oregon Social Learning Center (Loeber et al., 1984; Reid et al., 1988). The rationale for the development of a school-based model was the desirability of identifying severe behavioral problems at early grade levels and being able to provide appropriate interventions in the early stages of developmental psychopathology rather than waiting until problems become extremely serious and resistant to alteration. The researchers involved in the early stages of this effort had noted that formal assessment and identification of students with severe behavioral disorders usually did not occur until about the middle school years, but a review of these students' behavioral records often found strong evidence for the existence of severe problems as early as kindergarten or first grade (H. Severson, personal communication, August 18, 1992).

The result of these efforts was the development of a multiple-gating procedure that showed strong evidence of several forms of reliability and validity and was found to have high classification accuracy in screening students with severe behavioral problems (Todis, Severson, & Walker, 1990; Walker, Severson et al., 1988, 1990). This multiple-gating system has since been revised and commercially published as the Systematic Screening for Behavior Disorders (SSBD) (Walker & Severson, 1992; Walker, Severson, & Feil, 2014). The SSBD is a three-gate system that includes teacher screening (using a rank-ordering procedure) of students with internalizing and externalizing behavioral problems (Gate 1), teacher ratings of critical behavioral problems (Gate 2), and direct behavioral observation of students who have passed the first two processes (Gate 3). The observational procedure used in Gate 3 includes academic behavior in the classroom and social behavior on the playground. The end result of the SSBD system is that students who are passed through all three gates become the focus of prereferral interventions and are potentially referred to the child study teams for formal assessment and special education classification. Figure 3.2 provides a diagram of the gates and procedures in the SSBD.

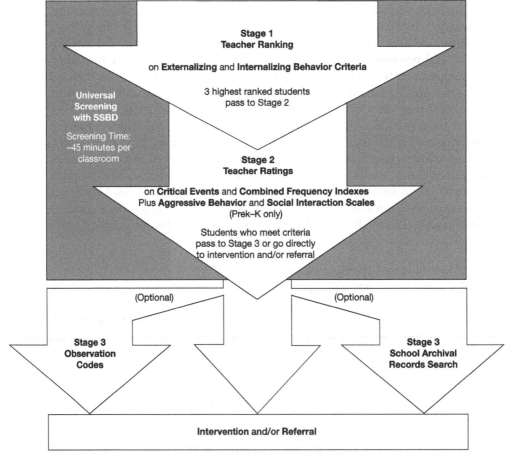

Figure 3.2 Diagram of the multiple gating stages of the Systematic Screening for Behavior Disorders

Source: From *Systematic Screening for Behavior Disorders, Second Edition*, by H. M. Walker, H. Severson, and E. Feil (2014). Eugene, OR: Pacific Northwest Publishing. Reprinted with Permission.

The complete SSBD package includes procedural, training, and technical manuals; normative data; recommendations for behavioral interventions; complete forms and protocols; and a video for training in the observational system. These materials are now also available online. It is a unique and exemplary system that shows some of the best possibilities of how school-based assessment and subsequent individualized support and/ or special education classification of students with severe behavioral and emotional problems can be accomplished.

SARS: Classification of Behavioral Problems Using Existing School Records

A fourth level of the SSBD, the School Archival Records Search (SARS) (Walker, Block-Pedego, Todis, & Severson, 1991) is also available. The SARS may be used as a fourth level in the multiple-gating SSBD system, or it may be used as a stand-alone tool. The SARS was designed to provide a systematic means of coding and quantifying existing school discipline records for the purpose of identifying students who may have externalizing or internalizing behavioral or emotional problems, and who may benefit from prevention or intervention programs. The SARS includes a four-page data entry form that provides spaces to enter information on students gleaned from existing school records in the following 11 areas: demographics, attendance, achievement test scores, number of grade retentions, academic and behavioral referrals, special education services, placement outside of regular classrooms, receipt of Chapter 1 academic services, frequency of referrals out of school, negative narrative comments (specified individually) from school discipline records, and disciplinary contacts outside of the classroom for the current school year. The SARS also includes a two-page Student Profile Form, which is used to code, in a more refined manner, much of the information obtained in the record form. The SARS manual provides instructions for converting this coded information into z scores and factor scores and suggested cutoffs for scores that are considered to indicate risk status in the following domains: Disruptive, Needs Assistance, and Low Achievement. The SARS scoring procedures and cutoffs are based on a regional sample of school records reviews from more than 300 students in Oregon.

Because the SARS is such a unique assessment tool, it is difficult to compare it with existing measures or traditional methods, and it should be evaluated on its own terms rather than by using traditional evaluation schemes. The information regarding the stability and effectiveness of the SARS presented in the technical manual and in subsequent published studies (Lane, Carter, Pierson, & Glaeser, 2006; Sugai, Sprague, Horner, & Walker, 2000; Tobin & Sugai, 1999; Tobin, Sugai, & Colvin, 1996) is impressive. The accumulated evidence indicates that the SARS provides a nonobtrusive means of gathering information from existing records that is highly predictive of existing behavioral risk categories and future behavior problems. It is a useful addition to the SSBD system and warrants use as a stand-alone tool. Because of increased concern regarding the failure of school personnel to pay close enough attention to existing indications of severe behavioral and emotional problems of students, tools such as the SARS designed to integrate and quantify school behavior files systematically are an important innovation in the field.

CONCLUDING COMMENTS ON ASSESSMENT AND CLASSIFICATION

Attempts have been made in this chapter to delineate suitable reasons for making diagnostic and classification decisions an important part of the assessment process, and to provide an overview of three major systems of classification: the *DSM*, special education service categories, and the emerging behavioral dimensions approach. In addition, it has been argued that there is scientific value using, and continuing to refine, our existing taxonomic classification systems. An important additional question to consider is: *How do classification activities help link assessment to the process of intervention?* Although attempts have been made to impress the reader with the necessity and advantages of conducting classification activities during the assessment process, the answer to this question is not yet as hopeful as we would like it to be. At present, the evidence supporting the treatment validity (usefulness in developing intervention or treatment plans) of current classification schemes is neither abundant nor compelling.

Although classification systems and activities serve several appropriate purposes, being able to take a given classification category and translate that automatically into a set intervention is seldom possible. Classifying human behavior is inherently easier than changing it. Because of the wide degree of individuality and variation in the biology, behavior, and temperament that humans exhibit, and in the conditions under which these characteristics are manifest, developing effective interventions for behavioral, social, and emotional problems requires a tremendous understanding of behavior–environment relationships and a great deal of clinical sensitivity on the part of interventionists. It remains an extraordinary challenge to the emerging generation of researchers and practitioners to develop classification systems that not only reliably codify a wide array of human characteristics, but also provide information that might translate directly into valid treatment planning.

On a somewhat more optimistic note, behaviorally oriented research scientists Scotti, Morris, McNeil, and Hawkins (1996) began a compelling argument for maintaining certain aspects of current categorical systems of classification and augmenting them with *functional* approaches to assessment when moving to treatment planning. These authors acknowledged that categorical classification systems that are limited to *structural assessment* of problems based on form (rather than function) of the concern are limited with respect to assisting intervention planning, but certain diagnostic systems may assist in delineating the *typical duration* and *developmental course* of specific clusters of related behavioral problems. For example, if we know that a child meets diagnostic criteria for the two *DSM* disorders Attention Deficit/Hyperactivity Disorder (ADHD) and Oppositional Defiant Disorder (ODD), we also know that they are at a higher risk than the general population for the development of Conduct Disorder (CD), which carries with it serious risks. This diagnostic information may help guide the assessment process toward the identification of protective and risk factors to target in an intervention plan. According to Scotti et al. (1996), assessment could take the form of a *funnel approach* that begins with a more traditional, structural assessment and moves to a more functional process as treatment planning increasingly becomes the focus.

Whether such a system and process offers a useful alternative to current categorically based systems remains an empirical question worthy of further research efforts. From the standpoint of problem solving, these systems seem worthy of exploration and careful evaluation. In addition, the use of multiple-gating procedures in assessment and classification is one development that shows promise in conducting systematic screening and assessment procedures that can be connected to various classification systems and subsequent programs of intervention.

On a final note related to classification are some thoughts related to the problem of classification or identification in relation to the stigmatizing effects that these processes may have on children and youth. Earlier in this chapter, a case was made for the practical and scientific importance of continuing to use and improve our systems for classifying human behavior. It is clear, however, that many professionals in the education and mental health fields do not share this view and would like to rid the field altogether of the use of diagnostic labels because of the stigmatizing effects such labels may have. Although there may be risks of stigmatization involved in appropriate diagnosis and classification practices, it is important to recognize that elimination of scientifically based systems of diagnosis and classification would not eliminate the stigmatization of children and youth with behavioral, social, and emotional problems: "Much worse than accurate diagnoses are the other labels that are applied to these children ... bad, unmotivated, dysfunctional, criminal, lazy, space-cadet, weird, etc." (Jensen, 2000, p. 2). Most human societies have a long tradition of stigmatizing individuals who have significant mental health and behavior problems (Kauffman, 2000). Eliminating labels and diagnostic categories might help reduce the discomfort that some professionals feel when they are presenting results to parents and teachers or making recommendations, but it would do little to reduce the stigma for children who are perceived as being different because of their behavior. Perhaps a better approach is to work toward improving current systems of diagnosis and classification, demanding that diagnoses be *data-driven,* and educating others regarding misconceptions and biases that lead to more difficulties for children who are already dealing with significant challenges in their lives.

CONCLUSIONS

Classification of behavioral, social, and emotional problems continues to be an important aspect of the overall assessment process. Although current psychological/psychiatric classification systems are imperfect, classification continues to be an important function because it can provide some common ground of understanding for professionals, and help provide access to services and remuneration for clients. Continuing to work with and refine present systems is a step in the right direction toward developing improved systems. Refining and improving our classifications that describe behaviors based on their form rather than their function is also consistent with the classification and taxonomic approaches that have typified the natural sciences for generations.

Differential diagnosis is a two-step process that involves making a decision regarding whether a problem is considered normal or abnormal and then reaching a decision regarding how to classify the problem. In making classification decisions, there are two major types of errors. A false-positive error involves making a determination that an individual has a particular disorder when in reality he or she does not, whereas a false-negative error involves failure to diagnose an individual with a particular condition or disorder that he or she in fact has. The stakes involved in making particular decisions determine which type of error is less onerous. The higher the risks and consequences are in a differential diagnosis and classification decision, the more conservative the approach to making the decision should be.

The *DSM* system, currently in its fifth edition, is the most widely used psychological/ psychiatric classification system in North America, and possibly the world. Historically, it has been based on the medical model, wherein emotional and behavioral disorders are viewed as *manifestations of an underlying disease process* residing within the individual. In more recent editions, the medical model outlook of the *DSM* has been tempered somewhat by the influence of behavioral psychology, and more attention is now given to the situational and environmental factors in diagnosing many types of disorders. Although the *DSM* system has been rightly criticized in the past for problems of unreliability and lack of treatment validity, there have been substantial improvements with the most recent editions. Continued future attention to behavior–environment relationships and the developmental and contextual aspects of behavioral and emotional problems will be useful in making the *DSM* system more sensitive and effective.

Within the public education system in the United States, the IDEA has substantial implications for assessment and classification of children and adolescents. Of particular interest to assessing social and emotional behavior in school settings is the IDEA special education eligibility category "emotionally disturbed." The definitional criteria for this category are broad enough to allow for classification of children with a variety of challenging social–emotional behaviors. One of the continuing controversies regarding the IDEA definition of ED is the so-called social maladjustment exclusion clause, which, similar to the definition of ED, has come under intense criticism but has not been changed by Congress, despite intensive lobbying efforts prior to the 1997 reauthorization. Efforts to move toward a general emotional–behavioral disorder definition that utilizes the behavioral dimensions (externalizing–internalizing) approach to identifying youth with emotional and behavioral disorders in school settings through the federal special education law hold promise.

A more recent approach to classification of child and adolescent social–emotional problems is what has been referred to as the behavioral dimensions approach. This approach, typified by the pioneering work of Achenbach and Quay, relies on sophisticated statistical models to derive empirically clusters or syndromes of child behavior.

A promising and innovative approach to assessment and classification of social–emotional problems of children and adolescents is school-wide and multiple gating. By using a sequential series of systematic and increasingly time-consuming screening procedures, multiple-gating methods allow for narrowing a large population down to a small group of candidates who are likely to exhibit behavioral and emotional problems to the point of needing further assessment and intervention. Multiple-gating approaches have been developed and validated for use in community and school settings. Although this methodology is time-consuming, multiple gating and sequential assessment theoretically may reduce error variance associated with using aggregated multiple assessment sources. Such efforts are promising and, with future refinements and improvements, may be utilized on a wide scale in providing universal screening of children and youth similar to what is advocated in the public health approach to disease prevention and health promotion. Despite the substantial improvements in classification systems for emotional and behavioral disorders of children and adolescents, many challenges remain. Perhaps the foremost challenge in this area is development of classification systems and categories that not only are reliable and scientifically taxonomic, but also have strong treatment validity. Although traditional classification systems may be useful as a starting point in developing intervention plans, by providing some general information about the structure of the problem, the function of the problem is also an essential element to be addressed in developing effective interventions.

REVIEW AND APPLICATION QUESTIONS

1. What are the primary purposes of classifying emotional and behavioral disorders of children and adolescents?

2. Define the term *differential diagnosis*, illustrating how it is used in the assessment and classification process.

3. Give examples of how *false-positive* and *false-negative* classification errors might occur in assessing behavioral, social, and emotional problems. Is one type of error less damaging than the other?

4. The *DSM* classification system has been widely criticized over the years but continues to be refined and is without question the pre-eminent classification system in North America. List the major positive and useful aspects of the *DSM* that have helped expand its influence.

5. What are some of the continuing problems with the *DSM* approach to classification? Reflect upon clinical cases you have discussed, observed, or conducted assessment, and consider the specific ways in which a *DSM* approach to classification has been helpful to the individual, as well as potentially harmful.

6. How defensible do you believe it is to restrict special education service eligibility as emotionally disturbed to students who are not "socially maladjusted"?

7. What are the assumptions and procedures behind the behavioral dimensions approach to classification, and how do they differ from those of other classification methods?

8. Two multiple-gating procedures for assessment and classification were described in this chapter. Identify the potential problems involved with instituting and using a multiple-gating procedure, and determine what steps could be taken to reduce these problems.

9. Using a multiple-gating procedure not only requires time and personnel to conduct the process, its results increase the likelihood that more referrals for assessment will be made to the multidisciplinary team. Assume your school or agency were considering starting a multiple-gating assessment procedure, discuss information you would present to support initiating a multiple-gating approach, its development, and maintenance.

10. One of the criticisms of classification and labeling systems for human behavioral and emotional problems is that they have little or no utility in development interventions or treatments. How much do you agree with this assertion?

11. Is limited intervention utility a big enough problem to justify moving away from classification taxonomies and into noncategorical service/eligibility systems?

4

DIRECT BEHAVIORAL OBSERVATION

This chapter provides a detailed introduction to the principles, specific uses, and problems of direct behavioral observation as a child assessment tool. This assessment technique is one of the primary tools of many clinicians and researchers who are involved in the assessment of behavioral, social, and emotional problems of children and adolescents, and it holds a prominent position as being one of the most empirically sound of these assessment techniques. In fact, behavioral observation is among the most frequently used assessment methods and may be the most commonly employed method among school psychologists (Wilson & Reschly, 1996). However, it is important for even the most ardent advocates of behavioral observation (including us) to recognize that this method of assessment does include several key challenges, and potential problems. Furthermore, there are major differences between anecdotal observation of behavior and systematic observational methods (e.g., Volpe & McConaughy, 2005), which cause us to contend that not all observational tools are equally useful and valid. This chapter first provides an overview of the basic principles and concepts of behavioral observation, then takes a detailed look at the general methods and typical coding procedures of behavioral observation. After the general foundations and methods of direct behavioral observation have been described, a review of several formal observational coding systems is provided. These systems were selected for inclusion in this chapter based on their general-purpose design and their utility in conducting assessments in school, home, and clinic settings. The chapter includes an analysis of some of the major problems and issues in behavioral observation. Issues ranging from the problem of observer reactivity to situational specificity of behavior are covered, and specific suggestions for overcoming these problems and limitations of behavioral observation are provided. The exploration of direct behavioral observation concludes with a discussion of how direct behavioral observation can be useful in making various decisions that are related to the assessment process.

BEHAVIORAL OBSERVATION: BASIC PRINCIPLES AND CONCEPTS

Direct observation of behavior is one of the cornerstone tools for the assessment of behavioral, social, and emotional problems exhibited by children and adolescents. Whether the observation involves formal behavioral recording in naturalistic settings, or whether it is done informally as part of other measurement strategies, behavioral observation provides the clinician with one of the most direct and objective assessment tools available. Direct behavioral observation is a procedure in which observers *develop*

DOI: 10.4324/9781315747521-5

operational definitions of the targeted behaviors of interest, observe the subjects, and systematically record their behaviors. Behavioral observation has the advantage of being linked to the development of interventions in a relatively straightforward manner.

The roots of behavioral observation are grounded firmly in behavioral psychology, as advocated by Watson, Skinner, and others. Since about the 1970s, there have been increased efforts at integrating behaviorism and direct observation into broader models of conceptualizing human behavior. To that end, direct observation has been found to be compatible with social learning theory (Bandura, 1977, 1978; Patterson, 1969), applied behavior analysis (Baer, 1982), and cognitive-behavior therapy (Meichenbaum & Cameron, 1982). Even an approach to treatment as different from behaviorism as Rogers's (1951) client-centered therapy relies on clinical observation by the therapist as an important part of understanding and treating the problems of the client, even though it is not as systematic as a solidly grounded behaviorist would prefer.

Keller (1986) noted that the unifying factor of various behavioral approaches appears to be "their derivation from experimentally established procedures and principles" (p. 355). As such, most methods of behavioral observation, and specifically those methods and techniques covered in this chapter, have a strong emphasis on sound empirical methodology and a high degree of treatment validity. Alessi (1988) noted that one of the crucial characteristics of observation methods for emotional and behavioral problems is that they permit a functional analysis of behavior and as such are intrinsically linked to the valid interpretation of assessment data and the development of systematic intervention plans. Direct behavioral observation methods are particularly suited to assessing the behavior of individuals as opposed to groups, although groups of individuals may be involved, because these methods are particularly adept at taking into account the unique context and the repertoire of responses exhibited by individuals (Alberto & Troutman, 2012; L. K. Miller, 1996; C. H. Skinner, Dittmer, & Howell, 2000; Sulzer-Azaroff & Mayer, 1991).

DIRECT BEHAVIORAL OBSERVATION AND ECOLOGICAL ASSESSMENT

Perhaps the foremost advantage of direct behavioral observation is that it allows the observer to gather functional information regarding not just individual behavior, but how this behavior exists as part of an interactive environment. This advantage of behavioral observation is particularly relevant to the theories of human behavior that were detailed in Chapter 1, namely social cognitive theory and the "triadic reciprocality" way of analyzing behavioral development and the ecological systems model of child behavior within varying contexts. Since the 1970s, substantial efforts by behavioral scientists have demonstrated that behavior is best understood, and predicted, when one takes into account the natural support systems within the environment that elicit and maintain the behavior because "those [behaviors] that run counter to natural support systems are less likely to prevail for very long" (Sulzer-Azaroff & Mayer, 1991, p. 46).

Take the case of an elementary-age student who exhibits aggressive and antisocial behavior in the various settings at school. A superficial observation of this student's behavior would merely define when, where, and how the problem behavior is occurring. In contrast, a systematic direct behavioral observation that takes into account the surrounding environment or ecology in which these behaviors exist, is more likely to provide information on conditions that elicit and maintain the problem behaviors, such as interactions between teachers and peers, the physical aspects of the classroom, or particular activities or individuals. A skilled clinician can use this type of information not only to describe and classify the behavior in detail, but also to develop intervention plans that may have a good chance of succeeding.

The notion of examining environmental antecedents and consequences of behavior and the ecological system in which behavior occurs, has existed for many years and has been continually refined. An influential article by Rogers-Warren (1984) more than 20 years ago referred to this notion as "ecobehavioral assessment," and the term *ecological assessment* also has been employed to reflect this notion. In the 1990s and later, this notion was infused with new energy through the proliferation of research and writing on the topic of functional behavior assessment (FBA) (Haynes & O'Brien, 1990; Horner, 1994; McComas & Mace, 2000; Reep, 1994; Vollmer & Northrup, 1996; T. S. Watson & Steege, 2003). FBA is discussed later in this chapter. In sum, researchers and practitioners who use direct behavioral observation should always consider that behavior does not occur "in a vacuum"; examining environmental relationships within the entire behavioral ecology should be a standard practice if the observation is meant to result in anything more useful than simple description of behavior.

GENERAL METHODS OF BEHAVIORAL OBSERVATION

Although there are many specific techniques and systems for observing and coding behaviors within direct observation, most can be subsumed in the three general categories of *naturalistic observation, analogue observation,* and *self-monitoring.* This section illustrates the main characteristics and uses of each of these three general methods.

Naturalistic Observation

The most direct way to assess child and adolescent behavior in most cases is through naturalistic observation in the setting in which the behavior typically occurs (Jackson, 2015; C. H. Skinner, Rhymer, & McDaniel, 2000; Whitley, Kite, & Adams, 2012). The essential elements of naturalistic observation were outlined by Jones, Reid, and Patterson (1979) more than 30 years ago, and include: (1) observation and recording of behaviors at the time of occurrence in their natural setting; (2) the use of trained, objective observers; and (3) a behavioral description system that requires only a minimal amount of inference by the observers–coders. Naturalistic observation differs from the other two general methods of observation in that there is a premium on obtaining observational data in typical, day-to-day situations, with strong efforts to minimize any obtrusiveness or reactivity caused by the presence of an observer. Analogue or self-monitoring methods require more inference than naturalistic observation in determining whether observed behaviors are representative of what actually occurs in the subject's day-to-day environment.

What type of observational settings can be considered to be naturalistic? Perhaps more than any other setting, school-based assessments offer many opportunities for naturalistic observation. Whether the observation takes place in the classroom, on the playground, during recess, in the cafeteria, in the halls between classes, or even on the school bus, the school environment has great potential for unobtrusive data collection in situations that are encountered by children and adolescents on a regular basis. For younger children who are not yet in school, other possibilities for naturalistic observation settings are day-care centers and play groups.

The home setting also offers opportunities for naturalistic observation but on a more limited basis. Observing a child interacting with his or her family in the home environment has the potential for being an excellent means of gathering data, but there are significant obstacles that must be overcome: the increased probability of obtrusiveness and reactivity and the physical circumstances of the home. Because most families are not used to having strangers enter their home and watch their ongoing activities, it is a given that they will behave differently under these conditions; most likely, they will make an effort to minimize the occurrence of any maladaptive or coercive behaviors by putting their "best foot forward." The design of most American houses and apartments, with the resulting lifestyles that are shaped, also creates considerable challenges for conducting observation. Many houses and apartments are sufficiently large and compartmentalized so that family members can distance themselves from each other (and from an observer) with relative ease by going into different parts of the home. In their pioneering efforts to develop valid home-based observation systems, investigators at the Oregon Social Learning Center (OSLC) (Reid, 1982; Reid et al., 1988) worked extensively on the problems of conducting effective naturalistic observations in home settings and developed methods of minimizing reactivity and physical barriers with their coding systems. A typical in-home observation by OSLC researchers is structured so that family members agree to stay in a common area of the home and do some activity together (other than watching television, which is considered too passive an activity to elicit sufficient family interaction) during the observation period. In a sense, conducting a home observation in this manner is contrived and is akin to analogue observation, but it still allows for highly effective observation and coding of family interactions in the home setting (Patterson, Ray, Shaw, & Cobb, 1969). More recently, the use of structured observation tasks in the homes has been linked to the development of contextually relevant, family-based interventions (Dishion & Stormshak, 2007). These observation tasks are often videotaped and then later used to give families feedback about the strengths and barriers in their interactions with one another (Smith, Dishion, Moore, Shaw, & Wilson, 2013). This direct feedback may not only help families to engage in intervention supports, but it also can help to reduce negative perceptions caregivers have about their children's behavior.

Analogue Observation

Unlike naturalistic observation methods, which are designed to capture behavior as and where it normally occurs, analogue observation methods are designed to simulate the conditions of the natural environment and to provide a highly structured and controlled setting in which behaviors of concern are likely to be observed (Hintze, Stoner, & Bull, 2000). Analogue assessment is considered to be an indirect measurement procedure that reflects "how an individual might behave in a real life situation" (p. 56). Analogue observation might occur in a clinic or a research laboratory, but the specific environment developed for the observation is structured to simulate everyday situations in the natural environment. In many cases, the participants in analogue observation might be requested to role play or engage in the observation activity in a specific way. Examples of situations that have been developed for analogue observation include parent–child interactions, family problem-solving approaches, and children's task orientation.

Analogue observation carries with it problems and obstacles. Compared with naturalistic observation, more inference is required in drawing conclusions about behavior and its generalization outside of the clinic or laboratory setting, and many questions are likely to arise concerning the validity of the observational data. Analogue observation offers enough advantages, however, that clinicians who conduct child and adolescent assessments are advised to become competent in its use. One of the chief advantages of the analogue method is that the observer can exert much greater control over the environment than with naturalistic observation, increasing the opportunities for eliciting important, but low-frequency, behaviors. For example, if one of the stated referral problems is noncompliance to teacher or parent directions, the observer can create many analogue situations in which the participants must react to directions. A related advantage that the control aspect of analogue observation offers is that extraneous stimuli—those things that are inconsequential to or detract from the behavior in question—can be reduced or eliminated. Overall, the analogue method offers many advantages and possibilities, if the observer considers its limitations.

One of the most important aspects of conducting an analogue observation is to structure the observational conditions so that they closely resemble those of the settings in which the problems are most likely to occur. By doing this, similarity in stimuli and responses between the two settings is maintained, and the observation is more likely to be conducive to the behavior in question. For example, if the assessment goal is to obtain observational data of interactions between a mother and her child, it would be important to have them engage in activities that they are likely to be doing at home, role play, or work with materials that they are likely to use at home. By carefully structuring the conditions of the analogue observation, the similarity between the natural environment is increased, and the resulting validity and usefulness of the observation data are enhanced.

Self-Monitoring
A third general method of observing behavior is self-monitoring. The essential feature of self-monitoring is that the participant or target child is trained in observing and recording his or her own behavior. The advantages of self-monitoring include its relatively low cost and efficiency, its utility in the measurement of covert or private events such as thoughts and subtle physiological changes, and its lack of intrusiveness (Cole, Marder, & McCann, 2000; Shapiro & Cole, 1994).

There are many drawbacks to self-monitoring, of which the reliability and validity of the self-monitored observations stand as major concerns (Gravina & Olson, 2009; Keller, 1986; R. O. Nelson & Hayes, 1986). It is difficult enough to train impartial observers–coders in the reliable use of observation technology, and when the observation is extended to include self-scrutiny by the participant (particularly with children), the implementation problems are likely to be increased. These potential reliability and validity problems can be decreased through specific procedures, including: (1) providing a sufficient amount of training to the subject; (2) using systematic and formal observation forms; (3) using self-monitoring procedures that require a minimum of time and energy by the subject; (4) conducting occasional reliability checks with the subject; and (5) reinforcing the subject for conducting accurate observations. Training should also include sufficient practice opportunities, so that the child is clear on when and how to self-monitor.

Self-monitoring tends to be used to a much greater extent in behavioral treatment programs than as part of a multimethod, multisource, multisetting assessment and, as such, is not addressed in any more detail in this book. For a more complete discussion of the use of self-monitoring procedures, readers are referred to works by Alberto and Troutman (2012), Cole et al. (2000), Cooper, Heron, and Heward (1987, 2007), Shapiro and Cole (1994), Sulzer-Azaroff and Mayer (1991), and the *Journal of Applied Behavior Analysis*. The first five sources are prominent texts that include many school-based applications of self-monitoring in assessment and treatment, whereas the last-mentioned source is the most prestigious scholarly journal related to applied behavior analysis and has included a large number and variety of articles over the years that detail many different uses of self-monitoring.

OBSERVATIONAL CODING PROCEDURES

Now that we have analyzed the general methods of behavioral observation, it is useful to look at the specific ways that behavioral observation data may be recorded or coded. As many as seven different observational coding procedures and useful combinations of procedures have been identified (Sulzer-Azaroff & Mayer, 1991), but in this chapter, the number of recording categories has been collapsed into four general types, which are illustrated as follows. A brief summary of these four observational coding procedures is found in Table 4.1. Note that for years observational coding was documented via paper and pencil formats. Although this is still a common mode of documentation, computer

Table 4.1 Guide to four basic observational coding procedures

Coding procedure	Definition	Example	Advantages and disadvantages
Event recording	Recording the number of times a specific behavior occurs during the length of an observational period	Number of times students leave their seats	A: Can be used to determine antecedents and consequences of behavior D: Not useful with behaviors that occur frequently
Interval recording	Dividing the observational period into intervals, and recording specified behaviors that occur at any time during the interval (partial interval) or during the entire interval (whole interval)	Number of intervals in which student is out of seat at any point (partial interval) or during entire time (whole interval)	A: Good choice for behaviors that occur at a moderate but steady rate D: Requires complete attention of observer
Time-sample recording	Dividing observational period into intervals, and recording if specific behavior occurs momentarily at interval	Number of intervals in which student is out of seat at exact point of interval	A: Requires only one observation per interval D: May miss some important low-frequency behaviors
Duration/latency recording	Recording how long a particular behavior lasts (duration), or how long from the end of one behavior to the beginning of another (latency)	How long students are out of seat (duration); how long students are out of seat after the teacher tells them to return to seat (latency)	A: Simple to do with a stopwatch or wall clock D: Difficult for behaviors without a clear beginning or end

software (e.g., iBAA or Behavioral Assessment Application available through iTunes and compatible with MacIntosh products) is consistently being developed and tested to make the input and analysis of behavioral observation data a more efficient process.

Event Recording

Event recording (also known as frequency recording) is a measure or count of how many times specified target behaviors occur during the length of the observational period. Event recording is best suited for use with behaviors that meet three criteria. The first criterion is that the *behaviors should have a clear beginning and end.* Within the behavioral domains of physical aggression or asking for help, it is normally quite simple to determine starting and stopping points, but with behaviors such as making noise, this task becomes more difficult. The second criterion is that *behaviors should last approximately the same amount of time each time they occur.* If the observer is recording a class of behaviors that vary considerably in time from occurrence to occurrence, another recording technique, such as duration recording, should be used. Because event recording yields a simple tally of how many times the behaviors occurred, it is not useful for gauging such aspects of behavior as intensity or length. The third criterion is that the *behaviors should not occur so frequently that it becomes difficult to separate each occurrence.* For example, if an observer was using event recording to measure self-stimulation behavior (e.g., hair twirling, rocking, or lip rubbing) of a child with severe disabilities, and these behaviors were occurring every few seconds, the event-recording procedure would become too cumbersome. Regarding this third criterion, the observer must make a decision if the frequency of the behavior is so high that event recording would be difficult to implement.

Certain techniques can be used with event recording to maximize its usefulness as an observational recording procedure. One way that the utility of event recording can be increased is to record events sequentially, or in the exact order in which they occur. By developing a sequential analysis of observed events, behaviors can be categorized according to *antecedents and consequences,* a task that may be helpful in better understanding the function of behavior and in developing intervention plans. A useful way of transcribing event recording into an analysis of behavioral antecedents and consequences is through the use of an A–B–C (antecedent–behavior–consequence) evaluation narrative, which follows these steps:

1. Divide a sheet of paper into three columns, one each for antecedents, behaviors, and consequences.
2. List the specific behaviors that were recorded in the middle column (behaviors).
3. Note what events or behaviors preceded the recorded behaviors (antecedents) in the left column and what events or behaviors followed the recorded behaviors (consequences) in the right column.

Using this A–B–C procedure requires some flexibility in the observation system—in some cases a targeted behavior that was recorded in the B column also will appear in the A column as an antecedent to another important behavior or event. The payoff of using this technique will come in the form of an ecologically sensitive observational recording system that has strong implications for treatment. An example of using the A–B–C breakdown sheet with event recording is provided in Figure 4.1.

The advantage of using a basic A–B–C breakdown sheet with event recording in observations (or with behavioral interviews) is that it allows one to *develop a testable*

A–B–C Event Recording Sheet

Antecedent	Behavior	Consequence
Teacher asks students to take out their workbooks	S does not take out workbook, talks to neighbor	Teacher reprimands S
Teacher reprimands S	S removes workbook from desk	Teacher focuses attention away from S
	S raises hand to ask question	Teacher works with another student
	S continues to raise hand	Teacher responds to S's question
Teacher responds to S's question	S puts head down on desktop	
S puts head down on desktop	S begins to tap leg against desk	Neighbor tells S to be quiet
Neighbor tells S to be quiet	S tells neighbor, "shut up"	Teacher tells S, "get back to work"
Teacher tells S, "get back to work"	S puts book in desk, places arms and head on desktop	Teacher again tells S to get back to work
Teacher again tells S to get back to work	S pounds hand on desk and swears at teacher	Teacher tells S to go to time-out chair in back of room
Teacher tells S to go to time-out chair in back of room	S kicks chair and goes to time-out chair	

Figure 4.1 An example of behavioral observation data that were collected using an event recording procedure and the A–B–C (antecedent–behavior–consequence) technique

hypothesis regarding the presumed functions that the problem behaviors may serve, which can then be evaluated and potentially used in developing an intervention (Crone & Horner, 2003).

Another way that the use of event recording can be fine-tuned to yield more useful data is to report the events in different ways, depending on the length of the observation period. Barton and Ascione (1984) suggested three length-based ways of reporting data:

1. If each observation period is of the same length, report the actual frequency with which each event occurred.
2. If the observation periods differ in length, the data should be reported by rates of occurrence, or the number of responses divided by the time period in which the observations took place.
3. Behavioral events that are supposed to follow specific cues (such as compliance with directions from the teacher) should be reported as a percentage of opportunities that the behavior occurred, as in three compliances for five commands.

Event recording in its most basic form is relatively easy to use, but by using some of these modifications, the observer will be able to make the observation more insightful and useful.

Interval Recording
The essential characteristics of interval recording involve: (1) selecting a time period for the length of the observation; (2) dividing the observational period into a number of equal intervals; and (3) recording whether the specified target behaviors occur during each interval. Interval recording is considered to be *a good choice for use with behaviors that occur at a moderate but steady rate* but is *not as useful for behaviors that occur with relatively low frequency*. It does not provide an exact count of behaviors but is a good choice for use with behaviors that occur on a frequent basis. An example of a typical interval-based observation would be a 30-minute observation period divided into 90 equal intervals of 20 seconds each.

Interval recording requires the complete attention of the observer and can be difficult to implement if the intervals are too short, the total observation time is too long, or the number of behaviors that are targeted for observation are too great. Interval recording may also be challenging with respect to obtaining high levels of interobserver reliability, and doing so may require extensive supervised training. In typical practice, an observational period is less than one hour long (20 to 30 minutes is typical in school-based practice), and the intervals are no more than 30 seconds long. The most simple form of interval recording involves using the procedure with one targeted behavior and recording a plus (+) or minus (–) in boxes that have been drawn for each interval to indicate whether the target behavior occurred. If the intervals are short, or if the number of behaviors that are targeted for observation are so many that it creates difficulty in making an accurate recording, brief recording intervals can be placed between each observation interval (Alberto & Troutman, 1998). For example, an observer might use ten-second intervals for the observation but place a five-second scoring interval between each observation interval, giving him or her the time to record accurately the behaviors and prepare for the next interval.

Whole-Interval or Partial-Interval Recording? Interval recording can be divided into two general types: whole-interval recording and partial-interval recording. With whole-interval recording, the behavior being coded must be observed *during the entire interval* in order to be recorded. The whole-interval method is a good choice if the behaviors being coded are continuous (such as on-task behavior) and the intervals are short to medium in length (Shapiro & Skinner, 1990). With partial-interval recording, the observer codes the target behavior in question if it occurs *at any time during the interval;* when a specific behavior has been coded, it is no longer necessary to monitor that behavior until the next interval begins. The partial-interval method is a good choice for recording behaviors without a clear beginning and end and that happen with such a high frequency that they are hard to count (Shapiro & Skinner, 1990). Figure 4.2 provides an example of a behavioral observation coding sheet used to code observations of social behavior in a playground setting, for a referred student, using the partial-interval method. Both types of interval recording, whole or partial, procedures may result in error.

Whole-interval recording tends to underestimate the behavior, whereas partial-interval recording tends to overestimate the behavior (Salvia & Hughes, 1990; Salvia &

Playground Social Behavior Recording Form

Name and Grade: *Justin T., Grade 4* Date: *October 17*
Location: *Central School Playground* Activity: *Morning Recess*
Observer: *Chris Thompson* Start/Stop Time: 10:05–10:18 A.M.
Interval Length/Type: 20 *seconds, partial interval*

Interval	PA	VA	INT	ISO
1				X
2				X
3				X
4			X	
5		X		
6		X		
7				X
8				X
9				X
10				X
11				X
12			X	
13			X	
14			X	
15		X		
16	X			
17			X	
18	X			
19				X
20				X

Interval	PA	VA	INT	ISO
21				X
22				X
23				X
24				X
25				X
26			X	
27			X	
28			X	
29			X	
30			X	
31				X
32				X
33				X
34				X
35			X	
36				X
37				X
38		X		
39		X		
40		X		

Coding Key:
PA = Physically Aggressive VA = Verbally Aggressive
INT = Appropriate Social Interaction ISO = Socially Isolated

Figure 4.2 An example of an interval-based coding system used to collect social observation data. This particular form was used for a playground-based observation of a referred student, using the partial-interval method, and focusing on social interaction and aggressive behavior

Ysseldyke, 2004). Which is the better of these two methods of interval recording? It depends on the behaviors being observed and the purposes for which the observation is being conducted.

A final consideration of interval recording is that to use it effectively, special timing devices may be necessary. If the observation intervals are long enough, and if the number of targeted behaviors is limited, it is possible to get by with the use of a phone or a digital watch with second timers. As the length of the time intervals decrease, or as the numbers of behaviors targeted for observation increase, using a typical watch with a second timer becomes increasingly frustrating (if not maddening), and the reliability and validity of the observation inevitably suffer as a result. Another option for the technologically savvy user would be to use programs such as GarageBand (MacIntosh application) to record audio cues onto an iPod at desired intervals, so that one doesn't have to visually keep track of intervals while simultaneously observing behavior.

Time-Sample Recording

Time-sample recording is similar to interval recording in that the observation period is divided into intervals of time. The essential difference between the two procedures is that with time sampling, *behavior is observed only momentarily at the prespecified intervals.* An additional difference between the two procedures is that with interval recording, the observation intervals are generally divided into equal units, whereas it is not unusual to divide the intervals randomly or in unequal units with time-sample recording. As with interval recording, time-sample recording is most useful for observing behaviors that occur at a moderate but steady rate.

Time-sample recording can be illustrated using assessment of on-task academic behavior as an example. The observation might occur during a 20-minute period of academic instruction that has been divided into 20 intervals of 1 minute each. As each minute ends, the observer records whether the target child was on-task. In this example, the time units were divided into equal intervals. These intervals do not need to be equal, however, and even could be generated randomly. If the intervals used in time-sample recording are short or highly variable, the type of electronic timing devices mentioned in the discussion of interval recording would be useful. Some innovative researchers and clinicians have developed electronic timing devices that randomly generate audible tones at varying time intervals.

A major advantage of time-sample recording procedures is that they require only one observation per interval and are less subject to the very real problems of getting "off-track" that are easily encountered with interval recording. If the intervals are large enough, the time-sampling method may free up the observer to engage in other activities. For example, a teacher could still go about directing an instructional activity while conducting an observation using time-sample recording, provided that the intervals are large enough and the recording is simple. The major advantage of time-sample recording is closely related to its most glaring drawback. Because time-sample recording allows for recording of behavior that occurs only occasionally, an observer may end up not recording many important behaviors, and conclusions may be reached based on sketchy or incomplete information (C. H. Skinner, et al., 2000). The longer the interval used with time-sample recording, the less accurate the data; as the interval increases, the sample of behavior decreases. Reaching an appropriate balance between the length of the interval needed and the necessity of freeing up the observer for other activities is the most reasonable way to use time-sample recording.

Duration and Latency Recording

Event recording, interval recording, and time-sample recording all have the similarity of focusing on obtaining exact or approximate counts of targeted behaviors that occur during a given time frame. Two additional techniques, duration and latency recording, differ from the first three because their focus is primarily on the temporal aspects of the targeted behaviors rather than on how often the behaviors occur. Duration and latency recording are best used with behaviors that have a discrete beginning and end and last for at least a few seconds each time they occur. Common examples of these behaviors include out-of-seat behavior, self-stimulating or stereotypic behavior, and tantrumming.

Duration Recording In duration recording, the observer attempts to gauge the amount of time that a target child engages in a specific behavior. In other words, the most critical aspect of the observation is how long the behavior lasts. For school-based assessment, a good example of how duration recording might be used is provided by the observation of out-of-seat behavior. If a student leaves his or her workspace during an instructional activity to wander around the classroom, it may be useful to know how long the out-of-seat behavior lasts. There is a big difference between a student who gets out of his or her seat three times during a 30-minute observation, who is still academically engaged for most of the period, and a student whose out-of-seat behavior occurs only once during the observation but who stays out-of-seat for most of the period. For clinic-based assessment, a good example of the use of duration recording is provided by observation of child temper tantrums. The parent of a six year old who engages in temper tantrums two to three times per week but whose tantrums last for 20 minutes or longer can provide the clinician with valuable information by measuring the length of the tantrums. As a practical matter, a treatment that reduces the average number of tantrums from three per week down to two per week might be less valuable than a treatment that does not change the average number of tantrums but reduces their duration to no more than five minutes each.

Latency Recording In latency recording, the observer attempts to gauge the *amount of time from the end of one behavior to the beginning of another.* The most critical aspect of the observation is *how long it takes for the behavior to begin.* A typical example of how latency recording could be used comes from observation of a child referred for noncompliant behavior. In this case, it might be important to observe how long it takes from the parent or teacher request for action to the enactment of the noncompliant behavior. Treatment progress could be gauged through seeing a consistent trend of a decreased amount of time between the request and the compliance.

EXAMPLES OF OBSERVATIONAL CODING SYSTEMS

This section provides overviews of several observational coding systems that are relatively general in orientation and focused primarily on social–emotional behaviors. Observational coding systems that are useful for highly specific purposes, such as the measurement of hyperactivity or social withdrawal, are reviewed in Chapters 9 to 13. Volpe, DiPerna, Hintze, and Shapiro (2005) conducted an excellent review of observational coding systems. This review includes some of the same coding systems described in this book, but also includes others that are focused more on academic behavior rather than general social–emotional behavior. The eight observational coding systems described in this section, which are summarized in Table 4.2, are divided into three types—school based, home based, and clinic based—with a few representative coding systems selected for each category. With the exception of the Direct Observation Form (DOF) of Achenbach's ASEBA system, these observation coding systems are not commercially published products. Most of these coding systems were originally reported in professional journals as one part of the

Table 4.2 Characteristics of eight selected general-purpose observational coding systems

Code name	Setting	Measures	Uses
Direct Observation Form	School	96-item rating scale, event recording, interval recording	Internalizing and externalizing behavior problems and on-task behavior
Behavior Coding System	School	eight categories, interval recording	Coercive and aggressive behavior
Social Interaction Scoring System	Home	12 categories, continuous event recording	General social–behavioral problems
Family Interaction Code	Home	29 categories, interval recording	Aversive family behavior
Child's Game and Parent's Game	Clinic	seven parent behavior and three child behavior categories, coded in 30-second intervals	Child noncompliance, behavior problems during interactions with parent
Teacher Behavior Code	Clinic/Home	nine categories, interval-based "teaching trials"	Change in parent teaching behavior following training
Behavioral Observation of Students in Schools	School	momentary time sampling, interval recording	Academic engagement and off-task behaviors
Coders Impression Measure	Clinic	59-item rating scale and six-item addendum	Parents' use of discipline, skill encouragement, problem-solving, positive involvement, and monitoring

research methodology employed in a study, and in some cases, these systems have become popular among other researchers and clinicians. To obtain complete information on most of these observational systems, readers need to locate the reference cited with them and may benefit from conducting a computer-assisted literature search using the name of the observational system as a keyword. These observational coding systems are included to provide illustrative examples. Although these systems are not being advocated as the "best of" coding systems available, they were selected because of their innovative designs and sound empirical base. You might also notice that each of these coding systems has been around for several years. They have stood the test of time and are among the more widely cited observational coding systems that have been developed.

School-Based Observation Systems

The Direct Observation Form (DOF)   The Direct Observation Form (DOF) was developed by Achenbach (1986, 2009) and his colleagues as the child observational component of the ASEBA. It was developed specifically for use in classrooms and in other group activities. The DOF, in contrast to many observational coding systems, is at least partially based on rating scale technology because it includes 96 items rated on a 4-point scale following a ten-minute observation period. The rating scale items are completed based only on what was observed during the observation period and not on a rater's general knowledge of a target child. In addition to the rating format, the DOF merges the use of event recording and time-sample recording. The event-recording aspect of the DOF is included by having the observer write a narrative description of the child's behavior as it occurs during the observation period. The time-sampling aspect of the DOF is included by having the observer record whether the subject was on-task at the end of each 1-minute interval.

Another characteristic of the DOF that sets it apart from most other observational coding systems is that it is a norm-referenced instrument—a norm group of 287 non-referred children aged five to 14 was used as the basis for comparing individual observation scores. The norm-group data also were used to develop a factor structure for the 96 rating items on the DOF, which, in addition to a total-problems score, includes internalizing and externalizing scores, consistent with the other measures in the CBCL system. Six additional narrow-band factor scores also are available through the use of an optional computer-scored profile.

The DOF, like the other components of the ASEBA system, is a thoroughly researched instrument that represents an empirically sound approach to assessment of behavior problems. It is easy to use and, unlike many other systematic observation systems, requires only a modest amount of training. The recommended observation and scoring procedure for the DOF allow for the obtaining of social comparison data with two observed control children on the checklist and on-task ratings. The psychometric properties of the DOF are good to excellent, with acceptable levels of inter-rater reliability and discriminant validity (Achenbach, 2001b; McConaughy, Achenbach, & Gent, 1988). The DOF is a good choice for group-based observations in which serious behavioral or emotional problems are likely to be observed in short time periods. It is not particularly useful for observing children or adolescents in individual or solitary situations and is not a good choice for assessing low-frequency behaviors that are unlikely to occur within a ten-minute period.

Behavioral Observation of Students in Schools (BOSS) The Behavioral Observation of Students in Schools (BOSS) coding system (Shapiro, 2003, 2011, 2013) was designed to measure the academic engagement and off-task behaviors of target students. The BOSS uses momentary time-sampling to measure whether an observed student is actively engaged, passively engaged, or not engaged in instruction. Additionally, observers use a partial interval recording system to determine different types of off-task behaviors. Student behaviors could be coded as off-task motor (OFT-M), off-task verbal (OFT-V), and off-task passive (OFT-P). OFT-M includes behaviors that are not associated with the academic task at hand and may include pencil tapping, random page turning, rolling on the carpet, etc. OFT-V includes verbal behaviors that are not permitted in class, such as whistling, talking to a peer, etc. OFT-P behaviors may be slightly more difficult to code and include passive behaviors such as staring out the window. Observers record the type of instruction being observed and collect peer comparison data during every fifth interval of observation. The BOSS is a user-friendly system that enables observers to gather useful information about student engagement. It is a familiar tool to many, who collect behavioral observation data.

The Behavior Coding System (BCS) Developed by Harris and Reid (1981), the Behavior Coding System (BCS) was designed to measure patterns of coercive behavior and aggression in classroom and playground settings. The BCS uses an interval-recording system with eight behavioral categories. The coding system of the BCS is easy enough to use so that para-professionals or trained undergraduate students could be effective observers. The reported psychometric properties of the BCS are strong, with interobserver agreement at 93% in classroom settings and 86% on playground settings. Harris and Reid also reported satisfactory consistency in behavioral categories across different settings. An interesting aspect of the BCS is that it not only provides a general observational measure of aggressive and coercive behaviors, but also provides data on the stability of these behaviors across different settings. As such, the BCS might be effective in helping to determine whether aggressive behavior problems are setting specific or whether they appear to generalize across settings.

Home-Based Observation Systems

Social Interaction Coding System (SICS) Designed to assess family interaction behaviors along various dimensions and on general classifications, the Social Interaction Coding System (SICS) (Weinrott & Jones, 1984) provides an interesting and useful format for conducting home-based observations. The SICS uses a continuous event-recording procedure wherein 12 different behavioral categories are targeted. The methodology employed in field testing the SICS was unique; the reliability of the coding system was studied using covert and overt observation techniques. In both cases, the reliability of the SICS proved to be adequate to good, although it was higher for overt observations (0.91) than for covert observations (0.73). While this is an interesting measure, there are fewer references in the literature mentioning its use, making it hard to know the extent to which this system is actually used.

Family Interaction Code (FIC) Another observational recording system developed by Weinrott and Jones (1984) for home-based observation and discussed in the same research report as the SICS, is the Family Interaction Code (FIC). Although the FIC was field tested along the same dimensions as the SICS (overt versus covert observations), its focus is different, and its design and use vary considerably. The FIC uses a six-second interval-recording system wherein 29 different behavioral categories are targeted. As such, the complexity and difficulty of use of the FIC is great, and it should be used by experienced trained observers. The general area measured through the FIC is family interactions, with its specific focus being aversive family behaviors. Similar to the SICS, the reliability level was higher on the FIC for overt (0.87), rather than covert (0.69) observations.

Clinic-Based Observation Systems

The Coders Impression Measure (CI) The Coders Impression Measure (CI) (DeGarmo, Patterson, & Forgatch, 2004) was developed to measure family interactions and parenting practices. This measure stems from a body of research in which Patterson (1982) and his colleagues developed the notion of coercive family practices, those that encourage the development and maintenance of antisocial behaviors by consistent and increasingly adverse interactions between parents and children. This research has expanded to include a related intervention approach, Parent Management Training Oregon (PMTO) (Forgatch & DeGarmo, 2002), which focuses on giving parents the skills to improve their positive parenting practices. Central to PMTO is the CI, which has enabled researchers and clinicians the opportunity to observe parenting behaviors. The CI globally measures parents' use of *discipline, skill encouragement, problem-solving, positive involvement,* and *monitoring.* Coders observe videotaped interactions between parents and children that occurred in a clinic or research facility. These interactions are prompted through specific tasks, such as a play task, during which a parent is asked to follow a child's lead in playing a game; a clean up task, in which parents are to encourage the child to clean up a game or toys; a problem-solving task in which families are encouraged to remember a recent problem that occurred in the family and discuss ways in which the problem could have been solved. The coders rate parents' behaviors on a Likert scale, and reliability estimates have ranged between 0.67 and 0.94 in previous studies (Forgatch, DeGarmo, & Beldavs, 2005). More recently, researchers (Stora, Hagtvet, & Heyerdahl, 2013) utilized generalizability theory to better understand the reliability between data collectors, observers and sources of measurement error on the CI. This is important to consider as sometimes the data collection is conducted by clinicians/researchers who are different from those that code videos. In this study, it was found that coders that analyzed all families from data collected, versus different coders for each family, yielded different reliability estimates; with a higher (and likely inflated) generalizability estimate for coders that analyzed all families.

Child's Game/Parent's Game An innovative coding procedure useful for observing parent–child interactions in clinic settings was developed by Forehand and his colleagues (Forehand & McMahon, 1981; Forehand et al., 1978). This coding system has not been formally named but is referred to herein as the Child's Game/Parent's Game because of its tasks and focus. The setting that is recommended for use of this observational coding system is a sound-wired clinic playroom that has a supply of toys and is equipped with a one-way window, from which an observer codes parent–child interactions from an adjoining room. Alternatively, observations could be videotaped and coded at a later time. Parent–child pairs are observed in two different situations that may last five or ten minutes each. The first situation is referred to as the Child's Game, which is an unstructured or free-play setting in which the child chooses the activity and rules. The second situation is the Parent's Game, in which the parent is instructed to choose an activity and rules. The Parent's Game is a situation in which the parent delivers commands to the child.

For both games, parent and child behaviors are coded using frequency counts in 30-second intervals. The only exception is inappropriate behavior, which is coded as occurring or not occurring during each interval. Six parent behavioral domains are coded, including rewards, attends, questions, commands, warnings, and time out. Three child behavioral domains are coded, including compliance, noncompliance, and inappropriate behavior. These codes are later summarized into rate per minute of various parent behaviors and percentages of child behaviors to various parent commands. An additional summary statistic includes the percentage of parental attention that was contingent on child compliance.

Several studies have shown the Child's Game/Parent's Game coding system to have adequate technical properties, including an average interobserver agreement rate of 75% (Forehand & Peed, 1979), strong stability over time (Peed, Roberts, & Forehand, 1977), sensitivity to treatment effects (McMahon & Forehand, 1984), and discriminant validity for differentiation of clinic-referred and non-referred children (Griest, Forehand, Wells, & McMahon, 1980). In sum, this clinic-based observational coding system is relatively easy to implement, requires a small amount of parent and child time, is unobtrusive, and seems to be a reliable and valid method of conducting behavioral assessment.

The Teacher Behavior Code (TBC) Unlike other observation systems reviewed in this chapter, the focus of the Teacher Behavior Code (TBC) (Weitz, 1981) is on the parent or caregiver, rather than the child. Specifically, the TBC was designed to be used in assessing the amount of change in "teaching behavior" by parents who have participated in a parent-training program. Although developed specifically for use with parents of children with developmental disabilities, there is no reason why the TBC could not be used as a measure for parents of children with different types of problems. The TBC was selected for review in this chapter for a pragmatic reason; in the clinical treatment of children with behavioral, social, or emotional problems, the parent is often the mediator or initial target of treatment. As such, it is important to have a measurement technique to assess the parent's responsiveness to consultation or parent training, rather than focusing on only the resulting child behavior.

The TBC can be used in home and clinic settings and includes nine targeted behavioral categories that are recorded using an interval measurement system during "teaching trials." The TBC can be used by trained graduate students, and perhaps even trained paraprofessionals, and by experienced observers. The reported technical properties of the TBC are adequate to good, with an average interobserver agreement of 87% and a range across categories from 69% to 98%. The TBC is a unique observation system that is worthwhile for consideration by clinicians or researchers who provide consultation or training to parents and who desire a formal system for assessing the level of change in parent's behaviors.

TECHNOLOGY ADVANCES IN BEHAVIORAL OBSERVATION

With the onslaught of laptops, tablets, and smartphones in our workplaces, it is essential that we begin to develop an understanding of how technology can be applied to behavioral observation. Cohen and Rozenblat (2015) call researchers and practitioners to consider this particular aspect of behavioral assessment and review some of the advantages and disadvantages of incorporating technology into applied behavior analysis, with a specific focus on data collection (i.e., direct observation). With a smartphone, for example, observers can collect a large sample of behavioral data efficiently. Observers can quickly observe changes over time with repeated measurement and can compute interobserver agreement easily, without having to rely on an arduous paper and pencil method. Further, observational codes that are programmed into an application in advance may make it easier to observe multiple topographies of behavior at the same time and may make observation of multiple behaviors more reliable. On the other hand, utilizing new technology applications may take practice to reliably code behaviors, and software may be subject to viruses and glitches. This section includes examples of behavioral observation codes, primarily used in schools, which highlight some of the rapid advances in technology that we have seen over the last few years. While there are a number of technology applications available, we have chosen to share four that may be used to observe students in school settings.

BehaviorSnap
BehaviorSnap (BehaviorSnap 2016, Version 2.3.1) is an application developed by SuperPsyched LLC and can be downloaded on Apple Products and Android products

for $9.99. This download enables users to make up to 12 observations before being prompted to choose a subscription plan. BehaviorSnap represents four separate tools in one application, which enables interval recording, ABC data collection, duration recording, frequency recording, and peer comparison data collection. This application can be used to help professionals target concerning behaviors, understand relevant antecedents and consequences, and collect ongoing data to monitor behavioral progress. Data collected can be downloaded into a csv file on a computer, which then can easily be summarized and incorporated into behavioral assessment reports.

BOSS (Behavioral Observation of Students in Schools)

The BOSS (Behavioral Observation of Students in Schools 2015, Version 1.2.0) is an application available on iTunes and Google Play for $29.99. It is a tool published by Pearson and developed by the late Dr. Edward Shapiro. This tool mirrors the paper and pencil version and allows observers to set the duration of the observation session and then track off-task (motor, verbal, passive) and student engagement (active, passive) through momentary and partial-interval time sampling. Data are compiled and graphed and can be emailed to the observer for future use.

!Observe

!Observe (Psychsoft 2015, Version 2.0.1) is an application available on iTunes and Android products for $9.99 and is available in 16 languages. There is also an !ObserveLite available for free with some reduced functionality of !Observe. This application allows observers to record data on one behavior or a class of behaviors. It records duration of behavior and analyzes data in terms of average duration of behavior and rates per minute. Data are saved and can easily be transferred right into Dropbox for later review. !Observe allows for peer comparison data to be taken as well.

iObserve

iObserve (2016, Version 1.4.3) is available from iTunes and Android stores for $64.99. This tool is appropriate for educators as well as persons in other professions in which behavioral observations are required (e.g., coaches, inspectors). This tool enables users to develop their own observational criteria and can also utilize audio and video functions. Users can also timestamp the observation, review the observation with students/teachers being observed, and then save the data.

RELIABILITY AND VALIDITY ISSUES IN DIRECT BEHAVIORAL OBSERVATION

Despite the strong empirical support and practical utility of using behavioral observation as a primary means of assessment, there are many potential limitations, problems, and cautions that should be kept in mind. Although there have been some significant developments in methodology and technology for child behavior observation during the past two decades, there are still many challenges and unanswered questions regarding this assessment method. It is important to consider that the jury is still out regarding how well traditional psychometric principles apply to direct behavioral observation methods (Hintze, 2005). Even the strongest advocates of observational assessment concede that the accuracy, validity, and reliability of behavioral observation data are often not adequately established, and there are various potential threats to the integrity of observational data (Briesch, Chafouleas, & Riley-Tillman, 2010; Hintze, 2005; C. H. Skinner, Dittmer, & Howell, 2000; C. H. Skinner, Rhymer, & McDaniel, 2000; Sulzer-Azaroff & Mayer, 1991). In this vein, it is worthwhile to consider that practitioners who develop observational codes should identify a "bottom line" of reliability, validity, and overall quality of their observational systems and seek to keep above this line in conducting observational assessment. It may be helpful to consider the seven "essential quality indicators" that have been proposed by Hintze (2005) with respect to direct observation methods, which include *internal-consistency reliability, test–retest reliability, interobserver agreement, content validity, concurrent and convergent validity, predictive validity,* and *sensitivity to change.* Observational systems that meet all of these quality indicators should certainly be the end goal, but it is important to realize that many practitioners may be using systems that are lacking in one or more areas. This section addresses some of the issues surrounding the use of behavioral observation that are potentially problematic, with a particular emphasis on issues that may impact reliability and validity of observational assessment data.

Defining the Observation Domain

One of the first tasks in developing an observational coding system or in using an existing system is defining what types of behaviors are important to target in the observation and then developing appropriate operational definitions for those behaviors. In defining behaviors to target, the domain of behavior can be viewed as a continuum, with broadly defined behaviors on one end and narrowly defined behaviors on the other end. Although defining each behavioral domain in a highly narrow manner may seem to make empirical sense, it may be impractical when it comes time to conduct the observation. For example, if aggressive behavior is of particular importance in an observational assessment, and the general category of "aggressiveness" is broken down into 15 different subcategories of behavior, the observational coding system will probably be cumbersome and of little use for all but the most esoteric scientific purposes. Conversely, defining a behavioral domain too broadly might increase the ease of coding by the observer but will tend to reduce the validity and reliability of the observational system (Epps, 1985; Skinner, Rhymer, & McDaniel, 2000). Using the example of the general category of aggressive behavior, it is easy to see how two behaviors that are qualitatively different might be coded in the same way if the domain of "aggressiveness" is defined too broadly. Arguing with and physically attacking another person are generally considered to be forms of aggression, but coding them as the same may not be particularly helpful for the assessment or for intervention planning.

To reduce the potential problems associated with defining the behavioral domain to be observed, care should be taken to ensure that the observational coding categories are defined neither too broadly nor too narrowly; the scope of the behavioral definition should be linked to the specific purposes of the observation, and treatment implications should be considered in creating definitions if the purpose of the assessment is to evaluate a problem and develop an appropriate intervention. If the observational domain must be defined broadly, *the validity of the assessment can be increased by employing multiple measures.* The use of multiple measures allows for the measurement of a broad range of behaviors, while avoiding the practice of equating behaviors that are related but still qualitatively different (Kent & Foster, 1977).

Observer Training and Reliability

One of the universes of generalization in behavioral assessment in Cone's (1978) classic and widely influential conceptualization of a *Behavioral Assessment Grid* is referred to as *scorer generalization*. This term indicates that behavioral assessment data may vary because of differences between persons who score or code the data. When the observational system has been developed or selected, it is imperative that the individuals who actually will be conducting the observations are properly trained, so that the resulting observational data are reliable and valid. Failure to train observers properly in the use of specific coding systems and procedures may result in behavioral assessment data that are of questionable use.

After the observers are trained properly in the reliable use of an observational coding system, there is still potential for scorer generalization problems. It was shown years ago that over time there is a tendency for observers to depart gradually from their original definitions of how to score or code particular behaviors (e.g., Kent, O'Leary, Diament, & Deitz, 1974), a phenomenon that is referred to as *observer drift*. This phenomenon is just one element of the generalizability challenges that are inherent in direct behavioral observation (Hintze, 2005; Hintze & Matthews, 2004). As is the case for observations carried out by observers who are poorly trained in the first place, a great deal of observer drift will produce observational data that are of questionable utility. To reduce the tendency of different observers to "drift" from original definitions of behavior, it is suggested that retraining or reliability checks of observers be conducted from time to time (Kazdin, 1981; Reid, 1982). Common procedures that might be used in observer retraining might include: (1) periodic group meetings; (2) conducting observations on actual sets of events ("live" or using videotaped situations); (3) calculating the rate of interobserver agreement (agreements divided by agreements plus disagreements); (4) discussing points of disagreement and coming to common decision rules; and (5) practicing until an acceptable criterion of reliability is reached. A simple procedure for calculating interobserver agreement, expressed as a formula, is:

$$\frac{\text{number of agreements}}{\text{number of agreements} + \text{number of disagreements}}$$

Although the problem of observer drift can be dealt with through the steps that have been noted, these steps are seldom possible for practitioners who work independently. Clinicians who employ direct-observation procedures in assessment who work under more solitary conditions can overcome this disadvantage in several ways. Enlisting the assistance of a colleague to act as a reliability check is one possibility. Other possibilities include doing an occasional self-check on observational reliability by videotaping observational situations, and striving to keep aware of new information pertinent to the observational techniques that are being used.

Use of Social Comparison Data

During the observational process, the target of the assessment is generally a specific child or adolescent who has been referred because of academic or behavioral concerns. Naturally the observation should focus on that particular individual. If the observation does not also include the use of social comparison data, however, the results may lead to inappropriate conclusions about the nature and severity of problems, and the validity of the observation might be jeopardized. The use of *social comparison data* is important to determine whether the problem behaviors exhibited by a particular subject deviate significantly from those of his or her peers who are in similar situations (Skinner, Rhymer, & McDaniel, 2000). In practice, obtaining social comparison data can be a simple part of the observation. The observer might randomly pick two or three non-referred subjects in the same setting and alternate the observation between the referred subject and the social comparison subjects on a rotating basis. The social comparison data obtained from rotating the alternate observation intervals may be considered to represent the behavior of a "typical" peer in a situation similar to the target subject's.

Alessi and Kaye (1983) suggested that obtaining observational social comparison data from the referred person's peer group may serve as a basis for identifying individuals whose behavioral problems are severe enough to warrant intervention. This suggestion is still a good starting point for practice. An important factor to keep in mind in obtaining social comparison data is *the type of setting* in which the behavior was observed. For example, if the assessment was conducted in a school setting in which the referred student was placed in regular education and special education classroom settings, it would be important to obtain social comparison data in both settings because the behavioral norms in the two settings might vary considerably (Walker, 1982). Reaching an inappropriate conclusion on the basis of observational data without social comparison information could threaten the overall validity of the observational system.

Observer Reactivity

Anyone with experience in observing child and adolescent behavior in naturalistic settings can attest that the presence of an observer may influence the behavior of the subjects, a problem that is referred to as *observer reactivity*. Often with uncanny perceptiveness, children seem to understand and react to the presence of a "stranger" in the observational setting, sometimes with amusing results. In my own experiences conducting behavioral observations in classroom settings, the target subject, on several occasions, has walked directly over to me and said something to the effect of "you're here to watch me, aren't you?" Other examples of children being aware of the presence of an observer are more subtle but equally illustrative of the reactivity problem. For example, it is common for a particular child who is not the target of the observation to spend a good deal of time during the observational period staring at the observer, asking questions like "what are you doing here," and even showing off or trying to impress or gain the attention of the observer. These examples illustrate the fact that obtrusiveness by the observer can cause a change in subject performance, simply as a result of the presence of a new person in the environment (Kazdin, 1981; Skinner, Dittmer, & Howell, 2000).

In situations in which there is a high degree of obtrusiveness in the observation, it is unwise to interpret the observational data without taking into account possible reactivity effects. In cases in which the presence of the observer has created significant reactivity, the data should be used with extreme caution, and attempts should be made to gather observational data that is more valid, if possible. As with other threats to observational validity, the use of data obtained under conditions of significant observer reactivity might result in reaching unwarranted conclusions.

Several steps may be taken to reduce the potential effects of observer reactivity. One possibility is to select observational settings in which the presence of the observer does not create an unusual circumstance. For example, observations in playground settings can be done in a way so that the targeted subjects might not even be aware of the presence of the observer, whereas observations in the home setting are likely to result in significant reactivity—the more private the observation setting, the more likely that observer reactivity will become a factor. In classroom observation situations, where the observation is usually considered to be naturalistic in character, the fact that subjects are being observed doing routine tasks is by itself a factor in reducing reactivity. Other commonsense measures can be employed to reduce the potential reactivity in classroom observations, such as (1) entering the classroom at the end of a recess period or other activity rather than during the middle of instructional time, (2) conducting the observation in an inconspicuous location such as the back of the room, (3) avoiding any unnecessary use of observational equipment that might attract the attention of the students, and (4) observing informally for a short period in order for the students to adjust to the observer's presence before the formal observation is conducted (Merrell, 1989).

Situational Specificity

The concept of *situational specificity* of behavior is central to assessment from the behavioral perspective and has certain implications for conducting behavioral observations. In the formative years of modern behavioral observation methodology development, Kazdin (1979, 1981, 1982) wrote extensively on this topic and regarded the essence of situational specificity as behavior exhibited by an individual in one particular setting that may or may not parallel their behavior in other settings. In other words, the ecological differences and varied stimulus control between settings may create specific conditions for behavior. For example, a student might behave differently in two different classrooms in which he or she is placed. Classroom rules, teacher expectations and management style, composition of students, and physical circumstances of the two classrooms might vary considerably, creating differences in the overall ecology of the classrooms that elicit, shape, and maintain behaviors in a different manner.

The idea of situational specificity of behavior has been supported by findings from several research projects. Wahler (1975) found that child behavior tends to "cluster" between school and home settings. Even when deviant or antisocial behaviors are present in the school and the home setting, the specific types of deviant behavior tend to differ. Stokes, Baer, and Jackson (1974) found that subject responses tended to be specific to the presence of individual experimenters and observers. The important point from both of these studies is that changes in setting were found to lead to different behavior patterns, indicating that generalization of behavior needs to be programmed into assessment and intervention strategies (Baer, Wolf, & Risley, 1968).

The problems related to situational specificity occur during behavioral observation assessment under two conditions: (1) when generalized inferences are drawn based on behaviors observed in specific settings; and (2) when the observer selects a setting for the observation that is inappropriate and does not adequately represent the behavioral responses exhibited in other settings. Both of these problems can be minimized when observations occur in multiple settings and when caution is used in making behavioral inferences based on what was observed in only one setting.

Inappropriate Recording Techniques

Earlier in this chapter, four general observation coding procedures were discussed—event, interval, time-sample, and duration or latency recording. Some authors (e.g., Barton &

Ascione, 1984) have suggested that there are six or more distinct categories of recording techniques. Whether or not one collapses or expands the categories of recording procedures, observation data can be recorded using at least four and possibly more procedures.

In addition to looking at specific recording procedures, behaviors can be categorized according to the dimensions under which they occur, which tend to correlate with specific recording techniques of choice. Alberto and Troutman (1998, 2003) identified six specific dimensions under which behaviors may occur, including (1) rate, (2) duration, (3) latency, (4) topography, (5) force, and (6) locus. The various dimensions under which behavior occurs might be expressed differently than these six categories, but the overall concept is still the same: Behaviors occur under several dimensions. There is also a general similarity between systems for recording behavior and systems for explaining behavior, which leads to the conclusion that a specific category of behavior is probably best chronicled through the use of a related recording system.

A potential threat to the validity of an observation may occur when the observer chooses a system for recording the behavior that is incongruent with that behavior. Low-frequency, but important behavioral occurrences, are normally best recorded using event recording techniques. Use of interval or time-sampling techniques probably would result in these behaviors not even being recorded. The dimension under which the behavior occurs and the recording system must mesh to a reasonable degree, or inappropriate conclusions may be reached.

Biased Expectations and Outside Influence
An additional potential threat to the validity of data obtained through direct behavioral observation may occur as a result of the observer, or someone who might influence the observer, expecting behavior to occur or change in a specific manner. Little has been written on this potential problem, but it nevertheless should be considered as a real threat. There is a humorous (but all too real) adage regarding biased expectations in behavioral science research and in life in general: "I wouldn't have seen it if I hadn't believed it." An observer who expects to see a target child engaging in aggressive behavior is more likely to record the behavior as being aggressive, even if the observational coding system used is quite objective. In this scenario, subtle biases in perceptions may occur wherein behavior that is a borderline or questionable fit with a particular coding category may be coded in that direction because the observer believes it should fit. One of my former students related to me an example of the subtle way in which this problem emerges. Having been asked to conduct an observation of a fourth-grade student in a general-education classroom setting, the observer (my former student) had been primed by the teacher and parent that the target student had serious problems with off-task behavior, inattentiveness, over-activity, and the like. Having never before met the target child, the observer asked the teacher to point him out from the back of the room, in a nonintrusive way. The observer conducted a 30-minute observation, and noted many instances of off-task and impulsive behavior. However, a later discussion with the teacher caused the observer to realize, in great embarrassment, that he had been observing the wrong student. The target child was actually one row of desks up from the child he had actually observed!

Another situation that may lead to biased results in observational data is when a researcher, supervisor, or some other person with a vested interest in the outcome of the observational assessment communicates to observers his or her satisfaction, disappointment, or annoyance with the content of behavioral observation data or his or her expectations regarding the child's behavior. In making plans for an observer to come into the classroom to assess a particular child, a teacher might make a comment such as "Karen is always off-task at least two or three times as much as other students in my class," with an empathic emphasis on "always." Or a supervisor might mention to the observer that the referral source for a specific case "almost always exaggerates how bad a problem is," setting up a situation in which the observer may feel pressure to not observe and code substantial problem behavior. This type of communication may set up a situation in which the observer feels some pressure to satisfy the stated expectations, which in turn might subtly bias the way that observed behavior is coded.

This particular threat to validity has no simple solutions. About the only actions that can be taken to reduce this threat are for the observer to make overt efforts to maintain their objectivity, to be scrupulously precise in the way they objectively code behavioral data, and to resist pressures toward a specified given outcome.

In sum, although there are several potential threats to the reliability and validity of systems for observing behavior directly, there are also many potential solutions. The major threats to validity, their potential consequences, and some possible solutions are presented in brief in Table 4.3.

Becoming aware of what problems might be encountered as part of direct behavioral observation and taking the appropriate preventative steps greatly enhance the usefulness of the obtained behavioral assessment data.

Table 4.3 Some potential threats to the validity of behavioral observations

Problem	Potential consequences	Possible solutions
Poorly defined observational domains	Observational recording system is either too cumbersome or too vague	Carefully define and select behaviors to be observed based on assessment problem and intervention goals
Unreliability of observers	Observers drift from original definitions; inter-rater reliability decreases	Provide high-quality initial training; conduct periodic reliability checks and retraining
Lack of social comparison data	Interpretations of behavior are not based on a normative perspective; deviancy may be under- or overestimated	Include typical or randomly selected subjects in the same setting for behavioral comparison
Observer reactivity	Subject behavior is influenced by the presence of the observer	Select and participate in observational settings in a discrete, unobtrusive manner
Situational specificity of behavior	Interpretations of observational data may not represent the larger picture	Conduct observations in multiple settings; don't overgeneralize from limited data
Inappropriate recording techniques	Behaviors are not adequately depicted; inappropriate conclusions are reached	Select recording systems carefully to match the behavioral domain
Biased expectations of the observer	Borderline behaviors may be systematically coded in a biased manner	Resist pressure to confirm expectations of persons with vested interests; remain scrupulously objective in coding behavior

BEHAVIORAL OBSERVATION AND FUNCTIONAL BEHAVIOR ASSESSMENT

In the 1990s, there was a strong general increase in attention to the notion of using functional behavioral assessment procedures to identify behavior and academic problems of children and youth and to link these problems to effective interventions. This increased interest has been particularly evident in the fields of special education and school psychology, primarily because of new requirements for assessment practice that were added to the IDEA as part of the 1997 congressional reauthorization (P.L. 105–17) of the law. The language in this reauthorization of the IDEA required that FBA be conducted for students engaging in behaviors that interfere with the educational process. In practice, the FBA requirement means that school personnel must conduct preintervention assessments of the functional relationships between a student's behavior and the suspected causes of that behavior. Following the FBA process, school personnel must develop intervention plans based on the obtained information (J. A. Miller, Tansy, & Hughes, 1998).

It is important to recognize that the actual process of FBA was not defined in P.L. 105–17. As a result, there has been confusion and frustration among practitioners and researchers concerned with child misbehavior regarding what FBA is and how it should be used within the overall processes of assessment and intervention. Because of the increased prominence of FBA over the past decade and its obvious relationship to direct behavioral observation, this section is included to provide some context to the issue. This section is necessarily brief and is not intended to be a comprehensive treatment of FBA or how direct behavioral observation fits into the process. Readers who desire additional information on this topic are referred to the following excellent works on FBA: Crone, Hawken, and Horner (2015), Horner (1994), Horner and Carr (1997), McComas and Mace (2000), O'Neill, Albin, Storey, Horner, and Sprague (2014), and Steege and Watson (2003).

FBA procedures may have been developed initially as a way of linking assessment to intervention with individuals having severe disabilities. As progress was made with FBA technology, however, its potential applications became more broad. The basis for FBA is relatively straightforward, although certain types of implementation may require a great deal of time and expertise in using the tools of applied behavior analysis. In its most simple description, functional assessment is merely a way of assessing problems to identify the particular functions of these problems. In other words, it is assumed that most problem behaviors serve some kind of a purpose in the child's or adolescent's world and that these purposes sometimes may maintain the problems. FBA also seeks to determine relationships between the problem behaviors or characteristics and any environmental antecedents that may elicit or bring forth the problems. The primary goal of FBA is to develop hypotheses about probable functions that the problem behaviors serve and to test these hypotheses by implementing an intervention. The experimental manipulation and evaluation of the treatment hypotheses is a separate phase or process and is referred to as functional analysis rather than functional assessment (McComas & Mace, 2000; J. A. Miller et al., 1998). Common functions of problem behavior include, but are not limited to, escape or avoidance of unpleasant or difficult tasks, social attention, self-stimulation, and access to desired items or activities. Although these common possible functions of problem behavior are frequently noted in discussions on this topic, it is important to recognize that for some complex behavior problems, the functions those behaviors serve may be very challenging to identify.

Because FBA focuses on obtaining assessment information that is as direct as possible, direct behavioral observation is usually a natural part of the process. Typically, the observation of behavior will occur in a naturalistic setting such as the school, but clinic-based analogue observation also has been shown to be an effective method in FBA. During the assessment process, careful attention is paid to the antecedents, the consequences, and the general environmental context of the targeted problem behavior. J. A. Miller et al. (1998) suggested that in practice, the first phase of FBA (description of the problem) should focus on the following aspects:

- settings in which the behavior occurs;
- frequency of the behavior;
- intensity of the behavior (e.g., consequences of the behavior for the student, peers, and immediate surrounding environment);
- duration of the behavior (how long the behavior lasts at a given time, how many days in a row it is observed);
- previous interventions attempted;
- educational impact of the problem behavior.

Although it may be possible to obtain information on these aspects of the behavior using methods other than direct observation (e.g., through interviews or rating scales), there are many advantages to using direct behavioral observation.

After the initial assessment data are gathered during the description process, the next phase (function) is to use the information to form hypotheses regarding the presumed functions of the behavior and to use these hypotheses to guide intervention planning. This phase is potentially difficult because in some circumstances there are no apparent explanations for the function of the behavior, and in other circumstances, there may be many competing explanations. Consider the potential functions that aggressive behavior may serve. Engaging in aggressive behavior toward peers may involve certain payoffs (reinforcement), such as getting what one wants. The inevitable attention that a child receives for engaging in aggressive behavior, even if it is negative attention, may serve as a reinforcing function. There also may be cognitive or affective contributions to the aggressive behavior. A youth may be depressed, which increases his or her irritability and helps to set up a chain of events that make aggressive interactions more likely. He or she may have distorted cognitions (e.g., inaccurate attributions of the intentions of others), which also may serve to increase the probability of aggressive behavior. There may be issues such as communication needs, frustration with the educational curriculum or expectations, physiological or constitutional issues, family issues, modeling, and more that may help to explain when the problem behavior is more or less likely to occur. In this process, the most plausible functions are identified based on the hypotheses that have been generated. These identified functions serve as the basis for an intervention plan. Ideally the intervention should be monitored carefully so that additional decisions may be data based. Although it is possible that the FBA process may end here, a complete or comprehensive FBA also should include a functional analysis phase, wherein the hypotheses that have been generated are evaluated empirically and fine-tuned as they are implemented. FBA and functional analysis are related concepts but not the same and not interchangeable.

In sum, FBA is an increasingly important process for guiding assessment and intervention of problem behaviors, and it is particularly relevant to working with students in school settings, where its use is mandated in some instances. Although FBA procedures do not rely on a single behavioral assessment method, direct behavioral observation has a potential role to play that is extremely important. The processes and coding systems related to naturalistic and analogue observation of behavior, which were described previously in this chapter, may be especially useful in successful implementation of FBA.

HOW MANY OBSERVATIONS ARE NEEDED?

An additional consideration regarding direct behavioral observations is the increasingly asked question, "How many observations are needed to get a reliable assessment of child behavior?" This question was not even considered a significant issue two decades ago, but a small number of research studies have indicated that it is a potentially serious issue with extensive implications for practice. With other primary methods of assessment—particularly with behavior rating scales, sociometrics, self-report instruments—the typical practice is to conduct the assessment at one time to gather a snapshot of the behavioral data. Although the issue of repeated assessments with these methods does raise some occasional questions regarding technical issues, best practice in the field overwhelmingly convinces practitioners and researchers to conduct one assessment with each tool or method and leave it at that. The same thinking has been true in most regards with direct behavioral observation, although with less certainty. It is typical practice for a school-based assessment professional to conduct one classroom or playground observation of a referred or identified child, and use the results from the single observation session to provide a snapshot of behavior in the naturalistic setting.

Given that naturalistic observation of behavior is known to be impacted by situational specificity or unique setting characteristics, some practitioners and researchers—including me—have argued that multiple observations, and observations across settings, may be a wise step. In fact, previous discussion in this chapter, as well as the recommendations found in Table 4.3, argue in favor of multiple observations, especially observations across multiple settings. But what of the issue of observations within a single setting? Is more than one observation within a single setting a requirement for obtaining reliable observational assessment data? Increasingly, there is evidence supporting this notion. An intriguing study by Doll and Elliott (1994) found that with preschool-age children observed in a free-play setting, at least five observations over time were required in order to reliably represent the behavior of individual children. Because this study was conducted in a free-play setting, and because it has been presumed that the behavior of younger children is particularly sensitive to changes in environment, it has been unclear whether these results are applicable to older children who are observed in academic settings. Interestingly, a more recent study by Hintze and Mathews (2004) dealt directly with this question and produced intriguing results. Conducting observations of on-task/off-task behavior during instructional time with individual students in a general-education fifth-grade classroom (two observations a day for ten school days), these researchers applied generalizability (G) theory to the data in an attempt to explain individual variance in behavior and to evaluate reliability of these observational data. It was determined that adequate levels of reliability of behavior could not be achieved even with a very straightforward on-task/off-task behavior definition. Follow-up analyses indicated that "for adequate levels of reliability to be assumed, participants would have had to be observed four times per day for four school weeks" (Hintze & Matthews, 2004, pp. 266–267).

Without question, it is simply not feasible for practitioners to devote such extensive amounts of time as may be needed to obtain reliable data within a specific setting with a particular child. Although these two studies with relatively small numbers of subjects are far from definitive, in tandem they raise a serious question and argue in support of the notion of the multimethod, multisource, multisetting assessment design that was introduced in Chapter 1. As Hintze and Mathews (2004) stated, "Clearly, systematic direct observation—although an important part of behavior assessment—cannot be used in isolation and must be combined with other forms of assessment (e.g., interviews, informant reports) in the decision-making process" (p. 268).

DIRECT BEHAVIORAL OBSERVATION AND DECISION MAKING

As has been stated several times in this chapter, the most important and powerful contribution that direct behavioral observation assessment methods can make to psychoeducational decision-making processes is in the area of intervention and treatment planning. Essentially, this use of assessment data places it within the context of a problem-solving process (Skinner, Rhymer, & McDaniel, 2000). Because behavioral observation has the capability, if done with great care, of being an ecologically valid assessment method, fewer inferences and intervening steps are potentially needed in translating the observational data to intervention planning because of the functional type of data that result from such an observation. Given that observation data may be capable of not only pinpointing specific problem behaviors, but also gauging the antecedent stimuli and controlling consequences of these behaviors, this assessment method can provide a great deal of information relevant to modifying the environment for the purpose of behavioral change.

Various forms of direct observation can be used within system-wide behavioral response to intervention (RtI) efforts. In terms of screening and assessment decisions, direct behavioral observation is potentially useful, but it may be too costly (in terms of professional time) to use on a large scale with several individuals. For example, observational data obtained during the course of a formal assessment may provide clues that further types of assessment are warranted, but using direct observation during the initial stages of a large-scale screening typically would be unmanageable and too costly. Direct observation could feasibly be used as a screening tool if the unit of analysis is larger, such as an observation of a classroom or recess period. During the initial screening stages of assessment for individuals, however, a quicker method, such as behavior rating scales, is desirable.

In making individual diagnosis or classification decisions, behavioral observations may provide useful information but probably will be insufficient alone. Two problems are likely to emerge if observational data are used exclusively in making diagnostic decisions:

1. Child behavior tends to be variable across situations and time, and an observational picture of child behavior may be incomplete.

2. To be used most effectively in making reliable diagnostic decisions, direct behavioral observation would need to occur in several settings and over several time periods, which could be an expensive and difficult proposition.

Situational specificity of behavior appears to be an increasingly important issue with respect to direct behavioral observation.

For making placement decisions with children and adolescents, observational data are often necessary. In implementing the IDEA, several states have required that direct behavioral observations must be conducted before placing a student in a more restrictive educational setting. For making placement decisions that involve psychiatric hospitalization or residential treatment facilities, few (if any) credible institutions would consent to such placements without having a staff member or associate first obtain a direct assessment of the referred child's behavior through observation.

Direct observation may be appropriate for progress monitoring behaviors targeted for intervention, but conducting regular, lengthy, systematic direct observations may not be the best use of staff time. Direct behavior ratings (DBRs) can serve as a more efficient method for progress monitoring behaviors targeted for intervention across contexts (Christ, Riley-Tillman, & Chafouleas, 2009). DBRs are viewed as a hybrid between systematic direct observation and indirect behavior ratings (see Chapter 5 for more information on behavior rating scales). These ratings are direct in that regular direct observations of behaviors in context are taken. DBRs target specific behaviors (e.g., academic engagement, disruption), and they require an adult (or sometimes the child) to rate the observed behavior at a particular moment in time (e.g., morning, math class). This method is promising in terms of its utility. It does not require substantial staff time but it aims to provide objective behavioral data that can both aid in monitoring intervention effectiveness and serve as a communication tool between school and home environments (Chafouleas, Riley-Tillman, & Christ, 2009).

CONCLUSIONS

Direct behavioral observation is one of the key assessment tools of scientifically minded clinicians and researchers. Grounded in the tradition of behavioral psychology, particularly the work of B. F. Skinner and the field of applied behavior analysis, direct behavioral observation is potentially useful in many situations, without respect to the theoretical orientation of the observer.

Perhaps the greatest advantage of direct behavioral observation is the fact that it can be highly functional or, in other words, be used to identify important antecedent stimuli and controlling consequences of behavior. In the hands of a skilled and theoretically grounded observer, direct observation data can be used to help in planning and implementing interventions. Essentially, high-quality direct behavioral observation assessment can be "ecobehavioral assessment."

There are three major types of direct behavioral observation: naturalistic observation, analogue observation, and self-monitoring observation. Naturalistic observation, or observing subjects in their natural environment and using an objective and impartial coding procedure, is the preferred method for most purposes. Analogue observation, or simulating the circumstances of the natural environment within a laboratory or clinic, has some advantages for research and may be used when naturalistic observation is not possible. Self-monitoring observation is a process whereby the subject is trained to monitor and record his or her own behavior. Self-monitoring has the advantage of being strongly linked to intervention and may serve to change behavior in, and of, itself. It is difficult to maintain reliability and objectivity over time with self-monitoring, however.

Several types of coding systems have been developed for use in direct behavioral observation. In this chapter, these types of coding systems were circumscribed into four general areas: event recording, interval recording, time-sample recording, and duration and latency recording. Each of these types of coding systems is useful for different purposes, and the choice of a specific system should be guided by the characteristics of the behavior under observation.

Six formal observation coding systems were reviewed in some detail. These six systems are representative of the variety found in direct behavioral observation and show how specific observational systems may be developed for specific purposes. In contrast to some other types of assessment methods, most direct behavioral observation systems are not commercially produced or norm referenced. They tend to be developed for specific purposes and settings. Skilled clinicians may develop their own observational systems to address the specific problems and situations they encounter.

Although, at its best, direct behavioral observation is highly ecologically valid and functional, several potential threats to the validity of observational data must be considered. These threats include poorly defined observational data, unreliability of observers, lack of social comparison data, observer reactivity within observation settings, situational specificity of behavior, use of inappropriate recording techniques, and biased observer expectations. Specific practices may be employed to reduce these various threats to observational validity. Perhaps the most important practice in reducing threats to observational validity is simply to consider these various threats when planning and implementing the observation and taking specific steps to counter problems as they arise.

FBA has emerged as an important process in behavioral assessment and intervention for children and adolescents in school settings, particularly when problem behaviors are extremely challenging and disrupt the educational process. FBA is an approach to integrating assessment with intervention and not a separate assessment method. Rather, FBA relies on various assessment methods to help describe objectively the problem behavior and its presumed functions, and to assist in forming hypotheses regarding functions that may be useful in developing interventions. Direct behavioral observation has an obvious natural role in conducting FBA and should be considered one of the first-line assessment methods to use.

Direct behavioral observation data may be used in various ways in making decisions regarding the delivery of psychological or educational services. Perhaps the greatest advantage of direct observation in this regard is use of ecologically valid and functional information for intervention planning and implementation. Direct observation procedures are typically so time-consuming and costly that they are best used in the later stages of the classification process. In doing so, it is crucial to consider the potential problems of situational specificity of behavior and unreliability of behavior over time, and the increasingly important notion that several observations may be required in order to reliably represent child behavior.

REVIEW AND APPLICATION QUESTIONS

1. Define the term *ecobehavioral assessment.* What practices should be considered and implemented in behavioral observation to make the resulting data functional and ecologically valid?

2. Three types of general observational procedures were outlined: naturalistic observation, analogue observation, and self-monitoring. For each of these three types, describe an appropriate and inappropriate situation for using it.

3. Define functional behavior assessment (FBA) and describe how direct observation of behavior may serve as an important foundation of FBA.

4. What are some of the most potentially useful ways that direct behavioral observation data may be used in decision making? Conversely, in what situations will direct behavioral observation data be less useful in decision making?

5. The issue of the number of observations required to reliably represent child behavior is increasingly being raised. Given the current state of knowledge regarding this issue, what is the recommended best practice in using direct behavioral observation data in decision making?

6. Measuring behavior through observation requires operational definitions of target behaviors that are neither too broad, nor too narrow. Consider the following common behavioral terms and brainstorm how you would define each to increase the likelihood that an accurate and useful measurement will be taken:
   - withdrawn;
   - depressed;
   - hyperactive;
   - inattentive;
   - reluctant or avoidant;
   - out of control;
   - impulsive.

7. You are leading a research project whereby observational data must be collected in an elementary school classroom. You are interested in measuring "student engagement" and have determined four aspects of this concept to measure. Eventually you would like to publish your study in a peer-refereed journal and you know that the editor will look for the use of an inter-rater observer procedure in your study. Describe how you will protect against observer drift, while utilizing an inter-rater observer procedure.

8. You are a psychologist working in a community mental health clinic, seeing clients for 50-minute sessions. A ten-year-old child is brought to an initial appointment by his mother, who reports the child chronically "back talks" and is frequently noncompliant. After speaking with the child, along with the mother, you note that he has answered all of your questions in a polite and thoughtful manner. Which observational phenomenon might this behavioral discrepancy represent and what observational methods could you consider to measure the behaviors of concern?

9. Perhaps the best way to integrate one's understanding of the best uses of various types of observational and coding procedures is to work on cases requiring the development of various methods and procedures. For each of the five scenarios listed below, do the following:
   - Select and specify one setting that would be appropriate for conducting a 20-minute observation.

- Select what you consider to be the most appropriate observation method (naturalistic, analogue, or self-monitoring observation).
- Select what you consider to be the most appropriate coding procedure (event, interval, time-sample, duration and latency recording).
- Provide a rationale or justification for the methods and procedures you select. Consider threats to validity and how you would address these.
- List what behavior(s) you would specifically target for observation.

Scenarios

- Observation of a primary-grade student who was referred because of frequent off-task behavior, difficulty "staying put," and problems completing academic work.
- Observation of a four-year-old child who was referred because of severe social withdrawal, significant interpersonal communication problems, and stereotypic self-stimulating behavior (rocking, twirling, and hand flapping). The child attends a developmental preschool three hours per day.
- Observation of an adolescent who was referred because of self-reported depression. This client has made two suicide gestures or attempts in the past six months (cutting wrists, ingesting a bottle of aspirin).
- Observation of a ninth-grade student who was referred because of severe acting-out and aggressive behavior at school, including attacking other students and throwing chairs or other objects. These types of behaviors are reported to occur an average of three to five times per week.
- Observation of a fifth-grade student who was referred because of peer relationship problems, including teasing classmates, difficulty making friends, and being rejected by other students.

5

BEHAVIOR RATING SCALES

The popularity and use of behavior rating scales as a method of assessing behavioral, social, and emotional problems and competencies of children and adolescents has increased dramatically since about the mid-1980s. Behavior rating scales are now employed frequently as a primary component of an assessment battery, as a key means of obtaining information on a child or adolescent before implementing an intervention, and as a tool for monitoring the effectiveness of interventions and programs. As behavior rating scales have become more widely used, there have been numerous advances in research on rating scale technology that have strengthened the desirability of using this form of assessment (Elliott, Busse, & Gresham, 1993; Merrell, 2000a, 2000b).

The purpose of this chapter is to acquaint readers with the theoretical, technical, and applied aspects of using behavior rating scales as a method for assessing behavioral, social, and emotional concerns of children and adolescents. First, a brief discussion of the nature and characteristics of rating scales is presented. Sections on advantages and problems of rating scales and some of the measurement and technical issues involved in rating scale technology follow to assist readers in developing a broader understanding of some important measurement issues. After the initial foundation-laying part of the chapter, reviews and discussions of some of the most widely used general-purpose problem behavior rating scales for children and adolescents are provided. Next, some recommended practices in using rating scales are presented. The chapter ends with a discussion of the use of behavior ratings in making various decisions related to the assessment process.

CHARACTERISTICS OF BEHAVIOR RATING SCALES

Definitions and Foundations

Behavior rating scales provide a standardized format for the development of *summary judgments* regarding a child's or adolescent's behavioral characteristics by an informant who knows the child or adolescent well. The informant is usually a parent or teacher, but other individuals who are familiar with the child or adolescent might legitimately be a source for behavior rating scale data, including work supervisors, classroom aides, day-care providers, temporary surrogate parents, and extended family members.

As an assessment methodology, behavior rating scales are less direct than behavioral observation or structured behavioral interviewing because they measure *perceptions* of specified behaviors rather than provide a first-hand measure or direct observation of the existence of the behavior. Rating scales are an objective method, however, and yield more

DOI: 10.4324/9781315747521-6

reliable data than either unstructured clinical interviewing or projective–expressive techniques (R. P. Martin et al., 1986; Merrell, 2000a). As behavior rating scales began to be more widely used during the late 1970s, they typically were viewed with suspicion and used as a "last resort" by behaviorally oriented clinicians (Cone & Hawkins, 1977), but as the research base and technological refinements in rating scales became more advanced, there was a concurrent increase in their acceptance among researchers and clinicians.

Rating Scales Versus Checklists It is useful to differentiate *rating scale* from a related term *checklist*. A checklist format for identifying behavioral problems or competencies lists a number of behavioral descriptors, and if the rater perceives the symptom to be present, he or she simply "checks" the item. After completing the checklist, the number of checked items is summed. Checklists are thus considered to be *additive* in nature, because the obtained score is a simple additive summation of all the checked items. Rating scales, like checklists, allow the rater to indicate whether a specific symptom is present or absent. However, rating scales also provide a means of estimating the *degree to which a characteristic is present.* A common 3-point rating system (there are many variations of this) allows the rater to score a specific behavior descriptor from 0 to 2, with 0 indicating the symptom is "never" present, 1 indicating the symptom is "sometimes" present, and 2 indicating the symptom is "frequently" present. Because rating scales allow the rater to weight the specified symptoms differentially, and each weighting corresponds with a specific symbolic numerical value and frequency or intensity description, rating scales are said to be *algebraic* in nature. Conners and Werry (1979) defined rating scales as an "algebraic summation, over variable periods of time and numbers of social situations, of many discrete observations" (p. 341). In general, the algebraic format provided by rating scales is preferred to the additive format provided by checklists because it allows for more precise measurement and differentiation of behavioral frequency or intensity (Merrell, 2000a, 2000b). The differences between the additive nature of a checklist format and the algebraic character of a rating scale format are illustrated by the sample items in Table 5.1. A wider range of possible scores and variance is possible using the algebraic rating scale format as opposed to the less sophisticated checklist format, which seems to have continually lost favor over time.

Table 5.1 Example of differences between checklist and rating scale formats for assessing child behavior problems

Behavioral descriptor	Checklist	Format	Rating	Scale	Format
1. Is noticeably sad or depressed	Y	N	0	1	2
2. Feels hopeless about his or her problems	Y	N	0	1	2
3. Wants to be left alone	Y	N	0	1	2
4. Has had a change in eating or sleeping habits	Y	N	0	1	2
5. Is irritable or disagreeable	Y	N	0	1	2

Note: Key to checklist format: Y = symptom is present; N = symptom is not present.

Key to rating scale format: 0 = never occurs; 1 = sometimes or to some degree occurs; 2 = frequently or to a great degree occurs.

Advantages of Behavior Rating Scales

The widespread popularity of using behavior rating scales is not incidental—they offer many advantages for clinicians and researchers conducting child and adolescent assessments. The main advantages of behavior rating scales are summarized in the following six points:

1. In comparison with direct behavioral observation, behavior rating scales are less expensive in terms of professional time involved and amount of training required to use the assessment system.
2. Behavior rating scales are capable of providing data on low-frequency but important behaviors that might not be seen in a limited number of direct observation sessions. An example is violent and assaultive behavior. In most cases, these types of behavior do not occur on a constant or consistent schedule, so they might be missed within the constraints of conducting two brief observations. Nonetheless, it is extremely important to know about them.
3. As mentioned earlier, behavior rating scales are an objective assessment method that provides more reliable data than unstructured interviews or projective–expressive techniques.
4. Behavior rating scales can be used to assess children and adolescents who cannot readily provide information about themselves. Consider the difficulty in obtaining valid assessment data on an adolescent who is in a secure unit in a psychiatric hospital or juvenile detention center, and who is unavailable or unwilling to be assessed through interviews and self-reports.
5. Rating scales capitalize on observations over a period of time in a child's or adolescent's "natural" environments (i.e., school or home settings).
6. Rating scales capitalize on the judgments and observations of persons who are highly familiar with the child or adolescent's behavior, such as parents or teachers, and are considered to be "expert" informants.

With these six advantages of using rating scales illustrated, it is easy to see why they are so widely used: they get at the "big picture" of the assessment problem in a short amount of time, at moderate cost, and with a good deal of technical precision and practical utility.

Problems Associated with Using Behavior Rating Scales

Despite the several advantages behavior rating scales offer, there are some problems or disadvantages. The most sophisticated rating scales can help provide objective, reliable, and socially valid information on broad and narrow dimensions of behavioral, social, and emotional problems. The nature of rating scale technology contains several potential flaws, however, which are important to understand. At the onset of discussing problems associated with behavior rating scales, it is useful to remember that by their nature (i.e., assessing perceptions of problems), rating scales are capable of providing a portrait of a general idea or conception of behavior, but they do not provide actual observational data, even though their technical characteristics allow for actuarial prediction of behavior.

More than three decades ago, R. P. Martin et al. (1986) categorized the measurement problems of behavior rating scales into two classes: *bias of response* and *error variance*. These classes still represent an excellent way to understand some of the measurement challenges associated with rating scales.

Bias of response refers to the way that informants completing the rating scales potentially may create additional error by the way they use the scales. There are three

Table 5.2 Types of error variance found with behavior rating scales

Type of error variance	Examples
Source variance	Various types of response bias; different raters may have different ways of responding to the rating format
Setting variance	Related to situational specificity of behavior; eliciting and reinforcing variables present in one environment (e.g., Classroom 1) may not be present in a closely related environment (e.g., Classroom 2)
Temporal variance	Behavior is likely to change over time, and an informant's approach to the rating scale task may change over time
Instrument variance	Different rating scales may be measuring different hypothetical constructs; there is a continuum of continuity (ranging from close to disparate) between constructs measured by different scales

specific types of response bias, including: (1) *halo effects* (rating a student in a positive or negative manner simply because they possess some other positive or negative characteristic not pertinent to the rated item); (2) *leniency or severity* (the tendency of some raters to have an overly generous or overly critical response set when rating all subjects); and (3) *central tendency effects* (the proclivity of raters to select midpoint ratings and to avoid endpoints of the scale such as "never" and "always").

Error variance is related closely to, and often overlaps with, response bias as a form of rating scale measurement problems but provides a more general representation of some of the problems encountered with this form of assessment. Four types of variance that may create error in the obtained results of a rating scale assessment are outlined in Table 5.2.

These types of variance are summarized as follows: *Source variance* refers to the subjectivity of the raters and any of the idiosyncratic ways that they complete the rating scales. *Setting variance* occurs as a result of the situational specificity of behavior (Kazdin, 1979), given that humans tend to behave differently in different environments because of the unique eliciting and reinforcing properties present. *Temporal variance* refers to the tendency of behavior ratings to be only moderately consistent over time—partly as a result of changes in the observed behavior over time, and partly as a result of changes in the rater's approach to the rating task over time. Finally, *instrument variance* refers to the fact that different rating scales measure often related but slightly differing hypothetical constructs (e.g., aggressive behavior versus delinquent behavior), and a severe problem behavior score on one scale may be compared with only a moderate problem behavior score on a differing rating scale for the same person. Another problem that creates instrument variance is the fact that each rating scale uses different normative populations with which to make score comparisons, and if the norm populations are not stratified and selected in the same general manner, similar score levels on two different rating scales may not mean the same thing.

Although there are several problems inherent in using behavior rating scales, there are also effective ways of minimizing those problems. Notwithstanding the argument that in some cases it might increase error variance, the *aggregation principle* is particularly important to understand and implement in using behavior rating scales, and we consider this principle in some detail in the "best practices" later in this chapter.

Measurement and Technical Issues

So far I have reviewed some of the uses, advantages, and disadvantages of using behavior rating scales. This section provides a brief overview of some of the measurement and technical issues that can affect the psychometric properties of rating scales. One of the measurement characteristics of rating scales that can produce variation in the reliability and validity of a measure is the *time element* involved in making the rating. This is related to, but not the same as, the issue of temporal variance, which was already discussed. According to Worthen, Borg, and White (1993), there is a tendency for recent events and behavior to be given disproportionate weight when a rater completes a rating scale. This idea is based on the notion that it is easier to remember behavioral, social, and emotional characteristics during the previous two-week period than during the previous two-month period. Rating scales differ as to the time period on which the ratings are supposed to be based. For example, some rating scales specify that the rater should complete the rating items based on the observation of the child over the previous six-month period, whereas some other scales have a shorter time period (say, one month), and some scales do not indicate a time period. A related measurement issue raised by Worthen et al. (1993) is that it is easier for raters to remember unusual behavior than ordinary behavior. Typical uneventful behaviors may be assigned less proportional weight during the rating than novel, unusual, or highly distinctive behaviors.

Another measurement and technical variable that may affect the psychometric properties of rating scales is the construction of the rating format. The two rating formats that seem to be the most common for child behavior rating scales are 3-point and 5-point scales. An alternative scaling system that appears in some behavior rating scales is a 4-point scale, which reflects the middle ground between the two typical formats, but lacks an exact midpoint. These two or three typical formats are all capable of providing a reasonable and technically sound basis for behavior ratings, and there is no convincing evidence that one of these formats is necessarily better than the other.

Typically, each numerical value in the rating format is keyed or anchored to a descriptor (e.g., 0 = never, 1 = sometimes, 2 = frequently). As a rule, more accurate ratings are obtained when there is a tangible and understandable definition for each quality level. In terms of deciding how many rating points or levels of rating are appropriate in constructing a rating scale, Worthen et al. (1993) suggested that a common error in scale construction is to use too many levels; the higher the level of inference needed in making the rating, the more difficult it becomes to discriminate reliably among the rating levels. A good convention is for scale developers to use the fewest rating levels needed to make the rating discrimination and for scale consumers to avoid rating scales that include an extremely high number of inference points. It also is important to review carefully the descriptors or anchor points in a rating format to ensure that they are clear and meaningful before adopting a new behavior rating scale.

An interesting issue related to scaling of behavior rating formats is the wording of the descriptions or anchors that are connected to each potential rating item. In the examples that have already been provided for the most typical rating formats, the descriptors or anchors are usually somewhat generic and slightly subjective (e.g., 0 = never, 1 = sometimes, 2 = frequently). This traditional rating scale anchoring format has held up well over time and has not proven to present any insurmountable technical problems.

Some alternatives to the traditional rating scale formatting have begun to emerge, in which the anchors to specified numerical rating points are *very specifically connected to the estimated frequency of specified behaviors.* Although this emerging alternative format does not have a particular appellation at this time, I like to refer to it as the *frequency of behavior* format. Holland, Gimpel, and Merrell (1998, 2001) experimented with this format in the development of the ADHD Symptoms Rating Scale (ADHD-SRS), which is discussed in Chapter 10 and ultimately decided to use it in lieu of the traditional rating scale format. The specific frequency of behavior rating points and anchors from the ADHD-SRS are illustrated in Figure 5.1. In this illustration, we used a 5-point rating scale, ranging from 0 = "behavior does not occur/no knowledge of behavior" to 4 = "behavior occurs one to several times an hour." The main difference between this frequency of behavior rating format and traditional rating scale formats is that the anchors and rating points are tied to very specific time periods, such as months, weeks, days, and hours. In developing this format, they hypothesized that such an anchoring system might result in higher reliability and precision in ratings. The actual pilot-testing research in which they asked teachers and parents to complete child ratings using both formats, and then rate their preference for each, resulted in some interesting and unexpected findings. With respect to reliability and precision of ratings, they found that the two formats were both solid and essentially identical, negating their hypothesis that the frequency of behavior format would result in better precision and consistency. With respect to rater preferences, they found that there was a small but meaningful overall preference of teachers and parents for the frequency of behavior format over the traditional format. Given the essential similarity of the two rating formats with respect to the psychometric properties of the ratings, they opted to go with the frequency of behavior format, concluding that the higher preference for it among raters was a potentially important aspect of user acceptability and social validity. At that time, there had been no other studies of this ratings format scaling phenomenon, and this issue continues to represent a potentially important area for future investigations.

A final technical characteristic to consider regarding rating scales includes their directions for use. Some scales provide highly detailed instructions for completing the ratings, such as which persons should use the rating scale, the time period involved, and how to approach and interpret the items. Other scales may provide a minimum of directions or clarifications. It is recommended that users of behavior rating scales select instruments that provide clear and tangible directions for conducting the rating and

Directions: Read each item carefully and decide how often you think this child has demonstrated these behaviors in the past 3 months. Circle the number that best describes your choice. Please complete all items.

Behavior Does Not Occur/No Knowledge of Behavior	Behavior Occurs One to Several Times a Month	Behavior Occurs One to Several Times a Week	Behavior Occurs One to Several Times a Day	Behavior Occurs One to Several Times an Hour
0	1	2	3	4

Figure 5.1 An example of a "frequency of behavior" alternative rating scale format

Source: Reproduced by special permission from the ADHD Symptoms Rating Scale (ADHD SRS) by Melissa Lea Holland, Ph.D., Gretchen A. Gimpel, Ph.D., Kenneth W. Merrell, Ph.D., Copyright 2001 by Wide Range, Inc.

decision rules for interpreting blurred distinctions (Gronlund & Linn, 1999). In sum, the characteristics of rating scale technology that make behavior rating scales appealing also may negatively affect the consistency and utility of the measure. As with any type of measurement and evaluation system, consumers of behavior rating scales are advised to evaluate a potential instrument based on the important technical characteristics.

REVIEW OF SELECTED GENERAL-PURPOSE BEHAVIOR RATING SCALES AND SYSTEMS

Now that the technical foundation for understanding the technology, uses, and problems of rating scales has been covered, I take an in-depth look at a few selected behavior rating scale systems that are widely available and frequently employed as child assessment tools in school and clinic settings. The instruments or systems that have been selected for review and discussion include two rating scales from the Achenbach System of Empirically Based Assessment; the Behavior Assessment System for Children, Third Edition; and the Conners Rating Scale system. Besides the fact that these three systems are frequently used and widely available, they have been selected for inclusion because they are *general-purpose* behavior rating scale systems. That is, they provide parent and teacher rating forms to measure a variety of behavioral, social, and emotional problems. In many cases, these systems also include scales and subscales that measure adaptive competencies in addition to problem behaviors. Another reason these instruments have been singled out for inclusion as examples in this chapter is that they represent some of the best constructed and widely researched instruments currently available. Finally, these three systems can be completed by either parents or teachers and are useful in a variety of assessment and treatment settings.

Several other general problem behavior scales are available but not reviewed in this chapter because of space limitations and my own judgment regarding which scales or systems are most influential. The lack of a descriptive review in this book should not be interpreted as a condemnation of any assessment tool. In addition to the scales reviewed in this chapter, there is an ever-increasing array of general-purpose behavior rating scales available that are useful, have adequate or good technical properties, and are used on a wide-scale basis in assessing children and adolescents. Several other behavior rating scales have been developed for more specific purposes, such as assessing social skills, hyperactivity, depression, anxiety, antisocial behavior, and school-based behaviors, that could be referred to as specific-purpose or narrow-band instruments. Many of these instruments are reviewed and discussed in subsequent chapters of this book, when assessment of specific problems or constructs is discussed.

ASEBA: *Child Behavior Checklist and Teacher's Report Form for Ages 6 to 18*
Among the most sophisticated, well researched, and technically sound general-purpose problem behavior rating scales are those incorporated into the Achenbach System of Empirically Based Assessment (ASEBA). This collection of instruments incorporates several rating scales, self-report forms, interview schedules, and observation forms for children, adolescents, and adults. Several of these instruments—particularly those for use with school-age children and youth—use a common cross-informant system of similar subscales and items. Two of the instruments in this system, the Child Behavior Checklist

for Ages 6 to 18 (CBCL/6–18) (Achenbach, 2001a), and the Teacher's Report Form for Ages 6 to 19 (TRF/6–18) (Achenbach, 2001c), are conceptually similar and are reviewed herein. These two instruments are in many ways the historical core of the ASEBA system. Although the CBCL/6–18 and TRF/6–18 have different names and normative groups, the items and format are quite similar. In combination, these instruments are clearly the most widely researched parent and teacher behavior rating scales in existence for use with schoolchildren. In fact, there have been more than 8,000 publications from more than 100 cultures written by about 15,000 authors, and translations of the ASEBA tools have been made in over 90 languages to date. Without question, this volume of research dwarfs that of any similar assessment system. More than any other measures, the ASEBA child behavior rating scales have been the driving force behind the increased interest and acceptance of behavior rating scales and the advances in technical adequacy that have occurred since the late 1970s. The 2001 revisions of these two rating scales reflect minor content changes and new norming samples from the previous versions (Achenbach, 1991a, 1991b). A new user's guide and technical manual (Achenbach, 2001b) provides research documentation and user information for both rating scales. In addition to the updated materials released in 2001, the *Multicultural Supplement to the Manual for the ASEBA School-Age Forms and Profiles* was made available (Achenbach & Rescorla, 2007). This module provides users with norms for children in countries other than the United States. It also enables scores to be calculated in the following new scales: Obsessive-Compulsive Problems, Posttraumatic Stress Problems, and Sluggish Cognitive Tempo. The release of the *DSM-5* also required developers to update the *DSM*-Oriented Scales. This update was taken seriously and included having a number of experts from 30 societies rate the extent to which items were *not consistent, somewhat consistent*, or *very consistent* with *DSM-5* criteria that had changed. The *Anxiety Problems* and *Somatic Problems* scales were revised so that they are comprised of items most relevant to *DSM-5* (Achenbach, 2013). The ASEBA rating scales for use with young children are discussed in Chapter 13, and the Youth Self-Report version of the system is described in Chapter 7 and in other places in this book.

Description The CBCL/6–18 and TRF/6–18 both include 120 problem items: 118 items that reflect specific behavioral and emotional problems, and two items that are used for open-ended description of rater's concerns regarding the child's or adolescent's behavior. These items are rated on a 3-point scale, where 0 = *Not True*, 1 = *Somewhat or Sometimes True*, or 2 = *Very True* or *Often True* format. The 120 items on the two checklists have a high degree of continuity, with 93 items the same across the scales, and the remainder of the items more specific to the home or school settings. Downward extensions of both of these measures have been developed for use with younger children and are discussed in Chapter 13. In addition to the problem behavior rating scales on the CBCL/6–18 and TRF/6–18, both instruments contain sections wherein the informant provides information on the adaptive behavioral competencies of the subject. On the CBCL/6–18, this section includes 20 items where the parents provide information on their child's activities, social relations, and school performance. On the TRF/6–18, the competency items include sections for academic performance and adaptive functioning.

Scoring System and Scale Structure Raw scores for the CBCL/6–18 and TRF/6–18 are converted to broad-band and narrow-band scores that are based on a *T* score system (a normalized distribution with a mean of approximately 50 and standard deviation of 10), and that are grouped according to gender and age level (six to 11, 12 to 18). Both rating scales can be hand-scored using the test manual and appropriate versions of the hand-scoring profiles, which include scoring keys for the internalizing/externalizing total scores, plus the various subscales scores, and a graph to plot the scores. The hand-scoring process is somewhat tedious, taking at least 15 minutes for an experienced scorer and longer for a scorer who is not familiar with the system. Available hand-scoring templates make this job quicker and easier, however, and a computerized scoring program (ASEBA-PC software) or web-based scoring system (ASEBA-WEB) on the publisher's website are available at additional cost. These latter two scoring methods provide convenient and easy-to-read printouts of score profiles. For ASEBA users who use the CBCL/6–18 and TRF/6–18 on more than an occasional basis, it is well worth purchasing the Assessment Data Manager (ADM) computerized scoring programs.

For both instruments, three different broad-band problem behavior scores are obtained. The first two are referred to as Internalizing and Externalizing and are based on the behavioral dimensions breakdown of overcontrolled and undercontrolled behavior that were discussed in detail in Chapter 3. The third broad-band score is a total problems score, which is based on a raw score to T score conversion of the total ratings of the 120 problem behavior items. The total problems score is not obtained by merely combining the Internalizing and Externalizing scores because there are several rating items on each instrument that do not fit into either of two broad-band categories but are included in the total score. The CBCL/6–18 and TRF/6–18 scoring systems also provide T score conversions of the data from the competence portions of the instruments, which were discussed previously.

In terms of narrow-band or subscale scores, the CBCL/6–18 and TRF/6–18 score profiles both provide a score breakdown into eight common subscale or syndrome scores, which are empirically derived configurations of items. These eight "cross-informant syndromes" include the internalizing area scales of Anxious/Depressed, Withdrawn/Depressed, and Somatic Problems; the externalizing area scales Rule-Breaking Behavior and Aggressive Behavior; and three scales that are considered "other" problems (not specifically internalizing or externalizing): Social Problems, Thought Problems, and Attention Problems.

This broad-band and narrow-band configuration, which is consistent across the school-age measures of the ASEBA, are shown in Figure 5.2 in their hierarchical relationship structure. Like the 1991 version, the 2001 versions of the CBCL and TRF behavior profiles are based on different norms for boys and girls and by age group. The names of the narrow-band syndromes are constant, however, and the general item content within these syndrome scores is similar. For the narrow-band and broad-band scale scores of these measures, clinical cutoff points have been established, based on empirically validated criteria. In addition to the basic narrow-band and broad-band scales, the 2001 versions of both instruments include six optional *DSM*-oriented scales: Affective Problems, Anxiety Problem, Somatic Problem, Attention Deficit/Hyperactivity Problem, Oppositional Defiant Problem, and Conduct Problems. These *DSM*-oriented scales were added to the 2001 versions to enhance consistency with the *DSM* diagnostic criteria, and to aid in initial decision making regarding possible classifications to consider.

Development and Standardization The 2001 edition of the CBCL/6–18 includes a large new nationwide normative sample of 1,753 nonreferred child and adolescent cases,

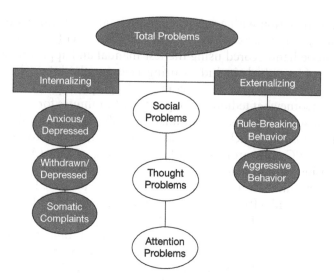

Figure 5.2 Diagram of scales and their relationship structure from the cross-informant scales of the CBCL/6–18 and TRF/6–18 of the ASEBA system

with 4,994 additional clinically referred cases used for construction of the narrow-band and *DSM*-oriented subscales, and establishment of clinical cutoff criteria. The test developers report that the normative standardization sample is representative of the 48 contiguous U.S. states for socioeconomic status, ethnicity, geographic region, and urban–suburban–rural residence patterns. The 2001 TRF/6–18 norming sample is based on ratings of 2,319 nonreferred students, with 4,437 additional cases of referred students used for establishing the subscale structure and developing clinical cutoff criteria. Like the CBCL/6–18, the TRF/6–18 norming sample is based on a broad sample that is generally representative of the larger U.S. population in several respects.

Psychometric Properties The psychometric properties of the two ASEBA child behavior rating forms are reported in the test manual and in hundreds of externally published research reports. Given that the 2001 revisions of these instruments are relatively slight in terms of item content and that the rating format remains the same as previous versions, the huge body of accumulated evidence from previous versions of the scales should be counted as supporting the reliability and validity of the current measures. In general, the psychometric properties of the current versions of the CBCL and TRF, as well as previous versions, range from adequate to excellent. In terms of test–retest reliability, most of the obtained reliabilities for the CBCL/6–18, taken at one-week intervals, are in the 0.80 to mid-0.90 range and are still quite good at three-, six-, and 18-month intervals (mean reliabilities ranging from the 0.40s to 0.70s at 18 months). On the TRF/6–18, the median test–retest reliability has been reported at 0.90 for seven-day intervals, and at 0.84 for 15-day intervals. The median TRF test–retest correlation at two months has been reported as 0.74 and at four months, 0.68. These data suggest that ratings from both the CBCL and TRF rating scales can be quite stable over short to moderately long periods.

Inter-rater reliabilities (between parents) on previous versions of the CBCL and TRF have been reported in many studies and were in part the topic of a highly influential article by Achenbach et al. (1987) on cross-informant reliability of scores within the

ASEBA system. Median correlation across scales of the two forms has been reported at 0.66. On previous versions of the TRF, inter-rater reliabilities between teachers and teacher aides on combined age samples have ranged from 0.42 to 0.72. Although lower than the test–retest reliabilities, the inter-rater agreement is still adequate. On a related note, Achenbach et al.'s (1987) meta-analytic study examined cross-informant correlations in ratings of child/adolescent behavioral and emotional problems and discussed in detail the problem of situational specificity in interpreting rating scale data. Based on the data from this study, *average cross-informant correlations across all forms of the ASEBA were found to be closer to the 0.30 range.*

Various forms of test validity on the CBCL/6–18 and TRF/6–18 and previous versions of these scales have been inferred through years of extensive research, and are cataloged in a staggering array of published studies. Through demonstration of sensitivity to theoretically based group differences, strong construct validity has been inferred for each instrument. The scales have been shown to distinguish accurately among clinical and normal samples and among various clinical subgroups. The convergent construct validity for both scales has been demonstrated through significant correlations between the scales and other widely used behavior rating scales. The factor analytic evidence regarding the validity of the eight-subscale cross-informant syndrome structure is presented in impressive detail in the test manual and has been replicated externally with independent samples for the CBCL (Dedrick, 1997) and the TRF (deGroot, Koot, & Verhulst, 1996).

Additional Comments Given the current focus on responsiveness to intervention (RtI), the *Brief Problem Monitor* (BPM) (Achenbach, McConaughy, Ivanova, & Rescorla, 2011) has also recently been made available. This measure is intended to monitor the behavioral progress of children exposed to intervention. Items parallel those from the CBCL/6–18, TRF, and Youth Self Report (YSR) and the 18–19 items can be quickly completed by parents (BPM-P), teachers (BPM-T), and children aged 11 and older (BPM-Y). Norms are based on gender, age and rater, and users can calculate scores based on Internalizing, Attention Problems, Externalizing, and Total Problems scales. This measure was developed based on Item Response Theory and has demonstrated technical adequacy (Chorpita et al., 2010).

The CBCL/6–18 and TRF/6–18, the most widely used ASEBA tools, have a great deal of clinical utility, given that they provide general and specific information on the nature and extent of a subject's rated behavioral, social, and emotional problems. Used in combination with parents and teachers, these rating scales have been shown to be powerful predictors of present and future emotional and behavioral disorders of children and adolescents (Verhulst, Koot, & van der Ende, 1994). It has been the opinion of several reviewers (e.g., Christenson, 1990; Elliott & Busse, 1990; Myers & Winters, 2002) that the ASEBA system is a highly useful clinical tool for assessing child psychopathology.

Despite their enormous popularity and unparalleled research base, the CBCL/6–18 and TRF/6–18 are more useful for some types of assessment purposes and problems than others and are not necessarily the best choice for routine assessment situations. Many of the behavioral symptoms on the checklists are quite psychiatric or clinical in nature (e.g., hearing voices, bowel and bladder problems, handling one's own sex parts in public) and certainly have a great deal of relevance in assessing childhood psychopathology. However, many of these more severe low-rate behavioral descriptions on the scales are not seen on a day-to-day basis in most children who have behavioral or emotional concerns, and some teachers and parents tend to find certain ASEBA items irrelevant for the children they are rating, if not offensive. In addition to limited sensitivity of these instruments to identify less serious problems, other weaknesses of the ASEBA cross-informant system for school-age children and youths have been pointed out, including limited (and perhaps misleading) assessment of social competence, possible bias in interpreting data regarding physical symptoms, and difficulties raised by combining data across informants (Drotar, Stein, & Perrin, 1995). Although Achenbach's empirically based assessment and classification system is without question the most widely researched child rating scale currently available for assessing substantial childhood psychopathology and has become a sort of de facto "gold standard" in this regard, and despite the fact that it has much to commend it as a rating scale for social skills and routine behavioral problems in home and school settings, it may not be the best choice. However, for assessing significant psychopathology or severe behavioral and emotional problems of children and adolescents from a cross-informant perspective, the school-age tools of the ASEBA system are without peer.

Behavior Assessment System for Children, Third Edition

The Behavior Assessment System for Children, Third Edition (BASC-3) (C. R. Reynolds & Kamphaus, 2015) is, as the title implies, a comprehensive system for assessing child and adolescent behavior. Over the last 20 years, the BASC system has continued to improve with each edition (see Reynolds & Kamphaus, 1992, 2004, 2015) and has been expanded. The BASC-3 system can be considered a family of assessments and intervention materials designed to assess and support the emotions and behaviors of children and adolescents. It takes a multi-dimensional, multi-method, multi-informant approach to best understanding the behavioral concerns of young people. The current edition includes a large age span (two to 25) and is aligned to *DSM-5* criteria and can also be used to understand disability under IDEA. Included in the BASC-3 are parent and teacher rating scales for preschool-age children (two to five years old), children (six to 11 years old), and adolescents (12 to 21 years old). These behavior rating scales are separately normed and unique across age range and informant versions but still share a common conceptual and practical framework and have many items in common across versions. Also included in the overall BASC-3 are comprehensive self-report forms (SRP) for children (aged six to seven and eight to 11), adolescents (aged 12–21), and college-age young adults (aged 18–25), a structured developmental history form (Structured Developmental History; SDH), and a student observation system (Student Observation System; SOS). There is a parenting questionnaire (Parenting Relationship Questionnaire; PRQ) as well as an intervention (Behavior Intervention Guide) and prevention guide (Behavioral and Emotional Skill-Building Guide). Finally, there is an updated screening system (Behavior & Emotional Screening System; BESS) associated with the BASC-3 and a system developed that enables progress monitoring (FLEX Monitor). These tools are all available by paper and pencil or Q-Global/Digital, a web-based assessment and intervention management system. The preschool versions of the BASC-3 are discussed in Chapter 14, and the self-report forms are discussed in Chapter 8. The screening and progress monitoring system is reviewed in Chapter 9. In this chapter, an overview is provided of the parent (PRS) and teacher (TRS) versions of the child and adolescent rating forms. Table 5.3 includes a breakdown of the TRS and PRS rating forms for children and adolescents by composites and scales and by number of rating items in each form.

Table 5.3 Composites and scales of the child and adolescent forms of the Teacher Rating Scales (TRS) and Parent Rating Scales (PRS) of the Behavior Assessment System for Children, Third Edition

Composites and scales	TRS-C	TRS-A	PRS-C	PRS-A
Composite				
Adaptive Skills	×	×	×	×
Behavioral Symptoms Index	×	×	×	×
Externalizing Problems	×	×	×	×
Internalizing Problems	×	×	×	×
School Problems	×	×	−	−
Primary				
Adaptability	×	×	×	×
Activities of Daily Living	−	−	×	×
Aggression	×	×	×	×
Anxiety	×	×	×	×
Attention Problems	×	×	×	×
Atypicality	×	×	×	×
Conduct Problems	×	×	×	×
Depression	×	×	×	×
Functional Communication	×	×	×	×
Hyperactivity	×	×	×	×
Leadership	×	×	×	×
Learning Problems	×	×	−	−
Social Skills	×	×	×	×
Somatization	×	×	×	×
Study Skills	×	×	−	−
Withdrawal	×	×	×	×
Content				
Anger Control	×	×	×	×
Bullying	×	×	×	×
Developmental Social Disorders	×	×	×	×
Emotional Self-Control	×	×	×	×
Executive Functioning	×	×	×	×
Negative Emotionality	×	×	×	×
Resiliency	×	×	×	×
Clinical Index				
ADHD Probability Index	×	×	×	×
Autism Probability Index	×	×	×	×
EBD Probability Index	×	×	×	×
Functional Impairment Index	×	×	×	×
Executive Functioning Index				
Attentional Control Index	×	×	×	×
Behavioral Control Index	×	×	×	×
Emotional Control Index	×	×	×	×
Overall Executive Functioning Index	×	×	×	×
Problem Solving Index	×	×	×	×
	×	×	×	×

Description The BASC-3 behavior rating scales are comprehensive instruments, designed to assess a variety of problem behaviors, school problems, and adaptive skills. These updated scales include approximately 32% new items, many added to reflect Developmental Social Disorder and Executing Functioning concerns (Psimas, 2015). The parent and teacher rating forms for school-age children and adolescents include the PRS-C (parent rating scale for ages six to 11), PRS-A (parent rating scale for ages 12–21), TRS-C (teacher rating scale for ages six to 11), and TRS-A (teacher rating scale for ages 12–21). These instruments are relatively long in terms of number of items, ranging from 139 to 160 items. Both instruments are available in English- and Spanish-language versions. The items are rated by circling adjacent letters indicating how frequently each behavior is perceived to occur, based on N = Never, S = Sometimes, O = Often, and A = Almost Always. The basic hand-scored form is self-scoring and easy to use. After the rating is completed, the examiner tears off the top perforated edge and separates the forms, which reveals an item-scoring page and a summary page with score profiles. Norm tables in the test manual are consulted for appropriate raw score conversions by rating form and age and gender of the child. A comprehensive web-based administration and scoring program (Q-Global) is also available, which can be used as a hybrid option for paper and pencil administration with digital scoring and reporting. This requires input of individual item responses and basic information about the respondent and child/adolescent, and which provides not only T score and percentile rank conversions of raw scores, but detailed information regarding score profile patterns, clinical significance of scores, and other useful interpretive information. Users can also opt to use a completely digital format in which administration, scoring, and reporting is all completed online.

Scoring System and Scale Structure Raw scores on BASC-3 rating scales are converted to T scores (based on a mean score of 50 and standard deviation of ten). Examiners may use any of several possible norming groups, including general, sex-specific, combined-sex clinical, ADHD, and learning disabilities. T scores for clinical scales are converted to five possible classification levels, ranging from *Very Low* (T scores of ≤ 30) to *Clinically Significant* (T scores of ≥ 70). Other classification levels include *Low*, *Average*, and *At Risk*.

In addition to the clinical and adaptive scales, the BASC-2 rating scales contain several validity indexes, which are designed to detect unusable, excessively negative, or excessively positive responses made by a teacher or parent.

The empirically derived scale structure of the BASC rating scales is relatively complex, consisting of composite and scale scores. Table 5.3 shows the specific composite and scale structure of the TRS and PRS forms, by age level. The composite scales are primarily focused on emotional and behavior problems, but also include adaptive skills and competencies. The clinical scale structures of the TRS and PRS are mostly similar. The primary difference in this regard is found in competency areas that are more specific to the school or home setting. The TRS includes three scales not found on the PRS, including Attention Problems, Learning Problems, and Study Skills, whereas the PRS includes an Activities of Daily Living scale that is not found on the TRS, and covers item content related to the parent's rating of their child's daily activities and routine. The composite scores of the BASC-3 are divided into four main areas of content and scale coverage— Adaptive Skills, the Behavioral Symptoms Index (a sort of a composite problem total score that includes critical emotional and behavioral problem symptom scales), Externalizing Problems, and Internalizing Problems. The School Problems composite is found only on the TRS version of the system. The content scales for both the TRS and PRS include Anger Control, Bullying, Developmental Social Disorders, Emotional Self-Control, Executing Functioning, Negative Emotionality, and Resiliency. New within the

BASC-3 are clinical probability indexes that allow users to understand ADHD Probability, Emotional Behavior Disorder Probability, Autism Probability, Functional Impairment, and General Clinical Probability. Additionally, research by Garcia-Barrera, Karr, and Kamphaus (2013) supported the incorporation of a new executive functioning index in the TRS and PRS. These indexes include the Problem Solving Index, Attentional Control Index, Behavioral Control Index, and Emotional Control Index.

Development and Standardization Extensive development procedures for the BASC-3 rating scales are detailed in the test manual. An initial item pool was developed based on the original BASC and BASC-2 as well as from information obtained through surveys of teachers, parents, and students. The Spanish forms were developed at the same time as the English forms. Experts reviewed the proposed items and gave feedback to researchers, which helped in rewording and dropping unnecessary items. Final item selection was determined empirically through basic factorial analysis and covariance structure analysis to determine appropriate item fit within their intended domain. Readability analyses and bias analyses also were conducted during the item development phase.

The various components of the BASC-3 system include extensive and well-stratified norm samples that are models of painstaking detail. The norming samples for the BASC-3 were gathered from April 2013 to November 2014 from testing sites in 44 states. The numbers of participants used in norming the entire system include more than 9,000, a mind-boggling figure by any standard. The TRS norms are based on a sample of 1,700 at all levels, whereas the PRS norms are based on an across-age sample of 1,800. The samples for the general norms were matched to the 2013 U.S. Census data, and were controlled for sex, race/ethnicity, geographic region, socioeconomic status, and inclusion of special populations. Although the numbers of participants in the clinical norming samples vary somewhat (TRS or PRS), they are high and acceptably stratified by nearly any standard, and are among the very best of any child assessment instrument.

Psychometric Properties The BASC-3 includes a detailed and comprehensive description of evidence of the psychometric properties of the various parts of the system. Given that the BASC-3 is a revision of the original BASC and BASC-2 and that the three versions are mostly similar, much of the accumulated evidence regarding psychometric properties of the first editions should also be considered in evaluating the BASC-3. Researchers have been interested in establishing internal consistency, temporal stability, inter-rater reliability and convergent validity of the BASC-3. Internal consistency reliability (coefficient alpha) estimates for the PRS-C, PRS-A, TRS-C, and TRS-A are impressive, ranging from 0.92 to 0.98 for the composites, and from 0.78 to 0.96 for the scale scores, and 0.83 to 0.96 for clinical indexes (e.g., ADHD Probability Index). Short-term and moderate-term test–retest coefficients were calculated for the TRS and PRS forms. The resulting temporal stability indexes are adequate to good, with values ranging from 0.77 to 0.94 for the composites, 0.76 to 0.93 for scale scores, and 0.82 to 0.93 for the clinical indexes. In general, longer retest intervals produced lower coefficients, which is typical for behavior rating scales and other social–emotional assessment tools.

Several inter-rater reliability studies of the BASC and BASC-2 have been conducted. As should be expected, cross-informant reliability of these rating scales varies considerably, depending on specific rater and setting pairs that were analyzed. As has already been noted, considerable variability of behavior rating scale scores across raters and settings is a known phenomenon and is attributable to both source and setting variance. Inter-rater reliability coefficients reported in the BASC-3 manual range from 0.47 to 0.84 for the TRS, and from 0.58 to 0.87 for the PRS, with some individual scale coefficients showing considerably lower cross-informant stability, and some producing higher coefficients. These values are generally consistent with the expected ranges for cross-informant comparisons reported by Achenbach et al. (1987) in their highly influential review. A review of the first edition of the BASC by Merenda (1996), although generally positive, was critical of the test–retest and inter-rater reliability of the measures within the system. It is my opinion, however, that Merenda's review did not adequately take into account the overall evidence regarding source and setting variance and expected reliability performance with behavior rating scales. Both of these areas of reliability for the BASC, BASC-2, and BASC-3 child and adolescent forms are in the expected range or higher compared with other widely researched behavior rating scales and taking into account the yield of evidence regarding cross-informant and cross-setting reliability of third-party ratings.

Validity evidence from a variety of studies is presented in the BASC-3 manual, which bolsters the evidence that was first presented in the original BASC and BASC-2 manuals and the external published research evidence that has accrued on the BASC since it was first published. The complex factorial structure for the scales was based on strong empirical evidence derived from extensive covariance structure analyses, and the empirically derived scale structure appears to be quite robust. Studies reported in the BASC-3 test manual showing correlations between the TRS and PRS with several other behavior rating scales (including the original BASC scales from the ASEBA system, and scales from the Conners 3) provide evidence of convergent and discriminant construct validity, as do studies regarding inter-correlation of scales and composites of the various TRS and PRS forms. BASC-3 profiles of various clinical groups (e.g., ADHD, learning disabilities, etc.), when compared with the normative mean scores, provide strong evidence of the construct validity of the TRS and PRS through demonstrating sensitivity and discriminating power to theory-based group differences. Again, the validity evidence presented in the BASC-3 manual should be considered as building on the basic foundation of evidence that had accrued for the original BASC and BASC-2 (which included several externally published studies), as the two versions are more similar than different.

Additional Comments As with the ASEBA system, the BASC-3 has also been expanded significantly to include a number of new assessment and intervention options. A screening tool entitled the *Behavioral and Emotional Screening System (BESS)* (Kamphaus & Reynolds, 2007) and a progress monitoring tool called the Flex Monitor (C. R. Reynolds & Kamphaus, 2016) will be described in more detail in Chapter 9. As was mentioned earlier, the BASC-3 system has also incorporated another scale, the Parenting Relationship Questionnaire (C. R. Reynolds & Kamphaus, 2015). This brief measure is intended to provide key insight into the parent or caregivers' perceptions of their relationship with their child, which serves to complement the PRS. The PRQ takes about ten to 15 minutes to complete and is appropriate for children aged two to 18. It includes Attachment, Communication, Discipline Practices, Involvement, Parenting Confidence, Satisfaction With School, and Relational Frustration subscales.

The BASC-3 Intervention Guide & Materials (BASC-3 Intervention) (Vannest, Reynolds, & Kamphaus, 2015) is a book that contains more than 70 interventions that aim to decrease the behavioral challenges derived from the BASC-3 assessment tools.

This book includes theoretical information, practical strategies, fidelity documentation checklists, and even parent/caregiver tip sheets related to the 11 categories of suggested intervention (i.e., academic problems, adaptability, aggression, anxiety, attention problems, conduct problems, depression, functional communication, hyperactivity, leadership/social skills, and somatization). Additionally, there is a prevention-oriented guide, the BASC-3 Behavioral and Emotional Skill-Building Guide, that includes skill-building lessons and activities for groups or classrooms of students. These intervention and prevention-oriented packages reflect genuine movement toward connecting behavioral assessment data to relevant and functional clinical strategies.

Although some other components of the BASC-3 system are not as strong as the TRS-C, TRS-A, PRS-C, PRS-A, and the BESS rating scales, overall, the system is impressive, and there is little room for significant criticism. These instruments were developed with the latest and most state-of-the-art standards and technology, have an impressive empirical research base, and are practical, if not easy to use. They represent the best of the newer generation of behavior rating scales. The original BASC was positively reviewed in the professional literature (e.g., R. Flanagan, 1995; Sandoval & Echandia, 1994), and the BASC-2 has been widely used. One of the few drawbacks of the BASC-2 rating scales was their extensive length (as many as 160 items), which may make these instruments difficult to use for routine screening work and a poor choice for frequent progress monitoring, which requires a much briefer measure. Routine screening and progress monitoring may require the use of shorter measures. The BASC-3 assessments have added even more items; however, developers clearly have attempted to address these limitations with the creation of screening, progress monitoring, and even intervention tools. For a thorough and comprehensive system of behavior rating scales, the BASC-3 is representative of the best of what is currently available. From the mid-1990s to the publication of the BASC-2 in 2004 and now the publication of the BASC-3, the original BASC had become extremely popular for use in schools, through a combination of design quality, user-friendly features, and aggressive marketing by the publisher. There is no doubt that the BASC-3 will continue and perhaps increase the widespread popularity of the system.

The Conners Rating Scales, Conners Rating Scales–Revised, the Conners 3, and the Conners Comprehensive Behavior Rating Scales

The Conners Rating Scales (Conners, 1990, 1997, 2008a) are referred to as a system because they form a set of several behavior rating scales for use by parents and teachers that share many common items and are conceptually similar. The original scales vary in length from 28 to 93 items. Several versions of these scales have been in use since the 1960s (Conners, 1969), and were originally developed by the author, Keith Conners, as a means of providing standardized objective behavioral assessment data for children with hyperactivity, attention problems, and related behavioral concerns. Research on the Conners scales has been widely reported in the literature over the years—several hundred studies involving these scales have been published. The scales also have found wide acceptance among clinicians. Although a broad range of behavioral, social, and emotional problem descriptions is included in the scales, they have been touted primarily as a measure for assessing attentional problems and hyperactivity, and historically they have been among the most widely used scales for that purpose. It was not until 1990 that the scales became widely commercially available and that a manual was published that integrated the description, use, and scoring of the four scales into one source.

In 1997, a revised, expanded, and completely restandardized version of Conners Rating Scales was published. This revision was considered to be a comprehensive behavior assessment system because it contained numerous parent and teacher rating scales and an adolescent self-report scale. The revised Conners scales were designed ultimately to replace the original Conners scales. The publisher, Multi-Health Systems, is no longer publishing and selling the 1997 versions of the scales, but is promoting the most recent version, The Conners 3 (2008a) and The Conners Comprehensive Behavior Rating Scales (2008b). This review focuses extensively on The Conners 3, the most widely used version, and concludes with a description of the Conners Comprehensive Behavior Rating Scales. However, I also believe that a review of the previous version is important for giving readers context for the changes that occurred in 2008.

The Conners Rating Scales–Revised (1997)   The Conners Rating Scales–Revised (CRS-R) (Conners, 1997) was a comprehensive revision and expansion of the original Conners scales. The CRS-R was designed as a comprehensive assessment system because it contains six main scales and five brief auxiliary scales, including adolescent self-report scales. In terms of general problem behavior rating scales, this discussion focuses on long and short forms of the Conners Parent Rating Scale–Revised (CPRS-R:L, 80 items, and CPRS-R:S, 27 items) and long and short forms of the Conners Teacher Rating Scale–Revised (CTRS-R:L, 59 items, and CTRS-R:S, 28 items). These instruments all are designed for assessment of children and adolescents aged three to 17.

The revised Conners scales were similar in many respects to their predecessors (the CTRS-39, CTRS-28, CPRS-48, and CPRS-93). Even though there is much similarity in item overlap between the original and revised rating scales, some items were added or deleted to make the revised scales specifically compatible with the *DSM-IV* diagnostic criteria for ADHD. The rationally derived subscale structure of the revised Conners scales also differed somewhat from that of the predecessor instruments. Specifically, in addition to the general subscales, the long-form scales contained the ten-item Conners Global Index (formerly referred to as the Hyperactivity Index), a 12-item ADHD index, and an 18-item *DSM-IV* Symptom Scale for ADHD. The Global Index was more recently specifically touted as a brief measure of psychopathology that would be useful for screening or progress monitoring. These ten items are embedded into the long-form rating scales and were available on a separate short scale for screening use. The ADHD index included critical items that were considered to be important in determining the existence of ADHD. The *DSM-IV* Symptoms Subscales, however, were used specifically in determining whether ADHD characteristics fall into the Inattentive or Hyperactive–Impulsive subtypes from *DSM-IV*. The ADHD and *DSM-IV* scales on the longer versions of the Conners scales were packaged separately as a specific ADHD assessment instrument, which is reviewed in Chapter 10. The long and short scales of the revised Conners system included the same 4-point rating format and the same *T* score/percentile rank score conversion format that were used with the original versions. Separate scoring norms were provided for boys and girls in three-year age span increments for the three to 17-year age range. Scoring of these instruments was accomplished by using the Quick Score hand-scoring forms provided or, with an additional cost, using computer-assisted administration scoring software or the publisher's online administration and scoring system. The CRS-R scales were available in English, Spanish, and French Canadian languages.

The standardization sample for the CRS-R system was very large, with more than 8,000 normative cases in aggregate and about 2,000 to 4,000 for the specific rating scales reviewed in this section. The normative sample was well stratified, including extensive samples from the United States and Canada. Extensive data were provided in the technical manual regarding gender and racial and ethnic breakdowns of the various samples and the effects of gender and ethnicity on CRS-R scores. Internal consistency reliability for all CRS-R scales was adequate to excellent. For example, the internal consistency coefficients for the CPRS-R:L subscales ranged from 0.73 to 0.94. The scales with lower reliability coefficients tended to be the scales with fewer items. Test–retest reliability at six- to eight-week intervals for the CPRS-R:L and CTRS-R:L had been shown to range from 0.47 to 0.88 for the various subscales. Extensive factorial validity evidence (including confirmatory factor analyses) for the CRS-R scales was presented in the technical manual. Additional validity evidence for the CRS-R scales was presented in the form of extensive convergent and divergent validity coefficients among various scales within the system and correlations with scores from the Children's Depression Inventory. Given that the CRS-R was based heavily on the already extensively researched original Conners rating scales, it is assumed that the developers did not consider it as essential to gather as extensive validity evidence as would be needed with a totally new system of instrumentation. Although it probably can be assumed that much of the existing validity evidence for the original Conners scales may have translated reasonably well to the revised scales, there is always a need to conduct a full range of reliability and validity studies.

In sum, the rating scales within the revised Conners system, which was available for over a decade, showed considerable utility. Reviews of these scales have been generally positive (e.g., Collett, Ohan, & Myers, 2003; Hess, 2001; Knoff, 2001; S. M. Snyder, Drozd, & Xenakis, 2004), despite some concerns noted regarding insufficient details in some aspects of the test manual and a paucity of externally published validity evidence. The extensive norming sample was impressive, as was the integration of *DSM-IV* criteria for ADHD into subscales on the long forms. These instruments were particularly useful in assessing children who have attention problems and hyperactivity, but they had broader applications as well. As Conners (1997) stated:

> The main use of the Conners Rating Scales–Revised will be for the assessment of ADHD. However, the CRS-R can have a much broader scope, as they also contain subscales for the assessment of family problems, emotional problems, anger control problems, and anxiety problems.

(p. 5)

Description of The Conners 3 Similar to the CRS-R, The Conners third edition is a comprehensive, multi-informant system that can aid in the assessment of ADHD and other externalizing problems such as Oppositional Defiant Disorder (ODD) and Conduct Disorder (CD) (Conners, 2008a). The Conners 3 represents a major revision of the CRS-R and includes many added features. This system was specifically aligned to diagnostic criteria included in the *DSM-IV-TR* and can also be linked to eligibility categories included in IDEA 2004. While this tool was originally aligned with the *DSM-IV-TR*, the developer also carefully reviewed the items while considering changes reflected in the *DSM-5* and updated the scoring and *DSM* symptom scales to reflect alignment with the *DSM-5* (Conners, 2014). The Conners 3 includes items that help to identify the extent to which behaviors impair one's functioning at home and in peer relationships. There are items that screen for depression and anxiety, as well as critical items that reflect severe behaviors in need of immediate attention. This system also includes validity scales that help to identify if the rater is answering in an overly positive, negative or inconsistent way.

The Conners 3 includes parent, teacher, and self-report forms that can be used for children aged six to 18. There are full-length forms including 99–110 items, a subset of items that constitute short forms including 41–45 items, and two ten-item index forms. The Conners 3 AI (ADHD Index) is a brief tool that can be used to screen for ADHD and the The Conners 3GI (Global Index) can be used to progress monitor treatment. These indices are embedded as subscales within the full-length forms as well.

Scoring System and Scale Structure in the Conners 3 Raw scores are converted to subscale scores using a *T* score distribution (i.e., mean scores of 50 and standard deviations of 10) for all scales in the Conners system. Total scores are typically not obtained and used with the Conners scales and are not part of the published scoring systems, although some investigators and clinicians have used a total score in their work. The basic factor structure and content scales of the Conners 3 have been adjusted and include A. Inattention, B. Hyperactivity/Impulsivity, C. Learning Problems, D. Executive Functioning, E. Defiance/Aggression, and F. Peer/Family Relations. *DSM-IV-TR* Symptom Scale scores are also derived to help identify symptoms of ADHD, ODD, and CD.

The rating scales in the Conners system are scored easily and converted to standardized subscale scores based on gender and age-level breakdowns, using an innovative two-sided "Quikscore" format that requires minimal time and reduces the chance of committing scoring errors. Online and software-based administration and scoring programs for the Conners scales are also available from the publisher. The computer programs provide not only administration and scoring possibilities, but also the generation of brief interpretive summary paragraphs related to individual score configurations and levels.

Development and Standardization of the Conners 3 The development of the first version of the Conners Rating Scales was started during the 1960s by clinicians at Johns Hopkins Hospital in Baltimore, Maryland. These clinicians, who were implementing and researching psychopharmacological and psychotherapeutic interventions in children, developed a set of rating scale items that were used informally and qualitatively to obtain further information from teachers. In discussing how the scales progressed from this earlier informal prototype to the standardized versions, Conners (1990) stated:

> When I compared data from normal children and clinical cases, it was clear that they differed on several different dimensions, not just in the number of total symptoms. Factor analysis confirmed that existence of stable clusters of items, . . . having much more clinical interest than a simple catalogue of problems.
>
> (p. vi)

Research on this first standard version of the scales was published by Conners in 1969, and this version was essentially the same as the CTRS-39. The Conners 3, in conjunction with the Conners Comprehensive Behavior Rating Scale and the Conners Early Childhood (EC) (Conners, 2009), however, represents an extensive update that occurred over the course of four years. The overarching goals of this update were: (1) to refine the CRS-R so that it is more ADHD-specific; (2) to create a separate tool that comprehensively addresses the social–emotional and behavioral issues experienced by children (CBRS); (3) to create a tool specific to early childhood; (4) to align items with current classification and diagnostic schemes; (5) to provide links between assessment and intervention; and (6) to update norms and technical properties.

The development of the Conners 3 occurred in three phases. After initial item development, pilot studies and normative studies were conducted and included a representative sample of over 7,000 children. Exploratory and confirmatory factor analyses were conducted and determined necessary items for inclusion/exclusion and the factor structure outlined above.

The Conners 3 Global Index (3CGI) consists of the same ten items that have been validated over the years; these items are included in the Conners 3 full-length forms, and provide measures of restlessness/impulsiveness and emotional lability. These items can be used as a stand-alone tool and Conners suggests they be used to monitor treatment effectiveness. The Conners 3 ADHD Index (3AI) was newly revised and also consists of ten items and has been found to distinguish samples with ADHD from samples without ADHD.

Based on responses given by the normative sample, Positive Impression, Negative Impression, and Inconsistency Indices were created. For the Positive (PI) and Negative Impression (NI) Validity scales, each of the items was analyzed and if less than 10% of the sample answered an item with a particular response choice, the item was given a score of 1 rather than a 0. Completed forms resulting in raw scores of 5–6 (4–6 for PI self-reports) should be analyzed with caution, as bias is likely a factor. The Inconsistency Index was developed slightly differently and involved analyzing items with the highest intercorrelations.

Anxiety and Depression screener items were chosen from the newly developed Conners Behavior Rating Scale. Based on information gathered from item-total correlations, representative items were chosen to screen children for symptoms of depression and anxiety. Critical items were identified through analysis of the normative data. These items suggested severe, concerning behaviors that would highlight a need for immediate attention/intervention. Finally, short forms were developed that are highly correlated with the full-length Conners 3 forms. These short forms include the PI and VI Validity scales, but they do not include the *DSM-IV-TR* Symptoms Scales, The Anxiety and Depression Screener items, the critical behavior items, the 3GI, the 3AI, or the Inconsistency Index.

Psychometric Properties Cronbach's alpha coefficients were used to assess the internal consistency of the parent, teacher, and self-report content scales and *DSM-IV-TR* symptom scales. Mean alphas across informants and scales ranged from 0.85 to 0.94. Mean alphas across informants for the validity scales were lower and ranged from 0.56 to 0.72. Mean test–retest coefficients were derived after a two to four week interval from the three types of informants and the content and *DSM-IV-TR* scales ranged from 0.76 to 0.89. Overall, the reliability information suggests that the internal consistency of items is high and the reliability of responses over time is relatively stable.

Evidence for several forms of validity for the various Conners scales has accumulated in many published research reports over the years. Several studies have documented the efficacy of the Conners scales in differentiating between distinct diagnostic groups— hyperactive and normal children (King & Young, 1982), learning disabled and regular education students (Merrell, 1990), boys referred to juvenile court and a normal control group (L. Berg, Butler, Hullin, Smith, & Tyler, 1978), and behavior disordered and non-special education students (Margalit, 1983). CTRS-39 ratings of children at age seven have been shown to be highly predictive of diagnoses of hyperactivity three years later, at age ten (Gillberg & Gillberg, 1983). Finally, the convergent construct validity of various versions of the Conners scales has been demonstrated through several studies that found significant correlations between them and other instruments, such as the Child Behavior Checklist (Edelbrock, Greenbaum, & Conover, 1985), the Behavior and Temperament Survey (Sandoval, 1981), the Behavior Problem Checklist (Campbell & Steinert, 1978), the School Behavior Survey, and the School Social Behavior Scales (Merrell, 1993a). Most of the validity studies cited have involved the use of the CTRS-39, and less is known about the properties of the CPRS-48. An annotated bibliography of more than 450 studies using the Conners rating scales was assembled by the publisher over a decade ago (Wainwright & MHS Staff, 1996), providing extensive documentation evidence for the many reliability and validity studies that have been conducted prior to the publication of the most recent version of the scales.

Similar to the earlier versions of the Conners system, the Conners 3 has begun to accumulate a range of validity evidence. In addition to the factorial validity that helped to determine the factor structure of the items, convergent validity has been established based on moderate to strong correlations between the Conners 3 and the CRS-R, BASC-2, the ASEBA, and the Behavior Rating Inventory of Executive Function (BRIEF). The Conners 3 has been found to discriminate between clinical and typically developing populations as well.

The Conners Comprehensive Behavior Rating Scale (CBRS) The Conners CBRS (Conners, 2008b) is a rating scale that aims to assess a wide range of childhood problems. This system also includes a parent form, a teacher form, and a self-report form for children aged six to 18 years. There are between 179–204 items across the forms. Scores are generated according to either *DSM-IV-TR* or *DSM-5* Symptom Scales, Empirical Scales, Rational Scales, and Validity Scales. *DSM* symptoms addressed are those pertaining to ADHD, CD, ODD, Major Depressive Disorder, Manic Episode, Generalized Anxiety Disorder, Separation Anxiety Disorder, Social Phobia, Obsessive-Compulsive Disorder, Autistic Disorder, and Asperger's Disorder. Items associated with the Empirical Scales are associated with Emotional Distress, Aggressive Behaviors, Academic Difficulties, Hyperactivity, Hyperactivity/Impulsivity, Separation Fears, Social Problems, Perfectionistic and Compulsive Behaviors. The Validity Scales are similar to those seen in the Conners 3 and pertain to Positive Impression, Negative Impression, and Inconsistency Indices. The Rational Scales are unique to the CBRS and help to identify students who might have the potential to commit violent acts or who suffer from physical symptoms. There are also critical items that help to identify concerning behaviors pertaining to bullying, enuresis, encopresis, panic, phobia, trichotillomania, trauma, etc. Finally, a Clinical Index is included and consists of 25 items that can be used to monitor treatment programming. As with the Conners 3, this measure was normed on a large sample. Reliability coefficients were moderate to strong and adequate convergent and divergent validity was established.

Additional Comments The CTRS-39, CPRS-48, Conners 3, and Conners CBRS have been and continue to be widely used in clinical practice and have been tested in various ways in many published studies. There is no question that the CTRS-39 is the particular version of the Conners scales for which there is the most externally published empirical evidence. Less has been demonstrated about the other Conners scales. There is a good deal of overlap between the different scales that comprise the Conners system, however, which should lend at least a substantial degree of "face validity" to the versions of the scales that have not been researched as extensively.

The 1990 publication of an integrated manual and standard scoring systems for the Conners scales filled a large void in the understanding and use of these instruments and resulted in their increased clinical use and paved the way for the 1997 and 2008 revisions. Because the short forms of the Conners 3, the CTRS-39 and CPRS-48 are relatively brief instruments (half as many or fewer items than the other scales reviewed in this chapter), they are an excellent choice for conducting initial screenings, but it is important that they be supplemented with other evaluation methods in conducting comprehensive clinical assessments. The Conners 3 and Conners CBRS represent an important step for the Conners scales. They contain information that is relevant to this particular time in the world of social and emotional assessment (e.g., alignment with IDEA 2004, subscales pertaining to bullying) and they include carefully constructed scales that can serve as an incredibly useful component of a comprehensive evaluation process. The large sample used to update norms and the structure of the assessment forms was a critical step forward for this behavior rating system.

BEST PRACTICES IN USING BEHAVIOR RATING SCALES

This chapter has included an overview of the uses, advantages, and cautions of behavior rating scales and reviews of several of the most widely used, commercially published general-purpose problem behavior rating scales. To use behavior rating scales effectively requires more than just a cursory understanding of their characteristics. Thus, three "best practices" are suggested for using rating scales in a useful manner.

The first suggestion is to *use rating scales routinely for early screening*. Effective screening practices involve being able to systematically and accurately identify children who are in the early stages of developing behavioral, social, or emotional problems. The identified subjects are evaluated more carefully to determine whether their problems warrant special program eligibility and intervention services. The purpose of screening for social–emotional problems is usually for secondary prevention, which is preventing the existing problem from becoming worse (Kauffman, 2000). Screening for early intervention is one of the best uses of behavior rating scales, given that they cover a wide variety of important behaviors and take little time to administer and score. For general screening purposes, it is recommended that children or adolescents whose rating scale scores are 1 or more standard deviations above instrument normative means in terms of problem behavior excesses be identified for consideration of further evaluation. This practice narrows the screening pool down to approximately 16% of the overall population, and this selected group can be evaluated more comprehensively.

The second suggestion is to *use the "aggregation principle."* This principle involves obtaining ratings from a variety of sources, each of which might present a slightly different picture. When using rating scales for purposes other than routine screening, obtaining aggregated rating scale data is recommended to reduce bias of response and variance problems in the assessment. In practice, using aggregated measures means obtaining rating evaluations from different raters in different settings and using more than one type of rating scale to accomplish this (Merrell, 2000a, 2000b).

A final suggestion is to *use behavior rating scales to assess progress during and after interventions*. It has been demonstrated that continuous assessment and monitoring of student progress after the initial assessment and intervention is important in successful implementation of behavioral interventions (Kerr & Nelson, 1989). Progress toward behavioral intervention goals can be assessed easily on a weekly or biweekly schedule using appropriate rating scales. Full-length behavior rating scales may be too long and time-consuming for teachers or parents to complete on a repetitive basis. For this reason, clinicians and researchers might consider identifying selected items from the rating scales, for which the initial ratings were high, and which are congruent with the intervention goals, and creating a very brief rating tool (ten to 15 items) based on these items, solely for the purpose of gauging perceptions of change and progress. In addition to identifying specific items that are aligned with individualized intervention goals, researchers have also become committed to developing technically adequate short forms of existing rating scales that can serve as general outcome measures of behavior change (Gresham et al., 2010; Volpe & Gadow, 2010). Although behavior rating scales may not be the best measurement choice for daily assessment data (unless they are shortened considerably), there are many other simple ways of assessing progress daily, such as using Direct Behavior Ratings (Chafouleas et al., 2009), performance records or brief observational data. Additional assessment after the intervention also can be a useful process. The main reason for follow-up assessment is to determine how well the intervention effects have been maintained over time (e.g., after three months) and how well the behavioral changes have generalized to other settings (e.g., the home setting and other classrooms). In practice, a follow-up assessment might involve having teachers and parents complete behavior rating scales on a child after a specified time has elapsed following the student's participation in a social skills training program. The data obtained from this follow-up assessment may be used to determine whether follow-up interventions seem appropriate and may be useful in developing future intervention programs if it is determined that social–behavioral gains are not being maintained over time or generalized across specific settings.

BEHAVIOR RATING SCALES AND DECISION MAKING

One of the major advances in the development and use of behavior rating scales over the past two to three decades is considered to be the effective use of such scales in decision making regarding children and adolescents (Elliott et al., 1993; Merrell, 2000a, 2000b). There are several potential ways that behavior rating scales may be used in decision making. Perhaps their most natural use involves decisions regarding screening and additional assessment. Behavior rating scales are an excellent choice for use in either individual or large-group screenings because they tend to be quick and easy to administer, and if the screening criteria are set low enough, they result in few false-negative errors (failure to identify children and adolescents who do meet behavioral criteria). For making decisions regarding additional assessment that may need to occur, behavior rating scales are capable of identifying specific dimensions or behavioral clusters that may need to be investigated in more detail. The multiple-gating systems described in Chapter 2 use rating scales as one of the important first steps in narrowing down a large population to a smaller population of potentially at-risk individuals before additional assessment methods are used. In actual screening practice, behavior rating scales completed by parents or teachers would be either the first or the second gate in the assessment process and would be followed by more time-intensive measures, such as direct behavioral observation and interviewing.

Although behavior rating scales should never be used alone for making classification or placement decisions, they are capable of providing some valuable information in this regard. Given the development of the behavioral dimensions approach to classification, and the application of sophisticated multivariate statistical techniques to rating scales, rating scales may be used to isolate specific dimensions of problem behaviors that would be useful in making classification decisions, particularly if used across raters and settings. Several state education agencies have recommended or required that local education agency personnel use behavior rating scales in systematic or prescribed ways in the identification of students for special education services under certain classification categories.

Behavior rating scales are increasingly being considered useful for making intervention planning decisions (Elliott et al., 1993; Merrell, 2000a). Primarily because they are quite effective at identifying specific areas of behavioral deficits or excesses a child or adolescent may exhibit, behavior rating scales may be used effectively in a general way for intervention planning. In terms of methods for effectively linking assessment results to intervention planning, data obtained through the use of behavior rating scales seem to line up most effectively with two specific intervention linkage strategies described by Shapiro (1996). The first of these strategies is referred to as the *Keystone Behavior Strategy,* which was described originally by Nelson and Hayes (1986). This strategy involves identification of a group or cluster of responses that appear to be linked to a particular disorder, then selecting interventions that are known to be functionally linked to impacting that particular problem or disorder. For example, if Child Behavior Checklist scores on a referred adolescent consistently showed him or her to have behavioral excesses in a cluster of items related to aggressive behavior and antisocial conduct problems, it would be logical to select one of the several contingency management interventions that have been found to be effective in altering this group of behaviors with antisocial–aggressive adolescents. Another potentially useful strategy in this regard that was discussed by Shapiro (1996) is referred to as the *Template-Matching Strategy,* originally described by Cone and Hoier (1986) and Hoier and Cone (1987). This strategy involves comparing objective behavioral data (i.e., rating scale data) on referred children with similar data obtained on children who have high functioning levels of the desired social–behavioral competencies. The areas of largest discrepancy between the two sets of data would become the prime targets for intervention. For example, suppose that BASC-3 ratings on a referred child were compared with those obtained from behaviorally high-functioning children, and the largest discrepancy area included items related to attention problems and off-task behavior. Appropriate behavioral strategies for increasing on-task and attentive behavior would be the obvious intervention choices.

In addition to these particular decision-making uses for behavior rating scales, it is important to consider their use in monitoring and modifying interventions that have been put in place. Behavior rating scales are an excellent choice for summative evaluation of intervention efficacy; if modified appropriately (i.e., using shortened versions), they may also be useful for monitoring intervention progress on a weekly (and perhaps daily) basis.

CONCLUSIONS

Behavior rating scales have become an increasingly prominent assessment method for measuring child and adolescent behavior. Particularly since the late 1970s and early 1980s, technical advances with behavior rating scales have enhanced their popularity and prominence considerably. Rating scales provide a structured format for making summary evaluative judgments regarding perceptions of child or adolescent behavior. Behavior rating scales do not measure behavior per se, but measure perceptions of behavior. The evidence regarding the validity of behavior rating scales in predicting behavior is extensive and impressive, however. The earlier generation of rating scales tended to use simple additive checklist formats. Beginning in the 1980s, use of an algebraic style rating scale became the standard, allowing for more precision in measurement of degree and intensity of behavior.

Child behavior rating scales offer many advantages for researchers and practitioners. Among these advantages are the low cost; efficiency; increased reliability and validity in comparison with other methods of assessment; opportunity for assessment input from parents, teachers, and other important social informants; and possibility of obtaining assessment data on individuals who are not in a position to be observed directly or to provide high-quality self-report information. Rating scales are not without their disadvantages, however. Foremost among the limitations and disadvantages of rating scales are various types of error variance (source, setting, and instrument variance) and response bias from raters, such as halo effects, leniency or severity effects, or central tendency effects. Many of these limitations and problems associated with behavior rating scales can be dealt with effectively by using rating scales as one part of a comprehensive assessment design and by obtaining aggregated ratings across sources, instruments, and settings. Careful attention to the technical aspects of measurement in designing rating scales can also reduce potential problems.

Several widely used, commercially published general-purpose problem behavior rating scales were reviewed and discussed. These instruments—including the Child Behavior Checklist/6–18 and Teacher's Report Form/6–18 from the Achenbach System of Empirically Based Assessment (ASEBA); the Behavior Assessment System for Children, Third Edition; and Conners Rating Scales—represent some of the best of what is currently available. Many other technically sound and clinically useful behavior rating scales that are not as widely known as these measures have been developed for various purposes. The CBCL/6–18 and TRF/6–18 of the ASEBA system are by far the most extensively researched of any child behavior rating scales. The validity of these measures has been well documented and they are useful for many purposes. They have been criticized, however, for not being as useful for routine behavioral concerns as they are for severe psychopathology. The Behavior Assessment System for Children, which recently was published in a third edition, is representative of a new generation of behavior rating scales linked to a comprehensive assessment system. The BASC-3 rating scales offer numerous advantages, and have become extremely popular among school-based clinicians. They are technically sound and potentially useful for varied research and clinical purposes. The various forms and versions of the Conners Rating Scales have been extensively researched and used clinically for nearly three decades. Although the reputation of these instruments was built largely through research and clinical applications with children who have ADHD characteristics, they are considered to have broader applications for assessing emotional and behavioral problems. The 1997 and 2008 revisions to the Conners scales have included several positive changes while building on the solid empirical tradition of the previous versions.

Three best practices in using behavior rating scales were recommended. First, behavior rating scales should be used extensively for screening and early identification purposes. Second, the aggregation principle of gathering rating scale data from multiple informants across multiple settings is encouraged to provide a comprehensive portrait of perceptions of child behavior. Third, the use of rating scales to monitor progress during and after interventions is encouraged to provide empirical evidence of the efficacy (or lack thereof) of planned interventions and to help guide formative changes in such interventions.

Behavior rating scales are potentially useful in clinical and education decision making, in several respects. Examples of the types of decisions that may be aided through the use of behavior rating scales include screening and assessment, classification and placement, and intervention decisions. Regarding intervention decisions, there appears to be an increasing acceptance of the usefulness of behavior rating scales for this purpose. Use of specific intervention linkage strategies, such as the Keystone Behavior Strategy and the Template Matching Strategy, may be helpful in making effective links between behavior rating scale data and subsequent intervention decisions.

REVIEW AND APPLICATION QUESTIONS

1. Describe the major differences between behavior rating scales and behavior checklists. What is considered to be the major advantage of using rating scales instead of checklists?
2. For each of the four types of error variance described in this chapter, describe at least one practical way to implement the assessment to minimize or overcome potential error.
3. Assume that the same behavior rating scale has been completed on the same child by three different teachers, but the obtained scores from the three sources are considerably different. What are some potentially effective ways of interpreting this pattern of data?
4. The Child Behavior Checklist and Teacher's Report Form comprise the most widely and well-researched combination of child behavior rating scales. They are probably not a good choice for some purposes, however. In what situations, or with what problems, would it be more advantageous to use a different rating scale?
5. Behavior rating scales may not be as effective for assessing internalizing problems (e.g., anxiety, depression, and somatic problems) as for externalizing problems (e.g., aggressive behavior, hyperactivity, and conduct problems). What are some reasons for this difference in rating scale utility across symptom domains?
6. Why is test–retest and inter-rater reliability of internalizing problem subscales of behavior rating scales typically lower than for externalizing problem subscales?
7. What are some ways that item-level data on behavior rating scales could be used to establish and monitor Individualized Education Program (IEP) goals? Provide some specific examples.
8. For screening purposes, a cutoff point on behavior rating scales of 1 standard deviation or higher is recommended. If two separate rating scales are used for screening, and they

produce differing results (one meets screening criteria, one does not), how can a screening decision be made, and what are the risks and advantages of making yes/no decisions?

9. What is the Template-Matching Strategy, and how might it best be implemented using data obtained through behavior rating scales?

10. Consider and describe 2 assessment questions that may be answered by the BASC-3.

11. Consider the following assessment questions and associated settings and choose the behavior rating scale/s that could provide the best data and discuss the rationale for your choice:

- A 10-year-old African American male has been referred by his teacher to the school psychologist because of concerns with daydreaming, poor work completion, nail-biting, and clearing his throat with high frequency that it is distracting to other students. There is no history of prior evaluations.

- A 7-year-old Spanish-speaking-only female is attending an intake session with her mother at a community healthcare clinic. The girl was referred by her pediatrician because of frequent daytime urinary accidents, outbursts, and noncompliant behavior. Following the intake, the psychologist recommends an assessment and a few follow-up therapy sessions.

- A 16-year-old Caucasian male has been referred by his parents to a psychologist in private practice, following years of "underachievement" and diminished interest in schoolwork. They are concerned that their son will not be admitted to college, although he has always "flown under the radar" and his teachers have not voiced any concerns this school year.

- Researchers from a major university are interested in studying the frequency and intensity of acts of bullying on middle-school campuses and their effects on identified victims over time.

6

INTERVIEWING TECHNIQUES

Whether one is meeting informally with the teacher of a referred student, conducting a problem identification interview with a parent, or undertaking a diagnostic interview with a child or adolescent, interviewing is a widely used and valuable assessment method. The popularity of interviewing is due to the many advantages it offers to clinicians. Some surveys have indicated that interviewing is the most commonly used assessment method among clinical psychologists (Watkins, Campbell, Nieberding, & Hallmark, 1995), and it is certainly one of the most popular assessment methods in other areas of professional psychology as well. This chapter provides a broad overview of interviewing children and adolescents, including problem identification and developmental history interviewing with the parents of children and adolescents. The chapter also makes specific recommendations for procedures and techniques that may be useful in conducting effective interviews.

The type of interviewing emphasized in this chapter has been termed *clinical interviewing*, or the *child clinical interview*. These terms encompass a broad range of interview techniques. For additional clarification of this terminology and the types of techniques encompassed by it, readers are referred to McConaughy and Whitcomb's (2022) treatment of this topic. To help understand the essential features of this sort of interviewing, it is important to recognize that the term *clinical* in this case refers to a purpose rather than a place. Clinical interviewing is conducted in a variety of settings: schools, hospitals, homes, detention centers, and clinics. The purpose reflected in the word *clinical* is to gather specific information regarding behavioral, social, and emotional functioning, particularly regarding deficits or problems in functioning that may be occurring in any of these areas. McConaughy (2000a) noted that "clinical assessment interviews usually cover specific content areas . . . and are limited to one or two sessions" (p. 170). In contrast to other methods of assessment that may be used for these same purposes, clinical interviewing is unique in its emphasis on direct face-to-face contact and interpersonal communication between the clinician and the client. As such, it places some unique demands on the clinician. As Sattler stated in his text on interviewing children and their families:

> Clinical assessment interviewing is a critical part of the assessment process. And even more than other assessment techniques, it places a premium on your personal skills, such as your ability to communicate effectively and your ability to establish a meaningful relationship.
>
> (1998, p. 3)

DOI: 10.4324/9781315747521-7

This chapter begins with a discussion of the role of the interview as an assessment method, including sections on developmental issues in interviewing, factors or contexts that affect overall interview quality, and how to select specific interview methods for specific purposes. Much of this chapter is devoted to discussions of three types of interviews: the traditional or unstructured interview, behavioral interviewing, and structured or semistructured diagnostic interviews. Because the clinical interview is the most useful assessment technique for working with children and adolescents who are suicidal, a specific section is devoted to this topic. Before the summary and review questions, the chapter concludes with a brief discussion of how interviews can be used in decision-making processes.

THE ROLE OF INTERVIEWS IN ASSESSING CHILDREN AND ADOLESCENTS

There is no question that as an assessment method, clinical interviewing holds a place of prominence in psychology, psychiatry, social work, and counseling. This venerated attitude toward the interview process has been perpetuated in popular media and has strongly shaped the beliefs of the public. Public beliefs and attitudes regarding clinical interviewing are often shaped (with help from popular media) to the point of distorting and nearly mystifying what is actually done and accomplished in the interview process. Many psychologists and psychiatrists have experienced this unwarranted public elevation of the interview process and the supposed diagnostic powers possessed by clinicians, sometimes to the point of absurdity. Even when conducting such mundane business as standing in line at the supermarket, getting a haircut, or having a major appliance serviced, when clinicians are queried by strangers as to what their occupation is, the answer frequently draws responses such as "Are you analyzing me now?" or "Oh no, you'll figure out what all my problems are by talking to me!" An honest reply to such questions is usually disappointing to the professional and those inquiring about their skills. Both would like to believe that the clinician's prowess in interpersonal communications allows him or her more insight (if not prescience) than is usually the case.

If the process of clinical interviewing is not a mystical conduit to the inner life of the person being interviewed, then what is it? Essentially, interviewing is structured communication, mainly verbal, but nonverbal as well. Martin (1988) noted that an interview resembles a conversation but differs from day-to-day conversation in that it: (1) is purposeful; (2) is usually "controlled" by the interviewer through the initiating of interchanges and the posing of questions; and (3) has unity, progression, and thematic continuity. In other words, clinical interviews should have direction and structure and are driven by specific goals related to obtaining relevant information and using it to make decisions. Putting a practical spin on the definition of interviewing, La Greca (1990, p. 4) notes that, "Interviews are critical for obtaining information, appreciating children's unique perspectives, and establishing rapport."

Interviews come in several forms, ranging from unstructured "stream of consciousness" exchanges to formalized and highly structured interview schedules used for exploring specific problem areas. Although the purposes, underlying theories, and level of structure among different types of interviews may vary, all forms of clinical interviewing share some commonalities and have specific advantages compared with other assessment methods. Perhaps the most salient advantage of interviewing as an assessment method is the *flexibility* it provides. Throughout the course of an interview, the clinician has the opportunity to shorten or lengthen it, to change direction when needed, and to focus on specific aspects of the client's thought, behavior, or emotion that emerge as being most important at the time. With other methods of assessment, this type of flexibility is rarely, if ever, possible. Another advantage of clinical interviewing is that it provides the clinician with the *opportunity to observe the client directly under structured conditions.* Client characteristics such as social skills, verbal ability, insight, defensiveness, and willingness to cooperate can all be assessed to a degree throughout the course of an interview. When interviewing children, the observational advantage of the interview process is particularly important because their limited experiences and typically unsophisticated verbal medi- ation skills make it difficult for them to express directly their concerns, needs, and problems. In cases in which the client is not available or otherwise incapable of providing high-quality information in an interview context (a typical concern with young children), interviews can be conducted with individuals who know them well, such as parents or teachers. Finally, the process of interviewing can be an important bridge in the therapeutic process. In contrast to any other method of assessment, clinical interviewing provides the opportunity to establish rapport, trust, and security with clients, all of which may be crucial to the eventual implementation of an intervention plan.

Similar to other methods of assessment, clinical interviewing does have its flaws or weak- nesses. It is wrong to think of clinical interviewing, or any other assessment method for that matter, as the "gold standard" of assessment (McConaughy & Whitcomb, 2022). Perhaps the most easily criticized feature of interviewing is that the flexible, nonstandardized nature of many interviews, which also is considered to be an advantage, may lead to unreliability or inconsistency over time and between interviewers. Another potential problem with inter- viewing is that to be effective, it requires a great deal of training and experience. In addition, there are some important limitations in clinical interviewing related to distortion and bias. Clinicians and clients may have personal biases that may result in selective or faulty recall of information, lack of attention to important details, and subtle cues from the clinician that may lead clients to distort the information they provide (Sattler, 1998). Finally, clinicians need to be vigilant regarding the possibility of deliberate distortion or lying on the part of the child or adolescent who is being interviewed. Distortion or lying by the interviewee may occur for a variety of reasons and is common (McConaughy & Whitcomb, 2022).

DEVELOPMENTAL ISSUES IN INTERVIEWING

The process of interviewing children or adolescents differs from interviewing adults. Although the basic tasks of interviewing children versus adults may have some superficial similarity, a qualitatively different approach is required to obtain a useful and informative verbal report. As children develop and mature in their physical, cognitive, and social– emotional functioning, their ability to respond to the tasks required of them in an interview format likewise changes. To interview children and adolescents in an effective manner, interviewers must have knowledge of some of the basic aspects of these developmental issues. This section provides a general discussion of some basic developmental issues that may affect the interview process, some of which are summarized in Table 6.1. For a more complete discussion of developmentally sensitive interviewing, readers are referred to

Table 6.1 Developmentally sensitive interviewing: Considerations and suggestions

Developmental period	Developmental considerations		Suggested practices
	Cognitive functioning	Social–emotional functioning	
Early childhood	May be confused by appearance–reality distinctions; memory not fully developed; some difficulty understanding perspective of others	Actions may be considered right or wrong based on consequences; limited ability to describe range of emotions; learns to initiate tasks; some difficulty in self-control	1. Use combination of open and closed questions 2. Don't attempt to maintain total control of interview 3. Reduce complexity of questions 4. Use toys, props, manipulatives 5. Establish familiarity and rapport
Middle childhood	Increased capability for verbal communication; simple logic attained; mastery of increasing cognitive challenges	May view right or wrong based on rules and social conventions; industry versus inferiority struggle based on how well new challenges are mastered; peer group becomes increasingly important	1. Avoid abstract 2. Rely on familiar settings and activities 3. Avoid constant eye contact 4. Provide contextual cues (pictures, examples) and request language interaction 5. Physical props in context may be useful
Adolescence	Ability for abstract reasoning and formal logic usually emerges; systematic problem solving usually begins	May develop postconventional moral reasoning; possibility of identity confusion and experimentation; high emotional intensity and lability not unusual; peer group tends to become extremely important	1. Consider the possibility of emotional lability and stress 2. Avoid making judgments based solely on adult norms 3. Show respect

book chapters by Bierman (1983) and Hughes and Baker (1990) that are specifically devoted to this topic.

Preschool-Age and Primary-Age Children

Young children tend to be particularly difficult to interview and pose what is perhaps the greatest challenge to the interviewer. As Bierman noted:

> Young children are able to describe their thoughts and feelings, but they require specialized interview techniques to do so. Moreover, characteristics of conceptual organization and information processing associated with cognitive and linguistic development result in a phenomenological world for the young child that is qualitatively different from the adult's world. Clinicians who are unfamiliar with the thought processes associated with various developmental levels are likely to find children's reasoning extremely difficult to follow or comprehend. To conduct effective child interviews, clinicians must acquire an understanding of the characteristics of developing social–cognitive processes, and they must make some major adjustments in their interviewing techniques and strategies.

(1983, pp. 218–219)

One of the pioneers in the field of child development, the late Jean Piaget (1896–1980), developed an incredibly influential stage theory of child development. Although some of the explicit assumptions of Piaget's theory have been shown over time to underestimate the cognitive abilities of children, the general framework is still an interesting approach that may be potentially useful—if used with caution—in considering developmental aspects of children and adolescents that might impact their abilities to be an effective interview informant. In Piagetian terms, children between the ages of about two and seven are in the *preoperational* stage of cognitive development, which is characterized by the child's being able to represent things with words and images, but still quite lacking in logical reasoning abilities (Piaget, 1983). Many (and perhaps most) children in this age range may be confused by distinctions between reality and appearance, find it easier to follow positive instructions ("hold the blocks carefully") than negative ones ("don't drop the blocks"), and may have difficulty understanding the viewpoint or experience of another person. Piaget referred to this latter tendency as *egocentrism*, meaning that many young children have difficulty viewing situations from anything but their own experience or perspective. Children in this developmental stage may have difficulty recalling specific information accurately because they are still developing complex memory retrieval strategies (McNamee, 1989). Many preoperational children may focus on just one feature of a problem, neglecting other important aspects, a tendency referred to in Piagetian terms as *centration*. They may exhibit difficulty understanding that actions can be reversed. These cognitive aspects of early childhood may lead many young children to provide incomplete accounts of past events and make them particularly susceptible to acquiescing to "leading" questions from an interviewer, such as "does your mom get really mad at you?" (Saywitz & Snyder, 1996).

To many young children, behavioral actions are considered to be right or wrong depending on their consequences ("stealing is wrong because you get put into jail"). Kohlberg (1969) referred to this type of moral reasoning as being at a *preconventional level.* In terms of emotional development, most younger children may experience a wide range of emotions and affect but typically can describe these experiences only along a limited number of verbal dimensions (i.e., happy or sad, good or bad, mean or nice) because their abilities to verbally express what they are experiencing are still developing.

As was indicated previously, some of the formerly absolutist aspects of developmental stage theories with young children—not only with Piaget's theory but with Kohlberg's theory—have been questioned and disputed. Hughes and Baker (1990) reviewed several studies from the 1970s and 1980s demonstrating that the apparent cognitive limitations of young children are often artifacts of the way they are questioned or the way that tasks are presented to them. It is now known that young children are capable of producing higher quality self-report information than was previously considered to be possible (Measelle, John, Ablow, Cowan, & Cowan, 2005). It has been demonstrated that many young children are highly capable of engaging in prosocial or altruistic behavior (e.g., Eisenberg et al., 1999; Zahn-Waxler & Radke-Yarrow, 1982), and that they can be empathetic toward others (e.g., Strayer & Roberts, 2004; Zahn-Waxler, Radke-Yarrow, Wagner, & Chapman, 1992).

The chances of obtaining high-quality interview information from young children are increased if they are comfortable in the interview situation and are questioned by an interviewer who understands cognitive development and appropriately modifies interview tasks for them (Gelman & Baillageon, 1983). It has been shown that providing specific training regarding how to recall and elaborate on details may be important for obtaining a more accurate interview with younger children (Dorado & Saywitz, 2001). Because social–emotional assessment in early childhood poses many singular challenges and requires a high level of specific skills, this topic is treated separately in this book. Specific techniques and recommendations for increasing the quality of interviews with young children are presented in Chapter 13.

Elementary-Age Children

As children move from the preschool and primary years into the elementary years, their capabilities for verbal communication tend to increase dramatically. Although conducting an effective interview with elementary-age children is a challenging endeavor that requires special understanding and methodology, the probability of obtaining high-quality interview information is substantially better than it is with younger children.

In developmental terms, elementary-age children tend to be in what Piaget (1983) referred to as the *concrete operations* stage of cognitive development, which extends from roughly seven to 11 years. Children at this developmental stage are typically able to use simple logic, but generally can perform mental operations only on images of tangible objects and actual events. During the concrete operations stage, many principles are mastered that were formerly elusive to children while they were younger. The notions that actions can be reversed, the ability to recognize that a change in appearance may not necessarily reflect a change in substance or volume, and an increasing ability to see the "big picture" rather than just one aspect of an event or object are among the characteristic cognitive changes that are evidenced in elementary-age children. Elementary-age children typically learn to develop simple hierarchical classification abilities but still may not have the ability to use formal logic or abstract reasoning, at least beyond a very limited basis. For example, a child at this stage of development may understand that anger is an emotion and that acting out is a behavior, but he or she may not necessarily have much insight into the connection between the two areas.

Elementary-age children are challenged by the task of learning to function socially beyond the family into a broader social realm, a developmental stage that Erikson (1963) referred to as *industry versus inferiority*. If they are able to master these new social challenges, elementary-age children develop a strong sense of self-competence. Lack of such mastery may lead, however, to feelings of low self-esteem and poor self-efficacy.

Most elementary-age children learn to make moral decisions in a more complex way than they did during the preschool and early primary grade years. Kohlberg (1969) suggested that most children in this age range reach conventional morality, wherein rules and social conventions are viewed as absolute guidelines for judging actions. For example, although a preschool-age child might respond to the statement "Why is it wrong to steal?" by stating something like "Because you will get in trouble" (a consequence-based explanation), a typical elementary-age child might respond by saying "Because it is against the school rules," an example of compliance with social conventions. Of course, Kohlberg's theory of moral reasoning is not a universally accepted convention, and there have been criticisms of it, but many aspects of this stage theory seem to hold up well for the typical elementary-age child.

Effective interviewing of elementary-age children can be facilitated greatly by using specific methods and techniques that are developmentally appropriate for this age level. Establishment of adequate rapport and familiarity with the child before the actual assessment has been found to be a crucial variable in influencing the amount and quality of responses presented in standardized assessment situations (Fuchs & Fuchs, 1986; McConaughy, 2013). Although elementary-age children generally have developed a reasonable mastery of language, the interviewer should avoid the use of abstract or symbolic questions, which probably would confuse the child (McConaughy, 2000a; McConaughy & Whitcomb, 2022). Hughes and Baker (1990) suggested that interviews with elementary-age children may be enhanced by: (1) relying on familiar settings and activities during the interview; (2) allowing them to use manipulatives and drawings during the interview; (3) avoiding constant eye contact (which elementary-age children typically are not used to); and (4) providing contextual cues (such as pictures, colors, and examples) with requests for language interaction. Use of physical materials and familiar contexts in interviewing children has been empirically studied. Priestley and Pipe (1997) found that the use of toys and other physical props in interviews with children may facilitate their accurate accounts of events they have experienced, particularly when many props are provided and the physical similarity of these objects is similar to what was experienced in the actual event. Use of toys, props, and other physical materials is likely to enhance the quality of interviews with preschool-age, primary-age, and elementary-age children.

Adolescents

By the time adolescence has been reached, which is typically around 12 to 14 years of age, children are usually capable of participating in an interactive interview situation to a much greater extent than are younger children. In some ways, the interview task becomes similar to that of interviewing an adult. Clinicians who assume, however, that interviewing adolescents is the same as interviewing adults risk reaching invalid conclusions or obtaining low-quality information, because of their lack of sensitivity to the unique developmental aspects of adolescence. It is much better to approach interviews with adolescents from the perspective that adolescence is a unique developmental stage that brings forth numerous unique circumstances, challenges, and tasks.

In terms of Piaget's stage theory, most individuals move toward the *formal operations* level of cognitive development at about age 12 (Piaget, 1983). This stage is characterized by the increasing ability to use formal logic and to apply mental operations to both abstract and concrete objects. Many adolescents tend to become more systematic in their problem-solving efforts, rather than using quick trial-and-error methods for attacking problems. It is important to consider that some individuals (i.e., individuals with impaired cognitive functioning or developmental disabilities) do not reach this advanced stage of cognitive functioning; there is no guarantee that because an interviewee is 17 years old, he or she will be able to think abstractly and logically. It is worth considering screening the youth's academic and intellectual history before the clinical interview.

During adolescence, many persons may reach what Kohlberg (1969) referred to as *postconventional* moral reasoning, a stage at which actions are more likely to be judged based on individual principles of conscience rather than potential consequences or social conventions. Some adolescents (particularly older adolescents) may make decisions regarding what is considered right or wrong behavior based on abstract internalized ideals, rather than conventional guidelines, such as school or family rules, or fear of consequences. Although there is not a great deal of empirical evidence regarding how many adolescents make decisions in postconventional terms, it can be generalized that this stage is more likely to be reached toward the end of adolescence, and many individuals do not reach this stage of moral reasoning development at all. In practical terms, an example of a postconventional response to the question "Why is stealing wrong?" might be "Because stealing violates the personal property rights of other people." Related to the area of moral reasoning, adolescence is a time when many individuals experience personal shifts in their values and beliefs, a developmental issue that sometimes may lead to significant stress in relationships with parents (Dusek, 1996).

Since the time of the industrial revolution in Western industrialized societies, prominent thinkers as disparate as the European philosopher Jean Jacques Rousseau and the pioneering American psychologist G. Stanley Hall have characterized emotional development during adolescence as a period of "storm and stress" because of the challenging adaptations that must be made. In his theory of psychosocial development, Erikson (1963) characterized adolescence as a time of *identity versus confusion* crisis, in which young persons struggle to find themselves and may experience a wide variation in emotional intensity. Teachers and clinicians who work frequently with adolescents (and those who are or have been parents of teens) usually agree with these assessments of age-related emotional stress. The empirical evidence regarding adolescence as a period of emotional storm and stress has been characterized, however, as being mixed or less than convincing (Dusek, 1996). One of the unfortunate aspects of adolescence in the United States is that compared with childhood, it is accompanied by substantial increases in suicidal ideation and suicide attempts (Dusek, 1996). As of 2014, suicide constituted the secondary cause of death for adolescents (Centers for Disease Control and Prevention, 2014). This evidence is often cited to characterize adolescence as a time of emotional difficulty. It is important to consider that even with this age-related increase, however, adolescent suicide rates are still low compared with older age groups (Weiten, 2000). Although it is still empirically unclear whether adolescence constitutes a developmental period of unique emotional turbulence, most parents of current, or former teens, are likely to conclude that the notion of emotional turbulence is indeed a key characteristic of adolescence, even for well-adjusted youths. Clinicians who interview adolescents should consider that adolescence is a time of many challenges and changes and be sensitive to and aware of these issues.

Conducting interviews with adolescents can be a rewarding experience. It is usually more authentic and less constrained or frustrating than interviewing younger children. Nevertheless, clinicians must consider the unique developmental aspects of adolescence to elicit useful interview information and to make sound inferences. Although many adolescents may be adult-like in their approach to the clinical interview and may enjoy the unique one-on-one attention that comes from this process, others may find the process annoying, intimidating, or upsetting. It is not unusual for troubled adolescents to become uncooperative or disengaged during an interview situation.

It is important to consider the possibility of intensely variable emotionality with adolescent interviewees. Although most *Diagnostic and Statistical Manual of Mental Disorders,* fifth edition (*DSM-5*) diagnostic categories may apply to adolescents and adults, clinicians still should exert extra care and caution in making significant inferences with adolescents. Any diagnoses of severe affective or behavioral problems should be tempered by the understanding of normal adolescent development, and adult standards of behavior and emotionality should not be exclusively applied. There is evidence that making decisions on an adolescent's social and emotional behavior in the same manner that is done with adults may lead to faulty conclusions. Archer (2005) noted that about 25% of adolescent participants responded to the original Minnesota Multiphasic Personality Inventory (MMPI) in a manner that would be suggestive of psychotic behavior when strictly interpreted according to adult norms. Regardless of whether one subscribes to the notion that adolescence is by its nature an emotionally difficult and variable period, this type of evidence compels us to consider adolescence as a time of unique challenges and adaptation.

FACTORS THAT MAY AFFECT THE QUALITY OF THE INTERVIEW

Knowledge of child development and methods of making interviews developmentally appropriate do not by themselves result in effective and useful interviews with children or adolescents. In addition to developmental issues and interview format, there are many other factors that may contribute to the overall quality of the interview. Several of these factors are discussed in this section.

The Interpersonal Context

Whether the interview is with a child, parent, or teacher, the interpersonal relationship established before and during the course of the interview may significantly affect the extent and quality of client's self-report data. One of the key tenets of humanistic psychology (particularly person-centered theory) is that the development of a positive relationship between the interviewer and the client is crucial to the quality of client self-disclosure and the effectiveness of counseling. Three core relationship conditions are considered essential: (1) *empathy,* or accurate understanding of the client's concerns; (2) *respect,* or positive regard for the client; and (3) *genuineness,* which can be described as congruence between the interviewer's verbal and nonverbal messages toward the client (Rogers, Gendlin, Kiesler, & Truax, 1967). Although these interpersonal considerations were first described and used within the context of person-centered therapy, they have value for other forms of interviewing and therapy as well.

Cormier, Cormier, and Cormier (1997) elaborated further on the relationship-building aspect of the interview and suggested that *expertness, attractiveness,* and *trustworthiness* are additional characteristics that enhance the interpersonal context of communication. Expertness is related to the client's perception of how competent the interviewer is, with an emphasis on characteristics of interviewer competence that are immediately evident to a client. Attractiveness goes far beyond the client's perception of the interviewer's physical characteristics and includes such attributes as friendliness, likability, and similarity to the client. Trustworthiness includes the interviewer's reputation for honesty; the congruence of the interviewer's nonverbal behaviors; and the amount of accuracy, openness, and confidentiality that is evident during the interview process. Clinicians who successfully incorporate these interpersonal characteristics and behaviors into their interviewing methods are likely to increase the value of their interviews with clients.

Children may have a different perspective than adults on what interpersonal qualities make a good and trusted interviewer. For example, take the concept of expertness. Although many adults might be swayed toward positive appraisal of a clinician who comes across as a highly knowledgeable expert, these same characteristics would not impress children as much, and in some cases may even hinder communication. Thompson and Rudolph (1992) stated that "adults are often too aggressive in trying to initiate conversations with children" (p. 33). Although some adults might respond well to a clinician who seems confident and eager to engage in conversation, this same behavior may be intimidating to many children. Likewise, consider how our perceptions of what constitutes expertness relate to professional dress standards. In American culture, a clinician who is dressed in relatively formal business-type attire might impress many adults as being groomed like a professional, but it is highly doubtful that the same effect would result with many children and adolescents, who might view the professional as being stiff, detached, and unapproachable. In attempting to develop an appropriate and effective interpersonal context for clinical interviews with children, a clinician should always consider these and other potential differences between children and adults and place a premium on helping the child client feel comfortable and safe.

The Ethnocultural Context

The United States is a uniquely diverse nation racially, ethnically, and culturally, and all demographic indicators point to this diversity increasing steadily over the next several decades. During the most recent major census, the U.S. Census Bureau (2010) found that the proportion of Americans who are White, non-Hispanic (sometimes referred to as European American) had shrunk to about 72% of the total population. Census updates have indicated that this percentage has continued to decline during the first decade of the twenty-first century, and that the percentage of Americans who are considered to be of European American ancestry is currently about 64%. It has been estimated that the percentage of Americans who are considered to be White, non-Hispanic will shrink to slightly over 50% by 2050 and that growth in the population of Hispanic Americans and Asian Americans will account for most of this ethnic or racial population shift (Rosenblatt, 1996). Given that American culture is increasingly pluralistic with respect to race, ethnicity, and culture, and given that one's cultural background may play an important role in interpersonal communication style, it is crucial for clinicians to consider cultural factors that may affect clinical interviewing.

In discussing information about differences between racial, ethnic, or cultural groups, it is important to consider that much of the information we have on group differences is based on *generalizations from studies of groups.* There are always individuals who do not fit the "typical" group characteristics. Caution is essential to avoid stereotypical overgeneralizations of group differences. I stress that the literature on group differences, whether based on gender or race/ethnicity, must be used with great care and caution because generalizing a characteristic from a group-based study, even if done with good intentions, may function as a way of stereotyping individuals and further exaggerating differences in how we categorize and classify individuals.

Two dimensions of the clinical interview that may have immediate cultural relevance include the *degree of eye contact* and the *amount of physical distance* between the interviewer and the client. Sue and Sue (2008) noted that White Americans make eye contact with the speaker about 80% of the time but tend to avoid eye contact about 50% of the time when speaking to others. This general trend has also been noted by Vasquez-Nuttall and colleagues (2003) and is in contrast to the eye contact patterns of many African Americans, who as a group tend to make greater eye contact when speaking and less frequent eye contact when listening. Indigenous Americans as a group are more likely to use indirect eye contact patterns when speaking or listening, whereas Asian Americans and

Table 6.2 Generalized between-group communication style differences among major ethnic groups in the United States: Some aspects of overt activity and nonverbal and verbal communication

Indigenous Americans	Asian Americans and Latinos	Whites	African Americans
1 Speak softly/slower	1 Speak softly	1 Speak loud/fast to control	1 Speak with affect
2 Indirect gaze when listening or speaking	2 Avoidance of eye contact when listening or speaking to high-status persons	2 Greater eye contact when listening	2 Direct eye contact (prolonged) when speaking, but less when listening
3 Interject less, seldom offer encouraging communication	3 Similar rules	3 Head nods, nonverbal markers	3 Interrupt (turn-taking) when can
4 Delayed auditory (silence)	4 Mild delay	4 Quick responding	4 Quicker responding
5 Manner of expression low-key, indirect	5 Low-keyed, indirect	5 Objective, task-oriented	5 Affective, emotional, interpersonal

Source: From *Counseling the Culturally Different* (3rd ed.), by D. W. Sue & D. Sue, 1999, New York: John Wiley & Sons, Inc. Reprinted by permission of John Wiley & Sons, Inc.

Hispanics, as groups, are more likely to avoid eye contact altogether when speaking to persons whom they perceive to have high status.

In terms of comfortable physical proximity or distance between persons, Sue and Sue (2008) and Vasquez-Nuttall and colleagues (2003) also noted that there may be important cultural differences. For Latino Americans, Africans, African Americans, Indonesians, South Americans, Arabs, and French, a much closer physical stance between communicators than most White/Anglo clinicians are comfortable with is normal. Degree of eye contact and physical proximity between interviewee and interviewer may be variables that can affect greatly the overall quality of the interview. Some culturally based aspects of interpersonal communication styles among U.S. cultural groups are reflected in the information presented in Table 6.2. Additionally, because cultural diversity is such a crucial issue in conducting effective social–emotional assessments, the topic is dealt with separately in Chapter 2.

The Behavioral Context

Some specific interviewer behaviors are likely to enhance or detract from the amount and quality of interview information that is obtained from a client during a clinical interview. Whether the interview has a structured or unstructured format, there is some evidence that by preparing the client and instructing him or her in desirable ways of responding, the interviewer will increase the amount, quality, and accuracy of self-disclosure by the client (Gross, 1984; Saywitz & Snyder, 1996). At the beginning of an interview with the parent of a referred child, the clinician might say something like "When you tell me about problems you are having with Sari, I would like you to be very specific—tell me exactly what she does that you see as a problem, how it affects you, and what you generally do about it." Advance instructions such as this appear to pose no danger of leading the client. Rather, this practice may help the clients to frame their responses in a way that is more objective, direct, and potentially linked to understanding antecedents and consequences of behavior.

Another interviewer behavior that may increase the quality of the interview is the use of reinforcement. With children and adults, the selective use of praise or appreciative statements has the effect of increasing the amount and quality of subsequent self-disclosure (Gross, 1984). A clinician who is interviewing a child about how the divorce of his or her parents has affected him might say something like the following:

> Steffen, you did a great job of telling me what it was like for you when your mom and dad got divorced. I know that was a hard thing for you to talk about, but you were able to tell how you feel about it in a way that really helped me to understand things. The more you can tell me about how you feel and what has happened to you, the better I can understand you and help you.

Other forms of reinforcement may also be effective with younger children. Edible primary reinforcers, such as raisins, nuts, or small pieces of candy, are one possibility, although they should be used with parent permission and with caution to avoid satiation effects and to avoid having the reinforcers take center stage during the interview. As an alternative to edible reinforcers, stickers are often popular with children, as are tokens that can be exchanged for small rewards after the interview.

Finally, the type of questioning used is another important interviewer behavior. The use of *closed questions* (those that can be answered with a one-word response) should be avoided except when specific information is needed. A barrage of closed questions from an interviewer may leave the client feeling as though he or she is being interrogated. With adults, adolescents, and older children, the use of *open-ended questions* (e.g., "Tell me about what you like to do with your friends") is generally preferred over closed questions (e.g., "Do you like to play with your friends?"). In general, any question that can be answered with a "yes" or "no" response is a closed question. There are exceptions to the convention of avoiding closed questions. With young children, it is generally most useful to use a combination of open and closed questions (Hughes & Baker, 1990). It also has been recommended that interspersing open questions with probes provides an effective means for obtaining interview information with children and adolescents (McConaughy, 2000a; 2005).

The Truth Context: Dealing with Lying

Any experienced clinician knows that whether interviewing children or adults, some aspects of what the client tells you may not be historically or objectively accurate. One possible explanation for this phenomenon is that the client may not understand the question or may be confused regarding what is wanted. Another possible explanation is that the client does indeed understand what the clinician is getting at with his or her question, but deliberately distorts or falsifies his or her response in order to spin it in the manner that he or she wishes to convey. McConaughy and Whitcomb (2022) noted that a surprisingly high percentage of children and adolescents are perceived by their parents or teachers as having lied in the recent past and that the percentages of youths who are perceived as having lied are higher for mental health or special education samples than for non-referred samples. In terms of children and adolescents own self-reports of whether they have lied in the recent past, the percentage of non-referred youths who affirm doing so ranged from 24% to 29% and the percentage of referred youths who endorsed having lied ranged from 43% to 52% (Achenbach & Rescorla, 2001). Of course, these figures raise an interesting conundrum: If respondents are known to have a reasonably high propensity to lie, then how much should we trust their self-report of lying?

Given that child or adolescent clients may sometimes respond to the interviewer's request for information in ways that appear to demonstrate lying or falsification, some commonsense practices should be considered. First, the interviewer should try to avoid questions that come across as inflammatory or pejorative and, thus, may be more likely to elicit a defensive or self-protective response from the client. Questions such as, "How often do you steal from other kids at school?" or "When was the last time you took illegal drugs?" both fall into this inflammatory or pejorative category. Without question, a clinician can get at this same information in a way that is more subtle, less combative, and more apt to eventually lead to accurate interview responses. Second, interviewers should tread carefully in situations where it appears the client is lying. Sometimes in an interview situation, the client may respond to the clinician's questions in a way that is obviously untrue. Should you confront the child or adolescent directly about this apparent lying? McConaughy (2013) thinks not, suggesting "Confronting children directly about suspected lies or exaggerations . . . is likely to be counterproductive, because it may lead them to tell more lies to save face or to defend themselves against accusations or punishments" (p. 30). Instead, it may be more effective to either skip that situation and come back to it later after more trust and rapport is built or approach the child or adolescent in a way that is less threatening, such as "Maybe you could tell me some more about that . . . you said you never steal, but your file has all these office referrals for stealing. Sometimes these questions can be really confusing or hard to answer. What do you think?"

The Physical Context

A final aspect of the interview that should be considered is the physical context of the interview setting and the physical or topographical aspects of communication. I have already discussed the degree of eye contact, which involves the physical context and the ethnocultural context. Related to degree of eye contact is physical proximity between clinician and client. With children, this issue may be particularly important. It is widely held that children prefer to talk to adults at the same eye level as they are, and it has been recommended that to increase their comfort during an interview, children should be allowed in most cases to control the distance between them and the interviewer (Thompson & Rudolph, 1992). Clinicians are encouraged to allow the child to determine how close he or she wants to sit to the interviewer in most situations and to be willing to sit lower to the ground to avoid intimidation of the child. With younger children, and children who are not comfortable in formal assessment situations, this advice may become especially crucial. Of course, there will be occasions when a child or adolescent client from a specific cultural background is not comfortable with these generally preferable arrangements. Clinicians should strive to be sensitive to such individual differences and should always strive to do what is best or most effective for their clients, rather than following rules rigidly, no matter how generally true those rules seem.

An additional aspect of the physical context is the seating arrangement for the clinical interview, or how to arrange tables, chairs, and desks for optimal comfort and effectiveness.

Although no empirical evidence has been reported regarding this issue, clinicians who are experienced in counseling children tend to agree that having a barrier such as a desk between the clinician and a child client tends to make the child see the clinician as an authority figure, which in some cases may inhibit communication. Also, having the clinician and child client seated directly across from each other with no physical barrier between them is seen as being problematic because it can be too intimidating for the child. Regarding appropriate seating arrangements for counseling and interviewing with children, Thompson and Rudolph recommended that the preferred arrangement is to:

> Use the corner of a desk or table as an optional barrier for the child, allowing them to retreat behind the desk or table corner or to move out around the corner when he or she feels comfortable doing so.
>
> (1992, p. 33)

These general guidelines may be useful as a starting point, but the optimal interview situation may vary from child to child and situation to situation. Clinicians are encouraged to pay complete attention to the comfort and level of disclosure of their client and to make modifications to the physical setup or interview technique as needed. Essentially, what works is what is best in any given situation, and that will certainly vary.

SELECTING AN APPROPRIATE INTERVIEW METHOD

In this chapter, clinical interviewing methods are divided into three general categories: traditional interview techniques, behavioral interviews, and structured or semistructured interviews. It is possible to divide or categorize interview methods into more classifications, but this three-part division provides a useful grouping into general methods that typically might be used in most clinical interviews.

The particular choice of the interview method depends on several factors, including: (1) the theoretical orientation of the clinician; (2) the level of training and experience the clinician has in conducting interviews; and (3) the overall goals and specific objectives for the interview. The clinician's theoretical orientation influences the choice of interview methods in that his or her personal beliefs and biases may limit the level of comfort he or she has in using different methods. For instance, a clinician who has a strong behavioral orientation may not be comfortable using a traditional, open-ended interview format with a client, perceiving that the type of information obtained will be of little use in identifying key elements and sequences of problem behaviors and in developing an intervention. Conversely, a psychodynamic-oriented or humanistic-oriented clinician may perceive that some highly structured diagnostic interview schedules are rigid and confining.

The clinician's level of training and experience may affect choice of methods. Being able to conduct a traditional, open-ended interview effectively and without a great deal of preimposed structure requires a significant amount of clinical expertise, which is gained only through training and more experience. Conducting an effective behavioral interview requires a solid grounding in behavioral theory, if the results are to be useful in identifying factors that elicit and maintain problem behaviors and subsequently developing an intervention plan. Some of the structured and semistructured interview schedules that are available require a high degree of specific training in that particular system, although some of these schedules can be used easily and effectively by paraprofessionals and laypersons with a minimal amount of training.

In addition to the clinician's theoretical orientation and level of training, the choice of interview techniques is also shaped by the specific purposes for conducting the interview. Traditional interview formats are useful when there is a premium on obtaining historical information and in establishing rapport with the client within the arrangement of a less formal, client-focused interview. Behavioral methods of interviewing are particularly useful when the pre-eminent goal is to conduct a functional behavior assessment or to develop an immediate intervention wherein the crucial behavioral variables can be identified and modified. If diagnostic or classification purposes are paramount for the interview, many of the semistructured or structured interview schedules are considered to be a good choice, particularly if the purpose is psychiatric diagnoses via the *DSM* system.

TRADITIONAL INTERVIEWING TECHNIQUES

What is referred to in this chapter as traditional interviewing is not really a specific format or type of interview. Rather, this term represents the broad range of clinical interviews that are relatively open-ended, less structured, and highly adaptable depending on the situation. Traditional interviewing techniques may include a wide range of specific types of approaches to interviewing, such as psychodynamic, case history, and psychosocial status. Within this discussion of traditional clinical interviewing techniques, two areas are covered that are relevant to virtually any type of interview: (1) gathering background information from parents and teachers; and (2) methods of developing the interview with child or adolescent clients.

Gathering Relevant Background Information from Parents and Teachers

In addition to identifying specific problems and developing intervention plans, both of which are covered in the Behavioral Interviewing section of this chapter, one of the main purposes for interviewing the parent or teacher of a referred child is to obtain a report of relevant background information. Why should background information be obtained? Although one could make an argument for using only information that is current and linked directly to the presenting problem, such an approach is short-sighted. By carefully reviewing important historical information, clues sometimes are provided to the causes of, and potential solutions to, child behavior or emotional problems. It is important to think of children, their parents, and their teachers as existing within a complex ecological network, such as Bronfenbrenner's ecological systems model that was introduced in Chapter 1. The more information clinicians have about how this network functions, the more effective they may be in developing and implementing solutions to problems. An additional advantage of obtaining comprehensive background information is that it can help to provide links to seemingly unrelated problems. For example, some behavioral or physical side effects of medications a child is taking may be misunderstood unless the clinician is aware that the medication is being taken in the first place. Another benefit of interviewing parents or teachers is that it creates an opportunity to build trust and rapport with them, which is a crucial ingredient when it is time to implement interventions.

What type of background information should be obtained? The answer to this question depends to some extent on the nature of the presenting problems, but there are some standard areas that typically are explored in the process. Table 6.3 includes five general areas of inquiry, each with some specific recommended areas of questioning. The general areas include medical history, developmental history, social–emotional functioning, educational progress, and community involvement. This format is not all-inclusive; other general areas and specific questions can be identified as the need arises. It is also important

Table 6.3 Recommended areas of questions for gathering background information

Medical history
Problems during pregnancy and delivery?
Complications shortly after birth?
Serious illnesses/high fevers or convulsions?
Serious injuries or accidents?
Serious illnesses in family history?
Allergies or dietary problems?
Current health problems or medications?
Vision and hearing OK?

Developmental history
Ages for reaching developmental milestones: crawling, talking, walking, toilet-training
Developmental delays (communication, motor, cognitive, social)?
Development in comparison with siblings or peers

Social–emotional functioning
Temperament as an infant/toddler
Quality of attachment to caregivers as infant/toddler
Quality of relationships with parents
Quality of relationships with siblings and peers
Discipline methods: what works best, who does he or she mind the best?
Behavioral problems at home or in community?
Number and quality of friendships with peers
Any traumatic/disturbing experiences?
Any responsibilities or chores?
Who provides after-school care?

Educational progress
Initial adjustment to school
Academic progress: delayed, average, high-achieving?
School grades and progress notes
Any school attendance problems?
Behavioral problems at school?
Quality of peer relations at school
Favorite subjects, classes, or teachers
Extracurricular activities

Community involvement
Belong to any organizations or clubs (e.g., Boys and Girls Club)?
Organized team sports?
Part-time job? (for adolescents)
Religious background/participation in church activities or spiritual practices
Relationships with extended family

to consider that the five general areas of inquiry presented here are not equally applicable to all adults with whom the clinician may be conducting an interview. Specific medical and developmental history may not be known to a foster caregiver or a teacher. Likewise, when interviewing a teacher, the focus on educational performance would be the major area of discussion.

A wide array of forms has been developed and is in use for obtaining developmental history information. These forms range from being self-produced to commercially produced, brief to long, informal to formal. An example of a comprehensive formal developmental history interview form that has been published commercially is the Structured Developmental History form from the Behavioral Assessment System for Children, Third Edition (C.R. Reynolds & Kamphaus, 2015). This form is a multipage tool that covers everything from prenatal history to family health history to adaptive skills of the child. In some cases, extensive and lengthy interview forms such as these may be useful. In other instances, it may be more desirable to conduct a brief and informal interview regarding background issues. The presenting problems and purpose of the interview should drive the format for obtaining background information.

Developing the Interview with Children and Adolescents

Interviewing a child or adolescent provides an opportunity for two important elements of the assessment: (1) directly observing behavior under structured conditions; and (2) obtaining self-report information regarding the interviewee's concerns, problems, goals, and hopes. The interview also provides an opportunity to develop rapport with the child or adolescent, which may prove to be especially important if the interviewer will also be functioning in an important role with the client after the completion of the assessment.

Areas for Observation Although the specific aspects of client behavior that are most important for the interviewer to observe depend to a great extent on the purpose of the interview and the nature of the presenting problems, there are four general areas that almost always are useful to target: (1) physical characteristics; (2) overt behavioral characteristics; (3) social–emotional functioning; and (4) cognitive functioning. Table 6.4 includes a more complete breakdown of child characteristics to observe within each of these four general areas. In some cases, the clinician may need to add to or subtract from this list, depending on the specifics of the interview.

Many clinicians who routinely conduct interviews as part of a broader assessment find it useful to make notes of the important characteristics that were observed during the interview so that they can be detailed in the report at a later time. Note taking should not take center stage during an interview, however, as it is likely to distract from the flow of communication and the establishment of good rapport with the child or adolescent.

Areas for Questioning As we have already discussed, the traditional child interview is amenable to some specific types of interviewing. We have also discussed the use of questioning strategies (e.g., open versus closed questions) and developmental considerations that must be considered when conducting clinical interviews with children and adolescents. Although traditional interview techniques for specific purposes and problems and with specific ages of clients vary to some extent, there are still some commonalities and some general areas of questioning that remain constant. Table 6.5 lists five general areas that are usually important to target when interviewing children or adolescents:

Table 6.4 Important child characteristics to observe during interviews

Physical characteristics
Unusual or inappropriate attire
Gang-related attire
Height and weight in comparison to same-age peers
Obvious physical difficulties
Direct signs of possible illness
Motor coordination
Tics (vocal, facial, motor)

Overt behavioral characteristics
Activity level
Attention span
Interaction with environment
Distractibility
Impulsivity

Social–emotional functioning
Range and appropriateness of affect
Mood state during interview
Reaction to praise
Reaction to frustration
Social skills with interviewer
Obvious anxiety or nervousness
Ease of separation from caregiver (for young children)

Cognitive functioning
Communication skills
Overall intellectual competence, estimated
Intrapersonal insight/self-awareness
Logic of reasoning
Time and space orientation
Level of organization in activities
Apparent planning ability

(1) intrapersonal functioning; (2) family relationships; (3) peer relationships; (4) school adjustment; and (5) community involvement. Within each of these areas, some specific areas for recommended questioning are provided, which can be increased or decreased as needed. When conducting traditional open-ended interviews, many clinicians find it useful to develop the interview and make notes according to a breakdown such as that shown in Table 6.5. This allows for a degree of structure and a logical progression in the interview while still leaving it flexible and open-ended.

BEHAVIORAL INTERVIEWING

Behavioral interviewing differs from traditional interview methods in the level of structure imposed by the interviewer and the purposes for conducting the interview. The roots of behavioral interviewing are found in behavioral psychology. As noted by Gross (1984) nearly four decades ago, it is still true that "the primary objective of behavioral assessment is to obtain descriptive information about problem behavior and the conditions maintaining it" (p. 62). The behavioral interview is viewed as a specific type of behavioral

Table 6.5 General areas of questioning for child/adolescent interviews

---

Intrapersonal functioning
Eating and sleeping habits
Feelings/attributions about self
Peculiar or bizarre experiences (e.g., hearing or seeing things)
Emotional status (e.g., depressed, anxious, guilty, angry, happy)
Clarity of thought/orientation to time and space
Insight into own thoughts and concerns
Defensiveness/blaming
Understanding of reason for interview

Family relationships
Quality of relationships with parents
Quality of relationships with siblings
Family routines, responsibilities, chores
Involvement with extended family members
Level of perceived support from family
Perceived conflicts within family

Peer relationships
Number of close friends
Preferred activities with friends
Perceived conflicts with peers
Social skills for initiating friendships
Reports of peer rejection and loneliness

School adjustment
Current grade, teacher, school subjects
General attitudes/feelings about school
Previous and current academic performance
Favorite or preferred subjects or teachers
Difficult or disliked subjects or teachers
Involvement in extracurricular activities
School attendance patterns
Perceived conflicts or problems at school

Community involvement
Involvement in clubs or youth organizations
Participation in community activities
Church attendance/religious or spiritual activities
Level of mobility within community
Part-time jobs (for adolescents)
Relationships with other individuals in the community

---

assessment, with the same objectives as other behaviorally oriented assessment methods. The clinician who conducts a behavioral interview is interested in pinpointing the problem behaviors and identifying variables that may have controlling or maintaining effects on those behaviors. In other words, behavioral interviewing may be focused to a great extent on understanding *functions* of behaviors. As such, the behavioral interview requires a relatively high degree of structure by the interviewer for the primary goals to be met. Because of the unique strengths and structure of behavioral interviewing, it is often an essential element in conducting a functional assessment of behavior, which is discussed in more detail in Chapter 4.

Table 6.6 Specific purposes of behavioral interviewing

1. Gather information about client concerns and goals
2. Identify factors that elicit and/or maintain problem behaviors
3. Obtain relevant historical/background information
4. Identify potential reinforcers within client's environment
5. Assess mediation potential of the client
6. Educate client regarding behavioral principles and the particular problem situation
7. Obtain informed consent from the parent/guardian of child or adolescent client (and obtain assent from the child or adolescent client)
8. Communicate about the goals and procedures of assessment and intervention

Several models of behavioral interviewing have been proposed, and each of them has a different level of emphasis of such variables as cognitive and verbal competency of the client, other within-client variables, analysis of the environment, and historical information. What these differing models of behavioral interviewing seem to have in common is their emphasis on description and clarification of the problem behaviors and the identification of antecedent stimuli and consequences of those behaviors.

Along these lines, Haynes and Wilson (1979) identified the essential elements of the behavioral interview as an organized interaction between the subject or a mediator and the behavioral interviewer for eight specific purposes ranging from gathering information about client concerns to communicating specifically about the procedures and goals of the assessment and any subsequent intervention. With the addition of some modifications provided by me, the eight specific purposes of behavioral interviewing originally outlined by Haynes and Wilson are listed in Table 6.6.

As a clinical interviewing technique, the behavioral method offers several advantages over other forms of assessment, including other interview techniques. Behavioral interviewing has been touted as an economical method of obtaining behavioral information (Wahler & Cormier, 1970), especially compared with direct observation. Given that interviews may be conducted with an informant who is familiar with the client, behavioral interviewing offers flexibility in the event that the child or adolescent client is not directly available to observe or interview or is not capable of providing detailed information. Another advantage of behavioral interviewing is that when conducted directly with the client, it allows the clinician to observe directly various social behaviors and communication skills of the client, which may be useful in developing intervention strategies. Additionally, conducting a comprehensive behavioral interview with a mediator (i.e., parent or teacher) allows the clinician to assess how receptive the mediator might be to the idea of implementing an intervention and to what specific types of intervention the mediator might be amenable (Gresham & Davis, 1988). Finally, in comparison with such behavioral assessment techniques as direct observation and rating scales, interviewing is flexible enough to allow the clinician the opportunity to expand or narrow the scope of the assessment, depending on what areas emerge as specific problems.

Implementing Behavioral Interviews with Parents and Teachers

When the client is a child or adolescent, it is almost always necessary and desirable to interview the parents as part of the initial assessment, and it is important to interview a teacher as well. "The interviewing of parents and teachers, in addition to the children themselves, has long been a standard component in assessing the behavior problems of children and adolescents" (Busse & Beaver, 2000, p. 235). Interviewing the parents or teacher of the referred child or adolescent can be an extremely important part of the assessment for several reasons: (1) they are a potential rich source of behavioral data because of their daily observations of the child's behavior in naturalistic settings; (2) they may be able to provide information on the child's behavior that is not available to the interviewer through other methods of assessment; and (3) because they often function as mediators in the intervention process, it is crucial to obtain their report and assess their ability to implement an intervention. Although conducting behavioral interviews of parents and teachers has been treated as a separate topic, the processes involved have much in common and are discussed together in this chapter.

Conceptualizing the behavioral interview process as part of an overall behavioral consultation model for working with parents and teachers, Gresham and Davis (1988) and Busse and Beaver (2000) identified three different types of behavioral interviews that might occur: (1) the problem identification interview; (2) the problem analysis interview; and (3) the problem evaluation or treatment evaluation interview. Because the problem or treatment evaluation interview phase is designed to be implemented after the implementation of an intervention, it is beyond the scope of this text. This chapter deals with only the first two types of behavioral interviews. Although it is possible to treat problem identification and problem analysis together, they are discussed individually, for purposes of conceptual clarity.

Problem Identification Interview Identification of the problem is considered to be the most important phase in the consultation process because it defines what will be focused on, and how the problem will be envisioned (Busse & Beaver, 2000; Gresham & Davis, 1988). In beginning the problem identification interview, a clinician typically starts by obtaining demographic information and asking general questions about the child ("What concerns do you have about your child?") but soon begins to probe into more specifics and in more depth ("How often does this student engage in aggressive behavior?"). The main idea is for the interviewer to assess the variety of problems reported, identify the problems that are of most concern, and obtain specific behavioral information relating to those problems.

Gresham and Davis (1988) identified six major objectives for the problem identification interview, as follows:

1. specification of the problem to be solved in consultation;
2. elicitation of an objective description of the target behavior;
3. identification of environmental conditions surrounding the target behavior;
4. estimation of the frequency, intensity, and duration of the problem behavior;
5. agreement on the type of data collection procedures that will be used and who will collect the data;
6. setting a date for the next interview, which will be a problem analysis interview.

In addition to identifying and gathering specific information on the problem behavior exhibited by the child or adolescent, Gross (1984) suggested that it is important to obtain information on the child's *behavioral assets*. By specifically asking the parents or teacher what behavior is desired in place of the problem behavior, the interviewer can work on assessing whether the child or adolescent has that behavior within his or her repertoire. Additionally, spending some time focusing on strengths and assets can also serve to help the adult interviewees, who are often frustrated by the child's behavior, to cognitively shift toward a more positive outlook. Another example of gathering information on behavioral assets involves the interview focusing on what things the child or adolescent finds particularly enjoyable or rewarding. This information could be used later in developing a menu of potential reinforcers.

There are several specific interview protocols that have been developed and adhere to the objectives laid out by Gresham and Davis (1988). Many are free and available online. One example is *The Functional Assessment Checklist for Teachers and Staff* (March et al., 2000).

Problem Analysis Interview Ideally, problem analysis occurs after a problem identification interview, which sets the stage for an appropriate plan for obtaining baseline data. Gresham and Davis (1988) identified four objectives for the problem analysis interview, as follows:

1. Validation or confirmation of the problem through an examination of the baseline data. If the problem is confirmed, this step also would include determining any discrepancies between the child's existing performance and what is desired.
2. Analysis of conditions surrounding the behavior. In other words, what are the antecedents, sequences, and consequences that affect the behavior, and what are the potential functions of the behavior?
3. Design of an intervention plan to alter the identified problem behavior. This objective includes developing general approaches and precise plans for how the interventions will be implemented.
4. Setting a date for the problem evaluation interview, assuming that an appropriate intervention plan has been developed and agreed upon.

It is often difficult to divide the problem identification and problem analysis aspects of the behavioral interview into two separate interview sessions, with the parent or teacher agreeing to gather appropriate baseline data between sessions. In practice, there are often strong time pressures, and needs, to develop interventions immediately that make it necessary to combine both aspects of the behavioral interview into one extended session. By doing this, however, there usually is no opportunity for the gathering of baseline data, and the clinician needs to rely on the verbal report of the client and rating scale data, then work on gathering progress data as the intervention is implemented and modified. The following interchange of dialogue between a therapist and the parent of a six-year-old boy illustrates how the elements of a problem identification interview and a problem analysis interview can be merged into one session:

THERAPIST: You've told me about several problems that are happening with Marcus. Which behavior do you see as being the biggest problem?
PARENT: The temper tantrums.
THERAPIST: Tell me, specifically, what Marcus does when he is having a tantrum.

PARENT: It usually starts out with screaming and yelling and sometimes crying. He'll call me names, make threats, and if it is a really bad one, he might kick the walls, push over furniture and lamps, and even try to kick me or hit me or someone else in the family.

THERAPIST: What kinds of things are usually going on just before Marcus behaves like this?

PARENT: It's usually when he wants something that I won't let him have or do, or when he has been in an argument with his older brother.

THERAPIST: And where does it usually happen?

PARENT: Always at home, and usually inside the house.

THERAPIST: Is it more likely to happen at particular times?

PARENT: Well, most of the time it's at night.

THERAPIST: And how long do these tantrums usually last?

PARENT: Oh, maybe 10 or 20 minutes, but a really bad one might go on longer.

THERAPIST: Tell me what kinds of things you do, both just before the tantrums happen, and then during or after them, as a way to stop them.

PARENT: It seems like when the arguments start that happen before the tantrums, I am usually tired or in a bad mood, and I might be kind of short with him. But not always. Once it gets started, it all depends on the situation and how I am feeling—it seems like if I'm worn-out and irritated, I yell back at him and sometimes even try to hold him still, or something like that. If I'm not so stressed, I might try and send him to the other room or just sit down and try to listen to him.

THERAPIST: And what seems to work best?

PARENT: Well, it does seem like the thing that works best is to not let the argument get so bad, like try and distract him by getting him to do something else, or to sit down calmly and listen to him. But I usually only do that when I'm not tired or stressed. Once it gets going, I know that the worst thing I can do is to get into it with him, but sometimes I don't really care. It seems like moving him into his room for a few minutes until he settles down works better than that.

The dialogue in this interchange shows how an interviewer/therapist can ask specific questions to pinpoint the greatest problem and determine its intensity, duration, locus, and environmental variables that might be eliciting or maintaining it. If conducting a functional behavioral assessment or developing an intervention plan is an important part of the behavioral interview, these techniques are necessary.

Implementing Behavioral Interviews with Children and Adolescents

Because behavioral interviewing techniques are associated strongly with the behavioral consultation model of problem identification and treatment, there is a definite emphasis on conducting the interview with parents and teachers, who ultimately serve as mediators in the intervention process. In many cases, however, the child or adolescent also can become an important participant in the behavioral interview process. As a general rule, the younger the child, the more difficult it is to obtain useful behavioral data in an interview, and the more important other behavioral assessment sources will be (e.g., parent interviews, direct observations, rating scales). Although interviews with young children may lead to the establishment of rapport and to the clinician being able to observe directly their social behavior, interviews with children younger than six years old typically provide little in the way of content information.

As children become older and more sophisticated in their use of verbal mediation skills, the likelihood increases that they will be able to provide valuable descriptive information in the behavioral interview process. When conducting a behavioral interview with a child who is capable of providing detailed information, it is important to move carefully from a general to a more specific level of questioning. The interview might start out with some general questions about why the client thinks he or she is being interviewed and might be an opportunity for the child to talk about his or her interests, but ultimately it should lead to specific probes of suspected problem behavior (e.g., "Tell me what usually happens before you get into fights"). As is true in the case of interviewing parents or teachers, it is important to ask questions pertaining to the child or adolescent's behavioral assets. Obtaining their perspective on what positive and appropriate behaviors they can do and what their strongest likes and dislikes are may be important when it is time to construct an intervention plan. For some students with limited communication skills, it may also be useful to conduct a more structured preference assessment as part of the interview process. Such assessments are available on www.interventioncentral.org and are useful when asking a child to point to or identify potential activities or tangible items that they prefer and that might be helpful reinforcers to use within an intervention plan (Wright, 2002). Furthermore, an example of a structured behavioral interview protocol to be used with older children and adolescents is The Functional Assessment Checklist for Students (March et al., 2000).

The following example illustrates some of the elements of conducting a semistructured behavioral interview directly with the child client. In this case, the client is an 11-year-old girl who has been referred for peer-relationship problems, and the clinician is a school psychologist, who is conducting a formal assessment:

PSYCHOLOGIST: Zoey, tell me what happens when you get into fights with the other girls you told me about.

ZOEY: Well, on Friday I got into a bad fight with Monica and Janeece. It was during recess, and I knew they were talking about me behind my back. I walked up to them and told them to just shut up.

PSYCHOLOGIST: You said you knew they were talking about you. Why did you think that?

ZOEY: I could see them talking, while they were walking away from me, and they were looking at me.

PSYCHOLOGIST: So you figured they were talking about you, even though you couldn't hear what they were saying. What happened next?

ZOEY: Well, Janeece told me to shut up, so I said, "You got issues." She called me a bitch, so I pushed her away, then Monica hit me and we started to really fight. The recess supervisor sent me to the principal's office, and I told her that I wasn't the one who started it, but she never believed me.

PSYCHOLOGIST: Do these kind of fights usually happen during recess?

ZOEY: Mostly. But sometimes during lunch and once while I was waiting for the bus.

PSYCHOLOGIST: But not during class?

ZOEY: No really, 'cause the teachers won't let me sit by kids who bother me all the time, and my homeroom teacher has my desk away from them. The teacher is usually there to stop it right away.

Similar to the previous example, this excerpt illustrates how the clinician can ask specific questions regarding the circumstances and the location of specific problem areas. Such information may prove to be invaluable in conducting a functional behavioral assessment or in developing an intervention plan.

An additional consideration of involving a child or adolescent in a behavioral-oriented interview is that it may be useful to conduct a brief joint interview with the adult and child. Particularly in the case of clinic-based assessments of child behavior problems, observing the parent and child together can provide the clinician with a rich source of direct observation data. Being able to observe the extent and quality of parent–child interactions and how they react to each other in positive and negative situations affords the opportunity for a valuable merging of behavioral interviewing and direct behavioral observation.

STRUCTURED AND SEMISTRUCTURED INTERVIEW TOOLS

Since about the 1970s, there have been several prominent efforts aimed at developing highly structured and standardized interview schedules for use with children and adolescents. Many of these structured or semistructured clinical interview instruments (or schedules, or protocols, as they sometimes are called) originally were designed for use in psychiatric settings or for epidemiology research, but they may be useful in other settings and for other purposes. These tools differ from other interview techniques because they are highly scripted, structured, and have specific purposes, such as assisting in making *DSM* diagnoses (McConaughy, 2000b, 2005, 2013; McConaughy & Whitcomb, 2022)). Frankly, most practitioners—especially school-based practitioners—will probably find that the most complex and highly structured interview tools are not practical for day-to-day use. These tools usually require extensive training and time, and are more suited for settings such as teaching hospitals, and for purposes such as research. Further, with the release of the *DSM-5*, many of the most frequently used clinical interview tools have yet to be adapted to reflect changes in diagnostic criteria, symptoms, symptom duration, and added specifiers (Leffler, Riebel, & Hughes, 2015). However, a good practitioner should be aware of what is available in this area, even if he or she does not use these tools, and some of the emerging semistructured interview tools may be useful in school-based practice. Two interview schedules that are representative of what is currently available are reviewed in some detail, and some comments on additional interview schedules that are available follow these reviews.

Schedule for Affective Disorders and Schizophrenia, School-Age Children

Also referred to as the Kiddie-SADS or K-SADS, the Schedule for Affective Disorders and Schizophrenia (SADS) for School-Age Children (Puig-Antich & Chambers, 1978) is a semistructured psychiatric diagnostic interview for children and adolescents in the six- to 17-year age range. It was developed as a downward extension of the SADS (Endicott & Spitzer, 1978). Although the title of this instrument implies that it is for the purpose of assessing affective and psychotic disorders, the K-SADS is a broad-based interview that has been used for eliciting information on a wide range of emotional and behavior problems, then classifying these problems according to *DSM* diagnostic criteria. The K-SADS has undergone extensive research and revision. The differences among previous versions have been described in detail by Ambrosini (2000).

At least three forms of the K-SADS have been developed. The Present Episode version (K-SADS-PE) was designed for use in assessing current or present (within the past year) episodes of psychopathology. The Epidemiologic version (K-SADS-E) was designed for use in assessing psychopathology that has occurred over the course of the subject's entire life. The Present and Lifetime version (K-SADS-PL) was updated in 2009 by Axelson, Birmaher, Zelazny, Kaufman, and Gill. This version integrates some components of the other two versions and includes many improvements, such as improved probes and anchor points, diagnosis-specific impairment ratings, *DSM-IV-TR* diagnostic classification linkage, and a wider variety of disorder screening capabilities. For example, extensive attention is given to bipolar disorders and pervasive developmental disorders. This review focuses on elements of the K-SADS that are common to all versions or are specific to the K-SADS-PL, given that it is a more recent version.

The K-SADS should be used only by experienced interviewers who have received specific training. The format is fairly complex and requires a degree of sophisticated judgment. All versions of the K-SADS first include a parent interview, then an interview of the child or adolescent. Each interview takes approximately one hour (or longer), so one must plan on two to three hours for the entire interview process. The interviews include a combination of unstructured or open-ended questions, and questions regarding highly specific symptoms, which are scored on a rating scale. The K-SADS allows for skipping certain areas of questioning that are not relevant for the particular client. In addition to providing specific open-ended and structured interview questions, the K-SADS provides a format for rating the overall behavioral characteristics and performance of the subject.

Data reported by Chambers et al. (1985) indicate that the K-SADS-PE has moderate test–retest reliability with parents and children over a 72-hour period (average = 0.54 across symptom categories), and adequate inter-rater reliability (.86 for parent interviews and 0.89 for child interviews) across symptom categories. A study of the validity of the K-SADS-E by Orvaschel, Puig-Antich, Chambers, Tabrizi, and Johnson (1982) compared K-SADS-E diagnoses of 17 subjects who were previously diagnosed using an earlier version of the K-SADS and found that 16 of the 17 subjects received the same diagnosis. More recent evidence on the K-SADS-PL indicates that it has good concurrent validity with diagnostic classification and standard self-report measures and has excellent test–retest reliability (Ambrosini, 2000; Kaufman, Birmaher, Brent, & Rao, 1997). In general, the evidence regarding the K-SADS indicates that it has adequate to good reliability and validity, and it has been recommended as one of the better structured interview schedules for use with children and adolescents (Hodges, 1993). To be better aligned with the *DSM-5*, the K-SADS does require some significant edits across particular diagnoses. For example, some diagnoses, such as Autism Spectrum Disorders, will require updates to symptom items, while conduct disorders will require updates to specifiers, since "with limited prosocial emotions" has been added to reflect behavior consistent with callous/unemotional traits (Leffler et al., 2015). The K-SADS may be a good choice for use in some situations in which *DSM* diagnostic criteria are important.

The Semistructured Clinical Interview for Children and Adolescents
The Semistructured Clinical Interview for Children and Adolescents (SCICA) (McConaughy & Achenbach, 2001), a more recently developed interview instrument than the three tools discussed previously, is part of the ASEBA. The SCICA, which is described in some detail by McConaughy (2000a, 2000b, 2005, 2013; McConaughy & Whitcomb, 2022), is a more recent addition to the ASEBA system and has undergone some fairly recent revisions that make it a promising clinical and research tool. In contrast to the other diagnostic interview schedules described in this chapter, which are designed to be used primarily as "stand-alone" tools, the SCICA is intended to be used as one component of a comprehensive assessment design, preferably with other parts of the ASEBA.

The SCICA is designed for use with children and adolescents aged six to 18. The method of administration and scoring within the SCICA is novel in comparison with the other structured and semistructured interview tools reviewed in this section. The interviewer conducts an open-ended interview of the child or adolescent, with questions in nine major areas, ranging from questions about activities, school, and job to questions about self-perception and feelings. Then, the interviewer evaluates the behavior of the interviewee using a standardized 120-item Observation Form and also evaluates the self-report content of the interview, using a 125-item Self-Report. The observation and self-report ratings are made using a 4-point scale, ranging from 0 (no occurrence of the problem) to 3 (definite occurrence with severe intensity of more than three minutes duration). Many of the SCICA items have direct or somewhat similar counterpart items on the CBCL and TRS components of the ASEBA system. A training videotape is available to assist users of the SCICA in learning scoring procedures.

Interviewer ratings on the SCICA are converted to *T* scores and percentile ranks using a standardized profile of problem scales. Five empirically based syndrome scales are used in deriving scores for problems observed by the interviewer: Anxious, Withdrawn/ Depressed, Language/Motor Problems, Attention Problems, and Self-Control Problems. In addition, three syndrome scales are used in driving scores for the problems reported by the child or adolescent during the interview process: Anxious/Depressed, Aggressive/ Rule-Breaking, and Somatic Complaints (for ages 12 to 18 only). Factor analysis of SCICA was used to produce an internalizing and externalizing broad-band grouping of score clusters, and there are also six optional scales that may be used to help cluster items into scores derived from *DSM-IV* diagnostic categories: Affective Problems, Anxiety Problems, Somatic Problems, Attention-Deficit/Hyperactivity Problems, Oppositional Defiant Problems, and Conduct Problems. Like other elements of the ASEBA system, the SCICA may be scored using hand-scoring profiles or by use of a computer software scoring program. Scores are aggregated by the six to 11 and 12 to 18 age groupings. Score distributions of both typical and clinic-referred youths were used by the authors to develop clinical cutoff scores.

Prior to the publication of the 2001 second edition of the SCICA, the senior author of this tool noted, "Although the SCICA does not have the extensive research base of the structured and semistructured diagnostic interviews, findings to date support its reliability and validity for multimethod assessment of children's problems" (McConaughy, 2000b, p. 343). Norms for the SCICA were derived from 686 children referred to a clinic setting and adequate test–retest reliability estimates were achieved (mean *r* across scales = 0.78). Some new research findings have been compiled since the 2001 revision, although it is fair to say that the amount of evidence for the SCICA is still limited and does not equal what is available for the three older structured interview systems that were reviewed previously. That said, the SCICA is recommended as an innovative semi-structured interview tool for use with children and adolescents. Although training is required for effective use of the SCICA, it is not as complicated as some other standardized interview systems, and clinicians who are already familiar with the other components of the ASEBA system should have little problem learning it, especially if the training videotape is used. One of the primary advantages of the SCICA is its connection to the ASEBA system, and the common platform for deriving scores from interview items, which is part of this connection. Future research may help to further establish the SCICA, but it presently appears to have sufficient technical integrity, user-friendliness, and usefulness to warrant its use as part of a multimethod assessment.

Concluding Comments on Formal Interview Schedules

As was stated earlier, these two interview schedules do not represent the entire domain of semistructured and highly structured interview tools that are available for use with children and adolescents. The National Institute of Mental Health Diagnostic Interview Schedule for Children (DISC-IV) (Shaffer, Fisher, Lucas, Dulcan, & Schwab-Stone, 2000) is a widely known structured interview schedule for use in assessing child and adolescent behavioral emotional problems, and it has been through several revisions over the years. Other structured interview schedules that have been reported in the child psychiatry and psychology literature include the Interview Schedule for Children and Adolescents (ISCA) (Sherrill & Kovacs, 2000), the Mental Health Assessment Form (MHAF) (Kestenbaum & Bird, 1978), and the Children's Interview for Psychiatric Syndromes (ChIPS) (Weller, Weller, Rooney, & Fristad, 1999). The two interview schedules reviewed in this chapter were featured because of factors such as availability, amount and quality of psychometric data, ease of use, and general purpose design.

Formal structured and semistructured interview schedules are an important development in the area of child and adolescent assessment, particularly in the arenas of psychiatry and mental health. For the most part, they represent high-quality attempts to integrate a stronger empirical base into the process of clinical interviewing. These tools appear to be particularly useful for assisting in generating *DSM* diagnoses, but many need revisions to be more consistent with *DSM-5*, and they are decidedly less useful for day-to-day assessment of child problem behaviors in school settings.

CLINICAL INTERVIEWING AND SUICIDAL IDEATION OR BEHAVIOR

Suicide is one of the most disturbing phenomena faced by mental health professionals. It is particularly troubling when a person who makes a suicide attempt is a child or adolescent. Many individuals simply cannot understand why a young person—someone with "his or her whole life ahead of them"—would even consider the possibility of taking his or her own life. To most individuals, suicide is an intensely irrational act. The evidence regarding suicide convinces us that it cannot be dismissed, however, and that children, especially adolescents, are not immune to it. Because suicide attempts and completions by children and adolescents seem to be increasing in the United States, and because clinical interviewing is the most widely used and direct method of assessing suicidal ideation (thinking about suicide) and potential suicidal behavior (specific behaviors aimed at suicide), this section is included. First, some facts regarding suicidal ideation and suicidal behavior among young people are provided. Second, recommendations for conducting clinical interviews with children and adolescents who may be suicidal are offered. This treatment of clinical interviewing and suicide is necessarily brief. Readers who desire a more in-depth treatment of the topic are referred to chapters by Brock and Sandoval (1997), McConaughy (2013), and Sattler (1998); books by Berman and Jobes (1991), Davis and Sandoval (1991), Erbacher, Singer, and Poland (2015) and D. N. Miller (2011); and articles by Peach and Reddick (1991) and Shaffer, Garland, Gould, Fisher, and Trautman (1988).

Facts Regarding Suicidal Behavior among Children and Adolescents

When we discuss statistics concerning suicide among young persons, it is important to recognize that there are many problems with the data, including the fact that most of the available data are a few years old, and that the data are in some cases contradictory. Many (perhaps most) suicide attempts go unreported, and many suicides are misinterpreted or reported as accidents. The available evidence does indicate, however, that suicide among children and adolescents is a significant problem in U.S. society. It appears that the rate of suicide among young people in the United States has increased since the 1990s. Statistics for younger children are virtually nonexistent. For elementary-age and middle school-age children (ages ten to 14), Curtin, Warner, and Hedegaard (2016) reported a suicide rate of 0.5 per 100,000 for females and 1.9 per 100,000 rate for males in 1990, compared to a 2014 female suicide rate of 1.5 per 100,000 and male suicide rate of 2.6 per 100,000. For ages 15–24, this report included a female suicide rate of 3.0 per 100,000 and a male rate of 16.8 per 100,000 in 1990. This is compared to 2014, when the female rate was 4.6 per 100,000 and 18.2 per 100,000 for males. Although these rates are not as high as the suicide rates for any adult age group in the United States, they are troubling, not only because of their mere existence, but also because of their continually increasing trend. More recent data from the Centers for Disease Control (2006) indicates that the increasing rates of youth suicide in the U.S. appear to have leveled off or even diminished since the 1990s, but they are still much higher than in the 1960s and 1970s, and the problem is considered to be unacceptable.

Although suicidal ideation and suicidal behavior potentially may affect young persons from virtually any demographic, there are clear demographic trends regarding who is more likely to make and complete suicide attempts. Regarding gender, girls are more likely than boys to make suicide attempts, but boys are more likely than girls to complete suicide attempts. Among adolescents of all racial and ethnic groups, girls were about twice as likely as boys to make a suicide attempt, but boys were about four times as likely as girls to die by suicide (Centers for Disease Control, 2006). There are some substantial group differences regarding race and ethnicity. According to the 2012 Statistical Abstract of the United States from the U.S. Census Bureau, non-Hispanic/White males account for 21.9 per 100,000 suicides, and Indigenous American/Alaska Native males account for 18.1 per 100,000 suicides. Further, LGBTQ are perhaps at most risk as 1 in 3 youth attempt suicide.

There are additional, numerous risk factors that may increase vulnerability among young people to suicidal ideation and behavior. Although these risk factors are complex and in many cases interactive, some of the major ones are thought to be the following:

- psychological disorders, particularly depression and conduct disorder;
- substance abuse;
- family history of suicide;
- family history of significant medical and psychiatric illness;
- chronic and debilitating illness;
- feelings of hopelessness;
- severe life stress, especially involving perceived losses.

These risk factors, when they exist in isolation, may be relatively weak predictors of suicide; however, they may have an interactive effect on each other. In other words, the presence of additional risk factors may increase vulnerability to suicide in more of a multiplicative than additive manner.

Experts on child and adolescent suicide have noted that although suicide attempts may occur suddenly after a single traumatic stressor, they usually are preceded by a number of signals or warning signs that may predict the suicide attempt (McConaughy, 2013). Although it is crucial to recognize that such warning signs may be numerous, complex, and weakly predictive in individual situations, they nevertheless should be scrutinized carefully. Some of the most commonly identified suicide warning signs include the following:

- suicide notes;
- suicide threats, suicidal statements, both direct and indirect;
- preoccupation with death and related themes;
- romanticizing and glorifying death;
- making final arrangements (e.g., saying goodbye, giving possessions away);
- feelings of helplessness and hopelessness;
- withdrawal from family and friends;
- loss of interest in activities that were previously important;
- heavy use and abuse of drugs, including alcohol;
- marked changes in temperament and/or behavior.

There is some overlap between the list of risk factors and the list of warning signs. Some characteristics or behaviors seem to serve both purposes. Most children and adolescents who become suicidal are not likely to be observed by persons who are highly familiar with the warning signs of suicide. It is more realistic to think that the persons most likely to observe suicide warning signs will be parents, friends, and teachers. Professional education and outreach activities regarding warning signs are imperative.

Recommendations for Clinical Interviewing

While sometimes controversial, many schools have begun to consider implementation of school-based suicide prevention screening and programming (Hamilton & Klimes-Dougan, 2015; Lazear, Roggenbaum, & Blasé, 2012; Schilling, Aseltine, & James, 2016). This work requires building school professionals' capacity to understand and notice student behaviors that may suggest risk as well as planned responses to students' self-reports of suicide risk. Although some good tools for screening for suicidal tendencies among adolescents have been developed, such as W. M. Reynolds' (1987) Suicidal Ideation Questionnaire, most clinicians use a more traditional interview format for such assessment. If this is the case, it is crucial that particular questions be asked and that particular areas of content be included in the interview. There should be *some strands of evidence* within the overall assessment or the content of the interview that first alert the interviewer that the client may be suicidal. Questions regarding the client's affect, level of engagement in activities, substance abuse, changes in routines and behavior, and especially feelings of helplessness and hopelessness may serve to drive hypotheses regarding potential suicidal characteristics. These areas of questioning may be part of a standard clinical interview but may be formed by analysis of other assessment data, such as self-report tests and behavior rating scales. Prior conversations with parents and teachers also may provide information that may help focus the content of the interview toward suicide assessment.

When the clinician has enough evidence to justify some concern or suspicion regarding the client's potential suicidal ideation or behavior, it is crucial simply to "jump right in" and conduct a suicide assessment interview. A common mistake that is made by inexperienced clinicians is that clients will be too hesitant to respond to questions regarding suicide or that they may become extremely upset if such questions are asked. In reality, the inexperienced clinician may be the one who is more likely to feel uncomfortable or upset by such questioning. On a personal note to back up this assertion, consider Merrell's own experience teaching an assessment class while in the process of revising this text for a previous edition. During the lecture and discussion on interviewing potentially suicidal youths, the class included an activity where graduate students in the class conducted practice interviews by following carefully scripted scenarios. The discussion following this activity was revealing and actually carried into the next week. Graduate students who had little or no prior experience interviewing suicidal clients were in several cases very upset by the scripted practice scenarios, and it was necessary for Merrell to spend a considerable amount of time debriefing after the exercise, following up with students individually, and discussing the issue of conducting this activity in real practice. While this may seem time consuming and perhaps uncomfortable, it is important to have the opportunity to practice such skills and to think through potential scenarios prior to engaging in this work in the "real world."

The experience of most clinicians who work with emotionally and behaviorally troubled children and adolescents is that they are relatively candid regarding suicidal thought and action and may be willing to discuss it because of their ambivalent feelings or desire to receive help. If there are reasonable concerns, the clinician should initiate a suicide assessment interview and take all statements regarding suicidal ideation and thought seriously. If there are no valid reasons for such concern, this will become manifest quickly enough during such an interview, and the clinician can move on to a more relevant topic.

There are many ways that suicide assessment questions may be asked, and these need to be modified depending on the developmental characteristics of the client. Certain areas of questioning are deemed crucial, however, in conducting a suicide assessment interview.

Thinking about Suicide The first area of questioning is to ask the child or adolescent if he or she has been thinking about killing himself or herself. For younger and less cognitively sophisticated clients, this area of questioning may need to be modified because the concept of death may be difficult for them to comprehend fully. In such cases, questions such as "Have you been thinking about wanting to be dead?" or "Do you sometimes wish you could make yourself be dead?" might be appropriate.

Suicide Plan If there is sufficient evidence that the client has been having suicidal thoughts, it is crucial to ascertain whether a particular plan for suicide is in place. Questions such as "Do you have a plan?" "Have you thought about how you might kill yourself?" or "Do you have specific ideas about how you might kill yourself?" may be useful in this regard. Clinicians should be particularly aware of how concrete or detailed such plans are. It is generally agreed that the more specific or detailed the plan, the more the individual has thought about suicide.

Means and Preparations for Suicide If the client indicates that he or she has a plan, the next area of questioning should be aimed at determining if the client actually has the means at hand (or specific preparations) to carry out such a plan. Questions such as "Do you have the means to carry out your plan, with you now, at school, or at home?"

might be used. If the plan is specific and, for example, involves a gun, the clinician simply should ask the child or adolescent, "Do you have a gun?" or "Is there somewhere you can get a gun?" At this point, it is crucial to become very specific. Clinicians should find out exactly where the lethal means are (e.g., "in my dad's gun cabinet in the basement").

Intended Place or Setting Assuming a suicide plan is in place, the clinician should ask where the client intends to commit the act. Such specificity in questioning has resulted in a prevented suicide on many occasions. It also may be helpful to ask whether the client has written a suicide note and, if so, what it says and where it is. A statement or question such as "You told me that you were seriously thinking about killing yourself, and that you would probably do it with the sleeping pills in your mother's medicine cabinet. Have you thought about where you might take the pills?"

Immediate Protective Action If one has proceeded through a suicide assessment interview and becomes convinced that the client has been seriously considering the possibility of killing himself or herself, ethics, law, and professional practice dictate that there is responsibility to take further action to support and protect the client. In the most serious cases, in which it is apparent that the client is clearly intent on killing himself or herself and has a plan and lethal means in place, immediate and direct action must be taken. First, the clinician *should never leave a suicidal client alone in an unsecured setting,* even for a short time. Second, clinicians should follow whatever protocol or policy is in place for such emergencies at their place of practice. Regarding this issue, Sattler (1998) stated, "If you decide there is a risk of imminent danger, notify the parents immediately, ask them to come to your office to get their child, and advise them to hospitalize their child" (p. 441). All U.S. states have provisions within licensing and certification laws regarding protecting clients from harming themselves. The clinician must be aware of the laws and policies in his or her area and be prepared to follow them in such emergency situations. In most areas, law enforcement officers may be called for assistance in situations in which there is clearly imminent danger and there is no reasonable means to get the in-danger person to the proper evaluation and treatment facility (i.e., the parents are not available or are not willing to provide assistance).

Suicidal Safety Planning Assuming that the clinician ascertains that a child or adolescent client has been thinking seriously about suicide, but there is no evidence of imminent danger, another set of supportive and protective actions is called for. Clinicians often elicit a promise or contract from the client that he or she will not engage in a suicide attempt or any related harmful behavior and that he or she will call the clinician (or their counselor/ therapist) if he or she begins to think seriously about it. Such contracts may be in formal written form or in the form of a verbal agreement. While clinicians often engage in this contract process, it has actually not been found to be effective (Matarazzo, Homaifar, & Wortzel, 2014). Instead, clinicians are encouraged to engage in more of a supportive safety planning process in which they help clients to identify their own warning signs; to build coping strategies; to consider social environments or people that might help them be distracted from feelings of distress; to identify people who can help; and to learn about who to call and where to go during a crisis (Matarazzo et al., 2014). In situations in which there is clear risk but no apparent immediate danger, it is important to discuss what resources the client may have to help him or her through this difficult time. Is there someone or something that would stop the client from making a suicide attempt? Is there someone with whom they are comfortable talking about their feelings? Have they talked to family or friends about their feelings? These types of questions help to set the stage for getting the client to think in terms of available support and appropriate courses of action to take when he or she is distressed.

Even if the child or adolescent client does not seem to be imminently dangerous to himself or herself, it is still recommended in most cases that the parents be called and asked to visit with the clinician. Although the clinician may have made an agreement with the client that their conversations would be held in confidence, danger of suicide is always considered an exception to confidentiality rules, and prudent clinicians make sure their clients understand this fact (and related exceptions to confidentiality) up front. The discussion with the parents should be frank and should assist in determining what support and resources the family is capable of providing and educating them regarding appropriate actions to take. Most parents in such a situation are fearful and upset and may need substantial confidence and support. Finally, it is crucial for clinicians to consult with other professionals (especially their supervisor) regarding suicidal clients and to determine jointly an appropriate course of action, such as follow-up plans or making a referral. The burden of clinical interviewing with a suicidal child or adolescent is simply too great to carry alone, and in this case, the old adage "when in doubt, consult" is particularly important.

In sum, clinical interviewing of children and adolescents who may be suicidal is a special circumstance and requires specific interviewing behavior and follow-up actions. Regardless of the setting in which they work, it is essential that clinicians who work with emotionally and behaviorally troubled youth become familiar with best practices for interviewing suicidal clients and that they establish and follow a practice or agency protocol for dealing with such situations. On a final note, be aware that this kind of work can be very taxing on the professional, and there are many ways for it to go wrong, even if all the proper steps have been followed. It may be useful to *agree to not be exceptional* at this difficult work.

INTERVIEWS AND DECISION MAKING

How useful are interviews when it comes to decision making? They can range from moderately useful to extremely useful, depending on the specific decision-making process. For making additional assessment decisions, interviewing can provide excellent information regarding specific additional areas that need to be assessed. During the process of interviewing, additional information may surface that will persuade the interviewer of the necessity for observation or other objective assessment in specific areas. Interview information can be important for diagnosis and classification decision making, although it seldom should be used alone. For special education classification, it is essential that decisions not be made based on a single assessment method. For making *DSM* diagnostic decisions, the interview normally serves as an important aspect, perhaps a keystone of a comprehensive assessment, although in some cases, *DSM* diagnoses can be made based on interview data alone. In making placement decisions, interview data can provide necessary clues and be used to support inferences drawn from additional information sources, but data alone are seldom sufficient to make the decision. One of the best uses of information obtained through interviews is for intervention or treatment decisions. If the interviews were structured carefully to identify specific problems and the environmental conditions eliciting and maintaining those problems (e.g., behavioral interviewing), there may be obvious implications for developing an intervention plan or at least for conducting a functional behavior assessment. In the case of developing prevention or intervention responses for suicidal youth, interviewing is likely the single best source of information.

CONCLUSIONS

Interviewing holds a place of prominence as an assessment method among mental health professionals. Even among the lay public, interview assessments by specially trained professionals are accorded high status and may even be the object of unrealistically high expectations. Although interviews appear simply to be special cases of a conversation, they are in fact much more complex in that they are goal-oriented and the interviewer attempts to shape or lead the direction of the conversation to fulfill specific information-gathering purposes. There are several methods of interviewing, ranging from being loose to tight in structure. Interviews have many advantages. They have disadvantages as well, however, and foremost among these disadvantages is the well-known problem of unreliability across interviewers.

Effective clinical interviewing of children and adolescents absolutely requires the clinician to have knowledge of developmental issues and to use this knowledge to inform the interviewing technique. Each of the three major developmental stages of early childhood, middle childhood, and adolescence includes major cognitive developmental milestones and changes and challenges in social–emotional functioning. Regardless of the chronological age of the child or adolescent client, it is essential to ascertain quickly his or her functioning in the various developmental areas and to build the interview format and activities based on developmentally appropriate expectations and tasks.

Several key factors may affect the overall quality of the interview. Perhaps most crucial among these factors is the interpersonal context, or the relationship that is established between the interviewer and the interviewee. One's culture may decidedly shape the interpersonal communication style and characteristics, and clinicians must show appropriate understanding of, and sensitivity to, race, ethnicity, and other cultural variables that may be important in establishing effective communication. Behavior of the client during an interview may be shaped by the clinician to optimize the validity of the interview through making specific requests and through modeling appropriate ways of responding. The physical context of the interview is an important factor in affecting interview quality. Clinicians should arrange and modify the physical circumstances of the interview setting to make the child or adolescent feel comfortable, safe, and secure.

Traditional interviewing techniques tend to be relatively unstructured and highly flexible and are probably the most commonly used of any of the interviewing techniques. In conducting traditional unstructured interviews, clinicians should strive to obtain appropriate relevant historical and developmental information from parents, develop the interview in a manner that meets their goals for interviewing, and carefully observe certain key behaviors of the interviewee. Traditionally, there are several specific areas of questioning that are useful to focus on in conducting clinical interviews.

Behavioral interviewing tends to be more structured than traditional interviewing and is aimed clearly at identifying crucial events and behaviors that elicit, shape, or maintain the presenting social–emotional problems. Behavioral interviews tend to involve parents and teachers in a consultation model of service delivery. Behavioral interviews may provide an important foundation for conducting a functional behavior assessment. Various models have been presented for conducting behavioral consultation interviews, but most are oriented toward identifying and analyzing the problem in behavioral terms and, most importantly, identifying possible intervention agents and factors to change problem behaviors.

Several structured interview schedules have been developed for use with children and adolescents. These structured interview schedules, such as the K-SADS and SCICA, in most cases tend to be scripted and time-consuming and require extensive interviewer training. In their better manifestations, such structured interview schedules can yield high reliability across interviewers, however, something that is notoriously difficult with less structured interview methods. Also, some of these structured interview methods, particularly the K-SADS, have been shown to have good diagnostic validity from a *DSM* diagnostic perspective. Some emerging interview tools, such as the SCICA, show a great deal of promise as alternatives to the traditional structured diagnostic schedules.

For assessing children and adolescents who may be suicidal, clinical interviewing is the pre-eminent method and offers many advantages over other methods, such as rating scales, self-report tests, and direct behavioral observation. Suicide among children and adolescents appears to be a significant phenomenon in U.S. society. It is essential that clinicians who work with troubled children and adolescents become knowledgeable in conducting a suicide assessment interview. Such an interview requires specific areas of direct questioning to ascertain if the individual may be suicidal, if he or she has a specific plan and lethal means in place, and what supports may be available to individuals to help them cope with suicidal feelings and thoughts. Ethically, there are specific obligations that professionals assume when interviewing a suicidal child or adolescent, specifically, the duty to protect. In the most serious cases, immediate protective action must be taken, which in some cases involves immediate hospitalization or asking for the assistance of law enforcement officers. In cases in which the threat of danger to the self seems less clear and imminent but is still probable, other precautionary and follow-up measures should be taken. When dealing with suicidal children and adolescents, it is often necessary to break the confidentiality of the communication and to notify other persons, particularly the child's parents. Working with suicidal clients is too great of a burden for one professional to deal with in isolation. Discussing suicidal cases with a supervisor is a given, and practices and agencies should have clear guidelines in place for such situations. Even for clinicians in solo private practices, it is crucial to consult with trusted colleagues regarding the appropriate course of action: "When in doubt, consult."

REVIEW AND APPLICATION QUESTIONS

1. Regarding physical circumstances of clinical interviews with children, what is the recommended optimal furniture and space setup to facilitate comfort and communication?
2. Several typical interpersonal communication styles and behaviors related to the racial or ethnic background of individuals were described in this chapter. How well do such

generalities predict individual behavior, and what are some problems related to overgeneralizing such inferences regarding group differences?

3. Regarding cognitive development of children and adolescents, how should our knowledge of developmental stages shape specific interviewing practices with preschool-age and primary-age children, with elementary-age children, and with adolescents?

4. Regarding social–emotional development of children and adolescents, how should our knowledge of developmental stages shape specific interviewing practices with preschool-age and primary-age children, with elementary-age children, and with adolescents?

5. What are some practical ways that behavioral interviewing might be useful in identifying possible functions of behavior and in developing future intervention plans?

6. For what purposes are structured and semistructured clinical interview schedules such as the K-SADS and SCICA most appropriate?

7. When should a statement by a child or adolescent regarding suicide be taken seriously?

8. If one is concerned that an interviewee may be suicidal, what are the most essential areas of questioning to pursue?

9. What prior preparations are recommended for breaking confidentiality between clinicians and minor clients in the case of suicidal ideation or behavior?

7

SOCIOMETRIC TECHNIQUES

Sociometric techniques include a variety of procedures used within social groups to measure such related constructs as social status, popularity, peer acceptance or rejection, and reputation. Sociometric techniques are not new; in fact, they have been used in educational–clinical practice and research since the 1930s. Several important research efforts in this area occurred between the 1960s and 1980s. These landmark studies (e.g., Cowen, Pederson, Babigan, Izzo, & Trost, 1973; Dodge, Coie, & Brakke, 1982; Roff, 1961) emphasized the importance of social functioning in childhood and underscored the importance of clinicians who work with children having a basic knowledge of sociometric assessment methods, regardless of whether they use these techniques on a regular basis.

This chapter begins with a discussion of the conceptual and historical foundations of sociometric assessment and some information about the validity of sociometrics for various clinical and research purposes. The largest section of the chapter is devoted to detailed overviews of four general types of sociometric methods: peer nominations, peer ratings, sociometric rankings, and alternative sociometric procedures. General and specific aspects of assessment using these four approaches are discussed, and numerous examples are presented. Following the overview of specific sociometric assessment techniques, some ethical and pragmatic issues regarding sociometric assessment are explored. The chapter ends with a discussion on how sociometric assessment can be used best in making various types of clinical and educational decisions.

SOCIOMETRICS: IMPORTANCE, HISTORY, AND EMPIRICAL BASE

Sociometric assessment procedures involve gathering information directly from within a peer group (usually in a classroom setting) concerning the social dynamics of that group. The key ingredient of sociometric assessment is that data on various aspects of social status of persons within the peer group are obtained *directly from its members*, rather than through observations or ratings by impartial outside evaluators. These procedures allow the assessor to tap directly into the ongoing social dynamics of a group, an obvious advantage because there are many aspects of social relationships within a group that are not easily discernible to the casual observer (Merrell & Gimpel, 1998; Worthen et al., 1993).

Sociometric assessment provides an avenue for measuring constructs such as level of popularity; peer acceptance or rejection status; and attribution of specific positive and negative characteristics such as leadership ability, athletic or academic prowess,

DOI: 10.4324/9781315747521-8

aggressiveness, and social awkwardness. In contrast to many other assessment methods, sociometric procedures are not usually norm-referenced, standardized, or commercially published. Instead, they tend to consist of different variations of a few relatively simple methods originally developed for use by researchers but capable of being translated into school or clinical practice.

Why Assess Social Status?

In 1917, C. R. Beery, a prominent educator, published a series of books titled *Practical Child Training*. In this series, Beery offered some practical advice to mothers who had children with few friends and difficulty approaching peers. Beery suggested that mothers could help these children by facilitating opportunities for peer interaction, such as a picnic that would include their children's classmates. He noted that these types of activities would help children to "have a royal good time" and further suggested that if a child shows fear in approaching other children, the mother should "not scold or make any scene, but simply appear to pay no attention to him" (cited in Asher & Parker, 1989, p. 5). Although advice to parents may now take a different form in contemporary contexts, this anecdote demonstrates that concern regarding the quality of children's social interactions with peers has been of academic and practical importance for many years.

As we see herein, the study of social status is important because peer relationship problems during childhood may have a potentially large and lasting impact on later adjustment in life, whether positive or negative. How extensive are peer relationship problems during childhood? Based on a classic study by Hymel and Asher (1977), wherein typical elementary-age children were asked to nominate their three best friends, Asher (1990) provided a conservative estimate that about 10% of all children experience significant peer relationship difficulties. This estimate is based on Hymel and Asher's finding that about 10% of the children in the study were not named as anybody's best friend. Asher (1990) noted that if the criterion of reciprocal friendship nominations is used, the estimated percentage of children with peer relationship problems is substantially higher. We can make a conservative estimate that at least 10% of all school-age children experience notable problems in developing friendships and in gaining social acceptance. Given the poor long-term prognosis that may follow many of these children, this figure is alarming.

The study and assessment of children's social status is also important because of the positive developmental purposes that children's friendships serve. Fine (1981) noted that children's friendships serve an important purpose by making a significant contribution to the development of their overall interactional competence. In other words, through the processes that friendship building requires and refines, children not only learn to interact effectively with their friends, but also develop social-interactional skills that may generalize to many other situations and persons. Fine specifically identified three functions of preadolescent friendships that contribute to general interactional competence. First, friendships provide a *staging area* for behavior. Friendships are situated in social environments that have implications for the acquisition of interactional competencies. Second, friendships are *cultural institutions,* and as such they provide didactic training. Third, friendships provide a *context for the growth* of the child's social self, a context within which he or she can learn the appropriate self-image to project in social situations (p. 49). Understanding some of these dynamics regarding the positive developmental aspects of children's friendships allows us to understand better why peer relationship problems in childhood can be so detrimental. Essentially the development of positive peer relationships via friendship making is a crucial aspect of a child's overall cognitive and social development.

Historical Development of Sociometric Assessment

The use of sociometric assessment procedures dates back to the 1930s, with the first clinical and research uses of these techniques being conducted by educators and sociologists. One of the first published works on sociometry was a highly influential book by Moreno (1934), ominously titled *Who Shall Survive?* The earliest attempts to use sociometric assessments were experimental and novel, but by the late 1930s and early 1940s, reports of the systematic use of sociometry began appearing in scholarly journals. The journal *Sociometry* began publication in the 1930s and included a mix of articles showing applications of sociometric techniques in educational practice and sociological research. Several research reports using sociometric assessment were published in the *Journal of Educational Psychology* in the early 1940s, as exemplified through articles by Bonney (1943) and Young and Cooper (1944).

By the 1950s, the state of sociometric assessment had advanced considerably, and many books were published on the topic (e.g., Cunningham, 1951; Laughlin, 1954; Taba, Brady, Robinson, & Vickery, 1951). During this period, and probably through the early to mid-1960s, sociometric procedures were used commonly as a means of measuring social adjustment in public school settings, in what can now be viewed as a kind of "golden age" of sociometry. Starting in about the mid-1960s, the use of sociometrics as a typical school-based assessment procedure appears to have declined. Possible reasons for the declining clinical or practical use of sociometrics may include the advancement of other forms of assessment (specifically behavior rating scales and objective self-report measures), emerging new ethical and legal standards regarding informed consent and assent, public and professional concerns that sociometric assessment may have some negative effects on some children, and the increasingly stringent nature of ethical guidelines for research and human subjects institutional review boards. Although concerns do exist about the potential negative effects of sociometric assessment, these concerns have not necessarily been substantiated through research. The ethical–professional concerns associated with sociometric assessment are discussed later.

Although sociometric techniques are still used widely by researchers in the fields of child development, education, sociology, and psychology, their use as a standard method for assessing social adjustment problems in schools appears to be less than it was in the 1970s and 1980s. Surveys of school psychologists during the 1980s (Goh & Fuller, 1983), 1990s (Hutton, Dubes, & Muir, 1992), and 2000s (Shapiro & Heick, 2004) indicated that sociometric procedures were used so seldom by practitioners that they did not even appear on tables of survey results.

One area in which sociometry has begun to gain momentum in education, however, is in use of statistical packages that support Social Network Analysis (SNA) methodology to "map" relationships within an organization (e.g., school, classroom). SNA is different from typical sociometric techniques that aim to better understand attributes of individuals (e.g., students) and how individuals are separated based on attributes. SNA, rather, is predicated on understanding shared attributes and relational ties between individuals to understand social influence, diffusion of ideas, and achievement of outcomes (Grunspan, Wiggins, & Goodreau, 2014). Whether there will be increased use of sociometric assessment in the future remains to be seen, but it is doubtful that sociometry, used to understand attributes and clinical concerns, will regain the level of popularity that it had during its heyday in the 1940s and 1950s, if for no other reason than because of the advent and refinement of so many other competing assessment procedures that were not available at that time, coupled with the challenges of obtaining informed consent and assent on a groupwide basis.

Validity of Sociometric Assessment

Dimensions of Social Status According to Landau and Milich (1990), early researchers in the use of sociometrics tended to view social status in a fairly unidimensional manner. More recent efforts in this area have led investigators to conclude, however, that the construct of social status is complex and multidimensional. In a landmark study, Coie, Dodge, and Coppotelli (1982) used peer preference questions in a sociometric technique with a large number ($N = 5,537$) of elementary-age and middle school-age children and analyzed the obtained data to develop five different social-status groups: popular, rejected, average, neglected, and controversial. An analysis of characteristics of the students indicated that although there was some overlap between categories, each category had some distinct features. *Popular* children were those who were rated by peers as being cooperative, having leadership ability, and engaging in little disruptive behavior. *Rejected* children were rated as frequently fighting and being disruptive and not being cooperative or having leadership traits. *Neglected* children were those who were largely ignored by other children and were seen as being socially unresponsive. The fourth nonaverage group, *controversial* children, tended to exhibit features of the popular and the rejected group, being considered disruptive and aggressive, but also as being assertive leaders. This widely cited and influential conceptualization of social-status ratings shows how complex social dynamics within peer groups can be and indicates that sociometric procedures can provide complex and compelling social assessment data.

Table 7.1 presents the four nonaverage groups from the Coie et al. (1982) study, with a listing of the social–behavioral characteristics pertinent for each group. In viewing this conceptualization of children's social-status groupings, it is important to recognize that this system is not without criticism.

Because Coie et al.'s system has been so widely influential, it has been adopted by researchers for various purposes in several investigations. Not all of these studies have

Table 7.1 Descriptions of four nonaverage child and adolescent social status

Group	Sociometric findings and social–behavior characteristics
Popular	Receive the most positive and fewest negative nominations; described by peers in prosocial terms and perceived as leaders
Rejected	Receive the most negative nominations; described by peers as being disruptive and likely to fight; perceived as having poor leadership skills and being uncooperative
Neglected	Receive few positive or negative peer nominations; described by peers as being shy and unassertive; perceived as having poor social skills
Controversial	Have characteristics similar to popular and rejected groups; described by peers as being active and assertive leaders, but also perceived as being disruptive, demanding, and frequently not liked

Note: Based on research by Coie, Dodge, and Coppotelli (1982).

produced results supportive of the classification system. Gresham and Stuart (1992) found that the categories in the Coie et al. system (particularly the Controversial category) were relatively unstable over a one-year interval and produced high reclassification errors. Foster, Bell-Dolan, and Berler (1986) maintained that the Coie et al. classification system produced subject selection bias and overlapped poorly with teacher nomination and assessment methods. These two studies do not negate the usefulness of the classification system but should serve to promote careful consideration and caution in its use.

Technical Adequacy of Sociometric Procedures The technical and psychometric aspects of various sociometric procedures have been investigated in numerous studies. In general, the yield of this research has shown favorable evidence of the technical adequacy of sociometrics, leading the authors of one comprehensive review of sociometrics to state, "We find clear evidence of the importance and utility of sociometrics" (McConnell & Odom, 1986, p. 275). Temporal stability of sociometric assessments has been shown to be relatively high at short-term and long-term stability periods (Hartup, 1983; Jiang & Cillessen, 2005; Roff, Sells, & Golden, 1972). Landau and Milich (1990) reviewed several studies of inter-rater correspondence in sociometric procedures and noted moderate to high levels of correspondence between raters. There is one interesting and peculiar finding in this regard, however: a gender difference on social convergence in ratings wherein *boys and girls tend to attribute more positive attributes to members of their own sex and more negative attributes to members of the opposite sex.* A methodologically sophisticated study on this topic by Hayden-Thomson, Rubin, and Hymel (1987) went a step beyond simply identifying the fact that boys and girls tend to provide more positive nominations and ratings to each other than to members of the opposite sex. In this study, gender biases in children's sociometric preferences were examined developmentally. The authors used a two-study cross-sectional design to obtain rating scale data from 195 girls and 191 boys in kindergarten through third grade and 91 girls and 88 boys in third grade through sixth grade. As expected, the results indicated that children at each grade level rated their classmates of the opposite sex significantly lower than same-sex peers. A significant linear trend for these gender biases was found, however, wherein the negative gender biases of boys and girls *increased with age.* This trend was particularly evident at the early grade levels. The generally strong inter-rater correspondence in sociometric assessment may not generalize well when cross-gender data are considered, particularly as children move from early childhood to intermediate elementary grades.

The role that context plays in understanding the stability of sociometric preferences has also recently been studied. Martin (2011) published an article in which he had surveyed the sociometric preferences of 522 students from the island of Tenerife. Surveys required students to state their most and least preferred classmates in academic settings and in leisure (recess) settings. About 50% of students' ratings changed depending on context. Ratings included children identified as *preferred, rejected, ignored, controversial,* and *unclassified.* Students rated as *rejected* had the most stable scores across settings while students rated as *controversial* in one setting were those that were most likely to receive a different rating in another setting.

Predictive Validity of Sociometric Assessment Predictive validity, or ability to predict future social outcomes of sociometric assessment procedures, has been established through several widely cited studies. Cowen et al. (1973) used the Class Play peer assessment procedure in their longitudinal study of 537 children who were tested in three different cohorts in either the first grade or the third grade. The children who were nominated more frequently for negative roles in the Class Play assessment were more likely to receive psychiatric services as adults, based on their names appearing on registers of psychiatric services.

Roff (1961) conducted a prospective study of 164 boys who were referred to child guidance clinics and who later served in one of the branches of the U.S. military. On the basis of a review of the participants' case histories as children and their adult service records, those who were reported to have poor peer adjustment were significantly more likely to receive bad-conduct discharges from the military than the children who were reported to have good peer relations. Approximately half of the subjects in this study ultimately received bad-conduct discharges. Another widely cited and highly influential study by Roff and his colleagues (Roff & Sells, 1968; Roff et al., 1972) used a longitudinal design in studying various social–behavioral characteristics of approximately 40,000 children who were enrolled in grades 3 through 6 in public schools in Minnesota and Texas. The sociometric assessment data for this study included peer nominations and teacher ratings. When records of delinquency were evaluated four years after the completion of the sociometric assessments, it was found that low-rated children were significantly more likely to appear on rosters of juvenile offenders in the corrections system. These classic studies from the watershed era of sociometric assessment indicate that important future social outcomes are associated strongly with sociometric assessment information obtained during childhood and adolescence.

Sociometric status also has been shown to be a significant factor in predicting school dropout patterns. Ullman (1957) studied peer and teacher sociometric ratings of students in 11 ninth-grade classes and found that positive sociometric ratings were predictive of being named on honor rolls at graduation, whereas negative sociometric ratings were predictive of the students' dropping out of school before graduation.

In sum, although sociometric assessment procedures tend not to be standardized or commercially published, like many other forms of assessment, they nevertheless have been shown to have favorable technical properties and should be viewed as a potentially useful method of assessing peer relations and social status. Understanding social networks could be incredibly helpful when planning targeted interventions aiming to support individual behavioral change or the overall dynamic of a group or classroom.

OVERVIEW OF SOCIOMETRIC ASSESSMENT PROCEDURES

Because most sociometric assessment procedures are nonstandardized and have a considerable amount of overlap with each other, it is difficult to divide them into distinct categories. There are some distinctive similarities and differences among various methods, however, that make a general categorization possible. This section provides an overview of some commonly used sociometric procedures based on a division into four common categories: (1) peer nomination procedures; (2) peer rating procedures; (3) sociometric ranking procedures; and (4) alternative sociometric procedures. In some cases, these categories involve general descriptions common to many methods within the category. In other cases, the categorical description is unique to a specific procedure.

Peer Nomination Procedures

The oldest and most widely used sociometric approach, and the basis for most other types of sociometric measures, is the nomination method, originally introduced by Moreno (1934). The essential characteristic of the peer nomination technique is that students are asked to nominate or name classmates they prefer according to specific positive criteria. This approach typically involves the students' naming one or more classmates with whom they would most like to study, play, work on a class project, or engage in some other positive way. For children with sufficient reading and writing ability, peer nomination procedures can be administered by an item-by-peer matrix or a questionnaire wherein they fill in names of classmates on blank lines following questions.

The item-by-peer matrix consists of having the names of all children in the class across the top of the page and the social interaction items listed vertically on the left side of the page. The students are instructed to put an X under the names of the other students to whom they think the item applies (e.g., "Which student would you most like to have as your best friend?"). Use of a questionnaire format accomplishes essentially the same thing (e.g., "Write the names of three students in your class that you would most like to have as your friends" followed by three numbered blank lines). Scoring of peer nominations typically is done by totaling the number of nominations that each child receives.

Worthen et al. (1993) suggested that the results of positive peer nomination procedures can be classified and interpreted according to a frequently used set of criteria. *Stars* are individuals who are frequently chosen. *Isolates* are individuals who are never chosen in the process. *Neglectees* are those who receive only a few nominations. The results also can be plotted graphically using a *sociogram,* which shows the patterns of choice for each student and helps to identify not only frequently and never nominated students, but also cliques or small groups. A *mutual choice* occurs when an individual is chosen by the same student that he or she selected. A *cross-sex choice* occurs when a boy chooses a girl or a girl chooses a boy. A *clique* is identified by finding a small group of students who choose each other and make few or no choices outside of that group. *Cleavage* is when two or more groups within the class or social unit are identified who never choose someone from the other groups. Using these scoring and classification criteria, one can see easily how a procedure as deceptively simple as the peer nomination method can yield information that is striking and complex. Figure 7.1 is an example of an anonymous item-by-peer matrix that could be used in a peer nomination assessment in a classroom setting and includes positive and negative items. Figure 7.2 is an example of a sociogram that was plotted based on a positive nomination procedure used with 15 elementary-age boys who were asked to select two boys with whom they would most like to be friends.

Although the peer nomination technique as described involves the use of positive items indicative of high social status, many researchers and some practitioners have used variations of this method by employing negative nominations, using items created to identify students who are socially rejected by peers (e.g., "Who would you least like to play with?" or "Who would you never want to be friends with?"). Negative nominations are scored and interpreted in a variety of ways, including finding specific patterns of social rejection within a group and identifying rejected students who receive a large number of negative nominations.

Scores of research studies have indicated that negative nominations may be a powerful predictor of later negative outcomes. When used in conjunction with positive nominations,

PLEASE LIST THE NAME OF YOUR TEACHER _____

WHAT GRADE ARE YOU IN? _____

I AM A (circle one): BOY/GIRL

DIRECTIONS: We are interested in finding out how well children are able to notice the behavior of other children. Please help us by answering some questions about the other children in your class. Follow along as the questions are read out loud, and try to answer each question the best you can. For each question, you will be asked to pick one student that you think the question is most like, and then put an X in the box under their name for that question. Remember, there are no right or wrong answers, and the way you answer these questions will not affect your grade. Your classmates and your teacher will not know how you answered the questions. If you don't understand what to do, or need help, please raise your hand.

	Tina	Jan	Cal	Ole	Ken	Tim	Kim	Sari	Jon	Tia	Kyle	Sue	Erin	Pat	Eli
Who would you most like to be best friends with?															
Who is angry or mad a lot?															
Who would you like to invite over to your home?															
Who gets in fights?															
Who gets along well with the teacher?															
Who is in trouble a lot?															

Figure 7.1 An example of an item-by-peer matrix for a peer nomination procedure that includes positive and negative items

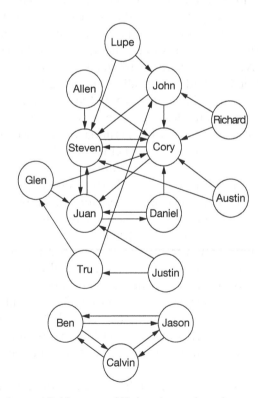

Figure 7.2 An example of a sociogram plotted for a group of 15 elementary-age boys who were asked to select the two boys in the classroom with whom they would most like to be friends

negative nominations can provide more detailed information about the subtle dynamics of social status within a group, as exemplified by Coie et al.'s (1982) division of social status into five different groups.

Peer Rating Procedures

The use of peer ratings, also referred to as the *roster rating method*, constitutes a form of sociometric assessment that is conceptually and psychometrically quite different from peer nominations. In the peer rating procedure, the children within a group are asked to respond to a sociometric question for each child in the group. A typical procedure for implementing the peer rating method involves providing each member of a group with a roster that has the names of all other group members and a list of sociometric questions, then rating each member of the group on each question using a 5-point scale (Connolly, 1983). For younger children, a variation of the 5-point scale is often used, which consists of a series of three or five faces ranging from frowning to smiling that are anchored to different scale values. Using this method, the children are asked to circle one of the faces in lieu of a numerical rating (Asher, Singleton, Tinsley, & Hymel, 1979). A sample peer rating assessment form is shown in Figure 7.3. This particular example shows a rating scale format for peer rating that might be used with children in grades 3 to 6.

Psychometrically and statistically, peer rating methods vary considerably from peer nomination methods. Each child's score is based on *an average of all the ratings he or she receives.* Because each child is rated by all of his or her classmates, a broader picture of the child's social status is obtained. Compared with peer nomination methods, ratings are *more stable within a group* and are *affected less by the size of the group* (Connolly, 1983). In general, peer ratings tend to yield higher reliability/stability coefficients than do nomination methods (McConnell & Odom, 1986), and with younger children, the increase in score stability with rating methods is particularly noticeable (Asher et al., 1979). Another measurement characteristic of peer ratings is that they tend to provide distributions that are less skewed than distributions provided by some other forms of sociometric assessment (Hops & Lewin, 1984).

In addition to having measurement qualities that differ from peer nomination procedures, peer rating methods differ conceptually and may measure a somewhat different construct. Peer ratings are thought to produce a measure of *average likability,* whereas peer nominations are thought to produce a measure of *popularity.* Although likability and popularity have obvious similarities, there are some subtle yet important differences between these constructs. For example, using the peer rating method, a child might receive scores that indicate an average amount of likability, yet it is possible that he or she might not receive any positive nominations. In this case, if the sociometric interpretation were based on the peer nomination data alone, the child might be considered to be socially isolated or neglected, which might not be the case. There is a relatively large degree of measurement overlap between these procedures; Oden and Asher (1977) reported a correlation of 0.63 between the two measures. In another study (Asher & Hymel, 1981) of 23 children who received no positive nominations, 11 received high positive ratings from their peers.

By combining the nomination and rating procedures in conducting a sociometric assessment, the obtained sociometric data may be more powerful in differentiating popular/likeable and unpopular/unliked children than would be single-source data (Asher & Renshaw, 1981). Another advantage of using peer rating procedures is that they

Rating Form

Please List the Name of Your Teacher: _____

What Grade Are You In? _____

I AM A (circle one): BOY / GIRL

DIRECTIONS: We are interested in finding out how much the students in your class would like to work with each other or play with each other. For each student on this list, circle one of the numbers to show how much you would like to play with them and circle one of the numbers to show how much you would like to work with them. This is what the numbers mean:

1 = NOT AT ALL (I definitely would not want to work or play with this person)
2 = NOT VERY MUCH (I don't think I would want to work or play with this person)
3 = DON'T CARE (It really wouldn't matter to me if I played with this person or not)
4 = SORT OF (I think I would like to work or play with this person)
5 = VERY MUCH (I definitely would like to work or play with this person)

Your teacher and the other students in the class will not know how you answered. There are no right or wrong answers, and the way you fill this form out will not affect your grade. If you have any questions, or if you need help, raise your hand.

NAME	WORK WITH?					PLAY WITH?				
1. _____	1	2	3	4	5	1	2	3	4	5
2. _____	1	2	3	4	5	1	2	3	4	5
3. _____	1	2	3	4	5	1	2	3	4	5
4. _____	1	2	3	4	5	1	2	3	4	5
5. _____	1	2	3	4	5	1	2	3	4	5
6. _____	1	2	3	4	5	1	2	3	4	5
7. _____	1	2	3	4	5	1	2	3	4	5
8. _____	1	2	3	4	5	1	2	3	4	5
9. _____	1	2	3	4	5	1	2	3	4	5
10. _____	1	2	3	4	5	1	2	3	4	5

Figure 7.3 A sample peer rating assessment form

can provide information regarding positive and negative social status without the use of negative questions; this can be done by wording questions positively or neutrally and looking at the distribution of scores. This advantage may be particularly important when one is attempting to obtain consent from parents or program administrators who are uncomfortable with the use of negative nomination methods.

In contrast to traditional sociometric procedures, sociometric instruments have been developed to assess specific social indices related to classrooms. A promising and alternative instrument for collecting sociometric data to assess the management needs of a classroom is what Doll, Zucker, and Brehm titled "ClassMaps" (2004). ClassMaps is a student survey modeled after sociometric rating procedures in which students rate classroom conditions and characteristics of their classmates that are related to academic engagement. Doll and colleagues make the argument that students can reliably and accurately gauge relationships within their classroom, thus providing evidence that students are a good resource for accurately describing their classroom's resilience.

In order to assess classroom resilience through a sociometric strategy, the authors developed a 55-question survey addressing six resilience characteristics: academic efficacy, academic self-determination, behavioral self-control, teacher–student relationships, peer relationships, and home–school relationships. All individual student ratings are aggregated to capture a general impression of classroom beliefs. Results of studies in elementary schools (Doll, Spies, LeClair, Kurien, & Foley, 2010) and middle schools (Doll, Spies, Champion, Guerrero, Dooley, & Turner, 2010) indicated that the survey's technical adequacy is fairly robust and consistent with the survey's conceptual framework. All in all, ClassMaps provides a cost-effective sociometric method to assess classroom resiliency, and, interestingly, combines both student perceptions of relationship dynamics and classroom context (Doll et al., 2004).

Sociometric Ranking Procedures

In contrast to the peer nomination and peer rating procedures that have just been reviewed, sociometric ranking procedures are designed to provide information on child social status and peer relations through data contributed by adults rather than peers. In most instances of sociometric ranking procedures that have been reported in the literature, the informant is a teacher and the peer group consists of same-grade classmates. It would also be possible, however, to implement sociometric ranking assessment procedures in nonschool settings, such as group homes, residential or day treatment programs, and perhaps clinic-based therapy groups.

Because the object of sociometric assessment is to obtain information on status and relations within a peer group, what advantage is there in going outside of the peer group to an adult informant to collect these data? Connolly (1983) noted that when using the peer group as a source of information, one must assume that children are capable of making accurate social distinctions. With typical children who are elementary age or older, this assumption seems to be valid. With younger children and perhaps with older children who have moderate to severe intellectual or social–emotional disabilities, however, the completion of sociometric tasks may be difficult and may result in lower reliability. Using teachers as sociometric informants may increase reliability in some instances (Foster et al., 1986; Hagborg, 1994). Another reason for employing teachers as sociometric informants is that they tend to be expert objective observers of child behavior and understand the social dynamics within their classroom. Additionally, educators are often understandably hesitant to commit blocks of academic time for nonacademic student tasks and might be more willing to provide sociometric ranking data themselves rather than have their students spend instructional time on it.

There are two general ways in which sociometric rankings can be completed by classroom teachers. The first method involves the teacher rank-ordering every student in the classroom according to some sociometric criteria, such as popularity with classmates or positive interactions with peers. Previous studies that have employed this type of ranking procedure have shown that the obtained data tend to be highly reliable and may correlate better with independent ratings and observations of child social behavior than do peer nominations or ratings (Connolly & Doyle, 1981; Greenwood, Walker, Todis, & Hops, 1979). When the object of interest is negative social interactions or peer rejection, teacher rankings have been found to correlate with independent ratings and observations of child behavior to a lower degree than negative peer nominations (Connolly, 1983).

A related method for obtaining teacher sociometric rankings involves first determining which students in a classroom fit a given social–behavioral description, then rank-ordering the students according to the severity or strength of how they fit those criteria. Using this method of ranking, not all students in a classroom are ranked, only those who are found to meet a given criterion. An example of this method of selective rank-ordering is found in Stage 1 of Walker and Severson's (1992, 2014) Systematic Screening for Behavior Disorders (SSBD), a multiple-gating screening and assessment procedure that was discussed in Chapter 3. This rank-ordering procedure involves teachers selecting ten students in their classrooms whose behaviors most closely match an objective description of internalizing behavior problems, then rank-ordering the students according to the severity of their symptoms. Examples from the description of internalizing problems include not talking with other children; being shy, timid, or unassertive; not participating in games and activities; and being unresponsive to social initiations by others. Following the rank-ordering along the internalizing dimension, a separate rank-ordering procedure is conducted in a similar manner for students who exhibit externalizing social–behavioral problems. Examples from the description of externalizing problems include arguing, forcing the submission of others, disturbing others, and stealing. The instructions for rank-ordering students with internalizing behavior problems are presented in Figure 7.4.

Research reported in the SSBD technical manual indicates that the Stage 1 rank-ordering procedures have adequate to strong inter-rater agreement between teachers and classroom aides (0.89 to 0.94 for the externalizing dimension and 0.82 to 0.90 for the internalizing dimension) and good test–retest reliability at ten to 30-day intervals (0.81 to 0.88 for the externalizing dimension and 0.74 to 0.79 for the internalizing dimension). The Stage 1 ranking procedure of the SSBD has also been found to have a strong degree of sensitivity in discriminating students with behavioral disorders from peers with normal levels of problem behaviors.

Alternative Sociometric Procedures

In addition to peer nominations, peer ratings, and sociometric rankings, other sociometric procedures have been developed that may have some similarities with one or more of these categories but are unique in many ways. Three of these alternative sociometric assessment procedures are reviewed in this section: picture sociometrics, the Class Play, and "guess who" techniques.

Picture Sociometrics Picture sociometric procedures involve individually presenting to each child in a classroom an arbitrary assortment of photographs of each child in the class, then asking the child to answer a series of questions by pointing to or selecting a photograph of a peer. This method is an adaptation of other peer nomination methods and is useful for work with preliterate subjects. Landau and Milich (1990) stated that it is the preferred method for preschool-age children through second-grade students. Examples of questions that have been used with this technique include "Whom do you like to play with the most?" and "Who is your best friend?" and "Who is the best student in your class?" As with most other sociometric techniques, specific questions can be developed on the basis of the clinical or research questions, and these questions can be produced to indicate either social acceptance or social rejection.

Stage 1 Screening for Internalizing Students
Rank Ordering on Internalizing Dimensions

Step 1. Carefully study the definition of internalizing behavior below and then review your class roster.

Internalizing refers to all behaviour problems that are directed inwardly (i.e., away from the external social environment) and that represent problems with self. Internalizing behavior problems are often self-imposed and frequently involve behavioral deficits and patterns of social avoidance. Non-examples of internalizing behavior problems would be all forms of social behavior that demonstrate social involvement with peers and that facilitate normal or expected social development.

Examples Include:

- Having low or restricted activity levels
- Not talking with other children
- Being shy, timid, and/or unassertive
- Avoiding or withdrawing from social situations
- Preferring to play or spend time alone
- Acting in a fearful manner
- Not participating in games and activites
- Being unresponsive to social initiations by other
- Not standing up for one's self
- Appearing depressed

Non-Examples Include:

- Initiating social interactions with peers
- Having conversations
- Playing with others, having normal rates or levels of social contact with peers
- Displaying positive social behaviour toward others
- Participating in games and activities
- Resolving peer conflicts in an appropriate manner
- Joining in with others

Step 2. In Column One, enter the five students whose characteristic behavior patterns most closely match the internalizing behavior definition.

Step 3. In Column Two, rank order students you have listed in Column One according to the degree or extent to which each displays internalizing behavior. The student who exhibits internalizing behavior to the greatest degree in ranked first and so on until all five students are rank ordered. The three highest ranked students will be rated on Stage 2 measures.

Column One List Internalizers	Column Two Rank Order Internalizers
Student and/or ID No.	Student and/or ID No.

Figure 7.4 Instructions for rank-ordering students with internalizing social–emotional problems, from stage 1 of the SSBD multiple gating system. A rank-ordering procedure for externalizing problems is also included in stage 1

Source: From *Systematic Screening for Behavior Disorders, Second Edition*, by H. M. Walker, H. Severson, and E. Feil (2014). Eugene, OR: Pacific Northwest Publishing. Reprinted with Permission.

The original picture sociometric technique and minor variations of it are scored on the basis of totaling the number of times each child was nominated by classmates in questions indicating positive social status. Using this scoring scheme, rejected or neglected children would have significantly lower scores than accepted children with higher social status. Variations in scoring procedure would be needed if there were any significant deviations in administration method from the original study by McAndless and Marshall (1957). Questions that reflect positive (e.g., "Whom do you most like to do schoolwork with?") and negative (e.g., "Whom are you afraid to be around on the playground?") social status could be mixed, and the scoring system could be divided into positive and negative status categories.

The use of picture sociometrics was first reported by McAndless and Marshall (1957) and has been used in many other published studies. The psychometric properties of picture sociometric techniques have been shown to be quite good, with relatively high inter-rater reliability, high short-term test–retest reliability, and adequate long-term test–retest reliability (Landau & Milich, 1990; Shin, Kim, Goetz, & Vaughn, 2014). Validity of the picture sociometric method has been shown by producing significant discriminations between groups of aggressive, aggressive–withdrawn, and normal boys (Milich & Landau, 1984). With young children, picture sociometrics have been shown to produce more effective discriminations of social status than information provided by teachers, particularly when negative ratings or nominations are involved. In this day of easy digital photography, it may be easier to physically prepare for picture sociometrics than was true in the past, but researchers and practitioners should consult appropriate administrators to first determine whether active parental consent is needed prior to taking such photographs of children.

Class Play The Class Play procedure first was used and described by Bower (1969), then was revised further by Masten, Morrison, and Pelligrini (1985). It is a frequently used sociometric technique that has been employed in several large-scale investigations, including the classic 11- to 13-year follow-up study of elementary-age children by Cowen et al. (1973). The basis of this procedure is that children are asked to assign their peers to various roles (usually positive and negative roles) in an imaginary play. The original Class Play described by Bower included positive (e.g., "someone who will wait his or her turn") and negative (e.g., "someone who is too bossy") roles but consisted of a scoring procedure wherein only a single score (negative peer reputation) was derived, which was done by calculating the number of negative roles given to a child and dividing that by the total number of roles given to the child. Large percentages are supposed to indicate a high degree of peer rejection, whereas low percentages are meant to indicate that the child has higher social status. As is the case with most sociometric approaches, the specification of roles in the Class Play procedure (and the method of scoring) can be manipulated by the clinician or researcher to suit specific assessment goals. The scoring system advocated by Bower has been criticized as being flawed (Landau & Milich, 1990).

The use of Class Play sociometric procedures is attractive for two reasons other than the measurement capabilities it may have. One advantage is that children seem to enjoy participating in make-believe plays and casting their peers into the various roles. The second advantage is that teachers and administrators seem to view this type of procedure more positively or at least with less suspicion than some other sociometric methods, and as such, it is more likely to be supported and approved than some other approaches. Masten et al. (1985) suggested that because of the diversity of roles needed in a play, this procedure would reduce any probability of disapproving labels on children with high negative scores by other children in the rating/casting process.

"Guess Who" Measures The "guess who" technique is a sociometric approach wherein brief descriptive statements are provided to students and they are then asked to write down names of a few other students (usually three or fewer) who they think best fit the descriptions. For example, the students might be asked to respond to descriptions such as "Guess who is often in trouble," "Guess who does the best job on schoolwork," "Guess who no one knows very well," or "Guess who is often angry at other children." The descriptions can be provided to the students verbally or in written format. The content of the "guess who" items can be made up by the teacher, clinician, or researcher on the

basis of specific characteristics they are interested in identifying. Scoring of these types of measures is done by making simple frequency counts of each question/description. More elaborate scoring methods are possible, such as grouping descriptions into categories of similar content (e.g., antisocial behaviors, helping characteristics, peer popularity) and obtaining frequency counts within each broader category.

An example of a "guess who" measure that has been used with a large number of students and has been investigated carefully is the Revised PRIME Guess Who Measure, which was developed for use in Project PRIME, a large-scale investigation of students with disabilities who had been integrated into regular education classrooms for part of their instructional day (Kauffman, Semmell, & Agard, 1974). The original instrument consisted of 29 questions/descriptions and was administered to more than 13,000 students in grades 3 through 5. Factor analytic procedures conducted on the instrument divided the items into four major factors, labeled *disruptive, bright, dull,* and *well-behaved.* A revised scale including 20 items (the five items contributing the most to each factor) was developed by Veldman and Sheffield (1979), who reported reliability coefficients ranging from 0.56 to 0.77 for each factor score and developed a satisfactory concurrent validity procedure for the instrument by correlating the instrument items with teacher ratings along similar dimensions.

In sum, the "guess who" technique is flexible, easy to administer, and easy to score; has been used in a large number of studies and projects; and has been found to have satisfactory technical properties. Clinicians and investigators desiring an adaptable, easy-to-administer sociometric measure may find "guess who" techniques to be a useful choice in assessment instrumentation.

ETHICAL CONCERNS IN USING SOCIOMETRIC PROCEDURES

Sociometric assessment approaches have a great deal of appeal to clinicians and researchers and have a long history of use in psychology, sociology, and education. These approaches are not without controversy, however. Many sociometric methods involve negative ranking or nomination procedures or having children single out peers based on negative characteristics. Largely because of the use of these negative nomination procedures, parents, teachers, and administrators may be hesitant or alarmed at the possibility of their children participating in sociometric assessments, for fear that some children may be singled out by peers and ostracized further because of the procedure. The use of negative criteria is the most controversial aspect of sociometric assessment (McConnell & Odom, 1986). The gist of this controversy is that there seems to be a common concern that children will compare their responses after the assessment to find out which children were singled out for negative nominations and that this process will end up in increased isolation or social exile for the children who were commonly perceived in negative terms. We are personally familiar with several separate research projects that had to undergo major methodological modifications or be stopped altogether because of threats by parents and some educators to "shut down the study" because of outrage over the use of negative peer ranking or nomination procedures.

Although concerns regarding negative effects from sociometric assessment are understandable, such concerns have never been substantiated through empirical evidence. Landau and Milich (1990) noted that several large-scale longitudinal investigations with at-risk children have been conducted wherein sociometric procedures have been employed (e.g., Pekarik, Prinz, Liebert, Weintraub, & Neale, 1976; Serbin, Lyons, Marchessault, Schwartzman, & Ledingham, 1987) with no reports of negative consequences to the participants. An ambitious and intriguing investigation by Hayvren and Hymel (1984) found that there were no observable negative consequences within peer groups immediately after the use of sociometric assessment procedures. This study was conducted with a population of preschool-age children, however, and it is unclear whether the same results would generalize to elementary-age or secondary-age schoolchildren.

More recently, an ambitious study was conducted by Mayeux, Underwood, and Risser (2007) to gauge children's long-term reactions to participating in sociometric assessment. In this study, 91 third-grade students were included in a sociometric assessment procedure. 15 weeks following the assessment period, students were interviewed about their experiences during and following assessment. In general, researchers found that children were not upset by the assessment procedure. They reported enjoying the experience and they did not feel as though their friends treated them differently following the assessment.

Mayeux et al.'s study is similar to that conducted by Iverson and Iverson (1996). In this study, 82 children in the fifth grade completed a positive and negative peer nomination procedure during the last week of the school year. After summer vacation, 45 of the participants (who were by then in the sixth grade) were interviewed individually to assess their reactions to the sociometric procedures. One-third of the participants indicated that they had discussed the measures with their peers, despite specific instructions that they were not to do so. The participants stated that they enjoyed participating in the sociometric procedure, however, particularly the positive nomination procedure. Because the original nomination procedure was used to assign participants to social status groups based on the five-category breakdown of average, controversial, neglected, popular, and rejected by Coie et al. (1982), the participants' responses were analyzed by group. No evidence of reactions indicating any harm to any of the participants was found.

The research which has specifically examined possible negative effects of sociometric techniques on participants (including additional studies by Bell-Dolan, Foster, and Christopher, 1992, and Bell-Dolan, Foster, and Sikora, 1989) has grown to the point where the body of evidence can be examined as a whole, rather than relying solely on individual studies. In commenting on the yield of research in this area, Hoza and colleagues stated:

> [Sociometric] procedures must be done while protecting the confidentiality of the target individual and addressing concerns about the effects of the measurement procedure on the peer group. *We find it important that numerous studies now document the lack of ill effects of administering sociometric procedures on the peer group* ... yet misconceptions and logistical constraints remain as impediments.
>
> (2005, p. 412, italics added for emphasis)

Given the combined evidence in this area to date, two things can be surmised. First, it seems likely that a substantial number of children who participate in sociometric procedures, perhaps one-third or more of participants, will discuss their choices with peers, even if they are instructed not to do so. Second, despite the reasonable possibility of children comparing their responses, there is no empirical evidence that negative nomination or rating procedures are harmful to individuals who participate in the assessment. In fact, there are several studies that have examined this issue specifically, and in no cases were ill effects identified. Concerns regarding the use of sociometrics may be reduced through not using negative criteria, but such a course of action may reduce the utility of sociometric assessment. Before deciding to do away entirely with the use of any negative criteria in sociometric assessment, the following quote from McConnell and Odom (1986) should be considered: "Because the efficiency of peer nomination assessments will decrease markedly when negative nominations are not used, it is imperative that they be included in the assessment process" (p. 233).

Whether or not concerns about the effects of sociometric assessment are founded, clinicians and researchers desiring to use sociometric approaches are advised to pick carefully the most appropriate method for their purposes, communicate closely and carefully with their constituent groups, and educate those involved on the purposes and procedures involved. Landau and Milich (1990) suggested that the use of positive nomination procedures or peer ratings instead of negative nomination procedures may be necessary (but not optimal) when working with systems or individuals who are suspicious of the use of sociometrics. In the meantime, additional research on any potential peer effects of sociometric measurement involving negative ranking or nomination would be extremely useful.

In addition to the potential ethical concerns and administrative difficulty in conducting sociometric assessments, there is a practical consideration that may create a significant challenge. Because the basis of sociometric assessment is that data are gathered from within an existing social group, it is necessary that the entire group (or most of the group) participate in the assessment, not just a few individual members of the group. In other words, if a clinician or researcher plans to conduct a sociometric assessment of children within a specific classroom, he or she needs to plan on including all of the children in the classroom in the assessment. If even a few children are left out of the assessment, some important or even vital data may be lost. The challenge here is that specific parental consent generally is required for each child who is to participate in the assessment. If the targeted classroom included 25 students, parental permission would need to be secured from parents or guardians of each of the students for full participation in the assessment. Clinicians, researchers, or teachers who have never been faced with the challenge of obtaining so many parental consent forms simultaneously may be surprised at how difficult and time-consuming a task it may be. Two potential problems may occur in this regard. First, for various reasons, some parents simply may refuse permission for their child to participate in the assessment, which is certainly their right. Second, some parents (usually a greater number than the first category) simply ignore the permission slips and do not sign and return them as requested. My own experience with this second issue is that a phone call, note, or other prompt to the parents usually results in some additional permissions being granted, but the process may be time-consuming, and even then, some parents simply will not follow through.

The reality is that in many or most cases of attempting to conduct sociometric assessment with large social groups of children, it may be difficult to ensure that the entire group will end up being able to participate. This situation raises the obvious question: "How many data are enough?" A novel study of this issue by Hamilton, Fuchs, Fuchs, and Roberts (2000) indicated that a minimum of 80% participation by children and classroom settings may be required for the obtained data to be reliable. Based on this study, participation rates of less than 80% are likely to result in unreliable information and threaten the overall validity of the assessment. Although this particular study is the only one of its kind to date, it employed sound methodology and should be considered a benchmark of sorts until new evidence accrues to convince us otherwise.

SOCIOMETRIC PROCEDURES AND DECISION MAKING

Perhaps the best use of sociometric assessment is in making decisions about screening and assessment. As a screening tool, various sociometric approaches can help quickly identify individuals who might be at heightened risk for developing social–behavioral problems. As part of a comprehensive assessment system, sociometric methods can help to confirm or disprove hypotheses about peer relationship problems or other social risk factors that have been developed through the use of other assessment methods.

Sociometric assessment may have some use as a means to identify individuals who might benefit from special social skills interventions, but if used for this purpose, it would be important to augment the sociometric approaches with other objective assessment methods. It also would be important to word the sociometric assessment questions or instructions carefully to match the type of intervention that is intended. For example, if a school counselor or psychologist were attempting to identify potential participants for an anger control group, a peer nomination question such as "List five students who lose their tempers" might be useful in conjunction with other selection data. For making specific intervention decisions, it is difficult to see how sociometric data would be very useful. It has been suggested by some researchers that a clear link between sociometric assessment and social–behavioral intervention is not clearly founded (Foster et al., 1986; Gresham & Stuart, 1992; Hagborg, 1994).

An intriguing potential use of sociometric assessment data is for grouping students together in classroom settings for maximizing cooperation and providing appropriate modeling. For example, a student who lacks social skills and comes out as socially neglected in a sociometric assessment might be paired strategically with another student with strong social competence and who is identified in the sociometric assessment as being well liked and accepting. Such a pairing might result in the socially neglected student being exposed to a positive social model and a potential source of social support. Likewise, a teacher who is assigned to teach an intact group of students but who does not yet know these students well might use a sociometric assessment to ensure that seat assignments and work group pairings include an appropriate mix of students and that students at heightened risk for engaging in negative social behavior (e.g., rejected and controversial students) are not clustered together.

Further, with increased use of SNA statistical packages, sociometric assessment and analysis could be used to better understand how social networks change (or remain stable) over time. Longitudinal SNA could serve to better understand the extent to which school-wide or class-wide behavioral intervention and prevention approaches impact social networks. For example, Sentse, Kiuru, Veenstra, & Salmivalli (2014) used SNA to understand the bullying behavior of adolescent social networks. They assessed students at three points in the school year, some of whom were provided with the Finnish KiVA bully prevention program and others who served as controls. Researchers found that students were less likely to like peers who engaged in a high level of bullying behavior, and that peers liked others with similar levels of bullying behavior (i.e., low levels). Interestingly, they also found no changes in peer ratings between intervention and control groups, suggesting that consideration may need to be given on how to best implement prevention efforts in secondary schools, where students are more mobile, and class climate initiatives may need to look different from those implemented in intact elementary classroom settings.

For making diagnosis/classification or placement decisions, sociometric assessment procedures seem to be less useful. These types of decisions tend to require objective information on whether an individual meets specific criteria. The only possible use of sociometrics in this regard would be as a means of confirming or disproving other data used in determining whether the criteria have been met.

In sum, sociometric assessment, similar to other forms of assessment used to gauge emotional and behavioral problems, is more relevant for certain types of decision-making processes. The decision-making process that seems to be most relevant to sociometric assessment is screening and assessment decision making. Sociometric assessment also may have some relevance when used, in conjunction with other forms of assessment, for making general decisions about interventions for peer relationship problems, but the current link in this regard is questionable.

CONCLUSIONS

Sociometric assessment comprises a collection of related measurement techniques that allow for the gathering of social information from within an intact peer group, such as students within a classroom. Social status, popularity, social acceptance or rejection, and average likability are the most common constructs that are assessed with sociometrics. Sociometrics is a potentially important assessment method because the constructs that are measured are important and highly predictive of future social and emotional outcomes. Sociometric assessment has a rich history within developmental psychology, education, and sociology and became widely used by the 1950s and 1960s. The use of sociometrics seems to have declined since that era, however, perhaps partly because of the increasing availability of other social assessment methods and partly because of increasing difficulty in obtaining acceptance and approval for using sociometrics.

The empirical base for sociometrics is generally quite solid. Numerous studies have been conducted over the years that have documented the reliability and validity of various sociometric procedures. Perhaps the most compelling of these studies supporting the use of sociometrics were the classic studies conducted by Cowen, Roff, Ullman, and their respective colleagues. These studies showed in a persuasive way that sociometric assessment not only is capable of having sound technical adequacy, but, more importantly, is also strongly predictive of important future social–emotional outcomes. Some studies have been conducted that have highlighted the shortcomings of sociometric assessment, but it has held up surprisingly well to some fairly intense scrutiny.

The peer nomination procedure is the oldest sociometric technique and provides the basis for most other sociometric techniques. Peer nominations involve presenting children with a series of positive and negative statements or questions—such as "Whom would you most like to play or work with?" or "Whom are you afraid to be around?"— and asking them to nominate someone from their peer group who they think best fits the specific question. In addition to the peer nomination procedure, other common sociometric techniques include peer rating scales and sociometric ranking procedures.

These methods vary in terms of how they best tap underlying constructs and their technical or psychometric properties. Additional alternative sociometric techniques, such as picture sociometrics, "guess who" techniques, and the Class Play, have been developed for use with specific populations and problems.

Since the 1970s and 1980s, there has been increasing concern regarding the ethics of using sociometric techniques for assessment of children. Prompted primarily by concerns regarding the use of negative criteria and the fear of children comparing their responses and then further ostracizing rejected or neglected children, many institutional review boards and school administrators have been reluctant to approve projects involving sociometric assessment. As a result, many practitioners or researchers do not view sociometry as a viable method or they compromise by removing all negative criteria, which has the effect of reducing the power and efficiency of sociometric assessment. These concerns are understandable but simply are not founded on empirical evidence. None of the several studies that have attempted to investigate negative effects resulting from participation in sociometric assessment have identified any short-term or long-term negative consequences for participants. If informed consent and full participation is not obtained for all or most of the members of a group, the validity of the sociometric assessment data may be questionable. To date, the best benchmark for a minimal level of participation for reliable and valid data is the 80% figure suggested by Hamilton et al. (2000).

Perhaps the best use of sociometric assessment to assist in psychoeducational decision making is for making decisions regarding additional screening and assessment. Sociometrics have been shown to have substantial accuracy in identifying at-risk children and adolescents who may be in need of additional assessment or intervention services. With increased use of statistical packages utilizing SNA, we may find an increased use of sociometry to understand networks and relationships among students, teachers, and teaming structures within organizations.

REVIEW AND APPLICATION QUESTIONS

1. What are some advantages of obtaining peer-referenced sociometric assessment data rather than relying solely on teacher ratings or observations of social interaction patterns?
2. Briefly describe some of the evidence attesting to the predictive validity of sociometric assessment.
3. Compare and contrast peer ranking and peer rating procedures. Under what circumstances might each procedure be best used?
4. Describe two ways of using positive nomination procedures. Under what circumstances might each procedure be best used?
5. What are some ways of implementing sociometric assessment procedures with children who cannot yet read or write?
6. Develop a list of five different "guess who" questions that you might use to help select the three students in a third-grade classroom who are most likely to benefit from participation in a social-skills training group wherein friendship-making and peer interaction skills will be stressed.
7. The use of negative peer nomination procedures and other negative criteria in sociometrics has generated a great deal of controversy. Regarding this issue, respond to the following

questions: (1) What are some of the possible negative outcomes of using negative nomination procedures? (2) What evidence exists attesting to the negative effects of these procedures? (3) What are some potential alternatives to negative nominations?

8. There may be practical and ethical challenges to obtaining informed consent for full group participation in a sociometric assessment. What is the recommended minimal percentage of group participation for sociometric assessment to be reliable and valid, and what are the risks of proceeding with the assessment if less than this level of participation is reached?

8

SELF-REPORT ASSESSMENT

This chapter addresses the development and use of a broad category of assessment instruments that are referred to herein as *objective self-report tests,* or simply *self-report tests.* This assessment category is linked inextricably to the field of personality assessment. Some assessment texts define self-report assessment separately from personality assessment, whereas other texts include additional categories of assessment methods in this vein. For this book, a decision was made to refer to this general category of assessment instruments as self-report tests because the term is descriptive of the type of activity the assessment involves and because many (if not most) of the self-report tests reviewed in this chapter and in later chapters are not designed to measure the broad construct of personality, but to assess specific aspects of social and emotional characteristics and behavior based on the child or adolescent's own perceptions.

Self-report assessment is conceptualized and viewed differently by various authors and researchers. For example, Eckert and colleagues (Eckert, Dunn, Codding, & Guiney, 2000; Eckert, Dunn, Guiney, & Codding, 2000) have described self-report assessment tools as "rating scale measures" and positioned them as being conceptually similar to behavior rating scales, with the primary difference between the two forms of assessment being the informant. Differences of opinion exist regarding how direct and objective self-report assessment is as a general method, with some authors considering it to be a direct form or process of assessment (Witt, Cavell, Heffer, Carey, & Martens, 1988) and other authors considering it to be an indirect form (Cone, 1978). Differences of opinion aside, it is important to view objective self-report assessment of children and adolescents as an increasingly prominent method that can play an important role and provide unique and valuable information as part of a broad-based assessment design.

This chapter provides a framework for understanding and using self-report assessment. The chapter begins with a broad examination of the important foundations of self-report assessment, including historical and psychometric considerations. Most of the chapter is dedicated to evaluative reviews and discussion of several self-report assessment instruments designed for use with children and adolescents. These instruments differ from the types of self-report measures that are reviewed in Chapters 10 to 13 because they are omnibus or general purpose assessment instruments designed for measuring overall personal adjustment and psychopathology. Conversely, the self-report instruments discussed in later chapters include instruments developed for assessing specific constructs, such as ADHD, depression, anxiety, social competence, and self-concept. The chapter ends with a discussion on how data from self-report tests can be used in making decisions regarding screening and assessment, classification, and intervention.

DOI: 10.4324/9781315747521-9

FOUNDATIONS OF SELF-REPORT ASSESSMENT

To best appreciate the uses of self-report tests in assessing behavioral, social, and emotional problems, it is first necessary to develop a general understanding of them. This section presents a historical and psychometric overview of the basis of objective self-report assessment. First, a brief historical account of the personality testing movement is presented, followed by some basic definitions and discussion of objective measurement. Then, information specific to methods of objective test construction and some associated measurement problems are presented.

Historical Foundations of Personality Testing

As was mentioned previously, self-report assessment is linked closely to, if not an integral part of, the field of personality assessment. As noted by McReynolds (1986), interest in personality assessment is older than the field of psychology. Primitive attempts to measure personality have been identified in antiquity, as exemplified by the work of some of the ancient Greek philosophers. Hippocrates originated the theory that one's personality or persona is based on four separate temperaments (*sanguine, choleric, melancholic, phlegmatic*). Galen expanded on Hippocrates' theory by positing that each temperament was related to one of four bodily fluids or humors: *blood, mucus, black bile,* or *yellow bile.* These notions of temperaments and the four humors survived for well over 1,000 years and were prevalent in Europe throughout the Middle Ages and well into the beginnings of the modern era. The idea of "blood letting" to treat certain maladies stemmed from the humoral notion of personality. Later, the eighteenth-century German philosopher Immanual Kant wrote extensively on the four temperament types and developed an axis to evaluate each type based on the feeling and activity.

The first formal efforts connected to assessing personality structure in the modern era were found in free-association techniques, such as those developed by Freud and Jung in their psychoanalytic work and Kraepelin's (1892) use of the technique in studying physiological effects of hunger, fatigue, and drugs (cited in Anastasi & Urbina, 1997). As advances in the study of personality continued in the early 1900s, there was more of a distinction between projective methods (such as the Rorschach test, apperception tests, and drawing tests) and objective methods of personality assessment, the latter of which are the focus of the remainder of this discussion.

Anastasi (1988) and Anastasi and Urbina (1997) noted that the prototype of the modern personality/self-report inventory was the Personal Data Sheet, which was developed by Woodworth during World War I as a test to screen men with serious emotional problems from military service. By the late 1920s and early 1930s, many objective personality questionnaires, surveys, and inventories had been developed for research and clinical purposes. Many of these early efforts did not meet the current criteria for being considered objective self-report measures, but they were objective in the sense that they incorporated methods that were distinctly different from associative and projective techniques. By the late 1930s and early 1940s, advances in personality theory, psychometric theory, and statistical analysis set the stage for major advances in objective personality assessment. In the first edition of his enormously influential book, *Essentials of Psychological Testing,* Cronbach (1949) noted that the publication of Berneuter's Personality Inventory in the 1930s resulted in an instrument that was based on four personality traits and was used widely in clinical and other applied settings. This assessment instrument became the prototype for many later objective self-report measures. The most notable of these later measures was the MMPI, which was first published in 1943 and which subsequently has been revised and updated. The MMPI was the first widely used instrument to use the sophisticated empirical criterion keying method of construction, a technique on which many later tests were constructed.

During the 1950s, 1960s, and 1970s, there were many challenges to the validity of traditional personality assessment. Some of these challenges arose from the increasing influence of behaviorism in graduate psychology training, which challenged many of the assumptions of personality assessment. The growth of humanistic psychology in the 1950s and 1960s also posed some challenges to traditional personality assessment because many humanistic practitioners considered personality assessment to be impersonal, mechanistic, and invasive. Some of the challenges to personality assessment during this era arose from the fact that many of the assessment instruments that were commonly used had poor psychometric/technical qualities and limited evidence of validity. During the 1970s, 1980s, and 1990s, the field of personality assessment underwent many changes but has not seen its demise, as some predicted. In fact, there has been a resurgence of interest in personality assessment since the 1980s (Anastasi & Urbina, 1997; Swann & Seyle, 2005). Currently, numerous professional organizations and scholarly journals are devoted specifically to the assessment of personality or social–emotional behavior. Some of the reasons for the apparent modern revitalization of personality assessment include: (1) increasing eclecticism among practitioners and researchers; (2) a decline in dogmatism and parochialism in specific schools or fields of psychology; and (3) the development and refinement of sophisticated mathematical models and statistical techniques for studying personality and developing self-report instruments. Regarding the relatively recent improvements in technical sophistication and research regarding personality assessment, Anastasi and Urbina stated:

> The 1990s have witnessed a resurgence of research that faced up to the complexities of personality assessment and sought innovative solutions to these long-standing problems. The period is characterized by significant theoretical and methodological advances. The earlier critiques of personality measurement undoubtedly had a salutary effect and in part stimulated the subsequent development in this area of psychometrics. We must, however, guard against the danger that, in the zeal to eradicate fallacious thinking, sound and useful concepts may also be lost. The occasional proposal that diagnostic personality testing and trait concepts be completely discarded, for example, indicates an unnecessarily narrow definition of both terms.
>
> (1997, p. 385)

Psychometric Foundations of Objective Test Construction

In Chapter 1, the notion of direct and objective assessment was introduced, and it has been touched on briefly in subsequent chapters. These concepts have not been addressed in detail at this point, however. Because the focus of this chapter is on objective self-report tests rather than projective–expressive techniques, it is appropriate and necessary to discuss objective assessment more fully in this section.

R. P. Martin (1988) proposed that there are four essential characteristics or criteria that must be present for an assessment instrument to be considered an objective test. These are listed as follows:

1. There must be *individual differences in the responses* of persons to the test stimuli, and these differences must be sufficiently consistent over time, across test items, and in different assessment situations.
2. The measurement must involve the *comparison of one person's responses with those of other individuals,* and the items must be presented to different persons in a consistent manner.
3. The assessment device must include normative data so that *individual scores can be assigned a place on a scale for purposes of comparison* against a larger group of persons.
4. The test responses must be shown to be *related to other meaningful behavior.* In other words, the measurement must be shown to be useful in predicting behavior. This criterion is referred to as the validity requirement.

By this definition, an objective self-report test is one in which the targets or participants respond to various items or questions about their own social–emotional behavior in a standardized manner, wherein their responses are compared with those of a normative group, and evidence is provided as to the psychometric properties (reliability and validity) of the measure. R. P. Martin's (1988) four criteria and the subsequent summation of these key points show that the assessment methods discussed in previous chapters (behavioral observation, rating scales, interviewing, and sociometric measures) are not usually considered to be objective self-report measures in the most strict sense of the term, although they sometimes meet several of the essential characteristics. To these four characteristics, it is useful to add a brief definition of how self-report responses are scored using objective procedures: Each possible response on an item is associated with a predetermined score, and there is no room (or very little room) for inference or individual judgment in the scoring process.

With regard to the first essential criterion of objective measurement (consistent measurement of individual differences), self-report personality/affective measures tend to have special difficulties when compared with tests that measure various forms of cognitive functioning, such as intelligence and academic achievement tests (Anastasi & Urbina, 1997). Part of the problem with the greater difficulty in obtaining high reliability coefficients on personality or behavioral measures is the stability of the underlying construct in general. Social and emotional behavior in humans tends to be less stable or predictable than human cognitive functioning (Brown, 1983). A second potential reason for psychometric problems on self-report tests noted by Brown is that these tests often have been accepted uncritically or used for purposes that were not intended. Given the differences in predictability between social–emotional and cognitive functioning in humans, the psychometric gap between the two areas may be reduced in time but perhaps never closed.

The characteristics measured by personality tests are also more changeable over time than those measured by tests of ability. The latter fact complicates the determination of test reliability because random temporal fluctuations in test performance are less likely to become confused with broad, systematic behavioral changes. Even over relatively short intervals, it cannot be assumed that variations in test responses are restricted to the test itself and do not characterize the area of nontest behavior under consideration. A related problem is the greater situational specificity of responses in the noncognitive than in the cognitive domain (Anastasi & Urbina, 1997, p. 385).

Three Approaches to Developing Objective Self-Report Tests

Experts in personality assessment agree that the number of approaches for constructing objective self-report tests is quite small, with most experts listing only three categories of test construction methods. In this regard, the only variable that differs to any significant extent is the name that is assigned to each category or type of approach. For a further analysis of the basic types of test construction categories and names, readers are referred to works by Anastasi (1988), Anastasi and Urbina (1997), Goldberg (1974), Gregory (2010), Kaplan and Saccuzzo (2012), Kline (2015), and Lanyon and Goodstein (1984, 1997). In the present text, the names assigned to the three basic categories of objective test construction include the *rational–theoretical approach*, the *factor analytic approach*, and the *empirical criterion keying* approach.

Rational–Theoretical Approach The rational–theoretical approach to developing self-report tests involves the assumption by the test developer that a given set of personality traits and behavioral correlates can be measured by developing a set of items or scales that appear to fit within the definitions for those traits and behaviors. If the test developer simply uses his or her own ideas about what constitutes appropriate items or scales, the test is said to have been *intuitively developed*. If the test developer uses the judgments of experts in developing and selecting items, the process is referred to as a *content validation method*. The development process is said to be *theory based* if the construction of items or scales is done according to a recognized theory of personality or personal social–emotional functioning.

The rational–theoretical approach can be illustrated using the example of developing a self-report test for measuring depression. A test developer might generate a list of items that he or she believes represent the construct of depression (intuitive), ask a group of mental health professionals to evaluate or generate potential items thought to measure depression (content validation), or develop potential items based on how closely they concur with an accepted theory of depression (theory based). In reality, these rational–theoretical test construction methods often are used in conjunction with each other. It is seldom the case that the content of a well-developed assessment tool was derived from only one practice within this approach. In many cases, an objective measure initially is developed using rational–theoretical methods, and then subjected to other forms of developmental validation.

The main advantage of the rational–theoretical approach is that if the item and scale development process proceeds thoughtfully, the end result is a group of items or scales that have strong face validity and seem to be psychologically meaningful and theoretically unified. The main disadvantage of this approach is that regardless of how much face validity they may seem to have, the resulting items or scales may not have acceptable psychometric properties or be able to differentiate between normal and abnormal behavior.

Factor Analytic Approach This approach to test construction is characterized by reliance on a sophisticated group of statistical procedures to sort and arrange individual test items into groups that are mathematically related or that have specific properties. The term stems from the factor analytic statistical technique. Other techniques are also used within this general approach, including cluster analysis, path analysis, structural equation modeling, item–response analysis, and hierarchical linear modeling, to name a few. Presumably the arrangement of test items into statistically related groupings allows for more precise measurement and interpretation of various personality or behavioral constructs. Normally the test developer also uses a rational–theoretical approach in developing the test items before subjecting them to factor analysis (or other techniques) and subsequent interpretation. Chapter 4 provides several examples of how factor analytic procedures were used in the development of some of the most commonly used behavior rating scales and how the obtained factor solutions are commonly interpreted. The same general procedures and practices are also true of factor analytic approaches to the development of self-report measures.

The major advantage of the factor analytic approach is that it is capable of producing mathematically precise groups of items and may bring a high degree of scientific precision to self-report measurement of behavioral, social, and emotional characteristics. This mathematical sophistication can also be a disadvantage. Even among psychologists who have received graduate training in measurement and psychometrics, few have the skills to understand the nuances of factor analysis and make consistently good decisions on factor analytic test data produced by computer programs. Factor analysis and related statistical techniques are difficult to understand fully and even more difficult to implement adequately in the development of a clinical test. The use of more recent statistical methods for testing or confirming factor structures presents additional challenges for clinicians and researchers who are not conversant in the latest statistical thinking (Crowley & Fan, 1997). If the test items themselves are constructed poorly, the mathematical sophistication offered by factor analysis is of little value in making the test useful and may only confuse matters. It is not unusual to find test items in the same factor that do not seem to have a great deal of clinical similarity based on their face validity. Factor analysis cannot enhance a test that was poorly constructed in the first place. As the old adage goes, "garbage in, garbage out."

The Empirical Criterion Keying Approach Anastasi and Urbina (1997) referred to the third major objective test construction method as empirical criterion keying. This term alludes to the development of scoring keys in terms of some external criterion. The manner in which this procedure is implemented typically involves administering a large number of test items to groups of persons who are known to differ in some psychologically meaningful way (e.g., those who are clinically depressed and those who are not clinically depressed or those who have conduct disorders and those who do not have conduct disorders). After the pool of items is administered, the items are analyzed to determine which ones reliably discriminate or differentiate between the two groups. The discriminating items are considered to be a scale that is used in predicting or classifying membership in the particular groups. The items that are initially administered to the two groups are not just random descriptions of behavior; they are typically developed carefully and selected using rational–theoretical construction methods.

The actual steps in the empirical criterion keying approach are more complex than this brief description might indicate. Readers who are interested in learning more about the specific steps in empirical criterion keying are referred to more thorough descriptions found in general texts on psychological test construction. Some of the most widely used and influential self-report measures (such as the various versions of the MMPI and the Millon inventories) are based on the empirical criterion keying approach.

The major strength of the empirical criterion keying approach is that it relies on the empirical properties of particular test items or scales rather than the presumed clinical expertise of the test developer or the observed behavior of the person who takes the test. With this approach, the clinical implications of the actual contents of items is less important than the fact that the items are known to "sort" meaningfully among different groups of persons. For example, if the item "I do not sleep well at night" is found to differentiate between persons who are highly anxious and those who are not, we do not actually know whether the anxious individuals have trouble sleeping. The important consideration is that they report not sleeping well, and this discriminates them from nonanxious persons. The same could be said for items that seem to lack any face validity, and yet consistently result in score differences between groups who are known to differ in some clinically important way.

The empirical criterion keying approach also has many drawbacks. R. P. Martin (1988) noted that the scales of many tests constructed in this fashion do not have high internal consistency, a statement that is illustrated by the surprisingly modest alpha coefficients on the clinical scales of the MMPI-2, MMPI-A, and the MMPI-A-RF. Another possible problem to consider is the precision with different diagnostic groups used to develop scales selected in the first place. For example, if the tests or other selection procedures used to identify depressed and nondepressed persons are unreliable or are reliable only within specific geographical and cultural constraints, the utility of an empirical criterion keying scale to differentiate these groups is suspect.

Response Bias and Error Variance

Although each of the three major forms of objective test construction has some advantages and disadvantages, trying to determine the "best" method typically is not a fruitful endeavor. There have been some empirical attempts to answer this question (Burisch, 1984; Hase & Goldberg, 1967), which have concluded that the psychometric properties and validity evidence of individual tests are more important markers of their usefulness than the method employed in their construction. Regardless of the approach or method to test construction, objective self-report measures invariably are subject to some degree of response bias on the part of the examinee, a phenomenon that leads to error variance.

Error variance was defined by R. P. Martin (1988) as "variation of responses that is uncorrelated with the trait being assessed and with any nontest behavior of interest" (p. 60). This problem is created by the response bias of the examinee, which can be defined as either conscious or unconscious attempts to respond to items in particular directions or to create a specific type of impression. So, response bias may be either deliberate or unconscious on the part of the examinee, but it can have the effect of increasing the error present in the assessment.

Response bias can take several forms. One of the best researched forms is *acquiescence*, which is a tendency of some test takers to answer true/false or yes/no items consistently in one direction. Acquiescence is particularly a problem when test items are ambiguous or unclear. A common method of attempting to control for acquiescence involves developing items and scales so that there are equal numbers of true/false or yes/no responses keyed into specific scales.

Another well-known type of response bias is the *social desirability* response set. This term refers to the conscious or unconscious tendency of most test takers to endorse items in a socially desirable direction. For example, virtually all test takers faced with the statement "Boys and girls should both be treated equally and fairly by teachers" would answer "True," regardless of their personal awareness or convictions regarding sexism, gender roles, and public policy. Well-adjusted and poorly adjusted persons tend to respond to items in the socially desirable direction, and their responses are usually not indicative of their true behavior or feelings (R. P. Martin, 1988). It is difficult to gauge how much, if any, error variance is created through this response set.

Another form of response bias is *faking*, which involves deliberate attempts by test takers to manipulate or distort their responses to test items to create a particular impression. Faking usually takes the direction of manipulation to create a favorable or positive impression (e.g., a test taker applying for a job or a person accused of a crime undergoing pretrial assessment), but it also can involve deliberate distortion by the examinee to create a negative impression or exaggerate their psychopathology (e.g., a "cry for help" or malingering). Several adolescent and adult self-report instruments incorporate sophisticated methods for detecting faking. The most notable example is the MMPI-A-RF, with various validity scales that are designed to detect falsification, random answering, defensiveness, and related styles of deliberate distortion. Other self-report tests for children (e.g., the BASC-3 self-report scales) include lie or fake detection scales, but these efforts generally are not as well researched or understood as are scales used with adults.

Another type of response bias is *deviation*, or the tendency to answer test items in unusual or unconventional ways. The deviation hypothesis was proposed by I. A. Berg (1967), who argued that deviation in test responses is content-free and can be found on either verbal or nonverbal tasks. Little is known about deviation as a form of response bias, and it is unclear how it contributes to error variance in self-report testing.

It thus far has been shown that several forms of response bias exist in testing and that they may contribute to the error variance found in a given assessment situation. We also have seen that test construction methods potentially can include efforts to reduce or control response bias. What is the probable overall effect of response bias? Although response bias in self-report assessment continues to be a problem, Anastasi (1988) contended that some aspects of it may be "a tempest in a teapot" (p. 554). Perhaps the best solution to reduce error variance through response bias is to make systematic efforts to detect response styles and response sets, then evaluate the examinee's responses to individual test items in terms of their motivations, cognitive ability, and social–emotional status.

REVIEWS OF SELECTED GENERAL-PURPOSE SELF-REPORT TESTS

Chapters 10 to 13 include reviews and comments regarding several self-report tests for children and adolescents that are designed for assessing specific types of behavioral and emotional problems. Several psychometrically sound and clinically useful self-report instruments for children and adolescents have been developed for assessing specific theoretical constructs and types of problems, such as depression, anxiety, social competence, and self-concept. Until more recently, there were few general-purpose self-report tests for children and adolescents that meet the criteria of acceptable psychometric and technical properties. With regard to the preadolescent age group (i.e., ages eight to 11), the dearth of good general-purpose self-report measures has been particularly noticeable. Research and development efforts in this arena have been encouraging, however. The number of technically sound and useful general purpose self-report instruments developed for use by children and adolescents has increased since about 1990 from barely a handful to several, and the supporting research evidence for these newer tools has begun to accrue.

This section includes descriptions, technical information, and evaluative comments regarding seven general-purpose self-report instruments, including the Adolescent Psychopathology Scale (APS); the child and adolescent self-report forms of the Behavior Assessment for Children, Third Edition (BASC-3); Minnesota Multiphasic Personality Inventory, Adolescent Version (MMPI-A) and Restructured Form (MMPI-A-RF); Conners 3-Self Report and Conners Comprehensive Behavior Rating Scales Self Report, and Youth Self-Report (YSR). These measures are included for review in this chapter as exemplars of what is available and technically adequate in the area of self-report instruments for children and adolescents. Each test is recommended, but each is differentially useful for various purposes. It also should be noted that a few of these measures have not been updated to reflect changes in *DSM-5*, but they still may be useful in practice. This section provides a framework for selecting among several potentially useful measures that have strengths and weaknesses in comparison with each other.

The Adolescent Psychopathology Scale (APS)

Description The Adolescent Psychopathology Scale (APS) (W. M. Reynolds, 1998) is a 346-item, broad-purpose self-report instrument designed for use with adolescents aged 12 to 19 to evaluate symptoms of psychological disorders and distress. The scale breakdown of the APS is presented in Table 8.1. The APS has many unique characteristics. Similar to many of the more recently developed social–emotional assessment instruments designed for use with children and adolescents, the APS also is based on the conceptual distinction between the internalizing and externalizing expression of problem symptoms. The APS self-report questionnaire is a 12-page booklet that groups items according to logical or similar clusters of characteristics. The publisher states that approximately 45 to 60 minutes are needed by most youths to complete this scale.

A unique aspect of the APS is that the items are rated in varying formats and according to varying time periods. Although most of the items are rated using a 3-point ("Never or almost never," "Sometimes," or "Nearly all the time") response format, some item clusters are completed as true/false statements, and a few are based on specific time periods in which behaviors may have occurred, such as never, once or twice a week, or three or more times a week. The response format for the APS items is highly sophisticated and sensitive to time and behavioral intensity, requires a computer program for scoring, and is available in limited or unlimited use options at varying price points. The items of the APS are converted into one or more of 40 scales (using a *T* score system) that measure Clinical Disorders (20 scales), Personality Disorders (5 scales), Psychosocial Problem Content Areas (11 areas), and Response Style Indicators (4 scales). Many of the scales of the APS are organized to be consistent with *DSM-IV* symptom classification, but the author of the scale cautions that the APS should be used to establish severity of symptoms associated with specific *DSM-IV* disorders and not to provide any formal diagnosis or classification.

Table 8.1 Adolescent psychopathology scale, listed by area and scales

Clinical disorders	Psychosocial problem content
Attention deficit hyperactivity disorder	Self-concept
Conduct disorder	Psychosocial substance abuse difficulties
Oppositional defiant disorder	Introversion
Adjustment disorder	Alienation–boredom
Substance abuse	Anger
Anorexia nervosa	Aggression
Bulimia nervosa	Interpersonal problems
Sleep disorder	Emotional lability
Somatization disorder	Disorientation
Panic disorder	Suicide
Obsessive–compulsive disorder	Social adaptation
Generalized anxiety disorder	
Social phobia	**Response style indicator**
Separation anxiety disorder	Lie response
Posttraumatic stress disorder	Consistency response
Major depression	Infrequency response
Dysthymic disorder	
Mania	Critical item endorsement
Depersonalization disorder	**Factor score**
Schizophrenia	Internalizing Disorders Factor Score
	Externalizing Disorders Factor Score
Personality disorder	Personality Disorder Factor Score
Avoidant personality disorder	
Obsessive–compulsive personality disorder	
Borderline personality disorder	
Schizotypal personality disorder	
Paranoid personality disorder	

Technical Characteristics Technical information on the development, standardization, and psychometric properties of the APS is documented in an impressive manner in a separate psychometric and technical manual. The items were developed carefully to tap specific content areas and were refined using extensive input from a panel of experts and from feedback obtained from adolescents during a field-testing procedure. The 40 scales of the APS were developed using a combination of rational–theoretical and factor analytic approaches. Initial standardization of the APS was based on responses from 2,834 adolescents from school settings and 506 from clinical settings, from several U.S. states. The final norming sample is based on a pool of 1,837 adolescents selected from the larger sample to approximate the 1990 U.S. Census with respect to gender, ethnicity, and age.

Internal consistency reliability of the APS scales is generally in the 0.80s or 0.90s, although a few of the smaller scales are in the 0.70s range or lower. A 14-day test–retest reliability study reported in the APS manual showed that most of the scales had short-term temporal stability coefficients of 0.80 or greater, with a small mean difference in obtained scores across the two administrations. Extensive evidence for the validity of the APS is presented with regard to within-scale relationships, content validity, and convergent and discriminant construct validity based on relationships between APS scores and several other established measures of adolescent personality, psychopathology, and well-being.

In addition, construct validity evidence is presented in the form of sensitivity to differences between clinical and nonclinical groups and among diagnosed psychiatric subgroups (Conduct Disorder, Major Depressive Disorder, and Substance Abuse Disorder).

The APS Short Form A separate short-form version of the APS (APS-SF) (W. M. Reynolds, 2000) is also available. The APS-SF includes 115 items from the APS. The APS-SF takes an average of about 20 minutes to complete compared with about 60 minutes for the APS. It includes 12 clinical scales and two validity scales. Of the clinical scales, six are associated with symptoms of specific *DSM-IV* disorders (Conduct Disorder, Oppositional Defiant Disorder, Major Depression, Generalized Anxiety Disorder, Posttraumatic Stress Disorder, and Substance Abuse Disorder), and the other six are based on clusters of items specific to areas of adolescent psychosocial problems and competencies, including Eating Disturbance, Suicide, Academic Problems, Anger/Violence Proneness, Self-Concept, and Interpersonal Problems. Because the APS-SF was derived from the APS, the same standardization sample, reliability and validity studies, and scoring system were used for both measures. The APS-SF may be a good choice in situations where a shorter screening battery is desired.

Evaluation The APS and APS-SF are impressive adolescent self-report instruments and, in my opinion, constitute one of the most innovative and promising developments of the past two decades in broad-band self-report assessment of adolescent psychopathology. The APS items and rating format were developed with great care, the scales cover all of the major areas of importance for screening adolescent psychosocial problems, the technical properties are impressive, and the user's manuals are models of clarity and detail. Although the APS does not have as extensive an externally published research base as some older measures, the exemplary evidence presented in the technical manual and the many strengths of this measure are notable. Readers should understand, however, that the norms are now almost twenty years old. Hopefully, updated norms and a revised edition of the measure will be made available soon.

The Behavior Assessment System for Children, Third Edition: Child and Adolescent Self-Reports

Description The Behavior Assessment System for Children, Third Edition (BASC-3) (C. R. Reynolds & Kamphaus, 2015), a comprehensive system of child and adolescent assessment instruments, was discussed in some detail in Chapter 5 and is addressed in other chapters as well. Of interest for this chapter are three instruments that are self-reports of personality included in the system: the self-report for children aged eight to 11 (SRP-C), the self-report for adolescents aged 12 to 21 (SRP-A), and a self-report form for college-age young adults, aged 18–25 (SRP-COL). The three BASC-3 self-report measures, like the behavior rating scales of the system, are comprehensive instruments that include a variety of items and scales reflecting clinical problems, interpersonal adjustment, and adaptive competencies. The SRP-C includes 137 items, the SRP-A includes 189 items, and the SRP-COL includes 192 items. Many of the items on these three instruments are similar, but they were developed specifically for differing age and developmental groups rather than being just slightly reworded. They can be considered separate instruments, although they share many common features.

The SRP-C, SRP-A, and SRP-COL take approximately 20 to 30 minutes to complete in most situations. Telepractice options are available for youth that need additional support with administration/completion of the form. The SRP items are completed by the examinee using a combination of T (true) or F (false) (for about one third of the items) and 4-point rating (for about two-thirds of the items, where N = Never, S = Sometimes, O = Often, and A = Almost Always) formats by the examinee. The forms are scored using scoring forms that tear off from the rating forms after they are completed. Q-Global Digital scoring is a web-based scoring system available from the publisher. Raw scores are converted to subtest scores within four general areas: School Problems, Internalizing Problems, Inattention/Hyperactivity, and Personal Adjustment. In addition, an Emotional Symptoms Index score (a global index of emotional distress) is derived. The SRP-COL forms do not include items related to School Problems, but there is an Alcohol Abuse scale unique to this particular form. Converted scores are all based on a T score system. The Composites and Scales of the two SRP forms are shown in Table 8.2. In addition to the SRP scale scores, these instruments include various validity scales. Both forms

Table 8.2 Composites and scales of the child and adolescent versions of the self-report form of the Behavior Assessment System for Children, Third Edition

Composite scores	Child (SRP-C)	Adolescent (SRP-A)
Emotional Symptoms Index	×	×
Inattention–Hyperactivity	×	×
Internalizing Problems	×	×
Personal Adjustment	×	×
School Problems	×	×
Primary scales		
Anxiety	×	×
Attention Problems	×	×
Attitude to School	×	×
Attitude to Teachers	×	×
Atypicality	×	×
Depression	×	×
Hyperactivity	×	×
Interpersonal Problems	×	×
Locus of Control	×	×
Relations with Parents	×	×
Self-Esteem	×	×
Self-Reliance	×	×
Sensation Seeking		×
Sense of Inadequacy	×	×
Social Stress	×	×
Somatization		×
Content scales		
Anger Control		×
Ego Strength		×
Mania		×
Text Anxiety		×
Functional impairment index	×	×

include an F index (designed to detect abnormally high levels of symptom endorsement), a V index (consisting of nonsensical items such as "I sleep with my schoolbooks" to help detect random responding or failure to understand the directions), and an L index, designed to detect "faking good" or a social desirability response set.

Technical Characteristics The voluminous BASC-3 manual is highly detailed, well written, and provides extensive information regarding the development, standardization, and supporting empirical base for the BASC-3 components. The general norm samples for the SRP-C and SRP-A (total = 900) were derived from larger tryout samples, are geographically diverse, and are similar to the general U.S. population in terms of racial/ethnic group, socioeconomic status, gender distribution, and special education participation. Additional clinical norm samples for both forms were obtained to assist in validity research and the establishment of clinical cutoff score points. While the young adults representing the SRP-COL are significantly represented in the manual, it is likely that the standardization for this group is ongoing.

Internal consistency reliability coefficients of the SRP forms are acceptable to strong, with data from the general norm samples showing median coefficients for the composite scores ranging from the upper 0.80s to upper 0.90s, and individual scale scores mostly ranging within the 0.80s. Additional internal consistency studies with clinical subsamples produced alpha coefficients similar to or slightly lower than the reliabilities for the general norm sample. Test–retest reliability of both scales was evaluated with medium-size sub-samples at intervals ranging from 7 to 70 days between ratings. As should be expected, the resulting stability coefficients were somewhat lower than the internal consistency coefficients, but still adequate. Composite score stability coefficients are reported as generally being in the 0.60s to low 0.80s, with stability coefficients ranging from 0.59 to 0.86 for the individual scale scores. Not surprisingly, lower coefficients were reflected in scales that might be harder for young people to self-assess (e.g., self-reliance).

Various types of validity evidence for the SRPs are presented in the BASC-3 manual, including extensive factorial validity and covariance structure analysis studies, convergent and discriminant validity correlations with scores from the ASEBA Youth Self-Report, Conners 3 Child Self-Report Scale, Conners 3 Adolescent Self-Report Scale, Delis Rating of Executive Functions (D-REF), Children's Depression Inventory 2, Revised Children's Manifest Anxiety Scale Second Edition, Beck Youth Inventories-II, Beck Depression Inventory-II, MMPI-A, MMPI-A-RF, and the BASC-2 Self-Report forms. In addition, SRP profiles of mean scores from clinical group samples (ADHD, Autism Spectrum Disorder, Emotional/Behavioral Disturbance, Hearing Impairment, Specific Learning Disorder, Speech or Language Disorder) that completed the SRP-C or SRP-A are presented, with the results providing construct validity evidence regarding sensitivity to theory-based group differences. Although there are some differences between the BASC-3 and original BASC and BASC-2 SRP forms, the modest externally published research base from the original version of the scales also bolsters the reliability and validity evidence of the SRP-C and SRP-A.

Evaluation The SRP-C and SRP-A of the BASC-3 are *exemplary* child and adolescent self-report instruments in every respect. Based on the great popularity of the original BASC and BASC-2, the BASC-3 tools, which include some significant and positive improvements, will continue to be among the most widely used child and adolescent self-report measures and probably are as close to being a "standard work" for school-based assessment as exists. The SRP-C continues to fill a void in the relatively small number of general-purpose self-report instruments available for children aged eight to 11. Although the SRP-A does not fill as large of a void for adolescent self-report instruments because several other good-quality measures exist, it is definitely a positive addition and should be considered seriously against other available instruments. These self-report tools of the BASC-3 are practical, easy to use, and psychometrically strong, and they have many other positive qualities to support them. The externally published research base for these measures is still growing and provides additional supporting technical evidence to the extensive information found in the BASC-3 manual. Practitioners and researchers should have confidence in using the SRP-C and SRP-A for a variety of purposes.

The Minnesota Multiphasic Personality Inventory–Adolescent Version and Restructured Form (MMPI-A, MMPI-A-RF)

Description The Minnesota Multiphasic Personality Inventory–Adolescent (MMPI-A) (Butcher et al., 1992; Graham et al., 2006) is the adolescent-specific version of the MMPI, which is the most widely used objective self-report measure of personality and psychopathology in existence. The original MMPI was first published in the 1940s and was revised (the MMPI-2) in 2001. An adolescent version (the MMPI-A) was developed in early 1992 and revised in 2006. Although the original MMPI had been used routinely with adolescents, with special norms and interpretation guides developed for this purpose, the MMPI-A was the first version of the instrument designed specifically for use with youth. The clinical applications, research uses, and psychometric properties of the MMPI system in general have been the subject of an astounding number of published research studies (more than 10,000) and professional books (more than 100). It is arguably the most widely used and researched psychological assessment instrument of any type in existence. A tremendous knowledge base exists in support of specific clinical and research applications of these tools. Because the focus of this text is on assessment of children and adolescents, the MMPI-A and the more recently developed, MMPI-A-RF (restructured form) (Archer, Handel, Ben-Porath, & Tellegen, 2016) are discussed here, but it is important to recognize that this instrument is part of a larger system and a rich tradition.

The MMPI-A contains 478 true/false items, a reduction of nearly 100 from the MMPI and MMPI-2. The items in the MMPI-A are based on the original MMPI, but with items, scales, and norms specific to adolescents. The items that are specific to the MMPI-A involve areas considered crucial in adolescent assessment, such as alcohol and other drug use, school adjustment problems, family conflict, and maladaptive eating behaviors. As in the case of the MMPI-2 revision, several of the items of the MMPI-A that were retained from the original MMPI were reworded to make them more applicable and relevant in contemporary society. Many of the features of the original MMPI were retained in the MMPI-A, such as the L and K validity indicators and slightly revised versions of the F validity scale and the basic clinical scales. Many significant changes in scale structure from the other tools are found in the MMPI-A, however, including some validity scales and 15 "content" scales that were developed to reflect content that is highly specific to adolescent concerns and problems. In addition to the basic validity–clinical scales and the content scales, the MMPI-A includes a virtual plethora of optional scale possibilities, including:

- 6 supplementary scales;
- 27 Harris–Lingoes subscales that are similar to those developed for the MMPI and MMPI-2;
- 31 Content Component scales (including, for example, the ever popular "Misanthropic Beliefs" scale);
- 5 PSY-5 scales, which are based on the "Big 5" personality trait theory (Aggressiveness, Psychoticism, Disconstraint, Negative Emotionality/Neuroticism, Introversion/Low Positive Emotionality);
- 3 special indices related to response styles and percentages.

Although the optional or supplemental scale possibilities for the MMPI-A seem overwhelming, they are not needed or used in most cases except by the most ardent students and practitioners of the MMPI system. In general, the basic content and validity scales of the MMPI-A are sufficient for most assessment purposes with adolescents. The breakdown of these basic scales from the MMPI-A is presented in Table 8.3.

Similar to the MMPI and MMPI-2, the MMPI-A may be scored several ways, including: (1) hand-scoring with acetate scoring keys; (2) prepaid mail-in scoring services; (3) Q Local, allows the user to score and store results on a personal computer; and (4) computer scoring through Q-Global online administration or keyboard entry of completed answer forms. In addition to basic scoring options, Pearson, the publisher, provides a range of report options, which includes detailed interpretive information based on the configuration of validity, clinical, and supplemental scales from the publisher. These reports include a Correctional Interpretive Report, General Medical Interpretive Report, Inpatient Mental Health Interpretive Report, Outpatient Mental Health Interpretive Report, School Interpretive Report, and Drug/Alcohol Treatment Interpretive Report.

Technical Characteristics The MMPI-A was designed specifically for use with adolescents aged 14 to 18, and the instrument norms reflect this age group composition. These norms are based on a representative nationwide sample of 805 boys and 815 girls aged 14 to 18. Additionally, a clinical sample of 420 boys and 293 girls aged 14 to 18 was obtained, recruited from clinical treatment facilities in Minnesota. The items are written at about a sixth-grade reading level. The publisher has noted that the MMPI-A may be used with 13-year-old adolescents who have sufficient reading ability and cognitive maturity to understand the items. As is the case with the MMPI and MMPI-2, the adolescent version of the instrument includes separate norms for boys and girls, and uses a T score system. The basic clinical scales of the MMPI-A and other versions of the MMPI were developed using the empirical criterion keying approach. The MMPI-A manual is comprehensive in detail and provides substantial evidence regarding the psychometric properties of the test, which are adequate. The test–retest reliability studies presented in the manual show strong evidence of short-term temporal stability of MMPI-A scores, although the internal consistency coefficients of some of the scales are disappointingly low (in the 0.40 to 0.60 range in some cases).

The evidence presented in the manual regarding clinical sensitivity of MMPI-A scores is impressive, however, and the hundreds of studies of this instrument that have been

Table 8.3 Basic and content scales of the MMPI-A

Scale abbreviation	Scale name
Basic validity scales	
VRIN	Variable Response Inconsistency
TRIN	True Response Inconsistency
F1	Infrequency 1
F2	Infrequency 2
	Infrequency
L	Lie
K	Correction
Basic clinical scales	
Hs	Hypochondriasis
D	Depression
Hy	Hysteria
Pd	Psychopathic Deviate
Mf	Masculinity-Femininity
Pa	Paranoia
Pt	Psychasthenia
Sc	Schizophrenia
Ma	Hypomania
Si	Social Introversion
Content scales	
A-anx	Anxiety
A-obs	Obsessiveness
A-dep	Depression
A-hea	Health Concerns
A-aln	Alienation
A-biz	Bizarre Mentation
A-ang	Anger
A-cyn	Cynicism
A-con	Conduct Problems
A-lse	Low Self-Esteem
A-las	Low Aspiration
A-sod	Social Discomfort
A-fam	Family Problems
A-sch	School Problems
A-trt	Negative Treatment Indicators

published since its introduction in 1992 have bolstered the validity claims of the publisher in a substantial way. In sum, the MMPI-A has exemplary technical properties and an impressive array of evidence supporting its validity as a measure of personality and psychopathology for adolescents. Pearson continues to distribute this version of the MMPI but also markets the most up-to-date version, entitled the Minnesota Multiphasic Personality Inventory-Adolescent-Restructured Form (MMPI-A-RF).

The Minnesota Multiphasic Personality Inventory–Adolescent–Restructured Form (MMPI-A-RF)

The MMPI-A-RF (Archer et al., 2016) is structured in much the same way as the restructured form of the MMPI-2. It includes 241 items, 48 scales, and can be used with adolescents in a range of settings to identify problems, diagnose, and support treatment planning. The MMPI-A-RF takes about 25–30 minutes to complete on the computer and 30–45 minutes to complete by hand. The items are written at about a 4.5 grade reading level and forms are available in English and Spanish. Score reports include detailed information from six validity scales; Higher Order Scales that provide broad-band information about Emotional Internalizing Dysfunction, Thought Dysfunction, and Behavioral/Externalizing Dysfunction; Somatic/Cognitive and Internalizing Scales; Externalizing, Interpersonal, and Interest Scales; and updated PSY-5 scales. The norms for the MMPI-A-RF are taken from the normative sample of the MMPI-A. The 48 scales are empirically derived and users have the opportunity to customize reports so that individual scores are compared to relevant comparison groups (e.g., psychiatric inpatient, forensic correctional, school setting). Report options are the same for the MMPI-A-RF as they are for the MMPI-A (i.e., hand-scoring, mail-in, Q-local, Q-global).

Evaluation Since its introduction in 1992, the MMPI-A, and now the MMPI-A-RF, have become some of the most widely used instruments for self-report assessment of personality and psychopathology of adolescents. The technical and psychometric properties of the instrument are adequate to good, the heritage from the original MMPI is strong, and there is a vast and continually growing body of literature attesting to the validity of these measures for a variety of clinical and research purposes. Although the MMPI-A manual is detailed and provides clear instructions and suggestions for administration, scoring, and interpretation, there are several published books on this topic that are even better than the manual. Books by Archer (2005), Archer and Krishnamurthy (2001), Ben-Porath (1996), and Butcher, Williams, and Fowler (2000) are specifically recommended as the best available guides to using the MMPI-A.

Despite the enviable position of the MMPI-A and MMPI-A-RF, they are not a good choice in all situations and for all adolescents. There are two limiting factors to these measures in this regard: their length and the cognitive maturity and reading ability (though the MMPI-A-RF is more accessible) required to understand and complete it. They are a poor choice in situations in which a brief screening is needed (the full MMPI-A can take 90 minutes to complete) or in which the adolescent who is being assessed is a poor reader or has generally low cognitive ability. In situations where sufficient time is available and where the adolescent is a reasonably good reader, who is in the average or higher range of intellectual ability, the MMPI-A and MMPI-A-RF are excellent choices for a comprehensive assessment of personality and psychopathology.

The Conners 3 Self-Report

Description The Conners 3 Self-Report Form (Conners 3 SR; Conners, 2008a) is appropriate for youth aged eight to 18 years old. Like the other measures represented within the Conners 3 system, the Conners 3-SR includes a full-length form with 99 items, a short form with 41 items, and an ADHD Index form with ten items. Depending on the form used, administration time can take anywhere from five to 20 minutes, and the self-report forms range from a 3.0–4.6 grade reading level. While this tool taps a variety of constructs, it is primarily considered a comprehensive measure of ADHD. The rating scales in the Conners system are scored easily and converted to standardized subscale scores based on gender and age-level breakdowns, using an innovative two-sided "Quikscore" format that requires minimal time and reduces the chance of committing scoring errors. Online and software-based administration and scoring programs for the Conners scales are also available from the publisher. The computer programs provide not only administration and scoring possibilities, but also the generation of brief interpretive summary paragraphs related to individual score configurations and levels.

The Conners 3-SR content scales include Hyperactivity/Impulsivity, Learning Problems, Inattention, Defiance/Aggression, and Family Relations. The *DSM* symptom scales include ADHD Inattentive, ADHD Hyperactive-Impulsive, ADHD Combined, Conduct Disorder, and Oppositional Defiant Disorder. There are items that screen for anxiety and depression and also validity scales that aim to identify children that report in an overly positive, negative, or inconsistent way. There are items that target levels of impairment in schoolwork, friendships, and home life, and there are also critical items that reflect severe conduct.

Technical Characteristics The Conners 3 was developed in three phases. The structure of the various measures and the initial items were first developed, a pilot study was conducted, and then a larger normative study was completed. During the pilot study, 200 youth from a general sample and 54 from a clinical sample completed the Conners 3-SR. Data were analyzed to understand ceiling and floor effects, item discrimination, and overall factor structure. During the normative study, data were collected from 2,088 youth representative of the U.S. population. Reliability estimates for the content scales and *DSM-IV-TR* scales were calculated. Internal consistency coefficients ranged from 0.81 to 0.92 and test–retest coefficients ranged from 0.71 to 0.83. The Conners 3-SR was found to be moderately to highly correlated with the BASC-2 SRP, and the YSR from the ASEBA System, particularly with scales targeting inattention, hyperactivity, and other externalized behaviors.

Evaluation The Conners 3-SR is an excellent part of a multi-method, multi-source approach to assessment. The Conners 3 system is comprehensive, user-friendly, and has a history of quality research backing its use. Even though the Conners 3 was released prior to the release of the *DSM-5*, Dr. Conners released information in 2014 that highlights scoring and interpretative adjustments that have been suggested based on changes to the *DSM-5*. These adjustments are minor but are available from the publisher upon user request.

The Conners 3 Comprehensive Behavior Rating Scales Self-Report (CBRS-SR)

Description The Conners 3 CBRS-SR and the Conners Clinical Index (CI-SR) (Conners, 2008b) are integral to the CBRS assessment system. The CBRS-SR is appropriate for youth aged eight to 18 and includes 179 items. Similar to the Conners 3-SR, the CBRS-SR includes content scales, *DSM* scales, validity scales, impairment items, and critical items. The content scales for the self-report measure Emotional Distress, Defiant/Aggressive Behaviors, Academic Difficulties, Hyperactivity/Impulsivity, Separation Fears, Violence Potential Indicator, and Physical Symptoms. Other clinical indicators are also reflected and include Bullying Perpetration, Bullying Victimization, Panic Attack, Pervasive Developmental Disorder, Pica, PTSD, Specific Phobia, Tics, and Trichotillomania. The CI-SR is a short form with just 24 items and identifies Disruptive Behavior Disorder Indicator, Learning and Language Disorder Indicator, Mood Disorder Indicator, Anxiety

Disorder Indicator, and ADHD Indicator. With the teacher and parent report features, these self-reports can be useful in supporting diagnoses and/or educational classification, and for screening and treatment planning.

Technical Characteristics Similar to the Conners 3, the CBRS was developed in three phases—initial development, pilot study, and normative study. During the pilot phase, nearly 200 youth from the general population and 51 from clinical populations completed the CBRS-SR. Exploratory factor analyses were conducted and Other Clinical Indicators were selected. During the normative study, data were collected between 2006 and 2007 in the U.S. and Canada, and sampled from 2,057 youth. Internal consistency coefficients of the CBRS-SR ranged from 0.74 to 0.96 and temporal stability coefficients were 0.56 to 0.82. The CBRS-SR was compared to the self-report tools associated with the BASC-2, ASEBA system, Children's Depression Inventory, Multidimensional Anxiety Scale for Children, and previous Conners forms. Across these measures, the CBRS-SR converged and diverged with these measures in expected areas.

Evaluation The CBRS-SR and CI-SR are important contributions to the CBRS system. The Conners 3 and the CBRS are both exemplary and comprehensive assessment systems that have years of research supporting their development and iterations over time. The Conners 3 and CBRS self-reports are particularly helpful in that they are additional options for self-report measures that can be used with children under the age of 12.

The Youth Self-Report (YSR)

Description The Youth Self-Report (YSR) (Achenbach, 2001d) is the self-report component of the ASEBA. The most recent revision is an update of the 1991 YSR (Achenbach, 1991c). The YSR may be used alone, but it is intended for use as a "cross-informant" assessment instrument in conjunction with the CBCL and TRF, and was designed and normed for use by subjects aged 11 to 18. The YSR requires about a fifth-grade reading level to complete. The first section includes seven adaptive competency items where subjects provide information about their interests, hobbies, peer and family relationships, and school performance. These first seven items yield several competence scale scores. This section also includes four open-ended questions (e.g., "Please describe any concerns you have"). The major element of the YSR is 112 items, which are descriptive statements that are rated by the subject using a 3-point scale ("Not True" to "Very True"). Of these items, 101 are statements about various problem behaviors, whereas 11 items reflect socially desirable characteristics that are endorsed by most subjects. These socially desirable items are not scored but were placed in the checklist to provide a balance to the problem items and to help detect indiscriminate responding. The 101 problem items are scored along two broad-band scales (Internalizing and Externalizing), eight narrow-band syndromes, and a total problem score. The narrow-band cross-informant syndrome scores are the same as those used with the CBCL and TRF (see Chapter 4). All raw scores are converted to T scores in the scoring process, and the YSR can be scored using hand-scoring templates, a computer-based scoring program, or machine-readable scoring forms that require separate software and scanning devices. The scoring system provides separate score norms for boys and girls, although the same cross-informant subscale configuration is used with each gender.

Technical Characteristics The norms and clinical cutoff points for the YSR are based on a large standardization sample of 2,581 high-scoring (clinical) youths and 1,057 nonreferred youths. The standardization sample is nationally representative with respect to socioeconomic status, race, and urbanicity. Data reported in the YSR manual and in other sources indicate acceptable levels of test–retest reliability at one-week intervals (a median reliability coefficient in low 0.80s). In terms of internal-consistency reliability, the broad-band and total score alpha coefficients range from the low to upper 0.80s, and the range for narrow-band and competence scores is more variable (about 0.40 to the lower 0.80s range). Evidence of validity of the YSR presented in the manual includes sufficient factorial validity data and correlational data between the YSR, CBCL, and TRF (which are in the 0.40 range). Numerous independent studies using the current YSR and its processor have been published. It appears that the YSR is now the second most widely researched general-purpose objective self-report assessment tool for adolescents, next to the MMPI-A. Although the findings of these many studies have been mixed, they have demonstrated the technical adequacy and psychometric properties of the YSR as a self-report measure of problem behavior. The external research evidence on the YSR is far too extensive to review in this section. The many studies providing support for the validity of the YSR, among other things, have detailed its effectiveness in differentiating among clinical and nonclinical populations and various clinical populations, confirmed its factor structure, provided evidence of its sensitivity to changes wrought by intervention, and shown strong convergent construct validity in comparison with other measures. Among the studies that have raised questions regarding the validity of the YSR are some that have failed to detect score differences between differing clinical groups. In sum, the research evidence in support of the YSR is mixed, but at the same time it is primarily positive, and vast.

Evaluation Despite some potential cautions raised by a few researchers, the YSR has become widely used and well supported for good reasons. It appears to be valid for numerous clinical and research purposes, especially when used in conjunction with other forms of assessment. While the norms are somewhat old, *DSM-5* oriented scales have been developed to help guide users in current decision-making practices. The YSR has the distinct advantage of being part of the ASEBA, which is clearly the most comprehensive cross-informant assessment system for children and adolescents. One issue to consider regarding the YSR is that its items are very straightforward, even blunt at times. Items such as "I physically attack people," "I destroy things belonging to others," and "I swear or use dirty language" are not designed to be particularly subtle, and may raise defensiveness or denial in some youths. In contrast to most of the other tools reviewed in this chapter, it is for the most part a list of problem behaviors, and it lacks "validity scales" for determining how valid particular response patterns may be. It is my clinical experience and that of several colleagues that it is not unusual for adolescents with externalizing behavior problems (i.e., antisocial behavior and conduct disorders) to manipulate their responses on the YSR so that their scores tend to minimize any problems (i.e., they may look normal). Clinicians should be aware of this possible pattern. The YSR has many strengths and features that warrant its use, however, including an easy-to-use response format, a well-written manual with a great deal of technical information, a large and increasing body of research documentation, and the empirical connection between the YSR and the other components of the ASEBA.

SELF-REPORT TESTS AND DECISION MAKING

Objective self-report instruments can be useful for screening purposes and for making decisions about additional forms of assessment that may be warranted. Not only can the administration of self-report tests provide "red flags" that may be indicative of general social or emotional distress, but in some cases they can isolate specific areas of concern in which additional assessment is needed, or that may be entirely missed by direct behavioral observation or parent/teacher reports. Each of the general-purpose self-report tests reviewed in this chapter can provide specific information that can be used to generate hypotheses about additional assessment of depression, low self-esteem, anxiety, conduct problems, and even psychotic behavior. Anastasi and Urbina (1997) have emphasized that self-report personality inventories are best used as "an aid for describing and understanding the individual, identifying her or his problems, and reaching appropriate action decisions" (p. 385), a conclusion that I also endorse. In assessing children and adolescents, obtaining their own perspective through self-report assessment should be a crucial part of the assessment design and may yield information pertinent to decision making that is not possible through other sources.

Similar to most other forms of assessment, self-report tests should never be used by themselves to make diagnosis or classification and placement decisions. These types of decisions require a broad, multifactor assessment design wherein specific aspects of the decision process are weighed against specific pieces of evidence obtained through a carefully planned and implemented assessment process.

In terms of intervention or treatment planning decisions, self-report tests are normally used to generate broad hypotheses about what to do, in conjunction with other forms of assessment data, but seldom provide sufficient evidence by themselves to warrant the design and implementation of intervention plans. The possible exception—and I wish to emphasize the word *possible*—to this rule may be the use of the MMPI-A. Because of the vast history of research and clinical use of the MMPI and the extensive research base that has emerged specific to the MMPI-A, a great deal is understood about using actuarial assessment data from this instrument in developing treatment plans. There is a substantial amount of literature on the actuarial application of MMPI and MMPI-A data to treatment planning, and there is currently a great deal of interest in expanding and refining work in this area. A related decision-making use of self-report tests is their administration as treatment outcome measures. Several studies with the MMPI-A and other tools have shown that adolescent self-report measures may serve as sensitive indicators of subjective changes that may occur as a result of treatment. Readministration of a self-report test after treatment may provide some useful information regarding the efficacy of the intervention, at least from the client's own report of his or her symptoms.

In line with current RtI initiatives, self-report tests might also be useful to monitor the progress of individuals throughout treatment. Increasingly, studies are being conducted in which shorter and similarly reliable forms are being created from established rating scales. Through factor analytic techniques and use of change sensitive metrics, researchers are able to pull a smaller number of items with the highest factor loadings to create shorter scales that are sensitive to change (see Gresham et al., 2010; Volpe, Gadow, Blom-Hoffman, & Feinberg, 2009). A shorter form having good psychometric properties can be a reliable, valid, and efficient means by which to measure an individual's response to intervention and assist in making important decisions for alterations in treatment and maintenance of gains.

CONCLUSIONS

Although there has been interest in personality assessment since antiquity, empirical efforts at objective self-report assessment have been in place only since the early to mid-1900s. The Personal Data Sheet and Berneuter Personality Inventory of the 1920s and 1930s served as prototypes for modern objective self-report measures. The development and popularization of the MMPI in the 1930s and 1940s served as a model stimulus for developments in this emerging field. Although the area of objective personality assessment has faced many challenges, there has been increased interest in recent decades and important new technological developments.

Although there are many approaches to assessing behavioral, social, or emotional status through self-report means, there are specific technical criteria that must be in place for a test to be considered an objective self-report measure. In comparison with other forms of objective assessment, such as aptitude or ability testing, self-report assessment of social–emotional characteristics presents many unique challenges. Perhaps the greatest difference is that social–emotional characteristics of humans are much less stable and much more subject to variations through situations than are general cognitive characteristics.

Three major approaches to developing objective self-report tests have been identified: the rational–theoretical approach, the factor analytic approach, and the empirical criterion keying approach. There are substantial differences in how each approach is used to develop test items and scales. In reality, however, many test developers use combinations of these approaches, and it is difficult to identify any one approach as being superior. The characteristics and predictive power of particular tests are a better indicator of quality than the method used to construct the test.

Several types of response bias and error variance have been identified relative to self-report tests. Clinicians and researchers who use self-report tests should always consider the possibility of how these phenomena may affect obtained test scores, either overtly or subtly, and take these potential problems into consideration when interpreting results.

Descriptions and evaluative reviews of several illustrative general-purpose self-report tests for use with children and youth were provided in this chapter. These instruments include the Adolescent Psychopathology Scale, the child and adolescent self-report forms of the Behavior Assessment for Children, Third Edition, Minnesota Multiphasic Personality Inventory–Adolescent, Conners 3-SR, CBRS-SR, and YSR. Of these instruments, only four (the SRP-C, YSR, and Conners 3-SR and CBRS-SR forms) are aimed at the preadolescent population. These instruments represent the best of what is currently available, and they represent major advances in self-report assessment of adolescents. Before 1990, virtually nothing of value was available for children younger than age 11 or 12 in the way of psychometrically adequate general-purpose self-report forms. Although more instruments have been available for use with adolescents, the recent developments in this area have been encouraging as well. The field of self-report assessment of children and adolescents is substantially more advanced today than it was only a few years ago. Clinicians and researchers now are able to choose among several high-quality measures for specific assessment issues.

Self-report measures may provide information useful in making various decisions, such as screening, diagnosis, and treatment planning. An emerging decision-making use of self-report measures stems from their increasing use as treatment outcome measures. One caution that should be considered in making decisions with self-report data is the fact that these data sometimes are at odds with assessment data supplied from other sources, such as parent and teacher reports. Clinicians and researchers should include self-report assessment as one aspect of the assessment design and consider the overall picture provided by all sources of data when making decisions.

REVIEW AND APPLICATION QUESTIONS

1. What characteristics are considered to be essential for an assessment instrument to be considered an objective self-report test?
2. Compare and contrast the three major methods of objective test construction: rational–theoretical, empirical criterion keying, and factor analysis. Which, if any, of these is the preferred method for constructing self-report tests?
3. What are the major forms of *response bias* discussed in this chapter, and how may they be manifest in self-report assessment of children and adolescents?
4. You are a psychologist working in either a community-based clinic or a school. You are interested in using the Adolescent Psychopathology Scale with the population you serve. Discuss (1) the conditions under which this measure would be appropriate, and (2) advantages and disadvantages of this measure, given these conditions.
5. Of the several general-purpose self-report tests reviewed in this chapter, several (the SRP-C, YSR, Conners 3-SR and CBRS-SR) were developed for use with children younger than 12 years old. If one were determining which of these two instruments to administer to a nine- or ten-year-old child, how would the relative merits and drawbacks of each test play into the decision?
6. How might child and adolescent self-report tests be used best in making decisions regarding the effectiveness of treatment?
7. It is common for youth self-report instruments to yield data that differ—sometimes markedly so—from assessment data provided through other sources (i.e., parent and teacher reports). What are some realistic ways of treating these differences in assessment results?

9

PROJECTIVE–EXPRESSIVE ASSESSMENT TECHNIQUES

Projective and expressive assessment includes such techniques as drawing, storytelling, and sentence completion. Although projective and expressive assessment techniques are often at the center of a storm of controversy regarding reliability, validity, and appropriate uses, there is no question that these techniques continue to be popular among many clinicians. A review of the professional and scientific literature on projective–expressive assessment does not easily lead to a consensus regarding the current state of the art. On one hand, many researchers and clinicians who are concerned with assessment of children and adolescents view projective–expressive assessment techniques as an important feature of the clinical training of graduate students. This view is based on the notion that these techniques may offer a unique window into an individualized idiographic assessment of the "inner life" of children and adolescents. On the other hand, projective–expressive assessment has a small army of very vocal critics who view this area with disdain and rightly point out that the reliability and validity of many of these techniques fall short of professional standards as well as those of other forms of social–emotional assessment.

Survey research on assessment practices of school and clinical psychologists during the past two decades (e.g., Hojnoski, Morrison, Brown, & Matthews, 2006; Lubin, Larsen, & Matarazzo, 1984; Norcross, Karpiak, & Santoro, 2005; Watkins, Campbell, & McGregor, 1988; Wilson & Reschly, 1996) indicates that despite some of the controversies surrounding them, projective–expressive and related social–emotional assessment techniques remain popular among clinicians. For that reason alone, it is important to devote a chapter in this book to a treatment of the topic. We share some of the views of authors of related texts on psychological assessment of children (e.g., Groth-Marnat, 1997; Kamphaus & Frick, 2002) that projective–expressive assessment techniques are a unique method of assessing children, and in some cases may be a valuable component of a comprehensive assessment design. Because projective–expressive assessment techniques often do not meet the standards of technical adequacy of the primarily direct and objective techniques emphasized in other chapters of this text, I also share the view that these techniques should be used judiciously, cautiously, and rarely because of some of the unique psychometric and ethical concerns surrounding them (e.g., R. J. Cohen & Swerdlik, 1999; Groth-Marnat, 1997; Knauss, 2001). In fact, I agree with the opinion of Hojnoski et al. (2006), who stated, "Given issues of psychometric adequacy, treatment utility, and social validity, the continued use of projectives by school psychologists is puzzling" (p. 147). In short, I believe that a comprehensive chapter devoted to this topic is essential if for no other reason than to help readers evaluate the cautions and problems associated with projective–expressive assessment, so that they might make informed and defensible choices.

DOI: 10.4324/9781315747521-10

This chapter begins with a brief introduction to the theory and practice of projective–expressive techniques, and then includes sections on using thematic approaches, drawing techniques, and sentence completion tasks as methods of assessing social–emotional behavior of children and adolescents. The chapter concludes with a set of recommendations for best practice in using projective–expressive techniques, emphasizing appropriate and defensible practices. In making a determination of which projective techniques were most important to include in this chapter, some prominent techniques were left out because of space and practical considerations. One technique that is prominently missing from this chapter is the Rorschach Inkblot test. There are two reasons for this omission. First, the use of the Rorschach has evolved to the point where it is not as loosely projective as it once was, and the most widely used methods for scoring and interpretation treat it as a highly structured perceptual task (e.g., Bornstein, 2012; Exner & Weiner, 1994). Second, given the complexity of modern methods of using the Rorschach (i.e., the Exner system), readers should be advised that a cursory overview of the Rorschach in a general chapter would not prepare them even to begin administering this test. Rather, effective use of the Rorschach with subjects of any age requires intensive training and study. Clinicians who desire to become more familiar with it should refer to the appropriate comprehensive books, as well as some of the controversies regarding the use of the Rorschach.

PROJECTIVE ASSESSMENT: AN INTRODUCTION

According to Gregory (1996), the *projective hypothesis* was first formally detailed by Frank (1939) to describe a category of psychological tests designed to study personality through responses to unstructured stimuli. Use of assessment techniques that might be considered to be projective substantially predates the term itself, however, and some projective techniques were clearly in use with children and adults by at least the 1920s, if not earlier. The projective hypothesis is based on the assumption that "*personal interpretations of ambiguous stimuli must necessarily reflect the unconscious needs, motives, and conflicts of the examinee*" (Gregory, 1996, p. 511, italics added for emphasis). The basic task involved in projective assessment is to evaluate information and products (i.e., statements, drawings, key words) that are provided by the examinee in response to an ambiguous task, for the purpose of deciphering their underlying personality processes and social–emotional functioning. Without question, this task is formidable and, by the nature of the procedures designed to enable it, will often become a highly subjective and speculative pursuit. Within various projective methods, there is wide variation in how structured or unstructured the processes of elicitation and interpretation are.

The term *projective–expressive techniques* is used throughout this chapter. The addition of *expressive* to the constellation of projective techniques signifies that some methods that are often lumped together with projectives are not really projectives in the strict sense, given that they are not based singularly on the projective hypothesis. Expressive social–emotional assessment techniques are procedures in which examinees are allowed to express themselves in response to ambiguous or loosely structured stimuli, but their responses may not necessarily be used in a true projective manner. Examples of techniques that may be considered more expressive than projective include certain drawing tasks and specific sentence completion tests. Throughout this chapter, the term *projective–expressive* is used to denote a general category of assessment techniques that are based on similar assumptions and allow for individualized administration and interpretation by the clinician.

Many advocates of projective–expressive assessment have been influenced strongly by psychodynamic theory. Perhaps the most central psychodynamic tenet that is incorporated into projective–expressive assessment is the assumption that responses to ambiguous stimuli represent projections of the examinees' unconscious psychological processes. Within this psychodynamic–projective paradigm, the responses examinees make to ambiguous stimuli may be quite revealing (to the trained clinician) regarding their "inner processes," but the examinees may not be aware that the information is so revealing. Although psychodynamic theory has been in the forefront of projective testing, more recently humanistic theory also has been incorporated. In a strict sense, however, the purpose of the test is no longer truly projective when the psychodynamic theory is deemphasized. The major difference between psychodynamic and humanistic approaches to assessment is that humanistic-based techniques do not rely as much on the latent or hidden content of examinees' responses (i.e., the examinees' unconscious projections). Rather, assessment techniques that are underpinned by humanistic theory are more likely to view responses of examinees as direct statements about who they are as people. An example of a humanistic approach to this type of assessment would be human figure drawings for the purpose of identifying an examinee's overt body image. Although there are some psychodynamic and humanistic historical underpinnings to the area of projective–expressive assessment, this area also seems to be conceptually aligned with more recent ideologies, including postmodernism and constructivism.

Projective–expressive assessment seems to be as widely used with children and adolescents as it is with adults. Some projective techniques have been developed or adapted specifically to one age group or another, but many are adaptable across various age ranges. Some of the presumed advantages of using projective–expressive techniques with children and adolescents is that the examinees do not need to understand the specific purposes of the task and that they may be less suspicious and defensive when asked to engage in tasks such as drawing, finishing sentences, and telling stories about pictures than they might be when asked specific questions about their social–emotional behavior (Chandler & Johnson, 1991).

Like no other method of social–emotional or personality assessment, the use of projective techniques has been controversial (R. J. Cohen & Swerdlik, 1999; Hojnoski et al., 2006; Knauss, 2001; D. N. Miller & Nickerson, 2007). Most of the controversy regarding projective assessment has been from within the professional community rather than from the lay public (in contrast to the controversies surrounding IQ and academic achievement tests). There have been numerous points of contention regarding projectives, but the essential controversies involve two main issues. First, many psychologists and other professionals simply do not believe the argument that is evident in the projective hypothesis: that responses to ambiguous stimuli may reveal important information about the personality that is unconsciously projected. Second, and perhaps more important, projective–expressive assessment does not fare particularly well in comparison with more direct and objective assessment methods from the standpoint of scientific psychometric criteria (Gregory, 1996).

Despite years of controversy regarding projective assessment, these techniques continue to be popular, and in many cases are more popular than direct and objective methods that fare much better in terms of empirical evidence. Despite one recent survey of clinical psychologists indicating that projective assessment is used less frequently among clinicians than it was in the 1960s and 1970s (Norcross et al., 2005), studies by Hojnoski et al. (2006), Lubin et al. (1984), Watkins et al. (1988), and Wilson and Reschly (1996) all indicated that projective–expressive techniques are among the most widely used of all psychological assessment methods and that they show no sign of declining in popularity. In commenting on this paradox between evidence and use, Gregory stated:

> The essential puzzle of projective tests is how to explain the enduring popularity of these instruments in spite of their generally marginal (often dismal) psychometric quality. After all, psychologists are not uniformly dense, nor are they dumb to issues of test quality. So why do projective techniques persist?
>
> (1996, p. 512)

In answering his own question, Gregory proposed two explanations for the continued popularity of projective–expressive techniques. First, as humans, we are likely to cling to preexisting notions and stereotypes, even after we are exposed to contradictory findings. Second, there is a tendency toward *illusory validation* (Chapman & Chapman, 1967), a phenomenon that is best put into context by the deftly ironic statement "If I didn't believe it, I wouldn't have seen it." In essence, clinicians who believe strongly in using particular assessment methods are more likely to notice findings from those methods that confirm their hypotheses, while being likely to ignore findings that contradict their expectations. With this cautionary interpretation to the continued popularity of projectives as a preamble, this chapter provides a comprehensive overview of three of the most popular areas of projective assessment with children: thematic approaches, drawing techniques, and sentence completion tasks.

THEMATIC APPROACHES

Thematic approaches to assessing personality and psychopathology are based on the projective hypothesis, and their use became specifically associated with the study of *ego psychology* as advocated by H. A. Murray, Bellak, and their associates at the Harvard University Psychological Clinic in the 1940s. In a thematic-based assessment, the examinee is presented with a series of drawings or pictures showing unstructured ambiguous characters and situations and is asked to tell a story about each picture. The basis of interpreting responses to thematic storytelling tasks is that the examinee is assumed to project his or her needs, drives, conflicts, and emotions that form the foundation of the personality into the picture stimulus and the resulting story.

Many of the early clinical and research uses of thematic storytelling approaches were heavily oriented toward assessing creativity and imagination, and instructions to examinees typically encouraged them in this regard (Gregory, 2000). As thematic approaches became increasingly popular in the 1950s and 1960s, however, the emphasis on creativity and imagination was replaced with a stronger emphasis on personality assessment, particularly from a psychodynamic orientation.

Because there are so many thematic techniques available and because there are no dominant standardized methods of administration, scoring, and interpretation, it is best to refer to this category of assessment as thematic approaches rather than thematic tests.

In contrast to the other projective–expressive techniques discussed in this chapter, it is difficult to include a separate section on administration, scoring, and interpretation because there is so much variation from one clinician to another and among various thematic approaches (Gregory, 2000; Obrzut & Boliek, 1986; Teglasi, 2001; Worchel, 1990). There are some recent handbooks that focus on thematic approaches, should readers decide to pursue more information in this area (see Jenkins, 2008; Teglasi, 2010). This section provides information on administration, scoring, and interpretation within the description of three specific thematic approaches: the Thematic Apperception Test (TAT), the Children's Apperception Test (CAT), and the Roberts Apperception Test for Children (RATC). Following the description of these three approaches, additional sections on reliability–validity and concluding comments on using thematic approaches are provided.

Before proceeding with this discussion, it is important to recognize that this is a relatively cursory and limited overview and cannot possibly do justice to the vast body of literature on research and clinical applications of thematic approaches. Readers who desire to become highly familiar and skilled in the use of thematic approaches are referred to the recent volumes that have been written to provide in-depth explorations of thematic approaches (e.g., Bellak, 1975; Rabin, 1986; Teglasi, 1993, 2001, 2010).

The Thematic Apperception Test (TAT)

The Thematic Apperception Test (TAT) should be considered "the mother of all thematic approaches." Without question, the TAT is the most influential and widely researched thematic approach. Most other thematic approaches are modifications or extensions of the TAT. Developed by Henry Murray and his colleagues at the Harvard Psychological Clinic (Morgan & Murray, 1935; H. A. Murray, 1938), the TAT originally was designed to assess personality constructs such as *needs*, *press*, and *thema*, which were essential elements to Murray's personality theory. In this theory, needs include processes that organize thought, action, and behavior to be energized to satisfy underlying needs. Press refers to the power of environmental events that may influence a person. Themas are themes of combined needs and presses into a pattern that is played out in a story.

The TAT includes 31 black-and-white picture cards that contain a variety of unstructured and ambiguous characters, situations, and objects. The entire collection of cards is never administered to an examinee; an individualized administration battery ranging from ten or fewer cards to 20 cards is selected. The cards are numbered, and many cards include letters with the number, to identify cards that are recommended for specific use with boys (2), girls (G), adult males (M), and adult females (F), or some combination thereof (e.g., GF). Obrzut and Boliek (1986) recommended that when administering the TAT to children aged eight to 11, the following cards were particularly important: 1, 3BM, 7GF, 8BM, 12M, 13B, 14, and 17BM. For adolescents, Obrzut and Boliek recommended cards 1, 2, 5, 7GF, 12F, 12M, 15, 17BM, 18BM, and 18GF. Teglasi (1993) noted that cards 1, 2, 3BM, 4, 5, 6BM, 7GF, and 8BM were appropriate for use with children and adolescents of either gender. Other writers have expressed similar and differing preferences for constructing TAT batteries for child and adolescent use, but ultimately the clinician needs to select an appropriate set of cards from the TAT that make sense for use with the specific examinee. An important consideration in selecting an appropriate battery of TAT cards is the presenting issues and problems of the examinee. For example, if the examinee "appears depressed, those TAT pictures related to depression and suicide should be used" (Obrzut & Boliek, 1986, p. 178).

Administration instructions for the TAT tend to be nonstandardized, and many uses of the TAT tend to deviate from H. A. Murray's (1938) original directions, which emphasized creativity and imagination. Some writers have expressed the opinion that TAT directions should provide as few cues as possible, permitting the examinees great leeway in expressing themselves (Peterson, 1990). Teglasi (1993, 2001, 2010) argued, however, that TAT administrations with children and adolescents should include more structure because it allows for better follow-up questions by the examiner. Teglasi recommended the following general instructions from H. A. Murray (1943) for administering the TAT to children and adolescents:

Younger Children:
I am going to show you some pictures, and I would like you to tell me a story for each one. In your story, please tell: What is happening in the picture? What happened before? What are people thinking and feeling? How does it all turn out in the end? So I'd like you to tell a whole story with a beginning, a middle, and an ending. You can make up any story you want. Do you understand? I'll write down your story. Here's the first card.

Older Children and Adolescents:
I am going to show you some pictures, one at a time, and your task will be to make up a story for each card. In your story, be sure to tell what has led up to the event shown in the picture, describe what is happening at the moment, tell what the characters are feeling and thinking, and then give the outcome. Tell a complete story with a beginning, middle, and end. Do you understand? I will write your stories as you tell them. Here's the first card.

After each TAT card story, a series of clarifying questions is recommended so that the examiner will better understand the examinee's story. This process is referred to as the *inquiry phase* of administration. Questions may involve further clarification of the characters' thoughts and feelings and how the story was generated (e.g., whether the examinee created the story or adapted it from something he or she read, or watched on television). True to the unstandardized nature of the TAT, some writers have expressed a preference for conducting the inquiry phase only after all cards have been administered, so as to not interfere with the examinee's storytelling while it is happening (Bellak, 1975). If the clinician considers the TAT to be a true projective test, it should be considered that the more structure that is imposed on the administration process, the less projective or spontaneous will be the examinee's responses (Obrzut & Boliek, 1986).

Interpretation of the TAT tends to be even more nonstandardized than administration. Numerous interpretation approaches have been proposed, and it is beyond the scope of this chapter to review them all. In their review of using the TAT with children and adolescents, Obrzut and Boliek (1986) recommended the inspection technique as being "the simplest and, perhaps, most useful for TAT interpretation" (p. 179). This method is fairly straightforward and involves the clinician's simply treating the stories as being meaningful psychological communications from the child or adolescent examinee. Data that seem to be significant, specific, or unique are noted. This technique also incorporates the widely used suggestion of the original TAT authors to identify a *hero* (or main character) within each story, which is presumably the character that the examinee will identify with and project his or her unconscious motives and needs onto. "The motives, trends, and feelings of the hero; the forces within the hero's environment; the outcome of the stories; simple and complex themes; and interests and sentiments attributed to the hero" (Obrzut & Boliek, 1986, p. 180) are all considered to be important aspects of interpretation. Common themes among the stories should be identified, and the expressive manner in which the examinee relates the story should be noted carefully. This method of interpretation is simple, allows the clinician extensive leeway, and if used conservatively, should provide an effective bridge of understanding into the examinee's stories. Readers interested in practical strategies and applications of the TAT are referred to Aronow, Weiss, & Reznikoff (2013).

The Children's Apperception Test (CAT)

The Children's Apperception Test (CAT) (Bellak & Bellak, 1949) was developed as a downward extension of the TAT, specifically targeted for use with children aged three to ten. The CAT includes ten cards that depict animal characters (e.g., lions, bears, chimps, dogs) rather than human characters. The theory behind the use of animal characters by the authors of the CAT is that young children would be better able to relate to animal characters than human characters and might find them to be less threatening. A parallel form of the CAT (the CAT-H) was developed that includes human rather than animal figures (with the same picture scenarios as the CAT), which is thought to be more appropriate for older children and preadolescents.

Because the CAT is conceptually and theoretically similar to the TAT, the same general administration and general interpretation methods that were outlined for the TAT are recommended. Bellak (1975), the author of the CAT, recommended that interpretation of CAT stories should focus on identification of the following ten variables:

1. the main theme;
2. the main hero;
3. main needs and drives of the hero;
4. the conception of the environment;
5. how figures are seen;
6. significant conflicts;
7. nature of anxieties;
8. main defenses against conflicts and fears;
9. adequacy of superego as manifested by "punishment for crime";
10. integration of the ego.

Bellak's recommendations for interpretation are influenced heavily by psychodynamic and traditional psychoanalytic theories. Clinicians not so psychodynamically inclined who desire to use the CAT are advised to focus on the inspection technique of interpretation, focusing on the issues and variables in the story content with which they are most comfortable.

The Roberts Apperception Test for Children (RATC)

The Roberts Apperception Test for Children (RATC) (McArthur & Roberts, 1982), developed more recently than the TAT or CAT, is a thematic technique for children that is in wide use. The authors of the RATC intend for it to be used with children aged 6 to 15.

Its stated purpose is to assess child and adolescent perceptions of interpersonal situations, such as the thoughts, concerns, conflicts, and coping styles of examinees. The RATC includes 27 stimulus cards. Some cards are labeled specifically for use with boys or girls, and only 16 cards are administered at one time. The content of the RATC cards is more modern and less ambiguous than that of the TAT or CAT, depicting specific scenes involving such themes as parental discord and harmony, the observation of nudity, aggression, and peer rejection. A "Black" version of the RATC stimulus cards is available that depicts Black individuals in the same situations as on the standard cards.

Administration of the RATC is similar to that for the TAT and CAT. Scoring and interpretation is much more of a structured process for the RATC, however. The test includes a standardized T score scoring system and results in four areas of scores:

1. adaptive scales: reliance on others, support others, support child, limit setting, problem identification, and three types of problem resolution;
2. clinical scales: anxiety, aggression, depression, rejection, unresolved;
3. critical indicators: atypical response, maladaptive outcome, refusal;
4. supplementary measures: ego functioning, aggression, levels of projection.

The RATC seems to be a well-designed assessment technique that may be useful as a clinical tool when used with caution. The innovation and contribution of the RATC is its emphasis on a standardized scoring and interpretation system that is more empirically based than most thematic approaches (although the normative sample comprises only 200 cases). Worchel (1990) concluded that the RATC "appears to have significant benefits over its predecessors," while acknowledging that "the standardized scoring system is admittedly lacking in validity evidence compared to more objective personality tests" (p. 424). Several empirical studies on the RATC have been completed since it was published. During the preparation of an earlier edition of this text, a computer-assisted search located more than 40 studies (mostly unpublished doctoral dissertations) wherein the RATC was the primary topic or a major focus. A few more research studies on the RATC have appeared in the past ten years. Clinicians who are interested in using thematic approaches with children and young adolescents and who desire to use an objective scoring and interpretation approach may find the RATC to be a potentially useful addition to their assessment design. Clinicians who are not comfortable with the overt psychodynamic theoretical orientation of the TAT and CAT may find the RATC appealing because it is not expressively based on this theoretical approach.

A second edition of the RATC was published. The RATC-2 (G. E. Roberts, 2005) is designed to assess social understanding of children and adolescents, as they express it in free narrative. Thus, like the first edition, the RATC-2 does not include the explicit reliance on psychodynamic theory. The second edition includes several improvements on the original RATC, including updated test pictures that depict current hairstyle and clothing preferences; an extended age range (up to 18); three parallel sets of test pictures depicting White, Black, and Hispanic youths; and a new and larger norming sample that is generally representative of the U.S. population in terms of geographical region, ethnicity, and gender. The RATC-2 norming sample is based on a sample of 1,000 children and adolescents, aged six to 18, with an additional clinically referred sample of 500 youths. The scales of the RATC are somewhat different from those of the first edition, and include subscales within the following areas: Theme Overview, Problem Identification, Outcome,

Available Resources, Emotion, Resolution, and Unusual or Atypical Responses. The RATC-2 manual is generally well organized and includes some useful technical and psychometric information. Although there is currently limited externally published research evidence available on the RATC-2, it represents an improvement over the first edition, has received positive reviews (Flanagan, 2008), and will likely become popular over time as it attracts new users and as clinicians who are currently using the original RATC gradually switch to the second edition.

Reliability and Validity

The technical adequacy of thematic approaches has been difficult to evaluate, not only because there are numerous competing thematic techniques, but also because of the plethora of nonstandardized scoring and interpretation methods. In their review of psychometric properties of thematic approaches, Obrzut and Boliek (1986) stated that much less in this area has been investigated with children and adolescents compared with adults. They stated that the available evidence indicates thematic approaches have shown substantial reliability and evidence of clinical validity. Obrzut and Boliek's review is notable because of the bold assertion they made in several instances that traditional standards of reliability and validity are not particularly relevant with thematic approaches. Other authors have been less charitable in their assessment of the psychometric properties of thematic approaches: "In large measure, then, the interpretation of (thematic techniques) is based on strategies with unknown and untested reliability and validity" (Gregory, 1996, p. 523). Although thematic storytelling techniques for social–emotional assessment have many adherents, and a growing number of empirical studies have provided some evidence of convergent construct validity of various thematic approaches used in conjunction with other social–emotional assessment methods (Teglasi, 1993, 2001), there are also numerous concerns regarding technical adequacy of these measures (Hojnoski et al., 2006).

Concluding Comments on Thematic Approaches

Thematic approaches to personality assessment have a fascinating history and are interesting to administer and interpret. Child and adolescent examinees often seem to enjoy the process of making up stories to thematic stimulus cards and tend to find this assessment technique nonthreatening. One drawback to using thematic approaches with younger and less intellectually sophisticated children is that they often respond to the stimulus cards in a short, concrete, and unenlightening manner, making for difficult interpretation if one follows a true projective approach. As the review of psychometric properties of thematic approaches indicated, the evidence regarding reliability and validity is mixed, and even advocates of such techniques tend to be cautious in their appraisals. Caution is advised in using thematic approaches with children and adolescents, particularly regarding making strong interpretive statements in the absence of any additional supporting evidence. There are also some specific ethical concerns to consider regarding the use of these techniques in school settings (Knauss, 2001). A thematic approach to assessment may help facilitate communication and rapport with children and adolescents, who often find such activities to be fun and nonthreatening. Clinicians may find thematic approaches to be a useful part of a comprehensive social–emotional assessment design that may provide insight into young examinees from their own perspective and in their own words.

DRAWING TECHNIQUES

Drawing techniques are perhaps the oldest category of assessment procedures that can be placed in the general domain of projective–expressive assessment. Psychologically based drawing techniques have been in use nearly as long as the field of psychology has existed, as early as the 1890s by some accounts (Barnes, 1892). Historically, the first uses of psychologically based drawing techniques were not for assessment of social–emotional status or personality. Rather, the earliest uses of drawing techniques were focused primarily on intellectual and developmental assessment (Cummings, 1986). According to Hammer (1981), use of drawing techniques for projective–expressive assessment of children occurred gradually, as clinicians noted interesting qualitative differences in specific features of drawings (e.g., facial expression, size, position on page) produced by children. These qualitative differences in drawings did not result in differential scoring when intellectual or developmental screening procedures were being used, but led to interpretations by clinicians that such differences should be considered important emotional or affective expressions within the drawing. This type of reasoning led to the widespread clinical use of children's drawings for projective social–emotional and personality assessment.

In his excellent review of using projective drawings with children, Cummings (1986) stated that the literature indicates the use of four major functions for projective drawing tests:

1. to allow graphic, symbolic communication between a nonverbal child and a clinician;
2. to allow the clinician to develop an understanding of the inner conflicts, fears, family interactions, and perceptions of others from the child's perspective;
3. to provide a medium for understanding the child from a psychodynamic perspective (e.g., sexual identification, ego strength);
4. to assist in planning for further evaluation through the generation of hypotheses regarding the child.

As is true regarding virtually all projective–expressive techniques, a great deal of controversy exists regarding projective drawings, despite their widespread use. It is my opinion that many of the historical and current uses of projective drawing techniques with children are indefensible and that in general the technical properties (i.e., reliability and validity evidence) of such techniques tend to be vastly inferior to those of many of the more recently developed social–emotional assessment technologies that have been refined since the 1980s. It is also naive, however, to think that clinicians simply will abandon projective drawing techniques. As we see herein, these techniques remain enormously popular despite criticism, and supporting evidence that is mixed at best and abysmal at worst. Given this set of conditions, it is important to review the major projective drawing techniques for children in this chapter, with a specific focus on evaluating the supporting evidence and identifying the most appropriate uses for these techniques. This discussion includes separate overviews of three of the most widely used drawing techniques: The Draw-A-Person (DAP) technique, the Kinetic Family Drawing (KFD) technique, and use of the Bender-Gestalt Test (BGT) as a social–emotional screening device. Some related drawing techniques are discussed in less detail.

The Draw-A-Person Technique (DAP)

Without question, the most widely used drawing procedure in social–emotional assessment of children is the Draw-A-Person Technique (DAP). The pre-eminent position of this drawing technique was verified through Wilson and Reschly's (1996) national survey of assessment practices of school psychologists. The results of this survey indicated that in the 1980s and 1990s the DAP was not only the most widely used drawing technique for social–emotional assessment of children, but also the fourth most widely used psychological assessment technique overall. A more recent survey of projective test use among school psychologists by Hojnoski and colleagues (2006) found that although the DAP and related projective drawing tests were used less frequently among respondents than sentence completion tasks, they were still very popular.

The exact origins of human figure drawings (the predecessor to the current DAP technique) are unclear, but they have been in use by psychologists since the early part of the twentieth century. Although human figure drawings were formally used by Goodenough in the 1920s as a measure of cognitive development (Goodenough, 1926), they also appear to have been used clinically for social–emotional assessment during this time period (Chandler & Johnson, 1991). The first widely disseminated technique for using human figure drawings in social–emotional assessment was Machover's (1949) highly influential book *Personality Projection in the Drawing of a Human Figure*. This book was a major force behind the DAP as a social–emotional assessment technique, and it continues to be an influential foundation for current methods of using the DAP. Another book that has also been widely influential as a force behind the DAP for social–emotional assessment is Koppitz's (1968) *Psychological Evaluation of Children's Human Figure Drawings*, which was published two decades after Machover's seminal text.

The basis of using the DAP as a social–emotional assessment technique is similar to that of other drawing tests. Proponents of human figure drawings such as the DAP purport that the quality of drawings made by children through these tasks may provide important information regarding their psychosocial adjustment, including nonverbal symbolic communication of their conflicts, fears, family interactions, and so forth. The theoretical foundations and assumptions underlying DAP social–emotional assessment techniques are varied, but psychodynamic and humanistic theories have been in the forefront in this regard.

Administration, Scoring, and Interpretation Most advocates of DAP techniques suggest a similar administration method. The child is given a blank sheet of 8.5-inch-by-11-inch paper and a No. 2 lead pencil with an eraser. The child is instructed to "Draw a picture of a whole person" (Cummings, 1986, p. 202). Some variations on DAP instructions have been suggested by DAP devotees. Koppitz (1968) recommended that the examiner add the statement, "It can be any kind of person you want to draw. Just make sure that it is a whole person and not a stick figure or a cartoon figure" (p. 6). This clarification was suggested to discourage older children from quickly drawing a simple stick figure just to avoid the task. Another modification has been suggested by Chandler and Johnson (1991), who recommend that younger children (i.e., kindergarten-age and younger) be allowed to use a thick pencil, crayon, or felt-tip pen, for ease of drawing. Figure 9.1 is an example of a DAP produced by a child through this instructional procedure.

Most DAP advocates suggest that the examiner use the words *draw a person* rather than the less ambiguous instructions to draw a man, a woman, a girl, and so forth. The

Figure 9.1 A human figure drawing produced by a five-year-old girl, using standard DAP directions

ambiguity of the more general instructions has been considered to result in increased psychological projection regarding the subject's identification of gender, which has been the object of several empirical studies in and of itself (e.g., Dickson, Saylor, & Finch, 1990; Zaback & Waehler, 1994). Most advocates of the DAP favor having the child make two or more drawings, in a process where the second drawing is requested to be a person of the opposite sex of the person depicted in the first drawing (Cummings, 1986). The entire DAP process typically takes five to ten minutes to complete.

Scoring of the DAP tends to be nonstandardized and usually is done in conjunction with interpretation. The exception to this statement is Naglieri, McNeish, and Bardos's (1991) structured scoring system for using the DAP as a screening procedure for emotional disturbance, referred to as the DAP:SPED. The structured DAP:SPED system includes scoring templates and specific scoring rules for various features of drawings. Studies of the DAP:SPED have indicated that it can successfully distinguish students who receive special education from students who do not receive services (Matto, Naglieri, & Clausen, 2005), that it is moderately correlated with measures of social–emotional strengths (Matto et al., 2005), and that scores do not differ significantly across ethnic groups (Matto et al., 2005). However, most DAP advocates and users tend to favor a nonstandardized holistic manner of scoring that is connected directly to interpretation. Machover's (1949) and Koppitz's (1968) books provide general guidelines for scoring DAP figures and are still widely influential.

Interpretation of the DAP is a process that also tends to be nonstandardized and often is done in conjunction with a particular text or technique (i.e., Machover or Koppitz). Despite the influence of one interpretation technique or another, it has been our experience that many practitioners who use the DAP for clinical assessment use holistic, self-styled interpretation methods, occasionally borrowing from various interpretation guidelines that have been integrated during their career.

Machover's (1949) technique for interpretation of human figure drawings proposed that interpretation should be based on a combination of indicators rather than individual signs or characteristics. From this perspective, the social features of the drawing are symbolically represented in the head. For example, "Closed eyes may suggest an attempt to shut out the world" and "Large, accentuated eyes may be associated with hostility" (Cummings, 1986, p. 203). From this perspective, the *contact features* of a drawing (i.e., the fingers, hands, arms, toes, feet, and legs) are said to represent a child's interactions with his or her environment. For example, "A relative lack of attention to feet and legs or their omission may reveal a child's insecurity about his or her problems dealing with sexual impulses," whereas "irrelevant emphasis of pockets" in drawings is seen in "infantile and dependent individuals" (Cummings, 1986, p. 203). The Machover method also emphasizes such factors as figure size, placement of figures on the paper, and drawing themes.

The Koppitz (1968) method of interpretation is psychodynamically oriented and built on Machover's (1949) technique. One important difference in the Koppitz method is the increased emphasis on empirical identification of low-frequency emotional indicators through systematic investigation of clinical cases and normal cases. In the Koppitz system, a particular characteristic in human figure drawings is considered an emotional indicator if three criteria are met:

1. It must possess clinical utility through differentiating between drawings of children with and without emotional problems.
2. It must be unusual or, in other words, something that is infrequently found in the drawings of normal children.
3. It must not be related to developmental maturation.

Using these three criteria as a guide, Koppitz (1968) lists 38 emotional indicators, divided into the areas of *quality signs, special features,* and *omissions.* A summary of these emotional indicators is provided in Table 9.1. The Koppitz method of scoring and interpretation is complex and comprehensive, and requires a more in-depth study than simply referring to a table of emotional indicators.

A more recent system for scoring and interpreting the DAP is Naglieri et al.'s (1991) DAP:SPED method, which differs substantially from traditional methods of interpreting human figure drawings because of its emphasis on objective scoring and reliance on empirical criteria within a normative standardization group. Within this system, specific scoring indicators, such as legs together, placement of figure, various omissions, objects in mouth, fists, and nude figures, were developed through identification of low-frequency indicators that were significantly more likely to be found in clinical samples. Specific criteria are provided for the presence of these figures (including objective scoring keys), and each indicator is given a score of 1. The total raw score is converted to T scores and percentile ranks, based on gender and age breakdowns. Using this system, interpretation is based on "the higher the score, the more likely it is that emotional disturbance exists" (p. 64). Indicators are interpreted in a combined manner from a normative perspective, and individual indicators are not generally considered to have a great deal of clinical meaning in and of themselves.

Table 9.1 Summary of 38 emotional indicators for human figure drawings from the Koppitz (1968) Scoring and Interpretation System

Quality signs
Broken or sketchy lines
Poor integration of parts of figure
Shading of the face or part of it
Shading of the body and/or limbs
Shading of the hands and/or neck
Gross asymmetry of limbs
Figure slanting by 15 degrees or more
Tiny figure, 2 inches or less in height
Big figure, 9 inches or more in height
Transparencies

Special features
Tiny head, one-tenth or less of total height of figure
Large head, as large or larger than body
Vacant eyes, circles without pupils
Side glances of both eyes, both eyes turned toward one side
Crossed eyes, both eyes turned inward
Teeth
Short arms, not long enough to reach waistline
Long arms that could reach below kneeline
Arms clinging to side of body
Big hands, as big as face
Hands cut off, arms without hands and fingers
Hands hidden behind back or in pockets
Legs pressed together
Genitals
Monster or grotesque figures
Three or more figures spontaneously drawn
Figure cut off by edge of paper
Baseline, grass, figure on edge of paper
Sun or moon
Clouds, rain, snow

Omissions
Omission of eyes, nose, mouth, body, arms, legs, feet, neck

Reliability and Validity With the DAP and other specific types of human figure drawing techniques, there is no question that particular scoring systems can be used reliably across raters. In his review of the DAP, Cummings (1986) integrated the results of 13 inter-rater reliability studies, which revealed a range of agreement among judges from 75% to 95% (0.75 to 0.95), with a median reliability in the 80% range. Naglieri et al.'s (1991) test manual for the DAP:SPED also presents evidence as to internal consistency reliability, which was relatively modest, with coefficients ranging from 0.67 to 0.78 at various age and gender levels. Test–retest reliability of human figure drawings has been a more problematic area, with stability coefficients typically much lower than those obtained for behavior ratings scales and objective self-report tests. Naglieri et al. reported a test–retest reliability coefficient of 0.67 at a one-week interval with a sample of 67 children, using the DAP:SPED objective scoring system. Cummings (1986) integrated the findings of eight test–retest reliability studies from 1926 through 1978 with intervals ranging from one day to three months, with the resulting reliability coefficients ranging from 0.68 to 0.96. However, these studies were all based on Goodenough and Harris's scoring approaches for using human figure drawings to evaluate cognitive development and intellectual maturity. Few studies have been conducted wherein the more common use of the DAP as a social–emotional assessment technique was evaluated over time. In discussing the little evidence available in this area, Cummings (1986) commented that "drawings are subject to mood changes or a trait variable may be manifested by varying indicators" (p. 214). I would add to this restrained comment that children's drawings are also very likely to be influenced by a potentially large and complex array of other factors that are outside of the child but within his or her environment, such as the time of day, recent activities, environmental conditions, and peer behavior.

Validity evidence of using human figure drawings such as the DAP for social–emotional assessment of children is mixed at best. Koppitz's (1968) comprehensive book on children's human figure drawings was one of the first efforts to provide systematically empirical evidence for the validity of emotional indicators of DAP productions and reported several studies wherein specific types of emotional indicators were found to differ significantly among emotionally disturbed and normal children through chi-square analyses. Cummings's (1986) review of validity evidence of the DAP concluded that the evidence was mixed and sometimes contradictory regarding the ability of DAP drawings to differentiate among clinical and normal groups. In the manual for Naglieri et al.'s (1991) adaptation of the DAP, the results of four separate validity studies are presented, wherein DAP:SPED standard scores of various clinical groups were compared with those of normal children. Each of these studies showed statistically significant differences among groups, with the clinical groups always receiving higher scores. Taken in combination, these studies provide some support for the construct validity of the DAP:SPED scoring system. Several authors of more recent reviews and empirical investigations have provided evidence, however, that various adaptations of the DAP fail to discriminate accurately among clinical and nonclinical subjects (Bricceti, 1994; Feyh & Holmes, 1994; Klein, 1986), causing some writers to assert that DAP techniques are "tests in search of a construct" (Kamphaus & Pleiss, 1991, p. 395).

In addition, a study by Joiner, Schmidt, and Barnett (1996) examined reliability and validity of three commonly used indicators of emotional distress in children's projective drawings (size, detail, and line heaviness) and found that these indicators fared much more poorly than either self-report or thematic assessment techniques in converging with objective evidence of depression and anxiety among youths in an inpatient setting. These authors concluded that "in line with previous studies and reviews spanning almost five decades of work . . . the results of this study do not support the practice of interpreting individual drawing indices as indicators of emotional distress among children and adolescents" (p. 138). As evidence of the fierce devotion of many adherents of projective drawings, it is interesting to note that this study and the conclusions of its authors set off a maelstrom of controversy and "point–counterpoint" pieces in the next issues of the *Journal of Personality Assessment* (1996 and 1997), none of which convinced me that the conclusions of Joiner and colleagues should be dismissed.

Additional Comments The DAP technique and related human figure drawing tests are popular among clinicians and are currently among the most widely used social–emotional assessment procedures for children. The reliability and validity evidence for these procedures is mixed at best, however, and there will continue to be controversy surrounding their use, even as they continue in popularity and widespread use. Little is actually known regarding how clinicians use the DAP in practice. Some clinicians make the DAP and related techniques a centerpiece of their assessments and make sweeping interpretations of the child's social–emotional status based on little else. It is my experience, however, that many practitioners simply "throw" the DAP and related projective drawing tests into the assessment battery to build rapport with the child and form some tentative hypotheses, but they are actually quite conservative when it comes to clinical interpretation of these drawings.

An important but missing piece of evidence regarding social–emotional assessment with DAP is how they are actually used (and perhaps abused) in clinical practice. A final consideration in using DAP (or any other social–emotional assessment technique, for that matter) is how defensible the procedure might be if a clinician's assessment had to be defended in court or in a special education due process hearing. In respect to this troubling issue, Lilly (2001) concluded, using contemporary criteria for guidelines in forensic assessment, that the scoring procedures most commonly used for human figure drawing tests (global impressions and specific signs) do not meet admissibility criteria. If Lilly's conclusions are correct, then even casual or conservative uses of DAP should raise some concern among clinicians.

The Kinetic Family Drawing Technique (KFD)

Another adaptation of human figure drawings is the use of the Kinetic Family Drawing Technique (KFD). As a social–emotional assessment technique for children and adolescents, family drawings have been very popular with clinicians for decades and have been advocated since at least the 1930s (e.g., Appel, 1931). By the 1950s, the use of family drawings in psychological assessment of children had become widespread, as typified by widely cited articles during that period by Hulse (1951, 1952). The basic idea behind family drawings has always been that through the process of drawing a pictorial representation of their family, children may provide important information regarding their perspective on such issues as family dynamics, emotional relationships, and their place within the family.

In the 1970s, a major new approach to children's family drawings was introduced by Burns and Kaufman (1970, 1972), which was denoted the KFD technique. In contrast to earlier approaches to family drawings, which tended to provide a relatively open format for making the drawings, the KFD included a carefully circumscribed set of directions with a clear goal: *to draw everyone in the family doing something.* With the introduction of the KFD, which eventually became the most widely used family drawing technique, the emphasis was on actions. According to a critical review by Handler and Habenicht (1994), "This seemingly minor modification of the instructions results in some surprisingly revealing data concerning family dynamics, allowing a clearer picture to emerge of interpersonal interactions and emotional relationships among family members" (pp. 440–441). Compared with the DAP and House–Tree–Person techniques, the KFD has been said to "often reveal conflicts and difficulties when the other two procedures indicate the absence of problems" (Handler & Habenicht, 1994, p. 441). The hypothesized reason for the more revealing nature of the KFD is that it allows the clinician to view the child as the child feels he or she is reflected and expressed in the family, enabling the child to depict

Figure 9.2 A Kinetic Family Drawing produced by an eight-year-old boy

the family as an active unit and enabling the clinician to see the child's impressions of family interactions (Burns, 1982; Burns & Kaufman, 1970, 1972).

Administration, Scoring, and Interpretation The procedures for administering the KFD are simple. The examiner provides the examinee with a plain white sheet of 8.5-inch-by-11-inch paper and a No. 2 lead pencil with an eraser. The paper is set ambiguously on the table so that the child can determine whether to draw on it portrait or landscape. The examiner then gives the following directions: "Draw a picture of everyone in your family, including you, doing something. Try to draw whole people, not cartoons or stick people. Remember, make everyone DOING something—some kind of actions" (Burns & Kaufman, 1972, p. 5). An example of a KFD drawing produced by an elementary-age child is shown in Figure 9.2.

While the drawing is being completed, the examiner is expected to observe the examinee carefully, record verbal statements, and make other behavioral observations. There is no specified time limit for the KFD, and if the examinee asks questions regarding the procedure, the examiner is supposed to respond in a noncommittal manner.

After the drawing is completed, it is recommended that the examiner ask a series of postdrawing questions (the *inquiry phase*), for the purpose of finding out the child's perspective on additional information related to the drawings.

As recommended by Knoff and Prout (1985), the areas of questioning should attempt to find out who the figures in the drawing represent and what is the child's relationship to them; what the persons in the drawing are doing, feeling, and thinking; what is good and bad about each person; what the child was thinking about while he or she was drawing; what the drawing makes the child think of; what the weather is in the picture; and what the child would like to change about the picture.

Various scoring systems have been used for the KFD, including many derivations from what originally was proposed by Burns and Kaufman (1970, 1972). A variation on the original KFD scoring system was later proposed by one of the authors (Burns, 1982), is distinctly psychodynamic in nature, and includes four major scoring categories: actions; distances, barriers, and positions; physical characteristics of the figures; and styles. The *actions* category refers to the type of activity depicted for each figure, and Burns grouped possible actions into activities that are said to symbolize cooperation, communication, masochism, narcissism, nurturance, sadism, or tension. The *physical characteristics* category represents such formal aspects of the drawings as inclusion of essential body parts, the size of figures, the size of figures relative to other figures, the size of various body parts, and facial expressions. The *distances, barriers, and positions* category involves such things as numbers of barriers between key figures in the drawing, the direction each figure faces, and how far apart the figures are. The *styles* category involves the organization of figures on the page. Some of the style variables proposed by Burns to reflect psychopathology or emotional disturbance include intentional separation of family figures, encapsulation of figures by lines of objects, folding the paper into segments and placing each figure on individual segments, including more than one line across the entire bottom or top of the drawing, underlining individual figures, and presenting figures from an aerial or bird's eye view. In listing these scoring categories and major indicators, it is important to also note that the KFD scoring system is complex and requires careful study from the original sources for effective and meaningful interpretation.

Reliability and Validity When the original KFD technique was proposed in the early 1970s, it was criticized for having insufficient psychometric data available. Because the KFD has now been in widespread use for decades, reliability and validity studies have accrued, and much more is known about its psychometric properties. In terms of reliability, the yield of research on the KFD indicates that it has acceptable to excellent inter-rater reliability with specific scoring systems, but its test–retest reliability is often poor or marginal at best. In Handler and Habenicht's (1994) review, it was noted that median percentages of inter-rater agreement on the KFD typically ranged from 0.87 to 0.95 across studies, indicating that "the various KFD scoring systems can be scored with a high degree of inter-rater reliability" (p. 443). Test–retest reliability studies of the KFD have raised many questions and concerns, however. Many test–retest studies at short-term intervals (i.e., two weeks) have been conducted with specific scoring systems, and the reliabilities have ranged from the 0.40s to the 0.90s, which is a considerable spread. Test–retest reliabilities in the 0.40 and 0.50 range at short-term intervals with other types of social–emotional assessment procedures (e.g., objective self-report tests, behavior rating scales) would be construed as evidence of extreme inconsistency. With the KFD, poor to marginal test–retest findings have been interpreted in various other ways, however. For example, Mangold (1982) suggested that the KFD is sensitive to antecedent testing conditions, and performances may vary substantially depending on when and where it is administered. Cummings (1980) stated that the KFD is probably a state-dependent measure, in that it may tap a child's feelings, perceptions, and general affect for only a specific point in time. Other interpretations of the marginal test–retest reliability of the KFD are possible, but it is sufficient to observe that it is likely that children will produce qualitatively different drawings from one occasion to another.

In terms of test validity of the KFD, the evidence is equally mixed. In Handler and Habenicht's (1994) comprehensive review, it was noted that most of the validity studies on the KFD involved comparisons of drawings of children who had been identified as having some form of psychopathology or poor adjustment status with those of normal comparison children, and that various scoring systems have been used in these comparisons. In evaluating the yield of research of this type, it seems that many studies have shown significant differences among clinical status groups, whereas many others have not. There also have been a few studies wherein KFD scores were correlated with other types of social–emotional measures, such as self-concept tests, family relations tests, and behavior rating scales. Some of these studies have shown significant, but modest, correlations between the KFD and criterion measures, providing some evidence of construct and criterion-related validity.

Most of the validity studies of the KFD have used specific aspects of formal scoring systems, a practice that has come under closer scrutiny in recent years. According to Handler and Habenicht (1994), the best trend in KFD scoring is toward the use of a "holistic, integrative approach rather than one that emphasizes the mere addition of signs or symbols" (p. 458). Examples of these more "holistic" scoring systems are those used in studies by Cook (1991) and Tharinger and Stark (1990), both of which were able to differentiate clinical from nonclinical groups of children. The use of such systems necessitates a great deal of creativity and flexibility, given the statement of the latter authors that "the clearest sense of these characteristics can be gained through placing oneself in the drawing, preferably in place of the child" (Tharinger & Stark, 1990, pp. 370–371).

Kinetic School Drawing   One of the variations on the KFD is a technique known as the Kinetic School Drawing (KSD). This technique was first proposed by Prout and Phillips (1974), was refined by Sarbaugh (1983), and was integrated with the KFD by Knoff and Prout (1985). The basic premise of the KSD is similar to that of the KFD, in that a child who draws him- or herself within his or her school environment in an action-oriented manner may provide important information on relationships and other dynamics within the school environment.

The directions for the KSD are similar to those for the KFD. The examiner provides the child with a standard-size piece of white paper and a No. 2 lead pencil with an eraser, and states:

> I'd like you to draw a school picture. Put yourself, your teacher, and a friend or two in the picture. Make everyone doing something. Try to draw whole people and make the best drawing you can. Remember, draw yourself, your teacher, and a friend or two, and make everyone doing something.
>
> (Cummings, 1986, p. 229)

As with the KFD, various procedures have been proposed for interpreting the KSD, and formal scoring systems and qualitative–holistic methods of interpretation are possible. Much less is known about the psychometric properties of the KSD in relation to those of the KFD, however, because much less research has been reported. In general, the KSD does not seem to have caught on to the extent that the KFD has. Because the tasks are so similar and because there is similar variation in scoring and interpretation methods, it probably can be assumed that the KSD has psychometric characteristics and problems relatively similar to the KFD. Although the use of the KFD has become popular among many clinical child psychologists and school psychologists, it remains to be seen whether the KSD will attain this level of use.

Additional Comments Although the reliability and validity evidence regarding the KFD is mixed to say the least, perhaps the most salient issue is "For what purposes is the KFD valid?" rather than whether it is valid per se. As with any of the drawing and other techniques reviewed in this chapter, some uses are clearly indefensible, whereas other uses may be prudent and helpful in rapport building, or perhaps even in a diagnostic sense. In addition to basic reliability and validity evidence, Handler and Habenicht's (1994) review evaluated examinee variables that may strongly influence KFD production. Specifically, it was noted that age, gender, and culture/ethnicity all have been shown to be significant factors in the quality of children's drawings. Clinicians who desire to use the KFD should become familiar with the literature in this area and always take into account these factors in scoring and interpretation. Based on the current state of the art in using the KFD, it seems that there is definitely a trend toward the use of more naturalistic clinical methods of scoring and interpretation, and methods that integrate various scoring techniques rather than relying on single summative scoring systems. Although caution regarding the clinical use of the KFD is advised, there also seems to be some promise of improved clinical validity evidence in the future.

The Bender-Gestalt Test (BGT) as a Measure of Social–Emotional Status

Another drawing test that has been used for social–emotional assessment of children is the Bender-Gestalt Test (BGT), which also has been referred to as the Bender Visual–Motor Gestalt Test. The origins of this test stem from the foundation of Gestalt psychology. The BGT was developed by Lauretta Bender (1938, 1946), who adapted nine figures that were being used in perceptual experiments and added specific administration, scoring, and interpretation guidelines so that this drawing technique could be used as a standardized psychological test. The test was updated in 2003 by Brannigan and Decker. This test quickly became one of the most popular and widely used of all psychological assessment techniques, and it remains popular among the current generation of clinicians (Wilson & Reschly, 1996). This test is largely used for neuropsychological assessment but has been used for social–emotional assessment, too.

Because of its widespread use and continued popularity, numerous scoring and interpretation systems have been developed for the BGT. The most recent interpretation system is an update of the work by Elizabeth Koppitz and entitled the *Koppitz-2 Developmental Scoring System for the Bender Gestalt Test* (K2-BG) (C. R. Reynolds, 2007). This version includes updated norms based on scores from 3,500 individuals, an addition of six designs, and has been promoted mostly as a test of visual-motor perception and construction. In a review of this most recent update, Hartman states that

> neuropsychologists will find the phrase, "it's alive!" to be an appropriate description of the new K2-BG. Dr. Reynolds has resuscitated an old test and given it a new lease on life with a large normative base and excellent psychometrics. As a test of developmental visual–motor skill and a neuropsychological measure of visuoconstructional brain function, the test is better than it ever was and well worth using. Neuropsychologists can only hope the parts of the monster that caused its original burial—organicity screening and projective testing—do not reassert themselves and weaken the reputation of a very useful neuropsychological reincarnation.
>
> (2008, p. 95)

Most comprehensive scoring and interpretation systems are clearly not designed to aid in social–emotional assessment of children and are not discussed any further in this chapter. As stated above, the BGT has been used primarily as a measure of visual perception, visual–motor perception, and motor coordination, for such diverse purposes as screening for brain injury, assessing developmental motor coordination levels, and providing rough estimates of intellectual functioning. The major force behind the use of the BGT as a social–emotional assessment technique for children was the work of Koppitz. In her two-volume series of books, *The Bender Gestalt Test for Young Children* (Koppitz, 1963) and *The Bender Gestalt Test for Young Children, Volume II: Research and Application, 1963–1973* (Koppitz, 1975), Koppitz outlined the theory and practice of using the BGT to screen for *emotional indicators* (EIs). These EIs are defined as drawing characteristics that tend to occur primarily with emotionally disturbed and behaviorally disordered children and that are associated with specific types of emotional–behavioral problems, such as impulsivity, mental confusion, and low frustration tolerance. Other social–emotional or psychopathology methods have been developed for the BGT, but none has been nearly as influential for social–emotional assessment of children as the Koppitz method. This next section is devoted exclusively to a brief description and overview of the Koppitz method for EIs.

Administration, Scoring, and Interpretation Koppitz (1963, 1975) suggested that the original administration method advocated by Bender (1938, 1946) be used. This method of administration is straightforward and easy to follow. The examiner provides a sheet of 8.5-inch-by-11-inch white paper (more than one sheet may be used if needed) and a No. 2 lead pencil to the child, and sits with the child at a table suitable for drawing. The examiner states to the child that the task of this test is for him or her to carefully make copies on the paper of the figures that will be shown to him or her. The examiner then presents the child the nine BGT figures, one at a time in succession as he or she completes them. There is no time limit for this test, although it has been noted that most children complete the task in about six minutes (Koppitz, 1975). The examiner should provide minimal direction for the child, allowing him or her to copy the drawings any way he or she wants, while carefully observing his or her behavior during the testing task. An example of a child's reproduction of the BGT figures is shown in Figure 9.3.

With the Koppitz system, it is recommended that the developmental scoring system and identification of possible emotional indicators be used by the examiner. Because the developmental scoring system is not a primary concern of this text, it is not discussed herein, and readers are referred to Koppitz's (1963, 1975) two volumes and C. R. Reynolds' more recent manual (2007) for more detailed instruction. Because Koppitz's system for identifying emotional indicators is the major emphasis of this section, it is briefly presented herein. Users of this book who desire to become proficient in the Koppitz EI identification method should carefully study the original texts and supporting evidence, however, and not rely on this chapter alone as a training guide.

In her 1963 book, Koppitz presented ten EIs for the BGT. In her 1975 book, the original ten EIs were presented, with new supportive evidence, and two more indicators were presented, bringing the total number of EIs to 12. These EIs are described briefly as follows.

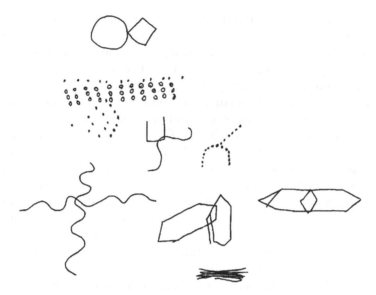

Figure 9.3 Bender-Gestalt Test designs produced by an 11-year-old boy

1. *Confused Order.* This EI is considered to be present if the designs are scattered arbitrarily on the paper and if there is no logical sequence or order to the drawings. Koppitz noted that confused order is associated with a lack of planning ability and poor organizational skills but emphasized that it is common among younger children (ages 5 to 7).

2. *Wavy Line in Figures 1 and 2.* If there are two or more abrupt changes in the direction of the lines of dots or circles in BGT Figures 1 or 2, this EI is considered to be present. Koppitz noted that Wavy Line appeared to be associated with poor motor coordination and emotional instability.

3. *Dashes Substituted for Circles in Figure 2.* If at least half of all the circles in Figure 2 are replaced with dashes 1/16-inch long or more, this EI is considered to be present. Koppitz noted that Substitution of Dashes for Circles in Figure 2 has been associated with impulsivity and lack of interest, particularly with younger children.

4. *Increasing Size of Figures 1, 2, or 3.* If the dots or circles of drawings of Figures 1 through 3 progressively increase in size until the last ones are three times as large or more than the first ones, this EI is considered to be present. Koppitz stated that increasing size on these BGT designs is associated with low frustration tolerance and explosiveness, particularly as children become older (e.g., age ten versus age seven).

5. *Large Size.* According to Koppitz, if the area covered by any one BGT figure drawing is at least twice as large as the design area on the stimulus card, this EI, which is said to be associated with acting-out behavior in children, is considered to be present.

6. *Small Size.* If the area covered by any BGT figure drawing is half as large or less than the original stimulus area on any of the figures, the Small Size EI, which is thought to be related to anxiety, withdrawal, timidity, and constriction in children, is considered to be present.

7. *Fine Line.* If the pencil line for any BGT figure drawing is so fine that it requires considerable effort to view the design, the Fine Line indicator is considered to be

present. Koppitz noted that this EI is associated with timidity, shyness, and withdrawal, specifically in young children.

8. *Careless Overwork or Heavily Reinforced Lines.* This EI is considered to be present if a design or part of a design is redrawn with heavy lines. This category is not scored if the drawing is erased and then redrawn or if it is corrected with careful lines that improve the drawing. Koppitz noted that Careless Overwork and Heavily Reinforced Lines have been associated with impulsivity, aggressiveness, and acting-out behavior.

9. *Second Attempt.* The Second Attempt EI is considered to be present if a BGT design or part of it is abandoned before or after its completion and a new drawing is made. This EI should be scored only if there are two distinct drawings from one design on two locations on the paper. Koppitz stated that the Second Attempt EI is associated with impulsivity and anxiety.

10. *Expansion.* The Expansion EI, which is said to be associated with impulsivity and acting-out behavior, is scored when two or more sheets of paper are used to complete the nine BGT drawings.

11. *Box Around Design.* Koppitz noted that this EI is quite rare, but suggested that children who exhibit it have "weak inner control; they need to be able to function in school and at home" (1975, p. 86). This EI is considered to be present when a box is drawn around one or more BGT designs after they have already been copied.

12. *Spontaneous Elaboration or Additions to Designs.* This EI is scored when a child makes spontaneous changes on BGT test figures that "turn them into objects or combine them into bizarre designs" (Koppitz, 1975, p. 88). Koppitz noted that:

> [This EI, which is also quite rare,] occur[s] almost exclusively on Bender Test records of children who are overwhelmed by fears and anxieties or who are totally preoccupied with their own thoughts. These youngsters often have a tenuous hold on reality and may confuse fact with fantasy.
>
> (p. 88)

When scoring and interpreting EIs on the BGT using the Koppitz system, it is important to consider some suggestions and warnings from the author (Koppitz, 1975). First, EIs "are clinical signs that should be evaluated individually like any other clinical symptom" (p. 89). Second, "EIs lack internal consistency and cannot, therefore, be added together into a meaningful total EI score" (p. 89). Finally, there is a concern that single EIs on BGT drawings are not always indicative of emotional problems. Koppitz noted that "three or more EIs are necessary before one can say with some degree of confidence that a child has serious emotional problems and will need further evaluation" (p. 89). With a process so tenuous as inferring emotional adjustment from a drawing task, these three recommendations should be considered an absolute minimum.

Reliability and Validity Ample evidence exists indicating that the BGT can be scored reliably across different scorers and is relatively stable over short periods. In her 1975 book, Koppitz summarized numerous studies showing that the inter-rater reliability validity of the BGT is often in the 0.80 to 0.90 range and that test–retest reliability of the BGT at short time intervals is often in the 0.70 to 0.80 range (although younger children often demonstrate less reliable performances). These generally strong findings regarding reliability of the BGT typically are based on overall developmental scoring system results and not just on the presence of EIs. The stability of EIs on BGT drawings is less clear.

In her 1975 book, Koppitz provided some empirical support for each of the 12 EIs. Given the 1975 publication date of this book, these supporting references all were based on research published in the 1960s and 1970s. A computer-based review of the PSYCHLIT database by Merrell revealed only a few additional studies regarding the validity of the Koppitz EI system. Most of the studies' support of the validity of EIs on BGT is based on methodology where frequency counts of specific EIs are compared between clinical and nonclinical groups, and the clinical groups evidenced a higher EI prevalence. In some of these studies, chi-square analyses were used to provide evidence of statistical significance of these differences, whereas other studies analyzed the frequency counts qualitatively. Many of these studies are in the form of unpublished Master's thesis and doctoral dissertation projects from the 1960s and 1970s and are virtually impossible to obtain for evaluation. It is difficult to form strong conclusions regarding the validity of the BGT as a social–emotional assessment procedure.

Additional Comments The Koppitz system for using the BGT for social–emotional assessment has some supporting evidence, but most of this evidence is substantially dated and does not meet current research standards for providing evidence of clinical validity (i.e., large effect sizes among clinical and nonclinical groups, use of multiple regression and structural modeling analyses for prediction purposes). Caution is advised in using the BGT for social–emotional assessment of children. Although the BGT is still popular, even as a social–emotional assessment technique, research on this particular use of the test seems to have diminished substantially in the years after the publication of Koppitz's two books (1963, 1975). These books are well written, documented to a substantially greater degree than most related books, and quite interesting. Given that the BGT is easy to administer and is typically a nonthreatening if not enjoyable experience for children, it is no surprise that it continues to be widely used, even for social–emotional assessment. Potential users of the BGT for social–emotional assessment purposes are cautioned, however, that the state of the art in social–emotional assessment has advanced considerably during the past decades, and that the evidence supporting the BGT for this purpose has not kept pace with the burgeoning evidence supporting other methods, such as behavior rating scales, direct observation, and objective self-report tests.

Concluding Comments on Drawing Techniques In this section, the history, rationale, and theory of using drawing tests for social–emotional assessment of children and adolescents has been outlined, and an overview of three of the most popular techniques in this area has been provided. These three techniques include human figure drawing techniques (specifically the DAP technique), the KFD and a related school-based procedure, and the use of the BGT as a social–emotional assessment procedure.

In addition to these three techniques, various other drawing techniques are popular for social–emotional assessment. The so-called House–Tree–Person drawing technique continues to be a widely used procedure that has many conceptual and practical similarities to the DAP technique. Likewise, Burns, the most influential early proponent of the KFD, later expanded his work in this domain to what he refers to as *Family-Centered Circle Drawings*. These and other variations of projective–expressive drawing techniques were not included in this section because of space constraints and their overlapping content with the procedures that were reviewed, and because the quantity of use and research on these procedures appears to be substantially less than that for the DAP, KFD, and BGT. Many variations and adaptations of social–emotional drawing tests are possible, and they vary substantially in terms of their popularity and availability of supporting evidence.

For the foreseeable future, it seems that projective–expressive and other types of drawing tests will continue to be widely used by clinicians in the United States and throughout the world. During the early 1980s, R. P. Martin (1983), an authority in the field of social–emotional assessment of children, wrote a blistering and convincing article in which he asserted that the use of projective–expressive drawing techniques is unethical and that such practices reduce the overall reliability of an assessment and may serve to reinforce biases held by the clinician. Such arguments are not new. Two decades earlier, Roback (1968) made a similar assertion against some uses of projective–expressive drawing tests, stating that "many clinicians apparently entertain grandiose delusions that they can intuitively gain a great deal of information from figure drawings about the personality structure and dynamics of the drawer" (p. 16). Such criticisms and the questionable validity and mixed research base of many of these procedures have failed to crush the desire of clinicians to use such techniques, as evidenced by their continued widespread popularity among psychologists who work primarily with children and by surveys of school psychologists for the past two decades (e.g., Hojnoski et al., 2006; Wilson & Reschly, 1996). It seems futile to berate clinicians for continuing to use drawing tests for social–emotional assessment of children and adolescents, given that past efforts to do so have had little impact on curbing the appeal of these techniques. Perhaps a better approach is to focus on appropriate or best uses of these tests. That said, I concur with Joiner et al. (1996), who concluded, "We suggest, based on our data and a wealth of past work, that although drawings may be useful rapport-building devices, they are not useful measurement devices" (p. 139).

SENTENCE COMPLETION TASKS

Like thematic approaches and drawing techniques, sentence completion tasks appear to be widely used for social–emotional and personality assessment (Lubin et al., 1984). In fact, a recent survey of school psychologists' projective test use indicated that 60% of all respondents routinely used this method (Hojnoski et al., 2006). In a sentence completion task, the examinee is presented a list of sentence stems (the beginning of a potential sentence) with a blank space after each stem. The task of the examinee is to complete the sentence. The typical way to conduct sentence completion tasks is for the examinee to read the stems and then provide a written response, but oral administration and response also is an option. Sentence completion tasks may range from only a few items (ten to 15) to 50 or more items. The basis of all sentence completion tasks is that either qualitative or systematic inspection of an examinee's responses may provide insight into their self-image, developmental characteristics, interpersonal relations, needs, and perceived threats (Chandler & Johnson, 1991). A sample sentence completion task with 20 stems is presented in Table 9.2. These stems are representative of the range of stems found in various sentence completion tasks that have been advocated for use with children and adolescents. There are several recurring types of stem content in these sample items.

Table 9.2 20 sample stems typical of the content of sentence completion tasks advocated for use with older children and adolescents

1. I wish . . .	11. I often feel . . .
2. Most people are afraid of . . .	12. Girls seem to . . .
3. I usually get mad when . . .	13. I am most proud about . . .
4. If I could only . . .	14. My mom . . .
5. At school . . .	15. I feel worse when . . .
6. Other kids think I . . .	16. Kids should . . .
7. I feel best when . . .	17. Teachers usually want you to . . .
8. I am the . . .	18. The worst thing that could happen . . .
9. The best thing about school . . .	19. My dad . . .
10. When Mom and Dad are together . . .	20. When I go to sleep . . .

Most advocates of sentence completion tasks recommend making inferences on clusters of items rather than on individual items or responses in isolation.

There has been some debate regarding how best to conceptualize and use sentence completion tasks. Some advocates of this assessment technique support a holistic, qualitative method of analyzing and interpreting responses (Chandler & Johnson, 1991), whereas other advocates contend that scoring and interpretation is best done using standardized systems (Hart, 1986).

There has been substantial disagreement regarding how sentence completion tasks should be conceptualized (Koppitz, 1982), and they have been alternately described as projective, semiprojective, and nonprojective techniques (Hart, 1986). Regardless of how these tasks are conceptualized and used, it is evident that they have been and continue to be used widely with older children and adolescents and that many clinicians value this method.

Sentence completion tasks appear to have been in use since the early 1900s. Similar to drawing techniques, the first uses of sentence completion tasks were for mental ability testing, but interest in this use gradually waned and gave way to personality assessment (Hart, 1986). Most of the early sentence completion tasks were developed for use with adults and older adolescents. The Rotter Incomplete Sentences Blank (Rotter & Rafferty, 1950) is perhaps the most influential of all sentence completion tasks in terms of the amount of research published on it and the influence it maintained in shaping subsequently developed sentence completion tasks. This test, which includes high school, college, and adult forms, has 40 items, has an objective scoring system, yields a single adjustment score, and has been shown to have exceptionally high reliability (Gregory, 1996).

Although older adolescents have been targeted specifically for development and use of sentence completion tasks since the early days of this procedure, specific extensions of such tasks to children occurred much later. One of the challenges in administering sentence completion tasks to children is that a certain reading level is required. In this regard, McCammon (1981) found that by the sixth grade, most children are capable of reading sentence completion tests and that oral administration is probably not necessary. Another challenge is that preoperational children (i.e., most preadolescent children) tend to think in a concrete manner and tend to provide factual, concrete responses to sentence completion stems, possibly defeating the projective–expressive purpose of the technique. Despite this history and the stated limitations, many clinicians use sentence completion tasks as a projective method with children and adolescents. Most of the sentence completion tasks in use by practitioners are nonstandardized and not commercially published or widely available (Gregory, 2000). They also tend to be used in a qualitative, nonobjective manner.

In addition to the general orientation on sentence completion tasks that has just been provided, this discussion includes sections on administration, scoring, and interpretation procedures; a brief overview of reliability and validity evidence; short descriptions of two sentence completion tasks that have been widely used with children (the Hart Sentence Completion Test [HSCT]) and adolescents (the Washington University Sentence Completion Test); and some concluding comments on the clinical uses of sentence completion tasks with children and adolescents.

Administration, Scoring, and Interpretation

Administration, scoring, and interpretation of sentence completion tasks tends to be highly dependent on the specific test used. Some tests have highly structured procedures, whereas others provide only minimal guidelines and structure for clinicians. From a projective psychodiagnostic perspective, a frequently used administration technique involves the clinician reading the sentence stem to the examinee, who is encouraged to complete the stem verbally with whatever words come to mind (Hart, 1986). If such an approach is used, the clinician is encouraged to record carefully the responses of the examinee and observations of behavior during the task. An inquiry phase often follows the initial administration technique, in which the clinician asks about the content of the response. Such inquiry is for the purpose of clarifying meaning, identifying reasons an examinee responded in a particular way, and "tracking feelings or perceptions to deeper levels and causes" (Hart, 1986, p. 252).

Various approaches to interpreting sentence completion tasks have been proposed. The most structured tests include standardized scoring systems that are linked directly with specific interpretative criteria. A common approach to interpretation has been rating each response according to the degree of conflict apparent (e.g., negative to neutral to positive), using a weighted scoring system such as that proposed for use in the Rotter Incomplete Sentences Blank. Many (if not most) clinicians tend to score and interpret sentence completion task responses in a subjective and qualitative manner, by reviewing each item to develop clinical impressions about the underlying dynamics of the response and to cluster sentence stems with similar content, and then focusing on the specific impressions obtained from examining those item clusters.

Reliability and Validity

In terms of reliability or stability, sentence completion tasks share a common characteristic with other projective–expressive techniques discussed in this chapter: They tend to have good to excellent inter-rater reliability with specific scoring systems but poor stability of children's responses over even short-term time intervals. Reliability of sentence completion tasks has been reviewed by Gregory (2000) and by Hart (1986), both of whom noted that interscorer or inter-rater reliability in the 0.70 to 0.90 range with specific tests and structured scoring systems is common. Test–retest reliability of sentence completion tasks is typically not reported, however, and the few studies that have investigated this phenomenon have found that children's responses are quite unstable over time. It is best to view sentence completion tasks as a means of eliciting information from a child that may be meaningful at that moment but probably will not generalize over time. Validity of sentence completion tasks is also an area of inquiry that has yielded mixed results.

Sentence completion tasks tend to have low convergence with other types of social–emotional assessment data. Numerous investigations with adult-focused sentence completion tasks have found them to differentiate among clinical and nonclinical groups, however, at least to a modest degree (Gregory, 2000). There is some support for the construct validity of sentence completion tasks. It is difficult, however, to generalize this validity evidence across the many tests that have been developed because they tend to vary greatly in terms of purpose, procedures, and scoring and interpretation methods.

The Hart Sentence Completion Test (HSCT) for Children

The Hart Sentence Completion Test (HSCT) (Hart, 1972, 1980; Hart, Kehle, & Davies, 1983) is a 40-item sentence completion task for children and adolescents aged six to 18. According to the author of this test, it was developed for two reasons: (1) to provide a sentence completion task developed specifically for children and adolescents rather than modifying adult sentence completion tasks for child use: and (2) because "other child-oriented sentence completion tests had poorly developed scoring systems or no standardized scoring systems at all and little documentation of any reliability and validity data" (Hart, 1986, p. 257). The HSCT was developed based on a four-dimensional theory of areas that are important to child social–emotional adjustment: family environments, social environments, school environments, and intrapersonal or internal conditions. The HSCT seems to have been developed with a great deal of care and is clearly the most objective, comprehensive, and clinically useful sentence completion task for children currently available. Two scoring approaches are used with the HSCT: a scale rating system and an item-by-item rating system. Information provided in the test manual and research reports in the public domain indicate that the HSCT has shown excellent inter-rater reliability; moderate test–retest reliability; and evidence of construct validity, including significant differentiation of responses of emotionally disturbed, learning disabled, and regular education students. For clinicians who desire a relatively objective, well-documented sentence completion task for use specifically with children, the HSCT seems to be peerless. This test is currently not available, however. The author of the HSCT does not consider it to be complete at present and is not distributing it publicly until such a time when additional research efforts are conducted for validation purposes (D. H. Hart, personal communication, April 25, 1997). Such efforts do not appear to be forthcoming. Researchers and clinicians interested in the HSCT will have a difficult time obtaining it but may desire to study the references provided in this section for more information on its development, structure, and use.

The Washington University Sentence Completion Test

The Washington University Sentence Completion Test (Loevinger, 1976, 1979) has been used widely with adults and adolescents. It is considered to be the most theory driven of all the sentence completion tasks (Gregory, 2000) because of its stated purpose of assessing ego development. Using a relatively objective scoring system, responses are classified according to seven stages of ego development, including presocial and symbiotic, impulsive, self-protective, conformist, conscientious, autonomous, and integrated. Merrell's computer-assisted review of the literature indicated that more scholarly journal articles had been published using Loevinger's sentence completion test than any other sentence completion task with adolescents. Consistent with the stated purposes of this test, most of the published studies using it involved the assessment of adolescent and adult ego development from a psychodynamic perspective. Although this sentence completion test is one of the best constructed and most widely researched, little is known regarding its ability to differentiate between emotionally disturbed or behaviorally disordered and normal adolescents.

Concluding Comments on Sentence Completion Tasks

Although sentence completion tasks have been among the most widely used projective–expressive assessment techniques of the twentieth century, theoretical and research interest in them seems to have waned. Most of the seminal research and development efforts and important literature on sentence completion tasks occurred in the 1940s, 1950s, and 1960s. Since the 1980s, there has been little in the way of new innovations with sentence completion tasks. One of the few potentially valuable innovations during this period has been the development and dissemination of the HSCT for Children, a tool designed to consider the unique characteristics of childhood. This test also has the advantage of good standardization and an objective scoring and interpretation scheme. Research and development efforts on the HSCT have waned, however, and it is no longer available in the public domain. Clinicians who desire to develop or modify sentence completion tasks to meet their own needs and use them in a qualitative–holistic manner may find them to be an interesting addition to their assessment design, particularly when results are interpreted in a conservative manner.

BEST PRACTICES

This chapter has provided an overview of theory, practice, and research regarding some of the most popular projective–expressive assessment techniques for use with children and adolescents, including thematic approaches, drawing techniques, and sentence completion tasks. After reading this chapter, two facts should be obvious: (1) projective–expressive techniques have been and continue to be an extremely popular and widely used form of social–emotional assessment among clinicians; and (2) there continues to be considerable controversy regarding the use of these techniques, primarily because of a combination of extremely mixed psychometric evidence and the vagueness or difficulty operationalizing some of the constructs purported to be measured by these techniques. It also seems there have been relatively few new innovations in this area during the past decades. In my opinion, most of the cutting-edge developments in assessing psychopathology and personality of children during the past decades have been in the realm of empirically based multiaxial assessment techniques, as illustrated by research and innovation and such areas as behavior rating scales, objective self-report measures, and multiple gating systems. Projective–expressive techniques are in a unique and paradoxical position, being among the most popular assessment techniques used by clinicians, but also becoming increasingly outdated and perhaps archaic.

Because of these issues and related concerns, prominent authors in the area of social–emotional assessment of children have issued strong statements against the continued use of projective–expressive techniques, in some cases calling for a moratorium on their use (R. P. Martin, 1983). In this vein, Wilson and Reschly (1996), commenting on the results of their survey of assessment practices of school psychologists, stated:

> The persistence of using measures with poor technical adequacy and dubious relationships to psychological constructs and to current child disability classification

systems criteria is difficult to explain, other than to note that some psychologists seem to be tied to poor assessment instruments. The Bender-Gestalt and Draw-A-Something projective measures have poor technical adequacy, and, if used as a primary basis for any decision, render the psychologist vulnerable to challenge in legal proceedings such as due process hearings. Use of these measures, especially in personality assessment, is difficult to justify from ethical as well as psychometric grounds.

(pp. 18–19)

Despite such strong and clearly defensible statements, it is naive to think that projective–expressive assessment techniques will just go away or that clinicians will simply abandon them. There is something about these techniques that appeals to many clinicians and that they must find to be useful. After looking at all the evidence, it seems the problem with projective–expressive assessment techniques may not be in the techniques themselves, but rather in how they may be used. Much of the heated dialogue regarding the pros and cons of projective–expressive assessment has stemmed from proponents who blindly argue for the merits of these techniques without regard to the evidence, or from opponents who are diametrically opposed to their use on virtually all grounds. Little has been written about how these tools are actually used, or how to make the best use of these assessment techniques that are popular and under close scrutiny. This chapter concludes with some basic suggestions for best practices in using projective–expressive techniques in an appropriate and defensible manner.

One appropriate use of projective–expressive techniques in social–emotional assessment of children and adolescents is to establish rapport with the examinee. As a general rule, children find these assessment procedures to be safe and nonthreatening and in many cases find them to be fun or enjoyable. Projective–expressive techniques such as thematic approaches, drawing techniques, and sentence completion tasks may serve the purpose of helping the examinee feel comfortable during the initial stages of the assessment and helping to establish a positive relationship between the clinician and the child.

Another appropriate and potentially effective use of projective–expressive techniques is to use them as a means of communication with extremely shy or verbally reluctant children, or young children who are not yet verbally sophisticated enough to engage in such processes as meaningful interviews. Even the most experienced and skilled clinicians have difficulty from time to time in getting some children to communicate with them through traditional means such as a clinical interview. Drawing techniques may be especially useful in this regard, given that they make few or no demands on the child to engage verbally with the clinician, yet provide the opportunity for observation under structured conditions. This latter area may prove to be highly advantageous in some cases; observing a child's behavior under the semistandardized and structured conditions of completing a drawing technique allows for making observations regarding comparison with the behavior of numerous other children who may have been observed under the same conditions.

If projective–expressive techniques have been used to fulfill either of the first two general purposes just stated, another possible use would be to help form hypotheses about the child's social–emotional functioning for additional assessment with more direct and objective approaches. For example, children sometimes are referred for assessment without a clear assessment problem or stated objective, and such children or the referral source sometimes are not particularly helpful in pinpointing specific areas to target in the assessment. In situations such as this, recurring themes found in nonthreatening projective–expressive assessment results may provide a basis for shaping future assessment directions (i.e., whether to target the internalizing or externalizing domain or whether to include specific objective self-report measures within the battery).

Some clinicians find projective–expressive assessment techniques to be helpful in developing an understanding of their child or adolescent client, particularly from the examinee's own worldview and personal perspective. Perhaps this sort of experiential understanding of the child may be helpful in forming counseling goals or in developing the rapport that will be useful in future counseling sessions.

Finally, it is important to articulate clearly and directly the inappropriate uses of projective–expressive assessment techniques. Perhaps the most egregious use of these techniques (and the use that continues to raise the most controversy) is to make factual inferences based on inconclusive "signs." For example, let's say that a 6-year-old girl produces a kinetic family drawing in which she is separated from her father by a thick barrier of some kind. Let's also suppose that her picture of herself in this drawing includes supposed signs of powerlessness (i.e., thin, weak arms) and that her picture of her father includes some supposed signs of hostility or anger (i.e., large arms, large sharp teeth). Suppose that in the final report, the clinician states, "This child feels weak, alienated, and separated from her father, whom she views as domineering and aggressive." In the absence of any corroborating defensible evidence, this type of use of projective–expressive techniques is unsupportable at best and inflammatory and unethical at worst. In our view, this is the worst and most indefensible use of projective–expressive techniques, yet it seems to happen routinely.

A related misuse of projective–expressive techniques is to use them as the sole basis for making a diagnosis or classification decision. Although various ethical and legal guidelines for assessment state that no single test or technique should be the basis for such a decision, using assessment techniques, which have questionable reliability and validity, for this purpose puts the clinician even further at risk. Such inappropriate uses of projective–expressive techniques should be avoided at all costs.

CONCLUSIONS

Although projective–expressive techniques differ substantially from the primarily direct and objective methods of assessment that are emphasized in this book, they are among the most widely used of all social–emotional assessment methods and have an important place in the history of social–emotional assessment. The basis of projective–expressive techniques is that examinees may "project" their subconscious motives, conflicts, and needs either verbally or in drawings when they are presented with ambiguous stimuli and tasks. Most of these techniques are influenced heavily by psychodynamic theory. Although projective–expressive techniques are popular among clinicians, they have been associated with controversy because of the difficulty in defining specific constructs they may purport to assess and because of psychometric properties that are often tenuous.

Thematic approaches to personality assessment are among the most widely used projective–expressive techniques and have a long and storied history. The Thematic Apperception Test (TAT) is among the oldest and most widely used techniques and is the basis for most other thematic approaches. The Children's Apperception Test (CAT) was the first downward extension of the TAT for use with younger children and includes pictures of animal characters for use with very young children. The Roberts Apperception Tests for Children (RATC and RATC-2) is a more recently developed thematic approach that includes less ambiguous stimulus cards and a relatively objective scoring system. The evidence regarding thematic approaches is mixed, but they continue to be popular among clinicians and have the potential advantage of facilitating communication with shy or reluctant examinees.

Drawing techniques for projective–expressive assessment have been in existence nearly as long as the field of psychology. The Draw-A-Person (DAP) technique for personality assessment is a later variation on human figure drawing tests, which originally were developed for cognitive and developmental assessment. Numerous methods have been articulated for interpreting DAP drawings, including some more recently developed objective methods of scoring and interpretation. The Kinetic Family Drawing system (KFD) is a relatively recent technique for drawing members of a family in action situations. The KFD has been purported to provide revealing information on the child's perception of the inner dynamics and conflicts of a family constellation. The Bender-Gestalt Test (BGT) has been used primarily for perceptual motor and intellectual screening, but also has been advocated as a projective–expressive test of social–emotional functioning. The most influential BGT technique in this regard is that proposed by Koppitz (1963, 1975). Overall, projective–expressive drawing techniques remain popular with clinicians. They evidence good inter-rater reliability using specific scoring systems, but evidence of test–retest reliability and construct validity has been less convincing.

Sentence completion tasks as a projective–expressive technique peaked in popularity in the 1940s and 1950s, and little has occurred in the way of new innovations during the past few decades. The most acclaimed sentence completion task specifically for children is the Hart Sentence Completion Test for Children (HSCT), but it was never considered fully complete by its author, is not currently available in the public domain, and likely will not be available in the future. The Washington University/Loevinger Sentence Completion Test is currently the most widely used sentence completion task with adolescents. It is privately published by its author and may be difficult to obtain. Most clinicians who use sentence completion tasks clinically develop their own lists of stems and interpret them in a qualitative manner.

In sum, projective–expressive assessment techniques are among the most popular forms of social–emotional assessment currently used, but they still exist in a maelstrom of controversy because of their occasional misuse and because of their technical properties, which are often weak according to traditional psychometric conceptions. Projective–expressive techniques likely will be in use for the foreseeable future, however, and do seem to have certain advantages and benefits. Clinicians who use them should focus on the recommended best practices that were provided in this chapter and avoid their misuse.

REVIEW AND APPLICATION QUESTIONS

1. What is the projective hypothesis? How can this hypothesis be operationally defined in assessment practice?
2. How can the continuing popularity of projective assessment be explained in the face of questionable empirical evidence?

3. If using the Thematic Apperception Test with an adolescent girl, what would be recommended stimulus cards?

4. How is the inspection technique best used in interpreting the Thematic Apperception Test and other thematic approaches?

5. How can the accumulated reliability and validity evidence regarding thematic approaches to assessment be best characterized?

6. For interpretation of the Draw-A-Person test and other human figure drawing tests, what should be considered when attempting to determine if a specific characteristic is a significant emotional indicator?

7. In comparison with the Draw-A-Person test, what is the active nature of the Kinetic Family Drawing test purported to predict?

8. How can the accumulated reliability and validity evidence regarding human figure drawing tests as social–emotional measures be best characterized?

9. What evidence exists to support the validity of Koppitz's emotional indicators on the Bender-Gestalt test?

10. How reliable over time are sentence completion tasks?

11. What are the most defensible and empirically supportable uses of projective–expressive assessment techniques?

Part II

ASSESSMENT OF SPECIFIC PROBLEMS, COMPETENCIES, AND POPULATIONS

10

ASSESSING EXTERNALIZING PROBLEMS

The domain of externalizing problems and its related symptoms is a particularly troubling area for parents and teachers. By their nature, externalizing behavior problems are difficult to overlook, they are usually annoying and disruptive, and they may be dangerous at times. These behaviors also create problems for other individuals who are in the same environments as the children or adolescents who exhibit them. Externalizing behavior problems can be effectively assessed, and some of the assessment methods may be useful in developing intervention plans.

This chapter begins with an overview of externalizing problems, including discussions of specific disorders from the behavioral dimensions and *DSM* approaches to classification. After this introduction to the externalizing domain, some of the prevalence, etiology, developmental course, and prognosis indicators associated with externalizing disorders are reviewed. The bulk of the chapter is devoted to discussions of how various methods of assessment may be used best in evaluating the externalizing domain of problems. This chapter also includes a brief discussion on how well the five methods of assessment are linked to developing interventions to externalizing disorders and problems.

EXTERNALIZING DISORDERS: AN OVERVIEW

Experts in child psychopathology have long agreed that the behavioral dimension of externalizing disorders includes a broad array of aggressive behavior, antisocial characteristics, and hyperactivity (e.g., Cicchetti & Toth, 1991). Other terms that have been used to identify this behavioral dimension include *undercontrolled, antisocial,* and *outer-directed* behavior. The essential characteristics of this domain, regardless of the name used to describe it, include aggressive, acting-out, disruptive, defiant, antisocial, oppositional, and hyperactive behaviors. A child or adolescent who exhibits externalizing problems may not show all of these behaviors, but the congruence or relatedness among such symptoms has been well established.

The area of externalizing behavior problems has received significantly more attention than internalizing problems in the research literature, perhaps because of the debate over the reliability and long-term implications of internalizing disorders (Cicchetti & Toth, 1991) and because of the practical consideration that externalizing problems are seldom difficult to overlook. Many historically important empirical studies have provided solid support for the construct of an externalizing dimension of behavior problems (e.g., Achenbach, 1985; Ackerson, 1942; Coie, Belding, & Underwood, 1988; Ivanova

DOI: 10.4324/9781315747521-12

et al., 2007; Robins, 1966; Sroufe & Rutter, 1984). In addition to the types of externalizing symptoms that were noted at the beginning of this section, most of these sources identified another commonality of externalizing disorders: *peer rejection* that stems from aggressive behavior.

The Behavioral Dimensions Approach to Classifying Externalizing Disorders

Several prominent researchers have developed empirical behavioral dimensions classification taxonomies of externalizing behavior disorders (see Chapter 3 for more details). Quay's model for externalizing disorders has been particularly influential and has had a major influence on other researchers for many years. Quay (1986a) reviewed more than 60 studies that applied multivariate statistical approaches to the classification of child psychopathology. These studies commonly identified several narrow-band dimensions of symptoms, with each area of symptoms consisting of core behaviors and characteristics that were replicated at least several times. Under the broad-band domain that we refer to as externalizing, Quay isolated three major narrow-band dimensions of disorders, including *undersocialized aggressive conduct disorder*, *socialized aggressive conduct disorder*, and *Attention Deficit Hyperactivity Disorder* (ADHD). These three disorders are discussed briefly in this section. Table 10.1 provides examples of specific behaviors that fit within these domains.

Undersocialized Aggressive Conduct Disorder The narrow-band externalizing dimension that Quay (1986a) referred to as undersocialized aggressive conduct disorder includes a cluster of behaviors that involve aggression, violation of rules, temper tantrums and irritability, attention seeking and impertinence, and a variety of other negative and oppositional behavioral characteristics. Quay noted that this particular domain had emerged in multivariate classification studies "almost without exception" (p. 11), indicating that it is a relatively stable confluence of associated behaviors. In addition to a pattern of aggressive, disruptive, and noncompliant behaviors, the undersocialized aggressive conduct syndrome includes two other noteworthy features. The first feature is that hyperactive and restless behaviors (but usually not full-blown ADHD) often occur concomitantly with this syndrome, indicating an element of motor overactivity within the domain but not attentional problems. The second noteworthy feature is that "stealing has not been found at all central to this dimension" (Quay, 1986a, p. 11). Instead, stealing behaviors are more central to socialized aggressive conduct disorder.

Socialized Aggressive Conduct Disorder The second type of conduct disorder identified in Quay's (1986a) review and analysis is socialized aggressive conduct disorder. This cluster of behaviors is seen less frequently than undersocialized aggressive conduct disorder but still has received strong empirical support (Loeber & Schmaling, 1985). The principal features of this narrow-band dimension include involvement with peers in illegal or norm-violating behaviors. Some of the specific characteristic behaviors of socialized aggressive conduct disorder include having "bad" companions, truancy from school and home, stealing (at and away from home), lying, and gang activity. The essential feature of the behavior problems in this disorder is that they occur as a way of maintaining social acceptance within a deviant or antisocial peer group. Given that these conduct problems are often aimed at violating the rights of other persons and social institutions, delinquent behavior and involvement with juvenile justice systems often results. The onset

Table 10.1 Major characteristics of three domains of externalizing behavior disorders derived from Quay's (1986a) classic literature review

Undersocialized Aggressive Conduct Disorder
Assaultive behavior (fights, hits)
Disobedient and defiant behavior
Temper tantrums
Destructive behavior
Impertinent or "sassy"; uncooperative
Attention seeking
Domineering/threatening behavior
Demanding/disruptive behavior; loud and boisterous
Irritable and explosive
Negativity and refusal
Restlessness, hyperactivity
Dishonest and undependable

Socialized Aggressive Conduct Disorder
"Bad" companions
Truancy from home and school
Gang membership
Steals with others; steals at home
Lies and cheats
Stays out late at night
Loyalty to delinquent friends

Attention Deficit Hyperactivity Disorder
Poor concentration, short attention span, distractibility
Daydreaming
Poor coordination and clumsiness
Stares into space; preoccupied
Passivity and lack of initiative
Fidgeting and restless behavior
Fails to complete tasks
Lazy or sluggish behavior, drowsiness
Impulsivity
Lack of interest, general boredom
Hyperactive motor behaviors

of socialized aggressive conduct problems typically occurs at a later developmental stage than the undersocialized variety, usually in late childhood or early adolescence (Quay, 1986a). Another feature of this disorder is that it is much more likely to occur with males and it often is accompanied by deficits or lack of development in moral reasoning (Smetana, 1990).

Attention Deficit Hyperactivity Disorder (ADHD) The third narrow-band dimension of externalizing behavior disorders identified by Quay (1986a) is Attention Deficit Hyperactivity Disorder (ADHD), characterized by notable problems in maintaining concentration and attention, and often including associated behavior features such as impulsivity, clumsiness, and passivity. Overt motor overactivity (what we commonly think of as hyperactivity) is not always a feature of this disorder; behaviors that are characteristic of underactivity are often a prominent feature. Essentially, ADHD is a diverse group of behaviors and characteristics, and there are extremes in how the level of motor activity is manifest in individual cases. Some children who exhibit this disorder are constantly "on the move," fidgety, and restless, and may be at heightened risk for developing other conduct problems. The disorder may be exhibited in children who are more withdrawn and passive and who seldom engage in aggressive or antisocial behaviors. As such, this particular disorder does not fit into the broad band of externalizing problems as neatly as undersocialized and socialized aggressive conduct disorders. ADHD more often has been lumped in with the externalizing than the internalizing broad-band dimension, based on statistical and clinical evidence. One of the principal problems in classification of the behavioral symptoms of ADHD has been in distinguishing them from conduct disorders, owing to the existence of so many overlapping behaviors (Campbell & Werry, 1986). There is strong evidence that active and aggressive behaviors usually coexist at an early developmental stage (Campbell, 1991).

The DSM *Approach to Classifying Externalizing Disorders*

Although Quay's behavioral dimensions approach to classification of externalizing disorders is empirically supportable and has enjoyed wide influence among researchers, the *DSM* system of classification is the most widely used among practitioners in the United States and Canada. The *DSM-5* includes four major categories of externalizing behavior disorders relevant to children and adolescents. ADHD is found in the *DSM* under the general heading of *Neurodevelopmental Disorders*, and Conduct Disorder, Oppositional Defiant Disorder (ODD), and Intermittent Explosive Disorder are found under the heading of *Disruptive, Impulse-Control, and Conduct Disorders*. These four categories of externalizing behavior problems are reviewed briefly in this section. Two additional *DSM-5* classification categories, *Other Specified Disruptive, Impulse-Control, and Conduct Disorder* and *Unspecified Disruptive, Impulse-Control, and Conduct Disorder*, are also used to classify or diagnose externalizing behavior problems. These categories are not an integral part of the domain of externalizing behavior disorders, however, and are not discussed further in this chapter.

Attention Deficit Hyperactivity Disorder (ADHD) The *DSM-5* diagnostic criteria for ADHD are shown in Table 10.2. The major behavioral characteristics of this disorder are similar to the major characteristics identified through Quay's (1986a) behavioral dimensions approach, although more detailed, comprehensive, and specific. Perhaps the most notable difference between the current *DSM* criteria and earlier editions of the *DSM* is that ADHD is categorized with other neurodevelopmental disorders (e.g., learning disorders, intellectual disabilities, autism). This is partially due to the persistence observed within all of these disorders, common associated delays and risk for poorer outcomes, and also the changes in neural development (Nigg & Barkley, 2014). Symptoms of ADHD are separated into two major groups (inattention and hyperactivity), with the resulting implication that the two symptom areas may be independent to some extent. A previous *DSM* edition (*DSM-III-R*) (APA, 1987) did not separate symptoms into clusters by type, but simply required that a diagnosis be based on the presence of a minimal number of symptoms out of a larger broad symptom list. Current thinking on ADHD is that this disorder is often manifest as a distinct pattern of either inattentiveness or hyperactivity–impulsivity, although many individuals exhibit characteristics of both types (Barkley, 1997a, 1997b, 1997c; Holland et al., 1998; Nigg & Barkley, 2014). Another significant

Table 10.2 Diagnostic criteria for Attention Deficit Hyperactivity Disorder from *DSM-5*

A. A persistent pattern of inattention and/or hyperactivity-impulsivity that interferes with functioning or development, as characterized by (1) and/or (2):

1. **Inattention:** Six (or more) of the following symptoms have persisted for at least six months to a degree that is inconsistent with developmental level and that negatively impacts directly on social and academic/occupational activities.

   Note: The symptoms are not solely a manifestation of oppositional behavior, defiance, hostility, or failure to understand tasks or instructions. For older adolescents and adults (aged 17 and older), at least five symptoms are required.

   a. Often fails to give close attention to details or makes careless mistakes in schoolwork, at work, or during other activities (e.g., overlooks or misses details, work is inaccurate)
   b. Often has difficulty sustaining attention in tasks or play activities (e.g., has difficulty remaining focused during lectures, conversations, or lengthy reading)
   c. Often does not seem to listen when spoken to directly (e.g., mind seems elsewhere, even in the absence of any obvious distraction)
   d. Often does not follow through on instructions and fails to finish schoolwork, chores, or duties in the workplace (e.g., obvious distraction)
   e. Often has difficulty organizing tasks and activities (e.g., difficulty managing sequential tasks; difficulty keeping materials and belongings in order; messy, disorganized work; has poor time management; fails to meet deadlines)
   f. Often avoids, dislikes, or is reluctant to engage in tasks that require sustained mental effort (e.g., schoolwork or homework; for older adolescents and adults, preparing records, completing forms, reviewing lengthy papers)
   g. Often loses things necessary for tasks or activities (e.g., school materials, pencils, books, tools, wallets, keys, paperwork, eyeglasses, mobile telephones)
   h. Is often easily distracted by extraneous stimuli (for adolescents and adults, may include unrelated thoughts)
   i. Is often forgetful in daily activities (e.g., doing chores, running errands; for older adolescents and adults, returning calls, paying bills, keeping appointments)

2. **Hyperactivity and impulsivity:** Six (or more) of the following symptoms have persisted for at least six months to a degree that is inconsistent with developmental level and that negatively impacts directly on social and academic/occupational activities.

   Note: The symptoms are not solely a manifestation of oppositional behavior, defiance, hostility, or failure to understand tasks or instructions. For older adolescents and adults (aged 17 and older), at least five symptoms are required.

   a. Often fidgets with or taps hands or feet or squirms in seat
   b. Often leaves seat in situations when remaining seated is expected (e.g., leaves his or her place in the classroom, in the office, or other workplace, or in other situations that require remaining in place)
   c. Often runs about or climbs in situations where it is inappropriate (in adolescents and adults, may be limited to feeling restless)
   d. Often unable to play or engage in leisure activities quietly
   e. Is often "on the go," acting as if "driven by a motor" (e.g., is unable to be or uncomfortable being still for extended time, as in restaurants, meetings; may be experienced by others as being restless or difficult to keep up with)
   f. Often talks excessively
   g. Often blurts out an answer before a question has been completed (e.g., completes people's sentences; cannot wait for turn in conversation)
   h. Often has difficulty waiting his or her turn (e.g., while waiting in line)
   i. Often interrupts or intrudes on others (e.g., butts into conversations, games, or activities; may start using other people's things without asking or receiving permission; for adolescents and adults, may intrude into or take over what others are doing)

(continued)

Table 10.2 Diagnostic criteria for Attention Deficit Hyperactivity Disorder from *DSM-5 (continued)*

B. Several inattentive or hyperactive–impulsive symptoms were present prior to age 12 years.

C. Several inattentive or hyperactive–impulsive symptoms are present in two or more settings (e.g., at home, school, or work; with friends or relatives; in other activities).

D. There is clear evidence that the symptoms interfere with, or reduce the quality of, social, academic, or occupational functioning.

E. The symptoms do not occur exclusively during the course of schizophrenia or another psychotic disorder and are not better explained by another mental disorder (e.g., mood disorder, anxiety disorder, dissociative disorder, personality disorder, substance intoxication or withdrawal).

Specify whether:

314.01 (F90.2) Combined Presentation: Of both Criterion A1 (inattention) and Criterion A2 (hyperactivity–impulsivity) are met for the past six months.

314.00 (F90.0) Predominantly Inattentive Presentation: If Criterion A1 (inattention) is met but Criterion A2 (hyperactivity–impulsivity) is not met for the past six months.

314. 01 (F90.1) Predominantly Hyperactive/Impulsive Presentation: If Criterion A2 (hyperactivity–impulsivity) is met and Criterion A1 (inattention) is not met for the past six months.

Specify if:

In partial remission: When full criteria were previously met, fewer than the full criteria have been met for the past six months, and the symptoms still result in impairment in social, academic, or occupational functioning.

Specify current severity:

Mild: Few, if any, symptoms in excess of those required to make the diagnosis are present, and symptoms result in no more than minor impairments in social or occupational functioning.

Moderate: Symptoms or functional impairment between "mild" and "severe" are present.

Severe: Many symptoms in excess of those required to make the diagnosis, or several symptoms that are particularly severe, are present, or the symptoms result in marked impairment in social or occupational functioning.

Source: Reprinted with permission from *Diagnostic and Statistical Manual of Mental Disorders, Fifth Edition* (pp. 59–61). Copyright 2013 by the American Psychiatric Association.

change from previous editions in the *DSM* criteria for ADHD is the requirement that symptoms must be pervasive and persistent (Hinshaw, 1994). This change apparently was intended to ensure that ADHD would not be diagnosed unless the associated problems were substantial and observed across multiple contexts. The *DSM-5* also requires that symptoms be present before the age of 12. It has been argued, however, that no specific research support exists for this age of onset criterion and that the primary symptoms of ADHD may be present in very young children but that the six month requirement for persistence of symptoms may be too short for young children (Barkley, 1997a, 1997b, 1997c; Barkley & Biederman, 1997; Nigg & Barkley, 2014).

Conduct Disorder The *DSM-5* diagnostic criteria for Conduct Disorder are presented in Table 10.3. In *DSM* terms, Conduct Disorder falls under the broad domain of Disruptive, Impulse Control, and Conduct Disorders. The essential feature of this disorder is "a repetitive and persistent pattern of behavior that violates the rights of others or in which major age-appropriate societal norms or rules are violated" (APA, 2013; Kimonis, Frick, & McMahon, 2014, p. 146). In other words, Conduct Disorder is characterized by high levels of antisocial behavior. In contrast to Quay's (1986a) behavioral dimensions approach to classification of conduct disorders, the current *DSM* criteria do not differentiate among various possible subtypes (other than age of onset and severity).

Table 10.3 *DSM-5* diagnostic criteria for Conduct Disorder

A. A repetitive and persistent pattern of behavior in which the basic rights of others or major age-appropriate societal norms or rules are violated, as manifested by the presence of at least three of the following 15 criteria in the past 12 months from any of the categories below, with at least one criterion present in the past six months:

Aggression to people and animals
1. Often bullies, threatens, or intimidates others
2. Often initiates physical fights
3. Has used a weapon that can cause serious physical harm to others (e.g., bat, brick, broken bottle, knife, gun)
4. Has been physically cruel to people
5. Has been physically cruel to animals
6. Has stolen while confronting a victim (e.g., mugging, purse snatching, extortion, armed robbery)
7. Has forced someone into sexual activity

Destruction of property
8. Has deliberately engaged in fire setting with the intention of causing serious damage
9. Has deliberately destroyed others' property (other than by fire setting)

Deceitfulness or theft
10. Has broken into someone else's house, building, or car
11. Often lies to obtain goods or favors or to avoid obligations (i.e., "cons" others)
12. Has stolen items of nontrivial value without confronting a victim (e.g., shoplifting, but without breaking and entering, forgery)

Serious violations of rules
13. Often stays out at night despite parental prohibitions, beginning before age 13 years
14. Has run away from home overnight at least twice while living in the parental or parental surrogate home, or once without returning for a lengthy period
15. Is often truant from school, beginning before age 13 years

B. The disturbance in behavior causes clinically significant impairment in social, academic, or occupational functioning
C. If the individual is age 18 years or older, criteria are not met for Antisocial Personality Disorder

Specify whether:
312.81 (F91.1) Childhood-Onset Type: Individuals show at least one symptom characteristic of conduct disorder prior to age ten years.
312.82 (F91.2) Adolescent-Onset Type: Individuals show no symptom characteristic of conduct disorder prior to age ten years.
312.89 (F91.9) Unspecified Onset: Criteria for a diagnosis of conduct disorder are met, but there is not enough information available to determine whether the onset of the first symptom was before or after age ten years.

Specify if:
With limited prosocial emotions: To qualify for this specifier, an individual must have displayed at least two of the following characteristics persistently over at least 12 months and in multiple relationships and settings. These characteristics reflect the individual's typical pattern of interpersonal and emotional functioning over this period and not just occasional occurrences in some situations. Thus, to assess the criteria for the specifier, multiple information sources are necessary. In addition to the individual's self-report, it is necessary to consider reports by others who have known the individual for extended periods of time (e.g., parents, teachers, co-workers, extended family members, peers).
Lack of remorse or guilt: Does not feel bad or guilty when he or she does something wrong (exclude remorse when negative consequences of his or her actions). For example, the individual is not remorseful after hurting someone or does not care about the consequences of breaking rules.

(continued)

Table 10.3 *DSM-5* diagnostic criteria for Conduct Disorder *(continued)*

Callous-lack of empathy: Disregards and is unconcerned about the feelings of others. The individual is described as cold and uncaring. The person appears more concerned about the effects of his or her actions on himself or herself rather than their effects on others, even when they result in substantial harm to others.

Unconcerned about performance: Does not show concern about poor/problematic performance at school, at work, or in other important activities. The individual does not put forth the effort necessary to perform well, even when expectations are clear, and typically blames others for his or her poor performance.

Specify current severity:

Mild: Few if any conduct problems in excess of those required to make the diagnosis are present, and conduct problems cause relatively minor harm to others (e.g., lying, truancy, staying out after dark without permission, other rule breaking).

Moderate: The number of conduct problems and the effect on others are intermediate between those specified in "mild" and those in "severe" (e.g., stealing without confronting a victim, vandalism).

Severe: Many conduct problems in excess of those required to make the diagnosis are present, or conduct problems cause considerable harm to others (e.g., forced sex, physical cruelty, use of a weapon, stealing while confronting a victim, breaking and entering).

Source: Reprinted with permission from *Diagnostic and Statistical Manual of Mental Disorders, Fifth Edition* (pp. 469–471). Copyright 2013 by the American Psychiatric Association.

Previous versions of *DSM* have included various typologies for conduct disorders, however. For example, the *DSM-III-R* (APA, 1987) included code types for group type and solitary aggressive type, two categories that roughly correspond to Quay's typology of socialized aggressive conduct disorder and undersocialized aggressive conduct disorder. Within the current *DSM* system, to make a diagnosis of Conduct Disorder, a minimum of three symptoms from a diverse list of 15 symptoms must be present. Such generality in classification precision presents some obvious challenges. One such classification issue is the required existence of three (as opposed to, say, four or five) symptoms in the absence of any compelling empirical evidence to justify the criterion of three (Kazdin, 1995). Another issue exists regarding the diversity of symptoms on the list of 15 and the lack of any developmental anchors for these symptoms. As Kazdin has noted:

> The symptoms are delineated in a fixed way so that they are applied equally across the full period of childhood to adolescence. Yet perhaps symptoms required to meet the diagnosis should vary with age. It is unlikely that a four-year-old child would steal or confront a victim or force sex on someone. Does this mean that Conduct Disorder does not emerge before the age of four years or that the criteria for a four-year-old child ought to be different?
>
> (p. 26)

These have been commonly stated concerns among scholars. The *DSM-5* does account for developmental variation and intensity of symptoms with the inclusion of new specifiers. Those diagnosing are now able to specify whether onset occurs during childhood, adolescence, or at an unspecified time period. Further, one can specify if individuals present *with limited prosocial emotions* such as *lack of remorse or guilt, callous—lack of empathy, unconcerned about performance,* and/or *shallow or deficient affect* and whether symptoms are considered *mild, moderate,* or *severe.* Despite ongoing concerns regarding the previous, and even current, *DSM* approach to classifying Conduct Disorder, it still results in identification of adolescents who, as a group, tend to show remarkable distinguishing behavioral characteristics and tend to have a much poorer prognosis for general life adjustment and success when compared with "normal" youth (McMahon & Estes, 1997; Walker, Colvin, & Ramsey, 1995; Walker, Ramsey, & Gresham, 2004).

Oppositional Defiant Disorder (ODD) The *DSM-5* diagnostic criteria for Oppositional Defiant Disorder (ODD) are listed in Table 10.4. There is no parallel behavioral dimensions category corresponding to ODD, but its symptoms seem to be subsumed under the undersocialized aggressive conduct disorder category. ODD is characterized by angry/irritable mood, argumentative/defiant behavior, and vindictiveness (APA, 2013). Although some researchers and clinicians may doubt the existence of ODD as an empirical category that is unique from Conduct Disorder (some have derisively referred to ODD as a "weeny conduct disorder"), *DSM-5* considers the angry/irritable dimension and

---

Table 10.4 *DSM-5* diagnostic criteria for Oppositional Defiant Disorder

---

A. A pattern of angry/irritable mood, argumentative/defiant behavior, or vindictiveness lasting at least six months as evidenced by at least four symptoms from any of the following categories, and exhibited during interaction with at least one individual who is not a sibling.

Angry/irritable mood
1. Often loses temper
2. Is often touchy or easily annoyed
3. Is often angry and resentful

Argumentative/defiant behavior
4. Often argues with authority figures or, for children and adolescents, with adults
5. Often actively defies or refuses to comply with requests from authority figures or with rules
6. Often deliberately annoys others
7. Often blames others for his or her mistakes or misbehavior

Vindictiveness
8. Has been spiteful or vindictive at least twice within the past six months.

Note: The persistence and frequency of these behaviors should be used to distinguish a behavior that is within normal limits from a behavior that is symptomatic. For children younger than five years, the behavior should occur on most days for a period of at least six months unless otherwise noted (Criterion A8). For individuals five years or older, the behavior should occur at least once per week for at least six months, unless otherwise noted (Criterion A8). While these frequency criteria provide guidance on a minimal level of frequency to define symptoms, other factors should also be considered, such as whether the frequency and intensity of the behaviors are outside a range that is normative for the individual's developmental level, gender, and culture.

B. The disturbance in behavior is associated with distress in the individual or others in his or her immediate social context (e.g., family, peer group, work colleagues), or it impacts negatively on social, educational, occupational, or other important areas of functioning.
C. The behaviors do no occur exclusively during the course of a psychotic, substance use, depressive, or bipolar disorder. Also, the criteria are not met for disruptive mood dysregulation disorder.

Specify current severity:
   Mild: Symptoms are confined to only one setting (e.g., at home, at school, at work, with peers).
   Moderate: Some symptoms are present in at least two settings.
   Severe: Some symptoms are present in three or more settings.

Source: Reprinted with permission from *Diagnostic and Statistical Manual of Mental Disorders, Fifth Edition* (pp. 462–463). Copyright 2013 by the American Psychiatric Association.

argumentative/defiant dimension to hold up as factors that are distinct from Conduct Disorder, while vindictiveness overlaps considerably and could be thought of as a developmental precursor to Conduct Disorder. To be clear, *DSM-5* does consider ODD and Conduct Disorder to be mutually exclusive classifications, however. If symptom criteria for both disorders are met, Conduct Disorder should be the appropriate classification. Making a differential diagnosis between the two disorders would be a problem because of their apparently hierarchical relationship. Perhaps the most salient feature that might separate ODD from Conduct Disorder is the absence of overtly aggressive behavior, which also is a major predictor of future problems.

Intermittent Explosive Disorder Intermittent Explosive Disorder has been incorporated in versions of the *DSM* since 1980 (Coccaro, 2012). It is a disorder characterized by behavioral outbursts that include verbal or physical aggression that either persist over time but do not cause physical damage or harm, or they occur on at least three occasions within a year and do cause harm (APA, 2013). This disorder is often diagnosed in late childhood or adolescence and is mostly considered a categorical disorder versus a dimensional one (Coccaro, 2012). Intermittent Explosive Disorder cannot be diagnosed if it can be better described as another disorder, but it does often co-occur with a number of disorders such as depression, anxiety, ADHD, Conduct Disorder, and ODD.

Subdimensions of Externalizing Problems: Classification Studies

In addition to the classic behavioral dimensions efforts and the *DSM* approaches to classifying externalizing problems, some more recent classification efforts by prominent researchers have shed additional light on this area and help us understand better the shape and complexity of the externalizing domain. Regarding ADHD, the hyperactive–impulsive and inattentive subtypes from *DSM-5* that are based on earlier behavioral dimensions efforts have been verified by more recent multivariate studies using large data sets. It seems that the two subdimensions of ADHD are stable and emerge consistently across varying samples. In research reports detailing the factor structure and psychometric properties of newly developed ADHD assessment tools, DuPaul and colleagues (DuPaul et al., 1997; DuPaul, Anastopoulos, et al., 1998) and Holland et al. (1998) found a robust and consistent division of ADHD-related behaviors into the hyperactive–impulsive and inattentive subtypes.

It seems that the ADHD dimension of the externalizing domain can be divided clearly into these two subtypes; however, there is evidence to suggest that subtypes are not particularly stable over time (Lahey, Pelham, Loney, Lee, & Willcutt, 2005; Lahey & Willcutt, 2010). Regarding the subdivision of the Conduct Disorder and ODD *DSM* divisions of the externalizing domain, there has been less consistency among more recent research findings than with ADHD, indicating that these behavioral clusters are complex and of varying stability. One of the more widely influential investigations in this regard was conducted by Frick and colleagues (1993, cited in Frick, 1998), who did a meta-analysis of teacher and parent ratings of child behavior that used multidimensional scaling. This meta-analysis reviewed more than 60 factor analytic studies and involved ratings of more than 28,000 children. The results were presented in a grid with two bidirectional and bipolar axes: a vertical axis that included *destructive behavior* at one end and *nondestructive behavior* at the other and a horizontal axis that included *covert behavior* at one end and *overt behavior* at the other. Using the resulting four quadrants with their associated behavioral clusters as a guide, these researchers identified four subdomains of conduct problems:

1. property violations (cruel to animals, sets fires, steals, engages in vandalism, lies), a dimension that falls along the destructive–covert segment of the quadrant;
2. aggression (assault, is spiteful, is cruel, blames others, fights, bullies), which falls in the destructive–overt quadrant;
3. status violations (runs away, plays truant, engages in substance use, breaks rules, swears), which falls in the nondestructive–covert quadrant;
4. oppositional (is touchy, argues, is angry, is stubborn, shows temper, defies, annoys), in the nondestructive–overt quadrant.

Another important recent development in understanding subtypes of externalizing problems is the work of Frick and colleagues regarding the identification and characteristics of the *callous–unemotional* trait among youths (e.g., Barry et al., 2000; Frick & Ellis, 1999; Frick, Lilienfeld, Ellis, Loney, & Silverfeld, 1999; Kimonis, Ogg, & Fefer, 2014). As described by these researchers, the callous–unemotional trait appears to be related to a *combination of impulsivity and antisocial behavior.* Many of the youths who fit this profile have received *DSM* diagnoses of both Conduct Disorder and ADHD. What seems to make the callous–unemotional group unique is that children high on these traits tend to show a lack of fearfulness and anxiety, as well as low levels of responsiveness to rewards (Marini & Stickle, 2010). They also are not easily aroused and show little distress regarding the results of their behavior problems. In other words, the callous–unemotional trait reflects a form of psychopathy common among persons who feel little or no guilt or remorse, have a low general level of arousal and emotionality, are indifferent to the pain they may cause others, and have a shrewd approach to getting what they want through antisocial means. Research also suggests that youth with callous–unemotional characteristics may differ from others in terms of the severity of their antisocial behaviors and deficits in processing not only social scenarios but the affective component of social interactions (Marini & Stickle, 2010; Stickle, Kirkpatrick, & Brush, 2009). The "With Significant Callous–Unemotional Traits" specifier for the diagnosis of Conduct Disorder is an important addition to the *DSM-5*, especially considering the research of Kahn, Frick, Youngstrom, Findling, and Youngstrom (2012) that suggested 10% to 50% of youth with Conduct Disorder would meet criteria for the *DSM* specifier. The research that has identified and articulated this trait has been extremely influential during the past few years and is widely accepted among researchers in the areas of developmental psychopathology and antisocial behavior.

These important efforts by Frick, Stickle and their respective colleagues have made a substantial contribution to understanding of conduct problems and the externalizing domain in general. Future efforts may help to clarify further the subdomains of conduct problems, especially under varying conditions and across widely varying groups of adolescents.

PREVALENCE, DEVELOPMENT, AND PROGNOSIS OF EXTERNALIZING DISORDERS

Prevalence

Prevalence estimates for externalizing disorders vary depending on definitional criteria, specific populations studied, and assessment methodology. There is a general consensus, however, that externalizing problems tend to be quite common. Most research suggests ADHD may be increasing in prevalence with it being diagnosed in up to 8.7% of U.S. children aged eight to 15 (Froehlich et al., 2007). More recently, however, Nigg and Barkley (2014) have noted that more sophisticated analyses that enable researchers to take into account the variability in assessment and diagnostic procedures may result in true prevalence being closer to 2–3%. ADHD is known to occur much more frequently in boys than in girls, with prevalence ratios for the genders ranging from 2:1, depending on the type of setting.

Regarding Conduct Disorder, *DSM-5* states that in the child and adolescent population, the prevalence rate ranges from 2% to 10% and that it is observed in boys more often than girls. These rates are similar to what B. Martin and Hoffman (1990) cited in prevalence studies that placed the range of estimation for conduct disorders from about 4% to 8% in the entire school-age population, with boys outnumbering girls at about a 3:1 ratio on average. More conservative figures were noted by McMahon and Estes (1997), who listed the prevalence of conduct disorders in the 2% to 9% range and noted that there has been comparatively little research on the development and prevalence of conduct disorders in girls.

Less information is available regarding the prevalence of ODD. *DSM-5* provides a wide range (1% to 11%) for the estimate of prevalence and notes that it is more likely to be observed in pre-pubertal males than in females, but the rates are probably more similar following onset of puberty (APA, 2013). In contrast with what is known about the prevalence and gender features of ADHD and Conduct Disorder, relatively little evidence exists in the professional literature regarding ODD. When viewed as a whole, the prevalence estimates for externalizing disorders indicate that this band of disorders is relatively common in school-age children, boys are more likely than girls to exhibit them, and Conduct Disorder is more common than ADHD.

Comorbidity

A well-known finding that has emerged from the literature on externalizing disorders in children is that they tend to occur in a *comorbid* pattern, meaning that two or more of these disorders coexist in a substantial percentage of cases. This finding has been verified with respect to the relationship between ADHD and Conduct Disorder (Hinshaw, 1987, 1994; Kazdin, 1995; Larson, Russ, Kahn, & Halfon, 2011; Loney & Milich, 1982; McMahon & Estes, 1997; Paternite & Loney, 1980), Conduct Disorder and ODD (Biederman, Faraone, Milberger, & Jetton, 1996; Kazdin, 1995), and ODD and ADHD (Biederman et al., 1996; Nock, Kazdin, Hiripi, & Kessler, 2007). Although the existence of one of these disorders does not mandate the presence of another (remember that a diagnosis of Conduct Disorder precludes a diagnosis of ODD), they have been linked through theory and research for many years. Loeber (1985a) posited an interesting speculation on the link between ADHD and Conduct Disorder, suggesting that ADHD symptoms (particularly hyperactive behavior) may be a necessary precursor for the development of severe forms of Conduct

Disorder in many children. This speculation is certainly consistent with the more recent work of Frick, Stickler, and others regarding the connection between impulsivity, antisocial behavior, and the callous–unemotional trait. In addition, several researchers have considered ODD a developmental precursor to Conduct Disorder, while others have found that ODD and Conduct Disorder develop through parallel pathways (Diamantopoulou, Verhulst, & van der Ende, 2011). Whatever the relationship among the various externalizing disorders, it is clear that they share extensive common ground. The substantial comorbidity or co-occurrence of specific forms of externalizing disorders "raises questions about the categories themselves and about what is the most meaningful and useful way to delineate disruptive behaviors" (Kazdin, 1995, p. 25).

It is important to consider that the opposing categories of externalizing and internalizing are not necessarily mutually exclusive. McMahon and Estes (1997) and Kimonis, Frick, and McMahon (2014) stated that the presence of internalizing problems in children and adolescents who have conduct problems is higher than would be expected by chance and that the conduct problems typically precede the internalizing problems in a developmental pathway. Barkley (1997c) noted the same general relationship between ADHD and internalizing disorders. More recently, researchers have also observed that more intense externalizing behaviors are often associated with increases in internalizing behaviors for younger children (Gilliom & Shaw, 2004), and there is also the hypothesis that adolescents who are genetically predisposed to one dimension may also be predisposed to the other (Cosgrove et al., 2011).

Etiology and Development
The development and etiology of externalizing disorders has been the focus of much speculation and research. The major models for explaining causation have been social learning, biochemical/neurological, and familial/genetic approaches, or variants thereof. Hinshaw (1994), in his excellent overview of the various competing etiological models for ADHD, noted that researchers are "actively searching for unifying themes that could account for the symptomatology, associated features, and course of the disorder" (p. 51). With respect to ADHD, Campbell and Werry (1986) noted that although there has been a tremendous amount of speculation that a biological basis for the disorder exists, "specific conclusions remain elusive" (p. 116). If there is a biological basis for ADHD, as Deutsch and Kinsbourne (1990) contend, it may be obscured because of its heterogeneous nature and by the fact that there may be differing causal factors and risk factors for diverging subgroups of children with ADHD (Hinshaw, 1994). A more recent theory regarding the etiology of ADHD, one that promises to be highly influential, has been postulated and continuously studied by Barkley (1997a, 1997b, 1997c, 2011), who argued that the root of this disorder is not attentional, but rather a developmental problem of self-control or a deficit in behavioral inhibition. It is anticipated that the tremendous surge of interest regarding ADHD will result in continued theoretical developments and empirical advances regarding etiology.

With respect to conduct disorders (including Conduct Disorder and ODD), there has been increasing speculation of a biologically based etiology (Dick et al., 2011; Kazdin, 1995; Werry, 1986), but specific conclusions are difficult at this point. Similar to ADHD, conduct disorders may have a familial/genetic connection (Deutsch & Kinsbourne, 1990; Plomin, Nitz, & Rowe, 1990). Even with the inclusion of some well-designed twin studies and adoption studies, however, ferreting out the specific contributions of social learning and genetics has been problematic (Deutsch & Kinsbourne, 1990; Hetherington & Martin, 1986; Meier, Slutske, Heath, & Martin, 2011; Werry, 1986).

Despite the increasing amount of attention and interesting evidence regarding the possible biochemical or neurological basis for conduct disorders, the social learning model may offer a more elegant and substantiated developmental model at present. For example, researchers at the Oregon Social Learning Center have conducted numerous high-quality studies and published many reviews of their research showing that such factors as *harsh and inconsistent discipline practices, lax parental monitoring, coercive behavior in families,* and *exposure to adult models of antisocial behavior* are all powerful predictors of the development of aggressive and antisocial behavior in children (e.g., Capaldi, DeGarmo, Patterson, & Forgatch, 2002; Lahey et al., 2008; Lorber & Egeland, 2011; Patterson, 1976, 1982, 1986, 2002; Patterson & Bank, 1986; Patterson & Dishion, 1985; Patterson et al., 1992; J. Snyder & Stoolmiller, 2002). Another influential social learning–based model of the development of childhood conduct problems was proposed by Wahler and colleagues in the 1980s and 1990s (Wahler, 1994; Wahler & Dumas, 1986). This model includes many of the features identified by Patterson and colleagues but takes a different approach, focusing on *social continuity* and *predictability* of coercive interactions between parents and children as key variables in developing and maintaining antisocial–aggressive child behavior. Despite efforts to identify single essential variables that lead to development of conduct disorders, researchers who investigate this area seem to be focusing less on specific sole etiological factors and are viewing these possible causes as being risk factors or factors that increase vulnerability to the development of the disorders. Perhaps the most useful method of approaching the etiology of Conduct Disorder and ODD for assessment purposes is to integrate the various findings and speculations into a reciprocal determinism model consistent with Bandura's (1986) social–cognitive theory. It is likely that behavioral, environmental, and personal factors all contribute to development of externalizing disorders and that they work together in an interactive fashion.

Developmental Course and Prognosis
There is more evidence regarding developmental patterns and long-term implications of externalizing disorders than for internalizing disorders (Cicchetti & Toth, 1991; Mash & Terdal, 1997). The general developmental course of ADHD seems to include several components, including onset in infancy or early childhood; continuation during childhood and adolescence with concomitant academic, behavioral, and social problems; and marginal adjustment to the disorder during adulthood (Barkley, 1997c; Campbell & Werry, 1986; Hinshaw, 1994). "Overall, ADHD is far from a benign disorder: It carries significant risk for antisocial outcomes and for continuing patterns of disinhibited behavior, cognitive dysfunction, and interpersonal difficulties" (Hinshaw, 1994, p. 87). Longitudinal studies of ADHD (Weiss, 1983; Weiss, Hechtman, Perlman, Hopkins, & Wener, 1979) have shown that although individuals with ADHD may exhibit less impulsivity, restlessness, and antisocial behavior as adults than they did as adolescents, they are more likely to be "underemployed" than individuals without ADHD. These same studies have indicated that ADHD by itself is not predictive of severe psychopathology later in life. A related review of studies by Whalen and Henker (1998) concluded that although adults who were diagnosed with ADHD as children may have continuing problems with ADHD symptoms and related externalizing problems, there is no compelling evidence that children with ADHD are at increased risk for later development of internalizing disorders, such as mood

or anxiety disorders. More recent work does suggest, however, that females who are diagnosed with ADHD in childhood are more likely to have conflictual relationships with their mothers, fewer romantic relationships, and more experiences with symptoms of depression than females without ADHD (Babinski et al., 2011). If ADHD during childhood is accompanied by other externalizing disorders, substance abuse, familial discord, and low levels of intelligence and academic achievement, however, the long-term prognosis is poorer, and there is a greater likelihood of criminal behavior and psychiatric problems (Barkley, 1990, 1997c; Whalen & Henker, 1998).

With respect to conduct problems (including Conduct Disorder and ODD from the *DSM* system), their developmental course and long-term prognosis seem to be related strongly to the amount and intensity of aggressive behavior that is present and the time of the onset of symptoms. Quay (1986b) suggested that aggression is more likely to be a major characteristic of unsocialized rather than socialized types of conduct disorders and that the best prognosis for long-term adjustment is likely with individuals who have socialized aggressive conduct disorder in conjunction with high intelligence and good social skills. Previous research on aggressive behavior resulted in findings that indicate reasonably strong stability over time. The likelihood that children's aggressive behavior will persist into adulthood increases with age. In other words, there is a modest probability that very young children (e.g., preschoolers) who exhibit persistent patterns of aggressive behavior also will exhibit aggressive behaviors as adults, but if these children are still exhibiting the same pattern of behavior by age ten or 12, the probability is that aggressive behavior as adults increases significantly. This pattern of continuity was shown in a classic review of the literature from 1935 to 1978 by Olweus (1979), who found that stability of aggressive behavior was almost as strong over ten-year periods (0.60) as that of intelligence (0.70). Quay (1986b) suggested that the pattern of persistence of aggressive behavior is stronger for males than for females. Whether aggressive and antisocial conduct results in involvement with the justice system (i.e., reported delinquent and criminal behavior) seems to be related strongly to whether the child or adolescent has a parent who was convicted of a crime before the child reached age ten (Farrington, 1978). The long-term developmental course of Conduct Disorder leads to the conclusion of a poor prognosis: "Longitudinal studies have consistently shown that Conduct Disorder identified in childhood or adolescence predicts a continued course of social dysfunction, problematic behavior, and poor school and occupational adjustment" (Kazdin, 1995, p. 69).

There have been substantial research and writing efforts to illuminate what seem to be two distinct developmental pathways for severe conduct problems, an "early starter" pathway and a "late starter" pathway (for example, several decades of research on this issue at the Oregon Social Learning Center are summarized in Patterson & Yoerger, 2002). In their excellent review of these constructs, McMahon and Estes (1997) noted several key characteristics that define each pathway. The early-starter pathway is characterized by the onset of conduct problems in early childhood and by a high degree of continuity of these problems throughout childhood and into adolescence and adulthood. The late-starter pathway begins during adolescence rather than early childhood and is less likely to persist into adulthood. The strongest paths that predict outcomes for late starters include poor parental monitoring, association with deviant peers, and conflict with parents (Patterson & Yoerger, 2002). Fewer children are involved in the early-starter pathway than the late-starter pathway, but the early-onset variety of conduct problems tends to be more overt, serious, and intractable than the late-starter variety. In fact, early starters (as indicated by the presence of several risk factors by fourth grade) have an astonishingly high probability of being arrested prior to age 14 (14 times higher than their peers who score low on risk factors) and are likely to exhibit patterns of social maladjustment, occupational problems, involvement with the justice system, and relationship problems throughout their early adult life (Patterson & Yoerger, 2002).

Although considered to be a less severe disorder than Conduct Disorder, ODD also seems to have a poor long-term prognosis, primarily because it is considered to be either a developmental antecedent or developmental parallel to Conduct Disorder. The amount and intensity of aggressive behavior that develops over time may be a key to understanding the long-term prognosis. The change in development from childhood to adolescence to adulthood of children who develop and maintain patterns of antisocial behavior is additive. That is, these children usually "do not change the types of behaviors they display but instead add the more severe conduct problem behaviors" (Frick, 1998, p. 215). To sum up our discussion on the long-term implications of conduct problems, it is important to consider two major findings: (1) Present aggressive behavior is the most important variable in the prediction of future aggressive and antisocial behavior (Quay, 1986b; Robins, 1966); and (2) although almost all adults with antisocial aggressive behavior exhibited these same patterns as children, many antisocial children do not become antisocial adults (Frick, 1998; B. Martin & Hoffman, 1990; Robins, 1974). A diagnosis of Conduct Disorder, although often associated with a poor prognosis for future adjustment, does not mandate such a prognosis, particularly if the onset of symptoms occurs later rather than in early childhood and involves more covert rather than overt antisocial behaviors.

METHODS OF ASSESSING EXTERNALIZING PROBLEMS

Each of the major direct and objective assessment methods emphasized in this book can be used successfully to measure externalizing problems of children and adolescents. In terms of the state of the art and the utility of each method for day-to-day assessment of externalizing problems, direct observation and rating scales have received more attention in the literature. In terms of interview techniques, the behavioral interview with parents or teachers offers a great deal in the assessment of externalizing problems, and some structured and semistructured interview schedules have shown promise. Sociometric techniques have been shown to be extremely strong predictors of externalizing behavior disorders but may not be implemented as easily in routine assessment designs. Objective self-report assessment also may be used to evaluate externalizing problems, but it does seem to be more limited in scope and utility than observation, rating scales, and interviews. Each of these five methods is discussed in this section.

Behavioral Observation
There is widespread professional agreement that direct behavioral observation is one of the most useful procedures for assessing externalizing behavior disorders (Alessi, 1988; Patterson & Forgatch, 1995; Reid et al., 1988). McMahon and Forehand (1988) suggested that behavioral observation is "the most reliable and valid assessment procedure for obtaining a functional analysis of conduct disorders in children" (p. 138). Although direct observation is not without limitations (such as the number of observations needed for

reliability, as well as issues of training observers reliably), there is no question that it has proven useful in assessing externalizing problems.

There are two major reasons that direct behavioral observation is a preferred method for assessing externalizing problems. The first has to do with the nature of externalizing disorders. In contrast to internalizing disorders, which often involve highly subjective perceptions and internal states, externalizing disorders are characterized by overt behavior patterns that are easy to observe, such as excessive motor activity, physical aggression, and verbal intimidation and opposition. Behavioral observation is an assessment method that easily measures externalizing target behaviors and is highly objective. The second reason for preference of direct observation in assessing externalizing disorders has to do with behavior–environment interactions and the need to identify aspects of the environment that may be modified usefully in a treatment plan. Similar to internalizing problems, externalizing behavior problems do not occur in a vacuum; they are elicited and maintained in a complex interaction between the person, the behavior, and the environment, as illustrated in Bandura's (1977, 1978, 1986) notion of reciprocal determinism. In contrast to internalizing problems, these interactive relationships in externalizing behavior problems are easier to observe directly. Specific interactions and environmental variables that may play a role in the development of interventions are relatively easy for a skilled observer to identify, which is the reason that direct observation is the key method in conducting functional behavior assessments. Studies suggest, for example, that direct observation is a preferred method of assessment by most school psychologists and that practitioners appreciate the ease with which direct observation data can be linked to effective and targeted intervention practices (Landau & Swerdlik, 2005; Riley-Tillman, Chafouleas, Briesch, & Eckert, 2008; Shapiro & Heick, 2004).

Chapter 4 includes a detailed discussion of general observation methods and coding procedures, including examples of systems useful in clinic, home, and school settings and a description of the process of conducting functional behavior assessments. This information is not repeated in this chapter. Provided in this section is an example of a direct observation system that has been used successfully to assess externalizing disorders in clinic settings. Although home-based observation and school-based observation systems for externalizing problems have been demonstrated successfully (see Chapter 4 for examples), our focus is on a clinic-based example in this section because this is a setting that can be used easily by most clinicians on a daily basis.

Although mental health, pediatric, or school psychology clinics are usually not considered to be naturalistic settings for conducting observations, these clinic environments can be effective settings for observing externalizing behavior problems (H. M. Hughes & Haynes, 1978). Clinic observations are usually analogue in nature because they can create conditions in which behavior can simulate the home setting or the school setting (Hintze et al., 2000). A major advantage of clinic-based observation is that it is more efficient and cost-effective and less obtrusive than home-based observations (McMahon & Forehand, 1988).

The Dyadic Parent–Child Interaction Coding System (DPICS) An example of an excellent clinic-based observation system is Eyberg and Robinson's (1983) Dyadic Parent–Child Interaction Coding System (DPICS), a coding procedure developed more than three decades ago that has proved to be a highly reliable and valid method for assessment of externalizing problem behaviors of children, and that is still in wide use. Now in its fourth edition, DPICS is particularly interesting in that it goes beyond simply focusing on child behavior problems and assesses these behaviors in the context of parental interactions in the parent–child dyad (Eyberg, Chase, Fernandez, & Nelson, 2014). The DPICS requires observation of the parent–child dyad in three different situations in the clinic: a free-play situation (child-directed interaction), a situation in which the parent guides the child's activity (parent-directed interaction), and a situation referred to as clean-up, in which the parent attempts to get the child to clean up the toys in a playroom. The observations occur for five minutes in each of the three settings using a continuous frequency recording system, for a total of 15 minutes of direct behavioral observation. Parent behaviors are coded along 12 domains, including direct and indirect statements, descriptive and reflective statements, descriptive and reflective questions, acknowledgment, irrelevant verbalization, unlabeled and labeled praise, positive and negative physical interactions, and critical statements. Child behaviors are coded along seven different domains, including cry, yell, whine, smart talk, destructive, physical negative, and change activity. The authors of the DPICS (Robinson & Eyberg, 1981) also developed composite behavioral coding variables (total praise, total deviant, total commands, command ratio, no opportunity ratio, compliance ratio, and noncompliance ratio), which consist of specific combinations of individual coding domains.

Results of several studies have shown the DPICS to have solid psychometric properties. The inter-rater reliability of the DPICS has been found to range from 0.65 to 1.00 (Aragona & Eyberg, 1981; Eyberg & Matarazzo, 1980), with mean reliability coefficients of 0.91 and 0.92 for parent and child behaviors in the standardization study (Robinson & Eyberg, 1981). Although the DPICS has been used primarily in clinic-based observations, one investigation (Zangwill & Kniskern, 1982) found overall cross-setting interobserver agreement of 0.68 and 0.69 between home and clinic observations.

In terms of validity evidence, Robinson and Eyberg (1981) showed that the DPICS can discriminate accurately between groups of children with conduct disorders from their siblings and from normal children and that it has a high correct classification rate for each of these child groups and their families. This finding has been replicated through other studies (Forster, Eyberg, & Burns, 1990). Additional studies have shown the DPICS to be sensitive to treatment effects (Eyberg & Matarazzo, 1980; Webster-Stratton, 1984). It appears to be relatively easy to implement with trained observers and to provide assessment data that are not only descriptive of problems, but also can be used to construct treatment plans.

The DPICS is just one example of a clinic-based coding procedure that has proved useful in assessing externalizing problems. Many other clinic-based systems that have been validated empirically for assessing externalizing disorders have been reported in the literature. More information about the comprehensive manual for the DPICS, updated in 2000, 2005, and 2014, is currently available online at www.pcit.org/measures.

One of the main advantages of behavioral observation is that the methodology is flexible and tailored easily to the specific assessment problem in question. Observational coding systems that have been well researched offer certain advantages, but clinicians and researchers who understand the dynamics of observational assessment are able to develop systems that are uniquely suitable for the settings in which they are working. If the referred child or adolescent client is reported to exhibit serious behavioral problems at school and at home, it may be necessary to observe directly in the classroom, using an observation system similar to the school-based examples that we looked at in Chapter 4.

As McMahon and Forehand (1988) have suggested, the therapist usually does not have the option of observing teacher–child interactions in the clinic, and naturalistic observation in the classroom may be warranted. If the problem behavior is related to a school-based referral, direct observation in the classroom should be a high priority, if not an essential part of the assessment.

Behavior Rating Scales

Behavior rating scales are potentially one of the most useful methods of assessing externalizing behavior problems. Because externalizing behavior is often overt and directly observable, an informant who knows the child or adolescent well may be in a position to provide a comprehensive rating of a wide variety of problem behaviors. Similar to direct observation, rating scales can provide relatively objective measurement, yet they are much less time-intensive to use. As a method of initial screening of problem behaviors and subsequent hypothesis generation, behavior rating scales may be one of the best choices. Theoretically, there are some important differences between even the best rating scales and direct observation, and these differences usually indicate the need for using both types of measures. Rating scales usually provide a retrospective method of assessment, given that a parent or teacher rates child or adolescent problem behaviors according to his or her observations and perceptions over a past time period, say, the preceding six months. Direct observation provides a format for measuring behaviors as they occur over a limited period. Rating scales seldom provide information on environmental variables relating to problem behaviors, whereas direct observation over short periods is likely to miss low-frequency but important behaviors. The multimethod, multisource, multisetting assessment model that was described in Chapter 1 provides a format for overcoming the limitations of individual assessment sources and still using their strengths.

For assessment of general externalizing problems or conduct problems, the general-purpose problem behavior rating scales or systems that were illustrated in Chapter 5 (the Behavior Assessment System for Children, Third Edition; the Child Behavior Checklist; the Teacher's Report Form; the Conners 3; and the Conners Comprehensive Behavior Rating Scales) are all excellent choices for screening externalizing behavior problems. These rating scales all have many items and scales specific to the externalizing domain. The School Social Behavior Scales and Home and Community Social Behavior Scales, which are discussed in Chapter 13, also may prove useful in assessing certain externalizing problems. The antisocial behavior scale of these instruments provides a specific format for measuring aggressive, disruptive, and antisocial behavior, in conjunction with a rating of social skills from their co-normed social competence scales. The Preschool and Kindergarten Behavior Scales, Second Edition, which are discussed in Chapter 14, provide an excellent means for screening externalizing behavior problems with preschool-age and kindergarten-age children.

Narrow-Band Rating Scales for Attention Deficit Hyperactivity Disorders

Although the four general-purpose behavior rating scales reviewed in Chapter 5 are all excellent choices for screening and assessing general externalizing behaviors and conduct problems, they may have some limitations when it comes to assessing ADHD, a specific narrow-band cluster of the externalizing domain. Although each of these general-purpose tools provides screening items and scales for assessing ADHD symptoms, it may be useful or necessary to screen for ADHD characteristics using a narrow-band scale developed specifically for this purpose. Such narrow-band instruments typically include a greater range of items designed specifically for evaluating ADHD characteristics and symptoms than would be found on a general-purpose behavior rating scale. This section includes brief reviews of four such narrow-band instruments that have been developed specifically for assessing ADHD. These instruments, which are representative of the several available instruments in this area, include the ADHD Rating Scale-5, Attention Deficit Disorders Evaluation Scales, ADHD Symptoms Rating Scale, and the Conners ADHD Scales (Conners 3AI). These four instruments all are parent and teacher rating scales designed for assessing the behavioral symptoms of ADHD specifically based on the *DSM-IV* or *DSM-5* diagnostic criteria. As such, they include certain advantages over general-purpose behavior rating scales when assessing ADHD symptoms. Additionally, another tool that is often associated with assessment of behaviors associated with ADHD will be reviewed. This is the Behavior Rating Inventory of Executive Functioning, Second Edition. Any of these instruments may prove to be a valuable addition to an assessment design in situations in which attention problems, impulsivity, and hyperactivity are a major focus of concern.

The ADHD Rating Scale-5 (ADHD-5) The brief (18-item) ADHD Rating Scale-5 (ADHD-5) (DuPaul, Power, Anastopoulos, & Reid, 2016) is designed for use by parents and teachers for diagnosing ADHD symptoms and assessing treatment response in children aged five to 18. Measures are available in both English and Spanish, and the 18 items are linked specifically to the *DSM-5* symptom descriptors and are based on the classification system organization of ADHD symptoms into the Inattention and Hyperactivity–Impulsivity domains (nine items each). This two-domain structure of the ADHD-5 is also empirically validated based on factor analytic research. To be consistent with changes to ADHD diagnostic criteria in the *DSM-5*, authors updated this measure in two primary ways. First, they created two slightly different, developmentally appropriate forms: one for children and another for adolescents. Second, they added questions to help reflect the level of impairment symptoms cause in a child/adolescent's life (e.g., in getting along with family, completing schoolwork). The items on both forms are rated using a 4-point scale ("Never or rarely" to "Very often"). The two domain scores and a total score are converted to percentile ranks based on separate gender and age groupings. These score conversion tables are based on national norms, with approximately 2,079 well-stratified cases for the parent norms and 1,070 for the teacher norms represented in the national standardization sample.

Psychometric evidence is presented in the ADHD-5 manual and in separate published studies (DuPaul & Stoner, 2015). The scale has been shown to have strong internal consistency reliability (0.89 to 0.95) and test–retest reliability (0.61 to 0.93) at six-week intervals for the symptom items and strong test–retest reliability for the impairment items (0.62 to 0.92). Inter-rater agreement between parents and teachers has been shown to range from 0.01 to 0.77 for symptom items and –0.06 to 0.77 for impairment items, which is in the expected range for cross-informant reliability across settings. Evidence of convergent and discriminant construct validity for the ADHD-5 includes correlational comparisons with other behavior rating scales and comparisons with direct observations of student behavior in classroom settings. The scale also has been shown to discriminate effectively between children with and without ADHD, and to show sensitivity to treatment effects of children with ADHD who receive stimulant medication.

The ADHD-5 offers many advantages, is easy to use, and is psychometrically sound. The brief 18-item format might be considered a disadvantage (i.e., not providing as much evaluation depth as scales with larger item pools), but the brevity is advantageous in some situations, such as when used for tracking treatment progress and for conducting initial screening when a more in-depth assessment is not possible.

The Attention Deficit Disorders Evaluation Scales (ADDES-4) The Attention Deficit Disorders Evaluation Scales–Fourth Edition (ADDES-4) (McCarney & Arthaud, 2013) include a set of instruments designed specifically for measuring the behavioral character-istics of ADHD in children and adolescents aged four to 18, and for making program planning and intervention decisions. The scales originally were published in 1989, with a second edition published in 1995 to reflect changes in the scales based on the changes in ADHD diagnostic criteria from the *DSM-IV*. The fourth edition reflects changes within the *DSM-5*.

Two versions of the ADDES-4 are available: (1) a 46-item home version designed to be completed by parents; and (2) a 60-item school version designed to be completed by teachers and other school-based professionals. The items of the ADDES-4 are descriptions of a variety of behaviors reflecting inattentiveness and hyperactivity–impulsivity. The items are divided into two sections and scales consistent with this *DSM-5* symptom area breakdown. The items are rated using a unique 5-point scale in which each rating point is anchored to a specific time element under which the behaviors may occur (0 = "does not engage in the behavior," 1 = "one to several times per month," 2 = "one to several times per week," 3 = "one to several times per day," and 4 = "one to several times per hour"). Raw scores are converted to standard scores (with a range of 0–20 and representing a mean of 10 and standard deviation of 3) and percentile ranks based on the two subscale breakdowns and a total score. These scores are keyed to three different diagnostic levels (normal score, some problems, and serious problems), based on standard deviation units from the normative population. These scales are easily hand-scored, but a computer-assisted scoring problem is also available, as is a Spanish-language version for home or parent raters.

The technical manuals for the home and school versions of the ADDES-4 provide a variety of information on the technical properties of each instrument. All versions of the ADDES were normed on large nationwide population samples. The ADDES-4 School Version was normed on 3,356 students. The stability of the ADDES across time, settings, and raters seems to be good. Test–retest reliability at 30-day intervals has been measured in the low 0.90 range for the total scores, with ranges from the upper 0.80s to mid-0.90s for the subscales. Reported inter-rater reliabilities and internal consistency of the ADDES-4 forms and its predecessors are very high. The factor/subscale structure of the instruments is very consistent with the *DSM-5* symptom area breakdown of ADHD. Diagnostic validity data gathered during the standardization of the ADDES show that each version of the instrument can discriminate between groups of children who have been diagnosed as having ADHD and randomly selected comparison subjects. Strong convergent construct validity evidence for both versions has been found with a variety of other ADHD and problem behavior rating scales.

The ADDES-4 is recommended as a narrow-band behavior rating scale for screening and assessment of children and adolescents in whom ADHD symptoms are the sole or primary concern. Parents and teachers likely will find the scales easy to use, and clinicians likely will find both versions of the ADDES-4 to be practical. The addition of some externally published research studies supporting the ADDES-4 would bolster the confidence with which researchers and clinicians might use these instruments, however, and would bolster their reputation within the professional community.

The Conners 3 ADHD Index (Conners 3AI) The Conners ADHD Index is part of the third edition of Conners comprehensive system for behavioral assessment that was overviewed in Chapter 5 (Conners, 2008a). The ADHD Index includes three forms: Conners 3AI-P (parent), Conners 3AI-T (teacher), and Conners 3AI-SR (self-report). The forms are appropriate for children aged six to 18 (eight to 18 for self-report). Each of these forms includes ten items and can be used as stand-alone behavioral measures. They are particularly useful in determining whether a more extensive evaluation is warranted or to monitor intervention progress over the course of time. The Conners 3AI is easy to score and, in addition to *T* scores, probability scores can be generated. For example, for youth receiving a probability score of 80% or higher, the likelihood that their behaviors are similar to those of youth with ADHD is very high. The reliability estimates provided in the manual suggest excellent internal consistency (0.83 to 0.93) and solid temporal stability (0.79 to 0.93). The Conners 3AI was carefully developed and has proven to discriminate between children with and without ADHD. It is an excellent tool for assessment situations in which the referral questions are specific to attentional problems, hyperactivity, or both, and for which there is no indication of coexisting conduct or affective problems.

The Behavior Rating Inventory of Executive Function, Second Edition (BRIEF-2) While not a measure specific to the assessment of ADHD, the Behavior Rating Inventory of Executive Functioning, Second Edition (BRIEF-2; Gioia, Isquith, Guy, & Kenworthy, 2015) is a tool that was first developed in 2000 and has experienced exponential growth in terms of its use. This growth mirrors the growth that has been observed in the study of executive functioning over the last 20 years. Since the development of the original scale in 2000, there have been over 800 peer-reviewed articles published and approximately 40 clinical trials including the BRIEF, and it has been translated into 60 languages. The BRIEF-2 includes parent, teacher, and self-report forms, and assesses weaknesses in executive functioning in children and adolescents (aged five to 18). This tool takes about ten minutes to complete (approximately 60 items), and there is a 12-item screening tool that takes approximately five minutes to complete.

Three factors have emerged from analyses, including a Behavior Regulation Index, Emotional Regulation Index, and Cognitive Regulation Index. Items from the Behavior Regulation Index reflect an individual's ability to self-monitor and appropriately inhibit behavioral responses. Emotion Regulation Index items include one's ability to transition between activities easily and handle emotions appropriately. Finally, the Cognitive Regulation Index includes multiple concepts such as one's ability to plan, organize, initiate and monitor tasks. This second edition includes new norms generated from a sample of over 3,500 children and adolescents. Reliability coefficients range between 0.80 to 0.90 and the BRIEF-2 is correlated with behavior rating scales such as the CBCL, BASC-2, Conners 3 and IQ measures such as the Weschler Intelligence Scale for Children, Fourth Edition (WISC-IV) and Weschler Adult Intelligence Scale, Fourth Edition (WAIS-IV).

Overall, the BRIEF-2 is a widely used and well-developed tool that is quickly becoming the gold standard for measurement of executive functioning skills and abilities of children and adolescents. While executive functioning, as a construct, is related to a wide range of behaviors, including internalized behaviors like anxiety and depression, I included it here as children with poor executive functioning skills also often engage in impulsive and externalized behaviors.

INTERVIEWING TECHNIQUES

Of the interviewing techniques discussed in Chapter 6, the behavioral interview appears to be a particularly appropriate approach for assessing externalizing problems. Although traditional (i.e., unstructured) interviewing techniques may be useful in obtaining a general appraisal of the cognitive and affective status of the client or informant, they are not as likely to result in a clear picture of the specific problems that are occurring. Given that child and adolescent conduct problems tend to be conceptualized in terms of inter-action with others (McMahon & Forehand, 1988), the behavioral interview should include input from parents and input from teachers if the conduct problems are present in the school setting. The characteristics of externalizing disorders may make conducting an effective interview directly with the child or adolescent client difficult. For conduct disorders, characteristic problems such as lying, defiance of authority, and oppositional behavior may result in the child or adolescent client providing information that is suspect. Children or adolescents with ADHD may not show such overt defiance to the interviewer but still may provide poor-quality data because of typical difficulties in concentration, self-awareness, and behavioral self-control. Behavioral interviews with parents and teachers are an important first step in assessing externalizing disorders.

Whether the externalizing problems in question involve conduct disorders, ADHD, or some combination thereof, the effectiveness of the behavioral interview is enhanced greatly by the specificity of questions. For assessing ADHD, DuPaul (1992) and DuPaul and Stoner (1994, 2003, 2015) suggested using a semistructured behavioral interview format in which teachers and parents are asked questions pertaining to the presence or absence and intensity of symptoms from the *DSM* criteria. Such an interview format is simple, yet potentially effective in ruling in or out various diagnostic criteria. An example of this type of interview was provided by Forehand and McMahon (1981), who described the use of the *Problem Guidesheet,* a semistructured format for conducting behavioral interviews to assess child conduct problems. This interview format, which is shown in modified format in Figure 10.1, assists the clinician in structuring questions so that specific information on the frequency, duration, and parent or child responses to the problem behaviors can be obtained. The *Problem Guidesheet* also provides a format for asking questions about problem behaviors in specific settings and at specific times (e.g., mealtime, public places). This tool is not intended to be a standardized interview instrument but simply a format to help clinicians structure behavioral interviews so that effective information about conduct problems can be obtained.

In terms of using standardized structured and semistructured interview schedules to assess externalizing problems, the instruments that were overviewed in Chapter 6 may be useful. These instruments were designed to assess a broad range of child disorders along the lines of *DSM* criteria and are not specifically designed for assessing externalizing problems. Conduct Disorder, ODD, and ADHD are all mainstay childhood disorders in the *DSM-III-R, DSM-IV/DSM-IV-TR,* and *DSM-5* and various characteristics of these disorders are covered within the K-SADS and SCICA.

Name of Child: Name of Interviewee(s):		Interviewer: Date of Interview:			
Setting/ Time	Description	Frequency	Duration	Parent Response	Child Response
At bedtime					
At mealtime					
At bath time					
With parent on the phone					
With visitors at home					
When visiting others					
Traveling in the car					
In public places					
At school					
With siblings					
With peers					
With other parent/ relative					
Disciplinary procedures					
Other					

Figure 10.1 Forehand and McMahon's (1981) Problem Guidesheet, a tool for conducting behavioral interviews to assess child conduct problems

Source: Reprinted with permission.

The National Institute of Mental Health Diagnostic Interview Schedule for Children (Fisher, Wicks, Shaffer, Piacentini, & Lapkin, 1992; Shaffer et al., 2000), currently in its fourth revision (DISC-IV) is another structured interview schedule that seems to be highly relevant for assessing externalizing problems. The DISC-IV is an interview schedule for use with children aged nine to 17 and their parents. This interview schedule originally was designed as a screening instrument for research purposes, but its clinical uses are currently being refined and investigated. The DISC-IV provides scores in 27 symptom areas that are outlined according to *DSM* classification criteria. The child version of the DISC-IV has more than 200 items and requires 40 to 60 minutes to administer, whereas the parent version includes more than 300 items and takes 60 to 70 minutes to administer. Both versions are highly structured and include specific codes for each item. The DISC-IV requires little training to administer and score, although interpretation is a more difficult task. Edelbrock and Costello (1988) reviewed several studies of previous versions of this tool and noted that it has strong inter-rater reliability, fair to adequate test–retest reliability, and modest agreement between parent and child forms. The DISC-IV also has been shown to have strong concurrent validity with the DICA-R and weaker but still significant concurrent validity with the parent version of the Child Behavior Checklist (Costello, Edelbrock, Dulcan, & Kalas, 1984).

A comprehensive user's manual and computerized diagnostic program are available. Another innovation has been the development of the computerized Voice DISC, which was released in 1999. This version allows interviewees to listen to the interview questions through headphones rather than face to face with an interviewer and to respond to the questions (which appear simultaneously on a computer screen) by using a computer keyboard. The computerized Voice DISC does not require a trained interviewer and relies primarily on the verbal comprehension skills of the adolescent who is being interviewed. The advantage of this method of administration is that it may elicit more honest responding from adolescents, who are able to avoid the potential embarrassment of personally answering a highly sensitive question from an adult they do not know. Overall, the DISC-IV seems to offer several advantages. It is relatively easy to use, it is highly structured, and it should be a particularly good choice for assessing adolescents with externalizing problems.

An additional semistructured interview tool to consider for use in assessing adolescents aged 12 to 18 with externalizing conduct problems is the Hare Psychopathy Checklist: Youth Version (PCL:YV) (Forth, Kosson, & Hare, 2003). This instrument was identified to help assess some of the main markers of "psychopathy" or antisocial traits, including cheating, fighting, bullying, and other antisocial acts. The PCL:YV uses a semistructured interview format as well as adjunct information to derive dimensional scores that are designed to predict the seriousness of problems and their likelihood of continuing into adulthood. Completion of the PCL:YV interview takes from 1.0 to 1.5 hours, with an additional hour required for gathering and entering collateral information. This tool was standardized with interview data from 2,438 youths in three nations. One of the interesting aspects of the norming sample is that there are data on 19 different samples of adolescents (e.g., institutionalized offenders, youths on probation, community samples, etc.) which allow for comparisons of individual scores with very specific group subsets. Raw scores for the PCL:YV are converted into dimensional scores in the Interpersonal/Affective and Social Deviance areas. Research data presented in the PCL:YV manual indicate that it has sound psychometric properties, including internal consistency coefficients ranging from the mid-0.80s to mid-0.90s across various settings, and sensitivity in differentiating various subgroups of adolescents with high accuracy. A fair amount of externally published research on this instrument has been published (e.g., Corrado, Vincent, Hart, & Cohen, 2004; Poythress, Dembo, Wareham, & Greenbaum, 2006), which provides additional supporting evidence regarding the construct validity and uses of the PCL:YV.

This instrument appears to be very well designed and psychometrically sound, and may be an interesting assessment interview choice for clinicians who work primarily in settings that serve antisocial and delinquent youths. It will be interesting to see if publishers continue to offer these measures and also to note if newer versions are made available that are specifically aligned to the *DSM-5*.

Sociometric Techniques

In Chapter 7, four types of sociometric assessment techniques were examined in detail, including peer nomination, peer rating, sociometric ranking, and alternative procedures such as picture sociometrics, the Class Play, and "guess who" measures. If properly applied, any one of these sociometric procedures is potentially an excellent choice for screening and assessing externalizing disorders.

The utility of sociometrics for assessing externalizing problems depends on two things: (1) the specific design of the sociometric question or task; and (2) the purposes for which the sociometric assessment will be used. To be most effective in assessing conduct disorders or ADHD, the sociometric tasks need to be structured carefully so that the peer or teacher informants will make selections based on the most salient behavioral characteristics. For instance, negative ranking or rating procedures in which participants are asked to list or rate peers who "fight a lot" will likely be more effective in externalizing assessment than procedures in which participants are asked to list or rate peers who "don't get along with other students." The latter example could have a great deal of correlation with internalizing problems. Sociometric assessment of externalizing problems is generally a more useful procedure for screening purposes or research than it is for individual assessment. Conducting a sociometric procedure as part of an individual assessment in the classroom of a referred student might provide some useful data on that student, but the amount of time and intrusiveness involved in doing this rarely would be warranted.

Because Chapter 7 provided an overview of the specifics of conducting sociometric assessments, that information is not repeated here. Some examples of studies employing sociometric procedures to assess externalizing characteristics and outcomes are provided, however. In their review of studies documenting the predictive validity of sociometrics, McConnell and Odom (1986) cited several investigations in which sociometric procedures were employed in the assessment of externalizing problems. One of the most frequently cited of these studies is a classic longitudinal investigation by Roff et al. (1972) of peer and teacher ratings of 40,000 children. One of the interesting findings of this classic study was that children rated least liked by their peers were significantly more likely to appear on registers of juvenile delinquency than children who were rated most liked by peers. Other longitudinal studies have found that peer ratings or nominations of classmates as mean, noisy, or quiet (Victor & Halverson, 1976) and troublesome or dishonest (West & Farrington, 1973) were significantly related to conduct problems and juvenile delinquency at a later age. Roff (1961) conducted a prospective study of 164 boys who were referred to child guidance clinics and later served in the military and found that children whose records indicated poor peer adjustment were significantly more likely to receive bad-conduct discharges from military service than children with good peer relations. Other studies documenting the utility of sociometric procedures in assessing externalizing problems could be cited, but these four classic studies provide sufficiently strong evidence. In sum, sociometric assessment procedures have been shown to be highly effective in the assessment of a variety of externalizing conduct problems and are particularly useful for screening and research purposes.

Self-Report Instruments

As shown in Chapter 11, the use of objective self-report instruments is often the primary method of choice for assessing internalizing problems. A much different picture of the usefulness of self-report assessment emerges, however, when it is applied to the measurement of externalizing behavior disorders. There are three measurement problems that emerge in using self-report tests for assessing antisocial behavior, conduct disorders, and ADHD. First, externalizing problems usually are assessed best through direct measurement and unbiased reporting by objective observers or informants (McMahon & Estes, 1997; McMahon & Forehand, 1988). Second, children and adolescents with externalizing disorders may not always be reliable or insightful reporters of their own behavior because of social perception distortions or because of oppositional defiance to the assessment process (McMahon & Estes, 1997), which may include efforts to deliberately and consciously distort or falsify information. Third, the nature of most objective self-report tests requires that a fair amount of inference be used in applying the results to actual behaviors exhibited, particularly with conduct problems. Although objective self-report tests may be extremely useful in the assessment of internalizing problems, they present some substantial challenges in assessing externalizing behavioral problems.

Despite the apparent limitations of using self-report instruments in assessing externalizing problems, there are times when it is highly desirable to include a suitable self-report instrument in an assessment battery. For instance, a clinician may want to gather systematic data on a child or adolescent client's perceptions of his or her behavior, or compare the client's personality profile with that of a normative or clinical group. Another possible advantage of self-report assessment of adolescents with externalizing disorders exists with regard to obtaining their own report of *covert* conduct problems (e.g., vandalism, theft, drug use) that may not be observed easily by third-party informants (Kazdin, 1995).

There are a few standardized self-report instruments that are a potentially valuable addition to the multimethod, multisource, multisetting assessment design for measuring externalizing disorders. The general-purpose self-report instruments that have been discussed in previous chapters—Adolescent Psychopathology Scale, child and adolescent self-report forms of the Behavior Assessment System for Children (BASC-3), Minnesota Multiphasic Personality Inventory–Adolescent (MMPI-A) and the restructured form (MMPI-A-RF, the Conners 3, and Conners Comprehensive Behavior Rating Scales (CBRS), and Youth Self-Report (YSR)—all may be useful to some extent in assessing externalizing problems and their correlates. Each of these instruments includes subscales that are associated with externalizing and antisocial behavior problems, such as the Psychopathic Deviate and Conduct Problems scales of the MMPI-A; the Impulse Control and Societal Conformity scales of the MMPI; and the Aggressive Behavior, Attention Problems, and Delinquent Behavior scales of the YSR. The APS and MMPI-A are best described as measures of personality that may be useful in predicting psychopathology. The YSR, BASC, and Conners require that adolescents rate their own levels of specified problem behaviors. Regarding the personality-related measures, it is important to draw the distinction between assessing information regarding a specific behavior and assessing response styles that may be associated with those characteristics. For example, many investigations have shown that the MMPI-2 and MMPI-A 2-point code type of 4 to 8 or 8 to 4 is a common pattern among individuals who have been incarcerated for severe antisocial acting-out behavior. Yet the MMPI-A does not assess antisocial and violent behavior directly; the vast amount of research on the instrument merely has identified response patterns that are correlated with these behaviors on the basis of group research.

In addition to the general-purpose self-report instruments just described, this section also provides brief evaluative reviews of another instrument that was designed expressly or primarily for self-report assessment of youth with externalizing behavior problems. This includes the Jesness Inventory (JI). This tool is described here. Again, a revision of this measure could not be found at the time of this publication. It will be interesting to see if a newer version is developed and aligned to *DSM-5*. At this time, the JI is still available for purchase from Multi-Health Systems.

The Jesness Inventory–Revised (JI-R) The Jesness Inventory–revised (JI-R) (Jesness, 2003) is the result of an extensive effort to update and restandardize previous versions of the scales, which have also been referred to as the Jesness Adolescent Personality Inventory (Jesness, 1962, 1996). This test originally was developed in the early 1960s and was based on outcome research with adolescents identified as delinquent in California (Jesness, 1962, 1963, 1965). The newer JI includes many characteristics of the previous versions, but has a greatly expanded norm sample and age span. The JI and its predecessors are among the oldest and most widely used self-report instruments specifically developed for assessing attitudes of adolescents with conduct disorders and antisocial or delinquent behaviors.

The revised instrument is a 160-item true/false questionnaire designed to measure attitudes and personality characteristics associated with antisocial and delinquent behavior. This tool is designed to be used across youth and adult age spans, and includes separate subscale norms for the following age groups: eight to 11, 12 to 14, 15 to 17, and 18 to 35. The 160 items yield *T* scores on nine personality scales, 11 subtype scales, two *DSM-IV* scales, and two validity scales. The scale structure of the JI is detailed in Table 10.5. As with all arbitrarily named test scales, the scales on the JI may not measure characteristics that a literal interpretation of the scale name might suggest. For example, the poorly named Autism scale does not measure characteristics of autism. Rather, it is designed to evaluate distortion of reality or superficial self-enhancement.

Normative data for the revised JI are based on samples of 4,380 individuals aged eight to 35 from North America, including a sample of 3,421 nondelinquents and 959 delinquents. Reviews of the revised JI (Rhoades, 2005; Yetter, 2005) have noted that there are no delinquent or antisocial youth under the age of 12 specifically represented in the sample, and that there are significant differences in the demographics of the delinquent and nondelinquent samples. Whereas the nondelinquent sample is more than 80% White, the delinquent sample is more than 70% non-White. In addition, the delinquent sample was derived primarily from one correctional site and is not geographically representative of the larger population.

Internal consistency estimates for the JI scales reported in the test manual range from 0.61 to 0.91, and should be considered as generally adequate to good. Test–retest reliability of the JI was evaluated with a sample of 131 delinquent individuals at eight- to 12-month intervals, with stability coefficients ranging from 0.35 to 0.67 across personality scales.

Table 10.5 Scale structure of the Jesness Inventory–Revised

Personality Scales
Social Maladjustment
Asocial Index
Withdrawal–Depression
Value Orientation
Manifest Aggression
Immaturity
Social Anxiety
Alienation
Denial
Repression
Autism

Subtype Scales
Unsocialized, Aggressive/Undersocialized Active
Unsocialized, Passive/Undersocialized Active
Immature Conformist/Conformist
Cultural Conformist/Group-Oriented
Manipulator/Pragmatist
Neurotic Acting-Out/Autonomy-Oriented
Neurotic Anxious/Introspective
Situational Emotional Reaction/Inhibited
Cultural Identifier/Adaptive

***DSM-IV* Scales**
Conduct Disorder
Oppositional-Defiant Disorder

Validity Scales
Random Response Scale
Lie Scale

Validity of the revised JI has been documented through studies showing that several of the scales reliably differentiate between subsamples of offenders and nonoffenders. In addition, research on previous versions of the JI has provided additional reliability evidence and has indicated that the instrument has strong convergent validity with other personality measures, is sensitive to treatment changes, and can reliably differentiate delinquent from nondelinquent groups (e.g., Jesness & Wedge, 1984; Kahn & McFarland, 1973; G. Roberts, Schmitz, Pinto, & Cain, 1990; Shark & Handel, 1977; Shivrattan, 1988).

The JI can be recommended as an objective self-report test for assessing personality and attitudes of antisocial children, youth, and young adults, although with some reservations and cautions. The recent revision was a welcome and needed change, and the new norming sample (despite its geographical, racial, and other limitations) is vastly better than the previous samples. Perhaps the most important caution to consider is that the JI was designed to assess *attitudes and attributes* of antisocial individuals; it does not actually assess conduct problems. Despite its limitations, the JI is a unique tool with a rich tradition and research base, and will likely continue to be a valued assessment instrument for many years.

LINKING ASSESSMENT TO INTERVENTION

Each of the five general methods for assessing externalizing disorders that I have discussed in this chapter have their own advantages and limitations, and are useful for various purposes and situations. When it comes to linking assessment data to interventions for externalizing problems, however, it is fairly clear that the five methods are not equal. Direct behavioral observation, particularly observational coding systems that take into account environmental variables and interactions between the subject and significant others, is the method that is potentially of most use in developing function-based hypotheses and intervention plans. Behavioral interviewing with parents and teachers of the referred child or adolescent client is another assessment method that allows for collection of the same type of function-based assessment data, albeit in a less direct fashion.

Behavior rating scales have many advantages and uses in assessing externalizing problems, but may be less useful than direct observation or behavioral interviews in generating hypotheses regarding functions of behavior and in designing function-based behavior supports, despite their psychometric superiority to these more direct methods. If rating scales completed by different raters in different settings consistently portray certain behaviors or situations as significant problems, the clinician will have some salient clues as to what specific behaviors or situations to focus on in the intervention plan. The Keystone Behavior Strategy (R. O. Nelson & Hayes, 1986) is an intervention selection strategy for which behavior rating scales may be useful. This strategy is based on the idea that identification of a group of crucial behaviors or responses linked to a particular disorder, something that is quite possible with rating scales, leads to the immediate targeting of those responses as "keystone" behaviors for intervention.

Sociometric assessment of externalizing problems is a highly reliable and valid descriptive method for screening or research, but it offers a much weaker link to intervention planning. Objective self-report tests also provide a tenuous link to treatment planning for externalizing disorders, owing to the fact that they assess responding and personality patterns rather than actual behaviors. There have been some attempts to link MMPI-A profile types to treatment planning, but these efforts cover only one specific self-report instrument and are based on actuarial prediction with groups and may not prove to be useful with all individuals who exhibit particular profiles. In sum, externalizing disorders by their nature are distinctly suited to the most direct methods of assessment, which in turn are capable of providing the most useful links to function-based intervention planning.

It is important to view the idea of linking assessment to intervention for externalizing behavior disorders within a realistic perspective. The more direct approaches to assessment (i.e., direct observation, behavioral interviews, behavior rating scales) offer the promise of linkage to intervention planning. A large body of evidence clearly indicates, however, that externalizing behavior disorders present many challenges for effective intervention. Reviews of the treatment literature on antisocial behavior and conduct disorders (Frick, 1998; Kazdin, 1995; McMahon & Estes, 1997; Reid & Eddy, 2002) and ADHD (Hinshaw, 1994; Whalen & Henker, 1998) point to a consensus that although there are several promising psychological treatments for externalizing disorders, they typically do not produce extremely large and long-lasting effects because these disorders tend to be relatively intractable. Treatment of externalizing disorders should be viewed in many cases as more of a long-term management strategy than as a "cure," and interventionists should be realistic in understanding that lasting change of significant externalizing problems will require significant and often resource-intensive approaches.

CONCLUSIONS

The area of externalizing disorders is perhaps the most clearly defined and extensively researched broad-band domain of child psychopathology. Externalizing disorders, which typically are thought of as being behavior problems rather than emotional problems (although the two categories are not exclusive), involve a variety of acting-out, aggressive, antisocial, disruptive, and overactive behaviors. This domain of behavioral problems has been referred to as undercontrolled and outer-directed in nature.

The two major approaches to classification of child psychopathology have resulted in similar, although slightly differing, diagnostic and classification categories, all of which tend to co-occur with each other in a large percentage of cases. Quay's behavioral dimensions classification scheme for the externalizing disorders includes three categories: (1) undersocialized aggressive conduct disorder; (2) socialized aggressive conduct disorder; and (3) ADHD. The *DSM-5* includes the major diagnostic categories of ADHD, Conduct Disorder, and ODD. Refinements in the *DSM* classification system for externalizing disorders of children have occurred from the two previous editions and likely will continue as better empirical evidence mounts.

Externalizing disorders often begin early in life, with the developmental antecedents sometimes present as early as infancy (difficult temperament) and early childhood (attention-seeking and acting-out behavior). There are many competing theories regarding the etiology of these disorders, ranging from biological to behavioral, but most recent notions of causality tend to view specific etiological components as risk factors rather than sole causes. With respect to conduct disorders, earlier development and the presence of aggressive behavior tend to be associated with a poorer long-term prognosis, whereas later onset, less aggressive behavior, the presence of good social skills, and higher levels of intelligence tend to be associated with a better prognosis. With ADHD, the presence of other externalizing disorders, substance abuse, and antisocial–aggressive behavior tends to be associated with a poorer long-term prognosis. All forms of externalizing behavior disorders tend to present substantial challenges for long-term adjustment.

Behavioral observations are one of the hallmark methods for assessing externalizing problems because they tend to be readily observable and because observation may be linked more functionally to intervention than some other methods. Behavior rating scales are another potentially useful method for assessing externalizing problems, for many of the same reasons as behavioral observation and because of their superior psychometric properties. Each of the general-purpose behavior rating scales discussed in Chapter 5 is potentially useful in assessing externalizing problems, as are the externalizing-specific rating scales discussed in this chapter. Interviewing, particularly behavioral interviewing and structured interview schedules, is another excellent assessment for externalizing problems. The advantage of behavioral interviewing for this purpose is that it allows for identification of possible behavior–environment relationships that may be useful in treatment planning. Sociometric assessment techniques have a long history of successful use with externalizing problems but often are impractical to use as part of individual assessment; their best uses in this regard tend to be for research and for general screening. Self-report instruments are probably the most tenuous of the five assessment methods for externalizing problems, but even this method has some advantages, such as obtaining self-report of covert conduct problems that may not be readily observed by parents, teachers, or observers. The general-purpose self-report instruments discussed in Chapter 8 all seem to have some degree of relevance for assessing externalizing problems, as do the externalizing-specific self-report instruments discussed in this chapter.

Although treatment for externalizing disorders tends to be difficult and is usually more of a long-term management proposition rather than a short-term "cure," there are some promising treatment modalities. Linkage between assessment and effective treatment of externalizing problems is most direct when using behavioral observation, behavioral interviewing, and behavior rating scales.

REVIEW AND APPLICATION QUESTIONS

1. What are some possible reasons the externalizing domain of child psychopathology is more easily defined and well documented than the internalizing domain?
2. Contrast Quay's behavioral dimensions approach to classifying externalizing disorders with the *DSM* approach. Does either approach present any salient advantages for assessment or treatment planning?
3. In recent years the callous–unemotional subtype or trait among children with externalizing problems has been identified and researched. What are the major characteristics associated with this trait, and why are these characteristics particularly troubling?
4. For children with conduct disorders, what characteristics tend to be associated with the poorest long-term prognosis? What characteristics tend to be associated with a more favorable long-term prognosis?
5. Substantial research efforts have been directed at identifying specific etiologic factors in the development of externalizing disorders. Why do you suppose that the current trend is to view specific possible causes as risk factors rather than as a sole causal explanation?
6. If one were to design an optimal observation coding system for detecting the broad band of externalizing disorders, what crucial observable behaviors would need to be coded?
7. Contrast the narrow-band behavior rating scales for assessing ADHD discussed in this chapter with the general-purpose rating scales presented in detail in Chapter 5. Under what circumstances would an assessment design be enhanced by one of these more focused instruments?
8. Regarding covert conduct problems, such as vandalism, stealing, drug use, and so forth, what advantages do interviews and self-report instruments offer over direct observation, parent or teacher interviews, and behavior rating scales? How much confidence should a clinician have regarding the truth or accuracy of self-report statements obtained from an adolescent with serious conduct problems?
9. What are the crucial components needed to link assessment of externalizing problems most effectively to intervention planning?

11

ASSESSING INTERNALIZING PROBLEMS

Internalizing problems, which include a broad domain of characteristics or symptoms related to depression, anxiety, social withdrawal, and somatic complaints, are an intriguing and sometimes problematic area for assessment. As will be discussed in greater detail later, internalizing problems can be difficult to detect, and the symptoms of various specific internalizing disorders often are mingled together. For these reasons, one expert has referred to internalizing problems in children as *secret illnesses* (W. M. Reynolds, 1992a). After carefully reading this chapter, readers will gain a greater understanding of the complexity and various dimensions of internalizing problems and how various assessment strategies are used in the investigation, identification, and classification process.

This chapter begins with a discussion of the nature of internalizing problems, including overviews of each major area of syndrome. This introductory overview is followed by discussions of the implications of developing internalizing problems and how this broad band of symptoms is related to self-concept. The chapter then provides detailed information on direct and objective methods of assessing internalizing problems, using behavioral observation, rating scales, interview techniques, sociometric approaches, and self-report tests. A special assessment section also is provided for methods of measuring self-concept. The chapter ends with a brief discussion of the challenges of linking assessment of internalizing problems to intervention.

INTERNALIZING PROBLEMS: AN OVERVIEW

As indicated in Chapters 3 and 10, efforts at creating sophisticated and empirically sound taxonomies of child psychopathology (i.e., the behavioral dimensions approach) have tended to sort general types of behavioral and emotional problems along two broad dimensions, usually referred to as internalizing (overcontrolled) and externalizing (undercontrolled) disorders (Cicchetti & Toth, 1991).

The domain of internalizing problems or disorders includes a seemingly broad array of symptoms, such as dysphoric or depressive mood states, social withdrawal, anxious and inhibited reactions, and the development of somatic problems (physical symptoms with no known organic basis). Although these various internalizing conditions at least superficially may appear to be distinct symptoms, there has long been strong evidence that they often tend to exist together in a *comorbid* or *co-occurring* relationship (Ackerson, 1942; Fish & Shapiro, 1964). There is a large and growing body of evidence that strongly indicates a great deal of behavioral covariation between the characteristics of mood

DOI: 10.4324/9781315747521-13

disorders, anxiety disorders, and somatic complaints (e.g., Achenbach & McConaughy, 1992; Maser & Cloninger, 1990). The chances may be quite high that a child or adolescent who presents the obvious symptoms of depression also may experience anxiety, social inhibition and withdrawal, and physical concerns (Merrell, 2008). It is useful, if not necessary, to study the assessment of these types of problems together within a common framework.

Behavioral Dimensions Classification

Consistent with previous discussions of the behavioral dimensions classification approach (see Chapters 3, 5, and 10), specific areas of internalizing problems have been identified using multivariate statistical techniques. Quay (1986a) identified the two major dimensions that coincide with internalizing problems as *Anxiety–Withdrawal–Dysphoria* and *Schizoid–Unresponsive*. The major characteristics of these two internalizing behavioral dimensions are listed in Table 11.1. There is a fair amount of overlap in characteristics between the two major internalizing domains from this perspective.

Other researchers have described the domains within internalizing problems in a different manner (e.g., Achenbach, 1982b; Achenbach & McConaughy, 1992; Compas, 1997; Ebmeier, Donaghey, & Steele, 2006), but Quay's description serves to illustrate the point of overlapping characteristics within types of internalizing problems.

The DSM Classification

The *DSM* system includes several general diagnostic categories that fit specifically within the internalizing domain, such as Depressive Disorders, Anxiety Disorders, Obsessive-Compulsive and Related Disorders, Trauma- and Stressor-Related Disorders and Somatic Symptoms and Related Disorders. An overview of the major *DSM-5* diagnostic categories for internalizing disorders is presented in Table 11.2. More details on some of the major *DSM-5* diagnostic categories for internalizing disorders are presented later in this chapter. The classification categories presented in Table 11.2 do not include the more general "not otherwise specified" categories, and they do not include several classification categories that are not primarily internalizing in nature but may have specific internalizing manifestations, such as Dissociative Disorders, Eating Disorders, Bipolar Disorders,

Table 11.1 Major characteristics of two dimensions of internalizing problems identified through Quay's (1986a) Review of Multivariate Classification Studies

Anxiety–Withdrawal–Dysphoria	Schizoid–Unresponsive
Anxious, fearful, tense	Won't talk
Shy, timid, bashful	Withdrawn
Depressed, sad, disturbed	Shy, timid, bashful
Hypersensitive, easily hurt	Cold and unresponsive
Feels inferior, worthless	Lack of interest
Self-conscious, easily embarrassed	Sad
Lacks self-confidence	Stares blankly
Easily flustered and confused	Confused
Cries frequently	Secretive
Aloof	Likes to be alone
Worries	

Table 11.2 Major diagnostic categories of internalizing disorders from *DSM-5*

Depressive Disorders

Disruptive Mood Dysregulation Disorder	Major Depressive Disorder
Persistent Depressive Disorder	Premenstrual Dysphoric Disorder
Substance/Medication-Induced Depressive Disorder	Depressive Disorder Due to Another Medical Condition
Other Specified Depressive Disorder	Unspecified Depressive Disorder

Anxiety Disorders

Separation Anxiety Disorder	Selective Mutism
Specific Phobia	Social Anxiety Disorder
Panic Disorder	Panic Attack Specifier
Agoraphobia	Generalized Anxiety Disorder
Substance/Medication-Induced Anxiety Disorder	Anxiety Disorder Due to Another Medical Condition
Other Specified Anxiety Disorder	Unspecified Anxiety Disorder

Obsessive Compulsive and Related Disorders

Obsessive-Compulsive Disorder	Body Dysmorphic Disorder
Hoarding Disorder	Trichotillomania
Excoriation	Substance/Medication-Induced Obsessive Compulsive and Related Disorder
Substance/-Medication Induced OCD and Related Disorder	OCD and Related Disorder Due to Another Medical Condition
Other Specified OCD and Related Disorder	Unspecified OCD and Related Disorder

Trauma- and Stressor-Related Disorders

Reactive Attachment Disorder	Disinhibited Social Engagement Disorder
Posttraumatic Stress Disorder	Acute Stress Disorder
Adjustment Disorders	Other Specified Trauma- and Stressor-Related Disorder

Somatic Symptom and Related Disorders

Somatic Symptom Disorder	Illness Anxiety Disorder
Conversion Disorder	Psychological Factors Affecting Other Medical Conditions
Factitious Disorder	Other Specified Somatic Symptom and Related Disorder
Unspecified Somatic Symptom and Related Disorder	

Schizophrenia and Psychotic Disorders, Neurodevelopmental Disorders, and Tic Disorders. Many of these other disorders are discussed in Chapter 12. In contrast to the externalizing disorders discussed in Chapter 10, these *DSM*-based classification categories for internalizing disorders bear little resemblance to the corresponding behavioral dimensions classification categories discussed previously and presented in Table 11.1. This lack of similarity among the major classification approaches to internalizing disorders indicates that this domain is still amorphous or difficult to define precisely to clinicians and researchers.

Prevalence

Prevalence rates for internalizing disorders of children and adolescents have been much more difficult to ascertain accurately than prevalence estimates for externalizing disorders. These rates tend to vary considerably from one investigation to another depending on the particular disorder under investigation and the diagnostic criteria that were used (Michael & Merrell, 1998). Examples of prevalence rates from epidemiologic studies average about 4.8% or higher for adolescent depression and 2.5% for childhood depression

(Beauchaine & Hinshaw, 2013). Prevalence rates for Separation Anxiety Disorder are about 3.9%, 6.7% for specific phobias, 2.2% for social phobia, and 1.7% for Generalized Anxiety Disorder in children. For adolescents, the average estimate of overall anxiety disorders are at 11% with 6.6% for specific phobia, 5.0% for social phobia, 2.3% for separation anxiety, 1.9% for Generalized Anxiety Disorder, and 1.1% for Panic Disorder (Beauchaine & Hinshaw, 2013). The *DSM-5* provides some general prevalence estimates for specific internalizing disorders, but these data tell researchers nothing about the prevalence of such problems in children and adolescents. There are many young people who are significantly affected by internalizing symptoms, but whose problem characteristics do not fit neatly into a specific diagnostic category. The *DSM* system does not have a category for Childhood Internalizing Disorder. Reviews (e.g., Dopheide, 2006) that address prevalence estimates do not necessarily clarify the picture, and indicate widely varying estimates of percentages of children and youth who experience functional impairment from internalizing problems.

Despite the lack of precision of current prevalence rates for internalizing disorders in children and adolescents, even the more conservative estimates are cause for concern.

For example, assume that there is a median prevalence rate of about 5% of the general school-age population that either has a specific internalizing disorder or has significant enough internalizing symptoms to interfere with their academic and personal adjustment. This figure would represent an average of one or two children in each class of 30 who are so afflicted. Perhaps most distressing is the fact that in contrast to children with externalizing disorders, many of these internalizers are overlooked or not identified as needing help. Even if effective interventions are available, the lack of detection and attention result in continued and unnecessary difficulties for many children and adolescents.

Gender Issues in Prevalence

Most prevalence estimates for internalizing problems and disorders indicate that they occur with greater frequency in girls than in boys, particularly in the case of depression, and especially following the onset of puberty. These adult gender prevalence patterns seem to be true for adolescents also, and it seems that "girls show an enhanced susceptibility for a number of internalizing disorders" (W. M. Reynolds, 1992b, p. 314). Most recent research suggests that girls and women experience both depression and anxiety twice as often as males (Beauchaine & Hinshaw, 2013; Maeng & Milad, 2015). Gender characteristics of internalizing disorders among younger children are much more speculative, however, with some studies showing no gender difference, some studies showing a higher prevalence among boys, and some studies showing a higher prevalence among girls (Merrell & Dobmeyer, 1996). In general, most descriptive studies indicate that internalizing disorders are more common in girls than in boys after the onset of puberty, but the evidence is still lacking in some respects, particularly with respect to prepubertal gender differences (e.g., Merikangas, Cui, & Kattan, 2012; Merrell, 2008; Twenge & Nolen-Hoeksema, 2002; Zahn-Waxler, Shirtcliff, & Marceau, 2008).

SYMPTOMS OF MAJOR INTERNALIZING DISORDERS: DEPRESSION, ANXIETY, AND RELATED PROBLEMS

To identify and more clearly define the major subcomponents of internalizing problems, this section includes brief discussions of symptoms based on a breakdown into three areas: depression, anxiety, and related problems. When using this three-part breakdown of internalizing problems, it is important to consider that there is more confusion among researchers over terminology and classification subtypes for internalizing problems than for externalizing problems (Merrell, 2008; Merrell, Crowley, & Walters, 1997). Any categorical breakdown in the internalizing domain will have some level of imprecision. This section follows a hybrid of behavioral dimensions and *DSM* approaches to categorization. This discussion of general characteristics of internalizing disorders addresses etiology and developmental course of specific problems only at a superficial level; a thorough treatment is beyond the scope of this book. Some useful sources for a comprehensive treatment of various internalizing problems include books or chapters by Barrios and Hartmann (1997), Beauchaine & Hinshaw (2013), Compas (1997), Lewis and Miller (1990), Mash and Barkley (2014), Merrell (2008), W. M. Reynolds (1992a), Schwartz, Gladstone, and Kaslow (1998), and Silverman and Ginsburg (1998).

Depression

To understand better what the target is when assessing depression, some definitions and distinctions are needed. The term *depression* may be construed to indicate a broad range of behaviors, characteristics, and symptoms. This broad and imprecise use of the term has been a problem in the research literature, resulting in many studies that have used the same basic terminology to describe differing facets of behavioral and emotional functioning. Cantwell (1990) noted three common uses of the term *depression*: depression as a *symptom*, depression as a *syndrome*, and depression within the context of a *depressive disorder*.

Depression as a Symptom As a symptom, depression involves a dysphoric mood state—feeling unhappy or sad, being "down in the dumps," feeling miserable, or feeling melancholic or "blue." These subjective states are only a smaller part of the syndrome or disorder of depression. Depressive symptoms are typical across the life span of most persons, are typically transient, and are usually not part of a depressive disorder or serious problem. It also is possible that depressive symptoms may exist as part of other disorders. Symptoms of depression alone usually do not provide the impetus for conducting an assessment of depression.

Depression as a Syndrome The term *syndrome* is used to describe something that is more than a dysphoric mood state. This term usually is understood to describe the coexistence of behavioral and emotional symptoms that often occur together and are not simply associated by chance. Cantwell (1990) noted that a depressive syndrome commonly involves not only mood changes, but also additional changes in psychomotor functioning, cognitive performance, and motivation. These additional changes usually occur in a negative direction, reducing the functional capacity of the person who experiences them. Depression as a syndrome is less common than depression as a symptom. It may be brought on by certain types of life stress, exist concurrently with various medical problems, or occur in conjunction with psychological and psychiatric disorders, such as disruptive behavior disorders, schizophrenia, and anxiety disorders. Depression as a syndrome also may occur as the primary problem, with no preexisting or co-occurring problems. Depressive syndromes also may be a part of depressive disorders, such as what the *DSM-5* has called Persistent Depressive Disorder (Dysthymia).

Depression as a Disorder The distinction between depressive syndromes and depressive disorders is not as clear as the distinction between depressive symptoms and depressive syndrome. Although depressive syndromes typically are part of depressive disorders, more is usually implied by the latter term. By saying that a depressive disorder exists, there is an implication not only that a depressive syndrome exists, but that the syndrome has occurred for a specified amount of time, has caused a given degree of functional incapacity, and has a characteristic outcome such as duration and responsiveness to treatment (Cantwell, 1990). The most common way of referring to depression as a disorder is within the context of the *DSM* classification system. As seen in Table 11.2, the *DSM-5* has several general categories for diagnosis of depressive disorders, including three categories for the diagnosis of depressive disorders. To make a diagnosis of a Major Depressive Episode, which is the most commonly considered way of looking at depression, at least five out of nine possible specified symptoms (ranging from a depressed mood to recurrent thoughts about death) must have occurred within a two-week period, one of which must be depressed mood or loss of interest or pleasure, in addition to certain exclusionary criteria being met, as is shown in Table 11.3.

One of the major challenges of using standard criteria such as the *DSM* system for diagnosing depressive disorders with children and adolescents is that these systems may not be equally effective or useful across various age ranges (Carlson & Garber, 1986).

Table 11.3 *DSM-5* diagnostic criteria for Major Depressive Episode

A. Five (or more) of the following symptoms have been present during the same two-week period and represent a change from previous functioning; at least one of the symptoms is either (1) depressed mood or (2) loss of interest or pleasure. *Note:* Do not include symptoms that are clearly attributable to another medical condition.

  1. Depressed mood most of the day, nearly every day, as indicated by either subjective reports (e.g., feels sad or empty) or observation made by others (e.g., appears tearful). *Note:* In children and adolescents, can be irritable mood
  2. Markedly diminished interest or pleasure in all, or almost all, activities most of the day, nearly every day (as indicated by either subjective account or observations made by others)
  3. Significant weight loss when not dieting or weight gain (e.g., a change of more than 5% of body weight in a month) or decrease or increase in appetite nearly every day. *Note:* In children, consider failure to make expected weight gains
  4. Insomnia or hypersomnia nearly every day
  5. Psychomotor agitation or retardation nearly every day (observable by others, not merely subjective feelings of restlessness or being slowed down)
  6. Fatigue or loss of energy nearly every day
  7. Feelings of worthlessness or excessive or inappropriate guilt (which may be delusional) nearly every day (not merely self-reproach or guilt about being sick)
  8. Diminished ability to think or concentrate or indecisiveness nearly every other day (either by subjective account or as observed by others)
  9. Recurrent thoughts of death (not just fear of dying), recurrent suicidal ideation without a specific plan, or a suicide attempt or a specific plan for committing suicide

B. The symptoms cause clinically significant distress or impairment in social, occupational, or other important areas of functioning

C. The episode is not attributable to the physiological effects of a substance or another medical condition.

D. The symptoms cause clinically significant distress or impairment in social, occupational, or other important areas of functioning.

  Note: Criteria A–C represent a major depressive episode.

Note: Responses to a significant loss (e.g., bereavement, financial ruin, losses from a natural disaster, a serious medical illness or disability) may include the feelings of intense sadness, rumination about the loss, insomnia, poor appetite, and weight loss noted in Criterion A, which may resemble a depressive episode. Although such symptoms may be understandable or considered appropriate to the loss, the presence of a major depressive episode in addition to the normal response to a significant loss should also be carefully considered. This decision inevitably requires the exercise of clinical judgment based on the individual's history and the cultural norms for the expression of distress in the context of loss.

E. The occurrence of the major depressive episode is not better explained by schizoaffective disorder, schizophrenia, schizophreniform disorder, delusional disorder, or other specified and unspecified schizophrenia spectrum and other psychotic disorders.

F. There has never been a manic episode or a hypomanic episode.

Note: This exclusion does not apply if all of the manic-like or hypomanic-like episodes are substance-induced or are attributable to the physiological effects of another condition.

Coding and recording procedures

The diagnostic code for major depressive disorder is based on whether this is a single or recurrent episode, current severity, presence of psychotic features, and remission status. Current severity and psychotic features are only indicated if full criteria are currently met for a major depressive episode. Remission specifiers are only indicated if the full criteria are not currently met for a major depressive episode.

In recording the name of a diagnosis, terms should be listed in the following order: major depressive disorder, single or recurrent episode, severity/psychotic/remission specifiers, followed by as many of the following specifiers without codes that apply to the current episode.

Specify:
With anxious distress
With mixed features
With melancholic features
With atypical features
With mood-congruent psychotic features
With catatonia
With peripartum onset
With seasonal pattern

Source: Reprinted with permission from the *Diagnostic and Statistical Manual of Mental Disorders, Fifth Edition* (Copyright © 2013). American Psychiatric Association.

Assessment of depression as a disorder in children and adolescents requires particular care, skill, and caution given that particular symptoms may be more frequently observed in children with depression versus adults (e.g., somatic complaints, irritability, social withdrawal). Although *DSM* notes that depression may present differently in children than in adults, there is still no alternative method of classification for children, and the *DSM* system does not typically include any of the internalizing disorders in separate categories usually first diagnosed in infancy and childhood. One of the new categories presented in the *DSM-5*, however, seems to be intended specifically for children as an alternative to a diagnosis of bipolar disorder or depression (Hammen, Rudolph, & Abaied, 2014). Disruptive Mood Dysregulation Disorder (DMDD) includes symptoms that focus on irritability and temper outbursts. In my clinical experience, I think of these as the children that are often angry and seem uncomfortable in their own skin. While this disorder has very limited research behind it at this point, it will be interesting to see how DMDD is differentiated from depression and bipolar disorders in children and adolescents.

Causal Factors Given that entire volumes have been devoted to the etiology of depression, treating these topics in such a short space is highly presumptuous, to say the least. The purpose of this discussion is simply to provide a brief description of some of the key findings on causal factors. Reviews of the literature on etiology of childhood depression by Beck (2008), Compas (1997), S. M. Miller, Birnbaum, and Durbin (1990), and Schwartz et al. (1998) have articulated some of the crucial psychosocial variables or issues such as parental influences, life events, and family interaction patterns that are associated with depression in children. A relationship has been found to exist between what is commonly referred to as "loss" and childhood depression, with this relationship most readily verified by studies of parent loss due to death or family separation. Children of parents who are depressed themselves have been shown to be at heightened risk for developing depression and other psychological disorders. High rates of parental stress and family conflict also have been found to be associated with childhood depression. There is some evidence that negative events that occur outside the family context in the lives of children, such as school and friendship problems, contribute to depression.

Children who become depressed may develop maladaptive or unhealthy cognitive styles and concurrent impaired coping skills. The learned helplessness model, first proposed by Seligman (1974), posits that some forms of depression may occur under learning conditions where the child does not recognize a relationship between his or her actions and the consequences of these actions. Lewinsohn (1974) proposed a highly influential model in which he suggested that the disruption of pleasurable and otherwise reinforcing events may predispose a person to depression, an idea that is worth considering when conducting a comprehensive child assessment wherein environments and behavioral characteristics are evaluated.

Additionally, there is strong evidence emerging in the psychobiology literature indicating that some forms of childhood depression are related to biological variables, such as the interrelated areas of family genetics and brain chemistry (Schwartz et al., 1998). For example, some research suggests that hyperreactivity of the amygdala can contribute to differences in how one perceives negative events (Beck, 2008), and that a certain version of a serotonin transporter gene (5-HTTLPR) can create increased reactivity of cortisol when an individual is faced with stressful events (Uher & McGuffin, 2010). Another interesting theory that has become prominent in recent years is the *kindling hypothesis*, first proposed by Post (1992). Although this theory is not specific to depression, it has often been cited as a supportive explanation with biological implications. The essence of the kindling hypothesis is that repeated or successive shocks or traumas (such as episodes of depression and antecedents associated with depression) predispose individuals to more easily develop the problem in the future, precipitated by even a moderate amount of stress or difficulty. As with small, dry pieces of kindling that have been set to start a fire, even a small spark may be enough to ignite the flames. It has been posited that repeated episodes of depression or other disorders might actually create permanent changes in neural pathways that lead to optimum conditions for easier onset of the problem in the future.

Anxiety

Anxiety is a class of internalizing responses that may involve subjective feelings (e.g., discomfort, fear, dread), overt behaviors (e.g., avoidance, withdrawal), and physiological responding (e.g., sweating, nausea, general arousal). Anxiety is related closely to two other areas: fears and phobias. Although anxiety, fears, and phobias have a great deal of overlap, there have been some historical distinctions drawn between these three categories. Fears have been described as "reactions to perceived threats that involve avoidance of the threatening stimuli, subjective feelings of discomfort, and physiological changes" (Barrios & Hartmann, 1988, p. 197). Fears usually are distinguished from anxiety because the former involves distinctive reactions to specific stimuli (e.g., darkness or noise), whereas the latter tends to involve a more diffuse type of reaction (apprehension) to stimuli that are not as specific in nature. Phobias are similar to fears in that they involve intense reactions to specific stimuli but are differentiated from fears in the sense that they are more persistent, maladaptive, and debilitating (Barrios & Hartmann, 1988, 1997; Morris & Kratochwill, 1983). Because the focus of this section is a general discussion of the subject, anxiety is the topic of this overview, rather than the more specific categories of fears and phobias.

The topic of anxiety in children has often been overlooked. Particularly in view of evidence that a significant portion of child clients at mental health clinics are treated for anxiety disorders (S. M. Miller, Boyer, & Rodoletz, 1990) and that childhood anxiety may be predictive of adult psychopathology (Bowlby, 1973), the topic deserves attention. One of the reasons that anxiety in children may be overlooked is the belief that it is common and transient (Wolfson, Fields, & Rose, 1987). In reality, many anxiety problems experienced by children are quite stable, with the combined literature indicating that 20% to 30% of anxiety disorders diagnosed during childhood show strong stability over intervals of two to five years (Silverman & Ginsburg, 1998).

With the publication of the *DSM-IV* in 1994, significant changes were made in the *DSM* classification criteria for anxiety disorders in children and adolescents. Perhaps the most significant of these changes was the elimination of the *DSM-III* and *DSM-III-R* broad diagnostic category *Anxiety Disorders of Childhood and Adolescence*. From this former diagnostic category, Overanxious Disorder was incorporated into the adult General Anxiety Disorder, and Avoidant Disorder was removed. The only childhood-specific anxiety disorder that remained from *DSM-III-R* was Separation Anxiety Disorder, but this category also was reclassified under another broad category, *Other Disorders of Childhood and Adolescence*. It is unclear what prompted the changes between *DSM-III-R* and *DSM-IV* with regard to child and adolescent anxiety disorders, but these changes may have some unintended effects. Silverman and Ginsburg (1998) noted that although research regarding anxiety in youth historically has lagged behind comparable research with adults, "research interest in anxiety in youth burgeoned with the establishment of the broad diagnostic category, Anxiety Disorder of Childhood and Adolescence" (in *DSM-III* and *DSM-III-R*) (p. 239). Although it is still too early to tell, it would be unfortunate if the elimination of youth-specific diagnostic categories for anxiety disorders in the *DSM* resulted in less research in the area. The *DSM-5* general and specific categories of anxiety disorders, all of which may potentially pertain to children and adolescents, are outlined in Table 11.2. Few changes were made in this area from the previous edition.

The current *DSM* classification categories for anxiety disorders, as shown in Table 11.2, are extensive and broad, yet also specific and narrow in some cases. Clinicians who work extensively with young children probably would use the diagnostic category of Separation Anxiety Disorder at least occasionally, and clinicians working with children and adolescents of various ages undoubtedly occasionally would encounter a specific type

Table 11.4 Diagnostic criteria for Generalized Anxiety Disorder from the *DSM-5*

A. Excessive anxiety and worry (apprehensive expectation), occurring more days than not for at least six months, about a number of events or activities (such as work or school performance).
B. The person finds it difficult to control the worry.
C. The anxiety and worry are associated with three (or more) of the following six symptoms (with at least some symptoms present for more days than not for the past six months).

Note: Only one item is required in children.

1. Restlessness or feeling keyed up or on edge
2. Being easily fatigued
3. Difficulty concentrating or mind going blank
4. Irritability
5. Muscle tension
6. Sleep disturbance (difficulty falling asleep or staying asleep, or restless unsatisfying sleep)

D. The anxiety, worry, or physical symptoms cause clinically significant distress or impairment in social, occupational, or other important areas of functioning.
E. The disturbance is not attributable to the direct physiological effects of a substance (e.g., a drug of abuse, a medication) or another medical condition (e.g., hyperthyroidism).
F. The disturbance is not better explained by another mental disorder (e.g., anxiety or worry about having panic attacks in panic disorder, negative evaluation in social anxiety disorder (social phobia), contamination or other obsessions in obsessive–compulsive disorder, separation from attachment figures in separation anxiety disorder, reminders of traumatic events in posttraumatic stress disorder, gaining weight in anorexia nervosa, physical complaints in somatic symptom disorder, perceived appearance flaws in body dysmorphic disorder, having a serious illness in illness anxiety disorder, or the content of delusional beliefs in schizophrenia or delusional disorder).

Source: Reprinted with permission from the *Diagnostic and Statistical Manual of Mental Disorders, Fifth Edition* (Copyright © 2013). American Psychiatric Association.

---

of anxiety disorder. Realistically, however, most clinicians who work with anxious children and adolescents probably would classify most cases of anxiety under the more general category of Generalized Anxiety Disorder, which is presented in Table 11.4.

Causal Factors Although a fair amount of effort has been devoted to exploring the etiology of depression, comparatively little has been done in this area related to the development of anxiety, particularly in relation to children. One of the problems in making a few general statements about the causes of anxiety in children is that they have been viewed differently by professionals from differing theoretical orientations, such as psychoanalytic, behavioral, and cognitive perspectives (S. M. Miller, Boyer, & Rodoletz, 1990). A review of etiologic perspectives by Silverman and Ginsburg (1998) divided the major areas of etiologic research into genetic biology, neurobiology, psychosocial, psychoanalytic, behavioral, cognitive, family, and peer influence and indicated that with the exception of psychoanalytic, there is at least a small body of empirical evidence to support each perspective.

While more empirical work has recently been devoted to the causes of anxiety in children, perhaps the most appropriate statement about causation is old, but is one that is compatible with the overall perspective of this book, is that "the child's temperamental characteristics, in combination with early socialization experiences and the nature of the current ... environment, probably account for the development (of anxiety-related problems)" (Kauffman, 1989, p. 334).

Related Internalizing Disorders

In addition to the characteristics of depression and anxiety, the broader category of internalizing disorders includes many other associated behavioral, social, and emotional problems. This section discusses some of the more prominent of these associated problems.

Social Withdrawal One of the major correlates of depression and anxiety is social withdrawal or isolation. As Kauffman (2000) has noted, social isolation can result from either behavioral excesses (e.g., aggression or hyperactivity) or behavioral deficits. The category of behavioral deficits is linked most closely with internalizing disorders. Children who are socially isolated or withdrawn because of behavioral deficits tend to lack responsiveness to the social initiations of others—in other words, they lack the specific social skills to make and keep friends. Often a severe lack of social skills is accompanied by immature or socially inadequate behavior that compounds the problem further by making the child an easy target of ridicule (Kauffman, 2000). Internalizing social withdrawal and isolation seems to be related not only to exposure to incompetent adult social models, but also to a temperamental characteristic referred to by Kagan, Reznick, and Snidman (1990) as *behavioral inhibition to the unfamiliar*. When present, this characteristic seems to emerge in infants at about age eight months and leads to a tendency to become inhibited or withdrawn when presented with unfamiliar stimuli. There may be biological contributions to this temperamental characteristic, but it probably interacts with behavior and environment in a complex manner to result in characteristic social withdrawal.

Somatic Problems Another common correlate of internalizing disorders is a broad range of physical symptoms and problems that collectively are referred to as somatic complaints. There is a strong probability that persons who experience significant depression or anxiety have concurrent physical symptoms. These somatic symptoms associated with internalizing characteristics presumably are based on a psychological origin, although physical infections or injuries may cause similar symptoms. The Child Behavior Checklist and Youth Self-Report of Achenbach's ASEBA system include several items that reflect somatic complaints and that are within the internalizing broadband scale, including "feels dizzy," "overtired," and "physical problems without known medical cause." This last item has seven possible specifications, including aches and pains, headaches, nausea, problems with eyes, rashes or other skin problems, stomachaches or cramps, and vomiting. Any or all of these physical symptoms may be reported by children who are experiencing depressive, anxious, or withdrawn symptoms. The congruence of somatic complaints and anxious–depressed–withdrawn characteristics in psychological assessment even predates the use of factor analytic assessment techniques.

The first three of the MMPI-A clinical scales (formally referred to as Hypochondriasis, Depression, and Hysteria), sometimes referred to as the *Neurotic Triad*, all contain items relating to physical complaints and statements about depressive, anxious, and withdrawn symptoms. First developed in the 1940s using empirical criterion keying procedures, these three scales have been shown to differentiate reliably among different psychiatric groups in numerous studies.

An additional health issue to consider within the context of internalizing disorders is that of obesity. It is well known that obesity rates among Americans have soared during the past three decades, and that childhood and adolescence are by no means exempt from obesity or from problems associated with being overweight. Although much has been written in the scientific and popular media regarding physical health problems associated with obesity or overweight in children, social–emotional and psychological problems are also a significant concern. Some of these problems—such as a lessened overall quality of life and increased absences from school—are not necessarily thought of as internalizing problems, but there is often a clear pattern of increased depression that goes along with this pathway. For example, a widely cited study by Mustillo and colleagues (2003) published in the journal *Pediatrics* found that depression was a significant correlate of obesity among a large cohort of boys that were studied longitudinally for more than eight years. Given that anxiety and other internalizing problems are associated with depression, it seems likely that children who are overweight may be at increased risk for these concerns as well. Although the exact nature of the relationship between obesity and internalizing problems is not yet fully understood, it is clear that there is a link.

Fears and Phobias Fears and phobias, a more specific group of characteristics that relate to anxiety, were briefly touched on earlier. What is commonly referred to as school phobia deserves some additional discussion, however, because it is a set of problems commonly encountered by mental health professionals who work with children and adolescents. The *DSM-5* does not have a separate diagnostic classification for school phobia but considers it one of the nine key features of Separation Anxiety Disorder. Traditional thinking considers that fears of, and subsequent refusal to attend, school are internalizing problems that relate to a child's inner state of anxiety. More recently, this traditional anxiety-based view of school phobia has come under criticism, and the problem has been reconceptualized as school refusal, a broader term that indicates the possible heterogeneity of symptoms. Pilkington and Piersel (1991) conducted a comprehensive review of the literature on school phobia and criticized the separation anxiety-based theory on three grounds: (1) methodological problems of the research; (2) lack of generalizability concerning pathological mother–child relationships; and (3) lack of emphasis on possible external or ecological variables. With respect to this third criticism, an alternative conceptualization of school phobia has been presented, in which many cases of refusal to attend school can be explained as "a normal avoidance reaction to a hostile environment" (Pilkington & Piersel, 1991, p. 290). Realistically, avoidance of or refusal to attend school probably includes a more heterogeneous group of conditions than once was thought, and anxiety problems and avoidant behavioral reactions are both likely explanations. What is often seen in clinical practice is that school refusal co-occurs with an emerging or pre-existing generalized anxiety disorder or separation anxiety disorder, or it is a manifestation from stressful environmental factors, such as bullying or school performance anxiety. The implication of this conceptualization of school phobia is that clinicians should consider assessing the school environment and child characteristics when refusal to attend school is a presenting problem. This implication is compatible with the transactional–interactional model within social learning theory and may indicate that the refusal to attend school may be explained by an interaction of parent and child characteristics, coupled with environmental and behavioral conditions at school.

Other Problems There are a few additional conditions that often are part of the larger internalizing syndrome. Obsessive thought processes and compulsive behavioral rituals are related closely to the anxiety disorders, but in *DSM-5*, Obsessive–Compulsive Disorder is now included in a diagnostic category under the broad category of Obsessive–Compulsive and Related Disorders rather than Anxiety Disorders. Various forms of eating disorders, including anorexia nervosa, bulimia, pica, and rumination disorders, also appear to be related to the broad internalizing syndrome (Kauffman, 2000). Some stereotypical movement disorders, such as motor tics, also may co-occur with internalizing problems, although tic disorders are widely conceptualized as a neurological phenomenon. Finally, elimination disorders (enuresis and encopresis) may occur with other internalizing problems, although there also are many physiological causes for these problems. Some of these problems are discussed in more detail in Chapter 12.

Implications of Internalizing Disorders
There has been some disagreement in the developmental psychopathology literature as to the potential long-term consequences of internalizing disorders, and more research in this area is needed. At present, there seems to be general agreement in the field that serious internalizing symptoms of childhood are not brief and transient and may persist for long periods, perhaps two to five years (Merrell, 2008; Quay & Werry, 1986; Silverman & Ginsburg, 1998). In terms of the persistence of these characteristics into adulthood, there is much less agreement. Quay and Werry (1986) stated that symptoms of anxiety–withdrawal "do not have the rather foreboding prognosis that is associated with undersocialized conduct disorders" (p. 101) and cited Robins' (1966) long-term follow-up research of children with neuroses as an example that internalizing symptoms during childhood may not predict accurately the presence of internalizing problems during adulthood. Other researchers have found evidence, however, for a less optimistic prognosis for children with internalizing disorders. Social withdrawal and inadequate levels of social competence have been found to be associated with many later negative outcomes, although the evidence to date suggests that the prognosis is worse for aggressive than nonaggressive socially withdrawn children (Kauffman, 2000; Pullatz & Dunn, 1990). When childhood depression is the internalizing disorder of interest, there seems to be stronger evidence for persistence across the life span, particularly in the case of adolescent depression (Cantwell, 1990; McLaughlin & King, 2015). There may be some hope that the existence of internalizing disorders during childhood does not hold as poor a prognosis as do externalizing disorders, but nevertheless there is evidence to suggest the potential for negative outcomes later in life (Barrios & Hartmann, 1997; W. M. Reynolds, 1992b).

POSITIVE AND NEGATIVE AFFECTIVITY: A MODEL FOR UNDERSTANDING INTERNALIZING PROBLEMS

An interesting development in the 1980s and 1990s regarding the understanding of internalizing disorders is the research that has been conducted on cognitive and mood states of these disorders. The constructs of *positive and negative affectivity* (or affect) involve the positive or negative presentations of various mood symptoms. This conceptualization of affectivity is not considered to be a specific dimension of internalizing disorders, but it is considered to be an important characteristic that may help differentiate among various types of internalizing disorders. D. Watson and Tellegen (1985) originally proposed this two-dimensional model of affect in an attempt to discriminate empirically between depression and anxiety. Positive affect has been defined as "the extent to which a person avows a zest for life" (D. Watson & Tellegen, 1985, p. 221) and is reflected by such descriptors as *active, alert, energetic, enthusiastic, interested, joyful,* and *determined.* Conversely, descriptors such as *drowsy, dull, fatigued, lethargic,* and *sluggish* reflect low levels of positive affect. In contrast, negative affect has been defined as "the extent to which a person reports feeling upset or unpleasantly aroused" (p. 221). The terms *distressed, fearful, hostile,* and *nervous* reflect high levels of negative affect, whereas adjectives such as *calm, placid,* and *relaxed* reflect low levels of negative affect.

In various studies on expressions of affectivity with internalizing disorders (e.g., Blumberg & Izard, 1986; Carey, Finch, & Carey, 1991; Jolly, Dyck, Kramer, & Wherry, 1994; Mikolajewski, Allan, Hart, Lonigan, & Taylor, 2013; Stark, Kaslow, & Laurent, 1993; Tellegen, 1986; D. Watson, 1988; D. Watson & Clark, 1984), a general consensus has emerged, notwithstanding the fact that there have been some minor differences among findings. In general, it is understood that measures of depression and anxiety tap negative affectivity. Persons who report high symptoms of either depression or anxiety are reporting high levels of negative affect. There also seems to be a general consensus, however, that individuals with high levels of depressive symptoms are likely also to be low in positive affect, whereas individuals with high levels of anxiety but no depression are not necessarily low in positive affect. In cases in which anxiety and depression can be differentiated, it may be that the presence or absence of positive affect is a key distinguishing feature.

Although there is still much that is not understood regarding the role of affectivity in child emotional and behavioral disorders, it seems to be an important element, particularly with respect to the internalizing domain. Although including dimensions of affectivity within clinical assessment and diagnostic practices is an endeavor that is still experimental, future developments in this area may prove to be essential to furthering assessment and intervention practices with children and adolescents who exhibit internalizing problems. For example, recent work related to affectivity has included examination of emotion regulation and, specifically, use of the strategies labeled *reappraisal* and *suppression.* Hughes, Gullone, and Watson (2011) found that children and adolescents with significant symptoms of depression were less likely to "reappraise" a situation and think or feel more optimistically, and were more likely to "suppress" or hide depressive feelings that they were experiencing. Research related to intervention processes that aim to boost positive affect and healthy emotion regulation will likely be incredibly helpful.

INTERNALIZING PROBLEMS AND SELF-CONCEPT

Because internalizing problems sometimes have been thought of as being self-related or inner directed, a psychological construct that is particularly relevant to this discussion is self-concept. The constructs of depression and self-concept have been linked clearly in the professional literature because diminished self-esteem is often a prominent feature of depression (Kazdin, 1988), particular styles of self-esteem beliefs are likely to increase substantially the risk of depression (Hammen, 1995), and irrational beliefs regarding self-worth often constitute a clear target for cognitive treatment of depression (Merrell, 2008; Swallow & Segal, 1995). Although less is known regarding specific links between other variations of internalizing problems (e.g., anxiety, social withdrawal, and somatic problems) and self-concept, it is logical to assume that self-concept and internalizing symptoms in general may be negatively associated, given the strong overlap among various internalizing symptoms and disorders.

In considering the connection between self-concept and internalizing symptoms, it is important to understand that the association is well established and is moderately strong. The directionality of this relationship is less clear, however. In other words, although it is known that self-concept is negatively associated with internalizing symptoms, it is not entirely clear whether there is a causal relationship. Does poor self-concept cause depression? Does depression cause poor self-concept? Or, do the two constructs coexist in some kind of symbiotic relationship? Answers to these questions are sparse and tentative. There have been a few attempts to understand the directionality of this relationship. For example, Sowislo and Orth (2013) conducted a meta-analysis of 77 studies including participants with depression, and found that self-esteem more strongly predicted depression than the other way around. Although one could argue convincingly that poor self-concept is a risk factor for developing depression or other internalizing problems, it is still also possible that depression causes low self-esteem. Martin Seligman (1998), a former past president of the American Psychological Association, argued (with substantial empirical support) that a healthy self-concept or self-esteem is the result of what one does and that interventions designed to improve self-esteem in the absence of any positive behavior changes are misguided and potentially dangerous.

As is true with internalizing symptoms, there is some evidence for gender differences in self-concept. The strength of these gender differences tends to be substantially weaker for self-concept than for internalizing problems, however, and the direction of these differences tends to be much less systematic. A comprehensive meta-analysis of the research on gender differences in child and adolescent self-concept found that with respect to specific domains of self-concept, there were more areas of similarity than difference between boys and girls, and the areas that did produce gender differences were about equally divided across gender (Wilgenbusch & Merrell, 1999). There were about as many self-concept domains where boys were likely to have lower scores than girls as there were where girls were likely to have lower scores than boys. Where significant gender effects were found, they tended to produce small to modest effect sizes, usually less than half a standard deviation. The findings of this meta-analysis do not support the notion that girls tend to experience a plummeting of self-esteem when they reach adolescence, a pop psychology idea that has become widely accepted through promotion in popular media.

Harter (1990, 1999) noted that self-concept might have many different definitions depending on the theoretical framework that is adopted. The definition of self-concept that is used in this book is that of *multidimensional* self-concept. When defined from a multidimensional viewpoint, self-concept includes not only a person's overall self-evaluation and level of self-esteem, but also his or her self-evaluation of particular aspects of functioning, such as physical appearance and skills, academic competence, and social–emotional functioning. In a multidimensional framework, a person's overall self-concept is not merely a summation of how he or she feels about or evaluates any of these different aspects of life. Rather, the evaluation of a particular aspect of self-functioning may contribute to his or her overall view of the self, but each dimension of the self may operate independently. A person might have a negative evaluation of some particular dimensions of the self (e.g., physical appearance and athletic competence) but still have a relatively high global self-concept, or overall view of the self.

Earlier work in the area of self-concept, as typified by research and theoretical writing before the 1970s, tended to regard self-concept in a unidimensional fashion. The unidimensional view indicates that self-concept is assessed best by presenting the subject with many different items that tap various aspects of self-functioning, giving each different aspect of the self-concept equal weight, then providing a global estimate of self-concept by simply summing the item responses. The assessment of self-concept from this unidimensional viewpoint is typified by two instruments originally developed during the 1960s, the Coopersmith Self-Esteem Inventory (Coopersmith, 1981) and the Piers–Harris Children's Self-Concept Scale (Piers & Harris, 1969), neither of which is reviewed in this text because they are based primarily on the older notions of self-concept and its assessment.

During the 1970s and 1980s, many researchers began to explore self-concept in a manner that identified specific domains of self-evaluation, which were thought to operate independently while correlating moderately with each other. This multidimensional approach to self-concept was typified during this period by the work of Harter (1985a, 1986) and Marsh (1987). Proponents of this view contend that individual areas of self-evaluation affect overall self-concept, but the contribution from each individual area is not the same. From a practical standpoint, viewing self-concept from a multidimensional perspective has important implications for a clinician who is conducting an assessment. For example, a child or adolescent might have a negative view of his or her academic competence, but not consider it to be important and feel okay about himself or herself in a general sense. A child or adolescent may see himself or herself as being competent and successful in most areas of functioning but assign great or undue weight to an unfavorable self-concept in the area of physical appearance and have a poor global self-concept, despite the many other areas in which he or she feels competent and successful.

Although the evidence regarding the relationship between self-concept and internalizing disorders still raises many unanswered questions, the overall evidence on self-concept is that it may play a strong mediational role in various aspects of human functioning. In this vein, Harter stated:

> There have also been concerns with the mediational role that self-worth may play in impacting both affective state, along a dimension of depressed to cheerful, and motivation, along a dimension of low to high energy. Our studies provide strong support for the impact that self-worth has on affect, which in turn influences the child's energy level. The implications of these findings for childhood depression as well as adolescent suicide have also been explored within this context.
>
> (1990, p. 319)

In sum, self-concept seems to be an important construct in the overall psychological and social functioning of children and adolescents, and it may have significant implications for youth with internalizing problems. Assessment of self-concept is an important clinical consideration.

METHODS OF ASSESSING INTERNALIZING PROBLEMS

Assessment of internalizing problems presents a challenge for clinicians and researchers. By definition and practice, internalizing problems tend to involve internal states and subjective perceptions. Assessing characteristics such as depression and anxiety using external methods (e.g., direct observation, sociometrics, and, to some extent, rating scales) can be problematic. Partly as a result of this problem, the research base on internalizing problems historically has lagged behind that of externalizing problems (Cicchetti & Toth, 1991). In terms of clinical practice with internalizing problems, this state of affairs has created similar problems. Because for the most part they are assessing internal and subjective states when evaluating internalizing problems, clinicians necessarily must rely on various forms of self-reporting as the primary method of assessment or as an important adjunct to other methods. Although this chapter discusses assessment of internalizing problems using each of the major methods of assessment, the larger focus is on the use of objective self-report tests and interview methods.

Behavioral Observation

Although assessment of internalizing problems through methods other than self-report presents many problems, some internalizing characteristics can be observed directly, and there has been some experimentation with the use of behavioral observation codes for assessment. In contrast to self-report methods, which assess client perceptions of internalizing symptoms, or rating scales, which assess third-party perceptions of internalizing symptoms retrospectively, the aim of direct behavioral observation is to assess these symptoms as they occur. Kazdin (1988) listed several symptoms of depression that are measurable through direct behavioral observation. Some of these include diminished motor and social activity, reduced eye contact with others, and slowed speech. Additional anxiety-related internalizing symptoms that might be assessed through direct observation include avoidance of feared or anxiety-provoking stimuli, facial expressions, physical proximity, crying, posture or stance, and trembling voice or lip (Barrios & Hartmann, 1997; S. M. Miller, Boyer, & Rodoletz, 1990). Using these characteristics as examples, it becomes clear how important some of the basic rules of conducting effective observations might be, such as defining the observation domain and selecting an appropriate recording system, which were discussed in Chapter 4.

An observational technique that has been used in the assessment of anxiety and related symptoms since the 1930s (Jersild & Holmes, 1935) is the Behavioral Avoidance Test (BAT). The BAT can be implemented in a variety of ways and is simple to use. The original BAT technique involved having the subject enter a room where the anxiety- or fear-provoking stimulus is present (e.g., an animal, insect, separation from parent, darkness), then having them approach the feared stimulus. The observational measures that can be taken include latency of approach, duration of time in the presence of the stimulus, and number of approaches completed (S. M. Miller, Boyer, & Rodoletz, 1990). A variation of the BAT involves having the subject imagine the feared stimulus or situation, then record his or her overt responses to the task. This variation of the BAT may be particularly useful for assessing overt responses to anxiety-provoking situations that cannot be contrived in a clinical setting, such as fear of imagined "monsters," injury or death of a caregiver, or clouds. In addition to the numerous variations of the BAT that have been used clinically or reported in the literature, there are several experimental observational systems for anxiety-related symptoms that have been described and reported in journal articles. For example, in their excellent review on assessing children's fears and phobias, Barrios and Hartmann (1997) identified several research-oriented experimental observation systems that had been used successfully with anxious children.

Kazdin (1988) listed three general classes of behavioral codes that could be used for direct observational assessment of childhood depression. These general codes are listed as follows, with types of specific target codes that might be included under each class:

1. *social activity*: talking, playing a game, participating in a group activity;
2. *solitary behavior*: playing a game alone, working on an academic task, listening and watching, straightening one's room, grooming;
3. *affect-related expression*: smiling, frowning, arguing, complaining.

These types of observational target codes have been used successfully in the measurement of depression and related internalizing problems in several studies. Williams, Barlow, and Agras (1972) found significant negative correlations with self-reports of depression and observations of verbal activity, smiling, and motor activity in depressed patients. Kazdin, Esveldt-Dawson, Unis, and Rancurello (1983) used behavioral codes from these three general categories to observe inpatient children (aged eight to 13) over a one-week period and found that those children who were high in depression engaged in significantly less social behavior and exhibited significantly less affect-related expression than other children. More recently, Mian, Carter, Pine, Wakschlag, and Briggs-Gowan (2015) developed an observational measure that targets anxiety in younger children. This tool, the Anxiety Dimensional Observation Scale (Anx-DOS) aims to measure children's responses to threat (e.g., spiders, loud sounds, separation from parents) and has seven codes including Fear Arousal, Physical Avoidance, Exaggerated Startle, Separation Distress, Proximity Seeking, Hypervigilance, and Dissociation. Researchers have worked to understand the reliability and validity of the Anx-DOS and have found that inter-rater reliability was generally very strong across codes. Hypervigilance had the lowest reliability coefficient of 0.37 and Dissociation had very few observations. Further, the Anx-DOS correlates with parent reports of anxiety. From these three studies, internalizing problems appear to be assessed effectively through direct observation. It is important always to consider, however, that the overt or easily observable characteristics of internalizing problems are only a part of the picture (and often a small part). The subjective emotional state and cognitive processes of the subject are also important, and these must be assessed primarily through client self-report. Because so many aspects of internalizing problems are subtle or covert, it is important to design the observation carefully, using procedures such as those outlined in Chapter 4.

Self-monitoring, a specific facet of direct behavioral observation, has not been researched widely as an assessment method for internalizing problems, but it seems to hold some promise in this regard. Because there is considerable evidence that children and adolescents can be trained to monitor and record their own behavior accurately (Cole et al., 2000; Gettinger & Kratochwill, 1987; Pincus, May, Whitton, Mattis, & Barlow, 2010; Shapiro & Cole, 1994), there is no obvious reason why they could not also be trained to monitor and accurately record internal or private events. For example, a clinician working with depressed adolescents might train them to record periodically the number of positive and negative internal self-statements they make and use this data to chart baseline rates and treatment progress. Likewise, children or adolescents could be trained to record their own perceptions of various somatic complaints, their pulse rate, engagement in pleasurable activities, or positive self-affirming thought processes. There may be some important limitations of self-monitoring observation with internalizing problems.

Self-monitoring may be reactive, in the sense that it may produce change in the subject (Kratochwill, 1982). Self-monitoring may be more useful in assessment during a follow-up or intervention period than during baseline data gathering. An obvious concern with self-monitoring of internalizing problems may surface when working with children or adolescents who exhibit obsessive–compulsive behaviors. It is logical and realistic to think that obsessive thoughts or compulsive behaviors potentially could be strengthened because of the increased focus placed on them. Despite these potential problems, self-monitoring of internalizing problems seems to be a plausible alternative to direct observation by an independent observer, although it has not been reported widely for these uses in the professional literature.

Functional Assessment and Internalizing Problems An additional issue to consider with respect to direct observation of internalizing problems is whether functional assessment techniques may be used effectively with this domain. In previous versions of this book, Merrell has taken the position that the clinical assessment technology is not sufficiently advanced to allow for reliable functional assessment of internalizing problems, and as a result, provided little or no coverage of the topic. In addition, he had serious questions regarding whether the same rules of behavior that allow for using assessment data to develop good working hypotheses regarding possible functions of behavior for externalizing problems even apply to the internalizing domain. During the past several years, he began to reconsider these issues, and came to the conclusion that it *is likely possible* to develop a reliable framework for functional assessment of internalizing characteristics. I am particularly intrigued by the role of discriminative stimuli (antecedents) in the development of depression and anxiety, as well as the possible reinforcing properties that may exist with some consequents of behaving in a depressed or anxious manner. In particular, the possible functional relationship between anxiety–depression and *escape/ avoidance* and *social attention* should be considered. Imagine, for example, a student who hesitates to initiate play with others during unstructured classroom time. This child often plays by himself or seeks attention/conversation from the teacher. The teacher could feasibly aid in reinforcing this boy's avoidance by engaging in conversation or by "allowing" him to continuously play on his own. One might be able to observe the child's frequency of alone time or of engaging with the teacher rather than peers. The observer may be able to identify contextual antecedents such as unstructured social time, too. At some level, however, professionals would need to rely on the child's verbal skills and self-report to truly understand the nature of the anxiety (e.g., he is afraid he won't know how to play). Although I am not convinced that such consequences provide a sufficient explanation for development of internalizing problems, they could have a strong link to effective intervention, and there are ample reasons to at least consider these possibilities. Recent work in the field of clinical behavior analysis has begun to directly take on the internalizing domain (e.g., Barnes-Holmes & Stewart, 2000; Bolling, Kohlenberg, & Parker, 2000; Dymond & Roche, 2009; Forsyth, 2000; Friman, Hayes, & Wilson, 1998), and may lead to additional efforts resulting in practical and reliable functional assessment methods.

Behavior Rating Scales

Each of the general-purpose behavior rating scales or rating scale systems that were discussed in Chapter 5 includes rating items and subscales specifically directed at measuring internalizing problems, and all of these instruments have been validated to some extent for this purpose. In addition, there are several other widely used general purpose rating instruments that are pertinent to the assessment of such varied internalizing symptoms areas as anxiety, depression, and social withdrawal. Although a few research instruments have been reported in the literature that are aimed at specific types of internalizing symptoms (see Barrios & Hartmann, 1997, and Compas, 1997, for a discussion of experimental behavior rating scales for assessing anxiety and depression), for the most part these behavior rating scales have not been validated sufficiently or are not in wide enough use to justify their inclusion in this chapter. The general-purpose instruments evaluated in Chapter 5 are recommended as the instruments of choice when objective third-party behavior ratings of internalizing problems are desired.

Another potentially useful behavior rating scale for assessing internalizing problems is the Preschool and Kindergarten Behavior Scales, which are discussed in Chapter 14. These scales include a broadband internalizing problems subscale with two internalizing problems subscales and may be useful for objective evaluation of internalizing problems of young children. Also, it may be useful to consider the use of any of the social competence rating scales or systems that are discussed in Chapter 13 (the Social Skills Improvement System, School Social Behavior Scales and Home and Community Social Behavior Scales, and Walker–McConnell Scales of Social Competence and School Adjustment) when there are concerns about assessing internalizing problems. Given that social withdrawal often accompanies depression and anxiety, and that deficits in social competence may be correlated with internalizing problems, such an assessment strategy may be useful.

Although the use of behavior rating scales is recommended as part of a comprehensive assessment design for evaluating internalizing problems of children and adolescents, this recommendation is not without caution. As has been mentioned numerous times in this chapter, many aspects of internalizing problems are not readily detectable to an external observer, even one who knows the child or adolescent relatively well. Because many of the core symptoms of internalizing disorders (such as cognitions and affect) are not externally observable in any reliable way, behavior rating scales should be used for this purpose with a great deal of caution. Because the evidence indicates that parent reports (and, by inference, teacher reports) may be more accurate for assessing externalizing problems, but child self-reports may be more accurate for assessing internalizing problems (Kolko & Kazdin, 1993), there always should be a strong assessment emphasis on the latter method when internalizing symptoms are concerned.

Interviewing

Whether structured, traditional, or behavioral in nature, the clinical interview is perhaps the most widely used method for the assessment of internalizing problems (S. M. Miller, Boyer, & Rodoletz, 1990). Virtually any of the interview techniques discussed in Chapter 6 can be useful in assessing depression, anxiety, social withdrawal, and related internalizing symptoms. In terms of structured or semistructured interview schedules, each of those discussed in Chapter 6 (e.g., K-SADS and SCICA) are directly relevant for assessing internalizing symptoms and include many areas of questioning that are specific to this area. As such, any of these interview schedules is worthy of consideration for assessing internalizing problems. An example of the utility of these structured interview schedules in assessing internalizing problems is a study by King (1997), who examined the diagnostic efficacy of one interview tool, the DISC (version 2.3), for diagnosing depressive disorders in a large sample of inpatient adolescents and found it to have strong concurrent validity for this purpose. This study found that the highest rates of diagnostic accuracy were obtained when results from parent and adolescent versions of the interview were combined. Another interesting facet of this investigation is that parents reported a higher prevalence of depressive symptoms in their children than the adolescents themselves reported.

An interview schedule that has been developed specifically for use in assessing depression is the Children's Depression Rating Scale (CDRS), which was originally developed by Poznanski, Cook, and Carroll (1979) but has since been revised and developed into a short form by some researchers. This instrument was developed as a downward extension and adaptation of the Hamilton Rating Scale for Depression, an interview rating instrument for use in assessing depression in adults. Although the CDRS-R may not be as widely used as the interview schedules reviewed in Chapter 6, it is of interest because of its specificity of design. The CDRS-R includes 17 symptom areas that cover a range of depressive symptoms, such as inability to have fun and the appearance of sad affect. The clinician, who conducts a semistructured interview, questions the child about each item but may consult other informants such as parents or teachers. Each interview item ultimately is rated for symptom severity by the clinician, using an 8-point scale (0 = unable to rate to 7 = severe symptoms). The research base on the CDRS-R is growing, and there have been some encouraging findings. For example, the CDRS has been found to have relatively high inter-rater agreement (coefficients of 0.75 and higher), high correlations with global clinical ratings of depression (0.85 and higher), high test–retest reliability at six-week intervals (low 0.80s), and good convergent validity with other diagnostic interview schedules. Additionally, some evidence has been gathered that suggests the CDRS-R is sensitive to change and can be used to monitor treatment for depression (Mayes, Bernstein, Haley, Kennard, & Emslie, 2010). This instrument seems to be useful for research purposes or as part of a comprehensive assessment battery when measurement of depressive symptoms is specified.

Sociometric Techniques

Similar to direct behavioral observation, sociometric approaches may be used to assess internalizing problems, but they pose some difficult challenges in the process. As is true in the case of behavioral observation, a major difficulty with the use of sociometric assessment for measuring internalizing problems is that subjective internal states, thought patterns, and other covert characteristics may not be observed easily, or otherwise perceived by peers. An additional difficulty surfaces when young children are being assessed. Given their experiential limitations owing to their age, very young informants may lack the maturity to make differentiations between subtle emotional characteristics. Although it may be relatively easy for a child to name three classmates who are likely to fight on the playground, the identification of peers who are sad, lonely, or nervous may become confounded with many other personality characteristics. With adults, sociometric assessment of internalizing characteristics is perhaps more effective, although not necessarily practical for day-to-day clinical use. Kane and Lawler (1978) reviewed 19 peer assessment studies in which the subjects were adults and concluded that several of the investigations were reasonably valid in measuring various internalizing-type characteristics.

Although sociometric approaches seldom would be the first method of choice for assessing internalizing problems, they nevertheless can and have been useful for this purpose. As an assessment component for internalizing problems, sociometric approaches probably are best used as a screening device for identifying potentially at-risk children who might be administered further assessments. Virtually all of the general sociometric assessment methods presented in Chapter 7 are flexible enough to be implemented appropriately in this manner. The teacher ranking procedure for internalizing problems from the Systematic Screening for Behavior Disorders (Walker & Severson, 1992; Walker, Severson, & Feil, 2014) that was discussed in Chapter 7 is an example of a sociometric type of method targeted specifically at internalizing characteristics. Typical peer nomination, rating, or ranking methods all could be used to target specific internalizing characteristics. As is true in using behavioral observation, it is necessary to define carefully the target characteristic for a valid assessment. For example, a nomination procedure used to screen for social withdrawal by wording the statement something like "Write down the names of three students who always seem to be alone" also might screen in children who are socially isolated because of their antisocial–aggressive behavior.

Despite the challenges inherent in doing so, several studies have shown that sociometric assessment approaches can screen effectively for internalizing problems in children. McConnell and Odom (1986) reviewed 46 investigations that used sociometric methods with children for various research purposes, and several of these studies directly assessed at least some internalizing characteristic, such as withdrawal or depression. Several of the studies reviewed by McConnell and Odom found that targeted subjects were likely to exhibit internalizing and externalizing symptoms. The distinction between these two domains of problems that has been found through behavioral dimensions research does not always exist in individual cases.

An additional sociometric assessment procedure that was used quite a bit in the 1980s and 1990s in the measurement of depression for research is the Peer Nomination Inventory for Depression (PNID) (Lefkowitz & Tesiny, 1980). The PNID consists of 20 statements that comprise three subscales (Depression, 14 items; Happiness, four items; and Popularity, two items). Individuals within a group (usually a classroom) are asked to identify to whom the statements apply. Examples of some of the statements on the Depression subscale include "Often plays alone," "Often sleeps in class," "Worries a lot," and "Often looks sad." Kazdin (1988) noted that the PNID has solid internal consistency (0.85), acceptable test–retest reliability at two- to six-month intervals, and adequate inter-rater agreement, and that normative data on the PNID have been gathered for more than 3,000 children in grades 3 to 5. Several validation studies of the PNID (e.g., Crowley & Worchel, 1993; Lefkowitz, Tesiny, & Gordon, 1980; Lefkowitz & Tesiny, 1985; Tesiny & Lefkowitz, 1982) have shown that it has relatively weak correlations with self-report and teacher ratings of depression but strong correlations with measures of school performance, self-concept, teacher ratings of social behavior, and other peer ratings of happiness and popularity. An interesting finding from the PNID validation research is that children who evidence greater depressive symptoms as measured by self-report instruments are more likely to rate other children as more depressed on the PNID (Crowley & Worchel, 1993). This instrument is an innovative assessment technique that is one of the few sociometric measures designed specifically or solely for assessing internalizing problems. At present, however, it probably is best used as a research or broad screening tool.

Narrow-Band Self-Report Instruments

In addition to the general-purpose self-report instruments discussed in Chapter 8, numerous self-report instruments have been developed for assessing specific internalizing

Table 11.5 Self-report instruments for assessing internalizing problems and self-concept: Summary of instruments reviewed in Chapter 11, listed in order of review

Instrument	Focus	Ages	Items and format	Norm sample
Children's Depression Inventory, Second Edition	Characteristics of depression	6–17	28 items, forced choice among three statements	1,100 (national)
Revised Children's Manifest Anxiety Scale, Second Edition	Characteristics of anxiety	6–17	49 yes/no statements	2,300 (national)
Reynolds Child Depression Scale, Second Edition	Characteristics of depression	8–12	30 statements responded to on a 4-point scale	(11 states)
Reynolds Adolescent Depression Scale, Second Edition	Characteristics of depression	11–20	30 statements responded to on a 4-point scale	3,300 (national)
State-Trait Anxiety Inventory for Children	State Anxiety and Trait Anxiety	9–12	2 scales with 20 items each; forced choice among 3 statements	1,554 (Florida)
Multidimensional Self-Concept Scale	Dimensions of Self-Concept	9–19	150 items rated using a Likert-type scale	2,501 (national)
Self-Description Questionnaire I	Dimensions of Self-Concept	8–12	76 items rated using a Likert-type scale	Over 1,000 (international)
Self-Description Questionnaire II	Dimensions of Self-Concept	13–17	102 items rating using a Likert-type scale	Over 1,000 (international)
Self-Perception Profile for Children	Dimensions of Self-Concept	9–14	36 statement pairs with two score options each	1,543 (Colorado)
Self-Perception Profile for Adolescents	Dimensions of Self-Concept	13–18	45 statement pairs with two score options each	651 (Colorado)

disorders and symptoms in children and adolescents. There are many more objective self-report instruments for assessing this area than can be addressed adequately in this chapter. Six of these self-report instruments have been selected for further discussion and evaluation in this chapter. Three of these instruments are designed specifically to assess symptoms of depression, two of them are designed to assess symptoms of anxiety, and one is designed to assess the broad range of internalizing symptoms and positive/negative affect. These six instruments were selected over other potential measures for inclusion because of their commercial availability, psychometric properties, ease of use, and amount or sophistication of available research evidence. Table 11.5 presents summary information on the major characteristics of each of these instruments.

The Children's Depression Inventory (CDI) and the Children's Depression Inventory-2 (CDI-2) The Children's Depression Inventory (CDI) (Kovacs, 1980–1981, 1991) is a 27-item self-report measure of depressive symptoms for use with school-age children and adolescents (aged six to 17). Without question, this instrument is the most widely used and researched child self-report depression scale, with several hundred studies using the CDI appearing in the professional literature by 2002. The CDI was developed as a downward extension of the Beck Depression Inventory and was first reported in the research literature in the early 1980s. For several years, the instrument and an accompanying unpublished manuscript were available in various versions from the author. In 1991, the CDI was commercially published and more easily available. In addition to the standard hand-scored, paper and pencil version of the CDI, the publisher also makes available a version that is computer administered and scored.

Each of the 27 items of the CDI has three statements about a particular depressive symptom, and the respondent chooses the statement that best describes his or her feelings during the past two weeks. Each item is scored 0, 1, or 2, with the statements reflecting the greater severity of symptoms receiving the higher value. The following is an item similar to those found in the CDI, to illustrate the structure of the items and how they are scored:

_____I feel very unhappy (scored 2)
_____I feel somewhat unhappy (scored 1)
_____I feel happy (scored 0)

The CDI is easy to administer and score, usually taking no more than ten to 20 minutes for the entire process. The CDI manual suggests that a cutoff score of 11 be used if the purpose of the administration is to screen for depression while making few false negative errors. If the purpose of the administration is to assess the presence of depression in children with behavioral and emotional problems, 13 is suggested as the appropriate cutoff score.

Normative data for CDI score conversions are based on a study by Finch, Saylor, and Edwards (1985), wherein CDI score norms for 1,463 Florida public-school children in grades 2 to 8 were reported. These normative data are broken down by gender and grade level. Previous versions of the unpublished CDI manual manuscript provided score norms based on a sample of 860 Canadian schoolchildren aged eight to 13.

Additional samples have been reported in the literature. Although the CDI total score is the measure of interest, various factor analyses of the CDI have been reported in the literature, wherein five to seven factors typically have been extracted. The current version of the CDI manual advocates a five-factor solution.

The psychometric properties of the CDI have been documented in many published research reports. Most studies have found the internal consistency of the CDI to be in the mid- to upper 0.80s. With some exceptions in which lower correlations were obtained, test–retest reliability of the CDI typically has been found to be in the 0.70 to 0.85 range at short (one week to two months) intervals and in the same general range at several-month intervals.

The most common method of determining the validity of the CDI has been through obtaining correlations of concurrent scores from other internalizing measures, and a plethora of studies have found the CDI to have significant relationships to other depression instruments and techniques purported to measure depression and related constructs. Other types of validity studies have included finding negative correlations between the CDI and measures of self-esteem (e.g., Kovacs, 1983) and social competence (e.g., Helsel & Matson, 1984), using CDI scores as a predictive measure of psychiatric diagnoses (e.g., Cantwell & Carlson, 1981; Hodges, 1990), and using CDI scores to predict future emotional and behavioral adjustment problems (e.g., Mattison, Handford, Kales, & Goodman, 1990). Also, the CDI has been used as a treatment outcome measure in many studies, and its ability to gauge change from treatment has been documented.

The CDI-2 was recently released (Kovacs, 2010) and includes much of the content from the original version with some added features. The self-report measure consists of 28 items and is appropriate for children aged seven to 17. Total scores, two scale scores (Emotional Problems and Functional Problems), and four subscale scores (Negative Mood/Physical Symptoms, Negative Self-Esteem, Interpersonal Problems, and Ineffectiveness) are derived from this measure. A short form, consisting of 12 items has also been developed for screening and progress-monitoring purposes. A parent form (17 items) and teacher form (12 items) are also available. Given that the normative data from the CDI were outdated, new norms have been established, based on data gathered from 1,100 children and adolescents from 26 states across all regions of the United States.

The CDI has the distinct advantage of being perhaps the most widely researched child self-report instrument in existence, and its psychometric properties and discriminant abilities are generally quite good. The CDI-2 should continue to have wide use in research. Until more research is conducted on this updated version, a conservative approach to the use of cutoff scores is recommended, given some previous criticisms of the predictive value of the cutoff scores.

The Revised Children's Manifest Anxiety Scale (RCMAS) and the Revised Children's Manifest Anxiety Scale, Second Edition (RCMAS-2) The Revised Children's Manifest Anxiety Scale (RCMAS) (C. R. Reynolds & Richmond, 1985) is a self-report instrument for use with children aged six to 17. It includes 37 statements that are responded to in a yes/no fashion and is designed to be a measure of trait anxiety (the tendency to be anxious over settings and time). Scoring the RCMAS simply involves summing the number of "yes" responses for each of three subscales (Physiological Anxiety, Worry and Oversensitivity, Concentration Anxiety) and a Lie scale and calculating a total score. The three RCMAS subscales were developed through factor analytic research (C. R. Reynolds & Paget, 1981), whereas the Lie scale consists of nine items that are socially desirable but almost never true (e.g., "I never say things I shouldn't").

Normative data for the RCMAS are from nearly 5,000 cases obtained in the United States, with each geographical region represented. These data first were reported in a study by C. R. Reynolds and Paget (1983) and include separate norm samples based on age, gender, and Black/White racial breakdowns.

Psychometric properties of the RCMAS as reported in the test manual and in numerous published studies are indicative of generally adequate levels of reliability and validity. Internal consistency reliability of the total RCMAS score has been reported at 0.79 for boys and 0.85 for girls in a study with kindergarten children (C. R. Reynolds, Bradley, & Steele, 1980). Internal consistency coefficients for the RCMAS subscales are at a troubling lower level than for the total score, ranging from 0.50 to 0.70 across groups for Physiological Anxiety and 0.70 to 0.90 for the Lie scale. One test–retest reliability study of the RCMAS found short-term reliability coefficients of 0.88 (one week) and 0.77 (five weeks) (Wisniewski, Mulick, Genshaft, & Coury, 1987), whereas another study found a coefficient of 0.68 at a nine-month interval (C. R. Reynolds, 1981). Evidence for the convergent validity of the RCMAS comes from a large number of studies comparing the RCMAS with other self-report measures of anxiety and related internalizing symptoms. Evidence for theory-based sensitivity to group differences of the RCMAS (an indicator of construct validity) comes from studies such as one that found the scores of gifted children to be lower than the scores of average children (C. R. Reynolds & Bradley, 1983) and one that found scores of learning-disabled children to be higher than those of average children (Paget & Reynolds, 1982). Many other studies have found RCMAS score elevations in children with various internalizing disorders.

The RCMAS-2 (C. R. Reynolds & Richmond, 2008) is similar to the RCMAS, and scores on each of the forms tend to be highly correlated with one another. The RCMAS-2 includes 49 items for children aged six to 19. Physiological Anxiety, Worry, Social Anxiety, and Defensiveness are scales derived from the items. The Social Anxiety scale includes ten additional items reflective of performance anxiety and takes the place of the Social Concerns/Concentration scale on the RCMAS. The Defensiveness scale is in place of the former Lie scale and there is also a new Inconsistent Responding index. A short form consisting of just ten items is also available. Updated norms were derived from a sample of 2,300 diverse individuals.

Although the internal consistency of the original RCMAS subscales is lower than desirable (although generally acceptable), this instrument can be recommended on several grounds. There are many published studies (approximately 200 at present) that attest to various properties and uses of the scale. The RCMAS-2 appears to improve upon some of the weaknesses noted in the original and also reflects norms that are up to date. The RCMAS is easy to use, has strong face validity, and can be recommended as part of a battery for assessing internalizing problems with children. Given the more marginal stability of the three RCMAS subscales as opposed to the total score, however, it is recommended that the total score be used for most assessment purposes and that subscale scores be interpreted with caution when they are used.

The Reynolds Child Depression Scale (RCDS) and the Reynolds Child Depression Scale, Second Edition (RCDS-2) The Reynolds Child Depression Scale (RCDS) (W. M. Reynolds, 1989) is a self-report measure of depression-related symptoms for use with children in grades 3 through 6 (ages eight to 12). It contains 30 items that are rated using a 4-point scale ("Almost never" to "All the time"). The 30 items primarily were developed based on depressive symptoms from the *DSM-III*. Some of these items are phrased to represent the presence of depressive symptoms (e.g., "I feel I am no good"), whereas others are phrased to reflect the absence of such symptoms (e.g., "I feel like playing with other kids"). The items are written at about a second-grade level and are administered orally to children in grades 3 and 4 and to older children who have reading problems. Scoring of the self-report protocol is done through an easy-to-use transparent overlay key that assigns values from 1 to 4 for each item, with higher scores reflecting item endorsement in the direction of depressive symptoms.

The RCDS was standardized with a group of more than 1,600 children from the midwestern and western United States. Technical information provided in the test manual indicates that the instrument has acceptable to excellent psychometric properties. Internal consistency of total score is 0.90 for the entire normative sample, with similar levels reported by grade, gender, and ethnic group breakdowns. Test–retest reliability estimates are reported at 0.82 at two-week intervals and from 0.81 to 0.92 at four-week intervals. A variety of information on the validity of the RCDS is presented in the test manual, including six studies correlating the RCDS with CDI and four studies correlating the RCDS with self-report measures of anxiety and self-esteem. Several other convergent construct validity studies also have appeared in the professional literature. Factor analytic research indicates the presence of a reasonably strong five-factor structure, although separate factor scores are not obtained in normal scoring of the RCDS. Interpretation of RCDS total scores is based on raw score to percentile score conversions and critical raw score values. The raw score value of 74 is considered to be the critical value for "clinical" level scores, and evidence presented in the test manual suggests that scores at this level have a high "hit rate" for identifying children who meet other criteria for having significant symptoms of depression.

The manual for the RCDS is exceptionally well written and documented, the research data presented therein are impressive, and the instrument has a great deal of face validity. It appears to be an excellent self-report instrument for assessing the symptoms of depression with elementary-age children, and it should be useful for research and clinical purposes.

The RCDS-2 reflects an updated version of the RCDS. The 30 items are similar to the original version but are also aligned with *DSM-IV* diagnoses. This new measure is now appropriate for children in grades 2 to 6, and a new short form is also available that can be completed in just two to three minutes. Updated normative data were derived from a sample of students from 11 states in the United States. While this measure is aligned to the *DSM-IV*, it is still used widely and provides extremely useful information, particularly since the definition for depression did not change dramatically in the *DSM-5*.

The Reynolds Adolescent Depression Scale, Second Edition (RADS-2) The Reynolds Adolescent Depression Scale, Second edition (RADS-2) (W. M. Reynolds, 2002) is a revision of the original RADS (W. M. Reynolds, 1986). This instrument is a self-report measure of depressive symptoms for adolescents and young adults aged 11 to 20. It is a companion instrument to the RCDS (the original RADS was the first of the two instruments to be developed), and it is similar in structure and format to the RCDS. Similar to the RCDS, the RADS-2 contains 30 items that are responded to in a 4-point format ("Almost never" to "All the time") that were developed to coincide with depressive symptoms from the *DSM*. The RADS-2 can be administered individually or with groups, and the items seem to be written at a low enough reading level that even most adolescents with reading problems should be able to understand them. The RADS-2 rating forms are hand-scored using a convenient scoring key.

The RADS-2 was standardized on a group of 3,300 adolescents and young adults from a variety of U.S. regions, reduced from an original sample of over 9,000 individuals. This norm sample is stratified to the 2,000 U. S. census estimates. There are three age divisions within the norming sample for scoring purposes, each with 1,100 normative cases: ages 11 to 13, 14 to 16, and 17 to 20.

Technical information provided in the RADS-2 test manual, and additional studies (e.g., Osman, Guiterrez, Bagge, Fang, & Emmerich, 2010) indicate that the instrument has acceptable to excellent psychometric properties. Internal consistency for the total sample is reported in the low 0.90s, with similar high levels reported by age and gender breakdowns. Test–retest reliability estimates are reported at approximately 0.80 for short-term retest intervals. Adequate validity information is presented in the RADS-2 test manual, and additional validity evidence has accrued through subsequent published studies using the RADS-2, as well as through its lineage from the very popular RADS. The manual, and several of these additional studies, have shown convergent validity evidence for the RADS-2 through correlational comparisons with other measures of depression and related internalizing symptoms. In correlational studies, the RADS-2 was compared with various adolescent self-esteem measures, with results showing a moderate to strong inverse relationship between RADS depression scores and self-concept scores.

Factor analytic research on the RADS-2 indicates the presence of a four-factor subscale structure. Interpretation of RADS-2 scores is based on raw score to T score and percentile score conversions, as well as critical raw score values, based on six items. Cutoff points for "clinical" level scores are provided, and evidence presented in the test manual suggests that scores at this level have a high "hit rate" for identifying adolescents who meet other criteria for having significant symptoms of depression.

Similar to the RCDS, the manual for the RADS-2 is exceptionally well written and documented, the research data presented therein are impressive, and the instrument has a great deal of face validity and usability. The RADS-2 items are related specifically and logically to adolescent concerns, the size of the standardization group is impressive, and the documentation of research evidence specific to adolescent populations is substantial and growing. The RADS-2 represents an excellent addition to the adolescent self-report instrumentation. The original RADS gained wide clinical and research acceptance, and there is little doubt that the RADS-2 will continue in this vein.

The Multidimensional Anxiety Scale for Children, Second Edition (MASC-2) The Multidimensional Anxiety Scale for Children, Second Edition (MASC-2; March, 2013) self-report is part of a multi-source rating system for children aged eight to 19. The MASC-2 is distributed by Multi-Health Systems and can be completed through a paper and pencil administration or online via the QuikScore. It takes about 15 minutes to complete and is written at about a second grade reading level. Total scores and Anxiety Probability Scores are generated as well as scale and subscale scores. Primary scales include Separation Anxiety/Phobias, Social Anxiety, GAD Index, Obsessions and Compulsions, Physical Symptoms, and Harm Avoidance. An Inconsistency Index is also available to screen for inconsistent responding. The technical manual is detailed and outlines changes made from the original MASC as well as updated normative data. The most recent normative sample involved 1,800 children in the United States and Canada with representation across groups including race/ethnicity, gender, parent education level, and age. A clinical sample was also recruited to help identify whether the MASC-2 is able to distinguish between clinical and normative populations. Internal consistency coefficients for the MASC-2 averaged at 0.92, while test–retest reliabilities ranged from 0.80 to 0.93. The MASC-2 converges moderately with the Beck Anxiety Inventory for Youth, and the Conners CBRS.

The MASC-2 self-report is a well-developed tool that is comprehensive in its measurement of the varying facets of anxiety. March recommends that it be used to screen and to progress monitor anxiety symptoms in children and adolescents. It can be used in a variety of settings and provides useful information that can add to a multi-pronged assessment process.

The State-Trait Anxiety Inventory for Children (STAIC) While it is an older measure, I feel it is necessary to continue to comment on the State-Trait Anxiety Inventory for Children (STAIC) (Speilberger, Edwards, Montuori, & Lushene, 1973). The STAIC is a self-report assessment of trait anxiety and state anxiety for children aged nine to 12. It was developed as a downward extension of the State-Trait Anxiety Inventory (Speilberger, Gorsuch, & Lushene, 1970), a self-report measure for adolescents and adults. The STAIC consists of two separate scales with 20 items in each: one to assess state anxiety (how anxious the child feels at the time the inventory is being completed) and one to assess trait anxiety (how anxious the child feels in general). The state anxiety items ask the respondents to determine how they "usually feel," whereas the trait anxiety items ask the respondents to rate how they feel "right now, at this very moment." The two scales can be administered separately or together. The STAIC may be administered individually or in groups and typically requires about ten minutes for each scale. Similar to the CDI, each item of the STAIC requires the participants to choose one of three statements that best describes how they feel. The items are scored 1, 2, or 3 points, with the higher score reflecting the statement indicating stronger symptoms of anxiety. Some of the STAIC items are reverse-worded and keyed, to control for the presence of acquiescent response sets. The most common version of the STAIC is a paper and pencil rating form with hand-scoring keys. A computerized version of the STAIC is also available.

The differentiation between state and trait anxiety is based on theoretical underpinnings previously postulated by Speilberger (1966, 1972). Children who are trait anxious tend to respond to a variety of situations as if they are threatening, whereas children who score high on the state anxiety scale but low on the trait anxiety scale are thought to feel anxious because of a specific situation or event. Previous reviews of the STAIC (e.g., R. P. Martin, 1988) have considered the theoretical orientation of the instrument to be a definite advantage.

Overall, the normative data of STAIC are old, but the tool has many qualities to recommend its use. The division of state and trait types of anxiety scales is interesting and useful from a theoretical standpoint, and many studies have validated the differential measurement properties of the two scales. Previous reviews of the STAIC (e.g., R. P. Martin, 1988) noted that the two major weaknesses of the instrument were a shortage of psychometric validation studies and a geographically limited normative population. The first weakness is now less of a problem because more than 200 studies have been published that used the STAIC as a primary measure and it continues to be used in research. The second weakness continues to be a problem. Not only is the norm sample limited to one state, but also the norms are now more than 35 years old. A current and nationally representative standardization of the STAIC would be of great use in increasing the confidence of obtained test scores and in ensuring the continued use of the test, which is deserved.

Concluding Comments on Internalizing Symptoms Self-Report Measures To conclude this section on self-report assessment of internalizing symptoms, it is important to recognize that self-report instruments designed to measure anxiety and depression have shown varying degrees of effectiveness in classifying children with internalizing disorders, despite the otherwise generally good psychometric properties of these measures. Historically, it is fair to say that classification studies have shown instruments for depression to be more effective than instruments for anxiety in differentiating among youth with the disorder in question. In commenting on this assessment problem regarding self-report measures of childhood anxiety, Silverman and Ginsburg stated that

> despite the advantages of children's self-rating scales . . . groups defined as anxious via these rating scales are not necessarily defined this way via diagnoses . . . specifically, it is not clear that these scales can differentiate children with anxiety disorders from children with other types of disorders.
>
> (1998, p. 254)

As was suggested in the discussion of positive and negative affectivity earlier in this chapter, perhaps the crucial problem in this regard is that most self-report scales may be assessing global negative affectivity rather than a specific internalizing disorder. Negative affectivity appears to be related to anxiety and depression, whereas the absence of positive affectivity appears to be related only to depression. Perhaps a newer generation of self-report measures that take into consideration the differential effects of positive and negative affectivity ultimately would be helpful in solving some of the diagnostic problems presented by internalizing disorders.

Self-Report Instruments for Assessing Multidimensional Self-Concept

An overview of five of the most widely used self-report instruments for measuring self-concept is provided in this section. In our earlier discussion of self-concept, it was made clear that the definitional focus for self-concept in this chapter would be a multidimensional, as opposed to a unidimensional model. The following overview precludes any of the several instruments designed to assess the latter view of the construct. The empirically demonstrated nature of self-concept necessarily precludes any assessment methods that rely on observations or perceptions of persons other than the target child or adolescent. Within the realm of self-report, the preferred assessment method is objective self-report tests rather than interviews because no structured or standardized interview methods have been developed yet to assess self-concept systematically. The self-report instruments presented in this section include Bracken's (1992) Multidimensional Self-Concept Scale, Marsh's (1992a, 1992b) Self-Description Questionnaires, and Harter's (1985b, 1988) Child and Adolescent Self-Perception Profiles. Harter and Pike (1984) developed a pictorial self-concept test for use with very young children; this instrument is reviewed in Chapter 14 (assessing young children). Although several other self-concept assessment tools for use with children and adolescents have been developed, the five instruments reviewed in this section generally outstrip the others in terms of sophistication, psychometric properties, and validity evidence.

The Multidimensional Self-Concept Scale (MSCS)

The Multidimensional Self-Concept Scale (MSCS) (Bracken, 1992) is a self-report instrument for assessing self-concept in a multidimensional fashion. The MSCS was developed for use by children and adolescents in grades 5 to 12 and includes 150 items. These items are rated by examinees on a Likert-type response scale, with 4 points ranging from "Strongly agree" to "Strongly disagree." The construction of MSCS items and the overall scale structure were theoretically driven, based on a view of self-concept as being "a behavioral construct, not a part of a larger cognitive self-system" (Bracken & Howell, 1991, p. 323). The items are divided into six subscales of 25 items each, based on Bracken's multidimensional factors and global self-concept theory: Affect, Social, Physical, Competence, Academic, and Family. A score also is produced for Global Self-Concept. For each of the seven possible score areas, raw scores are converted to standard scores with a mean of 100 and standard deviation of 15. Tables for T score conversions, percentile scores, and self-concept classifications are provided in the MSCS manual.

The MSCS was normed on 2,501 students in grades 5 to 12 in the United States, with adequate representation given to each U.S. geographical region. Strong internal consistency reliabilities are reported for the six subscales (0.85 to 0.90) and the total score (0.98). The MSCS also has been found to have strong stability over time, with subscale reliability coefficients ranging from 0.73 to 0.81 and a total score coefficient of 0.90 at four-week retest intervals. A body of externally published empirical evidence has begun to accumulate and has shown moderate to strong relationships between the MSCS and other multidimensional and unidimensional self-construct instruments, and convergent and discriminant support for the construct of multidimensional self-concept as measured by the MSCS. The MSCS manual is well written and documented, the instrument is easy to use, and it seems to be a well-designed and useful self-report instrument. While it is almost 25 years old at this point, a brief search of scholarly articles suggests that this tool continues to be widely used nationally and internationally, often in the context of research.

The Self-Description Questionnaire I (SDQ-I) The Self-Description Questionnaire I (SDQ-I) (Marsh, 1992a) is a 76-item self-report inventory that is designed to provide a multidimensional measure of self-concept for children and preadolescents (aged eight to 12). It may be administered individually or to groups and takes approximately 15 to 20 minutes for most children to complete. Australian researcher Herbert Marsh, an internationally recognized expert in the study of self-concept, developed the SDQ-I. This instrument has been in use in various versions internationally for years, including several years before the 1992 publication date. The 76 items of the SDQ-I load into 11 subscales in three domains: Academic (Mathematics, Reading, General-School), Non-Academic (Physical Abilities, Physical Appearance, Peer Relations, Parent Relations), and Global (Total Academic, Total Non-Academic, Total Self, General Self). The items are rated using a Likert-scale format, and the self-report rating form is hand-scored using a scoring profile.

In contrast to most of the other instruments reviewed in this book, which are intended for use primarily in the United States and Canada and standardized in these nations, the SDQ-I was standardized with a large sample of children who were primarily from Australia. Extensive research with the SDQ-I has been conducted internationally (including the United States), however, and the standardization and spelling differences should not pose a large barrier for use in the United States or Canada. Because of the extensive international use of the SDQ-I, researchers have translated it into several languages. Based on information presented in the test manual and in extensive externally published research reports, the psychometric properties of the SDQ-I are solid. Internal consistency of the scales generally has been found to be in the mid-0.80s to mid-0.90s range. Short-term test–retest reliability has been shown to be in the 0.70s to 0.80s range. The factor structure on which the scales are based is solid and has been shown to replicate well across various samples. Validity evidence is extensive and ranges from strong correlations with other measures, to strong associations with external criteria and outcomes, to sensitivity in detecting theory-based group differences. Most reviews of the SDQ-I have been positive, and one expert reviewer has championed it as being unquestionably the most validated self-concept measure available for use with preadolescent children (Byrne, 1996). The SDQ-I is a comprehensive and solid measure of multidimensional self-concept and continues to be used by clinicians and researchers.

The Self-Description Questionnaire II (SDQ-II) The Self-Description Questionnaire II (SDQ-II) (Marsh, 1992b) is a companion instrument to Marsh's SDQ-I, designed for use with adolescents (aged 13 to 17). This instrument may be administered individually or to groups. Like the SDQ-I, the SDQ-II is designed to provide a multidimensional assessment of self-concept. The 102 items of the SDQ-II load into 12 scales in three areas: Academic (Mathematics, Verbal, General-School), Non-Academic (Physical Abilities, Physical Appearance, Same Sex Peer Relations, Opposite Sex Peer Relations, Parent Relations, Emotional Stability, Honesty/Trustworthiness), and Global (Total Academic, General Self). The items of the SDQ-II have many similarities with the SDQ-I items but are written at a higher reading level and address many adolescent-specific concerns. The items are rated using a 6-point Likert scale, and the self-report rating form is hand scored using a convenient scoring profile.

The SDQ-II manual includes extensive information on reliability, validity, and other technical properties, and the instrument has been researched extensively with samples from various nations. It was developed in British English but has been translated and researched in several other languages. The SDQ-II was normed with a large, representative sample of adolescents from several English-speaking nations, primarily Australia. Because the SDQ-II has been in development and used internationally for several years and because numerous research standardization samples have been gathered, it is best to view it as having several norming samples rather than just the norming sample presented in the manual. An American standardization study by Gilman, Laughlin, and Huebner (1999) with a sample of 291 adolescents in the United States found the SDQ-II to have similar psychometric properties with this sample as have been reported in other samples. Internal consistency reliability of the SDQ-II scales has been shown to vary from the low-0.80s to mid-0.90s range. Short-term test–retest reliability has been shown to be strong, in the 0.70s to 0.80s range. The subscale or factor structure proposed by the author has been confirmed in several studies across various standardization groups. Validity evidence has accrued in several forms, including correlations with other measures, evidence of theory-based group differences in scores, and strong relationships to important criteria or outcomes. One expert recognized the SDQ-II as the most validated self-concept measure available for use with adolescents (Byrne, 1996), with favorable reviews from other authors as well (e.g., Keith, 1995). The SDQ-II is a comprehensive, extensively researched, and useful instrument that should be considered seriously as a choice for assessing self-concept in adolescents.

The Self-Perception Profile for Children (SPPC) The Self-Perception Profile for Children (SPPC) (Harter, 1985b, 2012) is a self-report instrument designed to assess multidimensional self-concept in children aged eight to 15. The SPPC includes 36 pairs of statements that reflect opposing views of particular aspects of self-concept (e.g., "Some kids wish their body was different, BUT Other kids like their body the way it is"). Examinees are asked first to choose which statement in the pair is most like them, and after they have made this initial choice they are asked to determine whether the statement they have chosen is really true or sort of true for them. Each test item is scored using a 4-point scale, with 1 reflecting the lowest and 4 reflecting the highest self-concept rating.

The 36 SPPC items are divided into six dimensions: Scholastic Competence, Social Acceptance, Athletic Competence, Physical Appearance, Behavioral Conduct, and Global Self-Worth. In contrast to the MSCS, the global self-worth scale is not a summation of the other subscales, but comprises six statements that reflect how the subject feels about himself or herself in an overall sense. Scoring the SPPC is done by determining the raw score mean value for each of the six dimensions, then comparing these scores with means and standard deviations of grade- and gender-specific score breakdowns from the normative group and plotting the mean scores on a pupil profile form where score levels are seen to be in the low, medium, or high range. Higher mean scores for each scale indicate higher perceptions of self-worth. The SPPC also includes two corollary instruments: a rating scale for teachers and an importance rating scale for subjects. The teacher rating scale provides a basis for comparing a child's responses with an objective rating, whereas the importance rating allows the examiner to determine if any discrepancies exist between the child's self-perception ratings and the importance of those ratings to the child's overall self-esteem. For example, a low score on athletic competence may or may not be cause for concern, depending on how important athletic competence is for the child.

The SPPC was originally normed in the 1980s and 1990s on four samples of children (1,543 total) from Colorado in grades 3 to 8. Tables of mean scores and standard deviations from the norm group are presented in the test manual based on gender and grade-level breakdowns. Internal consistency reliabilities on the SPPC range from 0.80 to 0.90 across a number of samples, and test–retest correlations across subscales have been found to range from 0.40 to 0.65 at one-month to one-year intervals (Harter, 1990). The factor structure of the SPPC seems to be sound, with items loading well into their respective factors and the six scales having only moderate intercorrelations. Gender differences in self-concept scores are reported in the SPPC manual, with the most systematic effects indicating that boys see themselves as significantly more athletically competent than girls, and girls see themselves as significantly better behaved than boys. Some additional significant gender effects were found in the areas of global self-worth and physical appearance, but these effects were not consistent across grade levels. An interesting finding in this regard is that at the elementary level there are no significant differences between boys' and girls' scores on these two dimensions, but at the middle school level, boys' scores in both areas are significantly higher than girls' scores.

The SPPC is a unique and innovative instrument and can be recommended on several grounds. Because it is a relatively brief measure (in comparison with the other measures reviewed in this section), it offers the advantage of brevity when a short screening tool is needed. There are some potential weaknesses, however, that warrant using it with caution. The SPPC norm group was taken from only one state, reducing the confidence with which score interpretations can be generalized. Although the accumulated research evidence regarding the SPPC is substantial (there were less than 75 studies by 1998), a large national norm sample would be extremely useful, as would raw score to standard score and percentile conversion tables.

The Self-Perception Profile for Adolescents (SPPA) Harter's (1988, 2012) Self-Perception Profile for Adolescents (SPPA) is a 45-item self-report instrument that is similar in design to the SPPC. The items and scales use the same type of rating and scoring format as the SPPC; only the SPPA characteristics that differ from those of the SPPC are discussed in this section. The items in the SPPA are mostly similar to those in the SPPC but are worded specifically for use by teenage subjects (e.g., "Some teenagers wish their physical appearance was different, BUT Other teenagers like their physical appearance the way it is"). In addition to the rewording of items from the SPPC, more items were added to the SPPA to reflect specific concerns of teenagers, such as job competence, close friendship, and romantic appeal. These three areas of concern appear as additional subscales on the SPPA, and the SPPA has a total of nine subscales instead of the six that are found on the SPPC. Like the SPPC, the SPPA includes an importance rating scale for examinees and a teacher's rating scale for assessing actual student behavior (e.g., "This individual is good looking OR This individual is not that good looking").

The SPPA was normed on a group of 651 students in grades 8 to 11 from four samples in Colorado. For each of the three grade levels, separate norms are provided for boys and girls. Internal consistency reliability of the SPPA is reported to range from 0.74 to 0.91. The factor structure of the SPPA appears to be adequate, and the generally moderate intercorrelations among the nine subscales suggest a basis for a multidimensional construction of self-concept. Like the SPPC, the SPPA has good face validity and offers an innovative and comprehensive method of assessing adolescent self-concept. A reasonable amount of external research evidence regarding this instrument has accumulated. The SPPA is also limited by the lack of a large nationwide norm sample and scant technical information in the manual. It has been the object of several external validity studies, has held up well over several years of research and clinical use, and offers a good alternative for a brief screening instrument.

LINKING ASSESSMENT TO INTERVENTION

In comparison with externalizing problems, in the domain of internalizing problems it is more difficult to establish a solid link between assessment and intervention. One of the major reasons that this link has been tenuous has to do with the nature of internalizing problems. Given that these types of problems often involve subjective individual perceptions and states, it is more difficult to identify tangible and directly observable behaviors to consider for intervention. For example, if a comprehensive assessment reveals that a child feels excessive sadness and has an extremely low opinion of himself or herself, a clinician should know that this child needs some attention. This type of assessment information does not give obvious clues, however, regarding what kind of attention would be best in ameliorating these symptoms. In contrast, comprehensive assessment data regarding externalizing problems often provide direct cues regarding what is needed because the problem behaviors are overt and defined easily as problems. Externalizing problems are a good choice for conducting a functional behavior assessment. As has been discussed previously in this chapter, functional behavior assessment methods are becoming more accepted but are still a challenge when used with internalizing problems. Although there is some promise in this regard, there is still not a standard methodology in place for functional assessment of internalizing problems.

This challenging state of affairs on linking assessment to treatment does not mean that effective treatment for internalizing disorders is not possible. On the contrary, reviews in this area have shown that although the number of controlled treatment studies are somewhat limited, there are several potentially effective interventions for a variety of internalizing problems of children and adolescents (e.g., Durlak et al., 2011; Hops & Lewinsohn, 1995; Mash & Barkley, 1989; Merrell, 2008; Schwartz, Gladstone, & Kaslow, 1998; Silverman & Ginsburg, 1998). The key problem is not the absence of effective interventions for internalizing problems. Rather, it is determining how to select, target, deliver, and monitor these interventions.

Despite the sometimes challenging link between assessment and intervention with internalizing problems, there is no question that carefully gathered assessment information can guide the development and delivery of effective interventions. It has been shown convincingly that comprehensive combined cognitive and behavioral treatment methods constitute the strongest evidence-based psychosocial approach to treating depression in children and adolescents (Merrell, 2008). Careful scrutiny of the assessment information, including a qualitative evaluation of individual self-report items and interview results, may be helpful in targeting and tailoring specific cognitive–behavioral techniques, such as identification of automatic negative thoughts, reduced engagement in positive activities, and distorted perceptions. Likewise, similar strategies may be used to link assessment information to cognitive–behavioral treatment techniques for anxiety. Specific behavioral information regarding anxiety symptoms, which might be obtained from rating scales and direct observation, might prove to be useful in forming hypotheses to design a behaviorally oriented intervention, such as systematic desensitization or relaxation training. The use of brief self-report measures of internalizing problems may be useful for monitoring intervention progress or response to treatment, whereas comprehensive self-report instruments may prove useful for evaluating the overall effects of an intervention at its conclusion. Finally, short forms of self-reports are becoming more commonly used in schools to screen universally and identify students at risk for developing depression and/or anxiety. Developing systems to support these practices are critical and can serve to prevent more serious internalizing problems from occurring. Students who score in an elevated range on screening measures may be eligible for targeted intervention and may show quicker improvement in symptoms than if screening never had occurred.

CONCLUSIONS

In contrast to externalizing problems, the domain of internalizing problems includes overcontrolled and inner-directed characteristics and is generally thought of as consisting of emotional rather than behavioral problems. The major areas within the internalizing domain are depression, anxiety, social withdrawal, and somatic problems. Specific classification paradigms, prevalence estimates, and division of symptoms have been more difficult to achieve with internalizing disorders than externalizing disorders, partly because of the more covert nature of internalizing symptoms and partly because the research in this area has lagged behind the research focused on the externalizing domain.

Although internalizing disorders of childhood may not have as negative long-term implications for later life adjustment as do externalizing disorders, they do pose serious problems for the children and their families who suffer from them. Not only do internalizing disorders create substantial barriers to present adjustment and success, but they also may persist for several years in some cases and may become lifelong debilitating problems. Research is increasingly indicating that internalizing disorders in childhood are not as benign as once thought; they seem to be associated with various negative outcomes later in life, particularly if they are left untreated.

A more recent development in understanding internalizing disorders is the articulation of the theory of positive and negative affectivity. These differing aspects of mood states appear to contribute to the development and classification of specific internalizing disorders. For example, persons who are depressed tend to have high levels of negative affectivity and low levels of positive affectivity, whereas persons who are anxious tend to have high levels of negative affectivity but normal levels of positive affectivity. Positive and negative affectivity may be useful in future paradigms of these disorders.

An inverse relationship exists between internalizing problems, particularly depression, and self-concept. That is, poor self-esteem or poor perceived self-competence is often an attribute or product of internalizing disorders. Assessment of internalizing problems also should take into account the possibility of self-concept assessment. The most sophisticated current self-concept theories are multidimensional in nature, meaning that they view global self-concept as something more complex than a simple summation of one's self-concept in specific areas.

Assessment of internalizing problems is uniquely suited for self-report methods, including clinical interviews and the use of self-report instruments. Increasingly, experts in this area consider obtaining the self-report of a referred child or adolescent with internalizing problems as an essential part of the overall assessment design. Clinical interviewing, whether unstructured or highly structured, provides an excellent means of assessing perceptions of internalizing problems, as do the many technically sound self-report instruments that have been developed in this area. Behavioral observation of internalizing problems is difficult because so many internalizing symptoms are not observed easily through external means. There are certain situations, however, in which direct observation may be helpful. Behavior rating scales suffer from some of the same drawbacks as direct observation as a means for assessing internalizing problems, but they typically are considered to be an important part of the overall assessment design, and improvements in this area have been encouraging. Sociometric assessment of internalizing problems also has similar limitations related to external observation of internalizing characteristics, but there have been some impressive developments in this area as well.

Although there are numerous intervention strategies that have proven to be effective in treating internalizing problems, it is often challenging to link assessment results directly to intervention planning in this area. Careful evaluation of assessment information may prove to be helpful, however, in targeting specific assessment techniques and in monitoring and evaluating intervention. Clinicians should be encouraged by findings regarding the potential efficacy of psychological treatments for depression, anxiety, and related internalizing problems.

REVIEW AND APPLICATION QUESTIONS

1. This chapter states repeatedly that internalizing disorders are more difficult than externalizing disorders to identify, empirically classify, and count. Beyond the obvious explanation that internalizing disorders are harder to observe through objective means than externalizing disorders, what are some other possible explanations for these difficulties?

2. Compare the behavioral dimensions approach to classifying internalizing disorders with the *DSM* diagnostic categories relevant to internalizing disorders. What do the large differences between the two approaches to classification imply about the current state of classification?

3. What are the major differences between depression as a symptom, depression as a syndrome, and depression as a disorder?

4. What is known regarding persistence and long-term implications of internalizing disorders?

5. What are some assessment issues to be considered, and what is known regarding differences between parent report and child self-report of internalizing symptoms of children and adolescents?

6. If you had to choose between conducting a clinical interview and using an objective self-report instrument with a child or adolescent who had significant internalizing symptoms, under which conditions would you choose each, and why would you choose them?

7. Characterize the state of the art regarding child and adolescent self-report instruments for internalizing problems compared with any other general category of problems. Related to this issue, what are some of the problems that still exist with internalizing self-report measures?

8. Discuss the idea of applying a function-based assessment to internalizing problems. Describe the questions you might ask the child or adolescent and how you would plan an intervention based on this information.

9. Ironically, assessment of externalization problems is linked more easily to intervention planning than is assessment of internalizing problems, yet the interventions for internalizing problems seem to be more effective than those for externalizing problems. What are some reasons for this state of affairs?

12

ASSESSING OTHER BEHAVIORAL, SOCIAL, AND EMOTIONAL PROBLEMS

Throughout this book, various behavioral, social, and emotional problems of children and adolescents have been discussed most frequently in terms of their place within the two broad dimensions of externalizing and internalizing psychopathology or disorders. This broad-band taxonomic division has become the standard paradigm among researchers who investigate developmental psychopathology. Not all childhood behavioral or emotional problems fit neatly within this model, however. Some disorders, as evidenced by some of the narrow-band cross-informant syndromes in the ASEBA, are considered to be mixed disorders. Within these syndrome scales, some items may load into the externalizing domain, other items may load into the internalizing domain, and some items may not load specifically into either of the two broad-band domains. Some severe problems, such as psychotic disorders and pervasive developmental disorders, occur with such low frequency in the general child population that it is difficult to justify even including relevant items for them in general screening instruments. Large-scale epidemiologic studies usually identify so few cases in which these low-frequency behaviors are present that it is difficult to ascertain accurately their appropriate classification dimensions.

This chapter discusses several of the problems and disorders that do not fit neatly within the externalizing–internalizing dichotomy, or that occur infrequently in general child populations. For lack of a better descriptive term, these are referred to in this chapter as "other behavioral, social, and emotional problems." Because the major emphasis of this text is on assessment and classification of more common externalizing and internalizing problems, the issues and disorders discussed in this chapter are not examined in substantial depth. Rather this chapter is intended to provide a brief general overview for understanding and assessment of the lower base-rate and more diagnostically nebulous problems that occasionally may be encountered by school psychologists, clinical child psychologists, and related professionals, particularly those working in generalist educational and mental health settings. Professionals who work in pediatric, psychiatric, or highly specialized education settings would encounter some of these problems more frequently than the generalists and likely would have developed a more comprehensive network of assessment, diagnostic, and intervention aids. School and clinical child psychologists (and related mental health professionals) who are more generalist in nature likely need to develop a network of contacts among their more specialized colleagues for purposes of consultation and referral when some of these other problems are encountered.

The format of this chapter differs from the chapters on assessment of externalizing (Chapter 10) and internalizing disorders (Chapter 11). The chapter begins with discussions of the two major approaches to classification and how they treat the various types of

DOI: 10.4324/9781315747521-14

problems in question. Because of the wide variety of characteristics and assessment needs of the various problems and disorders discussed in this chapter, each problem area is covered separately, including Autism Spectrum Disorder, Schizophrenia Spectrum Disorders, Psychotic Disorders, Tic Disorders (specifically, Tourette's Disorder), and Eating Disorders. Rather than including separate discussions of the major methods of assessment, as is the case in Chapters 10 and 11, details on assessment of specific problems and disorders covered herein (limited in some cases) are presented in conjunction with the general descriptions of these problems. The chapter concludes with a brief discussion on future directions in this area and some ideas for linking assessment to intervention.

CLASSIFICATION AND TAXONOMY

From the beginnings of psychology as a scientific discipline in the late 1800s, definition and classification of low-frequency and severe behavioral, social, and emotional problems have been a continuing problem. Because these disorders are relatively rare and because some of the classification categories have a fair amount of common or overlapping characteristics, the research base for classification and taxonomy in this area has lagged. Until about the 1960s, it was common for the generic term *childhood psychoses* to be used in the classification of all severe childhood disorders, although many other labels were used previously with some regularity, including *dementia precocissma, dementia infantilis, childhood schizophrenia, infantile autism, autistic psychopathy, symbiotic psychosis,* and *atypical child* (Howlin & Yule, 1990). Because the term *childhood psychoses* has no precise meaning, it is seldom used today, and most current classification paradigms are connected to the *DSM* system.

Behavioral Dimensions Classification
As mentioned in previous chapters, empirical efforts to establish a reliable classification taxonomy of severe and other low-frequency behavioral disorders were plagued by problems stemming from small sample sizes to overlapping behavioral and emotional characteristics. An early effort at developing a statistical taxonomy of the broad category of childhood psychoses was a study by Prior, Boulton, Gajzago, and Perry (1975), who used an analysis of 162 cases that ultimately led to a division into two categories: one subgroup with early onset of autistic-like features and the other subgroup with a later onset of symptoms and less debilitating impairment in social relationships. This study was never replicated, but the general idea of two similar divisions has caught on to some extent among researchers (Cantor, 1987; Howlin & Yule, 1990).

An effort at establishing a behavioral dimensions taxonomy for severe behavioral disorders was conducted by Quay (1986a), who through his analysis of 61 multivariate statistical studies described facets of child psychopathology. Although Quay (1986a) noted that "the problems associated with describing childhood psychosis have not readily yielded to clarification by multivariate statistical analysis" (p. 16), his effort resulted in an organization into two types of syndromes that are relevant for this chapter. One of these syndromes was labeled *schizoid–unresponsive*, with the most frequently identified behaviors being refusal to talk, social withdrawal, extreme timidity, and an aloof behavioral presentation referred to as "cold and unresponsive." The second of these two syndromes was labeled *psychotic disorder*, with the few key behavioral features identified including

Table 12.1 Major behavioral characteristics of two types of severe behavioral syndromes identified through Quay's (1986a) analysis

Schizoid–Unresponsive	Psychotic Disorder
Refusal to talk	Incoherent speech
Socially withdrawn	Repetitive speech
Shy, timid, bashful	Acts bizarre, odd, peculiar
Cold and unresponsive	Visual hallucinations
Lack of interest	Auditory hallucinations
Sad affect	Has strange ideas, behavior
Stares blankly	
Confused	
Secretive behavior	
Prefers to be alone	

incoherent and repetitive speech, bizarre behavior, auditory and visual hallucinations, and a group of odd characteristics referred to as "strange ideas, behaviors" (Quay, 1986a, p. 16). These two syndromes are listed with their characteristic behavioral symptoms in Table 12.1.

This taxonomy effort, which was conducted over three decades ago, was complicated by methodological difficulties and should be considered a preliminary or experimental effort.

The DSM Classification

The *DSM* classification system has evolved substantially. With regard to classification categories for some more severe and lower base-rate childhood disorders, changes over time have been particularly noticeable. Such continuing evolution provides evidence that the field of developmental psychopathology has evolved rapidly and that understanding of specific problems and disorders is likewise evolving.

The *DSM-5* includes several general classification categories, some with numerous specific diagnostic categories, that involve the "other" problems and disorders that are the focus of this chapter. For our purposes, the general categories from the *DSM-5* that are pertinent to this chapter include *Neurodevelopmental Disorders, Schizophrenia and Other Psychotic Disorders, Feeding and Eating Disorders*, and, to a limited extent, *Personality Disorders*. These general categories, with their more relevant specific diagnostic categories, are presented in Table 12.2.

There are additional general and specific categories within the *DSM* system that at times are associated with behavioral or emotional disorders of children, such as *Intellectual Disabilities, Substance-Related and Addictive Disorders, Elimination Disorders*, and *Disruptive, Impulse Control and Conduct Disorders*. Readers who desire a more detailed description of any of these categories that are beyond the scope of this book should refer to the *DSM-5* or specific books on psychopathology classification or developmental psychopathology.

AUTISM SPECTRUM DISORDER

Autism Spectrum Disorder falls under the broad category of Neurodevelopmental Disorders in the *DSM-5*. Autism Spectrum Disorder can constitute some of the most

Table 12.2 Some major diagnostic areas and categories from *DSM-5* that constitute severe, low base rate, or less differentiated types of behavioral, social, and emotional disorders among children and adolescents

Neurodevelopmental Disorders
Autism Spectrum Disorder
Motor Disorders (e.g., Tic Disorders and other movement disorders)

Schizophrenia Spectrum and other psychotic disorders
(Numerous types and subtypes of schizophrenia and other disorders are also listed)

Feeding and eating disorders
Pica
Rumination Disorder
Avoidant/Restrictive Food Intake Disorder
Anorexia Nervosa
Bulimia Nervosa
Binge-Eating Disorder
(Other specified and unspecified feeding or eating disorders)

debilitating psychological conditions of children. This disorder is not focused exclusively on the domain of behavioral, social, and emotional problems, which is the focus of this text; however, it is primarily characterized by deficits and impairments in social communication and by narrow interests and repetitive behaviors. These deficits and associated problems of social behavior can be severe and debilitating and certainly require an extensive system of supports and interventions, making Autism Spectrum Disorder an important part of this chapter. This section provides an overview of Autism Spectrum Disorder and specific information on assessment. Because several other disorders have been subsumed under Autism Spectrum Disorder or have been eliminated from the *DSM* altogether, I will describe previous disorders categorized under the *DSM-IV Pervasive Developmental Disorders*, but will provide much more detail on the history of autism and the changes to the *DSM-5* and characteristics of Autism Spectrum Disorder.

Rett's Disorder, Childhood Disintegrative Disorder, and Asperger's Disorder were added to the *DSM-IV* but were not included in *DSM-III-R* and are now not part of the *DSM-5*. Substantially less knowledge has accumulated regarding these disorders, which tend to have many features in common with autism, and their brief discussion in this section is a reflection of this fact. In addition to the discussion of each of these disorders, their major characteristics and associated features are summarized in Table 12.3. Readers are encouraged to take note of the significant overlap in characteristics that have defined these disorders. The classification and description systems for this cluster of disorders have undergone major changes and will continue to evolve significantly.

The best current estimates according to the Centers for Disease Control and Prevention (2016) indicate that approximately one in 68 children were diagnosed with an Autism Spectrum Disorder in 2012. This disorder has been found to occur at least four times more frequently in boys than in girls, and has also been found more often in Caucasian populations than in multiracial populations (CDC, 2016). In most cases, the Autism Spectrum Disorder has an onset before three years of age but often is not diagnosed until later, when more social demands and expectations for flexibility with routines are placed upon the child (Shattuck et al., 2009). Hence, some children are not identified until formally entering school, are interacting with similar-age peers, and are more objectively observed by multiple adults in the classroom.

Table 12.3 Some major characteristics and associated features of four primary pervasive developmental disorders that were in the *DSM-IV*

Autistic Disorder
Onset before age three years
Markedly impaired communication and social interaction
Markedly restricted repetitive stereotyped behavior
More common among males than females
Often associated with mental retardation

Rett's Disorder
Onset before age four years
Decreased head growth after normal growth for first five to 48 months
Stereotyped behavior and loss of hand skills at five to 30 months
Loss of social engagement skills
Decrease in gait/trunk motor coordination
Impaired language and psychomotor ability
Very rare
Reported to occur only among females
Associated with severe/profound mental retardation

Childhood Disintegrative Disorder
Onset between aged two and ten years
Loss of acquired skills after normal growth up to age two
Abnormal social interaction skills
Impaired language ability
Stereotypic and restricted behavior, activities, interests
Very rare
Appears to be more common among males
Associated with severe mental retardation

Asperger's Disorder
Onset during preschool years
Impaired social interaction
Restricted stereotyped behavior, interests, activities
Appears to be more common among males

Description

Autism Spectrum Disorder Psychiatrist Leo Kanner, a pioneer in the study of what is now called Autism Spectrum Disorder, first described 11 children in 1943 who fitted this general diagnostic picture. He noted that their fundamental disorder was the "inability to relate themselves in the ordinary way to people and situations from the beginning of life," and that a characteristic of this disorder is an aloneness that "disregards, ignores, shuts out anything that comes to the child from the outside" (Kanner, 1943, p. 243). This syndrome was labeled by Kanner as *early infantile autism* because it was noted that the tendency to display these characteristics seemed inborn and present from birth. For many years after Kanner's initial description, children with these characteristics were informally referred to as having Kanner syndrome (Newsom & Hovanitz, 1997). Howlin and Rutter (1987) noted that although there have been many changes since 1943 in the way that this disorder is conceptualized, Kanner's general description of autism is still fundamentally accurate.

Based on the *DSM-5* diagnostic criteria (Table 12.4), the major characteristics of Autism Spectrum Disorder include severe impairment in social communication and

Table 12.4 Diagnostic criteria for Autism Spectrum from the *DSM-5*

A. Persistent deficits in social communication and social interaction across multiple contexts, as manifested by the following, currently or by history (examples are illustrative, not exhaustive; see text):

1. Deficits in social–emotional reciprocity, ranging, for example, from abnormal social approach and failure of normal back-and-forth conversation; to reduced sharing of interests, emotions, or affect; to failure to initiate or respond to social interactions

2. Deficits in nonverbal communicative behaviors used for social interaction, ranging, for example, from poorly integrated verbal and nonverbal communication; to abnormalities in eye contact and body language or deficits in understanding and use of gestures; to a total lack of facial expressions and nonverbal communication.

3. Deficits in developing, maintaining, and understanding relationships, ranging, for example, from difficulties adjusting behavior to suit various social contexts; to difficulties in sharing imaginative play or in making friends; to absence of interest in peers

Specify current severity:
Severity is based on social communication impairments and restricted, repetitive patterns of behavior.

B. Restricted, repetitive patterns of behavior, interests, or activities, as manifested by at least two of the following, currently or by history (examples are illustrative, not exhaustive, see text):

1. Stereotyped or repetitive motor movements, use of objects, or speech (e.g., simple motor stereotypies, lining up toys or flipping objects, echolalia, idiosyncratic phrases)

2. Insistence on sameness, inflexible adherence to routines, or ritualized patterns of verbal or nonverbal behavior (e.g., extreme distress at small changes, difficulties with transitions, rigid thinking patterns, greeting rituals, need to take same route or eat same food every day)

3. Highly restricted, fixated interests that are abnormal in intensity or focus (e.g., strong attachment to or preoccupation with unusual objects, excessively circumscribed or perseverative interests)

4. Hyper- or hyporeactivity to sensory input or unusual interest in sensory aspects of the environment (e.g., apparent indifference to pain/temperature, adverse response to specific sounds or textures, excessive smelling or touching of objects, visual fascination with lights or movement)

Specify current severity:
Severity is based on social communication impairments and restricted, repetitive patterns of behavior.

C. Symptoms must be present in the early developmental period (but may not become fully manifest until social demands exceed limited capacities, or may be masked by learned strategies in later life).

D. Symptoms cause clinically significant impairment in social, occupational, or other important areas of current functioning.

E. These disturbances are not better explained by intellectual disability (intellectual developmental disorder) or global developmental delay. Intellectual disability and autism spectrum disorder frequently co-occur; to make comorbid diagnoses of autism spectrum disorder and intellectual disability, social communication should be below that expected for general developmental level.

Note: Individuals with well-established *DSM-IV* diagnosis of autistic disorder, Asperger's disorder, or pervasive developmental disorder not otherwise specified should be given the diagnosis of autism spectrum disorder. Individuals who have marked deficits in social communication, but whose symptoms do not otherwise meet criteria for autism spectrum disorder, should be evaluated for social (pragmatic) communication disorder.

Specify if:
With or without accompanying intellectual impairment
With or without accompanying language impairment
Associated with a known medical or genetic condition or environmental factor (Coding note: Use additional code to identify the associated medical or genetic condition).
Associated with another neurodevelopmental, mental, or behavioral disorders (Coding note: Use additional code(s) to identify the associated neurodevelopmental, mental, or behavioral disorder(s)).
With catatonia (refer to the criteria for catatonia associated with another mental disorder for definition) (**Coding note:** Use additional code 293.89 [F06.1] catatonia associated with autism spectrum disorder to indicate the presence of the comorbid catatonia).

Source: Reprinted with permission from *Diagnostic and Statistical Manual of Mental Disorders, Fifth Edition* (pp. 50–51). Copyright 2013 by the American Psychiatric Association.

interaction and a severely restricted and repetitive repertoire of activities and interests. These two primary symptom domains represent a significant change from the *DSM-IV*, which described autism as a three-pronged disorder involving deficits in social behavior, communication, and the presence of restrictive or repetitive behavior. The *DSM-5* does include specifiers that can be used to further describe the individual's specific clinical presentation, such as *with or without accompanying language impairment*, and there is also a *DSM-5* category of Social Communication Disorder, which may be a more appropriate diagnostic category for some higher functioning individuals. Specific characteristics that commonly are seen in children with autism are varied, but a common general pattern often is observed. In terms of severely impaired social relationships, individuals with Autism Spectrum Disorder may appear to be socially aloof and detached; they may fail to make eye contact, have a noticeably flat affect, shrink from physical contact, and often seem to relate to other persons as objects or conglomerations of parts rather than as people (Newsom & Hovanitz, 1997; Ornitz, 1989; Schreibman & Charlop-Christy, 1998). Additionally, individuals with autism often lack or fail to grasp the pragmatics of social or interpersonal communication, possibly because of an inability to interpret facial expressions, intonation, gestures, and other social cues (Prior & Werry, 1986). The severely restricted repertoire of activities and interests that is part of the disorder is characterized by stereotyped body movements (spinning, twisting, head banging, flapping the hands), a peculiar preoccupation with parts of objects (e.g., doorknobs, on–off switches), and exhibition of great distress when routines or insignificant parts of the environment are changed. Behaviors that are part of this second characteristic often take the form of obsession with routine and objects, such as a child repetitively dumping a pile of sticks on the floor and then lining them up in a particular manner. The additional specifiers in the *DSM-5* may be used to reflect individuals who may not engage in speech, or they may speak in a peculiar manner, such as using a robotic monotone voice, displaying an odd vocal rhythm and meter, or repeating words and phrases in a stereotypical manner (Howlin & Yule, 1990; Schreibman & Charlop-Christy, 1998). Individuals with autism may also experience a host of other challenges. For example, they may experience gastro-intestinal problems, sleep problems, immune system problems, social anxiety, aggression, ADHD, and OCD.

Aside from the major features of Autism Spectrum Disorder, there are some other correlates to consider. IQ scores of individuals with autism often are in the normal range or higher, but this is not always the case; many individuals with autism consistently test in the moderate to severely intellectually impaired range (Klinger, Dawson, Barnes, & Crisler, 2014; Prior & Werry, 1986). Autism Spectrum Disorder often may be associated with problems of sensory integration and perception (Kern et al., 2006; Klinger et al., 2014; Wing, 1969) and poor psychomotor development (Fulkerson & Freeman, 1980; Klinger et al., 2014). Because the combination of social impairment and low intellectual ability is often part of the picture, persons with Autism Spectrum Disorder may have significant difficulty learning new materials or tasks.

Kanner's (1943) early writings on autism considered that there was a strong probability that the disorder had a constitutional or biological origin. During this same seminal period of discovery, however, Kanner and others noted that parents of children with autism often showed a tendency toward emotional insulation, aloofness, or detachment toward the child. The notion was born and perpetuated by prominent writers (e.g., Bettelheim, 1967; O'Gorman, 1970) that autism may be due to abnormal family functioning. Although based on some important clinical observations, the problem with these theories was that they usually failed to take into account the reciprocal effect of parent–child interactions and placed too much weight on parent behaviors. The transactional–interactional approach would indicate that although parents of children with Autism Spectrum Disorder might respond at times in a manner that could be interpreted as emotionally detached, the characteristics of the child may have a great deal of influence on eliciting these behaviors. Despite this line of thinking, which was popular until about the 1970s, research efforts have failed to support the notion that autism is caused by abnormal parenting or family functioning (Howlin & Yule, 1990).

Although there is no conclusive evidence on the specific causes of Autism Spectrum Disorder at present, current thinking suggests that genetic and other biochemical influences are clearly involved in the disorder. In a large study, Ozonoff et al. (2011) found that there is indeed an increased risk for families with one child with autism to have multiple children with autism. Others have described a "broader phenotype" or the likelihood for family members to present with characteristics that may be consistent with Autism Spectrum Disorder, even if they don't necessarily meet criteria for disorder (e.g., poor social skills) (Klinger et al., 2014). The complexity of the biologically linked explanations for autism is captured in the following statement by Travis and Sigman:

> The etiology of autism is not well understood. Research has established that psychological or social stressors do not cause autism, focusing attention squarely on biological underpinnings. However, it now appears unlikely that autism is caused by any single organic factor. Rather, there is probably a heterogeneous set of biological factors and multiple causal paths that may result in autism. The search for biological underpinnings has revealed that autism is associated with a number of organic conditions, such as prenatal and obstetric complications, the onset of epilepsy in adolescence or adulthood, and two genetic disorders, tuberous sclerosis and Fragile X syndrome . . . The reasons for these links are not yet understood.
>
> (2000, p. 642)

The best evidence from follow-up studies of children with autism indicates that although some improvements may occur over time (particularly with intense early intervention efforts), many, if not most, individuals with the disorder will continue to exhibit some characteristic problem symptoms over the course of their life. Howlin and Yule (1990) noted that individuals with Autism Spectrum Disorder who have the greatest chance of achieving social independence and making satisfactory adjustment are those few with high IQ scores and reasonably good language skills and that "total social independence is gained by only a very small minority of autistic individuals" (p. 376). For many with Autism Spectrum Disorder, the long-term implications of the disorder are severe, and many require a high degree of personal, social, and occupational support throughout life.

Asperger's Disorder Asperger's Disorder is now subsumed under Autism Spectrum Disorder in the *DSM-5*. According to the *DSM-IV*, this disorder was described as the following: "The essential features of Asperger's Disorder are severe and sustained impairment in social interaction and the development of restricted, repetitive patterns of behavior, interests, and activities" (APA, 1994, p. 75). Based on this description, readers can begin to understand how there may be an overlap between what was previously defined as Autistic

Disorder and Asperger's Disorder. The major difference that clinicians and scholars considered between the two was that Asperger's Disorder did not include significant delays in language development and functioning. Also, Asperger's Disorder was characterized by the lack of clinically significant delays in cognitive development, self-help skills, and nonsocial adaptive behaviors. In several respects, Asperger's Disorder was already considered to be a form of "high functioning" autism (Mesibov, Shea, & Adams, 2001). Despite an upsurge of interest in this condition in the 1990s and 2000s, information regarding the prevalence of Asperger's Disorder is quite limited, but it was thought to appear more commonly in boys. It seemed to have a later onset than autism. Perhaps the most critical feature of Asperger's Disorder were the significant difficulties in social interaction. *DSM-IV* stated that "individuals with the condition may have problems with empathy and modulation of social interaction" (APA, 1994, p. 76). Asperger's Disorder seemed to follow a continuous developmental course, almost always throughout the life span. This disorder bore some similarity to the major characteristics of the schizoid–unresponsive behavioral dimension shown in Table 12.1. This disorder was named after Hans Asperger, who, according to Wolf (1989), was the first person to discuss the so-called schizoid disorders in the 1940s. These disorders were identified as separate diagnostic categories in *DSM-IV*, but they also had some similarity to Schizoid and Schizotypal Personality Disorders, which might be diagnosed in older adolescents. This general class of schizoid disorders is discussed later. There was a tremendous increase in interest in Asperger's Disorder in the 1990s, particularly since it was included as a separate diagnostic category in the *DSM-IV* in 1994 (Bashe & Kirby, 2001; Klin, Volkmar, & Sparrow, 2000; Myles & Simpson, 1998). There seemed to have been a significant increase in the number of diagnosed cases due to this category, which was either due to increased awareness or true increased prevalence.

Rett's Disorder A very rare condition, the most "essential feature of Rett's Disorder is the development of specific deficits following a period of normal functioning after birth" (APA, 1994, p. 71). These deficits include deceleration of head growth between the ages of five and 48 months, loss of previously acquired hand skills between five and 30 months, loss of social engagement early in the course of the disorder, poor motor coordination, and severe impairments in expressive and receptive language development (a major defining characteristic), coupled with severe psychomotor retardation. This is a very low-incidence disorder that has been reported only in girls. Exact prevalence estimates are unknown, but Rett's Disorder seems to occur much less frequently than autism. In most cases, affected individuals make some modest developmental gains, but the various difficulties they encounter tend to remain throughout their life span. Given that Rett's Disorder is no longer part of the *DSM*, there could be instances when individuals meet criteria for Autism Spectrum Disorder and have Rett's Disorder. In these cases, this could be specified as Autism Spectrum Disorder "associated with a known medical or genetic condition or environmental factor."

Childhood Disintegrative Disorder This pervasive developmental disorder is characterized by marked regression in several areas of functioning, after a period of two or more years of apparently normal development. With this disorder, the child shows a substantial loss of functioning in two or more of the following areas: expressive or receptive language, social skills or adaptive behavior, bowel or bladder control, play, or motor skills.

Children who develop Childhood Disintegrative Disorder typically exhibit some of the social, communication, and behavior features associated with autism. It is usually accompanied by severe mental intellectual impairment. Prevalence data for this disorder are limited. It does seem to be rare (occurring much less frequently than autism), however, and is probably more common among boys. The duration of the disorder is lifelong in most cases. Again, using *DSM-5* criteria, individuals may still be diagnosed with Autism Spectrum Disorder and Childhood Disintegrative Disorder would be identified as a specifier.

Assessment

Assessment of Autism Spectrum Disorder necessarily relies heavily on direct behavioral observation; clinical interviews with parents, caretakers, and teachers; and, in some instances, specialized behavior rating scales. In addition to behavioral and psychological assessment data, it is crucial to recognize that separate medical assessments of children with serious developmental disorders should be conducted by qualified behavioral pediatricians or specialists. With the exception of children and adolescents having adequate language and intellectual abilities, direct interviews with the child, self-report instruments, and sociometric techniques typically are not very relevant or useful for this class of problems. Most of the general-purpose behavior rating scales discussed in Chapter 5 would be useful for initial screening of Autism Spectrum Disorder symptoms. These general-purpose rating scales rarely contain more than a handful of items, however, that are directly relevant to the low-frequency problem behaviors that occur with Autism Spectrum Disorder.

Several behavioral observation coding systems, behavior rating scales, and structured interview schedules have been developed specifically for use in the assessment of autism, and several of them have been documented widely through research efforts. Brief reviews of several of these instruments are presented in this section.

The Autism Diagnostic Observation Schedule (ADOS) The Autism Diagnostic Observation Schedule (ADOS; Lord et al., 1989) is a standardized protocol for the observation of social and communicative behaviors that typically are associated with autism in children. The ADOS differs from most other standardized observation schedules in that it is interactive, requiring the observer to engage with the target child as an experimenter or participant on several standardized tasks that are designed to yield a better qualitative analysis of autistic behaviors than would be possible through simple observation and coding. The ADOS does not focus as much on specific autistic-type behaviors as some other observation schedules, but was designed to "facilitate observation of social and communicative features specific to autism rather than those accounted for or exacerbated by severe mental retardation" (Lord et al., 1989, p. 187). Through its interactive nature, emphasis on examiner behavior, and qualitative focus, the ADOS allows for assessment of some of the crucial features of autism that may distinguish the disorder from other severe developmental disorders.

The ADOS consists of eight tasks that are presented to the subject by the observer within a 20- to 30-minute timeframe. Two sets of materials are required for most tasks (a puzzle or pegboard and a set of familiar and unusual miniature figures), and the content and specific demands of these tasks can vary according to the age and developmental level of the subject. The eight tasks include construction, unstructured presentation of toys, drawing, demonstration, a poster task, a book task, conversation, and socioemotional questions. Within these tasks, 11 strands of target behaviors are coded, and general ratings are made after the interaction or observation according to a 3-point qualitative severity scale in four different areas: reciprocal social interaction, communication/language, stereotyped/restricted behaviors, and mood and nonspecific abnormal behaviors. Reliability and validity data presented by the authors of the ADOS are encouraging and have shown that the observation has adequate inter-rater and test–retest reliability and discriminant validity between autistic subjects and subjects with and without other types of developmental disabilities. Although the ADOS was developed as a research tool and is experimental, it seems to be an observational method that may provide a rich array of information on the qualitative aspects of autism.

The ADOS-2 (Lord et al., 2012) is similar to the original in that it includes a semistructured and standardized approach to the assessment of Autism Spectrum Disorder. This new version includes five modules, which vary based on the child's age and verbal fluency. The newest module is the Toddler Module and can be used with children aged 12 to 30 months, who do not fluently speak in phrases. Children are only administered one module, which takes about one hour. The ADOS-2 also includes updated algorithms that allow one to identify the range of concern (Toddler Module) or descriptive classifications (Modules 1–4) such as *Autism*, *Autism Spectrum*, or *Non-Spectrum*. These new algorithms have established predictive validity and increase the sensitivity of classification descriptions for many of the modules (Gotham et al., 2008). The ability to calculate a Comparison Score is also available with this version, which means that one will be able to understand how a child's scores compare to those of other children who are the same age, have similar language patterns, and already have been diagnosed with Autism Spectrum Disorder. This new version of the ADOS is often considered as a "gold standard" for the assessment of Autism Spectrum Disorder.

The Autism Diagnostic Interview (ADI) The Autism Diagnostic Interview (ADI) (Le Couteur et al., 1989) is a standardized structured interview schedule designed to assess the crucial characteristics of Autistic Disorder and to differentiate pervasive developmental disorders from other developmental disorders such as mental retardation. The ADI was developed for use by highly trained clinicians in conducting interviews with the principal caregivers of children who are at least five years old, with a mental age of at least two years. The ADI is considered to be an investigator-based rather than a respondent-based interview because it requires the interviewer to be familiar with the conceptual distinctions of pervasive developmental disorders and to actively structure the interview probes by providing examples and getting the interviewees to provide highly detailed qualitative information rather than simple yes/no responses.

The basic interviewing task is to obtain detailed descriptions of the actual behavior of the target subject in three general areas: reciprocal social interaction; communication and language; and repetitive, restricted, and stereotyped behaviors. The caregiver descriptions are scored according to a scale ranging from 0 to 3, where a score of 0 indicates the specified behavior is not present and 3 indicates that the behavior is present to a severe degree. Individual item scores are converted into three area scores and a total score, based on a scoring algorithm that was devised using the World Health Organization ICD-10 diagnostic criteria for autism. The length of time required for the interview varies according to the skill of the examiner and the amount of information provided by the caregiver, but the developers of the ADI note that test interviews conducted during initial research tended to last two to three hours.

Reliability and validity research reported by the authors of the ADI indicate strong psychometric properties. The ADI item, area, and total scores have been shown to have good reliability (generally in the 0.70 range), based on agreement between raters from an experiment with 32 videotaped interviews that were scored by four independent raters. The ADI area scores, total scores, and most individual item scores have been shown to differentiate between subjects with autism and subjects with intellectual disabilities to a significant degree, which indicates that the instrument is sensitive to qualitative differences in developmental problem patterns. The ADI item scores and many of the individual items also were found to have high sensitivity and specificity properties in differentially diagnosing autism and mental retardation. It should be assumed that the ADI would easily differentiate between autism and the milder developmental disorders (e.g., developmental delays and routine learning disabilities).

In sum, although there are few standardized interviews for autism, the ADI represents a strong preliminary step in this area. The ADI-R (Rutter, LeCouteur, & Lord, 2003) is the current available version and has been revised to be consistent with the *DSM-IV*. This newest version is shorter than the original and is appropriate for children with a mental age of 18 months and can be used through adulthood. It should be considered seriously by researchers conducting epidemiological studies and by clinicians who desire a structured method of obtaining information on autism from caregivers. Proper use of the ADI-R requires intensive training of interviewers and a considerable amount of time in administering the interview, so potential users should consider these constraints. It will be interesting to see if an updated version of the ADI-R, aligned with *DSM-5*, becomes available.

The Childhood Autism Rating Scale, Second Edition (CARS-2) The Childhood Autism Rating Scale, Second Edition (CARS-2) (Schopler, Van Bourgondien, Wellman & Love, 2010) consists of two brief (15-items) behavior rating scales designed to identify children with Autistic Disorder (CARS2-SF: Standard Form) and High-Functioning Autism or Asperger's Disorder (CARS2-HF: High-Functioning Form) and to distinguish them from children with other types of developmental disorders. They were designed to be completed by professionals who work with children in educational, medical, or mental health settings and can be used with children aged two and older. The behaviors on the CARS-2 are rated according to frequency, intensity, peculiarity, and duration. The item content of the CARS-2 is based on a broad view of autism (not just Autistic Disorder) from multiple diagnostic systems, including the *DSM*. The ratings may be based on a direct observation of child behavior within a given setting, a review of other relevant assessment data, or impressions of observations over time. After the child has been rated on each item on the standard form, a total score is obtained, and a percentile rank is given according to a normative sample of 1,034 children with Autism Spectrum Disorder. The CARS2-HF, new with this latest revision of the CARS-2, applies specifically to children aged six and older with more fluent verbal skills, and an IQ of 80 or higher. This form is based on a developmental sample of 994 children and assesses skills in the domains of Social–Emotional Understanding, Emotional Expression and Regulation of Emotions, Object Use in Play, Adaptation to Change/Restricted Interests, Fear or Anxiety, and Thinking/Cognitive Integration Skills. Unique to the CARS-2 is a Questionnaire for Parents or Caregivers (CARS-2-QPC). While this form does not derive quantitative data, it enables the family to provide important qualitative data that can help frame the results of the other forms.

In a recent review of the CARS-2 (Vaughan, 2011), technical adequacy data were reported. Internal consistency coefficients for the CARS2-ST (0.93) and the CARS-HF (0.96) were strong. The CARS-ST has been found to distinguish children with autism from children without autism, and the CARS-HF has similarly been found to distinguish children with high-functioning autism from children without. Concurrent validity data also suggest that both forms correlate moderately with the original ADOS (Lord et al., 1989).

In sum, the CARS-2 will likely follow its predecessor and become one of the most widely used and proven assessment instruments for autism. It has sound technical properties, is easy to use, and is one of the best available rating scales for screening and assessing children who exhibit symptoms of autism.

The Gilliam Autism Rating Scale, Third Edition (GARS-3) The Gilliam Autism Rating Scale, Third Edition (GARS-3) (Gilliam, 2013), is a recently published revision and expansion of the original two Gilliam Autism Rating Scales (Gilliam, 1995, 2006), which proved to be a very popular and widely accepted assessment tool. The GARS-3 is a behavior rating scale designed for use by teachers, parents, and professionals in identifying and diagnosing autism in individuals ages three to 22. The GARS-3 is aligned with the *DSM-5* criteria for Autism Spectrum Disorder and includes 56 items. There are six subscales including Restrictive/Repetitive Behaviors, Social Interaction, Social Communication, Emotional Responses, Cognitive Style, and Maladaptive Speech.

New normative data were collected for this edition in 2010 and 2011 and included 1,859 youth. Psychometric properties appear strong with internal consistency coefficients exceeding 0.85 for the subscales and 0.93 for the Autism Indexes. Inter-rater reliability ranged from 0.80 to 0.84, and the GARS-3 is correlated with other measures that target symptoms of autism. This measure is able to discriminate children with Autism Spectrum Disorder from those without.

In sum, the GARS-3 may be a good choice as a brief screening measure for assessing and screening children, adolescents, and young adults who have symptoms of autism. It has adequate technical properties, is easy to use, and seems to be valid for the purposes for which it was developed.

The Assessment of Basic Learning and Language Skills-Revised (ABLLS-R) The Assessment of Basic Learning and Language Skills-Revised (ABLLS-R) (Partington, 2006) is a criterion-based measure that is becoming more established, particularly in the fields of behavior analysis, developmental disabilities, and autism. This measure aims to assess the early learning, language, and functional skills of children and can be used to evaluate a child's current level of performance and progress made throughout an instructional program. The measure includes 544 items that are split across 25 domains such as Cooperation and Reinforcer Effectiveness, Visual Performance, Receptive Language, Vocal Imitation, Requests, Play and Leisure, Group Instruction, etc. In each domain, the beginning items are reflective of the simplest understanding of a skill area and become increasingly difficult with the introduction of each consecutive item. This measure includes a manual and a protocol book that outlines the procedures, tasks and materials needed to administer each item. The protocol book also includes a graph for each domain, so that those who are administering the assessment or who are charged with developing and implementing instruction can easily view the child's current skill level and logical next objective for instruction. Currently, there is also a web-based version of this graph (WebABLLS 2.0). Through this web-based application, consumers can enter data and track progress easily.

The manual for the ABLLS-R does not identify a specific age range for its use, and it can take a significant amount of time to administer; however, it is one of the few measures available allowing practitioners to easily link assessment data to intervention for children with developmental disabilities and autism. Limited research on the efficacy of ABLLS-R use is available at this time. I hope that research in this area develops, as this tool appears to be comprehensive and my clinical use of it suggests that it is a promising approach.

SCHIZOID DISORDERS

Description

As has previously been discussed, Quay's (1986a) exploratory attempt at developing a multivariate behavioral dimensions taxonomy for severe behavior disorders identified a classification category he labeled as schizoid–unresponsive (see Table 12.1). The exact meaning of the term *schizoid*, which was first coined by Asperger in the 1940s, is not precise. It generally is thought of as indicating "schizophrenic-like" (but not quite schizophrenic) symptoms. The term *unresponsive* was used by Quay to indicate not only detached and aloof peer relations, but also a general pattern of alienation and social withdrawal. These terms describe a cluster of behavioral, social, and emotional problems that have some things in common with autism and schizophrenia, but are generally subtler and less debilitating. Wolf (1989) noted that a perplexing number of terms have been used to describe the so-called schizoid disorders over the years, which has not helped to clarify the confusion that generally exists regarding them. Children and adolescents who exhibit the characteristics found in the schizoid–unresponsive category may not meet the diagnostic criteria for Autism Spectrum Disorder or Psychotic Disorders, but are likely to exhibit the following core characteristics: (1) solitariness; (2) impaired empathy and emotional detachment; (3) increased sensitivity (to external stimuli); (4) a rigid mental set; and (5) an odd or unusual way of communicating (Wolf, 1989).

Quay (1986a) suggested that the schizoid–unresponsive dimension may be the extreme of the personality style commonly referred to as *introversion*. As was discussed previously, this schizoid–unresponsive dimension bears some similarity to the characteristics of Asperger's Disorder. It also may be a counterpart of the *DSM-5* categories of Schizoid Personality Disorder and Schizotypal Personality Disorder. These two personality disorders are typified by various degrees and manifestations of social withdrawal, unresponsiveness, and peculiar or odd thought and behavior patterns. It would be highly unusual to diagnose a child with a personality disorder, but it is certainly possible by late adolescence.

The *DSM-5* states that the essential feature of Schizoid Personality Disorder "is a pervasive pattern of detachment from social relationships and a restricted range of expression of emotions in interpersonal settings" (APA, 2013). Individuals who fit this diagnostic picture do not desire or enjoy close social relationships, including familial relationships. They exhibit a highly restricted range of emotional behavior and come across to others as being cold and aloof. This disorder is one of the least researched within the *DSM* (Hummelen, Pedersen, Wilberg, & Karterud, 2015). Schizotypal Personality

Disorder is described as "a pervasive pattern of social and interpersonal deficits marked by acute discomfort with, and reduced capacity for, close relationships, as well as by cognitive or perceptual distortions and eccentricities of behavior" (APA, 2013). Although there is some common ground in the symptoms of these two personality disorders, there is a clear line of demarcation for differential diagnosis: Schizoid Personality Disorder does not include peculiarities of thought, behavior, and speech, whereas Schizotypal Personality Disorder is not so much characterized by the extreme voluntary social detachment of the former disorder.

Little is known about the prevalence of these disorders in the general population. The *DSM-5* states that the prevalence of both conditions is low. Some have estimated that Schizotypal Personality Disorder is at about a 4% prevalence with higher rates in men than in women (Rosell, Futterman, McMaster, & Siever, 2014). Although we can assume that these disorders are rare among adolescents, there is no benchmark to go by for determining how often they can be expected. Part of the problem in conducting an epidemiological study in this area is that it is difficult to define the boundaries between normal variations of personality and psychopathology (Wolf, 1989) and it can also be difficult to differentiate these disorders from high-functioning autism.

The essential features of these disorders most likely are present during early childhood, but differential diagnosis at this stage is difficult, given the overlapping symptoms that exist between them and several of the developmental disorders. Onset of the schizoid disorders tends to be clearest and well defined in middle childhood (Wolf, 1989).

There is no clear evidence at present as to the etiology of the schizoid disorders, but some interesting speculations have been offered. One prominent theory contends that a genetic link between the schizoid disorders and schizophrenia should be considered because about half of individuals with schizophrenia displayed schizoid characteristics before the onset of psychosis, children of schizophrenics often exhibit schizoid-like characteristics, and parents of children with schizoid disorders often exhibit similar behaviors (Blueler, 1978; Erlenmeyer-Kimling, Kestenbaum, Bird, & Hildoff, 1984; Wolf, 1989). Another theory is based on evidence that children who are at the highest risk for developing schizoid disorders may have suffered substantial neglect during early and middle childhood (Lieberz, 1989).

Based on Wolf and Chick's (1980) ten-year follow-up study of children with schizoid disorders, there is evidence that the essential features of the schizoid disorders carry on into adult life. Further evidence from Wolf's (1989) follow-up research with this cohort indicated that the intellectual ability of individuals with the disorder may be a crucial variable in the quality of their social adaptation over time:

> Our tentative impression is that the more gifted people are now less solitary, some having married, but their basic personality characteristics remain distinct. On the other hand, some of the less able and withdrawn people, while often working satisfactorily, remain single and excessively dependent on their families.
>
> (Wolf, 1989, p. 223)

Aside from this information, little is known about the long-term implications of the schizoid disorders. It is probably prudent to assume that children and adolescents who exhibit these characteristics to the point where their social and personal judgment is severely impaired will continue these struggles to some extent during adult life.

Assessment

Assessment of the broad constellation of problems subsumed under the schizoid–unresponsive behavioral dimension is a difficult challenge. The confusion in terminology, overlapping symptoms among a few *DSM-5* categories, and lack of substantial prevalence data all combine to create a situation in which there is little standard practice for assessment. Direct observation of behavior and general behavior rating scales likely would be useful in identifying patterns of severe social disengagement and peculiar thought or behavior patterns. The Child Behavior Checklist and Teacher's Report Form, in particular, have several items pertinent to these areas. Clinical interviewing likely would be helpful, not only in understanding the self-perceptions of the child, but also in allowing the clinician to observe social behavior of the client under standardized conditions. For youth who have sufficient cognitive maturity and reading ability (i.e., at least a sixth-grade level), certain adolescent self-report instruments may be helpful in screening for schizoid-like characteristics. Because of the breadth and depth of items and subscales relevant to clinical maladjustment in adolescents, the MMPI-A is recommended in this regard. Although neither one of these instruments contains specific scales developed to identify patterns of responding associated with the schizoid–unresponsive dimensions, it is possible that certain profile configurations or more than one scale may be helpful in generating or verifying hypotheses regarding these problems. The more recently developed Adolescent Psychopathology Scale (APS) seems to be particularly promising for assessing the symptoms of the schizoid disorders and associated personality disorders in adolescents. The APS includes five personality disorder scales (consisting of eight to 13 items each), including two that are specifically relevant here: an Avoidant Personality Disorder scale (consisting of ten items that measure social inhibition, shyness, feelings of inadequacy, and oversensitivity) and a Schizotypal Personality Disorder scale (consisting of 13 items that measure paranoid thoughts, odd beliefs and perceptions and the perception that one is behaving in a way that is "different" or inappropriate). Although it is a scale with less accumulated research evidence at present than the Millon Adolescent Clinical Inventory or MMPI-A, the APS seems to have all the qualities and characteristics to be an excellent choice for self-report assessment of youth who exhibit symptoms consistent with the schizoid disorders.

TIC DISORDERS

By definition, tic disorders are *disorders of movement*. Tics are defined as "a sudden, rapid, recurrent, nonrhythmic, stereotyped motor movement or vocalization" (APA, 1994, p. 100). Tics are often described by the affected person as urges that are very hard to control. However, many individuals find that they are able to suppress tic vocalization and/or movements for a time, only to experience a deluge of tic expression afterwards. All types of tics may be worsened by stress. Tic disorders are considered to have a neurological basis and should not be confused as having a behavioral, social, or emotional origin, despite the co-occurrence of these problems and worsening of tics when an individual is under stress. One specific tic disorder, Tourette's Disorder, is noteworthy in this regard, however, because it is often accompanied by behavioral and social adjustment difficulties and often co-occurs with disorders in these areas.

Description of Tourette's Disorder/Tourette Syndrome

Tourette's Disorder (otherwise known as Tourette Syndrome) is characterized by multiple motor tics and one or more vocal tics. The motor tics often involve the head and may involve other parts of the body such as the torso and limbs. Eye tics, such as blinking, eye rolling, or wide eye opening, are a common first motor tic symptom of Tourette's (Sallee & Spratt, 1998). The vocal tics that accompany Tourette's Disorder may include a variety of words and sounds, such as clicking noises, grunts, yelps, barks, sniffs, snorts, or coughs. One specific vocal tic that Tourette's has been associated with is *coprolalia*, which involves the seemingly uncontrollable uttering of obscenities. This unusual tic has become inaccurately associated among the public and some less astute professionals as a hallmark characteristic of Tourette's, perhaps because it is such an unusual and attention-getting activity. In reality, only a small percentage of individuals with Tourette's (perhaps 10%, according to Sallee and Spratt) exhibit coprolalia.

The average age of first onset for Tourette's Disorder is 8.1 years, and by definition, onset is always before age 18. The symptoms of this disorder are often misunderstood or attributed to other problems. About 0.19% of children in the U.S. are diagnosed with Tourette's Disorder. Consistently, this disorder is three times more common in boys than in girls. Although the duration of Tourette's is usually lifelong, it is common for the frequency, severity, and variability of symptoms to diminish during adolescence and early adulthood. In some cases, the symptoms disappear entirely (Sallee & Spratt, 1998). The etiology of Tourette's Disorder is not specifically understood at this time but is widely assumed to have a biological or genetic component (APA, 1994).

Perhaps the most relevant aspect of Tourette's Disorder for this book is that it frequently is accompanied by co-occurring behavioral disorders and social–emotional problems. According to the *DSM-5*, obsessive–compulsive behavior is the most common associated feature. Other common co-occurring symptoms include hyperactivity, distractibility, impulsivity, social discomfort, shame, extreme self-consciousness, and depression. As a result, it is not unusual for individuals with Tourette's to experience problems in academic, social, or occupational functioning. The major defining characteristics and related features of Tourette's Disorder are summarized in Table 12.5.

Table 12.5 Major characteristics and associated features of Tourette's Disorder

Multiple motor tics, often involving the head, upper body, and limbs
Vocal tics, which may vary considerably from person to person in presentation
Tics are chronic, occurring nearly daily in some form
Marked disturbance or impairment in adjustment and functioning
Onset before age 18, with median onset at age seven
1.5 to 3 times more prevalent in males than in females
Frequently accompanied by symptoms associated with attention deficit hyperactivity disorder and obsessive–compulsive disorder, with high rates of co-occurrence among these disorders
Frequently accompanied by social discomfort, self-consciousness, shame, and depressed mood
Frequently misdiagnosed or confused with other disorders
Frequently not diagnosed for several years after initial onset

Assessment

Assessment and accurate diagnosis of Tourette's Disorder can be a difficult proposition because some of the co-occurring symptoms may lead the clinician down the wrong path and because the core tic symptoms tend to be transient. Specific tic symptoms of Tourette's may not be noted directly through behavioral observation or in a clinical interview situation in most cases (Sallee & Spratt, 1998). Because of these difficulties, direct behavioral observation is often challenging and sometimes uninformative. General problem behavior rating scales may be useful for initial screening purposes but typically do not include enough specificity for accurate assessment of Tourette's symptoms.

It is crucial that assessment of children suspected of having Tourette's Disorder involve extensive clinical interviewing with the referred child or adolescent and parents. The interview should include an extensive developmental history, family history, and questions regarding specific and associated behavioral problems across various situations and settings. A referral for neurological or related medical examination of children suspected of having Tourette's Disorder may be helpful or even necessary, but it should be understood that "results of the neurological exam of patients with primary [Tourette's Disorder] are usually unremarkable with no focal or lateralizing signs" (Sallee & Spratt, 1998, p. 343).

Some assessment instruments specific to evaluation of Tourette's Disorder have been developed and reported in the literature. The Tourette's Syndrome Questionnaire (Jagger et al., 1982) is an interview instrument designed to obtain historical information regarding the development of tic symptoms and associated features of Tourette's. The Tourette's Syndrome Symptom Checklist (D. J. Cohen, Leckman, & Shaywitz, 1984) is a rating scale designed to be used on a daily and weekly basis to evaluate the presence and disruptiveness of major Tourette's characteristics. The Yale Global Tic Severity Scale (Leckman et al., 1989) is a semistructured interview instrument designed to provide an evaluation of the number, frequency, intensity, complexity, and interference of various Tourette's symptoms. These instruments are not of the commercially published, nationally norm-referenced variety, and the various citations in the research literature should be consulted for more information regarding their appropriate uses. Additionally, Kurlan (2010) reports that tic disorders are often diagnosed clinically and that it takes skill and expertise to identify them appropriately, as clients can often suppress tics during interviews but be more likely to engage in tic behaviors prior to entering or following leaving the interview context.

SCHIZOPHRENIA SPECTRUM AND OTHER PSYCHOTIC DISORDERS

The *DSM-5* diagnostic categories presented in Table 12.2 indicate that there are numerous classification categories of schizophrenia and related psychotic disorders. These categories have been developed almost exclusively based on research and clinical efforts with adults, however, and are not generally descriptive of psychotic disorders that occur among children and early adolescents. While schizophrenia often develops in late adolescence and into adulthood, early-onset schizophrenia can occur prior to the age of 18 and childhood-onset prior to age 13 (Kuniyoshi & McClellan, 2014). This section provides some general descriptive information on psychotic disorders of childhood and early adolescence, and recommendations and guidelines for conducting effective assessments of such youth.

Description

The term *psychosis* does not have an exact or universal meaning but generally is used to indicate a break with reality or a severe impairment of one's sense of reality and ability to perceive things and function as most other persons do. The terms *childhood psychosis* and *childhood schizophrenia* were used earlier in the twentieth century to indicate what we now refer to as Autism Spectrum Disorder, but the modern common understanding of these terms generally precludes autism. A defining feature of psychotic disorders is that the advent of the disorder causes a lowering or impairment of functioning from a previous level. Autism is considered to be a developmental disorder, in which the feature characteristics involve severe limitations in the normal course of development, whereas schizophrenia normally occurs after the early childhood developmental period and brings with it a loss of functioning.

The major diagnostic picture of schizophrenia includes the following symptoms: delusions of thought, prominent and lasting hallucinations, incoherence or a marked loosening of associations, catatonic behavior (severe restriction of motor activity that sometimes alternates with wild hyperactivity), and flat or grossly inappropriate affect. The delusions of thought in schizophrenia are typically bizarre and implausible, and hallucinations characteristically are pronounced, such as hearing voices for long periods. Along with these severe disturbances of perception, thought, and affect, a severe decline in personal and social functioning typically occurs, which might include significantly poor personal hygiene, inability to function effectively at school or work, and a severe impairment in social relationships. Using the *DSM* system, these characteristic symptoms must be present on a continuous basis for at least six months for a diagnosis to be made. Individuals with schizophrenia tend to display markedly peculiar behavior, such as talking to themselves in public, collecting garbage, and hoarding food or items that appear to be of little value. Schizophrenia often is accompanied by strange beliefs or magical thinking not in line with the cultural standard; the afflicted person might believe that their behavior is being controlled by another person or force, or that he or she has the power of clairvoyance.

Some characteristics of schizophrenia can be brought on by other conditions, such as severe affective disorders or the use of psychoactive substances. A true diagnosis of schizophrenia implies that the symptoms are pervasive and long-lasting, however, and not brought on by a temporary biochemical or affective change. Although the *DSM-5* criteria are the best working guidelines for schizophrenia currently available, it is important to consider that they may not always accurately describe the development of the disorder during childhood. Cantor (1987, 1989) noted that the *DSM* symptoms may not always be the most prominent features of schizophrenia that develops during childhood and that the childhood diagnostic picture is often complicated and clouded. Tolbert (1996) noted that when psychotic disorders are manifest in children, they are frequently accompanied by symptoms that are not always seen in adults. Some of these hallmark characteristics of childhood psychosis are presented in Table 12.6.

Because the trademark *DSM* symptoms of schizophrenia are rare before puberty, accurate prevalence estimates with children have been difficult to determine. For example, the child psychiatry division of the National Institute of Health has spent the last 20 years screening over 3,000 cases, with just 105 children meeting criteria for schizophrenia before the age of 12 (Addington & Rapoport, 2009). Reviews of evidence from the 1990s indicate, however, that the prevalence figure may be lower, closer to one in 10,000 children, and that only 0.1% to 1% of all cases of schizophrenia are manifest before age ten and only 4% before age 15 (Tolbert, 1996). It should be noted however, that studies of prevalence of schizophrenia across the lifespan result in widely variable estimates (El-Missiry et al., 2011), but that the CDC and NIMH both suggest a 1.1% 12-month prevalence in adults

Table 12.6 Behavioral, emotional, and cognitive symptoms associated with schizophrenia and related psychotic disorders in children

Severe speech problems
Difficulty distinguishing between dreams and reality
Hallucinations (visual and auditory)
Vivid and often bizarre ideas and thoughts
Confused thinking
Diminished interest in normal activities
Severe moodiness
Odd or peculiar behavior
Lack of inhibition
Believes that someone is "out to get" him or her
Behaves like a much younger child
Severe fears or anxiety
Confuses television programs with reality
Significant peer problems, difficulty making and keeping friends

in the U.S. With adults and older adolescents, schizophrenia tends to occur in similar numbers with males and females. With the preadolescent population (up to about age 14), the equal gender balance does not hold true, with males being diagnosed more often.

The cause of schizophrenia has been a controversial topic for centuries; explanations have run the gamut from demon possession to a weak constitution to poor parenting. In more recent years, a plethora of research has strongly suggested that schizophrenia has a biochemical basis. The neurotransmitter dopamine has been implicated as a crucial variable because drugs that block dopamine receptor sites tend to be highly effective at controlling the more severe symptoms of schizophrenia, such as delusions and hallucinations. Family studies and investigations of adoption conducted in the United States and Europe over the past several decades have provided additional evidence for a genetic explanation of schizophrenia, because the degree of genetic relatedness to an individual with schizophrenia is a strong factor in predicting the occurrence of the disorder (Gottesman, 1991). In cases in which one individual in a set of twins develops schizophrenia, the probability is almost four times greater that the other twin will develop the disorder when the twins are identical rather than fraternal. Although biochemical–genetic factors are prominent in explaining etiology, behavioral and environmental factors are likely to interact with the person variables to increase or decrease the likelihood of schizophrenia; if two individuals have an equal biochemical–genetic predisposition for developing the disorder, the individual with a dramatically higher level of psychosocial distress may ultimately be more likely to exhibit the symptoms.

The prognosis for children and adolescents who develop schizophrenia is variable and seems to hinge on such factors as age level, severity of symptoms, and family history. In his review on childhood psychoses, Tolbert (1996) stated that prognosis is poorest when the onset of the disorder occurs before age ten to 14 and for youth with a family history of psychotic disorders, and only about 25% of patients with adolescent-onset schizophrenia achieve a partial remission of symptoms. There seems to be wide variability in how schizophrenia affects individuals over the life span, and the availability of social support, medical care, and mental health services may be crucial factors in determining how debilitating the disorder becomes.

Assessment

Children and adolescents with schizophrenia and other psychotic disorders typically experience characteristic private or internal events (such as various disorders of thought and sensation) and exhibit characteristic overt and easily observed behaviors (such as psychomotor agitation or retardation, highly unusual verbal behavior, and wildly inappropriate social behavior). The assessment design for these youth must be planned carefully and must include techniques and instruments designed to evaluate overt and covert symptoms. In addition to the behavioral–psychological types of assessment covered in this text, assessment of children and adolescents with schizophrenia and other psychotic disorders should include appropriate medical assessment data, such as a physical examination, neurologic examination, and laboratory studies (Tolbert, 1996).

Behavioral Observation Behavioral observation generally proves to be valuable in assessing children and adolescents with psychotic disorders. Effective observational systems for this purpose require that the observation domain is defined carefully and that appropriate coding strategies are used. There are some specific problems with behavioral observation assessment that should be considered, however. Many of the characteristic problem behaviors in this domain are not overt or blatant, and they may be difficult to assess adequately with direct behavioral observation. For example, hallucinations, delusions, odd thought processes, and a desire to avoid other persons may be extremely difficult to observe unless they also are accompanied by overt behavioral signals, such as language, psychomotor agitation with explanatory language signs, or obvious social withdrawal. To design an effective observational system for assessing the characteristics of psychotic disorders, one must focus on the more overt aspects, operationally define them so that they can be observed and coded without question, and defer the assessment of the more internal or covert characteristics of the disorders to other methods (i.e., interviews, self-report, or rating scales completed by individuals who have observed the child over a long period).

Behavior Rating Scales Some of the general problem behavior rating scales reviewed in Chapter 5 may be helpful as screening tools. Specifically, the Child Behavior Checklist (CBCL) seems to be useful for initial screening of childhood psychotic disorders. The CBCL includes the Thought Problems cross-informant scale, which contains items pertinent to hallucinations, sensory distortions, and bizarre behaviors. The CBCL and other ASEBA instruments have shown sensitivity in discriminating among youth with psychotic disorders and youth with other types of disorders. Endorsement of items contributing to the Thought Problems scale can also be followed up with interview questions that probe these specific areas.

The Symptom Scale is an example of an experimental rating scale (or checklist) designed specifically for use in assessing the symptoms of schizophrenia in children and young adolescents (Cantor, 1987, 1989; Cantor, Pearce, Pezzot-Pearce, & Evans, 1981). This instrument consists of 18 checklist-style descriptors that were found through a review of the literature to be associated with schizophrenia in children and adolescents. Examples of these descriptors include "constricted affect," "perseveration," "inappropriate affect," "anxiety," "loose associations," "grimacing," and "incoherence." In one study, each of 54 children and adolescents with schizophrenia was rated by two clinical psychologists for the presence or absence of these 18 symptoms. The population was broken into three age groups: preschool ($N = 525$), latency ($N = 515$), and adolescent ($N = 514$). Most of the symptoms were found to be present in more than 50% of the subjects in each group, and a few of the symptoms were found to be present in more than 50% of the subjects in one or two groups, but three symptoms (clang associations, echolalia, and neologisms) were found to be present in less than 50% of the subjects in all three groups, indicating that they had relatively poor diagnostic validity. Although the Symptom Scale was not designed to be a norm-referenced diagnostic test, it may be useful in research or in validating behavioral characteristics of schizophrenia obtained from multiple assessment data. It is not commercially published and must be obtained by researching the references cited earlier in this section.

Clinical Interviews Most of the interview methods discussed in Chapter 6 can be used to some extent in assessing psychotic disorders. The specific choice of technique varies depending on the presenting problems exhibited by the referred child or adolescent; his or her age level, language capability, and social maturity; and the availability and cooperation of a parent or primary caregiver. The parent or caregiver behavioral interview is crucial if the child or adolescent is not capable of engaging in a traditional interview or if the referral necessitates the immediate development of a behavioral intervention plan. Traditional unstructured types of interviews with the child or adolescent may be of limited use in these cases but may provide some additional insights in cases in which psychotic features are emerging. Virtually any of the structured interview schedules reviewed elsewhere in this book are potentially useful in assessing youth with psychotic disorders. These structured interview schedules all include at least some items that are relevant to the severe behavioral and emotional disorders and include scoring algorithms that are designed to generate hypotheses about the existence of disorders from the *DSM*. An example of the utility of one of these structured interviews in assessing and diagnosing psychotic disorders is from research conducted by Haley, Fine, and Marriage (1988), who compared Diagnostic Interview Schedule for Children (DISC) data from psychiatrically hospitalized adolescents who were experiencing depression with or without psychosis symptoms. In this case, several strands of the DISC interview data were found to discriminate between the two groups because the subjects experiencing psychosis were more likely to have a history of sexual abuse, to have more serious depression, and to have more symptoms of hypomanic behavior than the subjects who were experiencing depression but no psychosis symptoms. Other research lending support to the use of structured interviews for assessing the severe disorders comes from an epidemiological study conducted by Cohen, O'Connor, Lewis, Velez, and Noemi (1987), who found that the DISC and Kiddie-Schedule for Affective Disorders (K-SADS) provided moderate to moderately high accuracy estimates of the prevalence of various *DSM* disorders. Another tool that still appears to be frequently used is the Positive and Negative Syndrome Scale (PANSS) (Kay, Fiszbein, & Opler, 1987). This is a well-operationalized structured interview tool that targets the presence and severity of positive and negative symptoms of schizophrenia. This tool includes a 35 to 45 minute interview and is followed by a rating of 30 symptoms on a 7-point Likert scale. While this tool, like many others in this section, was developed years ago, it still appears to be widely used.

A potential caution in conducting interviews for the assessment of psychosis involves making inquiries about low-frequency and bizarre symptoms, such as delusions, hallucinations, thought problems, and severe obsessive–compulsive behaviors. The clinician must word questions about these areas carefully and gauge the responses of children and parents with caution. Research by Breslau (1987) has helped to verify the notion that referred children and their parents may misunderstand structured interview questions about psychotic behavior and related characteristics and may provide answers that lead to high false positive errors. This research found that subjects often misunderstand the intent of these types of questions, and when appropriate follow-up questioning is introduced, many of the positive responses to questions are recoded as negative responses. A child might respond positively to a question such as "Do you ever see things that no one else can see," when he or she is thinking about seeing unique shapes in cloud formations or wallpaper designs rather than any visual hallucinations. When questioning about "the bizarre," it is important to follow up on affirmative responses and to obtain specific examples.

Sociometric Techniques Although sociometric techniques tend to be difficult to implement for basic clinical assessment of specific children and adolescents, they have been shown to be effective in identifying youth with psychotic disorders and may be of interest to researchers. Of the 20 studies cited by McConnell and Odom (1986) as providing evidence of the predictive validity of sociometrics, three were designed specifically to test sociometric assessment with schizophrenic or similar severity populations (Bower, Shelhamer, & Daily, 1960; Kohn & Clausen, 1955; Pritchard & Graham, 1966). These and other studies have proved that sociometric techniques that are designed and implemented specifically for assessing and predicting psychotic disorders can be effective.

Self-Report Instruments Depending on the type and severity of presenting symptoms, self-report instruments range in usefulness from not useful at all to highly useful in assessing children and adolescents with psychotic characteristics. In cases of severe and active psychotic behavior, the most serious manifestations of these problems usually make the self-reflective tasks involved in a self-report instrument impossible. For emerging, less active, or residual cases of schizophrenia, however, self-report instruments may be of some use. Some of the items and cross-informant scales of the Youth Self-Report (YSR) seem to have some utility in the assessment of psychotic symptoms. The cross-informant Thought Problems scale of the YSR is potentially useful in this regard, containing some items that are highly congruent with some of the characteristics of psychotic behavior, such as hoarding behavior (not to be confused with the hoarding of objects that is sometimes observed in Obsessive–Compulsive Disorder), sensory distortions, and disordered thought processes. As is discussed in Chapter 8, the YSR should be used cautiously because it contains no controls to detect manipulation or faking, and some research has suggested that it may not effectively discriminate groups of children and adolescents with severe psychopathology (e.g., Thurber & Snow, 1990). Another important consideration in using the YSR is that unusual responses on some of the items on the Thought Problems scales should be followed up with additional questioning; they are not always indicative of psychopathology. For example, it is common for adolescent respondents to endorse an item such as "I hear things that nobody else seems to be able to hear" when they are simply thinking of a favorite song continually repeating in their mind or to endorse an item such as "I store up things I don't need" to indicate a normal activity such as collecting stickers or baseball cards.

The MMPI-A is probably the best-documented and best-validated self-report instrument for use in assessing some of the characteristics of psychotic behavior with adolescents. With the MMPI-A, screening and classification accuracy for severe disorders of youth can be improved greatly through carefully interpreting code types and understanding the meaning of absolute score levels on individual scales. For example, extremely high T scores on scale 8 (Schizophrenia) usually are not indicative of psychotic behavior but are commonly reflective of intense, acute situational distress. Extreme elevations (T scores of 75 or higher) on scale 6 (Paranoia) typically identify persons with a psychotic degree of paranoid symptoms, such as paranoid schizophrenia and individuals manifesting paranoid states. Certain two-point code types also may be indicative of the types of serious psychopathology associated with psychotic behavior, most notably 6–8/8–6 (Paranoia–Schizophrenia), 8–9/9–8 (Schizophrenia–Hypomania), and 4–8/8–4 (Psychopathic Deviate–Schizophrenia). The MMPI-A manual contains correlates of the various scales for the normative and the clinical samples, and some interesting differences between the two groups are found on items from several scales, including 4, 6, and 8.

In addition to the MMPI-A, the more recently developed APS seems to be potentially useful for self-report assessment of youth who exhibit or are beginning to develop the symptoms or characteristics of psychotic disorders. Although less is known about the validity of the APS than the MMPI-A at present regarding its use for this purpose, it clearly was designed to take into consideration psychotic symptoms of youth and has obvious content validity in this regard. Among 20 clinical disorder scales, the APS includes a 27-item Schizophrenia scale, which, as the name suggests, was developed specifically for screening and assessment of the symptoms of schizophrenia.

EATING DISORDERS

The essential feature of eating disorders is severe disturbances in eating behavior. Anorexia Nervosa, Bulimia Nervosa, and now Binge Eating Disorder, are the three most common types of eating disorders and the focus of this section. These are not considered to be problems that usually first exist during infancy and childhood, rather they typically have a late adolescent or early adult onset. However, school-based clinicians (particularly those working with secondary school populations) and community-based clinicians who work extensively with adolescents often find these disorders to exist in alarming numbers among their clientele and to cause significant problems for many adolescents and their families. Previous research has indicated that these disorders seem to occur disproportionately in females. This is less true with Binge Eating Disorder, and may actually not be as extreme as once was thought for the other disorders, particularly since study of eating disorders in males is not as lagging as it once was (Von Ranson & Wallace, 2014). They also were historically more likely to be observed in the Western industrialized nations than in other parts of the world and have increased substantially in prevalence since about the 1950s and 1960s (Foreyt & Mikhail, 1997; Von Ranson & Wallace, 2014; Williamson, Bentz, & Rabalais, 1998). The major characteristics and associated features of these latter two disorders are summarized in Table 12.7.

Some experts (e.g., W. M. Reynolds, 1992a, 1992b) have included eating disorders under the general domain of internalizing problems. Behavioral dimensions approaches to classifying child and adolescent psychopathology have not consistently identified a separate eating disorders sector within the internalizing domain, however, even though they do have many characteristics in common, such as covert maladaptive behaviors,

Table 12.7 Major characteristics and associated features of the primary eating disorders

Anorexia Nervosa
Low body weight
Significant disturbance in self-perception of shape/size of body
Often resulting menstrual irregularities
Includes food-restricting and binge eating/purging specifiers
Often co-occurs with depression, obsessive–compulsive disorder, and personality disorders
May result in menstrual problems, heart problems, biochemical imbalances 5% to 10% long-term mortality rate

Bulimia Nervosa
Binge eating episodes
Inappropriate compensatory strategies
Self-evaluation excessively influenced by perceptions of body shape/weight
Individuals are usually within normal weight range
Often accompanied by excessive shame and depressed mood
Often co-occurs with mood disorders, substance-related disorders, and anxiety symptoms
May result in dental problems and biochemical imbalances

Binge Eating Disorder
Binge eating episodes
Often associated with obesity
Less focus on evaluation of body shape/weight
Often co-occurs with anxiety, mood disorders, substance-related disorders

diminished self-esteem, and mood disturbances. This topic is addressed in this chapter rather than in Chapter 11.

There are other types of eating and feeding disturbances, including Pica, Rumination Disorder, and Avoidant/Restrictive Food Intake Disorder, that are considered to be first evident in infancy or early childhood. Nevertheless, these problems are not discussed in this text because they have an extremely low base rate and tend to be dealt with in more specialized settings and by highly focused professionals, such as in children's medical centers by pediatric psychologists. Readers who desire more details on these problems should consult more specialized texts or the pediatric/pediatric psychology literature.

Description

Anorexia Nervosa The *DSM-5* definition for Anorexia Nervosa has changed substantially. This continues to be a disorder in which individuals restrict their food intake, fear gaining weight, and experience disturbance in their perceptions of their bodies. The changes with the *DSM* regard the low weight criterion and are worded as individuals having "significantly low body weight" (APA, 2013, pp. 338–339) rather than "a refusal to maintain body weight at or above a minimally normal weight for age and height" (APA, 1994, p. 554). Further, there is no particular weight cut off and individuals no longer require amenorrhea as criteria for diagnosis. There are specifiers that allow diagnosticians to clarify individual presentations such as "restricting type" or "binge-eating/purging type" and that allow to identify severity indicators based on body mass index.

Anorexia Nervosa often co-occurs with depressive disorders, obsessive–compulsive characteristics, and personality disorders (Gaudio & DiCiommo, 2011; Williamson et al., 1998). Prevalence studies among adolescent girls and young women indicated that 0.3%

to 1% of the population within the United States meet full criteria for Anorexia Nervosa, and there are many other individuals who exhibit symptoms but do not meet the full criteria threshold (e.g., Swanson, Crow, Le Grange, Swendsen, & Merikangas, 2011). Theories of etiology have focused on possible biologic underpinnings, psychosocial explanations, and sociocultural pressures for thinness, particularly among females. According to data based on *DSM-IV* diagnoses, the mean age of onset for Anorexia Nervosa is 17 years, with possible bimodal peaks at ages 14 and 18. Clinicians working with children in middle school or junior high school should become familiar with the disorder. In addition to the often co-occurring psychological problems, there are serious physical effects of Anorexia Nervosa, including heart problems, fluid and electrolyte imbalances, and death.

Bulimia Nervosa Bulimia Nervosa is characterized by ongoing episodes of binge eating followed by engaging in some type of compensatory behavior such as self-induced vomiting, use of laxatives, fasting, etc. (APA, 2013). Additionally, individuals with this disorder tend to evaluate themselves excessively by their own perceptions of body shape and weight. For a diagnosis of Bulimia Nervosa, the binge eating and maladaptive compensatory behaviors must happen on average at least once a week for three months. By definition, binge eating occurs in a circumscribed period of time wherein the individual consumes a substantially larger amount of food (often sweet, high-calorie foods such as desserts) than is normal. These episodes of binge eating often are characterized by a frenzied psychological state, a feeling of being out of control, and sometimes even a dissociative sensation. Binge eating episodes often are brought on by depressed mood states, interpersonal problems, or extreme hunger that is a result of dietary restraint. *DSM-5* includes specifiers to help describe the severity of individuals' behavior in terms of the average number of episodes occurring per week.

In contrast to the physical size of individuals with Anorexia Nervosa, individuals with Bulimia Nervosa tend to be within normal weight ranges, although it is common for them to be slightly overweight or slightly underweight. The prevalence of this disorder among individuals living in industrialized nations has been estimated to range from 1% to 1.6%, with a typical onset during late adolescence or early adulthood (Swanson et al., 2011). Etiological theories of Bulimia are the same as those referred to for Anorexia Nervosa (Williamson et al., 1998). Depressed mood states and feelings of extreme shame often follow an episode of binge eating, and it has been shown that individuals with Bulimia Nervosa have an increased incidence of mood disorders and substance abuse and dependence than individuals in the general population. Frequent purging episodes may lead to fluid and electrolyte imbalances, metabolic problems, permanent damage to the teeth through erosion of dental enamel, and noticeably enlarged salivary glands.

Binge Eating Disorder Binge Eating Disorder is characterized by weekly binge eating episodes without the purging or compensatory behaviors observed in Bulimia. It is often associated with a loss of control. Binge Eating Disorder was diagnosed in the Eating Disorder Not Otherwise Specified category in the *DSM-IV*. In the *DSM-5*, it is listed as its own disorder and research on this disorder has rapidly expanded (Von Ranson & Wallace, 2014; Wonderlich, Gordon, Mitchell, Crosby, & Engel, 2009). Binge Eating Disorder is most often associated with obesity, but this relationship appears complex and in need of further study (Wonderlich et al., 2009). Like other eating disorders, this disorder appears to co-occur with anxiety, specific phobias, social phobia, mood disorders, and substance-related disorders. While this Binge Eating Disorder most often begins in early adulthood, it can be observed in children (Von Ranson & Wallace, 2014).

Assessment

Assessment of Anorexia Nervosa, Bulimia Nervosa, and Binge Eating Disorder is typically difficult through direct behavioral observation and informant-based behavior rating scales because the major behavioral characteristics of these disorders tend to be covert or done in secret (i.e., binge eating, self-induced vomiting) and because other major characteristics tend to involve self-perceptions. However, two important aspects of Anorexia Nervosa may be externally observable at times by individuals who are close to the affected person: food restriction and excessive weight loss. The most effective and widely used methods of assessment for these eating disorders are clinical interviewing and self-report instruments. Clinical interviewing should focus not only on the core aspects of the maladaptive eating and compensatory behaviors, but also on possible coexisting psychosocial problems, such as depression, anxiety, distorted thinking patterns, and obsessive–compulsive characteristics.

The most widely used self-report instrument in this area is probably the Eating Disorders Inventory-3 (EDI-3) (Garner, 2004). This 91-item revision includes several new features, such as a computerized scoring program, T score and percentile score conversion profiles, a new normative sample ranging in age from 13 to 53, a short form brief self-report checklist, and the inclusion of separate clinical and nonclinical norm samples. This latest version of the EDI promises to continue the prominence of this instrument as the standard assessment tool for eating disorders. The items focus on various core and ancillary characteristics of eating disorders and a four-page symptom checklist. Raw scores are converted to 12 empirically derived subscales, which are based on a large normative sample. Various comparison norms (e.g., high school students, college students) are also provided in the test manual. The Eating Disorders Inventory–3 is a revision of the original Eating Disorders Inventory–2 and Eating Disorders Inventory, which were two of the first objective self-report measures developed specifically for evaluating eating disorders. Combined, the three instruments are the most widely researched self-report instruments for assessing eating disorders, with nearly 300 published studies to date. The psychometric properties, including the diagnostic validity of the instrument, are shown in the test manual and in several of the numerous published studies.

In addition to the standard psychological assessment methods that may be useful for evaluation of youth with eating disorders, physical assessments may be necessary. Because of the physical problems that may accompany eating disorders, "a complete medical exam is recommended for all persons with an eating disorder" (Williamson et al., 1998, p. 300). Direct measurement of daily caloric intake and eating diaries are strategies in treating eating disorders.

LINKING ASSESSMENT TO INTERVENTION

Virtually all of the categories of assessment data obtained in evaluating Autism Spectrum Disorder, schizoid disorders, tic disorders, psychotic disorders, and eating disorders of children and adolescents that are discussed in this chapter have direct utility for diagnostic purposes. Whether the assessment data are useful in intervention planning and implementation for these problems depends, however, to a great extent on the specifics of the assessment data, the problem, and the type of intervention that is needed. The emerging technology of functional behavior assessment has been proved to be useful for linking assessment to intervention for youth with pervasive developmental disorders, and it is likely that further refinements in this technology will increase its utility further. There have been minimal applications of functional behavior assessment reported thus far for assessment of children and adolescents who exhibit personality disorders, psychotic symptoms, eating disorders, and other conditions discussed in this chapter.

The most widely used and documented interventions for Autism Spectrum Disorder at present are behavioral in nature and tend to focus on altering either behavioral deficits (i.e., lack of communication and poor eye contact) or behavioral excesses (i.e., stereotypical behaviors such as echolalia and spinning) that tend to compound the social consequences of the disorder. Kauffman (2000) noted that early and intensive behavioral interventions are especially crucial for successful treatment of pervasive developmental disorders and that the prognosis for future adjustment is much better when early interventions are successfully employed. Interventions employing behavioral techniques (e.g., applied behavior analysis) have also been found to be most effective (Wilczynski, 2009). Most of the assessment methods for gauging the characteristics of Autism Spectrum Disorder and its related counterparts that have been described in this chapter are useful in pinpointing specific behavioral excesses and deficits that are cause for concern, and the ABLLS-R, in particular, has some promise for linking assessment data to specific intervention targets.

The "schizoid" disorders and related personality and social problems are notoriously difficult to treat effectively. Part of the problem in linking assessment data to interventions in an effective manner in these cases is that the individuals involved are often resistant to treatment, particularly when the treatment involves establishing a trusting relationship with a therapist in a one-to-one intervention setting. Self-report data from structured interviews and self-report tests may be useful in diagnosis but difficult to convert to an intervention plan with the schizoid disorders. Behavioral assessment data from observations, rating scales, and behavioral interviews with parents or caregivers are potentially useful in pinpointing target behaviors for intervention and, in some cases, in determining potential sources of reinforcement available within the immediate environment. Part of the clinical picture that usually is seen with the schizoid disorders is extremely poor social skills and peer rejection. In this regard, there is some hope that structured social skills training conducted in group settings might be an effective approach, although generalizing social skills training effects across settings and time is difficult and takes specific planning (Merrell & Gimpel, 1998). If a child or adolescent exhibits schizoid-like characteristics with severe social deficits and poor relationships, the assessment design could benefit from the inclusion of a specific social skills appraisal (see Chapter 13), which might help in identifying distinctive clusters of social skills deficits.

Children with Tourette's Disorder may benefit from pharmacologic interventions that reduce tics and in some cases ameliorate some of the related attentional problems. The assessment data that lead to appropriate diagnosis of Tourette's may provide the basis for making a medical referral. A comprehensive assessment of the child often identifies related or co-occurring problems, however, such as attentional problems, mood disturbances, social problems, and obsessive–compulsive symptoms. A thorough assessment often results in the identification of specific psychosocial problems that should be the focus of appropriate intervention planning. Functional behavior assessment (FBA) is often helpful in helping to identify antecedents to tic behaviors, and such behavioral assessment approach is often a first step in identifying the best course of intervention.

Linking assessment to intervention planning in cases of schizophrenic or other psychotic disorders can be a complex challenge. Kauffman (2000) stated that behavioral interventions have been highly successful with psychotic children in many research situations, but the results of these projects have not always provided direct and practical treatment implications for classroom teachers. Functional assessment data from observations or behavioral interviews might provide a basis for modifying the child's immediate environment to remediate specific behavioral excesses or deficits, but implementing these interventions outside of a highly controlled environment may be challenging. Smith and Belcher (1985) noted that such individuals often require considerable training in basic life skills, such as grooming, hygiene, and community living. For identifying specific areas for these life skills interventions, the use of behavior rating scales may prove to be useful. In most cases, effective management of psychotic disorders may involve medical referral and the possible use of neuroleptic (antipsychotic) medications. Medical referral and intervention is especially crucial in cases in which the child or adolescent is experiencing full-blown psychotic symptoms, such as hallucinations and delusions, or when there is an increased probability for him or her doing harm to himself or herself or others. Rating scales, interviews, observations, and in some cases self-report tests may be useful for identifying the overt symptoms of schizophrenia that warrant intervention. Because children with psychotic disorders (and pervasive developmental disorders) usually exhibit behaviors that are so blatantly maladaptive and different from those of their normal peers, the *template matching strategy* discussed by Shapiro (1996) may be useful in linking assessment to intervention. This strategy involves systematic comparison of the behavior of the troubled individual with behavior of well-adjusted youth, identifying the discrepancies between the two, then using the "normal" behavior as a template for targeting intervention.

Assessment of eating disorders must rely heavily on extensive clinical interviewing and self-report instruments because many of the core characteristics of these disorders are covert and may not be easily detectable through external methods of objective assessment. The various data obtained through assessment may be useful in selecting related areas to target for intervention. That is, the core targets for intervention will always be the maladaptive eating behaviors themselves, but there may need to be ancillary intervention targets, such as depression, distorted thinking patterns, obsessive–compulsive characteristics, and various other maladaptive behaviors and cognitions. Self-report instruments and clinical interviews may be helpful in identifying the appropriate ancillary targets and perhaps in determining how best to approach the core eating disorder symptoms with particular individuals.

CONCLUSIONS

Not all forms of child and adolescent psychopathology fit neatly within the broad externalizing and internalizing domains that have been well documented in the research literature. Some types of behavioral, social, and emotional problems are considered to be "mixed," given that the major characteristics may lead into either or both of the major broad-band domains. Other types of problems contain characteristics specific to either of the two major domains and stand alone in taxonomy to some extent. Additionally, some forms of child and adolescent psychopathology have such an extremely low base rate of prevalence that it is difficult to account for enough cases in large etiological studies to make broad-band classification possible or desirable.

This chapter provides descriptive information and brief comments on assessment methodology for several of these "other" domains of problems, including autism, the so-called "schizoid" disorders, Tourette's Disorder (a specific tic disorder that often has social–emotional overlays), schizophrenia and other manifestations of childhood psychoses, and the major eating disorders. Developing an adequate classification taxonomy for all of these disorders has been an ongoing problem. The behavioral dimensions approach to classifying severe childhood psychopathology (as illustrated by Quay's taxonomy system) has resulted in two clusters or subdomains of problems. The *DSM* approach to classification of severe problems seems to be in a continual state of flux, at least in part because of the low base rate for occurrence of many of the problems under consideration. Many of the *DSM* diagnostic categories are based on adult models of psychopathology (particularly in the case of schizophrenia and other psychotic disorders), even though there is evidence that childhood and early adolescent manifestations of these severe problems differ markedly from adulthood manifestations in many cases.

Autism Spectrum Disorder constitutes a class of severe problems that are first evident during infancy and childhood. It is manifest by age three and is typified by severe impairment in social communication and by the occurrence of stereotyped and markedly restrictive behaviors, activities, and interests. Three deletions from the previous *DSM* pervasive developmental disorders include Rett's Disorder, Childhood Disintegrative Disorder, and Asperger's Disorder. These three disorders are rare compared with autism, and little is known about prevalence and etiology. Many of the essential features of these other pervasive developmental disorders include symptoms similar to those found in Autism Spectrum Disorder but with specific and peculiar manifestations. Assessment of Autism Spectrum Disorder typically must rely heavily on direct behavioral observation, behavior rating scales, and clinical interviews with parents and teachers. Several widely researched instruments of these types have been developed for assessing autism.

The so-called "schizoid" disorders have been in and out of *DSM* throughout various editions but have been verified through behavioral dimensions research and have been of continual interest to researchers, particularly in parts of Europe. The schizoid disorders are characterized in general by extreme deficits in social interaction skills and by extreme difficulty in developing and maintaining close human relationships. Schizoid and Schizotypal Personality Disorders from *DSM-5* seem to be close parallels to the schizoid symptoms identified through behavioral dimensions research with children, even though these two personality disorders are not typically appropriate for childhood diagnoses. Asperger's Disorder, recently deleted from the *DSM*, overlaps quite a bit with characteristics of schizoid disorders. In some respects, Asperger's Disorder or high-functioning Autism seems to be a childhood parallel to Schizoid and Schizotypal Personality Disorder, in much the same way as Conduct Disorder is a childhood parallel to Antisocial Personality Disorder. Assessment of schizoid disorders is a difficult proposition, with few or no domain-specific instruments available. It seems that a broad assessment design is appropriate for assessment, which would include self-report measures such as the MMPI-A and YSR with adolescent clients who have adequate reading skills.

Tourette's Disorder is a specific type of tic disorder that is characterized by multiple and frequent motor and vocal tics, and that often includes social–emotional problems. Tourette's Disorder co-occurs with ADHD and OCD in a surprisingly large percentage of cases, and it is often misunderstood, misinterpreted, and misdiagnosed. This disorder usually occurs in early to middle childhood and often is characterized by an abating or lessening of symptoms by late adolescence or early adulthood. Assessment of Tourette's Disorder among children is accomplished best through a comprehensive assessment design that relies heavily on clinical interviewing of parents and the child in question. Some research interviews and rating scales have been developed specifically for use in assessing Tourette's Disorder. A particular assessment problem in this area is differential diagnosis and dual diagnosis, given the frequent co-occurrence of other disorders.

Schizophrenia Spectrum and other psychotic disorders rarely occur before mid-adolescence, with onset usually occurring in late adolescence or early adulthood. Psychotic episodes have been reported with children aged ten to 14 years, however, and as young as five or six years. The manifestation of psychotic symptoms among these younger subjects typically differs in important ways from the typical adult-oriented classification criteria of *DSM-5*. The effective assessment of psychotic behavior in children and adolescents requires a variable approach, depending on the age and developmental level of the youth in question. Each of the major assessment methods may prove to be useful or even essential for assessment and classification of psychotic disorders with specific clients, including self-report measures such as the MMPI-A with high functioning adolescents.

Although eating disorders sometimes have been lumped together with the broad band of internalizing psychopathology and do share some important characteristics and correlates, behavioral dimensions analyses have not placed them consistently as a subcategory of this area, so they are covered in this chapter rather than in Chapter 11. The three major eating disorders of interest for this chapter include Anorexia Nervosa, Bulimia Nervosa, and Binge Eating Disorder. The major diagnostic distinction between the disorders is that Anorexia involves low body weight, either through caloric restriction or a combination of food restriction and purging, while Bulimia tends to occur among individuals with normal body weight and involves binge eating accompanied by inappropriate compensatory strategies, such as self-induced vomiting. Binge Eating Disorder is characterized by binging without compensatory behaviors. Anorexia and Bulimia involve distortions in self-perceptions regarding body shape and size, tend to co-occur with mood disorders and other problems, and may have serious, even lethal, consequences. Binge Eating Disorder is associated with all of these characteristics, except the distorted perceptions of body weight. This aspect is less clear. Assessment of eating disorders through external objective means is difficult. Assessment must rely heavily on extensive clinical interviews and self-report instruments, such as the Eating Disorders Inventory, which is now in its third edition.

Linkage of these various "other" disorders to effective intervention strategies varies considerably across categories in terms of how easy and effective it is. For Autism Spectrum Disorder, functional assessment and analysis strategies are crucial, because intervention tends to be behavioral in nature and requires identification of antecedent–behavior–consequence relationships. Linking the assessment of the schizoid disorders to intervention is potentially problematic because of the often difficult-to-treat nature of these problems. Assessment of social skills is essential and may assist in planning social skills training interventions. Less is known regarding linkage of Tourette's Disorder to intervention, other than the necessity of making an appropriate diagnosis and the strong possibility of referring for medication intervention coupled with appropriate social–emotional support. Assessment of childhood psychotic disorders is difficult to link effectively to intervention, which usually requires a combination of medication and structured behavioral programming. For higher functioning adolescents, the MMPI-A may provide some empirically developed templates for selection of treatment strategies. Treatment of eating disorders tends to be eclectic, using a variety of behavioral and psychosocial strategies. Assessment of these disorders probably is linked best to intervention through identification of the key problems, which then are targeted for intervention.

REVIEW AND APPLICATION QUESTIONS

1. What are the most likely reasons why the "other" behavioral, social, and emotional problems discussed in this chapter do not fit neatly within the major domains of internalizing and externalizing psychopathology?

2. The *DSM-5* lists changes in its description of Autism Spectrum Disorder. Three disorders (all but autism) were deleted from the *DSM* in the fourth edition. Make an argument for these other three disorders (Rett's, Childhood Disintegrative, and Asperger's) being either separate disorders or just variations of autism.

3. In assessing a child with Autism Spectrum Disorder, what practices can be implemented to make the assessment as "functional" as possible in providing information useful for intervention planning?

4. Examine the characteristics of the schizoid disorders vis-à-vis the information on social skills assessment presented in Chapter 13. How could an assessment be designed to maximize the usefulness of the obtained information in addressing the most notable social–interpersonal deficits through intervention?

5. What are some of the major cautions that should be considered for interpreting parent and teacher general-purpose problem behavior rating scales that have been completed on a child who may have Tourette's Disorder?

6. In making a differential diagnosis with an elementary-age child who may have either Autism Spectrum Disorder or a psychotic disorder, what would be the key discriminating features to consider in making a diagnostic decision, and how could the assessment best be designed to be useful in this decision?

7. Individuals with eating disorders often are secretive regarding their maladaptive eating behaviors. Because effective assessment of these problems must rely heavily on clinical interviewing and self-report instruments, how can these assessments best be used so that the important problems and characteristics are not minimized or ignored?

8. Which factors are important in determining whether a self-report instrument may be a useful part of an assessment battery for an adolescent who may have psychotic symptoms?

13

ASSESSING SOCIAL SKILLS AND SOCIAL–EMOTIONAL STRENGTHS

Assessment of social skills of children and adolescents has been a topic of strong interest in the fields of education and psychology since the 1970s (Merrell & Gimpel, 1998, 2014). School and clinical child psychologists, special educators, and professionals from related fields who work with children and adolescents encounter numerous assessment and intervention questions that require a sound knowledge of the overall construct of social skills and effective methods of assessing these skills. Understanding one's skills from a strength-based perspective has also come to the forefront of research and practice as the "positive psychology" movement has gained momentum.

This chapter provides the reader with the prerequisite background knowledge needed to conceptualize appropriately various aspects of social skills of children and adolescents, conduct effective assessments of these skills with an emphasis on strength-based assessments, and use the obtained assessment information to develop sound intervention recommendations. The chapter begins with an overview of the broad construct of social competence and some of the domains that are hypothesized to comprise it. A theoretical model for conceptualizing the related constructs of social competence, social skills, and peer relations is reviewed as well as discussion of how emotional competencies may influence social development. Research by Merrell and colleagues regarding the development of a classification taxonomy for child and adolescent social skills is discussed, as is the research base regarding the importance and long-term implications of social skills and peer relations. Next, specific methods for assessing various aspects of social skills and peer relations are presented, particularly as they relate to the direct and objective assessment methods emphasized most prominently in this book. Included are assessments that specifically contribute to practice in their emphases on capturing the social and emotional strengths and assets of children and adolescents. The chapter ends with a discussion of best practices in using assessment data to develop effective interventions within an RtI model.

SOCIAL COMPETENCE: A COMPLEX CONSTRUCT

Although the terms *social skills* and *social competence* are often used interchangeably, these terms indicate differing but related constructs. Most expert definitions regard social competence as a broader construct that is superordinate to and inclusive of social skills (see Merrell & Gimpel, 1998, 2014, for a comprehensive review of theoretical definitions). Social competence has been conceptualized as a complex, multidimensional construct that consists of a variety of behavioral and cognitive characteristics and various aspects

DOI: 10.4324/9781315747521-15

of emotional adjustment that are useful and necessary in developing adequate social relations and obtaining desirable social outcomes. Characteristics related to social competence that are reflective of cognitive and emotional adjustment have drawn more attention in the research literature and include those indicating effortful control (the ability to inhibit or initiate a behavior purposefully; Rothbart & Bates, 2006), resiliency (the ability to respond flexibly and positively in adverse situations; Spinrad et al., 2006), social-information processing (the ability to appropriately encode a social message and respond prosocially; Crick & Dodge, 1994), emotion knowledge (the ability to identify emotions in oneself and others; Denham et al., 2003), and emotion expressiveness (the ability to accurately express activated emotions; Denham et al., 2003). Social competence transcends the divisions of internalizing and externalizing behaviors, which are discussed at length in Chapters 10 and 11. Peer relationship problems and deficits in social skills have been shown, however, to be a component of the internalizing and the externalizing domains (Kauffman, 2000; Merrell & Gimpel, 1998, 2014).

Several other constructs have a strong relationship to the domain of social competence. Three of these constructs—*adaptive behavior, social skills,* and *peer acceptance*—are particularly related to social competence and are discussed briefly in the following sections.

ADAPTIVE BEHAVIOR

Adaptive behavior as defined by the American Association on Intellectual and Developmental Disabilities (AAIDD, 2008) is "the conceptual, social, and practical skills that people have learned to be able to function in their everyday lives" (p. 2). Adaptive behavior is assumed to be a developmental construct, given that expectations for independent and responsible behavior vary, depending on mental and chronological age (AAIDD, 2008; Reschly, 1990). It also is important to consider that adaptive behavior must be viewed within cultural and environmental contexts because expectations and demands for independence and responsibility vary, depending on the specific culture or subculture in which the individual resides (AAIDD, 2008; Reschly, 1990).

Assessment of adaptive behavior is a crucial aspect of the classification of developmental delays and intellectual disabilities. The most recent definition of intellectual disabilities from the AAIDD prominently includes the construct of adaptive behavior (or adaptive skills) (AAIDD, 2008). In practice, the measurement of adaptive behavior includes assessing functional living skills, which tend to require a qualitatively different evaluation approach and are essential for individuals with pervasive intellectual disabilities and developmental disorders. Because these particular populations and assessment methods differ from those focused on in this book, this chapter does not discuss adaptive behavior assessment per se, but focuses specifically on the other two aspects of social competence: social skills and peer relationships. Readers desiring a more comprehensive treatment of the broader construct of adaptive behavior are referred to several other excellent sources, including AAIDD (2010), Kamphaus (1987), Reschly (1990, 1991), and Wehmeyer and Agran (2005).

Social Skills

Social skills have been explained and defined in many ways, including cognitive, behavioral, and ecological definitions (Merrell & Gimpel, 1998, 2014). There is no single or unitary definition of social skills that has been agreed upon by most experts in the field. In a comprehensive review of theories and definitions of social skills, Merrell found 15 different expert definitions. For purposes of this chapter, a good working definition of social skills is that they are specific behaviors, that when initiated, lead to desirable social outcomes for the person initiating them. From a behavioral standpoint, initiation of social skills increases the probability of reinforcement and decreases the probability of punishment or extinction based on one's social behavior (Gresham & Reschly, 1987a). According to Gresham and Elliot (2008), examples of behavioral classes representing social skills include communication, cooperation, assertion, responsibility, empathy, engagement and self-control.

Peer Relations

The construct of peer relations is also sometimes referred to as peer acceptance. Peer relations generally has been considered to be a subcomponent of social competence (Gresham, 1986) and often is considered to be a result or product of one's social skills. This view of peer relations is reasonable because social reputation and the quality of one's social relations are in great measure a result of how effectively one interacts socially with peers (Landau & Milich, 1990; Oden & Asher, 1977). Positive peer relations are associated with peer acceptance, whereas negative peer relations are linked with peer rejection.

Theoretical Model

Without a doubt, the constructs of social competence, adaptive behavior, social skills, and peer relations are interrelated. There have been varying viewpoints, however, on the direction or path of the relationship among these constructs. Two decades ago, Gresham (1986) proposed a hierarchical model of social competence (also outlined in Gresham, 1981a, and Gresham & Reschly, 1987a) and considered social competence to be a superordinate construct to adaptive behavior and peer acceptance or relations. At the present time, there have not been any large-scale multivariate studies that have answered definitely the question of how specifically these constructs are related and what the direction and strength of the paths are among them. To do so would require a carefully designed large-scale study using complex statistical techniques, such as structural equation modeling. Although no single study of this nature can be identified as a seminal or definitive work at this time, numerous studies conducted during the 1980s, 1990s, and 2000s shed additional light on the relationships among the constructs discussed in this section. Given the overall yield of research in this area, it is our opinion that the constructs of social competence, adaptive behavior, social skills, and peer relations are connected according to some specific hierarchical relationships and path directions.

It is proposed that adaptive behavior should be viewed as the overarching superordinate construct, of which social competence is one specific subordinate construct (along with other constructs, such as communication competency and motor skills). This is a modern view of adaptive behavior, a construct that has taken on significant importance in more recent years. As was indicated previously, the most recent definitions and discussion of intellectual disabilities from the AAIDD (2008, 2010) views social competence or social functioning as one component of the broader construct of adaptive behavior. This view also is supported through empirically derived factor structures of some adaptive behavior assessment instruments (Bruininks, Woodcock, Weatherman, & Hill, 1984; Harrison, 1987; Harrison & Oakland, 2000).

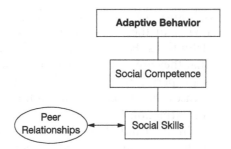

Figure 13.1 Outline of a proposed theoretical model of the relationships among the constructs of adaptive behavior, social competence, social skills, and peer relationships

Regarding the relationship between social competence and social skills, we contend that social competence is a broader superordinate construct that includes social skills in a subordinate position. This line of reasoning is illustrated clearly in a widely cited article by McFall (1982), who proposed that social competence is a summary or evaluative term based on conclusions or judgments regarding how adequately an individual performs social tasks. Social skills are specific social behaviors one must perform to be judged as competent on a given task. This operational definition of social skills was outlined earlier.

As for the relationship of peer acceptance or peer relations to these other constructs, Merrell proposes that it is a product or outcome of social skills rather than a separate component of adaptive behavior that is parallel with social skills. In essence, peer relations are determined by the quality and quantity of one's social skills. The relationship between peer relations and social skills is probably more complex, however, than being reduced to a simple existence–outcome formula. There is good evidence that the relationship between peer relations and social skills also is reciprocal in nature, or that the two constructs mutually influence each other. In other words, although the existence or nonexistence of social skills results in the outcome of good or poor peer relations, the quality of one's peer relations is also likely to influence the future development of social skills, by enhancing or decreasing opportunities for future observation and modeling of social skills.

To recap this model for understanding the relationship among the four constructs we have been exploring, adaptive behavior is viewed as the most broad and superordinate construct in the scheme. Social competence, an evaluative or summary term reflecting judgment regarding the overall quality of one's social performance, is a construct that is circumscribed within the broader construct of adaptive behavior. Social skills can be characterized as one of several important behavioral components that lead to social competence. Social skills, in turn, result in the quality of relationships one has with peers. Peer relations should be viewed as a product or outcome of social skills and something that reciprocally affects the development of social skills in the future. A graphic outline of this proposed model of relationships among social constructs is presented in Figure 13.1.

DIMENSIONS OF SOCIAL SKILLS

As research and clinical applications regarding children's social skills have increased in importance and volume since the 1980s, it is curious that relatively little work has been done related to identifying the specific underlying dimensions of social skills. In contrast to the area of child psychopathology, where there have been numerous empirical efforts aimed at developing and improving classification taxonomies, there has been a dearth of attention paid to developing a parallel taxonomy for social skills of children and adolescents. Perhaps one of the obstacles to such efforts is that the fields of child psychiatry and psychology traditionally have been pathology oriented, or focused on understanding behavior in terms of a medical model of disease and dysfunction.

To counter this lack of attention to such a potentially important endeavor, Caldarella and Merrell (1997) sought to develop an empirical taxonomy of child and adolescent social skills by employing a similar methodology to that used by Quay (1986a) in developing his widely influential empirical taxonomy for child emotional and behavioral disorders that is discussed in some detail in Chapter 3 and in other chapters in this volume. A brief overview of this social skills meta-analysis review is presented in this section. For more detail on the methodology or results of this investigation, the reader is referred to the full article.

Following an extensive literature search and study elimination process, 21 studies that used multivariate approaches to classifying social skills with more than 22,000 children and adolescents were included. The review and synthesis of these studies were accomplished by examining the name of each social skill factor derived in the studies and the underlying behaviors subsumed by the factor (the approach used by Quay, 1986a). For example, items composing a factor labeled "Peer Interaction" were examined to ensure that most of the items (at least 50%) were directly related to peers. If so, that factor would be grouped with other "peer-related" factors under a common dimension. The most common social skill dimensions, those noted as occurring in one-third or more of the studies, were identified. This method was used to eliminate outliers and study-specific findings. Using this methodology five primary dimensions of child and adolescent social skills were identified. These dimensions are labeled and described briefly in Table 13.1.

After the identification phase, the five dimensions presented in Table 13.1 were examined more closely to determine the most common social skills associated with each.

Table 13.1 The five most common dimensions of social skills, developed from a review and analysis by Caldarella and Merrell (1997)

Names of the most common social skill dimensions (in descending order of frequency)	Frequency (number of studies)	Percentage of studies
Peer Relations: social interaction, prosocial, interpersonal, peer preferred social behavior, empathy, social participation, sociability–leadership, peer reinforcement, general, peer sociability	11	52.38
Self Management: self-control/social convention, social independence, social competence, social responsibility, rules, frustration tolerance	11	52.38
Academic: school adjustment, respect for social rules at school, task orientation, academic responsibility, classroom compliance, good student	10	47.62
Compliance: social cooperation, competence, cooperation–compliance	8	38.09
Assertion: assertive social skills, social initiation, social activator, gutsy	7	33.33

This next step was accomplished by first listing the specific social skill components constituting each of the factors that composed the dimension. For example, all of the items constituting the first Peer Relations factor were listed. Then individual items of the next Peer Relations factor were listed, with similar items being grouped together. This process was carried out for all five of the most common dimensions. Similar social skills were grouped together to determine the principal behavioral characteristics (those occurring in one-third or more of the studies) associated with each dimension. These principal social skills were rank-ordered (based on frequency) as they appear in Table 13.1.

The *Peer Relations* dimension occurred in 11 (52.38%) studies. This dimension seems to be dominated by social skills, reflecting a child who displays positive behaviors and skills with his or her peers. Such skills as complimenting or praising others, offering help or assistance, and inviting others to play or interact seem to describe this dimension well. The *Self-Management* dimension also occurred in 11 studies. This dimension reflects a child who might be labeled by others as emotionally well adjusted. This dimension also reflects a child or adolescent who is able to control his or her temper, follow rules and limits, compromise with others, and receive criticism well. The *Academic* dimension occurred in ten (47.62%) studies reviewed. This dimension is dominated by social skills, reflecting a child or adolescent who might be called an independent and productive worker by his or her teacher. Such skills as accomplishing tasks or assignments independently, completing individual seatwork and assignments, and carrying out teacher directions all seem to describe this dimension well. The *Compliance* dimension occurred in eight (38.09%) studies reviewed. The picture that emerges here is a child who essentially gets along with others by following rules and expectations, using free time appropriately, and sharing things. Essentially, this dimension involves complying with appropriate requests made by others. The *Assertion* dimension occurred in seven (33.33%) studies reviewed. This dimension is dominated by social skills that reflect a child or adolescent who might be called "outgoing" or "extroverted" by others. Such skills as initiating conversations with others, acknowledging compliments, and inviting others to interact all seem to describe this dimension well.

These five most common dimensions of child and adolescent social skills have a strong base of empirical support, being derived in more than one-third of the studies reviewed, with two derived in more than half the studies. To date, no other research has been located that has done such an extensive review of empirically derived social skill dimensions of children and adolescents. This review could be said to have broken new ground by applying the influential research method used by Quay (1986a), which combines aspects of meta-analysis and qualitative review, to an area of crucial importance, child and adolescent positive social behaviors.

On the basis of the frequency with which these dimensions of social skills have been identified in 20 years of research, practitioners and researchers should consider focusing on these areas for assessment and intervention. Many of the social skills subsumed by these dimensions already have been incorporated into validated assessment and intervention strategies (see Durlak, Weissberg, Dymnicki, Taylor, & Schellinger, 2011; Walker, Colvin, & Ramsey, 1995; Walker, Ramsey, & Gresham, 2004). What this study provides is further empirical support for the five essential social skills dimensions composing the taxonomy. Gesten (1976) noted that competencies in clients must be identified and reinforced to maximize (treatment and research) outcomes. While this review is now almost 20 years old, the resulting taxonomy hopefully has helped to identify appropriate behaviors to reinforce and balance the scales between assessing for positive and negative behaviors in children and adolescents. The fields of psychology and psychiatry have long been pathology driven, and the worldview created by this focus perhaps has had the unfortunate effect of steering clinicians and researchers concerned with behavioral, social, and emotional assessment to take a pathology-confirming approach to assessment of children and adolescents. The fact that our present diagnostic and classification systems are disorder or disability oriented is evidence of this bias. In our view, it is time to begin to balance our emphases on adaptive and maladaptive behavior. The notion of focusing on positive outcomes or traits as opposed to a sole focus on pathology has gained attention in more recent years, as evidenced by the growing interest in the notion of positive psychology (Larson, 2000; Seligman & Csikszentmihalyi, 2000; Snyder & Lopez, 2001).

THE IMPORTANCE OF SOCIAL (AND EMOTIONAL) SKILLS

A growing body of literature in the fields of child development, education, and psychology collectively points to the conclusion that the development of adequate social skills and peer relationships during childhood has important and far-reaching ramifications. Some of the most influential studies from previous decades highlight these issues. It has been established that development of appropriate social skills is an important foundation for adequate peer relationships (Asher & Taylor, 1981). There also is evidence that childhood social skills and consequent peer relationships have a significant impact on academic success during the school years (Malecki & Elliot, 2002; Walker & Hops, 1976). In reviewing the literature on peer relations, Hartup (1983) showed that the ability to relate effectively to others is essential to the progress and development of the child.

More recently, researchers have been working to better understand how emotional competence relates to social development. It seems that having an ability to understand, regulate, and cope with emotions can be related to successful social behaviors and peer relationships. Children who acquire emotion knowledge and emotion regulation skills early in life may be able to respond prosocially to others and may demonstrate attentional control in the classroom (Denham et al., 2003; Denham & Weissberg, 2004; Trentacosta, Izard, Mostow, & Fine, 2006; Joseph & Strain, 2003). For example, Denham et al. (2003) found that preschoolers' emotion knowledge and expressiveness uniquely predicted social competence in kindergarten and that these skills also predicted overall preschool social competence. This relationship suggests that students who are able to understand the emotions of others may also be able to be more responsive to peers in the classroom.

Given that adequate social skills and peer relations are an important foundation for various types of success in life, it stands to reason that inadequate development in these areas is related to a variety of negative outcomes. A classic and frequently cited investigation by Cowen and colleagues (1973) involving an 11- to 13-year follow-up study of third-grade students provides convincing evidence that early peer relationship problems are strong predictors of mental health problems later in life. These researchers found that "peer judgment (using a negative peer nomination procedure) was, by far, the most sensitive predictor of later psychiatric difficulty" (p. 438). Other frequently cited studies have indicated that inadequate social skills and poor peer relations during childhood may lead to a variety of other problems later in life, such as juvenile delinquency, school dropout, being fired from jobs, conduct-related discharge from military service, chronic unemployment and underemployment, and psychiatric hospitalizations (Loeber, 1985a, 1985b; Parker & Asher, 1987; Roff, 1963; Roff & Sells, 1968; Roff et al., 1972).

As the literature on the social, emotional, and behavioral characteristics of children with disabilities continues to grow, it has become increasingly clear that these children are at significantly heightened risk for developing social skills deficits and experiencing peer rejection (e.g., Merrell & Gimpel, 1998, 2014). Students identified as having a learning disability have been found to experience high rates of social rejection by other children (Bryan, 1974; Cartledge, Frew, & Zacharias, 1985; Sater & French, 1989), to be rated by teachers as having poor interpersonal behavior (Gresham & Reschly, 1986), and to exhibit maladaptive social behaviors in instructional settings (Epstein, Cullinan, & Lloyd, 1986; McKinney & Feagans, 1984; McKinney, McClure, & Feagans, 1982). Students identified as intellectually impaired have been found to exhibit deficits in adaptive social competencies (Gresham & Reschly, 1987b), to experience high rates of peer rejection (Gresham, 1981b), and to receive inadequate amounts of social support (Park, Tappe, Carmeto, & Gaylord-Ross, 1990). Likewise, students identified as having behavior disorders have been found to be discriminated from students without disabilities by their maladaptive social–emotional behaviors (Merrell, Merz, Johnson, & Ring, 1992; Stumme, Gresham, & Scott, 1982; Vaughn, 1987) and to experience significant rates of social rejection by other children (Hollinger, 1987). Clinicians who work with children with disabilities and other at-risk children should be especially aware of the social problems these children face and keep up to date on appropriate methods of assessment of positive and negative social behavior.

METHODS OF ASSESSING SOCIAL AND EMOTIONAL SKILLS

Each of the five primary direct and objective assessment methods discussed in this book can be used in assessing social and emotional skills and peer relations. By contrast, projective–expressive techniques, the sixth assessment method covered in this book, may provide some clues for hypothesis building regarding social and emotional skills and peer relations of children, but it also requires a tremendous amount of inference and follow-up with one of the five more direct methods of assessment. Direct behavioral observation and behavior rating scales have been used most frequently for assessing social skills and peer relations in educational and clinical settings. Sociometric approaches also have been employed frequently in research on social skills and peer relations but are more limited in terms of day-to-day clinical use. Interview methods hold some promise for assessing social skills and peer relations but are used most commonly for other purposes, such as clinical diagnoses. The use of self-reports in assessing social competence is a relatively new endeavor with few exemplars, but it does show some promise. The use of each of these five direct and objective assessment methods in evaluating social competence is discussed in this section.

Direct Behavioral Observation

Many of the general behavioral observation techniques presented in Chapter 4 are highly relevant for assessing social skills and peer relations. In discussing behavioral observation as a method of assessing social skills, Elliott and Gresham (1987) optimistically stated that "analyzing children's behavior in natural settings . . . is the most ecologically valid method of assessing children's social skills" (p. 96). Although some recent research has illustrated some challenges in being able to reliably capture children's social behavior through a limited number of observations (e.g., Doll & Elliott, 1994; Hintze, 2005; Hintze & Mathews, 2004), direct observation of social skills is still an essential method, and clinicians who are serious about conducting valid assessments of child and adolescent social behaviors must master the basic methods of observational measurement, such as those reviewed in Chapter 4

Several other sources have provided reviews of methods for assessing child and adolescent social behavior through direct behavioral observation (e.g., Asher & Hymel, 1981; Gresham, 1981b; Hops & Greenwood, 1981; Leff & Lakin, 2005), but for this chapter it is useful to look at three examples of how behavioral observation techniques have been used for this purpose in published investigations, even though two of the three tools described are over 20 years old. The first example is an observation of social behavior observed within a system, whereas the second and third examples are interval-based coding systems for use with individual children in naturalistic settings.

The Student Interaction in Specific Settings Tool (SISS) As schools and school districts are beginning to think systemically about how to support the development of positive social behaviors and reduction of maladaptive behaviors, observation tools such as the Student Interaction in Specific Settings (SISS) can be useful. The SISS is a unique tool that allows researchers and practitioners to objectively gather system-wide social–behavioral data. Developed by Cushing and Horner (2003), this tool allows observers to record social interactions occurring within a hallway, during lunch periods in a cafeteria, or out at recess, for example. Observation "zones" are defined and all children that enter the zone are observed. Behaviors targeted are those that suggest: (1) Rule Violations/Low Intensity Behaviors; (2) Moderate Intensity Behaviors; and (3) High Intensity Behaviors. These types of behaviors are operationally defined, and observers code the behaviors observed as well as the consequence following the behavior. Consequences are considered to be: (1) Positive; (2) Negative; or (3) No Response (in addition to the manual, see Leff & Lakin, 2005 for further description of behaviors). Positive consequences are those that make the behavior more likely to occur in the future, while negative consequences are those that serve to diminish the behaviors. Gathering data in this way allows observers to determine the rate at which each type of behavior happens and the probability that the behaviors are followed by particular consequences. Essentially, this tool allows one to look "functionally" at the social behavior of a group. Studies have established the SISS as a reliable tool that moderately correlates with measures of school climate (Cushing, Horner, & Barrier, 2003). The SISS holds much promise for schools as they work to obtain a reliable "snapshot" of social behavior across school settings.

The Peer Social Behavior Code The Peer Social Behavior Code is the third and final stage or gate of Walker and Severson's (1992) and Walker, Severson, and Feil's (2014) Systematic Screening for Behavior Disorders (SSBD), the multiple gating screening system for use with children in grades 1 to 6 that was discussed in some detail in Chapter 3. Because the assessment method conducted at each successive gate results in a narrowing down of the population using increasingly intensive procedures, by the time the population has been narrowed after the direct observational process (the third gate), it should consist of children who are truly at risk for social behavior problems, including social skills deficits. The Peer Social Behavior Code observation system consists of a series of ten-second intervals. The actual number of intervals used in an observation is variable, depending on the situation. The recording forms each include spaces for 40 different intervals. Observations always are conducted during free-play situations (e.g., at recess), and a typical observation period might last 15 minutes.

Five different recording categories are included in the Peer Social Behavior Code: *Social Engagement* (SE), *Participation* (P), *Parallel Play* (PLP), *Alone* (A), and *No Codeable Response* (N). Behavior in the first two categories may be coded as either positive (1) or negative (2). Behavior in the PLP and A categories is coded by simply checking the appropriate box. No Codeable Response is coded with a check when the child is out of view and with a dot when the child is interacting with an adult rather than a peer. After the observation, the observational data are transferred from the recording forms (Figure 13.2) to an observational summary sheet (Figure 13.3).

Systematic Screening for Behavior Disorders
PEER SOCIAL BEHAVIOR RECORDING FORM

Student Name _____ Teacher Name _____

School _____ Grade _____ Observer _____

Reliability Observer _____ Date _____ Time Start _____

Time Stop _____ Length of Session _____

Interval Number	+ − SE	+ − P	✓ PLP	✓ A	• ✓ N	Interval Number	+ − SE	+ − P	✓ PLP	✓ A	• ✓ N
0–1						21					
2						22					
3						23					
4						24					
5						25					
6						26					
7						27					
8						28					
9						29					
10						30					
11						31					
12						32					
13						33					
14						34					
15						35					
16						36					
17						37					
18						38					
19						39					
20						40					

Figure 13.2 Peer Social Behavior Recording Form

Source: From *Systematic Screening for Behavior Disorders, Second Edition,* by H. M. Walker, H. Severson, and E. Feil (2014). Eugene, OR: Pacific Northwest Publishing. Reprinted with Permission.

Systematic Screening for Behavior Disorders
PEER SOCIAL BEHAVIOR
OBSERVATION SUMMARY SHEET

Student Name _____

School _____ Grade _____

Dates Observed _____ and _____
                        Session #1   Session #2

	Number of Intervals*	Observation #1**	Number of Intervals*	Observation #2**	Average of 1 and 2
1. Social Engagement (SE)	_____	_____ %	_____	_____ %	_____ %
2. Participation (P)	_____	_____ %	_____	_____ %	_____ %
3. Parallel Play (PLP)	_____	_____ %	_____	_____ %	_____ %
4. Alone (A)	_____	_____ %	_____	_____ %	_____ %
5. No Codeable Response (N)	_____	_____ %	_____	_____ %	_____ %
6. Social Interaction (SI)	_____	_____ %	_____	_____ %	_____ %
7. Negative Interaction (NI)	_____	_____ %	_____	_____ %	_____ %
8. Positive Interaction (PI)	_____	_____ %	_____	_____ %	_____ %
9. Total Positive Behavior	_____	_____ %	_____	_____ %	_____ %
10. Total Negative Behavior	_____	_____ %	_____	_____ %	_____ %

*Enter the number of intervals recorded for each category.

**Enter the percentage of time spent for each category by dividing the total number of intervals that you observed during the observation session into the intervals recorded under different categories and multiplying by 100.

Figure 13.3 Peer Social Behavior Observation Summary Sheet

Source: From *Systematic Screening for Behavior Disorders, Second Edition,* by H. M. Walker, H. Severson, and E. Feil (2014). Eugene, OR: Pacific Northwest Publishing. Reprinted with Permission.

The number of intervals recorded are entered for each category, then the percentage of time spent for each category is calculated by dividing the total number of intervals in the session into the intervals recorded under different categories and multiplying by 100. The SSBD manual contains thorough directions for interpreting Peer Social Behavior Code observation data using the normative tables provided. In addition, an excellent observer training tape is provided as part of the SSBD kit, which also includes an audio timing tape for accurately using the ten-second intervals. Extensive research went into the development of the Peer Social Behavior Code, and the validity evidence and technical properties reported in the manual and in other sources are impressive. The Peer Social Behavior Code is an exemplary interval-based coding procedure for direct observation of child social behavior and may serve as a model for constructing similar coding systems for more specific purposes.

The Target/Peer Interaction Code Several related studies of the development of antisocial behavior in boys (e.g., Shinn, Ramsey, Walker, Steiber, & O'Neill, 1987; Walker, Shinn, O'Neil, & Ramsey, 1987; Walker, Steiber, & O'Neill, 1990; Walker, Steiber, Ramsey, & O'Neill, 1993) used a variety of assessment methods, including direct observation, to assess positive and negative social behaviors. Of specific interest for this chapter is the use of an observational code for recording the social behavior of children in playground settings, the Target/Peer Interaction Code (TPIC). This direct observation coding system was developed by the researchers in these studies to help answer specific research questions. Because it is empirically sound and practical and was developed for use in a commonly accessible naturalistic setting (e.g., school playgrounds), it may be of interest to researchers and clinicians.

The TPIC requires coding of social behaviors of the target subject and interacting peers during continuous ten-second intervals. Although a complete description of the TPIC codes is beyond the scope of this chapter, certain aspects of the coding structure are of unique interest for assessing social skills and peer relations. One of the observational areas is target subject interactive behavior, which includes the behavioral classes of verbal behavior and physical contact. Within these response classes, behaviors are recorded as being positive or negative and initiated or noninitiated. Another observational category of interest is peer interactive behavior, which includes verbal and physical interactive behavior directed at the target child by his or her peers and is coded in a similar way as was described in the previous category of target subject interactive behavior. Additionally, under the peer interactive behavior category, target subjects' responses to the peer behaviors are coded according to whether they ignored, complied with, or appropriately resisted negative requests from peers.

Although each of the four studies cited in this section on the TPIC varied in overall methodology and findings, some generalized results were found to be consistent. Direct observations using the TPIC were extremely effective at discriminating subjects with antisocial behavior versus at-risk and normal control subjects, and certain components of the observational data were found to correlate significantly with teacher ratings of social skills. Finally, classroom observations of academic engaged time were also found to correlate significantly with teacher ratings of social competence, in some cases to a higher extent than the playground social–behavioral observations did.

Comments on Direct Observation of Child Social Behavior These examples of using the Student Interaction in Specific Settings Tool, Peer Social Behavior Code, and Target Peer Interaction Code illustrate how direct behavioral observation can be used to effectively assess social skills and peer relations of children and adolescents. Such observations may be conducted effectively in naturalistic and analogue settings. Many variations are possible in deciding which social behaviors to observe and which observational methods to employ. In using behavioral observation techniques to assess social skills and peer relations, two specific observational validity issues seem to be particularly important: defining the observation domain and obtaining social comparison data (see Chapter 4 for details). In defining which social behaviors to observe and how to code them, clinicians and investigators would do well to base their targeted behaviors and codes on established domains of social skills and peer relations and to define each class of behavior within the domains narrowly, in order to increase the specificity of the observation. Additionally, obtaining social comparison data is especially important for observations within these domains because it allows the observer to make inferences about whether the observed child's social skills and peer relations are effective or deficient. In the event that deficiencies are observed, increased specificity of behavioral definitions allows for targeted interventions and progress monitoring over time.

Behavior Rating Scales

Until the mid-1980s, most behavior rating scales or checklists were developed to be omnibus measures of problem behavior or to assess specific dimensions of problem behavior, such as hyperactivity. Few, if any, widely available rating scales were designed primarily for assessing children's social skills. In the 1980s and 1990s, there was a strong surge of interest in school-based assessment of social skills and providing training to children with social skills deficits. This increased interest stimulated the development of several commercially available social skills rating scales that have good standardization characteristics and psychometric properties. Two of these rating scales or systems are detailed in this section. Both instruments meet the criteria of having large, nationwide standardization samples and good psychometric properties. The Preschool and Kindergarten Behavior Scales (PKBS) (Merrell, 1994, 2002a), a social-behavior rating scale designed specifically for use with the early childhood/preschool population, is reviewed in Chapter 14. Although, the scales mentioned here are either entirely or partially comprised of items related to adaptive behaviors, two rating scales that are solely strength based and includes indicators of emotional adjustment will also be reviewed (for an extensive review of strength-based measures of social and emotional skills, see Jimerson, Sharkey, Nyborg, & Furlong, 2004, and Nickerson & Fishman, 2013).

The Social Skills Improvement System (SSIS)—Parent and Teacher Forms The Social Skills Improvement System (SSIS) (Gresham & Elliott, 2008) is a multicomponent social skills rating system focusing on behaviors that affect parent–child relations, teacher–student relations, and peer acceptance. This measure was recently updated from the Social Skills Rating System (SSRS) (Gresham & Elliott, 1990) and is part of a larger system that includes a Performance Screening Guide (described below), the SSIS Classwide Intervention Program, and the SSIS Intervention Guide for small groups and individuals. In 2017, the SSIS SEL (Social Emotional Learning) System will also be available. The availability of this overall package of assessment materials and intervention programs is timely, given that they can be used together to provide a comprehensive, tiered system of increasingly intensive social skills support to children and adolescents. The rating-scale system described here could ideally be used once a child is found to be "nonresponsive" to the classwide intervention program. This rating-scale system includes separate rating scales for teachers and parents and a self-report form for students, which is described later in this chapter. Each component of the system can be used alone or in conjunction with the other forms. Separate instruments and norms are provided for each of three developmental groups, which include preschool level (ages three to five), elementary level (grades K to 6), and secondary level (grades 7 to 12). Each form includes validity scales, and the parent forms now include Spanish translations. Because there is considerable overlap among the different rating forms of the SSIS, an overview of only the elementary-level teacher rating form is provided here as an example (the preschool forms are discussed in Chapter 14).

The elementary-level teacher rating form of the SSIS consists of 83 items divided over three scales: Social Skills, Problem Behaviors, and Academic Competence. For Social Skills and Problem Behaviors items, teachers respond to descriptions using a 3-point response format based on how often a given behavior occurs (0 = *never*, 1 = *sometimes*, and 2 = *very often*). On the Social Skills items, teachers are also asked to rate how important a skill is (on a 3-point scale) to success in the classroom. The importance rating is not used to calculate ratings for each scale but is used for planning interventions. On the Academic Competence scale, teachers rate students as compared with other students on a 5-point scale. Scale raw scores are converted to standard scores (M = 100, SD = 15) and percentile ranks. Subscale raw scores are converted to estimates of functional ability called Behavior Levels.

The Social Skills scale consists of 46 items used to rate social skills in the areas of teacher and peer relations. This scale contains seven subscales, including Communication, Cooperation, Assertion, Responsibility, Empathy, Engagement, and Self-Control. The Communication subscale includes items that reflect adaptive social communication (e.g., "Asks for help from adults"). The Cooperation subscale identifies compliance behaviors that are important for success in classrooms (e.g., "Finishes class assignments on time" and "Uses time appropriately while waiting for help"). The Assertion subscale includes initiating behaviors that involve making and maintaining friendships and responding to actions of others (e.g., "Invites others to join in activities" and "Appropriately questions rules that may be unfair"). The Responsibility subscale includes items that indicate ownership of behavior (e.g., "Takes responsibility for her or his own actions). The Empathy subscale reflects understanding of others (e.g., "Is nice to others when they are feeling bad"). The Engagement subscale indicates responsiveness to others (e.g., "Responds well when others start a conversation or activity"). The Self-Control subscale includes responses that occur in conflict situations such as turn-taking and peer criticism (e.g., "Cooperates with peers without prompting" and "Responds appropriately to teasing by peers").

The Problem Behaviors scale consists of 29 items that reflect behaviors that might interfere with social skills performance. The items are divided into five sub-scales: Externalizing Problems, Bullying, Hyperactivity/Inattention, Internalizing Problems, and Autism Spectrum. The Externalizing Problems subscale items reflect inappropriate behaviors that indicate verbal and physical aggression toward others and a lack of temper control (e.g., "Threatens or bullies others" and "Has temper tantrums"). The Bullying subscale reflects coercive behavior (e.g., "Keeps others out of social circles"). The Hyperactivity/Inattention subscale includes activities that involve excessive movement and impulsive actions (e.g., "Disturbs ongoing activities" and "Is inattentive"). The Internalizing Problems subscale includes behaviors that indicate anxiety, sadness, and poor self-esteem (e.g., "Shows anxiety about being with a group of children" and "Likes to be alone"). Finally, the Autism subscale primarily focuses upon social communication deficits and perseverative behaviors (e.g., "Uses odd physical gestures in interactions" and "Is preoccupied with object parts").

The third scale, Academic Competence, includes seven items that reflect academic functioning, such as performance in specific academic areas, student's motivation level, general cognitive functioning, and parental support (e.g., "In terms of grade-level expectations, this child's skills in reading are:" and "The child's overall motivation to succeed academically is:"). Behavior is rated on a 5-point scale that corresponds to percentages (1 = lowest 10% to 5 = highest 10%).

The SSIS is intended specifically to be linked to intervention ideas. Standard scores and percentile ranks are provided for the Social Skills, Problem Behaviors, and Academic Competence domains. In addition, behavior levels (Below Average, Average, and Above Average) are given for the subscale scores. If scores fall within the concerning range, the Model of Social Behavioral Strengths and Weaknesses can be used for further analysis.

This framework allows one to identify strengths, acquisition deficits, performance deficits, or behaviors that might compete with other skills within a child's repertoire.

The SSIS was standardized on a national sample of more than 4,700 children (when considering all forms combined) representing all four U.S. geographical regions and the U.S. population in terms of ethnic background, gender, and socioeconomic status. Given the overall large number of participants who were rated in the SSIS national standardization, however, it is assumed that the norms for each rating form in the system at the elementary and secondary levels were developed using a sufficient number of cases.

The overall psychometric properties obtained during scale development ranged from adequate to excellent. For the teacher scale, reliability was measured using internal consistency (i.e., coefficients ranged from 0.73 to 0.95), inter-rater and test–retest (i.e., 0.70 to 0.93 correlations across the three scales) procedures. Criterion-related and construct validity were established by finding significant correlations between the SSIS and other rating scales. Subscale dimensions were originally determined through factor analyses of each scale. Items that met a criterion of a 0.30 or greater factor loading were considered to load on a given factor.

The SSIS has the distinct strength of consisting of an integrated system of instruments for use by teachers, parents, and students, which is its major advantage (Demaray et al., 1995). The manual is well written, and the rating instruments are easily understood and used. The research base on the SSIS has grown since its publication and continues to expand. The sections of the instruments that measure social skills are comprehensive and useful. The sections measuring problem behaviors and academic competence are brief and should be considered as short screening sections to be used in conjunction with more appropriate measures of behavioral/emotional problems, when indicated. The SSIS Performance Screening Guide is also a strength of the SSIS assessment and intervention package. This tool is a very brief measure of students' prosocial behavior, motivation, reading, and math skills. Teachers can complete this form on students in preschool through high school. Skills are rated on a scale of 1 to 5 and can provide teachers with a quick estimate of which students need extra support in what areas. Test–retest reliability estimates of this scale were generally moderate, suggesting that the tool is likely appropriate for global screening purposes and might serve as an excellent way to gather data on all children within a RtI model.

The School Social Behavior Scales, Second Edition (SSBS-2)/Home and Community Social Behavior Scales (HCSBS) The School Social Behavior Scales, Second Edition (SSBS-2; Merrell, 2002b), a revision of the original School Social Behavior Scales (Merrell, 1993b), is a school-based social behavior rating scale for use by teachers and other school personnel in assessing social competence and antisocial problem behaviors of students in kindergarten through grade 12. It includes two separate scales (Figures 13.4 and 13.5) with a total of 64 items that describe positive and negative social behaviors that commonly occur in educational settings. Items are rated using a 5-point scale (1 = "never" to 5 = "frequently"). Each of the two scales of the SSBS yields a total score using a raw to *T* score conversion with a mean of 50 and standard deviation of ten. The two scales have three subscales each, with scores reported as four different *Social Functioning Levels*, including *High Functioning*, *Average*, *At-Risk*, and *High Risk*.

Scale A, Social Competence, includes 32 items that describe adaptive, prosocial behavioral competencies as they commonly occur in educational settings. The Interpersonal

	Scale A	Never	Sometimes			Frequently	Scoring Key		
1.	Cooperates with other sudents	1	2	3	4	5			
2.	Makes appropriate transitions between different activities	1	2	3	4	5			
3.	Completes school work without being reminded	1	2	3	4	5			
4.	Offers help to other students when needed	1	2	3	4	5			
5.	Participates effectively in group discussions and activities	1	2	3	4	5			
6.	Understands problems and needs of other students	1	2	3	4	5			
7.	Remains calm when problems arise	1	2	3	4	5			
8.	Listens to and carries out directions from teachers	1	2	3	4	5			
9.	Invites other students to participate in activities	1	2	3	4	5			
10.	Asks appropriately for clarification of instructions	1	2	3	4	5			
11.	Has skills or abilities that are admired by peers	1	2	3	4	5			
12.	Is accepting of other students	1	2	3	4	5			
13.	Completes school assignments or other tasks independently	1	2	3	4	5			
14.	Completes school assignments on time	1	2	3	4	5			
15.	Will give in or compromise with peers when appropriate	1	2	3	4	5			
16.	Follows school and classroom rules	1	2	3	4	5			
17.	Behaves appropriately at school	1	2	3	4	5			
18.	Asks for help in an appropriate manner	1	2	3	4	5			
19.	Interacts with a wide variety of peers	1	2	3	4	5			
20.	Produces work of acceptable quality for his/her ability level	1	2	3	4	5			
21.	Is good at initiating or joining conversations with peers	1	2	3	4	5			
22.	Is sensitive to feelings of other students	1	2	3	4	5			
23.	Responds appropriately when corrected by teachers	1	2	3	4	5			
24.	Controls temper when angry	1	2	3	4	5			
25.	Enters appropriately into ongoing activities with peers	1	2	3	4	5			
26.	Has good leadership skills	1	2	3	4	5			
27.	Adjusts to different behavioral expectations across settings	1	2	3	4	5			
28.	Notices and compliments accomplishments of others	1	2	3	4	5			
29.	Is assertive in an appropriate way when he/she needs to be	1	2	3	4	5			
30.	Is invited by peers to join in activities	1	2	3	4	5			
31.	Shows self-control	1	2	3	4	5			
32.	Is "looked up to" or respected by peers	1	2	3	4	5			
						Totals			
							PR	SM	AB

Figure 13.4 Scale A (Social Competence) of the School Social Behavior Scales

Source: From *School Social Behavior Scales, Second Edition*, by K. W. Merrell (2002b). Eugene, OR: Assessment-Intervention Resources. Copyright 2002 by Kenneth W. Merrell. Reprinted with permission.

	Scale A	Never	Sometimes		Frequently		Scoring Key		
1.	Blames others for his/her problems	1	2	3	4	5			
2.	Takes things that are not his/hers	1	2	3	4	5			
3.	Is defiant to teachers or other school personnel	1	2	3	4	5			
4.	Cheats on schoolwork or in games	1	2	3	4	5			
5.	Gets into fights	1	2	3	4	5			
6.	Is dishonest; tells lies	1	2	3	4	5			
7.	Teases and makes fun of other students	1	2	3	4	5			
8.	Is disrespectful or "sassy"	1	2	3	4	5			
9.	Is easily provoked; has a "short fuse"	1	2	3	4	5			
10.	Ignores teachers or other school personnel	1	2	3	4	5			
11.	Acts as if he/she is better than others	1	2	3	4	5			
12.	Destroys or damages school property	1	2	3	4	5			
13.	Will not share with other students	1	2	3	4	5			
14.	Has temper outbursts or tantrums	1	2	3	4	5			
15.	Disregards feelings or needs of other students	1	2	3	4	5			
16.	Is overly demanding of attention from teachers	1	2	3	4	5			
17.	Threatens other students; is verbally aggressive	1	2	3	4	5			
18.	Swears or uses offensive language	1	2	3	4	5			
19.	Is physically aggressive	1	2	3	4	5			
20.	Insults peers	1	2	3	4	5			
21.	Whines and complains	1	2	3	4	5			
22.	Argues or quarrels with peers	1	2	3	4	5			
23.	Is difficult to control	1	2	3	4	5			
24.	Bothers and annoys other students	1	2	3	4	5			
25.	Gets into trouble at school	1	2	3	4	5			
26.	Disrupts ongoing activities	1	2	3	4	5			
27.	Boasts and brags	1	2	3	4	5			
28.	Is not dependable	1	2	3	4	5			
29.	Is cruel to other students	1	2	3	4	5			
30.	Acts impulsively without thinking	1	2	3	4	5			
31.	Is easily irritated	1	2	3	4	5			
32.	Demands help from other students	1	2	3	4	5			
						Totals			
							HI	AA	DD

Figure 13.5 Scale B (Antisocial Behavior) of the School Social Behavior Scales

Source: From *School Social Behavior Scales, Second Edition*, by K. W. Merrell (2002b). Eugene, OR: Assessment-Intervention Resources. Copyright 2002 by Kenneth W. Merrell. Reprinted with permission.

Skills subscale includes 14 items measuring social skills that are important in estab-lishing positive relationships with, and gaining social acceptance from peers (e.g., "Offers help to other students when needed" and "Interacts with a wide variety of peers"). The Self-Management Skills subscale includes ten items measuring social skills relating to self-restraint, cooperation, and compliance with the demands of school rules and expectations (e.g., "Responds appropriately when corrected by teacher" and "Shows self-restraint"). The Academic Skills subscale consists of eight items relating to competent performance and engagement on academic tasks (e.g., "Completes individual seatwork without being prompted" and "Completes assigned activities on time").

Scale B, Antisocial Behavior, includes 32 items that describe problematic behaviors that either are other-directed in nature or are likely to lead to negative social consequences, such as peer rejection or strained relationships with the teacher. The Hostile–Irritable subscale consists of 14 items that describe behaviors considered to be self-centered and annoying and that will likely lead to peer rejection (e.g., "Will not share with other students" and "Argues and quarrels with other students"). The Antisocial–Aggressive subscale consists of ten behavioral descriptors relating to overt violation of school rules and intimidation or harm to others (e.g., "Gets into fights" and "Takes things that are not his or hers"). The Disruptive–Demanding subscale includes nine items that reflect behaviors likely to disrupt ongoing school activities and to place excessive and inappropriate demands on others (e.g., "Is overly demanding of teacher's attention" and "Is difficult to control").

Many studies and procedures are reported in the SSBS-2 manual and subsequent published articles concerning the psychometric properties and validity of the instrument. The scales were standardized on a group of 2,280 students in kindergarten through 12th grade from the United States, with each of the four U.S. geographical regions repre-sented in the standardization process. The percentage of special education students in various classification categories in the standardization group closely approximates the national percentages of these figures.

Various reliability procedures reported in the SSBS-2 manual indicate the scales have good to excellent stability and consistency. Internal consistency and split-half reliability coefficients range from 0.91 to 0.98. Test–retest reliability at three-week intervals is reported at 0.76 to 0.83 for the Social Competence scores and 0.60 to 0.73 for the Antisocial Behavior scores. Inter-rater reliability between resource room teachers and paraprofessional aides ranges from 0.72 to 0.83 for the Social Competence scores and 0.53 to 0.71 for the Antisocial Behavior scores.

Validity of the scales has been shown in several ways. Moderate to high correlations between the SSBS and five other behavior rating scales (including the Child Behavior Checklist, Conners Teacher Rating Scale–39, Teacher's Report Form, Waksman Social Skills Rating Scale, and the adolescent version of the Walker–McConnell Scale of Social Competence and School Adjustment) indicates that the scale has strong con-vergent and discriminant construct validity (Emerson, Crowley, & Merrell, 1994). Other findings indicate the scales can discriminate adequately between gifted and nongifted children (Merrell & Gill, 1994), between students with disabilities and regular education students (Merrell, 1993b; Merrell, Sanders, & Popinga, 1993), and between students with behavioral disorders and others receiving special education services (Merrell et al., 1992). The factor structure of the two scales is strong, with all items having a factor loading into their respective subscale of 0.40 or greater and no items being duplicated across subscales (Merrell, 1993b).

The SSBS-2 is a practical and easy-to-use school-based rating scale that provides norm-referenced data on positive social skills and antisocial problem behavior. It has satisfactory to good psychometric properties, it is easy to use, and the items and structure are highly relevant to the types of behavioral issues encountered by school-based professionals. The original SSBS has been reviewed positively in the professional literature (Demaray et al., 1995; Kreisler, Mangione, & Landau, 1997), and the minor revisions that went into the second edition of this instrument have only improved it. The Antisocial Behavior scale of the SSBS-2 is designed specifically to measure behavior problems that are directly social in nature or that would have an immediate impact on strained relations with peers and teachers. The scale was not designed to measure overcontrolled or internalizing behavior problems, such as those associated with depression and anxiety, and it was not designed to measure behavior problems associated with ADHD. If these types of problem behaviors are a significant issue on an assessment case, the assessment should be bolstered by the addition of an appropriate measure targeting these behaviors.

In addition to the revised SSBS-2, a cross-informant version of this instrument for use by parents and other home-based informants is available, the Home and Community Social Behavior Scales (HCSBS) (Merrell, 2002c). The HCSBS includes the same general rating format, social competence/antisocial behavior scale division, and items as the SSBS-R. Some of the items were reworded slightly, however, to reflect behaviors in home or community settings rather than school settings. The norming sample of the HCSBS includes more than 1,500 cases that were drawn from a national sample of more than 2,200 ratings of children and youth aged five to 18. The gender and ethnic/racial background of the norming sample is consistent with the 2000 U.S. Census. Findings from research to date on the HCSBS have indicated that this instrument has: (1) strong psychometric properties, as evidenced by high internal consistency coefficients (0.96 to 0.98 for the total scores) (Merrell & Caldarella, 1999); (2) the ability to differentiate accurately between at-risk and not-at-risk students (Merrell & Caldarella, 1999; Robbins & Merrell, 1998) and between students with learning and behavioral disorders and general education students (Lund & Merrell, 2001); (3) sensitivity to treatment outcomes (Snyder, Kymissis, & Kessler, 1999); (4) moderate cross-informant convergence with the SSBS (Robbins & Merrell, 1998); (5) the ability to differentiate between students with and without ADHD (Merrell & Boelter, 2001); and (6) strong convergent validity with several other child behavior rating scales (Merrell & Boelter, 2001; Merrell, Caldarella, Streeter, Boelter, & Gentry, 2001).

In sum, the HCSBS and SSBS together comprise a cross-informant behavior rating system for screening and assessing social and antisocial behavior of children and adolescents across school, home, and community settings. These instruments are easy to use, are practical, are aimed at routine or garden-variety social behaviors rather than psychiatric symptoms, and share strong psychometric properties and an expanding research base. They are designed to be useful in screening, classification, and development of interventions for at-risk children and adolescents.

The Social Emotional Assets and Resilience Scales—Teacher and Parent Reports (SEARS-T, SEARS-P) The Social Emotional Assets and Resilience Scales (SEARS; Merrell, 2011), a multirater assessment system, is a compilation of strength-based rating scales that can be completed by teachers (SEARS-T), parents (SEARS-P), children (SEARS-C) and adolescents (SEARS-A). These measures aim to describe the social and emotional strengths and assets of individual children and adolescents (aged five to 18) in a feasible and socially valid manner. Each SEARS measure also has a short form of approximately 12 items that can be used for screening and potentially for progress monitoring purposes. These measures include a 4-point Likert scale, and items reflect student strengths in peer relationships, empathy, responsibility, and awareness of cognitions and behavior. The SEARS forms are made of perforated, carbonless paper and once administered can be easily scored. Once raw scores are totaled, *T* scores and percentiles can be derived. Higher scores on each scale are reflective of more adaptive or "resilient" behaviors. The SEARS forms also include unique behavioral levels or descriptors that align with RtI tiered models of intervention. These include *Tier 1: Average to High Functioning*, *Tier 2: At Risk*, and *Tier 3: High Risk*. The SEARS-T and SEARS-P are described here and the SEARS-C and SEARS-A are described later in this chapter.

The SEARS-T is comprised of 41 items and takes very little time to complete. The technical properties of the SEARS-T were recently analyzed using a sample of approximately 1,500 teachers from diverse regions of the United States. Validity studies including both exploratory and confirmatory factor analyses resulted in four factors: Responsibility, Social Competence, Self-Regulation, and Empathy. Items reflective of Responsibility include "Is dependable, someone you can rely on" and "Makes good decisions." Social Competence item examples include "Other people see him/her as a leader" and "Asks others for help when he/she needs it." Self-Regulation items included "Thinks of her/his problems in ways that help" and "Can identify errors in the way he/she thinks about things." Finally, Empathy is described in items like "Cares what happens to people" and "Knows when other students are upset, even when they say nothing." Internal consistency coefficients ranged from 0.91 to 0.98, and test–retest reliability coefficients ranged from 0.84 to 0.94 in reliability studies. (Merrell, Cohn, & Tom, 2011). Furthermore, the short form of the SEARS-T (SEARS-SF-T) was found to be internally consistent and reliable with the long form.

The SEARS-P is very similar in format to the SEARS-T and consists of 39 items. In another study aiming to evaluate the technical adequacy of the SEARS-P (Merrell, Felver-Gant, & Tom, 2010), similar results were found. A three-factor structure emerged that included Self-Regulation/Responsibility, Social Competence, and Empathy. Strong internal consistency was demonstrated, ranging from 0.87 to 0.95, and strong test–retest reliability was established at a two-week interval (0.88 to 0.92). The SEARS-SF-P also correlated very well with the full-length form, and internal consistency estimates were strong.

While these are new measures, the SEARS is a comprehensive system that can provide a great deal of information about a child's strengths from a number of perspectives. Ideally, measures like the SEARS will be used more often in practice to guide development of strength-focused interventions and to monitor the progress of interventions in place. As data management systems that compile and track data of larger populations are becoming more of a norm, measures like the SEARS can be used as preventative screening tools that capture wellness and identify the strengths and needs of a population through a less pathology-oriented lens.

The Devereux Student Strengths Assessment (DESSA) The Devereux Student Strengths Assessment (DESSA) is a 72-item strength-based measure that can be completed by caregivers and teachers to assess the resilience and social–emotional competencies of children in grades kindergarten to 8 (LeBuffe, Shapiro, & Naglieri, 2014). The DESSA takes about ten minutes to complete and is written at a sixth-grade reading level. An overall Social Emotional Composite score is generated as well as subscale scores including Self-Awareness, Self-Management, Goal-Directed Behavior, Relationship Skills, Personal Responsibility, Decision Making, and Optimistic Thinking. A Protective Factor Index is also generated. Developers of the DESSA engaged in a multi-step process to develop the DESSA forms. They started with a pool of over 765 items that were developed on the basis of the social–emotional competencies identified by the Collaborative for Academic and Social Emotional Learning (www.casel.org) and then reduced the pool, based on redundancies, reading level, etc. A national pilot study was conducted, through which researchers were able to develop the final prototype for the measure.

Researchers conducted a national standardization study, through which they were able to generate national norms representative of the U.S. population (see Lebuffe et al., 2014). Internal consistency coefficients across forms and subscales were high and ranged from 0.82 to 0.99. Test–retest reliability was calculated based on scores generated from forms completed four to eight days apart. These coefficients were also high (0.84 to 0.94) but would be likely to decrease significantly with a longer retest window. Further, inter-rater reliability estimates were strong. In terms of validity, the DESSA has been shown to accurately discriminate between students who receive regular education versus those who are identified as emotionally disordered and receiving special education support. Additionally, the DESSA converges with the BASC-2 and the Behavioral and Emotional Rating Scale-Second Edition (BERS-2) (Epstein, 2004).

Overall, the DESSA is an impressive tool that effectively targets resiliency and social–emotional skills. There is also a brief screening tool (DESSA-mini; Lebuffe et al., 2014) that consists of eight items and can be used to identify children in need of further assessment or for classroom Tier 1 problem solving. What is most impressive is that the DESSA and DESSA-mini are just a few measures that are part of a much larger effort on the part of the Center for Resilient Children (see www.centerforresilientchildren.org) to increase these skills in children and adults. The Devereux Early Childhood Assessment has multiple forms targeting the development of these skills and competencies from infancy through preschool. These will be reviewed in Chapter 14. Further there are resources and supports to help practitioners, clinicians, and caregivers to use these data tools to plan prevention and intervention-oriented activities. This comprehensive, data-based approach to improving children's mental health will be very interesting to monitor as more studies are conducted in the years to come.

Interviewing Techniques

Direct assessment of social skills and peer relations is difficult at best to assess through interviewing techniques. The essence of these constructs are the behavioral skills a child or adolescent uses to initiate and maintain social communication, and the quality and nature of his or her resulting relationships with peers. In attempting to obtain high-quality information about a client's social skills or peer relations within the context of an interview, the clinician is in the position of having to rely on observations within an analogue environment, subjective and difficult-to-verify reports from the child or adolescent clients, or interview information obtained from parents or other informants. Elliott and Gresham (1987) noted that although behavioral interviews may be the most frequently used assessment method in the initial stages of intervention planning, they have not been investigated systematically as a social skills assessment technique. Little has changed in the three decades since that statement.

At present, there are no widely available structured or semistructured interview schedules that have been developed primarily for the assessment of social skills and peer relations. Accordingly, the use of less structured techniques is the only alternative for clinicians wishing to assess social skills and peer relations through interviews. Although this method may not be as desirable or direct as behavior rating scales or sociometric approaches, a good clinician still may find it useful in obtaining information on a client's social skills and peer relations.

Within the context of interviewing a child or adolescent client, there are several points and techniques that facilitate the process of obtaining good data on the client's social skills or peer relationships. One of the first points to consider is that when a child is experiencing strained peer relationships or rejection, his or her report may be colored by lack of insight, distorted perceptions, defensiveness, or hurt. The younger the subject, the more likely it is that the interview information may be influenced by these factors. As Boggs and Eyberg (1990) noted, children may not accurately or completely describe the events in their environment because of limited verbal skills or compliance with self-censoring rules they have learned. Clinicians who are skilled in interviewing children known to be experiencing severe rejection by peers often find that when subjects are asked to report on the amount and quality of their peer relations, most report having several friends and getting along with them well, and when asked to "name names," they even provide a detailed list of their "best friends." Clinicians conducting interviews in this manner need to use caution in corroborating the client's report with more objective data and are advised to conduct the interview in a structured, detailed manner to increase the objectivity of the results.

The use of role-playing within a child or adolescent interview, when combined with a careful observation of the client's behavior, can provide some potentially useful information on their level of social skills. Given a carefully structured analogue situation, the clinician may be able to obtain a direct observation within the interview session of such important social skills as eye contact, entering into a conversation, dealing with peer pressure or harassment, requesting help, and giving or receiving a compliment. The process of social skills observation during role-playing is relatively easy: the interviewer simply needs to set up the format and expectations, then observes the client functioning within his or her designated role. For example, the clinician might say something like the following:

> Let's pretend that I am a kid at your school who you might want to become friends with. I am going to act like I am sitting down in the cafeteria eating my lunch, and I want you to come up to me and start talking with me about anything you want. OK? Let's give it a try now.

Engaging in a role-play situation such as this may alert the interviewer to any potential social skills deficits the child or adolescent client has that may be negatively affecting their peer relations. The type of information obtained through this process not only can provide good assessment data, but also can be helpful in establishing an appropriate intervention after the assessment. Behavioral role-play techniques, such as the example just provided, may be considered to be a bridge between interviewing and direct behavioral observation because they use some traditional components of each method. Gresham (1986) noted that behavioral role-play interview techniques have several advantages for assessment, particularly when the interview setting is tightly controlled and simulated to be similar to the natural environment in which the child's normal social interactions occur. In this regard, it is crucial to consider that behavioral generalization and meaningful results are more likely to occur if the role-play situation is constructed to parallel the real environment (Stokes & Baer, 1977).

When conducting an interview with a parent of a child or adolescent client, useful social skills and peer relations information may be obtained by structuring the interview questions carefully and by providing the parent with specific guidelines on how to respond to questions. It is important to note that the behavior of the interviewer may have a significant impact on the responses of the client during the interview (Gross, 1984). Because the goal of the interview in this instance is to obtain specific information on the social skills and peer relations of the child, it is helpful for the interviewer to provide specific prompts to the parent to increase the quality of the interview data. The following scenario illustrates how an interviewer can maximize the quality of the information they obtain by carefully structuring questions and prompts:

INTERVIEWER: Tell me about how Jamie gets along with other children.

PARENT: Not very well.

INTERVIEWER: Can you tell me some more about that?

PARENT: Jamie doesn't have many friends . . . when she does have another child over to the house to play, they usually don't want to come back again because they get mad at her.

INTERVIEWER: Could you tell me specifically what kind of things the other kids seem to get mad at Jamie about?

PARENT: Usually, when they are playing with toys or a book or something, Jamie won't share with them . . . she wants to dominate everything and gets upset when they have something that belongs to her. She wants to take toys and things that they bring over and use them the whole time.

INTERVIEWER: So Jamie has a difficult time sharing with others and doing what they want to do . . . this seems to be a real problem for her in making friends.

PARENT: It's a real problem all right . . . if she could see the other kid's point of view, give in a little bit, and not be so jealous of her things, I think she could have a lot more friends to play with.

This interchange shows how the interviewer, by going from the general to the specific and by providing the parent with express prompts, is able to pinpoint specific types of social skills and peer interaction problems. The parent interview can vary from being open-ended to being highly structured; the specific level of structure should depend on the purpose of the interview. If the goal is to obtain useful information on the social skills and peer relations of the child, a higher degree of structure and prompting seems to be most useful.

Sociometric Approaches

Sociometric approaches are a valid method for assessing social skills and peer relations. In fact, the constructs of social skills and peer relations are perhaps more closely suited to assessment through sociometrics than any other constructs. Virtually any of the approaches discussed in Chapter 7 can be adapted easily for directly assessing different aspects of peer relations, which is their main purpose and use. Actual social skills tend be assessed less directly with sociometric approaches than do peer relations. Because peer relations are linked closely with social skills (Hartup, 1978), sociometric assessment should hold a great deal of heuristic interest for conducting social skills assessments as well. Because the general methods, techniques, and properties of sociometric approaches were discussed in detail in Chapter 7, this section focuses on a few issues and applications of sociometric assessment for measuring social skills and peer relations, rather than on duplicating the general information presented elsewhere.

Some discussion on the nature of the relationship between the two constructs of interest for this chapter—social skills and peer relations—may be useful at this point. Perhaps the best way of conceptualizing this relationship is to look at it as being reciprocal in nature. On one hand, peer relations are seen as being an outcome of social skills, in that the greater degree of adaptive social competency a person possesses, the greater his or her ability to develop positive and fulfilling relationships with other persons (Gresham & Reschly, 1987a). On the other hand, it also has been shown that to some extent peer relations are determinants of social skills, in that the social learning process involved in peer relationships contributes significantly to the development of social skills (Hartup, 1978, 1983). The relationship between these two subdomains of social competence is complex and is described best as being mutually influential or reciprocal. Figure 13.1 shows this theorized relationship between the two constructs. In one sense, peer relations may be considered an outcome of social skills, but in another sense, the constructs are mutually reciprocal in nature.

In preparing to conduct an assessment of social skills or peer relations using any of the sociometric approaches discussed in Chapter 7, the clinician or investigator must consider two aspects to make the assessment as useful as possible. The first area to be considered is which general technique to use. On the basis of Connolly's (1983) review, the choice of sociometric approaches at the general level is between using a peer nomination procedure and a peer rating procedure. Peer nomination procedures have been the traditional method of choice in sociometrics, but peer rating procedures may also be a useful alternative. The main difference between the two general types of procedures is that peer nominations tend to produce a measure of popularity, whereas peer ratings tend to produce a measure of average "likability" (Connolly, 1983). Although these two procedures seem to tap similar constructs, there is an important difference, which is illustrated by the example of a child who through peer ratings receives an average rating but is not positively or negatively nominated by any other children in the peer nomination procedure. Is this a typical child or a socially neglected child? It depends on which procedure you use and how you interpret it. A good compromise would be to use both types of sociometric approaches in the assessment if possible, which should strengthen the generalizability of your results. When practical considerations keep you from using both types of procedures in an assessment, it is important to define carefully what your intended goal or outcome for the assessment is and accordingly to select the general type of procedure to be used.

The second aspect to be considered is what specific procedure to use within your selected general method. Two needs will guide this decision. The first need to consider is the capability level of your subjects. When assessing younger or lower-performing children, it is necessary to select a procedure that will not require any extensive reading or writing. In such a case, McAndless and Marshall's (1957) picture board adaptation of the peer nomination procedure would be a good choice, as would the simplified pictorial rating scale procedure for peer ratings (Asher et al., 1979). The other need that will guide your decision regarding the specific procedure to use is the aspect of peer relations or social skills that you want to measure. In this regard, it is sufficient to say that you should evaluate carefully the face validity of the procedures you are considering (and formal validity properties) against the specific assessment needs you have and to choose accordingly.

In sum, the use of sociometric approaches is a time-honored empirically validated method of assessing peer relations that also has indirect validity in assessing social skills. Virtually any of the general methods and specific procedures discussed in Chapter 7, with proper selection and modification, may be of great use to the clinician or investigator in assessing these specific aspects of behavioral, social, and emotional problems.

Assessment with Self-Reports

At present, very little has been done in the area of developing a self-report assessment instrument for measuring social competence with children or adolescents. Perhaps one of the problems with developing effective self-report measures of social skills and peer relations is that children with deficits in these areas may not be reliable judges of their own behavior. It has been noted that youth with ADHD or conduct disorders, two groups that are extremely prone to exhibit social skills deficits and peer relation problems, have a tendency to perceive and interpret ambiguous information regarding the social behavior of other persons in a distorted manner (Merrell & Gimpel, 1998). Regarding the accuracy of self-perceptions of youth with social behavior problems, little empirical work has been conducted. Many clinicians have observed a tendency of these youth to perceive the effectiveness of their own social skills in more glowing terms than would be attributed by objective observers. Researchers and clinicians who obtain self-reports from at-risk children and adolescents regarding their own social skills and peer relations should be cautious regarding bias and distortions in their responses.

A few experimental or research instruments have been developed for self-report assessing of social skills, social emotional assets, or peer relations, but only a few instruments of this type are commercially published and widely available at present. These instruments, the self-report forms of the SSIS and SEARS, are reviewed in the following section.

The Social Skills Improvement System—Student Forms

As part of the larger, cross-informant Social Skills Improvement System that was described earlier in this chapter, there are two different self-report forms for a child or adolescent to use in assessing his or her own social skills. The Student (Ages 8–12) Form is designed to be used by children in grades 3 to 6, and the Student (Ages 13–18) Form is designed to be used for children in grades 7 to 12. Each form includes items rated on a 4-point scale. Both forms include two scales (Social Skills, Problem Behaviors) and 11 subscales (Communication, Cooperation, Assertion, Responsibility, Empathy, Engagement, Self-Control, Externalizing, Bullying, Hyperactivity/Inattention, and Internalizing), with the raw scores being converted to Behavior Levels and a total score, which is converted to a standard score (based on a mean of 100 and standard deviation of 15) and percentile ranking based on same gender norms. Three examples of items on the elementary form include "I make friends easily," "I do my homework on time," and "I ask classmates to join in an activity or game."

The Student Form–Secondary Level includes two sets of ratings. The first set of ratings is a "How True" rating, where the student rates how true each item is for him or her.

Similar to the elementary student version, the "How True" rating on the secondary student form is done according to the criteria of N = Not True, L = A Little True, A = A Lot True, and V = Very True. The second set of ratings is a "How Important" rating, where the student rates how important the specific behavior is in their relationship with others. This second set of ratings is also on a 0 to 2 scale, where 0 = Not Important, 1 = Important, and 2 = Critical. The inclusion of the importance ratings allows for a comparison on specific rating items for any discrepancies between the way a behavioral item was rated and how important it is to that student. For example, if a student rates *not true* on item 1, "I ask for information when I need it," yet his or her importance rating is *critical*, this discrepancy suggests that the student's perceived difficulty in asking for information is particularly painful for him or her.

The psychometric properties of the two student forms reported in the SSIS manual seem to be stronger than those from the original SSIS. They are generally in the acceptable range, particularly when considering that the student forms are designed to be used as part of a multirating system rather than by themselves. Internal consistency coefficients for the student scales range from 0.70 to 0.95. Reported test–retest reliability coefficients for the student forms ranged from 0.59 to 0.81. Convergent and discriminant validity of the student forms was assessed through correlations with the SSRS and BASC-2, and the obtained coefficients ranged from 0.25 to 0.58 on the Social Skills scale of the SSRS. The Problem Behaviors were not compared, as they were not included in the SSRS, and the correlations with the BASC-2 were all weak. These weak correlations probably have a great deal to do with the possibility that the BASC-2 measures different constructs.

Similar to the other components of the SSIS, the two student forms have the advantage of being part of an integrated social skills assessment structure and having been developed using a large, nationwide sample of respondents. These self-report forms, when used with appropriate caution, may be a useful adjunct to the teacher and parent rating forms in assessing social skills and may provide validity to the process of assessing social skills and peer relations by obtaining the student's own perspective.

The Social Emotional Assets and Resilience Scales—Child and Adolescent Forms (SEARS-C, SEARS-A) Similar to the SEARS-T and SEARS-P described earlier in the chapter, the SEARS-C and SEARS-A were developed by Merrell (2011) to measure the social and emotional strengths of students from the perspective of students. The SEARS-C is appropriate for children in grades 3 to 6 and the SEARS-A is for adolescents in grades 7 to 12. Scoring is similar to that described above and includes the same behavioral descriptors. The items on these forms are very similar to those seen on other forms and tap constructs such as empathy, self-regulation, responsibility, and social competence. That being said, factor analytic studies suggested that the SEARS-C items load on to one global factor, meaning that only one total score is derived. Items included on this measure are "I feel sorry for other people when bad things happen to them" and "I can name lots of different feelings." Internal consistency of the SEARS-C was measured at 0.92 and the SEARS-C-SF was less strong but still impressively stable with a coefficient of 0.85. The temporal stability of the SEARS-C was equally impressive (two week = 0.81, four week = 0.79, six week = 0.73). The SEARS-C also converged nicely with other measures of social and emotional health, the Internalizing Symptoms Scale for Children (Merrell & Walters, 1998 and the Behavior and Emotional Rating Scale (Epstein & Sharma, 1998).

The SEARS-A, appropriate for adolescents in grades 7 to 12, includes four subscales derived from factor analyses (Self-Regulation, Social Competence, Empathy, and Responsibility). The SEARS-A includes 35 items such as "I am comfortable talking to lots of different people" and "I am someone you can rely on." Internal consistency estimates ranged from 0.80 to 0.93 and temporal stability of total scores and subscales was moderate to strong across three occasions (two week = 0.63 to 0.83, four week = 0.72 to 0.81, and six week = 0.68 to 0.81). The internal consistency and temporal stability of the SEARS-A-SF were as strong, if not stronger, than those estimates derived from the long form. Convergent validity estimates suggested modest overlap with the SSRS (Gresham & Elliott, 1990) and the Student Life Satisfaction Scale (SLSS) (Huebner, 1991).

Overall, the SEARS-C and SEARS-A are unique measures that capture resilience and social and emotional health. While the SEARS-C and SEARS-A are newly published tools with limited research measuring their use in conjunction with strength-based intervention, we are hopeful that these tools will be used in this way. Developing a better understanding of how this tool can be best used to plan targeted interventions and progress monitor those interventions would be a useful contribution to the field.

LINKING ASSESSMENT TO INTERVENTION

In this chapter, the construct of social competence was defined, its importance was illustrated, and various methods and instruments for assessing social skills, social and emotional assets, and peer relations were reviewed. Although each of the five primary assessment areas covered in this chapter have some relevance for measuring social competence, behavioral observation, behavior rating scales, and sociometric approaches are particularly useful and have been reported widely in the research literature. Some summary information on the standardized assessment instruments that have been covered in this chapter is presented in Table 13.2. Assessing social competence is important for making classification and intervention decisions, but the specific link between social competence assessment data and effective social competence interventions is sometimes vague.

This chapter concludes with two suggestions for increasing the treatment validity of social skills assessment. The first suggestion is that recommended treatments should match identified problems. Over the course of several years serving individually as a school psychologist, teacher, educational consultant, program administrator, university educator of school psychologists, and clinical supervisor, I have read assessment reports in which certain social skills deficits and peer relations problems were identified, and the resulting recommendation from the clinician was that "social skills training should be provided." This generic type of treatment recommendation is akin to a physician diagnosing bronchial pneumonia in a patient, then recommending that the client needs "medical treatment for the pneumonia"; neither recommendation is particularly helpful in developing an effective treatment. One of the consistent findings over several years of research on effective interventions for children and adolescents with behavioral and emotional problems is that the closer the treatment matches the problem, the more chance the intervention has of being successful (Peacock Hill Working Group, 1991). An effective assessment of social skills, developmental assets, and peer relations may result in identifying some specific aspects of the child or adolescent's behavior that need some attention. A best practice is to identify the specific skills deficits or behavioral excesses that

Table 13.2 Summary of standardized assessment instruments for measuring social skills and peer relations

Name of instrument	Type	Rater	Number of items	Grade range
Social Skills Improvement System—Parent and Teacher Forms (Gresham & Elliott, 1990)	Behavior rating scale	School personnel and parents	83: 46 social skills, 29 problem behaviors, 7 academic competence	Pre-K–12
School Social Behavior Scales, Second Edition (Merrell, 2002b)	Behavior rating scale	School personnel	64: 32 social competence, 32 antisocial behavior	K–2
Home & Community Social Behavior Scales (Merrell, 2002c)	Behavior rating scale	Parents and community based informants	64: 32 social competence, 32 antisocial behavior	K–12
Social Emotional Assets and Resilience Scale	Strength-based social and emotional rating scale	School personnel and parents	41: teacher report 39: parent report 12: short forms	K–12
Devereux Student Strengths Assessment	Strength-based social and emotional rating scale	Parents and school personnel	72: parent/school forms 8: short forms	K–8
Social Skills Improvement System—Student Forms (Gresham & Elliott, 2008)	Self-report	Students	75 for secondary	3–6 and 7–12
Social Emotional Assets and Resilience Scale—Child and Adolescent Forms	Self-report	Students	35: SEARS-C and SEARS-A 12: Short forms	3–6 and 7–12

exist, to identify what the purpose of the current behaviors are, and to recommend prosocial interventions for those areas, rather than a generic treatment regimen that may or may not address the problems that have been identified. This method of using assessment results to inform or guide intervention is similar to the Keystone Behavior Strategy for academic skills interventions that was discussed by Shapiro (1996) nearly 20 years ago. This strategy essentially is based on the notion that assessment information may be linked to intervention planning through assisting in identification of the primary problems at hand, which then are targeted specifically for treatment. Several of the measures discussed in this chapter have been developed or improved upon across iterations to more explicitly address this issue. Additionally, many measures are now also developed or refined with the understanding that schools are moving toward implementation of RtI as it applies to behavior and mental health. As schools are examining their social climate and attempting to develop universally applied behavioral expectations that are being taught to students across multiple settings (e.g., Positive Behavior Interventions and Support; e.g., Horner, Sugai, Todd, & Lewis-Palmer, 2005), it is necessary that measures of social skills become a standard part of screening and treatment planning, so that students with more significant needs can be identified early and provided with support based on assessment data.

The second suggestion, which is aimed specifically at school-based practitioners, is that Individual Education Plan goals can be developed by modifying rating scale items or small clusters of items. One of the advantages of using rating scales is that the descriptions they contain are usually concise, well thought out, and specific in nature. As such, social skills rating scale items are often amenable to being developed into good intervention goal statements with a minimal amount of modification. For example, if a boy named Stefen consistently received "never" ratings on item 4 ("Offers help to other students when needed") and item 19 ("Interacts with a wide variety of peers") on the Interpersonal Skills subscale of the School Social Behavior Scales, these items could be reworded into general goal statements as follows:

1. Stefen will increase his level of providing help to other students when it is appropriately needed.
2. Stefen will increase his number of interactions with other students in the classroom and on the playground.

Of course, specific behavioral objectives would need to be developed after the statement of the general goals.

These two examples illustrate how clinicians may develop intervention recommendations using the actual data obtained during the assessment. Research on interventions for social skills deficits and peer relations problems was reported increasingly in the professional literature in the 1980s and 1990s, allowing us to make some generalizations about their effectiveness. Several meta-analyses of social skills training intervention research have been shown to be effective but still modest in terms of the amount of change they typically produce (Beelmann, Pfingsten, & Losel, 1994; Gresham, Sugai, & Horner, 2001; Mathur, Kavale, Quinn, Forness, & Rutherford, 1998). There still are numerous difficulties, however, in producing generalization across settings or maintenance over time with these changes. Two of the key aspects of promoting generalization and maintenance with social skills training include: (1) making the training setting and situation as similar to the naturalistic setting as is possible; and (2) involving parents and teachers in helping to promote practice opportunities for the new skills that are learned (Merrell & Gimpel, 1998). Consequently, any steps that can be taken to make the assessment of social skills and peer relations ecologically valid and to base intervention recommendations on specific assessment findings are especially important.

CONCLUSIONS

The terms *social competence* and *social and emotional skills* are often used interchangeably but in reality are considered to be separate, but related, constructs. Social competence is a summary term reflecting the judgment of the overall quality of one's social and emotional adjustment, whereas social skills are specific behaviors that lead to peer relations and social competence. Based on evidence and informed by the 2008 definitions of intellectual disability from the AAIDD, a theoretical model of the relationship among the constructs of adaptive behavior, social and emotional competence, and peer relations was proposed. In this model, adaptive behavior is considered to be the inclusive superordinate construct, with social and emotional competence and social skills constituting sequentially smaller links into adaptive behavior, and peer relations being considered a product or outcome of social skills and a mutually reciprocal agent that may influence the development of social skills.

Surprisingly little attention has been paid to the development of a classification taxonomy for child and adolescent social skills that is parallel to the several classification systems that have been developed for child and adolescent psychopathology. This lack of attention to a potentially important area was the stimulus for research by Merrell and colleagues, wherein a classification taxonomy for child and adolescent social skills was developed after an extensive review and analysis of multivariate studies of dimensions of social behavior. Using this methodology, five primary dimensions of social skills were identified: Peer Relations, Self-Management, Academic Skills, Compliance, and Assertion. This new classification taxonomy may have implications for the development of new assessment measures and treatment protocols.

A large body of research, some of it considered to be classic, has been generated regarding the importance and long-term outcomes of social skills and peer relations. Essentially, development of solid social skills early in life provides a foundation for later personal, social, academic, and occupational adjustment and is linked to many positive outcomes in life. Conversely, social skills deficits and peer relationship problems early in life are part of a pathway that may lead to a variety of negative outcomes, such as mental health problems, conduct-related discharge from military service, antisocial behavior and incarceration, and unemployment or underemployment. These striking outcomes underscore the importance of early detection of children who have social skills problems so that appropriate interventions may be implemented.

Direct behavioral observation is one of the most empirically validated methods for assessing child and adolescent social behavior. The Student Interactions in Specific Settings Tool, Peer Social Behavior Code, and Target/Peer Interaction Code all are examples of observational coding systems that are specifically relevant for assessing social skills. Clinicians and researchers can easily adapt various types of observational coding systems to target the crucial social skills behaviors they seek to assess.

Behavior rating scales are being used increasingly as a means of assessing social skills, and there have been some impressive developments in this area. The Social Skills Improvement System, School Social Behavior Scales, Second Edition, Home and Community Social Behavior Scales, the Social Emotional Assets and Resilience Scale, and the Devereux Student Strengths Assessment are examples of modern applications of rating scale technology to child and adolescent social skills assessment.

Interviewing is an assessment method that has been reported less frequently for assessing social skills but does seem to hold some promise in this regard. Specifically, behavioral role-playing during interviews may help to facilitate an analogue type of assessment of social skills of a child or adolescent client. If behavioral role-plays are used during an interview, it is crucial that they be designed to be as similar as is possible to the naturalistic setting that is being emulated.

Sociometric approaches to assessing child and adolescent social skills and peer relations have been in use for several decades. Most of the sociometric techniques described in Chapter 7 have some potential uses for social skills assessment. In conducting sociometric techniques for this purpose, it is important to recognize the overall goal for assessment and to plan accordingly. Peer nominations may provide a different kind of information than peer ratings. Sociometric assessment may be suited better for research purposes and screening than for individual assessment because of practical considerations.

Self-report instruments have only recently begun to be used on a large scale for assessing child and adolescent social skills. One of the possible reasons self-report assessment lags behind other types of assessment in this regard is that individuals with social skills deficits may not be highly reliable reporters of their own social behavior. Two self-report measures, the student report forms of the Social Skills Improvement System and Social Emotional Assets and Resilience Scales, are a potentially useful development in self-report assessment of social skills.

Social skills assessment data, if used carefully, may provide important information with which intervention planning may be informed. It is preferable to use assessment data to target specific areas for social skills training (the Keystone Behavior Strategy) rather than identifying deficits and simply recommending generic social skills training. Items from social skills rating scales are potentially useful for rewording into IEP goal statements. On the basis of the yield of research from social skills training interventions, assessment information may be helpful to the extent that it helps to identify important intervention targets and environments and to serve in progress monitoring of interventions.

REVIEWS AND APPLICATION QUESTIONS

1. Describe the difference between social competence and social and emotional skills, and state what types of practical assessment techniques are used to assess both of these constructs.
2. Describe how peer relations may be a product or outcome of social skills and a reciprocal influence for the future development of social skills.
3. In what ways might the development of a classification taxonomy for child and adolescent social skills be useful for social skills assessment and treatment?
4. Using the Peer Social Behavior Code as a guide, describe how this playground-based observational system could be used as a model for developing a classroom-based social behavior observation system.
5. What are some of the considerations and specific practices that should be used to make behavioral role-playing an effective means of social skills assessment during interviews?
6. In comparing the SSBS-2, SSIS, DESSA, and SEARS, what are the advantages, disadvantages, and best uses of each for assessing child and adolescent social behavior?
7. Why is it important to plan carefully the purpose of assessment before choosing between peer nomination and peer rating techniques for assessing peer relations?
8. What are some possible problems in using self-report instruments for assessing child and adolescent social skills?

14

ASSESSING SOCIAL AND EMOTIONAL
BEHAVIOR OF YOUNG CHILDREN

Commenting on the state of the art in assessing young children, Malcom (1993) stated, "A request to assess a child who has not reached school age often strikes fear in the hearts of psychoeducational diagnosticians" (p. 113). This statement may not be true for all clinicians, but it goes right to the center of the issue: there are often substantial challenges in assessing young children. In commenting on some of these challenges, Bracken (1987, 1994) noted that the technical adequacy of assessment measures for preschool-age children tends to lag behind that of measures for school-age children. With regard to social–emotional assessment technology for young children, the lag in technical adequacy appears to be more pronounced (Merrell, 1996a). The specific difficulties in conducting effective social–emotional assessments with young children are many and varied but can be summed up in general as follows:

1. In relation to what is available for use with school-age children and adolescents, there is substantially less assessment instrumentation and fewer specifically developed methods for assessing social and emotional behavior of young children.
2. The technical adequacy (standardization samples, reliability, validity) of many of the social–emotional assessment instruments available for young children is less than desirable, and in general their technical adequacy is not as strong as what typically is seen with instruments for school-age children and adolescents.
3. Some of the social–emotional assessment instruments available for use with young children are not sufficiently developmentally sensitive and specific to the early childhood age range; they are often simply downward-age extensions of tools developed for use with older children, sometimes developed as an afterthought.
4. Social and emotional behavior is exceptionally variable and inconsistent among young children, making it difficult to determine a standard normative perspective.
5. Social and emotional behavior of young children tends to be influenced tremendously by contexts and settings, which often results in undermining confidence in social–emotional assessment results obtained in specific situations at specific points in time.
6. Some of the standard methods of social–emotional assessment (i.e., interviews and self-report tests) commonly used with children and adolescents are extremely difficult and in some cases impossible to implement adequately with young children.

Despite these and other challenges inherent in assessing the social and emotional behavior of young children, there have been some encouraging developments in this area. There also is an increasing need for school psychologists, clinical child psychologists, and

DOI: 10.4324/9781315747521-16

early childhood special education diagnosticians to provide services to young children and their families, including comprehensive assessment services (Merrell, 1996a). This chapter serves a particularly important purpose as a resource for social–emotional assessment of young children. Many of the other chapters are relevant to this topic, but none is designed specifically to address assessment of young children, as this chapter is.

At the onset of this chapter, some definition of what is meant by the terms *young children* and *early childhood* as they are used herein is useful. There is no universally agreed-on definition of these terms. The focus of this chapter is for the most part on what is considered the preschool age range, which is typically ages three to five. It makes sense to focus on this age range because these are the young children who are the most likely to be in various settings where assessment referrals may be generated, such as developmental preschools, Head Start programs, medical clinics, and Child Find clinics. There are some areas within this chapter where the age focus extends down to the infant or toddler years or up to the kindergarten or first-grade level, but the three to five preschool-age focus is clearly my target.

This chapter begins with a review of an alternative diagnostic classification system for behavioral and emotional problems of young children. The largest section of the chapter is devoted to specific applications of the five primary direct and objective methods of assessment with young children. Additionally, recommended best practices for effective social–emotional assessment of young children are presented.

AN ALTERNATIVE DIAGNOSTIC CLASSIFICATION SYSTEM

In Chapter 3, diagnostic classification systems for behavioral and emotional disorders are presented, with a primary focus on the *DSM-5* and the behavioral dimensions approach to classification. One of the limitations of the *DSM* system is that many of the classification categories either have limited utility or are clearly inappropriate for use with young children, particularly those who are in the early stages of the preschool age range and younger. For example, ADHD, one of the most common childhood diagnoses, can be difficult to accurately diagnose in early childhood because there is a great deal of variability in behavior at this age, and many of the symptoms of ADHD (e.g., impulsive behavior) are fairly typical in young children. Further, challenging behaviors present in early childhood may reduce significantly over time. This can impact early diagnoses of Conduct Disorder, for example. In analyzing data from the Avon Longitudinal Study of Parents and Children in England, Barker and Maughan (2009) found that of the sample of young children with high levels of conduct problems, 60% of children showed minimal behavioral difficulties at adolescence. Both of these examples are worthy to consider, and the truth of the matter is that the younger the child, the more difficult and tenuous the diagnosis. Behavioral dimensions classification systems also have limitations with very young children, such as lack of age-proportional sampling in research programs and difficulties differentiating normal from abnormal development. Despite this difficult state of affairs, clinicians who work frequently with young children and their families still may desire to have at their disposal a diagnostic nomenclature appropriate for young children, for the same purposes that these systems are used with older children and adolescents.

As a response to these problems in diagnostic classification methodology for young children, an experimental diagnostic classification was initially released in 1994 by the

ZERO TO THREE National Center for Clinical Infant Programs, an interdisciplinary organization for leadership in infant development and early childhood mental health. This system was titled *Diagnostic Classification: 0–3 (DC: 0–3)* and subtitled *Diagnostic Classification of Mental Health and Developmental Disorders of Infancy and Early Childhood.* In 2005, a revised version of the system was released (*DC: 0–3R*), which maintained the same basic multiaxial structure as the initial version (with some wording changes), but included some minor to moderate modifications based on several years of research and user feedback, including changes to some of the Axis I diagnostic classifications. The authoring committee for the initial version stated that *"Diagnostic Classification: 0–3* is intended to complement existing approaches" (ZERO TO THREE, 1994, p. 15), and the *DC: 0–3R* authoring committee maintained the same complementary stance for the system, indicating that it is designed to be used in conjunction with, and to complement, existing diagnostic classification systems, particularly the *DSM* and *ICD* systems (ZERO TO THREE, 2005). The system initially caught on slowly, as would be expected, but it has gradually become accepted and known among clinicians who serve young children, and its diagnostic codes have been approved for use in obtaining third-party reimbursements by many healthcare insurance companies and health maintenance organizations (HMOs). It is clearly a comprehensive and well-designed system that was much needed and offers many advantages.

DC: 0–3R uses a multiaxial system for classification that is quite reminiscent of the *DSM-IV* system. The following axes, which are identified in more detail in Table 14.1, constitute the diagnostic framework:

1. Axis I: Clinical Disorders
2. Axis II: Relationship Classification
3. Axis III: Medical and Developmental Disorders and Conditions
4. Axis IV: Psychosocial Stressors
5. Axis V: Emotional and Social Functioning

The Clinical Disorders axis (Axis I) is designed to reflect the most prominent feature of the disorder. The Relationship Classification (Axis II) is designed to assist in understanding the quality of the parent–child relationship, which sometimes may be an important aspect of the overall presenting problem. Medical and Developmental Disorders and Conditions (Axis III) is used to note mental health or developmental diagnoses that have been made using other systems, such as *DSM-IV*, ICD-10, or specific classifications used by speech–language pathologists, occupational therapists, physical therapists, and special educators. Psychosocial Stressors (Axis IV) is simply a method of listing various forms and severity of psychosocial stress that seem to be influencing factors in childhood disorders. The Emotional and Social Functioning axis (Axis V) is used to denote or estimate age-expected functional developmental level. An appendix to *DC: 0–3R* provides a reproducible Functional Rating Scale that provides a format for rating the child or infant in six different areas, using a 1 to 6 rating system. Examples of some of the items on this scale include "Complex gestures and problem solving," "Use of symbols to express thoughts/feelings," and "Forming relationships/mutual engagement." Additionally, *DC: 0–3R* provides in another appendix, a Parent–Infant Relationship Global Assessment Scale, which is used to assess the quality of the infant–parent relationship. Specific descriptive anchor points are provided in 10-point increments ranging from 1–10 (documented maltreatment) to 91–100 (well adapted).

Table 14.1 Multiaxial organization of the *Diagnostic Classification: 0–3, Revised (DC: 0–3R)*

Axis I:	**Clinical Disorders**
100.	Posttraumatic Stress Disorder
150.	Deprivation/Maltreatment Disorder
200.	Disorders of Affect
210.	Prolonged Bereavement/Grief Reaction
220.	Anxiety Disorders of Infancy and Early Childhood
	221. Separation Anxiety Disorder
	222. Specific Phobia
	223. Social Anxiety Disorder
	224. Generalized Anxiety Disorder
	225. Anxiety Disorder NOS
230.	Depression of Infancy and Early Childhood
	231. Type 1: Major Depression
	232. Depressive Disorder Not Otherwise Specified
240.	Mixed Disorder of Emotional Expressiveness
300.	Adjustment Disorder
400.	Regulation Disorders of Sensory Processing
410.	Hypersensitive
	411. Type A: Fearful/Cautious
	412. Type B: Negative Defiant
420.	Hypersensitive/Underresponsive
430.	Sensory Seeking/Impulsive
500.	Sleep Behavior Disorder
510.	Sleep Onset Disorder (Protodyssomnia)
520.	Night Waking Disorder (Protodyssomnia)
600.	Feeding Behavior Disorder
	601. Feeding Disorder of State Regulation
	602. Feeding Disorder of Caregiver–Infant Reciprocity
	603. Infantile Anorexia
	604. Sensory Food Aversions
	605. Feeding Disorder Associated with Concurrent Medical Condition
	606. Feeding Disorder Associated with Insults to the Gastrointestinal Tract
700.	Disorders of Relating and Communicating
710.	Multisystem Developmental Disorder
800.	Other Disorders (*DSM-IV-TR* or ICD-10)
Axis II:	**Relationship Classification**
	Parent–Infant Relationship Global Assessment Scale
	Relationship Problem Checklist
Axis III:	**Medical and Developmental Disorders and Conditions**
Axis IV:	**Psychosocial Stressors**
Axis V:	**Emotional and Social Functioning**

At the time of publication of this book, Zero to Three is getting ready to release a new version of this system entitled the *DC: 0–5* (Zeanah et al., 2016). The new title reflects the fact that this classification system will be used with children aged zero to five. A task force was developed in 2013 to plan for this extensive revision. This task force began by soliciting feedback from over 20,000 researchers and practitioners worldwide. Through analysis of this feedback and an in-depth review of current research in early childhood mental health, this task force embarked on a process of revision. The *DC: 0–5* will maintain the multiaxial structure from the previous version, even though it was eliminated from the *DSM-5*. It is likely the axis structure will be changed significantly, however. Further changes reflect attempts to identify disorders that may be precursors to other disorders listed in the *DSM*. For example, Overactivity Disorder of Toddlerhood (OAD) reflects the extreme behaviors related to hyperactivity and impulsivity often seen very early in childhood (Gleason & Humphreys, 2016), and Early Atypical Autism Spectrum Disorder (EA-ASD; Soto, Giserman Kiss, & Carter, 2016) is for children between nine and 36 months that are displaying some symptoms associated with autism. While earlier classification is possible with some disorders, the *DC: 0–5* will also require functional impairment and severity ratings to help preclude diagnoses of disorders when behaviors may be truly reflective of a developmental or transient phase (Zeanah et al., 2016).

It is clear that the *DC: 0–3R* system and its predecessor, *DC: 0–3* have made major and much-needed inroads into mental health and developmental diagnosis of infants and young children, and that the system has become increasingly accepted among professionals and health care administration organizations. The *DC: 0–5* will provide users with an updated approach and will likely continue to offer several advantages over the *DSM* system, most notably that it is developmentally targeted and appropriate for use with infants and young children. It is comprehensive and well designed, and it is worthy of continued consideration and adoption by the professional community.

METHODS FOR ASSESSING YOUNG CHILDREN

With varying degrees of modification and effectiveness, each of the five primary direct and objective methods of assessment can be used to evaluate social and emotional behavior of young children. Projective–expressive social and emotional assessment techniques may be extremely problematic for use with young children because of the difficulty in determining whether unusual or aberrant responses are indicative of social–emotional functioning, cognitive maturity, or physical development (such as fine motor skills). Although it was noted in Chapter 9 that projective–expressive techniques have appropriate and helpful uses, these methods are highly questionable for use with young children and should be avoided in favor of direct and objective techniques that are developmentally appropriate and ecologically valid. At present, the most technically adequate methods of assessment in this domain for use with young children are direct behavioral observation and behavior rating scales. Both of these methods include a variety of empirically validated procedures, systems, and instruments designed specifically for use with young children. Assuming that appropriate modifications are made, sociometric assessment methods can be effective choices for use with young children, especially for screening and research purposes. Clinical interviewing has long been a popular method of assessing young children but, as shown in this section, requires special care and caution with young children, and is probably best used as a way to gather information about the child and his or her environment from another person, such as a parent or teacher. Objective self-report assessment is the least-validated and least-available method for assessing young children, although some interesting innovations have occurred in this area. This section includes comments, recommendations, and reviews of specific techniques and instruments for social–emotional assessment of young children. It concludes with a description of an innovative and comprehensive new multiple gating program for screening young children for behavioral and emotional disorders.

Direct Behavioral Observation

One of the most commonly used methods of assessing the social–emotional behavior of young children in naturalistic settings is systematic behavioral observation (Lehr, Ysseldyke, & Thurlow, 1987). Direct observation of preschool-age children in natural settings is a preferred strategy because it directly measures the behavior of interest, does not impose artificial test-room demands (to which young children are known to be highly reactive), and provides data that are less likely to be distorted by the expectations and biases of parents and caretakers (Doll & Elliott, 1994). Given the obvious advantages of direct behavioral observation with young children, coupled with the fact that some other methods of assessment would prove to be extremely questionable with this age group, each of the general methods and coding procedures of behavioral observation described in Chapter 4 is recommended for use with young children.

In addition to the general threats to reliability and validity of observational data that are described in Chapter 4, direct observation of preschool-age children may require some special precautions to ensure an adequate representativeness of the child's behavior. Because the social–emotional behavior of preschool-age children may change suddenly in response to situational variables (Wittmer & Honig, 1994), and because their developmental level and progress may influence the content of observed behavior strongly (Graham, 1980), it is commonly accepted that special care must be taken to attempt to conduct multiple observations in several settings. The issue of behavioral inconsistency with young children and the practical difficulty of conducting multiple observations pose some serious challenges to clinicians and researchers. One of the issues in this domain that is not fully understood yet is how much observational data should be collected when assessing young children. One of the few studies attempting to answer this question was conducted by Doll and Elliott (1994), who investigated the degree to which observations consistently described the characteristic social behaviors of 24 preschool-age children who were each observed nine times in free-play settings. By comparing partial and complete observational records, these researchers showed that *at least five observations were required to represent the children's social behavior reliably.* A similar finding was shared in a more recent study that observed the generalizability and dependability of systematic direct observations and direct behavior ratings of kindergarten children (Briesch, Chafouleas, & Riley-Tillman, 2010). In this study, researchers determined that three to five observations would likely be needed to obtain dependable direct observation data. In this study, the dependability of direct behavior ratings (DBRs) of young children was less clear, as there appeared to be some rater bias involved. It is unclear how much these results should generalize to routine assessment practice, but the implication is clear: To obtain consistent and representative social observational data with young children, you must be prepared to conduct several different observations across short to moderate periods of time. Clinicians and researchers who are relying heavily on single observations of young children to make inferences about their behavior may be in a precarious position.

Example: Early Screening Project (ESP) Social Behavior Observations Because direct behavioral observation systems tend not to be norm-referenced in the same manner as behavior rating scales, and because observational systems usually are developed and modified by researchers and clinicians for specific purposes and settings, there are few commercially produced observation systems available for general use with young children. One exception to this generalization is the Social Behavior Observations from the Early

Table 14.2 Categories and examples of antisocial and nonsocial behavior from the Social Observations of the Early Screening Project

1. A Negative Reciprocal Interchange, Either Verbal or Physical
    Negative Verbal Behavior
        name calling, bossy commands or statements, statements of rejection, possessive statements, accusations, highly critical or uncomplimentary statements, aggressive threats, pestering, taunts, demanding or quarrelsome behavior
    Negative Physical Behavior
        rough or harmful bodily contact, rough, painful, or irritating contact with objects or materials

2. Disobeying Established Classroom Rules

3. Tantrumming
        yelling, kicking, and/or sulking after a negative social interaction

4. Solitary Play
        not playing within three feet of another child, not exchanging social signals

Screening Project (ESP) (Walker, Severson, & Feil, 1995). The first tier of the ESP system is now part of the Systematic Screening of Behavior Disorders system (Walker & Severson, 1992; Walker, Severson, & Feil, 2014; Walker, Severson, Nicholson, Kehle, Jenson, & Clark, 1994), described in Chapter 15, but it is useful to focus more closely on its Social Behavior Observations component in this section to provide a specific example of a practical systematic behavioral observation system designed for use with young children. The ESP observations are designed to assess children's social behavior in free play or unstructured activities, with a more specific purpose being measurement of social adjustments and interactions with peers and adults. This system uses a duration coding procedure wherein the observer uses a timer to assist in recording the total amount of time that a child is engaged in a particular category of social behavior, antisocial behavior (negative social engagement, disobeying rules), or nonsocial behavior (tantrumming, solitary play). The resulting duration of time in these categories is calculated into a percentage of total time of the observation (which should be for at least ten minutes). Categories and examples of antisocial and nonsocial behavior are presented in Table 14.2. The ESP kit includes comprehensive training materials for use in observer training. Normative comparison data for antisocial or nonsocial behavior are presented in the ESP manual and provide ranges of percentages of engagement for specific groups. For example, with girls, engagement in antisocial or nonsocial behavior 37% to 45% of the time places them in the At-Risk group, whereas the ranges of 46% to 54% and 55% or more place them in the High Risk and Extreme Risk groups. The Social Observations are designed to be an optional part of the broader ESP screening process. Because normative data are available, however, and because the system has been tested comprehensively and possesses good technical properties, it seems appropriate for researchers or clinicians to use Social Observations separately from the system for specific purposes as needed. An updated version of this observation code is in process and will hopefully be released soon.

Behavior Rating Scales

In the 1980s and 1990s, there were few behavior rating scales designed for use with young children, most of them were not widely available, and few were developed with nationwide norming samples or possessed adequate technical properties and a solid research base. Within the past 15 years or so, there have been substantial new developments in this arena, and there are now several widely available and technically sophisticated behavior rating scales designed exclusively for use with young children. This section provides an overview of several such commercially published instruments that seem to be among the most widely researched and adequately developed of what is currently available for use with young children.

The Ages and Stages Questionnaires: Social–Emotional, Second Edition (ASQ:SE-2) The Ages and Stages Questionnaires: Social–Emotional, Second Edition (ASQ:SE-2; Squires, Bricker, & Twombly, 2015) is a highly innovative behavior rating instrument completed by parents to evaluate social–emotional competencies and problems of children aged one month to six years. The ASQ:SE-2 was designed to provide a low-cost, simple screening instrument that may be scored and interpreted by individuals with minimal training in standardized assessment and measurement, such as paraprofessionals, teachers, and child-care professionals. The ASQ:SE-2 uses a set of nine questionnaires for each of nine age levels (two, six, 12, 18, 24, 30, 36, 48, and 60 months). The rating forms increase in length for each age level, and the items for each age-level questionnaire were designed to be developmentally specific for that age. Each questionnaire can be used within about three months (for the two- through 30-month intervals) or six months (for the 36- through 60-month intervals) of the chronological age targeted by the questionnaire. The items are rated using a format that requires the parent to check one of three options for the specified behavior: Often or Always, Sometimes, and Rarely or Never. There is a separate section that parents may check if that behavior is a concern for them. The scoring process is simple, and only raw scores and percentiles are used. Additionally, developers added a "monitoring zone," which is near the cutoff score that would indicate an area of concern. The ASQ:SE-2 items are divided into seven behavioral areas: Self-regulation, Compliance, Communication, Adaptive functioning, Autonomy, Affect, and Interaction with people. English and Spanish language forms are available.

Standardization information and technical properties are described in a detailed technical report that constitutes a section of the ASQ:SE-2 manual and can also be downloaded from www.agesandstages.com (Squires, Bricker, Twombly, Murphy, & Hoselton, 2015). Over the years, normative groups were developed from a sample of more than 14,000 parent ratings of children from several U.S. states and stratified by gender and ethnicity. Typical and at-risk children were included in the norms for each level. Average internal consistency coefficients of the ASQ:SE-2 forms by age range was 0.84. The average test–retest coefficient was 0.89. Cutoff levels were developed to place children's ASQ:SE-2 scores into risk levels ("At-Risk" and "Okay"), and the evidence presented in the technical report regarding the correct classification rates for these risk levels is impressive, with respectable specificity and sensitivity percentages. The technical report provides evidence of strong associations between ASQ:SE-2 scores and those of comparison measures, and an ability to differentiate between typical and atypical or at-risk children. The ASQ:SE-2 has been found to specifically discriminate between groups of children with social–emotional disabilities versus those without. Also, the ASQ:SE-2 was able to identify those identified with autism as "at-risk" in 83.5% of the cases. This could be useful when clinicians are using the ASQ:SE-2 as a screening tool that helps them make decisions about cases in need of further assessment. Further studies of the original ASQ:SE (Squires, Bricker, & Twombly, 2004) also suggest that this tool can be more helpful than other strategies or tools available for screening for psychosocial concerns. Jee et al. (2010) found that the ASQ:SE was more sensitive in identifying children with psychosocial concerns than clinical judgment alone or developmental screening tools that were broader in scope (e.g., ASQ).

The ASQ:SE-2 has much to offer and is worthy of recommendation. The care the authors took in developing the ASQ:SE-2 based on developmental theory and the need for a simple and efficient screener is obvious, and the technical evidence presented in the manual is impressive. The ASQ:SE-2 is one of only a small handful and perhaps the most sophisticated and technically sound of available assessment tools that are useful for social–emotional screening with children ages one month to 72 months. For screening of young children—those who are too young to fall within the norming samples of the predominantly preschool-age measures that are reviewed in this section—the ASQ:SE-2 is an excellent choice and is perhaps the best tool available. Its unique features and developmental specificity make it a good potential choice for screening children in the preschool age range as well.

The Social Emotional Assessment Measure (SEAM) The Social Emotional Assessment Measure (SEAM) is a tool that was developed by the authors of the ASQ and ASQ:SE (Squires & Bricker, 2006). This tool is intended for use as a curriculum-based assessment measure, meaning that results from the SEAM can be logically linked to social–emotional intervention targets appropriate for young children. The SEAM includes two versions for children aged three to 18 months and 18 to 36 months, respectively. The SEAM can be used within a 5-step process that authors describe as Activity-Based Intervention: Social-Emotional (ABI:SE). The first step in the ABI:SE includes a questionnaire, the Environmental Screening Questionnaire, that caregivers complete and aims to help assessment professionals to screen the environment in which the child is developing. The second step includes completion of the SEAM measure. The SEAM is a comprehensive questionnaire that assesses a child's social–emotional competencies as well as the caregivers' strengths and weaknesses. The third step in the ABI:SE includes setting goals for intervention based on the assessment data gathered, and the last two steps include intervention implementation and evaluation. Squires et al. (2013) conducted a large psychometric study of the SEAM and found moderate to strong evidence of reliability and validity. Internal consistency coefficients ranged from 0.69 to 0.90, test–retest ranged from 0.97 to 0.99, and inter-rater reliability ranged from 0.64 to 0.95. The SEAM demonstrated strong convergence with other early childhood social–emotional measures (e.g., Devereux Early Childhood Assessment). Additionally, parents and early interventionists found that the SEAM was useful, clear, and gave meaningful information about children's social–emotional abilities. The SEAM serves as a functional, curriculum-based assessment tool and could potentially enhance current approaches to early intervention services for young children and families.

The Devereux Early Childhood Assessments (DECA) The Devereux Early Childhood Assessments include an infant and toddler measure (DECA-I/T; Mackrain, LeBuffe, & Powell, 2007) and a second edition of a preschool measure (DECA-P2; LeBuffe & Naglieri, 2012). These measures are behavior rating scales that are strength-based and measure resilience through report of three protective factors including Initiative, Self-Regulation, and Attachment/Relationships.

The DECA-I is a 33-item measure that can be used by parents, caregivers, and teachers of infants aged four weeks to 18 months, and takes about five to ten minutes to complete on paper and three to five minutes to complete electronically through a web-based platform (see www.e-deca2.org). There are English and Spanish forms available. Factor analyses indicated that Initiative and Attachment/Relationships are the two primary factors on this scale. A Total Protective Factors score is also generated and scores are reported as *T* scores and percentile ranks. This tool can also be used to compute a percentage delay, comparisons across sources, and at pretest and posttest. The toddler version, the DECA-T is appropriate for children aged 18 months to 36 months and has a similar structure as the DECA-I. There are 36 total items and three primary factors: Initiative, Self-Regulation, and Attachment/Relationships. Both the DECA-I and the DECA-T have excellent technical properties that were established through data collected from a sample of 2,183 children from 29 states in geographically diverse locations in the U.S. Internal consistency coefficients ranged from 0.80 to 0.94. Test–retest coefficients were obtained at 24- and 72-hour intervals for the infant measure, ranging from 0.83 to 0.94, while the DECA-T coefficients ranged from 0.72 to 0.99. Inter-rater reliability (between parents and teachers) was lower, which is not surprising. The DECA I/T do show evidence that they can discriminate between young children with and without social–emotional concerns.

The DECA-P2 targets preschool children aged three to five. This tool also is brief and consists of 38 items with the same factor structure as the DECA-T and an additional Behavioral Concerns subscale. Internal consistency coefficents were very high, ranging from 0.80 to 0.95. Test–retest reliabilities ranged from 0.88 to 0.95 for the subscale scores and inter-rater reliabilities were again lower as they reflect the differences in perceptions between caregivers and teachers. The DECA-P2 is able to discriminate between those with identified behavior disorders and those without.

Overall, the DECA behavior rating scales are well developed, brief, strength-based measures that target children as young as four weeks old. This assessment system, in combination with intervention and prevention resources available on www.centerfor resilientchildren.org, is another excellent example of a strength-based approach of linking assessment to intervention for the youngest children.

The Behavior Assessment System for Children, Third Edition (BASC-3) The Behavior Assessment System for Children, Third Edition (BASC-3) (C. R. Reynolds & Kamphaus, 2015) is the most recent version of the popular comprehensive system for assessing personality and behavior of children and adolescents. The BASC-3 includes parent and teacher rating scales, self-report forms, a structured observation form, a screening tool, and a developmental history interview form. The parent and teacher rating scales of the BASC-3 were reviewed in general in Chapter 5, and the self-report forms were reviewed in Chapter 8. Included in the BASC-3 rating scales are parent and teacher rating scales for use with children aged two to five, which were not discussed specifically in the previous chapters. These are reviewed herein.

The teacher rating scale for ages two to five (TRS-P) includes approximately 100 items that are rated according to four dimensions: never, sometimes, often, and almost always. The parent rating scale for ages two to five (PRS-P), designed and used in a similar way to the TRS-P, includes more than 100 items. The items on both forms represent a broad range of positive and negative behaviors of various types. These instruments have a complex and sophisticated structure that includes the following empirically derived subscales, listed alphabetically: Adaptability, Aggression, Anxiety, Attention Problems, Atypicality,

Depression, Functional Communication, Hyperactivity, Social Skills, Somatization, and Withdrawal. Content scales include Anger Control, Bullying, Developmental Social Disorders, Emotional Self-Control, Executive Functioning, Negative Emotionality, and Resiliency. Composite scores are also a part of the BASC-3 system, including a Behavioral Symptoms Index, Adaptive Skills, Externalizing Problems, and Internalizing Problems. Finally, there is a Clinical Probability Index, Functional Impairment Index, and an Executive Functioning Index (comprised of Attentional Control, Behavioral Control, Emotional Control). Raw scores in these areas are converted to T scores and percentile ranks. Additionally, the BASC-3 rating forms provide a means of evaluating unusual response patterns and critical items.

The national norm samples for the BASC are large and well stratified, and are quite similar in terms of ethnic-group breakdown to the 2013 U.S. Census Bureau American Community Survey (U.S. Census Bureau, 2013). The TRS-P general norms are based on teacher ratings of 500 children aged two to five, whereas the PRS-P norms are based on parent ratings of 600 children aged two to five. As stated in previous chapters, the BASC-3 manual is extensively documented, is well written, and details substantial reliability and validity evidence. Internal consistency reliabilities for the TRS-P are in the 0.75 to 0.92 range for the scale scores and in the 0.86 to 0.96 range for the composite scores. Short-term test–retest reliability for the preschool forms is high, with a median composite value of 0.90. Inter-rater reliability between teachers for the preschool form is reported and spans the 0.42 to 0.83 range. Convergent construct validity for TRS-P is shown in the manual through significant correlations with the Child Behavior Checklist and BASC-2, as well as the Autism Spectrum Rating Scales. Construct validity of the BASC rating scales is shown further in the manual through showing sensitivity to differences among various clinical groups, although it is unclear how much the preschool forms were represented in these studies. Reliability and validity coefficients for the parent forms were as impressive as those for the TRS-P. Although the BASC manual is extensively detailed, there has been little additional research published documenting the validity of the system for use with young children. One published study (McNamara, Holman, & Riegal, 1994) evaluated the usefulness of the BASC-2 in determining the mental health needs of a Head Start population and provided some additional supporting construct validity evidence.

In sum, the rating scale components of the BASC that are designed specifically for use with young children, the TRS-P and PRS-P, seem to be an excellent addition to the available rating scale instrumentation for this age group. The scales are well constructed, are comprehensive, and seem to have good technical properties. The only possible negative comment regarding the TRS-P and PRS-P is the modest size of the normative samples. If these instruments were introduced as separate tests rather than as part of the larger BASC system, it is likely that the modest norm samples would be a frequent criticism. On the basis of the overall strength of the BASC system, however, there is certainly enough supporting evidence to justify recommending the rating scales designed for assessment of young children.

The Early Childhood Rating Forms of the ASEBA System The comprehensive Achenbach System of Empirically Based Assessment offers two comprehensive rating scales for use with young children. The Child Behavior Checklist for Ages 1½–5 (CBCL/1½–5) (Achenbach & Rescorla, 2000) is the most recent revision of the Child Behavior Checklist for younger children (CBCL/2–3) (Achenbach, 1992). The Caregiver–Teacher Report

Form for Ages 1½–5 (C-TRF) (Achenbach, 2001a) is the most recent revision of this form, which previously extended downward only to age two. These instruments are discussed in this section.

The CBCL/1½–5 was designed to obtain parent ratings of child behavior using 99 problem items. Many of these items have counterparts on the CBCL for older children and youth, and some of the items were developed uniquely for the CBCL/1½–5, specific to the early childhood developmental period. The CBCL/1½–5 is designed to be completed by parents. Items are rated using a 3-point scale, ranging from 0 (Not True) to 2 (Very True or Often True). The individual items of this measure are added in various combinations into empirically derived clinical syndrome scores (subscales), broad-band scores (internalizing and externalizing), and a total problems score. The six cross-informant scales include Emotionally Reactive, Anxious/Depressed, Somatic Complaints, Withdrawn, Attention Problems, and Aggressive Behavior. Also included are five *DSM*-oriented scales, including Affective Problems, Anxiety Problems, Pervasive Developmental Problems, Attention Deficit/Hyperactivity Problems, and Oppositional Defiant Problems. Like the rest of the ASEBA system, raw scores on the CBCL/1½–5 are converted to *T* scores and percentile ranks, and hand-scoring forms and computer scoring programs are available. Additionally, Achenbach (2013) released a guide to interpretation of the *DSM*-oriented scales, given its revision to align with *DSM-5*. The computer scoring program takes less time and has the advantage of calculating agreement indices (referred to as Q correlations) between two parents who have rated the same child.

The CBCL/1½–5 includes an important and potentially useful change from the previous version of the instrument. Included with this scale is a Language Development Survey (LDS) for ages 18–35 months, a questionnaire that obtains information from parents about language development issues and problems of very young children. The LDS is a two-page form that includes eight general questions about the child's development, as well as a list of 310 words in 14 domains that parents are asked to review, and to circle if their child spontaneously uses the word.

The normative group for the CBCL/1½–5 consists of scores from a national sample of 700 children, derived from an initial norming sample of 1,728 child ratings. The norm sample is well stratified by race/ethnicity, gender, region, socioeconomic status, and urban–rural residence. Mixed gender norms are used. The manual for the CBCL/1½–5 provides adequate documentation of the technical properties of the test, which are generally quite good. Additional published research on the CBCL/1½–5 and its predecessor provide validity evidence in such areas as cross-cultural uses (Auerbach, Yirmiya, & Kamel, 1996; Leadbeater & Bishop, 1994), gender differences (van den Oord, Koot, Boosma, & Verhulst, 1995), relationships between child problem ratings and maternal depression, social support and stress (Leadbeater & Bishop, 1994), and group differences between children in and outside of daycare situations (Caruso, 1994).

The CBCL/1½–5 is a much-needed downward extension of the sophisticated ASEBA rating scale system on which it was based. This instrument is particularly useful because many of the items were developed specifically for the lower registers of the early childhood age range, and because the Language Development Survey provides opportunities for assessing language skills in early childhood that were not previously possible with the ASEBA system.

The C-TRF was designed to be a downward extension of the TRF and is designed for use by preschool and Head Start teachers, daycare center personnel, and kindergarten teachers. This instrument includes 99 problem items and contains the same cross-informant and *DSM*-oriented scales, as well as the same scoring and score conversion procedures that were described for the CBCL/1½–5. The norm group for the C-TRF includes 1,113 children who were rated by teachers or childcare providers, a sample derived from an initial pool of ratings of 1,192 children. This is a robust sample size for a limited age range and has the additional advantage of being well stratified. A guide for the test is available and provides information on development, reliability, validity, and applications. The C-TRF seems to be a promising instrument and, although the research base is still somewhat sparse in comparison with other components of the ASEBA system, can be recommended for use with young children.

The Preschool and Kindergarten Behavior Scales, Second Edition (PKBS-2) The Preschool and Kindergarten Behavior Scales, Second Edition (PKBS-2) (Merrell, 2002a) is a 76-item behavior rating scale designed to measure typical problem behaviors and social skills of children aged three to six. The PKBS-2 is an updated and revised version of the original PKBS (Merrell, 1994), including additional norm sample cases, an improved scoring system, and new research data. This instrument may be completed by teachers, parents, daycare providers, or others who are familiar with a child's behavior. The items are sufficiently generic that a common rating form is used across different informants and settings. The PKBS-2 was developed with a national normative sample of 3,313 children from across the United States, roughly comparable to the general U.S. population in terms of ethnicity, gender, and socioeconomic status. A Spanish-language version of the PKBS-2 is also available.

Rather than being a downward extension of an existing rating scale designed for use with older children, the PKBS-2 and its items were designed specifically for the unique social–behavioral aspects of the early childhood/preschool developmental period, and systematic item development and content validation procedures were employed. In other words, the initial PKBS item pool was developed after a systematic and comprehensive review of clinical and research literature describing the social, behavioral, and emotional problems of young children, particularly how these problems are manifested in preschool and kindergarten-age children.

The items on the PKBS-2 constitute two separate scales each designed to measure a separate domain: a 34-item Social Skills scale and a 42-item Problem Behavior scale. Each of these two scales includes an empirically derived subscale structure. The Social Skills scale includes the following subscales: Social Cooperation (12 items describing cooperative and self-restraint behaviors), Social Interaction (11 items reflective of social initiation behaviors), and Social Independence (11 items reflecting behaviors that are important in gaining independence within the peer group). The Problem Behavior scale includes two broad-band subscales, Internalizing Problems and Externalizing Problems. Consistent with the theoretical and empirical breakdown of the externalizing/internalizing problem dichotomy (see Cicchetti & Toth, 1991), the former broad-band scale includes 27 items describing undercontrolled behavioral problems, such as aggression, overactivity, and coercive antisocial behaviors, whereas the latter broad-band scale includes 15 items describing overcontrolled emotional/behavioral problems, such as social withdrawal, somatic problems, anxiety, and behaviors consistent with depressive symptoms. For the broad-band problem behavior scores of the PKBS-2, there are supplemental problem behavior subscales available which may be used to provide more details about the

Social Skills Scale				
	Never	Rarely	Sometimes	Often
1. Works or plays independently	0	1	2	3
2. Is cooperative	0	1	2	3
3. Smiles and laughs with other children	0	1	2	3
4. Plays with several different children	0	1	2	3

Figure 14.1 Social Skills Examples from the Preschool and Kindergarten Behavior Scales, Second Edition

Source: From *Preschool and Kindergarten Behavior Scales, Second Edition*, by K. W. Merrell (2002a). Austin, TX: Pro-Ed. Copyright 2002 by Pro-Ed. Adapted with permission.

Problem Behavior Scale				
	Never	Rarely	Sometimes	Often
1. Acts impulsively without thinking	0	1	2	3
2. Becomes sick when upset or afraid	0	1	2	3
3. Teases or makes fun of other children	0	1	2	3
4. Does not respond to affection from others	0	1	2	3

Figure 14.2 Problem Behavior Examples from the Preschool and Kindergarten Behavior Scales, Second Edition

Source: From *Preschool and Kindergarten Behavior Scales, Second Edition*, by K. W. Merrell (2002a). Austin, TX: Pro-Ed. Copyright 2002 by Pro-Ed. Adapted with permission.

breakdown of internalizing and internalizing problem symptoms. The Internalizing Problems broad-band scale includes two supplemental subscales (Social Withdrawal and Anxiety/Somatic Problems), whereas the Externalizing Problems broad-band scale includes three supplemental subscales (Self-Centered/Explosive, Attention Problems/Overactive, and Antisocial/Aggressive). Sample items from the PKBS-2 are presented in Figures 14.1 and 14.2.

Technical data reported in the PKBS-2 test manual and in other published sources provide evidence for adequate to excellent psychometric properties. Test–retest reliability estimates for the Social Skills and Problem Behavior total scores at three-month intervals were found to be 0.69 and 0.78. Child ratings by preschool teachers and teacher aides for the respective total scores have been shown to correlate at 0.48 and 0.59. Internal consistency reliability estimates for the Social Skills and Problems Behavior total scores were found to be 0.96 and 0.97. Content validity of the PKBS has been shown through the documentation of item development procedures and through moderate to high correlations between individual items and total scale scores. Discriminant convergent construct validity has been shown by examining relationships between the PKBS and four other established preschool behavior rating scales: the Matson Evaluation of Social Skills with Young Children, the Conners Teacher Rating Scale, the School Social Behavior Scales, and the Social Skills Rating System (Merrell, 1995a). Construct validity has been shown through analysis of intrascale relationships, factor analytic findings with structural equation modeling (Merrell, 1996b), and documentation of sensitivity to various group differences (Holland & Merrell, 1998; Jentzsch & Merrell, 1996; Merrell, 1995b; Merrell & Holland, 1997; Merrell & Wolfe, 1998).

Reviews of the PKBS and PKBS-2 in the professional literature have been positive (e.g., Bracken, Keith, & Walker, 1994, 1998; MacPhee, 1998; Riccio, 1995; Watson, 1998), and these scales have the advantage of being easy to use and well documented. In sum, the PKBS-2 is useful as a general problem behavior and social skills assessment tool for young children, particularly those exhibiting typical types of behavioral problems in typical types of settings such as Head Start programs and preschool or kindergarten classrooms. For assessing children with severe low-frequency behavior problems, such as might be exhibited by children in psychiatric treatment centers, instruments such as the Child Behavior Checklist may be more appropriate.

The Social Skills Improvement System (SSIS) The Social Skills Improvement System (SSIS) (Gresham & Elliott, 2008), which was reviewed in general in Chapter 13, is a comprehensive social skills assessment system for children and adolescents. The SSIS is updated from the widely recognized *Social Skills Rating System* (SSRS), and included in this update are improved measures of three- to five-year-old children's behavior. The SSIS system includes teacher and parent preschool-level rating forms for use with children aged three to five. These forms have been improved upon and include updated norms. Because these preschool level forms are highly relevant to the topic of social–emotional assessment of young children, and because they were not reviewed specifically in the previous general review, they are reviewed in this chapter.

The two SSIS preschool-level forms are similar to each other and contain many common items. The teacher form includes 30 social skills items that are rated on a 4-point scale based on how often the behaviors occur and how important they are for success in the particular setting. It also includes a brief ten-item problem behavior screen. The parent form includes 39 social skills items and ten problem behavior items, which are rated in the same manner as described for the teacher form. The main difference in content between the two forms involves the specificity of items across the home and preschool settings. The teacher form includes an item stating, "Appropriately questions rules that may be unfair," whereas the related item on the parent form states, "Appropriately questions *household rules* that may be unfair" (italics added). Given that these two forms are part of the general SSIS rating scale system, they were developed as downward extensions of the elementary and secondary parent and teacher rating forms, with minor item revisions, deletions, and additions to make them appropriate for use with young children. Similar to the other rating forms in the SSIS system, raw scores on the preschool level forms are converted to behavior levels, standard scores, and percentile ranks. Also like the other versions of the SSIS, the preschool-level forms include empirically derived Communication, Cooperation, Assertion, Responsibility, Empathy, Engagement, and Self-Control subscales within the social skills area and Internalizing, Externalizing, Bullying, Hyperactivity/Inattention, and Autism Spectrum areas within the problem behavior screening items.

The SSIS manual includes significantly more technical data regarding the psychometric properties for the preschool-level forms than the SSRS had. Factor analyses and normative data for the SSIS preschool forms were based on only 200 ratings for the teacher form and 400 ratings for the parent form, and the geographic, racial, mother's educational level, and education classification/diagnostic stratification of the preschool form norms generally matched U.S. population estimates in 2006. Coefficient alpha reliabilities for the subscales of the preschool forms range from the lower 0.70 to upper 0.90 levels, with total social skills score reliabilities in the high 0.90 range and total problem behavior score reliabilities in the mid 0.90 range for both parent and teacher forms. Test–retest reliability data are collapsed across age groups in the SSIS manual, with coefficients on the parent and teacher forms ranging from 0.72 to 0.93 across subscales. Convergent validity studies resulted in the SSIS preschool forms being moderately to highly correlated with the SSRS and the BASC-2 forms.

The external research base including use of the SSRS (previous version) preschool forms has expanded rapidly during the past few years, too. Convergent construct validity of the SSRS preschool version forms has been established by finding significant correlations with the Preschool and Kindergarten Behavior Scales (Merrell, 1995a) and the Behavioral Assessment System for Children (Flanagan, Alfonso, Primavera, & Povall, 1996). Additionally, cross-cultural validity evidence for the preschool forms of the SSRS has been reported (Elliott, Barnard, & Gresham, 1989; Powless & Elliott, 1993). Several studies have shown the usefulness of the SSRS preschool forms for identifying risk factors and theory-based differences among children in Head Start programs (Fagan & Fantuzzo, 1999; Fagan & Iglesias, 2000; Kaiser, Hancock, Cai, Foster, & Hester, 2000; Redden et al., 2001).

In addition to the rating forms described above, the SSIS manual also includes a *Performance Screening Guide*. This tool serves as a screener that can be used to efficiently measure student behaviors and academic performance class-wide. The preschool version of this tool specifically measures student performance as compared to grade level expectations in the areas of *prosocial behaviors, motivation to learn, early reading skills,* and *early math skills.* Teachers are asked to rate behaviors of each student in these areas on a scale of 1 to 5. Information can be used to identify students who may be in need of more targeted intervention or to progress monitor class progress based on the *SSIS Classroom Intervention Program.* Intraclass correlations derived within test–retest and inter-rater reliability studies suggested moderate to substantial correlations. The one area with a low coefficient in the inter-rater reliability study was in the area of *prosocial behaviors* (0.37).

In sum, the preschool level forms of the SSIS seem to be potentially useful in the assessment of social skills of young children and have the definite advantage of being part of the excellent and comprehensive SSIS system that is now linked to intervention programming, which is well designed and easy to use. With the updated normative and technical information, there is increasing external evidence to bolster reliability and validity claims.

Interviewing Techniques

In Chapter 6, there is some discussion of specific challenges, developmental issues, and recommendations regarding interviewing preschool-age and primary-age children. This section provides additional insights and suggestions regarding conducting interviews with young children. Perhaps the first issue that should be addressed in this area is the question, "How useful is it to interview young children?" The answer to this question depends on the purpose of the interview. It is well known that interviews with young children in which the intended purpose is to gather specific recollections of past events are problematic, to say the least. This problem becomes a particularly thorny issue when interviewing young children who may have been sexually abused, when the purpose of the interview is to gather evidence to document whether abuse occurred and to begin to identify a perpetrator (e.g., Boat & Everson, 1988; Coolbear, 1992).

In general, it is difficult for interviewers to obtain detailed and historically accurate information regarding events in a young child's life. A memory enhancement and interview preparation technique called Narrative Elaboration (NE) has shown considerable promise in enhancing the accuracy of recall in young children. The intervention teaches children to organize event-related information into relevant categories, such as actions, participants, settings, conversation, and so forth. Each category is represented to the child through the use of a generic drawing on a visual cue card. The card is used to remind the child to provide details according to each category. Before a recall interview in which the child is asked about a specific event, the child is provided with opportunities to practice using the cards to recall details about situations or stimuli that are not related to the pending interview situation. The visual cue cards are presented during the recall interview to remind the child of the categories of information and type of detail that he or she is expected to provide regarding the target event or situation.

The evidence of the effectiveness of NE in increasing accurate recall during interviews with children is promising. Children trained using the NE technique have been shown to increase the accuracy of their recall by more than 50% in comparison with control group children. NE originally was developed and researched by Saywitz and colleagues for use with elementary-age children (e.g., Saywitz & Snyder, 1996), but more recent studies by Dorado and Saywitz (2001) and Peterson, Warren, and Hayes (2013) showed impressive results with young (preschool- and elementary-aged) children. In sum, although obtaining accurate historical recall from interviews with young children has been a perpetual challenge, it seems that careful preparation and instructions may substantially enhance the accuracy of obtained information.

Children's competence in verbal communication gradually increases with age, and preschool-age children certainly tend to be less competent than school-age children. This fact does not mean, however, that young children cannot be assessed effectively in an interview situation. Hughes and Baker (1990) noted that researchers have shown that some of the supposed cognitive limitations of young children that were documented through Piagetian tasks are "artifacts of the way they (the children) are questioned" (p. 30). It is crucial to consider and remember that the skill and sensitivity of the interviewer will be a major determinant in whether an interview yields valid and useful results. Hughes and Baker also noted that when interviewing young children, adult interviewers often err in attempting to assume too much control in the conversation, usually by asking too many questions or by asking questions that are primarily forced-choice or closed-ended.

Given the current state of what is known regarding the cognitive and social developmental characteristics of young children, several techniques can be recommended to enhance the quality of clinical interviews. Hughes and Baker (1990) recommended that interviewers should: (1) use a combination of open-ended and direct questions; (2) not attempt to assume too much control over the conversation; (3) gain familiarity with the child's experience and use this understanding in developing questions; (4) reduce the complexity of interview stimuli to the greatest extent possible; and (5) reduce the complexity of the child's responses by allowing him or her to communicate with props or manipulatives at times. Regarding open-ended versus direct (closed-ended) questions, even open-ended questions can be misused with young children. A particular problem is referred to as leading questions, or asking a seemingly open-ended question in a manner that slants the content of the response. For example, asking a child a question such as "Tell me about what happens when your dad gets angry" in the absence of strong evidence to suggest this is even an issue will likely result in a response that confirms that dad is truly an angry person. Young children tend to want to please adults, and providing the kind of statements that they think an adult wants is one way of doing it. In terms of the issue of control over the conversation, clinicians should balance the natural tendency of children to move in and out of a specific topic with their own need to obtain information. A mental reminder before the interview that it is okay to have the interview seem directionless at times may help in this regard. The other suggestions made by Hughes and Baker are fairly self-explanatory.

An additional consideration for interviewing young children involves the difficulty many young children have in separating from their parents. If an interviewer prematurely requests the child to separate from the parent and go into the interview room with him or her, a likely effect will be a poor interview, and a possible effect may be elicitation of crying in the child. A technique that works well for many clinicians in working with young children is to invite the child and parent into the clinic room or office together first and invite them to engage in a nonthreatening activity, such as drawing pictures on a whiteboard or playing with a toy. After the child begins to show signs of feeling comfortable and secure, the clinician can matter-of-factly ask the parent to go into the other room to fill out forms or engage in some similar activity. If the child becomes upset, some empathy and gentle reassurance usually helps calm him or her. Statements such as "It's okay to feel scared when your mom is gone, but she will be back soon" and behaviors such as physically getting down to the child's level and engaging in a fun activity with him or her also help in this regard.

In sum, although clinical interviews with young children do possess inherent challenges, these challenges can usually be overcome with additional care, caution, and training. Assuming that the interview is only one part of a comprehensive assessment design, it can provide invaluable insights and information, even under less than ideal circumstances.

Sociometric Approaches

Each of the four general sociometric assessment methods illustrated in Chapter 7 (peer nomination, peer rating, sociometric ranking, alternative procedures) has been adapted and used with preschool-age children. Yet, despite their frequency of use with young children, these methods have been shown to have inconsistent psychometric properties and usefulness with this age group. Such findings, when considered in conjunction with some of the unique social development aspects of early childhood, have resulted in questions and cautions regarding the use of sociometric methods with young children (e.g., Connolly, 1983; Hymel, 1983). Despite some legitimate concerns regarding these cautions, it is my opinion that sociometrics can be used reliably and effectively with preschool-age and kindergarten-age children and that the overall evidence regarding validity of sociometric assessment with young children is supportive. This section adds to the material presented in Chapter 7 some particular comments regarding issues in using sociometrics with young children.

It is useful to understand the basis of concerns regarding the effective use of sociometrics with young children. In a comprehensive review on this topic, Hymel (1983) concluded that with regard to reliability, the data are less encouraging with children younger than four years old. Hymel also noted that there was a paucity of predictive validity evidence (as opposed to concurrent validity evidence) for sociometric measures obtained with preschool populations. Bullock, Ironsmith, and Poteat (1988) also reviewed the literature on sociometric assessment with young children, finding mixed evidence regarding the stability of measurement over time. Given these findings, we must ask the question why would the sociometric ratings of young children be less stable than those of older children? Perhaps the best answer to this question is that the constructs of friendship and peer popularity are probably less stable with young children. The review by Bullock et al. (1988) concluded that younger children's friendships tend to fluctuate more than those of older children. Related to this conclusion is a consistent finding that peer nominations and peer ratings tend to have more similarity with preschool-age children than with elementary-age children, indicating that in comparison with school-age children, younger children do not differentiate as much between being best friends with another child and simply liking that child. Any parent of young children can attest personally to these two findings. Preschool-age children may be quite likely to state that a child with whom they have played at preschool on one or two occasions is their "best friend," but fail to mention the same child only a few months (or days!) later if asked to name their best friends.

Despite the sometimes amorphous quality that young children's social relationships have and the resulting lowered temporal consistency with certain types of sociometric procedures, there is still much to be said for using them with this age group. Simple adaptations of basic sociometric methods, such as the use of picture sociometrics for peer nominations and the additional use of happy, sad, and neutral face drawings to serve as anchor points for peer rating procedures (see Asher et al., 1979), can make sociometric procedures useful with young children. Although some experts (e.g., Hymel, 1983) have recommended that rating scales should be used instead of nomination procedures with young children, others (e.g., Poteat, Ironsmith, & Bullock, 1986) have argued convincingly that with proper modifications, the two methods may both be reliable. The sociometric method of choice by a particular researcher or clinician in assessing young children should be based on the particular questions needing answers and the particular characteristics of the children being assessed. Although there is still more to be learned regarding effective use of sociometrics with young children, they can be recommended. The evidence is clear that negative nominations or ratings are associated with negative behavior, and positive nominations or ratings are associated with positive behavior. It is this demonstrated strong relationship between assessment results and actual behavior that continues to advocate for the use of sociometrics, and their use with young children should be no exception. Further, it will be interesting to observe if there is an increase in the use of sociometric procedures over time, as researchers and children are more and more savvy with the use of technology. In one recent study, researchers compared a traditional peer nomination approach with a computerized version, where preschool children could click on a happy, sad, or neutral face (Endedijk & Cillessen, 2015). They found that these approaches were comparable, and the computerized sociometric approach provided additional data and more evaluation possibilities.

Self-Report Tests

Self-report tests are seldom useful with young children, and very few are even available for use with this age group. As explained in Chapter 8, objective self-report tests typically require three prerequisite abilities: (1) the ability to read and understand test items; (2) the cognitive maturity or sophistication to make specific incremental judgments in responding to test items; and (3) the ability to translate these judgments correctly into the marking of the appropriate answer. Several self-report tests designed for social–emotional assessment of elementary-age children do allow for the examiner to read the items and mark the chosen responses for children who have difficulty reading, which might lead us to believe that they are appropriate for preschool-age and kindergarten-age children. This belief almost always is wrong. Even allowing for the examiner to read the test items to the children and to mark their answer forms for them does not solve the more fundamental problem of cognitive maturity or sophistication. Most preschool-age and kindergarten-age children simply do not possess the cognitive maturity needed to make appropriate discriminating judgments on self-report tests of social–emotional functioning. Most young children lack the intrapersonal insight regarding social and emotional functioning to understand adequately the concepts that they would be asked to evaluate in most self-report tests. It is best to assume that researchers and clinicians must rely on other means for assessing the social–emotional behavior of young children, with particular emphases on behavior rating scales, direct behavioral observation, and, where appropriate, sociometric approaches.

Despite the limitations of self-report methods for assessing social–emotional status of young children, there are a few ingenious self-report instruments that have been developed specifically to overcome the limitations that most self-report tests have for young children and that have been proven to be reliable and valid. The instruments reviewed in this section are examples of seminal self-report tests available for social–emotional assessment of young children, with a structure and approach to gathering information from young children that has been used to develop other measures in this area and in related areas.

The Pictorial Scale of Perceived Competence and Acceptance for Young Children The Pictorial Scale of Perceived Competence and Acceptance for Young Children (Harter & Pike, 1980, 1984) is a unique self-report test designed to evaluate the general self-concept and social acceptance of young children, according to their own perceptions. In contrast to most self-report social–emotional assessment instruments for children, this instrument does not require that the child subject either read or make detailed response discriminations. The examiner leads the child through the items with a series of picture plates, and the child is asked to make simple discriminations among paired items by pointing at the picture or symbol that is most like him or her.

Separate gender picture plates (one depicting male characters and the other depicting female characters) are used at two different developmental levels: one for preschool-age and kindergarten-age children and the other for children in first or second grade. The picture plates for the two different age levels are relatively similar but, for some items, depict children in activities that are developmentally appropriate at that specific level. For example, the preschool and kindergarten plates show children working on puzzles, and the parallel item for the first and second grade shows children working on number problems at school. There are 24 items in this test. The manner in which the items are presented to the child involves the examiner first showing a plate with two opposing pictures on it, then asking a simple question about it. For example, all children are shown a plate in which one picture shows a child who appears to be sad, and the other picture shows a child who appears to be happy. The examiner asks, "This girl (or boy) is usually kind of sad (points to the first picture), and this girl (or boy) is usually kind of happy (points to the second picture). Now I want you to tell me which of these boys/girls is most like you?" The child then responds by pointing to the picture within the pair that he or she selects as being most like him or her. Then the examiner asks the child how much the selected picture is like him or her, and the child responds by pointing to a large or small circle that is located directly below the picture. For example, if the child had originally pointed to the picture of the child who was usually sad as being most like them, the examiner would say "Are you always sad?" (points to the large circle) or "Are you usually sad?" (points to small circle). A value of 1 to 4 points is given for each item response, keyed so that the lowest value always indicates the lowest level of perceived competence or acceptance, whereas the highest value always indicates the highest level. Items are clustered into four subscales: Cognitive Competence, Physical Acceptance, Peer Acceptance, and Maternal Acceptance. The scales are scored by calculating a mean value for the items within that scale, then identifying the general level indicated by that value. For example, if a child received a mean score of 3.83 on Cognitive Competence, this score would be interpreted as a high level of perceived self-competence in the cognitive domain, whereas a score of 1.2 would be considered a low level. Scores for this test typically are interpreted in a criterion-referenced rather than norm-referenced manner.

Although the test manual provides no technical data on the uses and properties of this instrument, several publications have provided evidence that it is a potentially useful instrument for use with young children. Significant relationships have been shown between this test and measures of academic readiness (Anderson & Adams, 1985), self-perception items have been found to correspond with actual criterion behaviors and teacher ratings (Jongmans, Demetre, Dubowitz, & Henderson, 1996; Priel, Assor, & Orr, 1990), and interesting relationships between test scores and differences in the way that boys and girls tend to respond to other stimuli have been found (Harter & Chao, 1992). Additionally, the psychometric properties (i.e., basic reliability and validity) of this test have been shown to be acceptable (e.g., Cadieux, 1996; Holguin & Sherrill, 1990). Although the normative research base and psychometric properties of the Pictorial Scale of Perceived Competence and Acceptance for Young Children are not as strong and extensive as those available for many self-report instruments designed for use with older children and adolescents, this is virtually the only self-report instrument for young children that has been widely researched (with more than 50 published studies by 2002), and it must be considered that social–emotional behavior is typically a less stable trait in young children. As such, this instrument is particularly valuable as a research tool. Clinical use of the test with young children can be recommended, provided that it is done as part of a comprehensive battery and that hypotheses generated through evaluating scale scores are supported through other means. It seems, however, that this test is used most often in the context of research.

The Berkeley Puppet Interview (BPI) Additional measures have been developed that utilize a similar approach to Harter's scale. The ingenuity of this approach involves making the questions as concrete as possible and using pictures and props to help young children make meaning and answer reliably and validly. One measure that was originally developed in the 1990s is the Berkeley Puppet Interview (BPI) (Ablow & Measelle, 2003). This is somewhat of a combination of a self-report and interview approach in which children interact with puppets and answer a series of questions. There are two puppets that each make a statement, such as "I have lots of friends" and "I don't have lots of friends." Then, one of the puppets will say, "How about you?" This invites children to share their perceptions of their friendships with the puppets.

The BPI consists of three major domains and multiple subscales. The domains include the BPI Family Environment Scales, the BPI Academic and Social Scales, and the BPI-Social Scales. Additionally, items from multiple scales have been used in research to obtain children's self-perceptions on the *Big Five* personality factors (i.e., extraversion, agreeableness, conscientiousness, neuroticism, and openness) (Measelle, John, Ablow, Cowan, & Cowan, 2005). Researchers have actually found that young children can answer questions on dimensions of their personality as reliably as college students. The BPI is an impressive methodology that has been used in over 100 studies and has been translated into seven languages. It offers important information that can be considered when intervention planning for young children.

BEST PRACTICES

As has been shown throughout this chapter, social–emotional assessment of young children can be conducted using any or all of the five major assessment methods. To be done effectively with young children, however, such assessment must be conducted with particular precautions, modifications of design, extra care, and special sensitivity. At this point, it is important to emphasize particular recommendations for social–emotional assessment with young children that have an important bearing on research and practice.

One of the major recommendations for assessment of young children is that it is essential to include parents and teachers in the assessment process to the greatest extent possible. Although including parents and teachers is an important consideration in assessing all children and adolescents, it is especially crucial where young children are concerned. As has already been discussed, situational specificity of behavior is a particularly salient issue with young children. Obtaining multiple reports and normative perspectives across settings may help to clarify discrepancies in social–emotional behavior. Involvement of parents of young children is also important because they may not yet be experienced in dealing with professionals from educational and mental health systems. Parents who are dealing with such systems for the first time may feel intimidated by professional terminology and knowledge, unsure of the processes that they will encounter, and genuinely scared of what may be ahead for their child. In sum, they may need extra attention and reassurance.

Involving teachers in the assessment process and developing models to assess the classroom environment is also critical, given that newer intervention initiatives in education are focused on prevention of academic and social–emotional problems and that preschool teachers, in particular, are often the least trained and supported in our U.S. educational system. There have been several recent developments in this area, one of which is called the *Teaching Pyramid Model* (Fox, Hemmeter, Snyder, Binder, & Clarke, 2011; Hemmeter, Ostrosky, & Fox, 2006), which is very similar to conceptualizations of RtI. In this model, universally applied prevention efforts include an emphasis on teachers building nurturing relationships with children and designing clear, consistent and caring classroom environments. Secondary or more targeted support includes systematic teaching of social and emotional skills, and tertiary support includes intensive interventions that are functional and supportive of individual needs (Fox et al., 2011). One assessment tool that is specifically aligned with this model is called the *Teaching Pyramid Observation Tool* (TPOT) (Hemmeter, Fox, & Snyder, 2013). The TPOT is a rating scale that can be completed based on a two-hour observation in a preschool classroom. This tool has been described as a reliable and dependable measure and has been useful in measuring progress of *Teaching Pyramid* implementation over time (Fox et al., 2011).

Another recommended best practice for social–emotional assessment with young children is to use extra caution in the diagnosis/classification process and to avoid pathologizing children. Many *DSM-5* diagnostic categories for psychiatric disorders are simply not appropriate for young children. Making classification decisions regarding diagnostic categories that may be appropriate for young children is often extremely difficult because the way that behavioral problems are exhibited by them often differs markedly from that of older children. Given these diagnostic/classification concerns and other related concerns, it is especially important for clinicians to use extra caution and conservatism in making decisions that may have a lasting impact. Approaching referral issues from a functional and disconfirmatory perspective may be helpful in this regard. The referral should be approached from the standpoint of clarifying a possible problem and identifying what may be done to solve the problem. The clinician should not automatically assume that psychopathology exists.

A final best practice to consider in social–emotional assessment of young children is effectively linking such assessment results to intervention strategies. With older children and adolescents, there is typically a greater availability of empirically validated assessment and intervention technologies. Practitioners who work with young children are faced not only with fewer technically sound assessment methods and instruments, but also possibly more difficulty in selecting appropriate intervention strategies. Assessment that takes into consideration the important elements that will be needed to develop effective intervention has been referred to as intervention-based assessment (Barnett, Bell, Stone, Gilkey, & Smith, 1997). In this regard, Flugum and Reschly (1994) identified six quality indicators that have been related to successful interventions: (1) behavioral definition of the problem; (2) direct measurement of the targeted behavior in the natural setting; (3) detailed intervention plan; (4) intervention integrity; (5) graphing of intervention results; and (6) comparison of postintervention performance with baseline data. The link to intervention with young children would be enhanced by selecting methods, instruments, and an overall assessment design that allows for as much eventual intervention integrity as possible. Without a doubt, most of these characteristics could be used as benchmarks on which to develop and judge the efficacy of a planned assessment.

CONCLUSIONS

School psychologists, clinical child psychologists, special education diagnosticians, and other child-serving professionals are increasingly being asked to provide comprehensive services to young children, including social–emotional assessments. The state of assessment technology designed specifically for the unique needs of this age group lags behind what is available for use with older children and adolescents. An additional problem is that many clinicians have received minimal or no formal training in assessing young children, which requires special knowledge, care, and sensitivity to do effectively. Despite the problems and challenges involved in social–emotional assessment of young children, there have been numerous improvements and new developments in this area.

Traditional diagnostic classification systems for emotional and behavioral disorders of childhood (e.g., the *DSM-5*) are often of limited use with young children. An alternative diagnostic classification system designed specifically for use with young children, the *Diagnostic Classification: 0–3, Revised* and soon to be *Diagnostic Classification: 0–5*, is available to supplement the more traditional systems. This system uses a multiaxial classification format that is similar to that of *DSM-IV* but is designed to take into account the specific ways in which behavioral and emotional problems are manifest by young children. This system also is unique because of its strong focus on the quality of the relationship of the child and his or her parent.

Each of the five major assessment methods that are the focus of this book can be used with varying degrees with young children, assuming that certain modifications or precautions are taken into consideration. Direct behavioral observation has a long history of use for assessing social and emotional behavior of young children and offers the advantage of empirical assessment within naturalistic settings. Research has indicated, however, that the social behavior of young children is highly variable, and multiple observations of behavior may be needed to provide a reliable assessment. Developers of behavior rating scales for children historically have ignored the special characteristics and needs of young children, but this situation is changing. Rating scales such as the ASQ:SE-2, the SEAM, the DECA, the Behavioral Assessment System for Children, Third Edition, the preschool forms of the ASEBA, Preschool and Kindergarten Behavior Scales, Second Edition, and Social Skills Improvement System have helped to move rating scale technology for use with young children to increasingly higher standards of technical adequacy and usability.

Clinical interviewing of young children has been an extremely popular method of assessment, albeit one fraught with obstacles. Although even the best clinicians who employ interview methods with young children may have difficulty obtaining consistent or highly objective information, interviews can be used effectively for various purposes. With proper modifications and precautions, interviews can help clinicians better understand and gain rapport with the child, and may serve as a valuable component of comprehensive assessment design. Specific training and practice before the interview, using procedures such as Narrative Elaboration, may result in improved accuracy of recall. Although the research on using sociometric assessment approaches with young children has yielded mixed results, there is convincing evidence that such techniques may be useful and predictive of future behavior, particularly when appropriate modifications are made, such as using photographs of children and alternative picture-based response formats. Self-report methods of social–emotional assessment are challenging to implement with young children because they require the ability to read and make cognitive differentiations that are simply beyond the capabilities of almost all children younger than about second grade. There are exceptions, however, to the dearth of appropriate self-report assessment instruments for young children; these include the Pictorial Scale of Perceived Competence and Acceptance for Young Children and the Berkeley Puppet Interview.

For optimal effectiveness, certain practices should be incorporated into social–emotional assessment of young children, without regard to the type of design or methodology that is employed in the assessment. Among these practices and modifications, full participation and partnerships with parents, caution with respect to "pathologizing" child behavior, and developing effective linkages to interventions are especially recommended.

REVIEW AND APPLICATION QUESTIONS

1. What are some of the major difficulties in conducting adequate social–emotional assessments with young children?
2. How does the Zero to Three diagnostic classification system (DC: 0–3R/DC: 0–5) for young children compare with the major classification systems discussed in Chapter 3?
3. What is known regarding the reliability or stability of behavior of young children over time? How does this knowledge translate into practice in terms of conducting direct behavioral observations?
4. Five behavior rating scales or checklists for use with young children were reviewed in this chapter. In what circumstances or for what types of referral problems would each of these instruments be best used?
5. Given that interviewing with young children is problematic at best, what can be done to minimize the problems and enhance the validity and accuracy of interviews?
6. What are some explanations for the lower reliability over time of sociometric procedures with young children in comparison with school-age children? Does this lower reliability reduce validity of sociometric procedures with younger children?
7. What are some specific practices in assessment of young children that may be helpful to avoid "overpathologizing" them?

15

UNIVERSAL SCREENING IN SCHOOLS

With Kayla Gordon

The purpose of this chapter is to provide readers with an overview of methods and specific measures that can be used to screen populations for behavioral, social, and emotional risk and to target school-wide instructional priorities. While the concept of school-wide screening is certainly not new, implementing such practices is a large paradigm shift for many and requires organizational and systemic support to do effectively and efficiently. In this chapter, we provide readers with a conceptual overview of school-wide screening within a prevention model. We reflect on the purpose of screening for both externalizing and internalizing symptoms and we consider opportunities and challenges that emerge as school systems take on this approach. Multiple tools will be described with an emphasis placed on the technical adequacy and accessibility of these tools.

CONTEXT FOR UNIVERSAL SOCIAL–EMOTIONAL SCREENING

It is no secret that school professionals are currently called to engage in more than academic instruction. Approximately, 20% of American children and adolescents are struggling with social–emotional problems that warrant additional support, and few receive the support that they need (Costello, Mustillo, Erkanli, Keeler, & Angold, 2003). In fact, if they do receive counseling or intervention support, it is likely to happen within the school context. However, school-based mental health professionals cannot respond to the rising social–emotional needs of students alone. To effectively and efficiently address these concerns, school professionals are encouraged to think about preventatively assessing and teaching social–emotional skills as they would academics.

Scholarly work and practical applications related to prevention efforts have grown tremendously over the last several years, and are often organized within a Multitiered System of Support (MTSS) or Responsiveness-to-Intervention (RtI) framework (Costello & Angold, 2000; Merrell & Buchanan, 2006; Sugai & Horner, 2009). According to a National Association of School Psychologists (NASP, 2010) position statement, an MTSS framework includes three tiers of integrated academic and behavioral assessment and instructional supports that become increasingly intensive based on student needs. Tier 1 aims to prevent onset of academic or behavioral challenges through high-quality instruction and universal screening. Tier 2 reflects targeted interventions for students that are displaying some risk, and Tier 3 includes individualized and specialized interventions for students that have not responded to the Tier 1 and 2 supports offered. An MTSS model has been found to be particularly effective for students who may have

DOI: 10.4324/9781315747521-17

been vulnerable to risky or negative outcomes, such as suspension, dropout, etc. (Cortiella & Horowitz, 2014).

Based on years of accumulated research, NASP (2010) recommends particular practices to be incorporated into each tier within MTSS. For behavior in particular, Tier 1 includes providing students with high-quality instruction related to behavioral expectations, a continuum of positive feedback for meeting expectations as well as explicit redirection when expectations are not met (Sugai & Horner, 2009). Further, school professionals may engage in coordinated and planned instruction to help students access critical social–emotional learning skills (SEL) such as self-awareness, self-management, social awareness, responsible decision making, and relationship building (Durlak et al., 2011; Greenberg, Weissberg, Utne O'Brien, & Elias, 2003).

To plan Tier 1 instruction that is aligned with a school or district's particular circumstances (e.g., cultural, economic) and needs, it is recommended that schools develop an MTSS Tier 1 team that can work together to gather school-wide screening data that will help to drive Tier 1 instructional efforts. Additionally, Tier 2 teams, or problem-solving teams, can use these data to identify students in need of further assessment or more targeted support. These teams are not those that meet a handful of times to plan a set of practices that will be implemented once; rather, they are groups that develop a way of working in which data are consistently shared and used to monitor the effects of Tier 1 and Tier 2 instruction over time, as well as keep a finger on the pulse of students that may be emerging with social–emotional risk factors.

Schools are places that are often rich with extant data, which can be part of a universal screening effort. For example, schools that have methods to reliably collect office disciplinary data can use such data to understand and intervene around aspects of school-wide behavior. For example, if a school team identifies that most referrals include disrespect between peers on the playground then they can develop a Tier 1 instructional target to explicitly teach students about respectful and kind behavior at recess time. Further, many school teams use office disciplinary referrals as a method to identify students for Tier 2 interventions (Walker, Cheney, Stage, & Blum, 2005). In these cases, teams usually develop a data decision-rule (e.g., two or more referrals) to help determine when a student will be given additional intervention. While screening with office disciplinary information might be an efficient process, research suggests that this data source might not capture a complete picture of a school community's mental health (McIntosh, Campbell, Carter, & Zumbo, 2009). Office disciplinary referrals likely miss behaviors related to internalizing problems like symptoms of depression and anxiety. Given this limitation, schools have begun to turn toward use of further social–emotional screening methods and measures.

SOCIAL–EMOTIONAL SCREENING

Universal social–emotional screening in schools includes gathering brief amounts of information about the social–emotional functioning of all students in a school or district. This can take the shape of structured teacher nomination efforts, in which teachers learn to identify social–emotional symptoms and then can nominate students, about whom they have concerns, for further assessment and/or intervention (Walker, Severson, & Feil, 2014). Screening also includes brief teacher behavioral ratings or self-report methodology. In this chapter, we will primarily review behavioral rating screening tools.

While universal screening tools vary in terms of behavioral targets, response formats, and recommended frequency of administration (Glover & Albers, 2007), there are some standard considerations for those selecting instruments that we describe here. Glover and Albers (2007) suggest that users build an understanding of the appropriateness of a tool for its intended use, the technical adequacy of the measure, and feasibility of implementation of data collection and use. It is very important that users select a tool that includes social–emotional targets that are relevant to their school population. While screening is intended to be efficient, it is also intended to provide useful information that drives instruction and decision making.

As with any behavioral rating tool, having an understanding of the psychometric properties of a tool is a necessary consideration. Users should be aware of the normative sample, reliability, and validity of measures. For screening tools in particular, predictive validity is helpful to understand. For example, one should understand the *sensitivity* of a measure. The sensitivity index represents the proportion of those correctly identified as at risk that later turn out to be at risk. The *specificity* index, on the other hand, is the proportion of individuals who do not ultimately engage in at-risk behaviors and are not mistakenly identified as at-risk. These concepts are practically important for users because they don't necessarily want to over identify students and provide them with a great deal of unnecessary programming or intervention. On the other hand, users clearly would not aim to under identify students and then deprive them of needed support (Glover & Albers, 2007).

The final essential concept for school professionals to consider is the usability or feasibility of a screening measure (Glover & Albers, 2007). Screening efforts are not meant to be resource intensive. Schools need to consider how much they are willing to invest in terms of money, time, and personnel. Further, these considerations need to happen with the perspective that screening aims to support efficient Tier 1 decision making. Some of the measures that we describe in this chapter are freely available, while others are not. Some measures are incorporated into larger data management systems, which schools might be using anyway to screen and progress monitor academic skills (e.g., FastBridge). Others may require data entry and analysis. Finally, it is important for professionals to think through personnel time that will be needed to commit to training, administration, and analysis of screening data. While it is important for screening tools to be efficacious in accurately identifying concerning behaviors, it is also important for them to be effective, meaning that they can be feasibly used within a real-world setting (Levitt et al., 2007).

In this chapter, we have chosen to extensively review seven available screening measures/approaches. Given the scope of this chapter, we could not review every existing measure, but we did try to select tools that are emerging as effective and efficient. For a more comprehensive review of screening efforts, see Jenkins et al. (2014), and Lane, Menzies, Oakes, & Kalberg (2012). In addition to the seven reviews, we will also share an example of another tool with a research base that is in its infancy but holds promise for future practical application.

SCHOOL-WIDE SCREENING MEASURES

The Systematic Screening for Behavior Disorders, Second Edition (SSBD-2)

The first screening that we give here is not one tool; rather it is a well-established, systematic screening process. The Systematic Screening for Behavior Disorders, Second

Edition (SSBD-2) (Walker, Severson, & Feil, 2014) is an empirically validated multiple gating system for screening students in preschool through ninth grade for behavior disorders. This screening system was one of the first ever developed and has a large body of about 30 years of research supporting its use. The second edition was released in 2014, which updated the SSBD to an online format from its previous version (SSBD) (Walker & Severson, 1992) which was available solely in paper format. Additionally, the second edition includes assessment of preschool-aged children, which had previously been accomplished through a separate, though very similar method called the Early Screening Project (ESP) (Walker, Severson, & Feil, 1995). The ESP also represented an innovative multiple gating system designed to assist in screening preschool-age children (aged three to five) who were at high risk for developing significant emotional or behavioral disorders.

The SSBD-2, can be used to screen a class through a series of assessment and decision-making steps, which are successively refined and selective. An outline of the gating system is outlined in Figure 15.1. The first two stages in the SSBD rely on the judgment of teachers. Stage 1 involves a teacher nomination and rank ordering process to identify the children

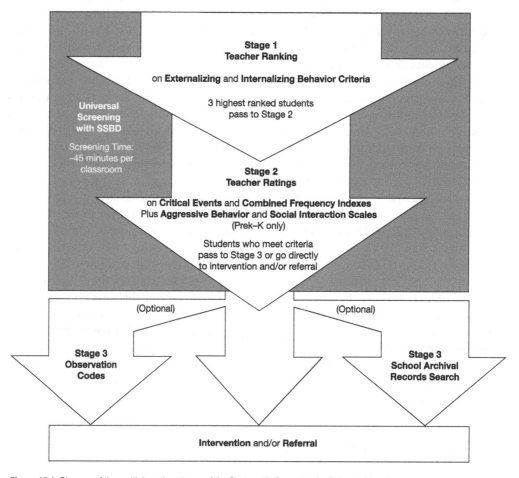

Figure 15.1 Diagram of the multiple gating stages of the Systematic Screening for Behavior Disorders

Source: From *Systematic Screening for Behavior Disorders, Second Edition*, by H. M. Walker, H. Severson, and E. Feil (2014). Eugene, OR: Pacific Northwest Publishing. Reprinted with Permission.

**Stage 1 Screening for Internalizing Students
Rank Ordering on Internalizing Dimensions**

Step 1. Carefully study the definition of internalizing behavior below and then review your class roster.

Internalizing refers to all behaviour problems that are directed inwardly (i.e., away from the external social environment) and that represent problems with self. Internalizing behavior problems are often self-imposed and frequently involve behavioral deficits and patterns of social avoidance. Non-examples of internalizing behavior problems would be all forms of social behavior that demonstrate social involvement with peers and that facilitate normal or expected social development.

Examples Include:

- Having low or restricted activity levels
- Not talking with other children
- Being shy, timid, and/or unassertive
- Avoiding or withdrawing from social situations
- Preferring to play or spend time alone
- Acting in a fearful manner
- Not participating in games and activities
- Being unresponsive to social initiations by others
- Not standing up for one's self
- Appearing depressed

Non-Examples Include:

- Initiating social interactions with peers
- Having conversations
- Playing with others, having normal rates or levels of social contact with peers
- Displaying positive social behaviour toward others
- Participating in games and activities
- Resolving peer conflicts in an appropriate manner
- Joining in with others

Step 2. In Column One, enter the five students whose characteristic behavior patterns most closely match the internalizing behavior definition.

Step 3. In Column Two, rank order students you have listed in Column One according to the degree or extent to which each displays internalizing behavior. The student who exhibits internalizing behavior to the greatest degree is ranked first and so on until all five students are rank ordered. The three highest ranked students will be rated on Stage 2 measures.

Column One List Internalizers	Column Two Rank Order Internalizers
Student and/or ID No.	Student and/or ID No.

Figure 15.2 Instructions for rank-ordering students with internalizing social–emotional problems, from stage 1 of the SSBD multiple gating system. A rank-ordering procedure for externalizing problems is also included in stage 1

Source: From *Systematic Screening for Behavior Disorders, Second Edition*, by H. M. Walker, H. Severson, and E. Feil (2014). Eugene, OR: Pacific Northwest Publishing. Reprinted with Permission.

in the class who exhibit the highest rates of internalizing and externalizing problems (see Figure 15.2). Five children from the classroom are selected to pass through the Stage 1 gate on to Stage 2. In this stage, the top three students with internalizing and externalizing problems are again rated by their teacher on two indices: the Critical Events Index and the Combined Frequency Index of Adaptive and Maladaptive Behavior, as well as an Aggressive Behavior and Social Interaction Scale for PreK and kindergarten students only. Students, who further exceed what would normally be expected, move along to stage three where direct observations are conducted, which are called the Screening, Identification, and Monitoring System (SIMS) Observation Codes.

Behaviors Targeted During the first stage, teachers are instructed to nominate their top five students displaying internalizing behaviors and the top five students displaying externalizing behaviors. The SSBD provides guidance on this by giving teachers examples and non-examples of what these behaviors entail. For internalizing behaviors, the examples given include not talking to other children, acting fearful, or appearing depressed. For externalizing behaviors teachers are asked to identify students who exhibit behaviors such as arguing, having tantrums, or being hyperactive. Out of these five students, the top three in each category pass through the first gate to Stage 2.

During Stage 2, a screening process through a series of questionnaires takes place. For students identified during Stage 1 behaviors, a Critical Events Index is completed by the student's teacher. This targets behaviors that have serious implications for long-term adjustment including stealing, reporting nightmares or sleep disturbance, and exhibiting a sad affect. Another questionnaire is also completed for each student by their teacher that assesses for adaptive and maladaptive behaviors including manipulating other children, completing classwork, and following the rules. Half of the items focus on adaptive student behavior and half focus on maladaptive. The teacher is asked to rate each child on each item on a 3-point Likert scale based on how often they have observed the student exhibiting that behavior this year. As was mentioned above, PreK and K students are also rated on aggressive behaviors and social interactions.

Students who receive scores on these measures that exceed normal limits pass through the second gate and move on to Stage 3. During Stage 3, a professional in the school conducts direct observations. These observations are conducted in both academic and other settings in order to assess both academic engaged time in the classroom and positive prosocial behavior.

Technical Adequacy The SSBD is validated for use in preschool through to grade 9 and is widely used as a multigated universal screening tool. It can reliably identify students displaying either internalizing or externalizing behaviors that may be in need of additional support. New norms were added in 2013 from 7,000 youth across the country in order to ensure that the measure was still reliable and relevant to today's youth. The technical manual for the SSBD is available for free online and includes additional specific information about the validation and reliability of the tool. The manual describes multiple studies that have accumulated evidence supporting the SSBD's reliability and validity since the 1980s. The original standardization sample included about 4,400 cases for Stage 2 and 1,300 cases for the SIMS Behavior Observation Codes. These participants were from eight states across all regions of the U.S. During initial pilot testing, the original inter-rater reliability coefficients for Stage 1 were low, so authors revised the descriptions of behaviors and saw improved coefficients, ranging from 0.82 to 0.94. Test–retest reliability ranged from 0.74 to 0.88. When initially testing the sensitivity of Stage 1, researchers found that 90% of students with behavior disorders were in teachers' lists of top three candidates. Over the next several years, multiple studies were conducted, where the reliability and validity of Stages 2 and 3 were further established.

The initial ESP national norm sample was large and diverse, consisting of 2,853 children aged three to six who were enrolled in a variety of typical and specialized preschool educational programs. The technical adequacy of the ESP has been solidly researched. Median inter-rater reliability coefficients were in the 0.70 range, and median test–retest coefficients at medium-length intervals were also in the 0.70 range. The ESP manual and subsequent published studies have documented various forms of test validity, based on correlations with specific assessment instruments and estimation of classification accuracy, among other procedures. The ESP has been shown empirically to result in relatively low false positive and false negative error rates in identification (Feil & Becker, 1993; Sinclair, Del'Homme, & Gonzalez, 1993) and to have strong construct validity when compared with other methods of assessment and when researched for accuracy of classification results (Jentzsch & Merrell, 1996).

Feasibility The SSBD takes less than an hour for a teacher to screen his or her entire classroom. As soon as teachers have completed their screenings, the individual student reports are automatically scored and generated by the SSBD online. Administrators and other professional support staff with administrative access can also see both the individual student reports and school level reports. The SSBD is available for purchase online (www.pacificnwpublish.com). It costs $550.00 per school for a 12-month subscription. Moving the SSBD to an online platform increases its feasibility tremendously, as now an individual or group of professionals are no longer needed to aggregate all of the data to be able to understand school-wide patterns and trends. The ingenuity and longevity of the SSBD is truly impressive, and it will be interesting to see how the online addition contributes to more widespread use.

The Student Risk Screening Scale—Internalizing and Externalizing (SRSS-IE)
The Student Risk Screening Scale Internalizing and Externalizing (SRSS-IE) is an empirically validated tool designed to be used for screening. It was initially developed as a universal screening tool for use at the elementary level, but it is now validated for use at the elementary, middle, and high school levels (Drummond, 1994; Lane, Kalberg, Parks, & Carter, 2008; Lane, Parks, Kalberg, & Carter, 2007; Schatschneider, Lane, Oakes, & Kalberg, 2014). The SRSS-IE is comprised of both the SRSS-E, or the externalizing composite of the SRSS, and the SRSS-I, or the internalizing composite of the SRSS.

All items on the SRSS are rated on a 4-point Likert scale indicating how often the behavior is likely to occur from never to frequently. On the externalizing scale, there are seven items, and the internalizing composite adds a total of five to six items to the SRSS-IE depending on the age of the students. For elementary school students, there are five internalizing items while at the secondary level there are six.

Behaviors Targeted The SRSS-E focuses solely on externalizing symptoms while the SRSS-I adds an internalizing symptoms component. Together, the SRSS-IE assesses risk for both externalizing and internalizing symptoms. A total score is also calculated that incorporates both internalizing and externalizing behaviors. The following risk factors are the externalizing symptoms measured by the SRSS-E: stealing, lying, cheating, and sneaking, behavior problems, peer rejection, low academic achievement, negative attitude, and aggressive behavior. For the SRSS-I, the items ask about internalizing symptoms such as a student being emotionally flat, shy or withdrawn, sad or depressed, anxious, and lonely. At the middle and high school level, the peer rejection item is moved from the externalizing scale to be a part of the internalizing scale.

The report produced by using the SRSS-IE shows if a student's level of risk is low, moderate, or high. This is based on the total score of all risk factors on either the internalizing or externalizing scales. It is not suggested that the individual items are predictive of a student's overall level of risk.

Technical Adequacy The SRSS has been validated for use at the elementary, middle, and high school levels (Drummond, Eddy, & Reid, 1998; Lane et al., 2008; Lane, Parks, Kalberg, & Carter, 2007). Lane, Kalberg, Lambert, Crnobori, and Bruhn (2010) examined the internal consistency estimates of the SRSS and found that they were 0.81, 0.82, and 0.81 at fall, winter, and spring administration time points, respectively. In addition, the authors examined test–retest reliability, which indicated that Pearson correlation coefficients ranged from 0.68 to 0.74. In terms of predictive validity, Lane et al. (2010) also found that the SRSS had similar accuracy to the SSBD for identifying externalizing disorders, but that it was less accurate at identifying students with internalizing characteristics.

Feasibility To use the SSRS-IE, each teacher rates each of their students on how often they exhibit the behaviors indicated by each item on a 0–3 scale. It is estimated that the SSRS-IE takes approximately 15–20 minutes to complete for an entire class. It is recommended that each teacher individually records each student's scores and then a coordinator or coach enters them into an online database to aggregate the data. The SRSS-IE is designed to be used three times per year.

The SRSS is a free screening tool for schools to use. Scoring sheets are available via an excel file online (www.ci3t.org). Responses should be entered by the SRSS coordinator, who should be selected by each school in order to enter and manage the data prior to using the SRSS. Once the data are entered, the excel file available online will automatically calculate the level of risk for each student as data are entered. In addition, the excel file will automatically color code the SRSS-E and the SRSS-I composite scores according to level of risk. The cell will remain white for low risk, yellow for moderate risk, and red for high risk. A total composite score is also calculated by the excel file encompassing both internalizing and externalizing symptoms. Two different excel files are available with one being only for elementary school students and the other being for use with middle and high school students.

The Strengths and Difficulties Questionnaire (SDQ)

The Strengths and Difficulties Questionnaire (SDQ) (Goodman, 1997) is a brief validated screening tool available for use with children and adolescents. Educator and parent forms are available online to be downloaded (www.sdqinfo.com) for children aged two to 17 years old. The SDQ has self-report forms available for individuals aged 11 to 17. There is also a self-report form and an informant report form for individuals aged 18 and over. The SDQ can be used for school-wide or program-wide screening, in addition to being used in clinic settings as part of an initial assessment. The SDQ can also be used in either clinics or schools to evaluate treatment effects before and after an intervention.

Behaviors Targeted The SDQ has three main components: a 25-item core questionnaire, an impact supplement, and a follow-up supplement. The items on the core questionnaire are divided among five subscales summarizing emotional symptoms, conduct problems, hyperactivity/inattention, peer relationship problems, and prosocial behavior (Goodman, 1997). Each subscale has five items. Four subscales, excluding prosocial behavior, are also added together to generate a total difficulties score. An internalizing symptoms composite, comprised of the emotional symptoms and peer relationship problems, and an externalizing symptoms composite, made up of conduct problems and hyperactivity/inattention symptoms, are also derived from the data (Goodman, Lamping, & Ploubidis, 2010).

The impact supplement asks the individual or informant to denote how much of an influence their impairments have on others. Specifically, these items ask about how long difficulties have occurred for, whether the client seems upset or distressed by the impairments, and whether the difficulties impact different areas of the client's life. The follow-up supplement asks questions about whether an intervention has reduced the problem or if it has found other ways to make the problem more bearable.

Technical Adequacy Norms for the SDQ are available from ten different countries. The current norms available on the SDQ website for the United States are from when the SDQ was included in the 2001 National Health Interview Survey (NHIS) Supplement. In total, 10,367 children between the ages of four and 17 participated in the study in order to obtain norms for the parent report form. In addition, Stone, Otten, Engels, Vermulst, and Janssens (2010) estimated the internal consistency scores for the SDQ to be between 0.53 and 0.76 for the parent report form with the total difficulties score having an internal consistency of 0.80. For the teacher report form, it is estimated that the subscales have a slightly higher reliability between 0.63 and 0.83 with an internal consistency score on the total difficulties composite of 0.85 (Stone et al., 2010). It is estimated that concurrent validity between the SDQ and the Child Behavior Checklist (CBCL) is between 0.52 and 0.71 for each of the parent reported subscales, and 0.76 for the total composite on the parent form. In comparison, on the teacher report form, the concurrent validity is estimated to be between 0.57 and 0.79 with the total composite concurrent validity also being a 0.76 (Stone et al., 2010).

Feasibility The SDQ is inexpensive to use, and parent, teacher, and self-report forms are available online. The core questionnaire can be completed by educators, parents, or clients in about five to ten minutes. Items are rated on a 3-point Likert scale where 0 = *not true*, 1 = *somewhat true*, 2 = *certainly true* to determine behavior during the last six months or during the current school year. The questionnaires are available to administer in over 80 different languages to accommodate most clients, educators, and families.

Scoring can currently be done either online or by hand through instructions provided online. The free online scoring website also generates reports to be used to summarize the data provided by the SDQ. Online scoring and transparent overlays for hand scoring are provided in many different languages. In addition, the SDQ website has syntax available to score the SDQ using SPSS, SAS, Stata, and R.

The Social, Academic, and Emotional Behavior Risk Screener (SAEBRS)

The Social, Academic, & Emotional Behavior Risk Screener (SAEBRS; Kilgus, von der Embse, Chafouleas, & Riley-Tillman, 2014) is a newly developed tool that is used to screen for social, emotional, and behavioral problems in students in kindergarten through grade 12. It is available online via the FastBridge data management system (www. fastbridge. org). The SAEBRS is a teacher report questionnaire comprised of 19 items on three scales. Each item is rated on a 4-point Likert scale where the respondent is asked to indicate how often the behavior occurred in the last month from never to almost always. The SAEBRS is designed to be used for universal screening to determine behavioral and emotional risk, which has been shown to be connected to academic success.

Behaviors Targeted The SAEBRS assesses risk for social behavior problems, academic behavior problems, and emotional behavior problems. These three types of behavior problems make up the three scales of the SAEBRS. The Social Behavior and Academic Behavior scales have six items each, while the Emotional Behavior scale has seven items. There is also a Total Behavior composite score that encompasses both the Social Behavior and Academic Behavior items for a total of 12 items (Kilgus et al., 2014; Kilgus, Eklund, Nathaniel, Taylor, & Sims, 2016). In addition to numerical scores, descriptors of "risk" or "no risk" are used to describe a student's current status.

Social behavior problems include behaviors that may limit a student's ability to maintain relationships with either peers or adults. Academic behavior problems may inhibit a student from being prepared for, engaging in, and benefiting from academic material that is taught. Emotional behavior problems are those that limit a student's coping mechanisms and appropriate responses to stressful and challenging events. In addition, students who display these concerns are likely to have a more difficult time adapting to change.

Technical Adequacy Kilgus et al. (2016) examined the current psychometric properties of the SAEBRS. They found that the internal consistency reliability at the elementary school level was estimated to be 0.83 through 0.92 on the three scales with the Total Behavior composite at 0.93. Sensitivity coefficients ranged from 0.79 to 0.97, and specificity ranged from 0.73 to 0.93. For middle school students, reliability ranged from 0.77 to 0.93 on the three scales with the Total Behavior reliability slightly higher than at the elementary school level at 0.94. Sensitivity coefficients ranged from 0.86 to 0.95 and specificity ranged from 0.73 to 0.92. The SAEBRS was also significantly correlated with the Behavioral Assessment System for Children, Third Edition: Behavioral and Emotional Screening System (BASC-3: BESS) on all scales and the total composite at both age levels (Kilgus et al., 2016).

Feasibility The SAEBRS is a tool that can be downloaded for free for paper and pencil administration or it can be purchased for online administration and scoring through FastBridge. It consists of a social–emotional rating scale with 19 items. Teachers can complete the rating scale online and it typically takes one to three minutes per student. Scoring is done automatically online, and the results are immediately available. The SAEBRS can be given multiple times per year. Educators may also complete the SAEBRS for individual students, all students in a classroom, across a grade level, or for an entire school or district. Reports are available at the individual student level, or teachers can select to see all of the students in their classroom to evaluate scores against local norms.

The Behavior Intervention Monitoring Assessment System (BIMAS)
The Behavior Intervention Monitoring Assessment System (BIMAS; McDougal, Bardos, & Meier, 2009) is a tool to assess social, emotional, and behavioral functioning in children and adolescents aged five to 18. The BIMAS can be used for universal screening, student progress monitoring, and program evaluation. There are teacher, parent, and clinician forms available for students aged five to 18 (grades K–12), and student self-report forms are available for students in grades 6 to 12 or 12–18 years old.

Behaviors Targeted The BIMAS has 34 items and 5 subscales. The scales are grouped into two categories: Behavioral Concern Scales and Adaptive Scales. The Behavioral Concern Scales include Conduct, Negative Affect, and Cognitive/Attention. On the Conduct scale, items relate to anger management, bullying, substance abuse, and deviance.

The Negative Affect scale items focus on anxiety and depression symptoms. The Cognition/ Attention scale examines behaviors related to attention, focus, organization, planning, and memory. The Adaptive Scales include social and academic functioning items that relate to communication with others, academic performance, attendance, and attitude toward learning.

The BIMAS is designed to be used within a multitiered model of support. At the universal level, the BIMAS Standard can be used to screen students for emotional and behavioral problems. At the advanced tiers, the BIMAS Standard and BIMAS Flex can be used for progress monitoring, treatment planning, and intervention and program evaluation.

Technical Adequacy The BIMAS is a research based and technically sound screening system with change-sensitive items that allow for treatment monitoring as well as universal screening. Normative data for the BIMAS includes 1,400 teacher ratings, 1,400 parent ratings, and 700 self-report ratings that are representative of the United States population as of the census data in 2000. In addition, 1,300 clinical cases were also collected. Internal consistency on subscales on all forms ranged from 0.75 to 0.91, and inter-rater reliability estimates ranged from 0.54 to 0.86, with lower coefficients on subscales comparing students with teachers and students with parents. Test–retest reliability at two to four weeks ranged from 0.79 to 0.91. Validity evidence has also been established as the BIMAS has been compared to all forms of the Conners Comprehensive Behavior Rating Scales. The BIMAS includes sensitivity coefficents that range from 0.76 to 0.84 and specificity coefficients that range from 0.69 to 0.86.

Feasibility It is estimated that the parent, teacher, clinician, and student report forms take about five to ten minutes each to complete per student. The Standard form has 34 items on the parent, teacher, and self-report forms. The clinician form has 31 items. It is available online and through a paper and pencil version. The BIMAS is available through MHS assessments (www.mhs.com). The manual costs $99.00 and the price for each questionnaire ranges from $2.00 to $4.00 depending on how many forms are purchased.

There are four report categories for the BIMAS, and they are all available online. Assessment reports can be generated at the individual student level, which can be particularly helpful for identifying students needing additional intervention, as well as at the multi-student level. Progress reports can compare multiple administrations of either the BIMAS Standard or Flex to progress monitor and detect changes over time. Comparative reports look at differences between results of different BIMAS assessments, such as between different raters. Demographic reports are used at the multi-student level to identify and plan prevention and intervention strategies around specific risk factors related to a class, grade, school, or district.

The BIMAS Flex In addition to the BIMAS Standard scales, the BIMAS Flex includes additional items that provide more specific information on each of the five scales that the standard BIMAS assesses. More specific behavioral items are included for each of the items on the standard form. Each item on the standard form has ten to 30 items associated with it on the BIMAS Flex. Items on the BIMAS Flex are available both positively and negatively worded, and a clinician can use the BIMAS Flex to customize treatment goals and evaluate the effectiveness of treatment.

The Behavioral Assessment System for Children, Third Edition: Behavioral and Emotional Screening System (BASC-3: BESS)

The Behavioral Assessment System for Children, Third Edition: Behavioral and Emotional Screening System (BASC-3: BESS) (Kamphaus & Reynolds, 2015) is a universal screening system for measuring behavioral and emotional strengths and weaknesses in preschool through high school. It is designed to be used by schools, mental health clinics, pediatric clinics, communities and researchers, and forms are available for administration for children and adolescents in preschool through grade 12. The teacher form has two levels available: Preschool (aged three to five) and Child/Adolescent (grades 3 to 12). There is a student self-report form that is available for children and adolescents in grades 3 to 12. A parent form is also available with two levels: Preschool (aged three to five) and Child/Adolescent (grades K–12). Any of these forms may be used individually or in combination. The BESS is available through Pearson on Q-Global.

Behaviors Targeted The BASC-3: BESS measures behavioral and emotional competencies across four domains which are internalizing problems, externalizing problems, school problems, and adaptive skills. The parent form has 29 items that assess these four domains, while the teacher form has 20 items and the self-report form has 28. Items that are both positively and negatively worded are included on the BASC-3: BESS. Items are rated on a 4-point Likert scale where the rater is asked to indicate whether the behavior never occurs, sometimes occurs, often occurs, or almost always occurs.

Technical Adequacy Scores are not provided for the scales individually, but a total Behavioral and Emotional Risk Index score is calculated for each client by each rater. For each scoring option, raw scores, T scores, and percentiles may be obtained. In addition, the report generated will produce a Behavioral and Emotional Risk Index score and a classification based on the T score. Scores of 0–60 indicate normal risk while scores between 61–70 depict an elevated risk. Scores 71 and higher indicate extremely elevated risk. If more than one form is completed for each client (i.e., a parent report form and a teacher report form), the scores are displayed side by side. Individual item responses are also recorded and indicated in the report that is generated. Validity indexes that identify responses that may be overly negative or inconsistent are also included in the report.

Much like all of the other measures within the BASC-3 system, the BESS includes impressive psychometric properties. Evidence of reliability and validity has grown since the original release of the BESS. Jenkins et al. (2014) summarized the psychometric properties of the BESS and found strong reliability coefficients with internal consistency ranging from 0.91 to 0.97, test–retest ranging from 0.79 to 0.96, and inter-rater ranging from 0.71 to 0.82. The BESS has also been found to appropriately converge and diverge with a range of other instruments (e.g., the ASEBA system).

Feasibility It is estimated to take approximately five to ten minutes to complete each BASC-3: BESS questionnaire. Teacher, parent, and self-report forms are available in both English and Spanish. Individuals may purchase a kit that includes both the manual and age-appropriate forms (parent and teacher for preschool students and all three for children and adolescents). The Preschool kit is $111.30 and the Child/Adolescent Kit is $136.30. Each kit includes a manual and 25 copies of each form. Additional forms may be purchased for an additional cost.

There are a few scoring options available for the BASC-3: BESS. It can be administered and scored either manually or through Q-Global. If an individual is selecting to administer and score electronically, they can order a comprehensive kit for $321.00 or they can choose a package that also includes intervention recommendations for $404.00.

The BASC-3 Flex Monitor The Flex Monitor is designed to monitor the effects of a behavioral intervention plan. It can be used as a progress monitoring tool and to track changes in behavioral and emotional functioning. The BASC-3 Flex can be used to monitor changes and progress in students who have been identified as needing additional support through the BASC-3: BESS after an intervention has been put in place. There are teacher, parent, and self-report forms available. Parent and teacher forms are available to track behaviors associated with ADHD, internalizing problems, disruptive behaviors, and developmental social disorders. Self-report forms can track both internalizing problems and school problems. Custom forms can also be created from a pool of over 600 items as teacher, parent, or self-report forms. Standard forms have five items, and custom forms may have up to 45. Standard forms take approximately five minutes to complete.

The Social Skills Improvement System—Performance Screening Guide (SSIS-PSG)
The Social Skills Improvement System—Performance Screening Guide (SSIS-PSG) (Gresham & Elliott, 2008) is a universal screener designed to be used with children aged three to18 years old in order to screen for social, motivational, and academic behaviors. Three different administration forms, preschool, elementary (grades K–6), and secondary (grades 7–12), are available to reach a wide age range. The SSIS-PSG is designed to be completed by each student's teacher three times per year to screen all students and monitor those receiving interventions.

The Social Skills Improvement System also has three other tools that can be used in combination with the SSIS-PSG. The Classwide Intervention Program is a ten-unit program covering five major prosocial behavior areas for preschool through secondary school students. It is designed to increase social skills including cooperation, assertion, responsibility, empathy, and self-control. The other two tools, the rating scale and the intervention guide were developed to be used for targeted assessment and intervention rather than school or classroom screening and intervention. The rating scales assess social skills, problem behaviors, and academic competence and are described in detail in Chapter 13. The Intervention Guide is designed to deliver interventions to students that are directly linked to their scores on the SSIS Rating Scales.

Behaviors Targeted The SSIS-PSG targets four main areas: prosocial behaviors, motivation to learn, reading skills, and math skills. Teachers rate each student within these four domains on a 5-point scale (4-point scale for preschoolers). After an educator fills out a form for each student in their classroom, the report indicates whether each student's score places them within a green, yellow, or red range for each domain, indicating various levels of risk or concern. The SSIS-PSG can be used within a multitiered system of support where interventions are provided for students whose scores place them in the yellow or red range for any of the four domains assessed. The SSIS-PSG is criterion-referenced and designed to measure students' skills against grade level expectations.

Technical Adequacy During the standardization for the SSIS Rating Scales, the SSIS-PSG data were collected from 138 teachers in PreK through high school classrooms, which meant that 497 students were screened. Test–retest reliability coefficients ranged from 0.53 through 0.74, with lower coefficients represented with the preschool sample. Inter-rater reliability ranged from 0.37 to 0.72. Internal consistency was not included as this is a criterion-referenced measure. In terms of validity evidence, the manual includes correlations of the SSIS-PSG with the SSIS Teacher Form (comprehensive rating scale).

Feasibility During the pilot study for the SSIS-PSG, authors also surveyed teachers about the usability of this brief measure. It takes approximately 20 minutes for a teacher to complete the SSIS-PSG booklet and materials are available through Pearson. Users felt that the directions and scores were easy to understand and it was easy to sort the information gained to best determine which students might need additional instruction or support.

Students' scores are placed into three categories: green, yellow, or red. Students who have a score of 1 (red) are identified as experiencing significant difficulty on that scale and having a high level of risk. Intervention should be provided for these students. For preschool students, a score of a 2 (yellow) indicates some level of risk, and this is indicated by a score of a 2 or 3 (yellow) for older students. For preschool students, a score of a 3 or 4 (green) indicates an average score and a low level of risk. For elementary and secondary students, this is indicated by a score of a 4 or 5 (green). Prevention and intervention for students should be tied to their level of risk and difficulty that they are experiencing and should be delivered within a multitiered model of support.

Additional Promising Tool

As universal screening efforts are gaining momentum in schools, more tools are regularly generated. One tool that puts an interesting spin on school-wide screening is the Protective Factor Index (PFI). The PFI is a screening tool that was developed based on Squire, Nailor, & Carey's (2014) review of constructs that are strongly related to academic achievement. These constructs include Motivation, Self-Direction, Self-Knowledge, and Relationships. The PFI is a 13-item measure that was developed collaboratively between a suburban school district and members of the Center for School Counseling Outcome Research and Evaluation at the University of Massachusetts Amherst. In an initial psychometric study of this measure, confirmatory factor analyses yielded 3 (not 4) factors, which were determined to be Academic Temperament, Self-Knowledge, and Motivation (Bass, Lee, Wells, Carey, & Lee, 2015).

While psychometric information on the PFI is in its early stages, the potential utility of the measure is what makes it most interesting. Through the partnership between the school district and university, the measure was incorporated into the school district's standards-based report card. This meant that teachers were rating students three times per year, when they were completing report cards. From an "implementation" perspective, this was quite innovative, as it did not require teachers to learn a new system or do different work than they were used to doing. They simply had replaced the behavioral domains previously used on the report card with the PFI. Data were then also analyzed by class, much like the SSRS-IE, to identify potential classroom concerns that could be instructional targets.

STRENGTHS AND IMPORTANCE OF SCHOOL-WIDE SCREENING

There are significantly more children in need of mental health services than those who receive them. Multitiered systems of support is a way to decrease the magnitude of needs through prevention. School-wide screening for social, emotional, and behavioral concerns is a major component of implementing a multitiered system of support (Burke et al., 2016). Systematic screening is essential for schools in order to support all students and identify those who may need additional support or intervention (Lane et al., 2012). Screening tools not only help to identify students in need of intervention early when unexpected or problem behaviors occur, but they also help to identify students in need of additional support early in their educational career (Schatschneider et al., 2014). In addition, as the role of mental health professionals including school psychologists, is changing from solely individual intervention to population-based prevention practices, school-wide screening is becoming even more essential (Dever, Dowdy, Raines, & Carnazzo, 2015).

When implementing a multitiered framework, it is important to have systematic ways of identifying students who are in need of support at the advanced tiers. Traditionally, teacher referral has been a common way of identifying students who need additional support (Eklund & Dowdy, 2014). While students spend the majority of their time in school with their teachers and teacher input is very valuable, this system alone is insufficient. Emotional and behavioral problems are often underreported, particularly internalizing symptoms, and a student must often display significant impairment prior to a referral being made. In addition, teachers have different backgrounds and abilities in terms of working with struggling students, which can lead to different rates of reporting depending on the teacher (Eklund & Dowdy, 2014). That is, a student who is identified by their teacher as needing additional support in one classroom would not necessarily be a student identified in another. Office discipline referrals have also traditionally been used for screening purposes, but they are far more effective at identifying externalizing problems than internalizing (McIntosh, Ty, & Miller, 2014).

Through an effective system for school-wide screening, schools can place more resources into prevention rather than crisis response (Eklund & Dowdy, 2014). It is well known that effective prevention and early intervention can have a huge impact on social and behavioral functioning (Burke et al., 2016; Lane et al., 2012). In addition to some of the validated measures discussed, schools can use data collected as part of regular school practices including report cards, curriculum based measurement, and office discipline referrals as secondary measures to identify students in need of more support (Lane et al., 2012). These are data that are already being collected within schools. In addition, many screening tools are free and time efficient to use. The benefits to school-wide screening outweigh the costs to stakeholders (Eklund & Dowdy, 2014).

IMPLEMENTATION CHALLENGES ASSOCIATED WITH SCHOOL-WIDE SCREENING

Despite the many benefits to school-wide screening, there are also challenges associated with the selection of appropriate measures, consistent implementation across multiple users, and use of data to make instructional decisions. School-wide change efforts are challenging and new practices take time to take hold. In their review of implementation science, Fixsen, Naoom, Blase, Friedman, & Wallace (2005) suggest that there are particular stages that organizations move through when they adopt a new practice or initiative. *Exploration and Adoption* reflects a readiness building stage in which individuals within an organization build an awareness of their needs and explore options for a new set of practices. In considering selection of new screening efforts, criteria for choosing tools for screening at the universal level is not widely available (Glover & Albers, 2007). While screening tools need to be reliable, valid, and able to measure progress (Lane et al., 2012), research on the efficacy of universal screening is emerging for elementary and middle schools and is minimal at the secondary school level (Chin, Dowdy, & Quirk, 2013; Lynne, Parks, Robertson, & Carter, 2007). Professionals tasked with selecting an appropriate measure must sift through the technical adequacy information available on a range of tools and consider the behavioral targets of tools to ensure that the tool chosen meets the needs of students in the current context.

The *Program Installation* stage reflects all that an organization might do to build the capacity for the implementation of a new set of practices. Schools are charged with having to think through the best methods for effective and efficient roll out of a school-wide screening effort. This might include consideration of the various systems needed to support staff in their implementation. This could involve thinking through the level of professional development that staff may need to understand the purpose and importance of universal screening, as well as to build their self-efficacy in being able to complete screening measures and use the data to make helpful decisions. During this phase, practices might be implemented in a limited way so that individuals can build an understanding of how the new practice works. For example, a small handful of teachers may implement screening in their classrooms to get a feel for administration and analysis. They might observe how long the screening process takes, and consider what additional resources may be needed to implement screening school-wide.

The *Initial Implementation* phase is complex, as it is a time when all are trying implementation for the first time, likely with varying levels of skill and understanding. During this time professionals are calibrating their practices, often experiencing doubts and frustration. I often describe this to schools, with whom I work, as the "awkward adolescent phase." In one school district in which I consult, teachers became accustomed to administering the SAEBRS three times per year during this phase, but had not reached a place where they knew what to do with the data and the data were not being shared back to them in an instructionally driven way. Given that this is also a time for troubleshooting and problem solving, the MTSS team in this school developed some procedural facilitators/ guidance documents to support their teachers in making class-wide Tier 1 observations about the data and instructional adjustments.

The *Full Operation* phase occurs within a system when the adopted practice becomes a routine "way of work." School professionals are regularly screening their students at established intervals and have the systems and structures developed (e.g., established MTSS teams) to take time to look at the data, analyze what the data suggest, explore Tier 1 instructional changes that may need to be made, and identify students with more specific intervention needs. Once practices have been implemented with fidelity, organizations then move into an *Innovation* phase, in which they are able to fine tune practices and generalize practices to other conditions or situations. Fixsen et al. (2005) suggest that innovation is different from "drift," where practices are fading or changing in a way that was not purposeful.

Finally, the *Sustainability* phase is one that is about "survival" of a practice. Schools are faced with consideration of how the practice will survive even when school priorities shift or funding streams diminish. In these last phases, schools must consider what elements of the screening effort have been and should continue to be institutionalized and what can be adapted based on the current context. For example, the function of teams who engage in data-based decision making may not change, but perhaps a new screening tool is needed to meet the needs of the current population. Overall, the adoption, implementation and sustainability of a new set of practices, such as school-wide screening, takes time, years even, in order for schools to actually know the extent to which it has been an effective and worthwhile pursuit.

CONCLUSIONS

In this chapter, we reviewed the concept of universal social–emotional screening in schools. We framed screening as being an important effort for schools to incorporate into their MTSS framework. Screening aims to prevent new social–emotional challenges from developing through implementation of efficient and effective measurement that enables targeted, population-wide instructional efforts. Screening also aims to help professionals identify students that might benefit from additional dosages of social–emotional and behavioral instruction, from more targeted instruction, and from increased monitoring and behaviorally specific feedback. We reviewed a number of screening systems and tools that are available and encourage readers to understand the variability that exists in terms of behaviors these tools target, technical adequacy of the measures, and usability of the measures within a school-wide implementation effort. Finally, we considered the many benefits of universal screening as well as the significant thought and perseverance that it takes to implement a school-wide screening effort well over time.

REVIEW AND APPLICATION QUESTIONS

1. Describe your understanding of where universal screening "fits" within a multitiered system of support in a school system. What might be some of the specific benefits and drawbacks to universal screening?
2. What are the practical implications of a screening measure with high sensitivity and low specificity?
3. Compare and contrast a multiple gating system like the SSBD from a universal screening tool like the SAEBRS? What are the pros and cons to each screening approach?
4. What is more important, the efficacy of a tool or the effectiveness/usability of a tool? Why?
5. Imagine you are a facilitator of your school's MTSS team. Your principal charged you with leading an effort to implement a new school-wide social–emotional screening approach within your school. Discuss some of the steps you would take to move this effort forward.

REFERENCES

Ablow, J. C., Measelle, J. R., & The MacArthur working group on outcome assessment. (2003). *Manual for the Berkeley Puppet Interview: Symptomatology, social, and academic modules (BPI 1.0).* MacArthur Foundation Research Network on Psychopathology and Development, Pittsburgh, KS: University of Pittsburgh Press.

Achenbach, T. M. (1982a). Assessment and taxonomy of children's behavior disorders. In B. B. Lahey & A. E. Kazdin (Eds.), *Advances in child clinical psychology* (Vol. 5, pp. 1–38). New York: Plenum.

Achenbach, T. M. (1982b). *Developmental psychopathology* (2nd ed.). New York: Wiley.

Achenbach, T. M. (1985). *Assessment and taxonomy of child and adolescent psychopathology.* Newbury Park, CA: Sage.

Achenbach, T. M. (1986, 2009). *The direct observation form of the child behavior checklist* (Rev. ed.). Burlington, VT: University of Vermont, Department of Psychiatry.

Achenbach, T. M. (1991a). *Manual for the child behavior checklist and 1991 profile.* Burlington, VT: University of Vermont, Department of Psychiatry.

Achenbach, T. M. (1991b). *Manual for the teacher's report form and 1991 profile.* Burlington, VT: University of Vermont, Department of Psychiatry.

Achenbach, T. M. (1991c). *Manual for the youth self-report and 1991 profile.* Burlington, VT: University of Vermont, Department of Psychiatry.

Achenbach, T. M. (1992). *Manual for the child behavior checklist/2–3 & 1992 profile.* Burlington, VT: University of Vermont, Department of Psychiatry.

Achenbach, T. M. (2001a). *Child behavior checklist for ages 6–18.* Burlington, VT: Research Center for Children, Youth, and Families.

Achenbach, T. M. (2001b). *Manual for the ASEBA school-age forms and profiles.* Burlington, VT: Research Center for Children, Youth, and Families.

Achenbach, T. M. (2001c). *Teachers report form for ages 6–18.* Burlington, VT: Research Center for Children, Youth, and Families.

Achenbach, T. M. (2001d). *Youth self-report for ages 11–18.* Burlington, VT: Research Center for Children, Youth, and Families.

Achenbach, T. M. (2013). *DSM-oriented guide for the Achenbach system of empirically based assessment (ASEBA).* Burlington, VT: Research Center for Children, Youth, and Families.

Achenbach, T. M., & Edelbrock, C. S. (1979). The child behavior profile II: Boys aged 6–12 and girls aged 6–11 and 12–16. *Journal of Consulting and Clinical Psychology, 47,* 223–233.

Achenbach, T. M., & Edelbrock, C. S. (1981). Behavior problems and competencies reported by parents of normal and disturbed children aged fourteen through sixteen. *Monographs of the Society for Research in Child Development, 46*(1, Serial No. 188).

Achenbach, T. M., & Edelbrock, C. S. (1983). Taxonomic issues in child psychopathology. In T. H. Ollendick & M. Hersen (Eds.), *Handbook of child psychopathology* (pp. 65–93). New York: Plenum.

Achenbach, T. M., & Edelbrock, C. S. (1984). Psychopathology of childhood. *Annual Review of Psychology, 35,* 227–256.

Achenbach, T. M., & Edelbrock, C. S. (1991). *Child behavior checklist.* Burlington, VT: University of Vermont, Research Center for Children, Youth, & Families.

Achenbach, T. M., & McConaughy, S. H. (1992). Taxonomy of internalizing disorders of childhood and adolescence. In W. M. Reynolds (Ed.), *Internalizing disorders of children and adolescents* (pp. 19–60). New York: Wiley.

Achenbach, T. M., McConaughy, S. H., & Howell, C. T. (1987). Child/adolescent behavioral and emotional problems: Implications of cross-informant correlations for situational specificity. *Psychological Bulletin, 101,* 213–232.

Achenbach, T. M., McConaughy, S. H., Ivanova, M. Y., & Rescorla, L. A. (2011). *Manual for the ASEBA brief problem monitor.* Burlington, VT: Research Center for Children, Youth, and Families.

Achenbach, T. M., & Rescorla, L. A. (2000). *Child behavior checklist for ages 1½–5.* Burlington, VT: Research Center for Children, Youth, and Families.

Achenbach, T. M., & Rescorla, L. A. (2001). *Manual for the ASEBA school-age forms and profiles.* Burlington, VT: Research Center for Children, Youth, and Families.

Achenbach, T. M., & Rescorla, L. A. (2007). *Multicultural supplement to the manual for the ASEBA school-age forms and profiles.* Burlington, VT: Research Center for Children, Youth, and Families.

Ackerson, F. (1942). *Children's behavior problems.* Chicago, IL: University of Chicago Press.

Addington, A. M., & Rapoport, J. L. (2009). The genetics of childhood-onset schizophrenia: When madness strikes the prepubescent. *Current Psychiatry Reports, 11*(2), 156–161.

AERA, APA, NCME (2014). *Standards for educational and psychological testing,* 11–31.

Alberto, P. A., & Troutman, A. C. (1998). *Applied behavior analysis for teachers* (5th ed.). Columbus, OH: Merrill.

Alberto, P. A., & Troutman, A. C. (2003). *Applied behavior analysis for teachers* (6th ed.). Upper Saddle River, NJ: Merrill/Prentice-Hall.

Alberto, P. A., & Troutman, A. C. (2012). *Applied behavior analysis for teachers* (9th ed.). Upper Saddle River, NJ: Merrill/Prentice-Hall.

Alessi, G. (1988). Direct observation methods for emotional/behavior problems. In E. S. Shapiro & T. R. Kratochwill (Eds.), *Behavioral assessment in schools: Conceptual foundations and practical applications* (pp. 14–75). New York: Guilford.

Alessi, G. J., & Kaye, J. H. (1983). *Behavior assessment for school psychologists.* Kent, OH: National Association of School Psychologists.

Ambrosini, P. J. (2000). Historical development and present status of the schedule for affective disorders and schizophrenia for school-aged children (K–SADS). *Journal of the American Academy of Child and Adolescent Psychiatry, 39,* 49–58.

American Association on Intellectual and Developmental Disabilities (AAIDD). (2008). *Frequently asked questions on intellectual disability and the AAIDD definition.* Washington, DC: Author.

American Association on Intellectual and Developmental Disabilities (AAIDD). (2010). *Intellectual disability: Definition, classification and systems of support* (11th ed.). Washington, DC: Author.

American Psychiatric Association. (1987). *Diagnostic and statistical manual of mental disorders* (Rev. 3rd ed.). Washington, DC: Author.

American Psychiatric Association. (1994). *Diagnostic and statistical manual of mental disorders* (4th ed.). Washington, DC: Author.

American Psychiatric Association. (2000). *Diagnostic and statistical manual of mental disorders* (4th ed., text revision). Washington, DC: Author.

American Psychiatric Association (2013). *Diagnostic and statistical manual of mental disorders* (5th ed.). Washington, DC: Author.

American Psychological Association (APA). (1990). *B. F. Skinner, PhD, keynote address, August 10, 1990, Boston, MA* [Videotape; Item 4500150]. Washington, DC: Author.

American Psychological Association (2017). *Ethical principles of psychologists and code of conduct.* https://www.apa.org/ethics/code/ethics-code-2017.pdf

Anastasi, A. (1988). *Psychological testing* (6th ed.). New York: Macmillan.

Anastasi, A., & Urbina, S. (1997). *Psychological testing* (7th ed.). Upper Saddle River, NJ: Prentice Hall.

Anderson, P. L., & Adams, P. J. (1985). The relationship of five-year-olds' academic readiness and perceptions of competence and acceptance. *Journal of Educational Research, 79,* 114–118.

Aponte, J. F., & Crouch, R. T. (1995). The changing ethnic profile of the United States. In J. F. Aponte, R. Y. Rivers, & J. Wohl (Eds.), *Psychological interventions and cultural diversity* (pp. 1–18). Boston, MA: Allyn & Bacon.

Appel, K. (1931). Drawings by children as aids to personality studies. *American Journal of Ortho-psychiatry, 1,* 129–144.

Aragona, J. A., & Eyberg, S. M. (1981). Neglected children: Mother's report of child behavior problems and observed verbal behavior. *Child Development, 52,* 596–602.

Archer, R. P. (2005). *MMPI-A: Assessing adolescent psychopathology* (3rd ed.). Mahwah, NJ: Lawrence Erlbaum Associates.

Archer, R. P., Handel, R. W., Ben-Porath, Y. S., & Tellegen, A. (2016). Minnesota multiphasic personality inventory-adolescent-restructured form (MMPI-A-RF): Administration, scoring, interpretation, and technical manual. Upper Saddle River, NJ: Pearson Education, Inc.

Archer, R. P., & Krishnamurthy, R. (2001). *Essentials of MMPI-A assessment.* New York: Wiley.

Arkes, H. R. (1981). Impediments to accurate clinical judgment and possible ways to minimize their impact. *Journal of Consulting and Clinical Psychology, 49,* 323–330.

Aronow, E., Weiss, K. A., & Reznikoff, M. (2013). *A practical guide to the thematic apperception test: The TAT in clinical practice.* Ann Arbor, MI: Routledge.

Asher, S. R. (1990). Recent advances in the study of peer rejection. In S. R. Asher & J. D. Coie (Eds.), *Peer rejection in childhood* (pp. 3–14). New York: Cambridge University Press.

Asher, S. R., & Hymel, S. (1981). Children's social competence in peer relations: Sociometric and behavioral assessment. In J. D. Wine & M. D. Smye (Eds.), *Social competence* (pp. 125–157). New York: Guilford.

Asher, S. R., & Parker, J. G. (1989). Significance of peer relationship problems in childhood. In B. H. Schneider, G. Attili, J. Nadel, & R. P. Weissberg (Eds.), *Social competence in developmental perspective* (pp. 5–23). Boston: Kluwer Academic.

Asher, S. R., & Renshaw, P. D. (1981). Children without friends: Social knowledge and skill training. In S. R. Asher & J. M. Gottman (Eds.), *The development of children's friendships* (pp. 273–296). New York: Cambridge University Press.

Asher, S. R., Singleton, L. C., Tinsley, B. R., & Hymel, S. (1979). The reliability of a rating sociometric method with preschool children. *Developmental Psychology, 15,* 443–444.

Asher, S. R., & Taylor, A. R. (1981). The social outcomes of mainstreaming: Sociometric assessment and beyond. *Exceptional Children Quarterly, 1,* 13–30.

Atkinson, D. R., Morten, G., & Sue, D. W. (1989). A minority identity development model. In D. R. Atkinson, G. Morten, & D. W. Sue (Eds.), *Counseling American minorities* (pp. 35–52). Dubuque, IA: Brown.

Auerbach, J. G., Yirmiya, N., & Kamel, F. (1996). Behavior problems in Israeli Jewish and Palestinian preschool children. *Journal of Clinical Child Psychology, 25,* 398–405.

Axelson, D., Birmaher, B., Zelazny, J., Kaufman, J., & Gill, M. K. (2009). *Schedule for affective disorders and schizophrenia for school-aged children: K-SADS-PL* (Working Draft). Pittsburgh, PA: Advanced Center for Intervention and Services Research (ACISR) for Early Onset Mood and Anxiety Disorders, Western Psychiatric Institute and Clinic.

Babinski, D. E., Pelham, W. E., Molina, B. S., Gnagy, E. M., Waschbusch, D. A., Yu, J., . . . & Karch, K. M. (2011). Late adolescent and young adult outcomes of girls diagnosed with ADHD in childhood: An exploratory investigation. *Journal of Attention Disorders, 15*(3), 204–214.

Baer, D. M. (1982). Applied behavior analysis. In G. T. Wilson & C. M. Franks (Eds.), *Contemporary behavior therapy: Conceptual and empirical foundations* (pp. 277–309). New York: Guilford.

Baer, D. M., Wolf, M. M., & Risley, T. R. (1968). Some current dimensions of applied behavior analysis. *Journal of Applied Behavior Analysis, 1,* 91–97.

Baio, J. (2012). Prevalence of autism spectrum disorders: Autism and developmental disabilities monitoring network, 14 Sites, United States, 2008. Morbidity and mortality weekly report. Surveillance summaries. *Centers for Disease Control and Prevention, 61*(3), 1–22.

Bandura, A. (1977). *Social learning theory.* Englewood Cliffs, NJ: Prentice-Hall.

Bandura, A. (1978). The self system in reciprocal determinism. *American Psychologist, 33,* 344–358.

Bandura, A. (1986). *Social foundations of thought and action.* Englewood Cliffs, NJ: Prentice-Hall.

Barker, E. D., & Maughan, B. (2009). Differentiating early-onset persistent versus childhood-limited conduct problem youth. *The American Journal of Psychiatry, 166,* 900–908.

Barkley, R. A. (1990). Attention deficit disorders. In M. L. Lewis & S. M. Miller (Eds.), *Handbook of developmental psychopathology* (pp. 65–75). New York: Plenum.

Barkley, R. A. (1997a). *ADHD and the nature of self-control.* New York: Guilford.

Barkley, R. A. (1997b). Attention-deficit hyperactivity disorder. In E. J. Mash & L. G. Terdal (Eds.), *Assessment of childhood disorders* (3rd ed., pp. 71–129). New York: Guilford.

Barkley, R. A. (1997c). Behavioral inhibition, sustained attention, and executive functions: Constructing a unifying theory of ADHD. *Psychological Bulletin, 121,* 65–94.

Barkley, R. A. (2011). *Barkley adult ADHD rating scale-IV (BAARS-IV).* New York: Guilford.

Barkley, R. A., & Biederman, J. (1997). Toward a broader definition of the age-of-onset criterion for attention-deficit hyperactivity disorder. *Journal of the American Academy of Child and Adolescent Psychiatry, 36,* 1204–1210.

Barnes, E. (1892). A study of children's drawings. *Pedagogical Seminary, 2,* 455–463.

Barnes-Holmes, D., & Stewart, I. (2000). A behavior-analytic approach to some of the problems of the self: A relational frame analysis. In M. J. Dougher (Ed.), *Clinical behavior analysis* (pp. 47–74). Reno, NV: Context Press.

Barnett, D. W., Bell, S. H., Stone, C. M., Gilkey, C. M., & Smith, J. J. (1997, August). *Defining intervention-based multifactored preschool assessment.* Paper presented at the meeting of the American Psychological Association, Chicago, IL.

Barnett, D. W., & Zucker, K. B. (1990). *The personal and social assessment of children.* Boston, MA: Allyn & Bacon.

Barrios, B. A., & Hartmann, D. P. (1988). Fears and anxieties. In E. J. Mash & L. G. Terdal (Eds.), *Behavioral assessment of childhood disorders* (2nd ed., pp. 196–262). New York: Guilford.

Barrios, B. A., & Hartmann, D. P. (1997). Fears and anxieties. In E. J. Mash & L. G. Terdal (Eds.), *Behavioral assessment of childhood disorders* (3rd ed., pp. 230–327). New York: Guilford.

Barry, C. T., Frick, P. J., DeShazo, T. M., McCoy, M. G., Ellis, M., & Loney, B. R. (2000). The importance of callous-unemotional traits for extending the concept of psychopathy to children. *Journal of Abnormal Psychology, 109,* 335–340.

Barton, E. J., & Ascione, F. R. (1984). Direct observation. In T. H. Ollendick & M. Hersen (Eds.), *Child behavioral assessment: Principles and procedures* (pp. 166–194). New York: Pergamon.

Bashe, P. R., & Kirby, B. L. (2001). *The oasis guide to Asperger syndrome.* Victoria, BC, Canada: Crown.

Bass, G., Lee, J. H., Wells, C., Carey, J. C., & Lee, S. (2015). Development and factor analysis of the protective factors index: A report card section related to the work of school counselors. *The Professional Counselor, 5,* 516–528.

Beauchaine, T. P., & Hinshaw, S. P. (2013). *Child and adolescent psychopathology* (2nd ed.). Hoboken, NJ: John Wiley & Sons, Inc.

Beck, A. T. (2008). The evolution of the cognitive model of depression and its neurobiological correlates. *American Journal of Psychiatry, 165,* 969–977.

Beelmann, A., Pfingsten, U., & Losel, F. (1994). Effects of training social competence in children: A meta-analysis of recent evaluation studies. *Journal of Clinical Child Psychology, 23,* 260–271.

Bellak, L. (1975). *The T.A.T., C.A.T., and S.A.T. in clinical use* (3rd ed.). New York: Grune & Stratton.

Bellak, L., & Bellak, S. (1949). *The children's apperception test.* New York: C.P.S.

Bell-Dolan, D. J., Foster, S. L., & Christopher, J. S. (1992). Children's reactions to participating in a peer-relations study: An example of cost-effective assessment. *Child Study Journal, 22,* 137–156.

Bell-Dolan, D. J., Foster, S. L., & Sikora, D. M. (1989). Effects of sociometric testing on children's behavior and loneliness in school. *Developmental Psychology, 25,* 306–311.

Bender, L. (1938). *A visual-motor gestalt test and its clinical use: Research monograph No. 3.* New York: American Orthopsychiatric Association.

Bender, L. (1946). *Bender motor-gestalt test: Cards and manual of instructions.* New York: American Orthopsychiatric Association.

Ben-Porath, Y. S. (1996). *Case studies for interpreting the MMPI-A.* Minneapolis, MN: University of Minnesota Press.

Berg, I. A. (1967). The deviation hypothesis: A broad statement of its assumptions and postulates. In I. A. Berg (Ed.), *Response set in personality assessment* (pp. 146–190). Chicago, IL: Aldine.

Berg, L., Butler, A., Hullin, R., Smith, R., & Tyler, S. (1978). Features of children taken to juvenile court for failure to attend school. *Psychological Medicine, 9,* 447–453.

Berman, A. L., & Jobes, D. A. (1991). *Adolescent suicide: Assessment and intervention.* Washington, DC: American Psychological Association.

Bettelheim, B. (1967). *The empty fortress: Infantile autism and the birth of the self.* New York: The Free Press.

Biederman, J., Faraone, S. V., Milberger, S., & Jetton, J. G. (1996). Is childhood oppositional defiant disorder a precursor to adolescent conduct disorder? Findings from a four-year follow-up study of children with ADHD. *Journal of the American Academy of Child and Adolescent Psychiatry, 35,* 1193–1204.

Bierman, K. L. (1983). Cognitive development and clinical interviews with children. In B. Lahey & A. E. Kazdin (Eds.), *Advances in clinical child psychology* (Vol. 6, pp. 217–250). New York: Plenum.

Blueler, M. (1978). *The schizophrenic disorders.* New Haven, CT: Yale University Press.

Blumberg, S. H., & Izard, C. E. (1986). Discriminating patterns of emotions in 10- and 11-year-old children's anxiety and depression. *Journal of Personality and Social Psychology, 51,* 852–857.

Boat, B. W., & Everson, M. D. (1988). Interviewing young children with anatomical dolls. *Child Welfare, 67,* 337–352.

Boggs, S. R., & Eyberg, S. (1990). Interview techniques and establishing rapport. In L. M. LaGreca (Ed.), *Through the eyes of the child* (pp. 85–108). Boston, MA: Allyn & Bacon.

Bolling, M. Y., Kohlenberg, R. J., & Parker, C. R. (2000). Behavior analysis and depression. In M. J. Dougher (Ed.), *Clinical behavior analysis* (pp. 127–152). Reno, NV: Context Press.

Bonney, M. E. (1943). The relative stability of social, intellectual, and academic status in grades II to IV, and the inter-relationships between these various forms of growth. *Journal of Educational Psychology, 34,* 88–102.

Bornstein, R. F. (2012). Rorschach score validation as a model for 21st-century personality assessment. *Journal of Personality Assessment, 94*(1), 26–38.

Bower, E. (1969). *Early identification of emotionally handicapped children in school* (2nd ed.). Springfield, IL: Thomas.

Bower, E. (1981). *Early identification of emotionally handicapped children in school* (3rd ed.). Springfield, IL: Thomas.

Bower, E. M. (1982). Defining emotional disturbance: Public policy and research. *Psychology in the Schools, 19,* 55–60.

Bower, E. M., Shelhamer, T. A., & Daily, J. M. (1960). School characteristics of male adolescents who later become schizophrenics. *American Journal of Orthopsychiatry, 30,* 712–729.

Bowlby, J. (1973). *Attachment and loss: Vol. 2. Separation.* New York: Basic Books.

Bracken, B. A. (1987). Limitations of preschool instruments and standards for minimal levels of technical adequacy. *Journal of Psychoeducational Assessment, 4,* 313–326.

Bracken, B. A. (1992). *The multidimensional self-concept scale.* Austin, TX: PRO-ED.

Bracken, B. A. (1994). Advocating for effective preschool assessment practices: A comment on Bagnato and Neisworth. *School Psychology Quarterly, 9,* 103–108.

Bracken, B. A., & Howell, K. K. (1991). Multidimensional self-concept validation: A three instrument investigation. *Journal of Psychoeducational Assessment, 9,* 319–328.

Bracken, B. A., Keith, L. K., & Walker, K. C. (1994). Assessment of preschool behavior and social–emotional functioning: A review of thirteen third-party instruments. *Assessment in Rehabilitation and Exceptionality, 1,* 259–346.

Bracken, B. A., Keith, L. K., & Walker, K. C. (1998). Assessment of preschool behavior and social–emotional functioning: A review of thirteen third-party instruments. *Journal of Psychoeducational Assessment, 16,* 153–159.

Brannigan, G. G., & Decker, S. L. (2003). *Bender visual-motor gestalt test, second edition.* Itasca, IL: Riverside Publishing.

Breslau, N. (1987). Inquiring about the bizarre: False positives in diagnostic interview schedule for children (DISC) ascertainment of obsessions, compulsions, and psychotic symptoms. *Journal of the American Academy of Child and Adolescent Psychiatry, 26,* 639–644.

Bricceti, K. A. (1994). Emotional indicators of deaf children on the draw-a-person test. *American Annals of the Deaf, 139,* 500–505.

Briesch, A., Chafouleas, S., & Riley-Tillman, T. (2010). Generalizability and dependability of behavior assessment methods to estimate academic engagement: A comparison of systematic direct observation and direct behavior rating. *School Psychology Review, 39*(3), 408–421.

Brock, S. E., & Sandoval, J. (1997). Suicidal ideation and behaviors. In G. C. Bear, K. M. Minke, & A. Thomas (Eds.), *Children's needs II: Development, problems, and alternatives* (pp. 361–374). Washington, DC: National Association of School Psychologists.

Bronfenbrenner, U. (1977). Toward an experimental ecology of human development. *American Psychologist, 32,* 513–530.

Bronfenbrenner, U. (1979). *The ecology of human development.* Cambridge, MA: Harvard University Press.

Bronfenbrenner, U. (1989). Ecological systems theory. In R. Vasta (Ed.), *Annals of child development* (Vol. 6, pp. 187–251). Greenwich, CT: JAI.

Brown, F. G. (1983). *Principles of educational and psychological testing* (3rd ed.). New York: Holt, Rinehart & Winston.

Brown, T. A., & Barlow, D. H. (2009). A proposal for a dimensional classification system based on the shared features of the DSM-IV anxiety and mood disorders: Implications for assessment and treatment. *Psychological Assessment, 21*(3), 256–271.

Bruininks, R., Woodcock, R. W., Weatherman, R. F., & Hill, B. K. (1984). *Scales of independent behavior.* Allen, TX: DLM Teaching Resources.

Bryan, T. (1974). Peer popularity of learning disabled children. *Journal of Learning Disabilities, 7,* 261–268.

Bullock, M. J., Ironsmith, M., & Poteat, G. M. (1988). Sociometric techniques with young children: A review of psychometrics and classification schemes. *School Psychology Review, 17,* 289–303.

Burisch, M. (1984). Approaches to personality inventory construction: A comparison of merits. *American Psychologist, 38,* 214–227.

Burke, M. D., Rispoli, M., Clemens, N. H., Lee, Y. H., Sanchez, L., & Hatton, H. (2016). Integrating universal behavioral screening within program-wide positive behavioral interventions and supports. *Journal of Positive Behavior Interventions, 18*(1), 5–16.

Burns, R. (1982). *Self-growth in families: Kinetic family drawings (K-F-D) research and application.* New York: Bruner/Mazel.

Burns, R., & Kaufman, S. (1970). *Kinetic family drawings (K-F-D): An introduction to understanding children through kinetic drawings.* New York: Bruner/Mazel.

Burns, R., & Kaufman, S. (1972). *Actions, styles, and symbols in kinetic family drawings (K-F-D): An interpretive manual.* New York: Bruner/Mazel.

Burr, E., Hass, E., & Ferriere, K. (2015). *Identifying and supporting English learner students with learning disabilities: Key issues in the literature and state practice* (REL 2015–086). Washington, DC: U.S. Department of Education, Institute of Education Sciences, National Center for Education Evaluation and Regional Assistance, Regional Educational Laboratory West.

Busse, R. T., & Beaver, B. R. (2000). Informant reports: Parent and teacher interviews. In E. S. Shapiro & T. R. Kratochwill (Eds.), *Conducting school-based assessment of child and adolescent behavior* (pp. 235–273). New York: Guilford.

Butcher, J. N., Williams, C. L., & Fowler, R. D. (2000). Essentials of MMPI-2 and MMPI-A interpretation (2nd ed.). Minneapolis, MN: University of Minnesota Press.

Butcher, J. N., Williams, C. L., Graham, J. R., Archer, R. P., Tellegen, A., Ben-Porath, Y. S., & Kaemmer, B. (1992). *Minnesota multiphasic personality inventory–adolescent: Manual for administration and scoring.* Minneapolis, MN: University of Minnesota Press.

Byrne, B. M. (1996). *Measuring self-concept across the lifespan: Methodology and instrumentation for research and practice.* Washington, DC: American Psychological Association.

Cadieux, A. (1996). Psychometric properties of a pictorial self-concept scale among young learning disabled boys. *Psychology in the Schools, 33,* 221–229.

Caldarella, P., & Merrell, K. W. (1997). Common dimensions of social skills of children and adolescents: A taxonomy of positive behaviors. *School Psychology Review, 26,* 265–279.

Campbell, S. B. (1991). Active and aggressive preschoolers. In D. Cicchetti & S. L. Toth (Eds.), *Internalizing and externalizing expressions of dysfunction* (pp. 57–89). Hillsdale, NJ: Lawrence Erlbaum Associates.

Campbell, S. B., & Steinert, Y. (1978). Comparisons of rating scales of child psychopathology in clinic and nonclinic samples. *Journal of Consulting and Clinical Psychology, 46,* 358–359.

Campbell, S. B., & Werry, J. S. (1986). Attention deficit disorder (hyperactivity). In H. C. Quay & J. S. Werry (Eds.), *Psychopathological disorders of childhood* (3rd ed., pp. 111–155). New York: Wiley.

Cantor, S. (1987). *Childhood schizophrenia.* New York: Guilford.

Cantor, S. (1989). Schizophrenia. In C. G. Last & M. Hersen (Eds.), *Handbook of childhood psychiatric diagnosis* (pp. 279–298). New York: Wiley.

Cantor, S., Pearce, J., Pezzot-Pearce, T., & Evans, J. (1981). The group of hypotonic schizophrenics. *Schizophrenia Bulletin, 7,* 1–11.

Cantwell, D. P. (1990). Depression across the early life span. In M. Lewis & S. M. Miller (Eds.), *Handbook of developmental psychopathology* (pp. 293–309). New York: Plenum.

Cantwell, D. P., & Carlson, G. A. (1981, October). *Factor analysis of a self rating depressive inventory for children: Factor structure and nosological utility.* Paper presented at the annual meeting of the American Academy of Child Psychiatry, Dallas, TX.

Capaldi, D., DeGarmo, D., Patterson, G. R., & Forgatch, M. (2002). Contextual risk across the early life span and association with antisocial behavior. In J. B. Reid, G. R. Patterson, & J. Snyder (Eds.), *Antisocial behavior in children and adolescents: A developmental analysis and model for intervention* (pp. 123–146). Washington, DC: American Psychological Association.

Carey, T. C., Finch, A. J., & Carey, M. P. (1991). Relation between differential emotions and depression in emotionally disturbed children and adolescents. *Journal of Consulting and Clinical Psychology, 59,* 594–597.

Carjuzaa, J., & Ruff, W. G. (2010). When Western epistemology and an Indigenous worldview meet: Culturally responsive assessment in practice. *Journal of Scholarship of Teaching and Learning, 10*(1), 68–79.

Carlson, G. A., & Garber, J. (1986). Developmental issues in the classification of depression in children. In M. Rutter, C. E. Izard, & P. B. Read (Eds.), *Depression in young people* (pp. 399–434). New York: Guilford.

Cartledge, G., Frew, T., & Zacharias, J. (1985). Social skills needs of mainstreamed students: Peer and teacher perceptions. *Learning Disability Quarterly, 8,* 132–140.

Caruso, G. A. L. (1994). The prevalence of behavior problems among toddlers in child care. *Early Education and Development, 5,* 27–40.

Castillo, E. M., Quintana, S. M., & Zamarripa, M. X. (2000a). Cultural and linguistic issues. In E. S. Shapiro & T. R. Kratochwill (Eds.), *Conducting school-based assessments of child and adolescent behavior* (pp. 274–308). New York: Guilford.

Castillo, E. M., Quintana, S. M., & Zamarripa, M. X. (2000b). Assessment of ethnic and linguistic minority children. In E. S. Shapiro & T. R. Kratochwill (Eds.), *Behavioral assessment in the schools* (2nd ed., pp. 435–463). New York: Guilford.

Celenk, O., & Van de Vijver, F. J. (2011). Assessment of acculturation: Issues and overview of measures. *Online Readings in Psychology and Culture, 8*(1), 1–22.

Centers for Disease Control and Prevention (2012). *Prevalence of autism spectrum disorders-autism and developmental disabilities monitoring network, 14 sites, United States, 2008.* Morbidity and mortality weekly report.

Centers for Disease Control and Prevention (2016). *CDC estimates: 1 in 68 school-aged children have autism; no change from previous estimate.* [Press Release]. Retrieved from https://www.cdc.gov/media/releases/2016/p0331-children-autism.html

Centers for Disease Control, National Center for Injury Prevention and Control (2006). *Suicide fact sheet.* Retrieved May 23, 2006, from www.cdc.gov/ncipc/factsheets/suifacts.htm

Centers for Disease Control, National Center for Injury Prevention and Control (2014). *Suicide fact sheet.* Retrieved April 12, 2017, from https://cdc.gov/violenceprevention/suicide/index.html

Chafouleas, S. M., Riley-Tillman, T. C., & Christ, T. J. (2009). Direct Behavior Rating (DBR): An emerging method for assessing social behavior within a tiered intervention system. *Assessment for Effective Intervention, 34*, 195–200. doi: 10.1177/1534508409340391

Chambers, W., Puig-Antich, J., Hersche, M., Paey, P., Ambrosini, P. J., Tabrizi, M. A., & Davies, M. (1985). The assessment of affective disorders in children and adolescents by semi-structured interview: Test–retest reliability of the K–SADS–P. *Archives of General Psychiatry, 42*, 696–702.

Chandler, L. A., & Johnson, V. J. (1991). *Using projective techniques with children.* Springfield, IL: Thomas.

Chapman, L. J., & Chapman, J. P. (1967). Genesis of popular but erroneous psychodiagnostic observations. *Journal of Abnormal Psychology, 74*, 271–280.

Chin, J. K., Dowdy, E., & Quirk, M. P. (2013). Universal screening in middle school: Examining the behavioral and emotional screening system. *Journal of Psychoeducational Assessment, 31*(1), 53–60.

Chorpita, B. F., Reise, S., Weisz, J. R., Grubbs, K., Becker, K. D., Krull, J. L. et al. (2010). Evaluation of the brief problem checklist: Child and caregiver interviews to measure clinical progress. *Journal of Consulting and Clinical Psychology, 78*, 526–536.

Christ, T. J., Riley-Tillman, T. C., & Chafouleas, S. M. (2009). Foundation for the development and use of direct behavior rating (DBR) to assess and evaluate student behavior. *Assessment for Effective Intervention, 34*, 201–213. doi: 10.1177/1534508409340390

Christenson, S. L. (1990). Review of the child behavior checklist. In J. J. Kramer & J. C. Conoley (Eds.), *The supplement to the tenth mental measurements yearbook* (pp. 40–41). Lincoln, NE: Buros Institute of Mental Measurements.

Cicchetti, D., & Toth, S. L. (1991). A developmental perspective on internalizing and externalizing disorders. In D. Cicchetti & S. L. Toth (Eds.), *Internalizing and externalizing expressions of dysfunction* (pp. 1–19). Hillsdale, NJ: Lawrence Erlbaum Associates.

Clark, M. L., & Dewry, D. L. (1985). Similarity and reciprocity in the friendships of elementary schoolchildren. *Child Study Journal, 15*, 251–264.

Cloth, A. H., Evans, S. W., Becker, S. P., & Paternite, C. E. (2013). Social maladjustment and special education: State regulations and continued controversy. *Journal of Emotional and Behavioral Disorders, 22*(4), 214–224.

Coccaro, E. F. (2012). Intermittent explosive disorder as a disorder of impulsive aggression for DSM-5. *American Journal of Psychiatry, 169*, 577–588.

Cohen, D. J., Leckman, J. F., & Shaywitz, B. A. (1984). The Tourette syndrome and other tics. In D. Schaffer, A. A. Erhardt, & L. Greenhill (Eds.), *The clinical guide to child psychiatry* (pp. 3–28). New York: The Free Press.

Cohen, E., & Rozenblat, R. (2015). Applied, behavioral, analytic and . . . technological: A current literature review on the use of technologies in behavior analysis. *European Journal of Behavior Analysis, 16*(2), 178–187.

Cohen, P., O'Connor, P., Lewis, S., Velez, C., & Noemi, S. (1987). Comparison of DISC and K–SADS–P interviews of an epidemiological sample of children. *Journal of the American Academy of Child and Adolescent Psychiatry, 26*, 662–667.

Cohen, R. J., & Swerdlik, M. E. (1999). *Psychological testing and assessment* (5th ed.). New York: Mayfield.

Coie, J. D., Belding, M., & Underwood, M. (1988). Aggression and peer rejection in childhood. In B. B. Lahey & A. Kazdin (Eds.), *Advances in clinical child psychology* (Vol. 2, pp. 125–158). New York: Plenum.

Coie, J. D., Dodge, K. A., & Coppotelli, H. (1982). Dimensions and types of social status: A cross-age perspective. *Developmental Psychology, 18*, 557–570.

Cole, C. L., Marder, T., & McCann, L. (2000). Self-monitoring. In E. S. Shapiro & T. R. Kratochwill (Eds.), *Conducting school-based assessments of child and adolescent behavior* (pp. 121–149). New York: Guilford.

Collett, B. R., Ohan, J. L., & Myers, K. M. (2003). Ten-year review of rating scales. V: Scales assessing attention-deficit/hyperactivity disorder. *Journal of the American Academy of Child and Adolescent Psychiatry, 42*, 1015–1037.

Compas, B. E. (1997). Depression in children and adolescents. In E. J. Mash & L. G. Terdal (Eds.), *Assessment of childhood disorders* (2nd ed., pp. 194–229). New York: Guilford.

Cone, J. D. (1978). The behavioral assessment grid (BAG): A conceptual framework and taxonomy. *Behavior Therapy, 9*, 882–888.

Cone, J. D., & Hawkins, R. P. (1977). *Behavioral assessment: New directions in clinical psychology.* New York: Bruner/Mazel.

Cone, J. D., & Hoier, T. S. (1986). Assessing children: The radical behavioral perspective. In R. Prinz (Ed.), *Advances in behavioral assessment of children and families* (Vol. 2, pp. 1–27). New York: JAI.

Conners, C. K. (1969). A teacher rating scale for use in drug studies with children. *American Journal of Psychiatry, 126,* 884–888.

Conners, C. K. (1990). *Conners Rating Scales manual.* Toronto, Ontario, Canada: Multi-Health Systems.

Conners, C. K. (1997). *Conners Rating Scales–Revised technical manual.* Toronto, Ontario, Canada: Multi-Health Systems.

Conners, C. K. (2008a). *Conners 3: Conners Third Edition.* Toronto, Ontario, Canada: Multi-Health Systems.

Conners, C. K. (2008b). *Conners Comprehensive Behavior Rating Scales.* Toronto, Ontario, Canada: Multi-Health Systems.

Conners, C. K. (2009). *Conners Early Childhood Behavior Rating Scales.* Toronto, Ontario, Canada: Multi-Health Systems.

Conners, C. K. (2014). Conners 3rd edition (Conners 3) DSM-5 update. Canada: Multi-Health Systems, Inc. Retrieved from: https://psychassessments.com

Conners, C. K., & Werry, J. S. (1979). Pharmacotherapy. In H. C. Quay & J. S. Werry (Eds.), *Psycho-pathological disorders of childhood* (2nd ed., pp. 336–386). New York: Wiley.

Connolly, J. A. (1983). A review of sociometric procedures in the assessment of social competencies in children. *Applied Research in Mental Retardation, 4,* 315–327.

Connolly, J., A., & Doyle, A. B. (1981). Assessment of social competence in preschoolers: Teachers versus peers. *Developmental Psychology, 17,* 451–456.

Cook, K. (1991). Integrating kinetic family drawings into Adlerian life-style interviews. *Individual Psychology: Journal of Adlerian Theory, Research, and Practice, 47,* 521–526.

Coolbear, J. (1992). Credibility of young children in sexual abuse cases: Assessment strategies of legal and human service professionals. *Canadian Psychology, 33,* 151–167.

Cooper, J. O., Heron, T. E., & Heward, W. L. (1987, 2007). *Applied behavior analysis.* New York: Prentice-Hall.

Coopersmith, S. (1981). *Self-esteem inventories.* Palo Alto, CA: Consulting Psychologists Press.

Corey, G., Corey, M. S., & Callanan, P. (1997). *Issues and ethics in the helping professions* (5th ed.). Pacific Grove, CA: Brooks-Cole.

Cormier, S., Cormier, L. S., & Cormier, W. H. (1997). *Interviewing strategies for helpers: Fundamental skills and cognitive-behavioral interventions* (4th ed.). Pacific Grove, CA: Wadsworth.

Corrado, R. R., Vincent, G. M., Hart, S. D., & Cohen, I. M. (2004). Predictive validity of the psychopathy checklist: Youth version for general and violent recidivism. *Behavioral Sciences and the Law, 22,* 5–22.

Cortiella, C., & Horowitz, S. H. (2014). The state of learning disabilities: Facts, trends and emerging issues. New York: National Center for Learning Disabilities.

Cosgrove, V. E., Rhee, S. R., Gelhorn, H. L., Boeldt, D., Corley, R. C., Ehringer, M. A., Young, S. E., & Hewitt, J. K. (2011). Structure and etiology of co-occurring internalizing and externalizing disorders in adolescents. *Journal of Abnormal Child Psychology, 39,* 109–123.

Costello, E. J., & Angold, A. P. (2000). Developmental epidemiology: A framework for developmental psychopathology. In A. J. Sameroff, M. Lewis, & S. M. Miller (Eds.), *Handbook of developmental psychopathology* (2nd ed., pp. 57–73). New York: Kluwer Academic/Plenum.

Costello, E. J., Edelbrock, C. S., Dulcan, M. K., & Kalas, R. (1984). *Testing of the NIMH diagnostic interview schedule for children (DISC) in a clinical population* (Contract No. DB-81–0027, final report to the Center for Epidemiological Studies, National Institute of Mental Health). Pittsburgh, PA: University of Pittsburgh, Department of Psychiatry.

Costello, E. J., Mustillo, S., Erkanli, A., Keeler, G., & Angold, A. (2003). Prevalence and development of psychiatric disorders in childhood and adolescence. *Archives of General Psychiatry, 60*(8), 837–844.

Council for Children with Behavioral Disorders (CCBD). (1991, February). New definition of EBD proposed. *Council for Children With Behavioral Disorders Newsletter.* Reston, VA: Council for Exceptional Children.

Cowen, E. L., Pederson, A., Babigan, H., Izzo, L. D., & Trost, M. A. (1973). Long-term follow-up of early detected vulnerable children. *Journal of Consulting and Clinical Psychology, 41,* 438–446.

Crick, N. R., & Dodge, K. A. (1994). A review and reformulation of social information-processing mechanisms in children's social adjustment. *Psychological Bulletin, 115*, 74–101.

Cronbach, L. J. (1949). *Essentials of psychological testing.* New York: Harper & Row.

Cronbach, L. J., & Gleser, G. C. (1965). *Psychological tests and personnel decisions.* Urbana, IL: University of Illinois Press.

Crone, D. A., Hawken, L. S., & Horner, R. H. (2015). *Building positive behavior support systems: Functional behavior assessment* (2nd ed.). New York: Guilford.

Crone, D. A., & Horner, R. H. (2003). *Building positive behavior support systems: Functional behavior assessment.* New York: Guilford.

Crowley, S. L., & Fan, X. (1997). Structural equation modeling: Basic concepts and applications in personality assessment research. *Journal of Personality Assessment, 68*, 508–531.

Crowley, S. L., & Worchel, F. F. (1993). Assessment of childhood depression: Sampling multiple data sources with one instrument. *Journal of Psychoeducational Assessment, 11*, 242–249.

Cummings, J. (1980). An evaluation of objective scoring systems for the kinetic family drawings (KFD). *Dissertation Abstracts International, 4*(6-B), 2313.

Cummings, J. A. (1986). Projective drawings. In H. M. Knoff (Ed.), *The assessment of child and adolescent personality* (pp. 199–244). New York: Guilford.

Cunningham, R. (1951). *Understanding group behavior of boys and girls.* New York: Bureau of Publications, Teachers College of Columbia University.

Curtin, S. C., Warner, M., & Hedegaard, H. (2016). Increase in suicide in the United States, 1999–2014. *NCHS Data Brief, 241*, 1–8.

Cushing, L. S., & Horner, R. (2003). *Student interaction in specific settings (SISS) measure, coding procedures and definitions.* Unpublished coding manual. (Available from Peabody College at Vanderbilt University, Box 328, Nashville, TN 37203).

Cushing, L. S., Horner, R. H., & Barrier, H. (2003). Validation and congruent validity of a direct observation tool to assess student social climate. *Journal of Positive Behavior Interventions, 5*(4), 225–237.

Dana, R. H. (1993). *Multicultural assessment: Perspectives for professional psychology.* Boston, MA: Allyn & Bacon.

Dana, R. H. (1994). Testing and assessment ethics for all persons: Beginning an agenda. *Professional Psychology Research and Practice, 25*, 349–354.

Dana, R. H. (1995). Impact of the use of standard psychological assessment on the diagnosis and treatment of ethnic minorities. In J. F. Aponte, R. Y. Rivers, & J. Wohl (Eds.), *Psychological interventions and cultural diversity* (pp. 57–72). Boston, MA: Allyn & Bacon.

Dana, R. H. (1996). Culturally competent assessment practice in the United States. *Journal of Personality Assessment, 66*, 472–487.

Dana, R. H. (1998). Multicultural assessment of personality and psychopathology in the United States: Still art, not yet science, and controversial. *European Journal of Psychological Assessment, 14*, 62–70.

Dana, R. H. (Ed.). (2000a). *Handbook of cross-cultural and multicultural personality assessment.* Mahwah, NJ: Lawrence Erlbaum Associates.

Dana, R. H. (2000b). Multicultural assessment of child and adolescent personality and psychopathology. In A. L. Comunian & U. P. Gielen (Eds.), *International perspectives on human development* (pp. 233–258). Lengerich, Germany: Pabst Science.

Dana, R. H. (2005). *Multicultural assessment: Principles, applications, and examples.* Mahwah, NJ: Lawrence Erlbaum Associates.

Dana, R. H. (2008). Clinical diagnosis in multicultural populations. In L. A. Suzuki, J. G. Ponterotto, & P. J. Meller (Eds.), *Handbook of multicultural assessment: Clinical, psychological, and educational applications* (3rd ed., pp. 107–131). San Francisco, CA: Jossey-Bass.

Davis, J. M., & Sandoval, J. (1991). *Suicidal youth: School-based intervention and prevention.* San Francisco, CA: Jossey-Bass.

Dedrick, R. F. (1997). Testing the structure of the child behavior checklist/4–18 using confirmatory factor analysis. *Educational and Psychological Measurement, 57*, 306–313.

DeGarmo, D. S., Patterson, G. R., & Forgatch, M. S. (2004). How do outcomes in a specified parent training intervention maintain or wane over time? *Prevention Science, 5*(2), 73–89.

deGroot, A., Koot, H. M., & Verhulst, F. C. (1996). Cross-cultural generalizability of the youth self report and teacher's report form cross informant syndromes. *Journal of Abnormal Child Psychology, 24*, 651–664.

Demaray, M. K., Ruffalo, S. L., Carlson, J., Brusse, R. T., Olson, A. E., McManus, S. M., & Leventhal, A. (1995). Social skills assessment: A comparative evaluation of six published rating scales. *School Psychology Review, 24*, 648–671.

DeMers, S. T. (1986). Legal and ethical issues in child and adolescent personality assessment. In H. Knoff (Ed.), *The assessment of child and adolescent personality* (pp. 35–55). New York: Guilford.

Denham, S. A., Blair, K. A., DeMulder, E., Levitas, J., Sawyer, K., Auerbach-Major, S., & Queenan, P. (2003). Preschool emotional competence: Pathway to social competence? *Child Development, 74*, 238–256.

Denham, S. A., & Weissberg, R. P. (2004). Social-emotional learning in early childhood: What we know and where to go from here. In E. Chesebrough, P. King, T. P. Gullota, & M. Bloom (Eds.), *A blueprint for the promotion of prosocial behavior in early childhood* (pp. 13–50). New York: Kluwer Academic/Plenum Publishers.

Deno, S. L. (1995). School psychologist as problem solver. In A. Thomas & J. Grimes (Eds.), *Best practices in school psychology III* (pp. 471–484). Bethesda, MD: National Association of School Psychologists.

Deutsch, C. K., & Kinsbourne, M. (1990). Genetics and biochemistry in attention deficit disorder. In M. Lewis & S. M. Miller (Eds.), *Handbook of developmental psychopathology* (pp. 93–107). New York: Plenum.

Dever, B. V., Dowdy, E., Raines, T. C., & Carnazzo, K. (2015). Stability and change of behavioral and emotional screening scores. *Psychology in the Schools, 52*(6), 618–629.

Diamantopoulou, S., Verhulst, F. C., & van der Ende, J. (2011). The parallel development of ODD and CD symptoms from early childhood to adolescence. *European Journal of Adolescent Psychiatry, 20*(6), 301–309.

Dick, D. M., Aliev, F., Krueger, R. F., Edwards, A., Agrawal, A., Lynskey, M. P., & Bierut, L. (2011). Genome-wide association study of conduct disorder symptomatology. *Molecular Psychiatry, 16*, 800–808.

Dickson, J. M., Saylor, C. F., & Finch, A. J. (1990). Personality factors, family structure, and sex of drawn figure on the Draw-A-Person Test. *Journal of Personality Assessment, 55*, 362–366.

Dishion, T. J., & Stormshak, E. (2007). *Intervening in children's lives: An ecological, family-centered approach to mental health care.* Washington, DC: APA Books.

Dodge, K., Coie, J., & Brakke, N. (1982). Behavior patterns of socially rejected and neglected adolescents: The roles of social approach and aggression. *Journal of Abnormal Child Psychology, 10*, 389–410.

Doll, B., & Elliott, S. N. (1994). Representativeness of observed preschool social behaviors: How many data are enough? *Journal of Early Intervention, 18*, 227–238.

Doll, B., Spies, R. A., Champion, A., Guerrero, C., Dooley, K., & Turner, A. (2010). The classmaps survey: A measure of middle school science students' perceptions of classroom characteristics. *Journal of Psychoeducational Assessment, 28*(4), 338–348.

Doll, B., Spies, R., LeClair, C., Kurien, S., & Foley, B. (2010). Student perceptions of classroom learning environments: Development of the classmaps survey. *School Psychology Review, 39*(2), 203–218.

Doll, B., Zucker, S., & Brehm, K. (2004). *Resilient classrooms: Creating healthy environments for learning.* New York: Guilford.

Dopheide, J. A. (2006). Recognizing and treating depression in children and adolescents. *American Journal of Health-System Pharmacists, 63*, 233–243.

Dorado, J. S., & Saywitz, K. J. (2001). Interviewing preschoolers from low- and middle-SES communities: A test of the narrative elaboration recall improvement technique. *Journal of Clinical Child Psychology, 30*, 568–580.

Drotar, D., Stein, R. K., & Perrin, E. C. (1995). Methodological issues in using the child behavior checklist and its related instruments in clinical child psychology research. *Journal of Clinical Child Psychology, 24*, 184–192.

Drummond, T. (1994). *The student risk screening scale.* Grants Pass, OR: Josephine County Mental Health Program.

Drummond, T., Eddy, J. M., & Reid, J. B. (1998). Follow-up study# 3: Risk screening scale: Prediction of negative outcomes by 10th grade from 2nd grade screening. *Unpublished technical report.* Eugene, OR: Oregon Social Learning Center.

DuPaul, G. J. (1992). How to assess attention-deficit hyperactivity disorder within school settings. *School Psychology Quarterly, 7*, 61–74.

DuPaul, G. J., Anastopoulos, A. D., Power, T. J., Reid, R., Ikeda, M., & McGoey, K. (1998). Parent ratings of attention-deficit/hyperactivity disorder symptoms: Factor structure and normative data. *Journal of Psychopathology and Behavioral Assessment, 20*, 83–102.

DuPaul, G. J., Power, T. J., Anastopoulos, A. D., & Reid, R. (2016). *ADHD rating scale–IV*. New York: Guilford.

DuPaul, G. J., Power, T. J., Anastopoulos, A. D., Reid, R., McGoey, K., & Ikeda, M. (1997). Teacher ratings of attention-deficit/hyperactivity disorder: Factor structure and normative data. *Psychological Assessment, 9*, 436–444.

DuPaul, G. J., & Stoner, G. (1994). *ADHD in the schools: Assessment and intervention strategies*. New York: Guilford.

DuPaul, G. J., & Stoner, G. (2003). *ADHD in the schools: Assessment and intervention strategies* (2nd ed.). New York: Guilford.

DuPaul, G. J., & Stoner, G. (2015). *ADHD in the schools: Assessment and intervention strategies* (3rd ed.). New York: Guilford.

Durlak, J., Weissberg, R. P., Dymnicki, A., Taylor, R., & Schellinger, K. (2011). The impact of enhancing students' social and emotional learning: A meta-analysis of school-based universal intervention. *Child Development, 82*, 405–432.

Dusek, J. B. (1996). *Adolescent development and behavior* (3rd ed.). Upper Saddle River, NJ: Prentice-Hall.

Dwyer, K. P., & Stanhope, V. (1997). IDEA '97: Synopsis and recommendations [NASP *Communique, 26(1)*, handout supplement]. Washington, DC: National Association of School Psychologists.

Dymond, S., & Roche, B. (2009). A contemporary behavioral analysis of anxiety and avoidance. *The Behavior Analyst, 32*, 7–28.

Ebmeier, K. P., Donaghey, C., & Steele, J. D. (2006). Recent developments and current controversies in depression. *The Lancet, 367*, 153–167.

Eckert, T. L., Dunn, E. K., Codding, R. S., & Guiney, K. M. (2000). Self-report: Rating scale measures. In E. S. Shapiro & T. R. Kratochwill (Eds.), *Conducting school-based assessments of child and adolescent behavior* (pp. 150–169). New York: Guilford.

Eckert, T. L., Dunn, E. K., Guiney, K. M., & Codding, R. S. (2000). Self reports: Theory and research in using rating scale measures. In E. S. Shapiro & T. R. Kratochwill (Eds.), *Behavioral assessment in schools: Theory, research, and clinical foundations* (2nd ed., pp. 288–322). New York: Guilford.

Eddings, J. (1997). Counting a "new" type of American: The dicey politics of creating a "multiracial" category in the census. *U.S. News and World Report, 123*, 22–23.

Edelbrock, C., & Costello, A. J. (1988). Structured psychiatric interviews for children. In M. Rutter, A. H. Tuma, & I. S. Lann (Eds.), *Assessment and diagnosis in child psychopathology* (pp. 87–112). New York: Guilford.

Edelbrock, C. S., Greenbaum, R., & Conover, N. C. (1985). Reliability and concurrent relations between the teacher version of the child behavior profile and the Conners revised teacher rating scale. *Journal of Abnormal Child Psychology, 13*, 295–303.

Eisenberg, N., Guthrie, I. K., Murphy, B. C., Shepard, S. A., Cumberland, A., & Carlo, G. (1999). Consistency and development of prosocial dispositions: A longitudinal study. *Child Development, 70*, 1360–1372.

Eklund, K., & Dowdy, E. (2014). Screening for behavioral and emotional risk versus traditional school identification methods. *School Mental Health, 6(1)*, 40–49.

Elliott, S. N., Barnard, J., & Gresham, F. M. (1989). Preschoolers social behavior: Teachers' and parents' assessments. *Journal of Psychoeducational Assessment, 7*, 223–234.

Elliott, S. N., & Busse, R. T. (1990). Review of the child behavior checklist. In J. J. Kramer & J. C. Conoley (Eds.), *The supplement to the tenth mental measurements yearbook* (pp. 41–45). Lincoln, NE: Buros Institute of Mental Measurements.

Elliott, S. N., Busse, R. T., & Gresham, F. M. (1993). Behavior rating scales: Issues of use and development. *School Psychology Review, 22*, 313–321.

Elliott, S. N., & Gresham, F. M. (1987). Children's social skills: Assessment and classification practices. *Journal of Counseling and Development, 66*, 96–99.

El-Missiry, A., Aboraya, A. S., Manseur, H., Manchester, J., France, C., & Border, K. (2011). An update on the epidemiology of schizophrenia with a special reference to clinically important risk factors. *International Journal of Mental Health and Addiction, 9*(1), 39–59.

Emerson, E. N., Crowley, S. L., & Merrell, K. W. (1994). Convergent validity of the school social behavior scales with the child behavior checklist and teacher's report form. *Journal of Psychoeducational Assessment, 12*, 372–380.

Endedijk, H. M., & Cillessen, A. H. N. (2015). Computerized sociometric assessment for preschool children. *International Journal of Behavioral Development, 39*, 383–388.

Endicott, J., & Spitzer, R. L. (1978). A diagnostic interview: The schedule for affective disorders and schizophrenia. *Archives of General Psychiatry, 35*, 837–844.

Epps, S. (1985). Best practices in behavioral observation. In A. Thomas & J. Grimes (Eds.), *Best practices in school psychology* (pp. 95–111). Washington, DC: National Association of School Psychologists.

Epstein, M. H. (2004). *Behavioral and emotional rating scale-second edition (BERS-2)*. Austin, TX: PRO-ED Inc.

Epstein, M. H., Cullinan, D., & Lloyd, J. W. (1986). Behavior problem patterns among the learning disabled: III. Replication across age and sex. *Learning Disability Quarterly, 9*, 43–54.

Epstein, M. H., & Sharma, J. (1998). *Behavioral and emotional rating scale (BERS)*. Austin, TX: PRO-ED Inc.

Erbacher, T. A., Singer, J. B., & Poland, S. (2015). *Suicide in Schools*. New York: Routledge.

Erikson, E. (1963). *Childhood and society*. New York: Norton.

Erlenmeyer-Kimling, L., Kestenbaum, C., Bird, H., & Hildoff, U. (1984). Assessment of the New York high risk project subjects in sample A who are now clinically deviant. In N. F. Watt, E. J. Anthony, L. C. Wynne, & J. E. Rolf (Eds.), *Children at high risk of schizophrenia* (pp. 227–339). Cambridge, England: Cambridge University Press.

Exner, J. E., Jr., & Weiner, I. B. (1994). *The Rorschach: A comprehensive system: Vol. 3. Assessment of children and adolescents* (2nd ed.). New York: Wiley.

Eyberg, S. M., Chase, R. M., Fernandez, M. A., & Nelson, M. M. (2014). *Dyadic parent-child interaction coding system: Comprehensive manual for research and training* (4th ed.). Gainesville, FL: PCIT International.

Eyberg, S. M., & Matarazzo, R. G. (1980). Training parents as therapists: A comparison between individual parent–child interaction training and parent group didactic training. *Journal of Clinical Psychology, 36*, 492–499.

Eyberg, S. M., & Robinson, E. A. (1983). Dyadic parent-child interaction coding system: A manual. *Psychological Documents, 13* (Ms. No. 2582).

Fagan, J., & Fantuzzo, J. W. (1999). Multirater congruence on the social skills rating system: Mother, father, and teacher assessments of urban Head Start children's social competencies. *Early Childhood Research Quarterly, 14*, 229–242.

Fagan, J., & Iglesias, A. (2000). The relationship between fathers' and children's communication skills and children's behavior problems: A study of Head Start children. *Early Education & Development, 11*, 307–320.

Fan, X., Wilson, V. T., & Kapes, J. T. (1996). Ethnic group representation in test construction samples and test bias: The standardization fallacy revisited. *Educational and Psychological Measurement, 56*, 365–381.

Farrington, D. (1978). The family backgrounds of aggressive youths. In L. A. Hersov, A. L. Berger, & D. Shaffer (Eds.), *Aggression and antisocial behavior in childhood and adolescence* (pp. 73–93). London: Pergamon.

Feil, E. G., & Becker, W. C. (1993). Investigation of a multiple-gated screening system for preschool behavior problems. *Behavioral Disorders, 19*, 44–53.

Feldman, D., Kinnison, L., Jay, R., & Harth, R. (1983). The effects of differential labeling on professional concepts and attitudes towards the emotionally disturbed/behaviorally disordered. *Behavioral Disorders, 8*, 191–198.

Feyh, J. M., & Holmes, C. B. (1994). Use of the draw-a-person test with conduct disordered children. *Perceptual and Motor Skills, 78*, 1353–1354.

Finch, A. J., Saylor, C. F., & Edwards, G. L. (1985). Children's depression inventory: Sex and grade norms for normal children. *Journal of Consulting and Clinical Psychology, 53*, 424–425.

Fine, G. A. (1981). Friends, impression management, and preadolescent behavior. In S. R. Asher & J. M. Gottman (Eds.), *The development of children's friendships* (pp. 29–52). New York: Cambridge University Press.

First, M. B. (2013). DSM-5 *handbook of differential diagnosis*. Arlington, VA: American Psychiatric Pub.

Fish, B., & Shapiro, T. (1964). A descriptive typology of children's psychiatric disorders: II. A behavioral classification. In R. L. Jenkins & J. O. Cole (Eds.), *American psychiatric association psychiatric research reports 18* (pp. 75–90). Washington, DC: American Psychiatric Association.

Fisher, P., Wicks, J., Shaffer P., Piacentini, J., & Lapkin, J. (1992). *NIMH diagnostic interview schedule for children user's manual*. New York: State Psychiatric Institute.

Fixsen, D. L., Naoom, S. F., Blase, K. A., Friedman, R. M., & Wallace, F. (2005). *Implementation research: A synthesis of the literature*. Tampa, FL: University of South Florida, Louis de la Parte Florida Mental Health Institute, The National Implementation Research Network (FMHI Publication #231).

Flanagan, D. P., Alfonso, V. C., Primavera, L. H., & Povall, L. (1996). Convergent validity of the BASC and SSRS: Implications for social skills assessment. *Psychology in the Schools, 33*, 13–23.

Flanagan, R. (1995). A review of the behavior assessment system for children (BASC): Assessment consistent with the requirements of the Individuals with Disabilities Education Act (IDEA). *Journal of School Psychology, 33*, 177–186.

Flanagan, R. (2008). Test review: Roberts, G. E., & Gruber, C. (2005). Roberts-2. Los Angeles: Western Psychological Services. *Journal of Psychoeducational Assessment, 26*, 304–310.

Flugum, K. R., & Reschly, D. J. (1994). Pre-referral interventions: Quality indices and outcomes. *Journal of School Psychology, 32*, 1–14.

Ford, R. T. (2005). *Racial culture: A critique*. Princeton, NJ: Princeton University Press.

Forehand, R., & McMahon, R. J. (1981). *Helping the noncompliant child: A clinician's guide to parent training*. New York: Guilford.

Forehand, R., & Peed, S. (1979). Training parents to modify noncompliant behavior of their children. In A. J. Finch & P. C. Kendall (Eds.), *Treatment and research in child psychopathology* (pp. 159–184). New York: Spectrum.

Forehand, R., Peed, S., Roberts, M., McMahon, R., Griest, D., & Humphreys, L. (1978). *Coding manual for scoring mother–child interactions*. Unpublished manuscript, Department of Psychology, University of Georgia, Athens.

Foreyt, J. P., & Mikhail, C. (1997). Anorexia nervosa and bulimia nervosa. In E. J. Mash & L. G. Terdal (Eds.), *Assessment of childhood disorders* (3rd ed., pp. 683–716). New York: Guilford.

Forgatch, M. S., & DeGarmo, D. (2002). Extending and testing the social interaction learning model with divorce samples. In J. B. Reid, G. R. Patterson, & J. Snyder (Eds.), *Antisocial behavior in children and adolescents: A developmental analysis and model for intervention* (pp. 235–256). Washington DC: American Psychological Association.

Forgatch, M. S., DeGarmo, D. S., & Beldavs, Z. G. (2005). An efficacious theory-based intervention for stepfamilies. *Behavioral Therapy, 36*(4), 357–365.

Forness, S. R., & Kavale, K. A. (2002). Emotional behavioral disorders: Background and current status of the E/BD terminology and definition. *Behavioral Disorders, 25*, 264–269.

Forness, S. R., & Knitzer, J. (1992). A new proposed definition and terminology to replace "serious emotional disturbance" in the Individuals with Disabilities Education Act. *School Psychology Review, 21*, 12–20.

Forster, A. A., Eyberg, S. M., & Burns, G. L. (1990). Assessing the verbal behavior of conduct problem children during mother–child interactions: A preliminary investigation. *Child and Family Behavior Therapy, 12*, 13–22.

Forsyth, J. P. (2000). A process-oriented approach to the etiology, maintenance, and treatment of anxiety disorders. In M. J. Dougher (Ed.), *Clinical behavior analysis* (pp. 153–180). Reno, NV: Context Press.

Forth, A. E., Kosson, D. S., & Hare, R. D. (2003). *Hare psychopathy checklist: Youth version*. North Tonawanda, NY: Multi-Health Systems.

Foster, S. L., Bell-Dolan, D., & Berler, E. S. (1986). Methodological issues in the use of sociometrics for selecting children for social skills research and training. *Advances in Behavioral Assessment of Children and Families, 2*, 227–248.

Fox, L., Hemmeter, M. L., & Snyder, P. (2008). *Teaching pyramid observation tool for preschool classrooms (TPOT) manual research edition*. Unpublished assessment.

Fox, L., Hemmeter, M., Snyder, P., Binder, D., & Clarke, S. (2011). Coaching early childhood special educators to implement a comprehensive model for promoting young children's social competence. *Topics in Early Childhood Special Education, 31*(3), 178–192.

Frank, L. K. (1939). Projective methods for the study of personality. *Journal of Psychology, 8,* 389–413.

Frey, W. H. (2019). *Declines in white youth population are countered by gains in other racial groups.* Brookings Institute. Retrieved from: https://www.brookings.edu/research/less-than-half-of-us-children-under-15-are-white-census-shows/

Frick, P. J. (1998). Conduct disorders. In T. H. Ollendick & M. Hersen (Eds.), *Handbook of child psychopathology* (3rd ed., pp. 213–237). New York: Plenum.

Frick, P. J., & Ellis, M. (1999). Callous-unemotional traits and subtypes of conduct disorder. *Clinical Child and Family Psychology Review, 2,* 149–168.

Frick, P. J., Lilienfeld, S. O., Ellis, S. M., Loney, B., & Silverthorn, P. (1999). The association between anxiety and psychopathy dimensions in children. *Journal of Abnormal Psychology, 27,* 383–392.

Friman, P. C., Hayes, S. C., & Wilson, K. G. (1998). Why behavior analysts should study emotion: The example of anxiety. *Journal of Applied Behavior Analysis, 31*(1), 137–156.

Froehlich, T. E., Lanphear, B. P., Epstein, J. N., Barbaresi, W. J., Katusic, S. K., & Kahn, R. S. (2007). Prevalence, recognition, and treatment of attention-deficit/hyperactivity disorder in a national sample of US children. *Archives of Pediatrics & Adolescent Medicine, 161*(9), 857–864.

Fuchs, D., & Fuchs, L. S. (1986). Test procedure bias: Ameta-analysis of examiner familiarity effects. *Review of Educational Research, 56,* 243–262.

Fulkerson, S. C., & Freeman, W. M. (1980). Perceptual-motor deficiency in autistic children. *Perceptual and Motor Skills, 50,* 331–336.

Garcia-Barrera, M. A., Karr, J. E., & Kamphaus, R. W. (2013). Longitudinal applications of a behavioral screener of executive functioning: Assessing factorial invariance and exploring latent growth. *Psychological Assessment, 25*(4), 1300.

Garner, D. M. (2004). *Eating disorders inventory–3.* Odessa, FL: Psychological Assessment Resources.

Gaudio, S., & DiCiommo, V. (2011). Prevalence of personality disorders and their clinical correlates in outpatient adolescents with anorexia nervosa. *Psychosomatic Medicine, 73*(9), 769–774.

Gelman, R., & Baillageon, R. (1983). A review of some Piagetian concepts. In P. H. Mussen (Ed.), *Carmichael's manual of child psychology* (pp. 167–230). New York: Wiley.

Gesten, E. L. (1976). A health resources inventory: The development of a measure of the personal and social competence of primary-grade children. *Journal of Consulting and Clinical Psychology, 44,* 775–786.

Gettinger, M., & Kratochwill, T. R. (1987). Behavioral assessment. In C. L. Frame & J. L. Matson (Eds.), *Handbook of assessment in childhood psychopathology* (pp. 131–161). New York: Plenum.

Gillberg, I. C., & Gillberg, C. (1983). Three-year follow-up at age 10 of children with minor neuro-developmental disorders: I. Behavioural Problems. *Developmental Medicine and Child Neurology, 25,* 438–449.

Gilliam, J. E. (1995). *Gilliam autism rating scale.* Austin, TX: PRO-ED.

Gilliam, J. E. (2006). *Gilliam autism rating scale* (2nd ed). Austin, TX: PRO-ED.

Gilliam, J. E. (2013). *Gilliam autism rating scale – third edition (GARS-3).* Austin, TX: Pro-Ed.

Gilliom, M., & Shaw, D. S. (2004). Codevelopment of externalizing and internalizing problems in early childhood. *Development and Psychopathology, 16,* 313–333.

Gilman, R., Laughlin, J. E., & Huebner, E. S. (1999). Validation of the self-description questionnaire II with an American sample. *School Psychology International, 20,* 300–307.

Gioia, G. A., Isquith, P. K., Guy, S. C., & Kenworthy, L. (2015). *Behavior rating inventory of executive function* (2nd ed.). Lutz, FL: Psychological Assessment Resources.

Gleason, M. M., & Humphreys, K. L. (2016). Categorical diagnosis of extreme hyperactivity, impulsivity, and inattention in very young children. *Infant Mental Health Journal, 37,* 476–485.

Glover, T. A., & Albers, C. A. (2007). Considerations for evaluating universal screening assessments. *Journal of School Psychology, 45*(2), 117–135.

Goh, D. S., & Fuller, G. B. (1983). Current practices in the assessment of personality and behavior by school psychologists. *School Psychology Review, 12,* 240–243.

Goldberg, L. R. (1974). Objective diagnostic tests and measures. *Annual Review of Psychology, 25,* 343–366.

Goodenough, F. L. (1926). *Measurement of intelligence by drawings.* New York: Harcourt Brace.

Goodman, R. (1997). The strengths and difficulties questionnaire: A research note. *Journal of Child Psychology and Psychiatry, 38,* 581–586.

Goodman, A., Lamping, D. L., & Ploubidis, G. B. (2010). When to use broader internalising and externalising subscales instead of the hypothesised five subscales on the strengths and difficulties questionnaire (SDQ): Data from British parents, teachers and children. *Journal of Abnormal Child Psychology, 38*(8), 1179–1191.

Gotham, K., et al. (2008). A replication of the autism diagnostic observation schedule (ADOS) revised algorithms. *Journal of the American Academy of Child & Adolescent Psychiatry, 47*(6), 642–651.

Gottesman, I. I. (1991). *Schizophrenia and genesis: The origins of madness.* New York: Freeman.

Graham, J. A., & Cohen, R. C. (1997). Race and sex as factors in children's sociometric ratings and friendship choices. *Social Development, 6*(3), 355–372.

Graham, J. N., Archer, R. P., Tellegen, A., Ben-Porath, Y. S., & Kaemmer, B. (2006). *Minnesota multiphasic personality inventory—adolescent manual supplement.* Upper Saddle River, NJ: Pearson Education, Inc.

Graham, P. (1980). Epidemiological studies. In H. E. Quay & J. S. Werry (Eds.), *Psychopathological disorders of childhood* (2nd ed., pp. 185–209). New York: Wiley.

Gravina, N., & Olson, R. (2009). Behavioral self-monitoring. *T and D, 63*(5), 18.

Gray, S. W. (1963). *The psychologist in the schools.* New York: Holt, Rinehart & Winston.

Greenberg, M., Weissberg, R., Utne O'Brien, M., & Elias, M. (2003). Enhancing school-based prevention and youth development through coordinated social, emotional, and academic learning. *American Psychologist, 58*(6–7), 466–474.

Greene, R. L. (1987). Ethnicity and MMPI performance: A review. *Journal of Consulting and Clinical Psychology, 55,* 497–512.

Greenwood, C. R., Walker, H. M., Todis, N. M., & Hops, H. (1979). Selecting a cost-effective screening measure for the assessment of preschool social withdrawal. *Journal of Applied Behavior Analysis, 12,* 639–652.

Gregory, R. J. (1996). *Psychological testing: History, principles, and applications* (2nd ed.). Boston, MA: Allyn & Bacon.

Gregory, R. J. (2000). *Psychological testing: History, principles, and applications* (3rd ed.). Boston, MA: Allyn & Bacon.

Gregory, R. J. (2010). *Psychological testing: History, principles, and applications* (6th ed.). Boston, MA: Allyn & Bacon.

Gresham, F. M. (1981a). Assessment of children's social skills. *Journal of School Psychology, 17,* 120–133.

Gresham, F. M. (1981b). Social skills training with handicapped children: A review. *Review of Educational Research, 51,* 139–176.

Gresham, F. M. (1986). Conceptual issues in the assessment of social competence in children. In P. Strain, M. Guralnick, & H. Walker (Eds.), *Children's social behavior: Development, assessment, and modification* (pp. 143–179). New York: Academic Press.

Gresham, F. M., Cook, C. R., Collins, T., Dart, E., Rasetschwane, K., Truelson, E., et al. (2010). Developing a change-sensitive brief behavior rating scale as a progress monitoring tool for social behavior: An example using the social skills rating system-teacher form. *School Psychology Review, 39*(3), 364–379.

Gresham, F. M., & Davis, C. J. (1988). Behavioral interviews with parents and teachers. In E. S. Shapiro & T. R. Kratochwill (Eds.), *Behavioral assessment in schools: Conceptual foundations and practical applications* (pp. 455–493). New York: Guilford.

Gresham, F. M., & Elliott, S. N. (1990). *The social skills rating system.* Circle Pines, MN: American Guidance.

Gresham, F. M., & Elliott, S. N. (2008). *The social skills improvement system (SSIS): Performance screening guide.* Minneapolis, MN: Pearson.

Gresham, F., Elliott, S., Cook, C., Vance, M., & Kettler, R. (2010). Cross-informant agreement for ratings for social skill and problem behavior ratings: An investigation of the social skills improvement system—rating scales. *Psychological Assessment, 22*(1), 157–166.

Gresham, F. M., & Gansle, K. A. (1992). Misguided assumptions of the *DSM-III-R:* Implications for school psychological practice. *School Psychology Quarterly, 7,* 79–95.

Gresham, F. M., & Reschly, D. J. (1986). Social skills deficits and low peer acceptance of main-streamed learning disabled children. *Learning Disability Quarterly, 9,* 23–32.

Gresham, F. M., & Reschly, D. J. (1987a). Dimensions of social competence: Method factors in the assessment of adaptive behavior, social skills, and peer acceptance. *Journal of School Psychology, 25*, 367–381.

Gresham, F. M., & Reschly, D. J. (1987b). Issues in the conceptualization, classification and assessment of social skills in the mildly handicapped. In T. Kratochwill (Ed.), *Advances in school psychology* (pp. 203–264). Hillsdale, NJ: Lawrence Erlbaum Associates.

Gresham, F. M., & Stuart, D (1992). Stability of sociometric assessment: Implications for uses as selection and outcome measures in social skills training. *Journal of School Psychology, 30*, 223–231.

Gresham, F. M., Sugai, G., & Horner, R. H. (2001). Interpreting outcomes of social skills training for students with high-incidence disabilities. *Exceptional Children, 67*, 331–344.

Griest, D. L., Forehand, R., Wells, K. C., & McMahon, R. J. (1980). An examination of differences between nonclinic and behavior-problem clinic-referred children and their mothers. *Journal of Abnormal Psychology, 89*, 497–500.

Gronlund, N. E., & Linn, R. L. (1999). *Measurement and evaluation in teaching* (8th ed.). New York: Prentice-Hall.

Gross, A. M. (1984). Behavioral interviewing. In T. H. Ollendick & M. Hersen (Eds.), *Child behavior assessment: Principles and practices* (pp. 61–79). New York: Pergamon.

Groth-Marnat, G. (1997). *Handbook of psychological assessment* (3rd ed.). New York: Wiley.

Grunspan, D. Z., Wiggins, B. L., & Goodreau, S. M. (2014). Understanding classrooms through social network analysis: A primer for social network analysis in education research. *CBE-Life Sciences Education, 13*(2), 167–178.

Hagborg, W. J. (1994). Sociometry and educationally handicapped children. *Journal of Group Psychotherapy, Psychodrama, and Sociometry, 47*, 4–14.

Haley, A. (1996). *The autobiography of Malcom X.* New York: Grove Press.

Haley, G. M., Fine, S., & Marriage, K. (1988). Psychotic features in adolescents with major depression. *Journal of the American Academy of Child and Adolescent Psychiatry, 27*, 489–493.

Hambleton, R., & Kang Lee., M. (2013). Methods for adapting and translating tests to increase cross-language validity. In D. H. Saklofske, C. R. Reynolds, & V. L. Schwean (Eds.), *Oxford handbook of child psychological assessment* (pp. 172–181). New York: Oxford University Press.

Hamilton, C., Fuchs, D., Fuchs, L. S., & Roberts, H. (2000). Rates of classroom participation and the validity of sociometry. *School Psychology Review, 29*, 251–266.

Hamilton, E., & Klimes-Dougan, B. (2015). Gender differences in suicide prevention responses: Implications for adolescents based on an illustrative review of the literature. *International Journal of Environmental Research and Public Health, 12*(3), 2359–2372.

Hammen, C. (1995). The social context of risk for depression. In K. D. Craig & K. S. Dobson (Eds.), *Anxiety and depression in adults and children* (pp. 82–98). Thousand Oaks, CA: Sage.

Hammen, C. L., Rudolph, K. D., & Abaied, J. L. (2014). Child and adolescent depression. In E. J. Mash & R. A. Barkley (Eds.), *Child psychopathology* (3rd ed., pp. 225–263). New York: Guilford.

Hammer, E. F. (1981). Projective drawings. In A. I. Rabin (Ed.), *Assessment with projective techniques: A concise introduction* (pp. 151–185). New York: Springer.

Handler, L., & Habenicht, D. (1994). The kinetic family drawing technique: A review of the literature. *Journal of Personality Assessment, 62*, 440–464.

Harrington, G. M. (1988). Two forms of minority group test bias as psychometric artifacts with animal models *(Rattus norvegicus). Journal of Comparative Psychology, 102*, 400–407.

Harris, A. M., & Reid, J. B. (1981). The consistency of a class of coercive child behaviors across school settings for individual subjects. *Journal of Abnormal Child Psychology, 9*, 219–227.

Harrison, P. L. (1987). Research with adaptive behavior scales. *The Journal of Special Education, 21*, 37–68.

Harrison, P. L., & Oakland, T. (2000). *Adaptive behavior assessment system.* San Antonio, TX: The Psychological Corporation.

Hart, D. H. (1972). *The Hart sentence completion test for children.* Unpublished manuscript, Educational Support Systems, Inc., Salt Lake City, UT.

Hart, D. H. (1980). *A quantitative scoring system for the Hart sentence completion test for children.* Unpublished manuscript, Educational Support Systems, Inc., Salt Lake City, UT.

Hart, D. H. (1986). The sentence completion techniques. In H. M. Knoff (Ed.), *The assessment of child and adolescent personality* (pp. 245–272). New York: Guilford.

Hart, D. H., Kehle, T. J., & Davies, M. V. (1983). Effectiveness of sentence completion techniques: A review of the Hart sentence completion test for children. *School Psychology Review, 12,* 428–434.

Harter, S. (1985a). Competence as a dimension of self-evaluation: Toward a comprehensive model of self-worth. In R. Leahy (Ed.), *The development of the self* (pp. 137–181). New York: Academic Press.

Harter, S. (1985b). *Self-perception profile for children.* Denver, CO: University of Denver, Department of Psychology.

Harter, S. (1986). Processes underlying the construct, maintenance, and enhancement of the self-concept in children. In J. Suls & A. Greenwald (Eds.), *Psychological perspectives on the self* (Vol. 3, pp. 137–181). Hillsdale, NJ: Lawrence Erlbaum Associates.

Harter, S. (1988). *Self-perception profile for adolescents.* Denver, CO: University of Denver, Department of Psychology.

Harter, S. (1990). Issues in the assessment of the self-concept of children and adolescents. In A. M. LaGreca (Ed.), *Through the eyes of the child* (pp. 292–325). Boston, MA: Allyn & Bacon.

Harter, S. (1999). *The construction of the self: A developmental perspective.* New York: Guilford.

Harter, S. (2012). *Self-perception profile for children.* Denver, CO: University of Denver, Department of Psychology.

Harter, S., & Chao, C. (1992). The role of competence in children's creation of imaginary friends. *Merrill–Palmer Quarterly, 38,* 350–363.

Harter, S., & Pike, R. (1980). *The pictorial scale of perceived competence and acceptance for young children.* Denver, CO: University of Denver, Department of Psychology.

Harter, S., & Pike, R. (1984). The pictorial perceived competence scale for young children. *Child Development, 55,* 657–692.

Hartup, W. W. (1978). Peer relations and the growth of social competence. In M. Kent & J. Rolf (Eds.), *Social competence in children* (pp. 150–172). Hanover, NH: University Press of New England.

Hartup, W. W. (1983). Peer relations. In E. M. Hetherington (Ed.), *Handbook of child psychology: Vol. 4. Socialization, personality, and social development* (pp. 103–198). New York: Wiley.

Harvey, E. A., Friedman-Weieneth, J. L., Miner, A. L., Bartolomei, R. J., Youngwirth, S. D., Hashim, R. L., & Arnold, D. H. (2009). The role of ethnicity in observers' ratings of mother–child behavior. *Developmental Psychology, 45*(6), 1497–1508.

Hase, H. D., & Goldberg, L. R. (1967). Comparative validity of differing strategies of constructing personality inventory scales. *Psychological Bulletin, 67,* 231–248.

Hayden-Thomson, L., Rubin, K. H., & Hymel, S. (1987). Sex preferences in sociometric choices. *Developmental Psychology, 23,* 558–562.

Haynes, S. N., & O'Brien, W. H. (1990). Functional analysis in behavior therapy. *Clinical Psychology Review, 10,* 649–668.

Haynes, S. N., & Wilson, C. C. (1979). *Behavioral assessment.* San Francisco, CA: Jossey-Bass.

Hayvren, M., & Hymel, S. (1984). Ethical issues in sociometric testing: Impact of sociometric measures on interaction behavior. *Developmental Psychology, 20,* 844–849.

Helsel, W. J., & Matson, J. L. (1984). The assessment of depression in children: The internal structure of the child depression inventory. *Behavior Research and Therapy, 22,* 289–298.

Hemmeter, M. L., Fox, L., & Snyder, P. (2013). *Teaching pyramid observation tool (TPOT) for preschool classrooms manual: Research edition.* NY, NY: Paul H. Brookes Publishing Company Incorporated.

Hemmeter, M., Ostrosky, M., & Fox, L. (2006). Social and emotional foundations for early learning: A conceptual model to intervention. *School Psychology Review, 35*(4), 583–601.

Henning-Stout, M. (1994). *Responsive assessment.* San Francisco, CA: Jossey-Bass.

Hernstein, R. J., & Murray, C. (1994). *The bell curve: Intelligence and class structure in American life.* New York: The Free Press.

Hess, A. K. (2001). Review of the Conners rating scales–revised. In B. S. Plake & J. C. Impara (Eds.), *The fourteenth mental measurements yearbook* (pp. 331–333). Lincoln, NE: Buros Institute of Mental Measurements.

Hesson, K., Bakal, D., & Dobson, K. S. (1993). Legal and ethical issues concerning children's rights of consent. *Canadian Psychology, 34,* 317–328.

Hetherington, E. M., & Martin, B. (1986). Family factors and psychopathology in children. In H. C. Quay & J. S. Werry (Eds.), *Psychopathological disorders of childhood* (3rd ed., pp. 332–390). New York: Wiley.

Hinshaw, S. P. (1987). On the distinction between attentional deficits/hyperactivity and conduct problems/aggression in child psychology. *Psychological Bulletin, 101*, 443–463.

Hinshaw, S. P. (1994). *Attention deficits and hyperactivity in children.* Thousand Oaks, CA: Sage.

Hintze, J. M. (2005). Psychometrics of direct observation. *School Psychology Review, 34*, 507–519.

Hintze, J. M., & Matthews, W. J. (2004). The generalizability of systematic direct observations across time and setting: A preliminary investigation of the psychometrics of behavioral observation. *School Psychology Review, 33*, 258–270.

Hintze, J. M., Stoner, G., & Bull, M. H. (2000). Analogue assessment: Emotional/behavioral problems. In E. S. Shapiro & T. R. Kratochwill (Eds.), *Conducting school-based assessments of child and adolescent behavior* (pp. 55–77). New York: Guilford.

Hodges, K. (1990a). Depression and anxiety in children: A comparison of self-report questionnaires to clinical interview. *Psychological Assessment, 2*, 376–381.

Hodges, K. (1993). Structured interviews for assessing children. *Journal of Child Psychology and Psychiatry and Allied Disciplines, 34*, 49–68.

Hoffman, T., Dana, R. H., & Bolton, B. (1987). Measured acculturation and the MMPI-168. *Journal of Cross-Cultural Psychology, 16*, 243–256.

Hoier, T. S., & Cone, J. D. (1987). Target selection of social skills for children: The template-matching procedure. *Behavior Modification, 11*, 137–164.

Hojnoski, R. L., Morrison, R., Brown, M., & Mathews, W. J. (2006). Project test use among school psychologists: A survey and critique. *Journal of Psychoeducational Assessment, 24*, 145–159.

Holguin, O., & Sherrill, C. (1990). The use of a pictorial scale of perceived competence and acceptance with learning disabled boys. *Perceptual and Motor Skills, 70*(3, Pt. 2), 1235–1238.

Holland, M. L., Gimpel, G. A., & Merrell, K. W. (1998). Innovations in assessing ADHD: Development, psychometric properties, and factor structure of the ADHD symptoms rating scale. *Journal of Psychopathology and Behavioral Assessment, 20*, 307–332.

Holland, M. L., Gimpel, G. A., & Merrell, K. W. (2001). *ADHD symptoms rating scale.* Odessa, FL: Psychological Assessment Resources.

Holland, M. L., & Merrell, K. W. (1998). Social–emotional characteristics of preschool-age children referred for child find screening and assessment: A comparative study. *Research in Developmental Disabilities, 19*, 167–179.

Hollinger, J. D. (1987). Social skills for behaviorally disordered children as preparation for main-streaming: Theory, practice, and new directions. *Remedial and Special Education, 11*, 139–149.

Hood, A. B., & Johnson, R. W. (1997). *Assessment in counseling* (2nd ed.). Alexandria, VA: American Association for Counseling and Development.

Hops, H., & Greenwood, C. R. (1981). Social skills deficits. In E. J. Mash & L. G. Terdal (Eds.), *Behavioral assessment of childhood disorders* (pp. 347–394). New York: Guilford.

Hops, H., & Lewin, L. (1984). Peer sociometric forms. In T. H. Ollendick & M. Hersen (Eds.), *Child behavioral assessment* (pp. 124–147). New York: Pergamon.

Hops, H., & Lewinsohn, P. M. (1995). A course for the treatment of depression among adolescents. In K. D. Craig & K. S. Dobson (Eds.), *Anxiety and depression in adults and children* (pp. 230–245). Thousand Oaks, CA: Sage.

Horner, R. H. (1994). Functional assessment: Contributions and future directions. *Journal of Applied Behavior Analysis, 27*, 401–404.

Horner, R. H., & Carr, E. G. (1997). Behavioral support for students with severe disabilities: Functional assessment and comprehensive intervention. *Journal of Special Education, 31*, 84–109.

Horner, R. H., Sugai, G., & Lewis, T. (2015, April). *Is school-wide positive behavior support an evidence-based practice?* Retrieved from www.pbis.org

Horner, R. H., Sugai, G., Todd, A. W., & Lewis-Palmer, T. (2005). School-wide positive behavior support: An alternative approach to discipline in schools. In L. Bambara & L. Kern (Eds.), *Individualized supports for students with problem behavior: Designing positive behavior plans* (pp. 359–390). New York: Guilford Press.

Howlin, P., & Rutter, M., with Berger, M., Hemsley, P., Hersov, L., & Yule, W. (1987). *Treatment of autistic children.* Chichester, England: Wiley.

Howlin, P., & Yule, W. (1990). Taxonomy of major disorders in childhood. In M. Lewis & S. M. Miller (Eds.), *Handbook of developmental psychopathology* (pp. 371–383). New York: Plenum.

Hoza, B., Mrug, S., Gerdes, A. C., Hinshaw, S. P., Bukowski, W. M., Gold, J. A., et al. (2005). What aspects of peer relationships are impaired in children with attention-deficit/hyperactivity disorder? *Journal of Consulting and Clinical Psychology, 73*, 411–423.

Huebner, E. S. (1991). Correlates of life satisfaction in children. *School Psychology Quarterly, 6*(2), 103–111.

Hughes, E. K., Gullone, E., & Watson, S. D. (2011). Emotional functioning in children and adolescents with elevated depressive symptoms. *Journal of Psychopathology and Behavioral Assessment, 33*, 335–345.

Hughes, H. M., & Haynes, S. N. (1978). Structured laboratory observation in the behavioral assessment of parent–child interactions: A methodological critique. *Behavior Therapy, 9*, 428–477.

Hughes, J. N., & Baker, D. B. (1990). *The clinical child interview.* New York: Guilford.

Hulse, W. (1951). The emotionally disturbed child draws his family. *Quarterly Journal of Child Behavior, 3*, 152–174.

Hulse, W. (1952). Childhood conflict expressed through family drawings. *Journal of Projective Techniques, 16*, 66–79.

Hummelen, B., Pedersen, G., Wilberg, T., & Karterud, S. (2015). Poor validity of the DSM-IV schizoid personality disorder construct as a diagnostic category. *Journal of Personality Disorders, 29*(3), 334.

Hutton, J. B., Dubes, R., & Muir, S. (1992). Assessment practices of school psychologists: Ten years later. *School Psychology Review, 21*, 271–284.

Hymel, S. (1983). Preschool children's peer relations: Issues in sociometric assessment. *Merrill–Palmer Quarterly, 29*, 237–260.

Hymel, S., & Asher, S. R. (1977, April). *Assessment and training of isolated children's social skills.* Paper presented at the biennial meeting of the Society for Research in Child Development, New Orleans, LA. (ERIC Document Reproduction Service No. ED136930.)

Ivanova, M., et al. (2007). The generalizability of the youth self-report syndrome structure in 23 societies. *Journal of Consulting and Clinical Psychology, 75*(5), 729–738.

Iverson, A. M., & Iverson, G. L. (1996). Children's long-term reactions to participating in sociometric assessment. *Psychology in the Schools, 33*, 103–112.

Jackson, M. F., Barth, J. M., Powell, N., & Lochman, J. E. (2006). Classroom contextual effects of race on children's peer nominations. *Child Development, 77*(5), 1325–1337.

Jackson, S. L. (2015). *Research methods and statistics: A critical thinking approach.* Belmont, CA: Cengage Learning.

Jacob, S., Decker, D. M., & Hartshorne, T. (2011). *Ethics and law for school psychologists* (6th ed.). Hoboken, NJ: Wiley & Sons.

Jacob, S., & Hartshorne, T. (2003). *Ethics and law for school psychologists* (4th ed.). New York: Wiley.

Jagger, J., Prusoff, B. A., Cohen, D. J., Kidd, K. K., Carbonari, C. M., & John, K. (1982). The epidemiology of Tourette's syndrome. *Schizophrenia Bulletin, 8*, 267–278.

Jee, S., Conn, A., Szilagyi, P., Blumkin, A., Baldwin, C., & Szilagyi, M. (2010). Identification of social-emotional problems among young children in foster care. *Journal of Child Psychology and Psychiatry, 51*(12), 1351–1358.

Jenkins, L. N., Demaray, M. K., Wren, N. S., Secord, S. M., Lyell, K. M., Magers, A. M., Setmeyer, A. J., Rodelo, C., Newcomb-McNeal, E., & Tennant, J. (2014). A critical review of five commonly used social-emotional and behavioral screeners for elementary and secondary schools. *Contemporary School Psychologist, 10.* doi: 10.1007/s40688-014-0026-6

Jenkins, S. R. (2008). *A handbook of clinical scoring systems for thematic apperceptive techniques.* New York: Erlbaum.

Jensen, P. S. (2000). What's in a name? The role of diagnosis and assessment of emotional and behavioral disorders. *Report on Emotional & Behavioral Disorders in Youth, 1*, 1–23.

Jentzsch, C. E., & Merrell, K. W. (1996). An investigation of the construct validity of the preschool and kindergarten behavior scales. *Diagnostique, 21*, 1–15.

Jersild, A. T., & Holmes, F. B. (1935). Children's fears. *Child Development Monograph, 20.*

Jesness, C. F. (1962). *The Jesness inventory: Development and validation* (Research Report No. 29). Sacramento, CA: California Youth Authority.

Jesness, C. F. (1963). *Redevelopment and validation of the Jesness inventory* (Research Report No. 35). Sacramento, CA: California Youth Authority.

Jesness, C. F. (1965). *The Fricot Ranch study: Outcomes with large vs. small living units in the rehabilitation of delinquents* (Research Report No. 47). Sacramento, CA: California Youth Authority.

Jesness, C. F. (1996). *The Jesness inventory manual.* North Tonawanda, NY: Multi-Health Systems.

Jesness, C. F. (2003). *The Jesness inventory, revised.* North Tonawanda, NY: Multi-Health Systems.

Jesness, C. F., & Wedge, R. F. (1984). Validity of a revised Jesness inventory I-level classification with delinquents. *Journal of Consulting and Clinical Psychology, 52*, 997–1010.

Jiang, X., & Cillessen, A. (2005). Stability of continuous measures of sociometric status: A meta-analysis. *Developmental Review, 25*, 1–25.

Jimerson, S. R., Sharkey, J. D., Nyborg, V., & Furlong, M. J. (2004). Strength-based assessment and school psychology: A summary and synthesis. *California School Psychologist, 9*, 9–19. Retrieved from http://education.ucsb.edu/school-psychology/CSP-Journal/index.html

Joiner, T. E., Jr., Schmidt, K. L., & Barnett, J. (1996). Size, detail, and line heaviness in children's drawings as correlates of emotional distress: (More) negative evidence. *Journal of Personality Assessment, 67*, 127–141.

Jolly, J. B., Dyck, M. J., Kramer, T. A., & Wherry, J. N. (1994). Integration of positive and negative affectivity and cognitive content-specificity: Improved discrimination of anxious and depressed symptoms. *Journal of Abnormal Psychology, 103*, 544–552.

Jones, R. R., Reid, J. B., & Patterson, G. R. (1979). Naturalistic observation in clinical assessment. In P. McReynolds (Ed.), *Advances in psychological assessment* (Vol. 3, pp. 42–95). San Francisco, CA: Jossey-Bass.

Jongmans, M., Demetre, J. D., Dubowitz, L., & Henderson, S. E. (1996). How local is the impact of specific learning difficulty on premature children's evaluation of their own competence? *Journal of Child Psychology and Psychiatry and Allied Disciplines, 37*, 563–568.

Joseph, G. E., & Strain, P. S. (2003). Comprehensive evidence-based social-emotional curricula for young children: An analysis of efficacious adoption potential. *Topics in Early Childhood Special Education, 23*(2), 65–76.

Kagan, J., Reznick, J. S., & Snidman, N. (1990). The temperamental qualities of inhibition and lack of inhibition. In M. Lewis & S. M. Miller (Eds.), *Handbook of developmental psychopathology* (pp. 219–226). New York: Pergamon.

Kahn R. E., Frick, P. J., Youngstrom, E., Findling, R. L., & Youngstrom, J. K. (2012). The effects of including a callous-unemotional specifier for the diagnosis of conduct disorder. *Journal of Child Psychology and Psychiatry, 53*(3), 271–282.

Kahn, M. W., & McFarland, J. (1973). A demographic and treatment evaluation study of institutionalized juvenile offenders. *Journal of Community Psychology, 1*, 282–284.

Kaiser, A. P., Hancock, T. B., Cai, X., Foster, E. M., & Hester, P. P. (2000). Parent-reported behavioral problems and language delays in boys and girls enrolled in Head Start classrooms. *Behavioral Disorders, 26*, 26–41.

Kamphaus, R. W. (1987). Conceptual and psychometric issues in the assessment of adaptive behavior. *Journal of Special Education, 21*, 27–35.

Kamphaus, R. W., & Frick, P. J. (2002). *Clinical assessment of child and adolescent personality and behavior* (2nd ed.). Boston, MA: Allyn & Bacon.

Kamphaus, R. W., & Pleiss, K. L. (1991). Draw-a-person techniques: Tests in search of a construct. *Journal of School Psychology, 29*, 395–401.

Kamphaus, R. W., & Reynolds, C. R. (2007). *Behavior assessment system for children – second edition (BASC-2): Behavioral and emotional screening system (BESS).* Bloomington, MN: Pearson.

Kamphaus, R. W., & Reynolds, C. R. (2015). *Behavior assessment system for children—third edition (BASC-3): Behavioral and emotional screening system (BESS).* Bloomington, MN: Pearson.

Kane, J. S., & Lawler, E. E. (1978). Methods of peer assessment. *Psychological Bulletin, 85*, 555–586.

Kanner, L. (1943). Autistic disturbances of severe contact. *Nervous Child, 2*, 217–250.

Kaplan, R., & Saccuzzo, D. (2012). *Psychological testing: Principles, applications, and issues.* Ontario, Canada: Nelson Education.

Kauffman, J. M. (1989). *Characteristics of behavior disorders of children and youth* (4th ed.). Columbus, OH: Merrill/Prentice-Hall.

Kauffman, J. M. (1997). *Characteristics of emotional and behavioral disorders of children and youth* (6th ed.). Columbus, OH: Merrill/Prentice-Hall.

Kauffman, J. M. (2000). *Characteristics of emotional and behavioral disorders of children and youth* (7th ed.). Columbus, OH: Merrill/Prentice-Hall.

Kauffman, J. M., Semmell, M. I., & Agard, J. A. (1974). PRIME: An overview. *Education and Training for the Mentally Retarded, 9*, 107–112.

Kaufman, J., Birmaher, B., Brent, D., & Rao, U. (1997). Schedule for affective disorders and schizophrenia for school-age children—present and lifetime version (K–SADS–PL): Initial reliability and validity data. *Journal of the American Academy of Child and Adolescent Psychiatry, 36*, 980–988.

Kay, S. R., Fiszbein, A., & Opler, L. A. (1987). The positive and negative syndrome scale (PANSS) for schizophrenia. *Schizophrenia Bulletin, 13*(2), 261.

Kazdin, A. E. (1979). Situational specificity: The two-edged sword of behavioral assessment. *Behavioral Assessment, 1*, 57–75.

Kazdin, A. E. (1981). Behavioral observation. In M. Hersen & A. S. Bellack (Eds.), *Behavioral assessment: A practical handbook* (pp. 101–124). New York: Pergamon.

Kazdin, A. E. (1982). *Single-case research designs: Methods for clinical and applied settings.* New York: Oxford University Press.

Kazdin, A. E. (1988). Childhood depression. In E. J. Mash & L. G. Terdal (Eds.), *Behavioral assessment of childhood disorders* (2nd ed., pp. 157–195). New York: Guilford.

Kazdin, A. E. (1995). *Conduct disorders in childhood and adolescence* (2nd ed.). Thousand Oaks, CA: Sage.

Kazdin, A. E., Esveldt-Dawson, K., Unis, A. S., & Rancurello, M. D. (1983). Child and parent evaluations of depression and aggression in psychiatric inpatient children. *Journal of Abnormal Child Psychology, 11*, 401–413.

Kea, C. D., Campbell-Whatley, G. D., & Bratton, K. (2003). Culturally responsive assessment for African-American students with learning and behavioral challenges. *Assessment for Effective Intervention, 29*(1), 27–38.

Keith, L. K. (1995). Self-concept instrumentation: A historical and evaluative overview. In B. A. Bracken (Ed.), *Handbook of self-concept: Development, social, and clinical considerations* (pp. 91–170). New York: Wiley.

Keller, H. R. (1986). Behavioral observation approaches to assessment. In H. Knoff (Ed.), *The assessment of child and adolescent personality* (pp. 353–397). New York: Guilford.

Kelly, E. J. (1989). *Clarifications of federal eligibility criteria for students identified as "seriously emotionally disturbed" versus exclusion for the "social maladjustment" from C.F.R. part 300.5 (i) (A–E) and (ii).* Nevada Clarifications. Las Vegas, NV: University of Nevada, Department of Special Education.

Kent, R. N., & Foster, L. F. (1977). Direct observational procedures: Methodological issues in naturalistic settings. In A. R. Ciminero, K. S. Calhoun, & H. E. Adams (Eds.), *Handbook of behavioral assessment* (pp. 279–328). New York: Wiley.

Kent, R. N., O'Leary, K. D., Diament, C., & Deitz, A. (1974). Expectation biases in observational utility of therapeutic change. *Journal of Consulting and Clinical Psychology, 42*, 774–780.

Kern, J. K., Trivedi, M. H., Garver, C. R., Granneman, B. D., Andrews, A. A., Savla, J. S., . . . & Schroeder, J. L. (2006). The pattern of sensory processing abnormalities in autism. *Autism, 10*(5), 480–494.

Kerr, M. M., & Nelson, C. M. (1989). *Strategies for managing behavior problems in the classroom* (2nd ed.). Columbus, OH: Merrill.

Kestenbaum, C. J., & Bird, H. R. (1978). A reliability study of the mental health assessment form for school-aged children. *Journal of the American Academy of Child Psychiatry, 7*, 338–347.

Kilgus, S. P., Eklund, K., Nathaniel, P., Taylor, C. N., & Sims, W. A. (2016). Psychometric defensibility of the social, academic, and emotional behavior risk screener (SAEBRS) teacher rating scale and multiple gating procedure within elementary and middle school samples. *Journal of School Psychology, 58*, 21–39.

Kilgus, S. P., von der Embse, N. P., Chafouleas, S. M., & Riley-Tillman, T. C. (2014). *Social, academic, and emotional behavior risk screener—teacher rating scale.* Unpublished document.

Kimonis E. R., Frick, P. J., & McMahon, R. J. (2014). Conduct and oppositional defiant disorders. In E. J. Mash & R. A. Barkley (Eds.), *Child psychopathology* (3rd ed., pp. 145–179). New York: Guilford.

Kimonis, E., Ogg, J., & Fefer, S. (2014). The relevance of callous unemotional traits when working with youth with conduct problems. *NASP Communique, 42*(5), 16–18.

King, C. A. (1997). Diagnosis and assessment of depression and suicidality using the NIMH diagnostic interview schedule for children (DISC–2.3). *Journal of Abnormal Child Psychology, 25*, 173–181.

King, C., & Young, R. D. (1982). Attentional deficits with and without hyperactivity: Peer and teacher perceptions. *Journal of Abnormal Child Psychology, 10*, 438–495.

Kistner, J. A., & Gatlin, D. G. (1989). Sociometric differences between learning disabled and non-handicapped students: Effects of sex and race. *Journal of Educational Psychology, 81*, 118–120.

Kistner, J., Metzler, A., Gatlin, D., & Risi, S. (1993). Classroom racial proportions and children's peer relations: Race and gender effects. *Journal of Educational Psychology, 85*, 446–452.

Klein, R. G. (1986). Questioning the clinical usefulness of projective psychological tests for children. *Developmental and Behavioral Pediatrics, 7*, 378–382.

Klin, A., Volkmar, F. R., & Sparrow, S. S. (Eds.). (2000). *Asperger syndrome.* New York: Guilford.

Kline, A. (2015). Under ESSA, states, districts to share more power. *Education Week, 35*(15), 10–12.

Klinger, L. G., Dawson, G., Barnes, K., & Crisler, M. (2014). In E. J. Mash & R. A. Barkley (Eds.), *Child psychopathology* (3rd ed., pp. 531–572). New York: Guilford.

Knauss, L. K. (2001). Ethical issues in psychological assessment in school settings. *Journal of Personality Assessment, 77*, 231–241.

Knoff, H. M. (1986). Identifying and classifying children and adolescents referred for personality assessment: Theories, systems, and issues. In H. M. Knoff (Ed.), *The assessment of child and adolescent personality* (pp. 3–33). New York: Guilford.

Knoff, H. M. (2001). Review of the Conners rating scales–revised. In B. S. Plake & J. C. Impara (Eds.), *The fourteenth mental measurements yearbook* (pp. 334–337). Lincoln, NE: Buros Institute of Mental Measurements.

Knoff, H. M., & Prout, H. T. (1985). *The kinetic drawing system: Family and school.* Los Angeles, CA: Western Psychological Services.

Kohlberg, L. (1969). Stage and sequence: The cognitive-developmental approach to socialization. In D. A. Goslin (Ed.), *Handbook of socialization theory and research* (pp. 347–380). Chicago, IL: Rand-McNally.

Kohn, M. L., & Clausen, J. A. (1955). Social isolation and schizophrenia. *American Sociological Review, 20*, 265–273.

Kohn, S. W., Scorcia, D., & Esquivel, G. B. (2012). Personality and behavioral assessment: Considerations for culturally and linguistically diverse individuals. *Handbook of multicultural school psychology: An interdisciplinary perspective*, pp. 289–307.

Kolko, D. J., & Kazdin, A. E. (1993). Emotional/behavioral problems in clinic and nonclinic children: Correspondence among child, parent, and teacher reports. *Journal of Child Psychology and Psychiatry, 34*, 991–1006.

Koppitz, E. M. (1963). *The Bender-Gestalt test for young children.* New York: Grune & Stratton.

Koppitz, E. M. (1968). *Psychological evaluation of children's human figure drawings.* New York: Grune & Stratton.

Koppitz, E. M. (1975). *The Bender-Gestalt test for young children: Vol. II. Research and applications, 1963–1973.* New York: The Psychological Corporation.

Koppitz, E. M. (1982). Personality assessment in the schools. In C. R. Reynolds & T. B. Gutkin (Eds.), *The handbook of school psychology* (pp. 245–271). New York: Wiley.

Kovacs, M. (1980–1981). Rating scales to assess depression in school-aged children. *Acta Paedapsychiatrica, 46*, 305–315.

Kovacs, M. (1983). *The children's depression inventory: A self-rated depression scale for school-aged youngsters.* Unpublished test manual.

Kovacs, M. (1991). *The children's depression inventory* (CDI). North Tonawanda, NY: Multi-Health Systems.

Kovacs, M. (2010). *The Children's depression inventory, Second Edition* (CDI-2). North Tonawanda, NY: Multi-Health Systems.

Kraepelin, E. (1892). *Über die Beeinflussung einfacher psychischer Vorgänge durch einige Arzneimittel.* Fischer, Jen.

Kratochwill, T. R. (1982). Advances in behavioral assessment. In C. R. Reynolds & T. B. Gutkin (Eds.), *The handbook of school psychology* (pp. 314–350). New York: Wiley.

Kreisler, T. A., Mangione, C., & Landau, S. (1997). Review of the school social behavior scales. *Journal of Psychoeducational Assessment, 15*, 182–190.

Kumabe, K. T., Nishida, C., & Hepworth, D. H. (1985). *Bridging ethnocultural diversities in social work and health.* Honolulu, HI: University of Hawaii.

Kuniyoshi, J., & McClellan, J. M. (2014). Early-onset schizophrenia. In E. J. Mash & R. A. Barkley (Eds.), *Child psychopathology* (3rd ed., pp. 573–592). New York: Guilford.

Kuperminc, G. P., Darnell, A. J., & Alvarez-Jimenez, A. (2008). Parent involvement in the academic adjustment of Latino middle and high school youth: Teacher expectations and school belonging as mediators. *Journal of Adolescence, 31*(4), 469–483.

Kupersmidt, J. B., DeRosier, M. E., & Patterson, C. P. (1995). Similarity as the basis for children's friendships: The roles of sociometric status, aggressive and withdrawn behavior, academic achievement, and demographic characteristics. *Journal of Social and Personal Relationships, 12*, 439–452.

Kurlan, R. (2010). Tourette's syndrome. *New England Journal of Medicine, 363*, 2332–2338.

La Greca, A. M. (1990). *Through the eyes of the child.* Boston, MA: Allyn & Bacon.

Lahey, B. B., Pelham, W. E., Loney, J., Lee, S. S., & Willcutt, E. (2005). Instability of the DSM-IV subtypes of ADHD from preschool through elementary school. *Archives of General Psychiatry, 62*, 896–902.

Lahey, B. B., Van Hulle, C. A., Keenan, K., Rathouz, P. J., D'Onofrio, D. M., Rodgers, J. L., & Waldman, I. D. (2008). Temperament and parenting during the first year of life predict future child conduct problems. *Journal of Abnormal Child Psychology, 36*, 1139–1158.

Lahey, B. B., & Willcutt, E. G. (2010). Predictive validity of a continuous alternative to nominal subtypes of attention-deficit hyperactivity disorder for *DSM-V. Journal of Clinical Child & Adolescent Psychology, 39*(6), 761–775.

Lamiell, J. T. (1998). "Nomothetic" and "idiographic": Contrasting Windelband's understanding with contemporary usage. *Theory & Psychology Journal, 8*, 23–38.

Landau, S., & Milich, R. (1990). Assessment of children's social status and peer relations. In A. M. Le Greca (Ed.), *Through the eyes of the child: Obtaining self-reports from children and adolescents* (pp. 259–291). Needham Heights, MA: Allyn & Bacon.

Landau, S., & Swerdlik, M. (2005). Commentary: What you see is what you get: A commentary on school-based direct observation systems. *School Psychology Review, 34*(4), 529–536.

Lane, K. L., Carter, E. W., Pierson, M. R., & Glaeser, B. C. (2006). Academic, social, and behavioral characteristics of high school students with emotional disturbance or learning disabilities. *Journal of Emotional and Behavioral Disorders, 14*, 108–117.

Lane, K. L., Kalberg, J. R., Lambert, W., Crnobori, M., & Bruhn, A. (2010). A comparison of systematic screening tools for emotional and behavioral disorders: A replication. *Journal of Emotional and Behavioral Disorders, 18*, 100–112.

Lane, K. L., Kalberg, J. R., Parks, R. J., & Carter, E. W. (2008). Student risk screening scale initial evidence for score reliability and validity at the high school level. *Journal of Emotional and Behavioral Disorders, 16*(3), 178–190.

Lane, K. L., Menzies, H. M., Oakes, W. P., & Kalberg, J. R. (2012). *Systematic screenings of behavior to support instruction.* New York: Guilford.

Lane, K. L., Parks, R. J., Kalberg, J. R., & Carter, E. W. (2007). Systematic screening at the middle school level score reliability and validity of the student risk screening scale. *Journal of Emotional and Behavioral Disorders, 15*(4), 209–222.

Lanyon, R. I., & Goodstein, L. D. (1984). *Personality assessment* (2nd ed.). New York: Wiley.

Lanyon, R. I., & Goodstein, L. D. (1997). *Personality assessment* (3rd ed.). New York: Wiley.

Larson, K., Russ, S. A., Kahn, R. S., & Halfon, N. (2011). Patterns of comorbidity, functioning, and service use for US children with ADHD. *Pediatrics, 127*, 462–470.

Larson, R. (2000). Toward a psychology of positive youth development. *American Psychologist, 55*, 170–183.

Laughlin, F. (1954). *The peer status of sixth and seventh grade children.* New York: Bureau of Publications, Teachers College of Columbia University.

Lazear, K. J., Roggenbaum, S., & Blasé, K. (2012). *Youth suicide prevention school-based guide – Overview*. Tampa, FL: University of South Florida, College of Behavioral & Community Services, Louis de la Parte Florida Mental Health Institute, Department of Child & Family Studies (FMHI Series Publication #218-OV-Rev 2012).

Leadbeater, B. J., & Bishop, S. J. (1994). Predictors of behavior problems in preschool children of inner-city Afro-Americans and Puerto Rican adolescent mothers. *Child Development, 65*, 638–648.

LeBuffe, P. A., & Naglieri, J. A. (2012). *The Devereux early assessment for preschoolers, second edition*. Users Guide and Technical Manual. Lewisville, NC: Kaplan.

LeBuffe, P. A., Shapiro, V. B., & Naglieri, J. A. (2014). *Devereux student strengths assessment*. Charlotte, NC: Apperson SEL+.

Leckman, J. F., Riddle, M. A., Hardin, M. T., Ort, S. I., Schwartz, K. L., Stevenson, J., & Cohen, D. (1989). The Yale global tic severity scale: Initial testing of a clinician-rated scale of tic severity. *Journal of the American Academy of Child and Adolescent Psychiatry, 28*, 566–573.

Le Couteur, A., Rutter, M., Lord, C., Rios, P., Robertson, S. Holdgrafer, M., & McLennan, J. (1989). Autism diagnostic interview: A standardized investigator-based instrument. *Journal of Autism and Developmental Disorders, 19*, 363–387.

Leff, S. S., & Lakin, R. (2005). Playground-based observational systems: A review and implications for practitioners and researchers. *School Psychology Review, 34*(4), 475–489.

Leffler, J. M., Riebel, J., & Hughes, H. M. (2015). A review of child and adolescent diagnostic interviews for clinical practitioners. *Assessment, 22*(6), 690–703.

Lefkowitz, M. M., & Tesiny, E. P. (1980). Assessment of childhood depression. *Journal of Consulting and Clinical Psychology, 48*, 43–50.

Lefkowitz, M. M., & Tesiny, E. P. (1985). Depression in children: Prevalence and correlates. *Journal of Consulting and Clinical Psychology, 53*, 647–656.

Lefkowitz, M. M., Tesiny, E. P., & Gordon, N. H. (1980). Childhood depression, family income, and locus of control. *Journal of Nervous and Mental Disease, 168*, 732–735.

Lehr, C. A., Ysseldyke, J. E., & Thurlow, M. L. (1987). Assessment practices in model early childhood education programs. *Psychology in the Schools, 24*, 390–399.

Lethermon, V. I., Williamson, D. A., Moody, S. C., Granberry, S. W., Lemanek, K. L., & Bodiford, C. (1984). Factors affecting the social validity of role-play assessment of children's social skills. *Journal of Behavioral Assessment, 6*, 231–245.

Lethermon, V. I., Williamson, D. A., Moody, S. C., & Wozniak, P. (1986). Racial bias in behavioral assessment of children's social skills. *Journal of Psychopathology and Behavioral Assessment, 8*, 329–337.

Levine, R. J. (1995). Adolescents as research subjects without permission of their parents or guardians: Ethical considerations. *Journal of Adolescent Health, 17*, 287–297.

Levitt, J. M., Saka, N., Romanelli, L. H., & Hoagwood, K. (2007). Early identification of mental health problems in schools: The status of instrumentation. *Journal of School Psychology, 45*, 163–191.

Lewinsohn, P. (1974). A behavioral approach to depression. In R. Friedman & M. Katz (Eds.), *The psychology of depression: Contemporary theory and research* (pp. 157–185). Washington, DC: U.S. Government Printing Office.

Lewis, M. (2000). Toward a development of psychopathology: Models, definitions, and prediction. In A. J. Sameroff, M. Lewis, & S. Miller (Eds.), *Handbook of developmental psychopathology* (2nd ed., pp. 3–22). New York: Kluwer Academic/Plenum.

Lewis, M., & Miller, S. M. (Eds.). (1990). *Handbook of developmental psychopathology*. New York: Plenum.

Lewis, T. J., & Sugai, G. (1999). Effective behavior support: A systems approach to proactive school-wide management. *Focus on Exceptional Children, 31*(6), 1–24.

Lezak, M. D. (2002). Responsive assessment and the freedom to think for ourselves. *Rehabilitation Psychology, 47*(3), 339–353.

Lieberz, K. (1989). Children at risk for schizoid disorders. *Journal of Personality Disorders, 3*, 329–337.

Lilly, S. J. (2001). Should human figure drawings be admitted into court? *Journal of Personality Assessment, 76*, 135–149.

Loeber, R. (1985a). Patterns of development of antisocial child behavior. *Annals of Child Development, 2*, 77–116.

Loeber, R. (1985b, November). The selection of target behaviors for modification in the treatment of conduct disordered children: Caretaker's preferences, key-stone behaviors, and stepping stones. In B. B. Lahey (Chair), *Selection of targets for intervention for children with conduct disorder and ADD/hyperactivity.* Symposium conducted at the meeting of the Association for Advancement of Behavior Therapy, Houston, TX.

Loeber, R., & Dishion, T. J. (1983). Early predictors of male delinquency: A review. *Psychological Bulletin, 94,* 68–99.

Loeber, R., Dishion, T. J., & Patterson, G. R. (1984). Multiple gating: A multistage assessment procedure for identifying youths at risk for delinquency. *Journal of Research in Crime and Delinquency, 21,* 7–32.

Loeber, R., & Schmaling, K. B. (1985). Empirical evidence and covert patterns of antisocial conduct problems. *Journal of Abnormal Child Psychology, 12,* 337–352.

Loevinger, J. (1976). *Ego development.* San Francisco, CA: Jossey-Bass.

Loevinger, J. (1979). Construct validity of the sentence completion test of ego development. *Applied Psychological Measurement, 3,* 281–311.

Loney, J., & Milich, R. (1982). Hyperactivity, inattention, and aggression in clinical practice. In M. Wolrach & D. Routh (Eds.), *Advances in behavioral pediatrics* (Vol. 2, pp. 113–147). Greenwich, CT: JAI.

Lorber, M. F., & Egeland, B. (2011). Parenting and infant difficulty: Testing a mutual exacerbation hypothesis to predict early onset conduct problems. *Child Development, 82*(6), 2006–2020.

Lord, C., Luyster, R. J., Gotham, K., & Guthrie, W. (2012). *Autism diagnostic observation schedule, second edition (toddler module).* Los Angeles, CA: Western Psychological Services.

Lord, C., Rutter, M., DiLavore, P. C., Risi, S., Gotham, K., & Bishop, S. L. (2012). *Autism diagnostic observation schedule, second edition.* Los Angeles, CA: Western Psychological Services.

Lord, C., Rutter, M., Goode, S., Heemsbergen, J., Jordan, H., Mawhood, L., & Schopler, E. (1989). Autism diagnostic observation schedule: A standardized observation of communicative and social behavior. *Journal of Autism and Developmental Disorders, 19,* 185–213.

Lorenzo-Blanco, E. I., Unger, J. B., Baezconde-Garbanati, L., Ritt-Olson, A., & Soto, D. (2012). Acculturation, enculturation, and symptoms of depression in Hispanic youth: The roles of gender, Hispanic cultural values, and family functioning. *Journal of Youth and Adolescence, 41*(10), 1350–1365.

Lubin, B., Larsen, R. M., & Matarazzo, J. D. (1984). Patterns of psychological test usage in the United States: 1935–1982. *American Psychologist, 39,* 451–455.

Lund, J., & Merrell, K. W. (2001). Social and antisocial behavior of children with learning and behavior disorders: Construct validity of the home and community social behavior scales. *Journal of Psychoeducational Assessment, 19,* 112–122.

Lynne, L. K., Parks, R., Robertson, K. J., & Carter, E. (2007). Systematic screening at the middle school level. *Journal of Emotional and Behavioral Disorders, 15*(4), 209–222.

Machover, K. (1949). *Personality projection in the drawing of a human figure.* Springfield, IL: Thomas.

Mack, J. (1985). An analysis of state definitions of severely emotionally disturbed children. In Council for Exceptional Children (Ed.), *Policy options report.* Reston, VA: Council for Exceptional Children.

Mackrain, M., LeBuffe, P. A., & Powell, G. (2007). *The Devereux early childhood assessment for infants and toddlers.* Assessment, Technical Manual, and User's Guide. Lewisville, NC: Kaplan.

MacPhee, D. (1998). Review of the preschool and kindergarten behavior scales. In J. C. Impara & B. S. Plake (Eds.), *The thirteenth mental measurements yearbook* (pp. 769–771). Lincoln, NE: Buros Institute of Mental Measurements.

Maeng, L. Y., & Milad, M. R. (2015). Sex differences in anxiety disorders: Interactions between fear, stress, and gonadal hormones. *Hormones and Behavior, 76,* 106–117.

Malcom, K. K. (1993). Developmental assessment: Evaluation of infants and preschoolers. In H. B. Vance (Ed.), *Best practices in assessment for school and clinical settings* (pp. 113–145). Brandon, VT: Clinical Psychology.

Malecki, C. K., & Elliot, S. N. (2002). Children's social behaviors as predictors of academic achievement: A longitudinal analysis. *School Psychology Quarterly, 17*(1), 1–23.

Mangold, J. (1982). *A study of expressions of the primary process in children's kinetic family drawings as a function of pre-drawing activity.* Unpublished doctoral dissertation, Indiana State University, Terre Haute.

March, J. S. (2013). *Multidimensional anxiety scale* (2nd ed.). New York: Multi-Health Systems.

March, R. E., Horner, R. H., Lewis-Palmer, T., Brown, D., Crone, D., Todd, A. W., et al. (2000). *Functional assessment checklist: Teachers and staff* (FACTS). Eugene, OR: Educational and Community Supports.

Margalit, M. (1983). Diagnostic application of the Conners abbreviated symptom questionnaire. *Journal of Clinical Child Psychology, 12,* 355–357.

Marini, V. A., and Stickle, T. R. (2010). Evidence for deficits in reward responsivity in antisocial youth with callous-unemotional traits. *Personality Disorders: Theory, Research, and Treatment, 1*(4), 218–229.

Marsh, H. W. (1987). The hierarchical structure of self-concept: An application of hierarchical confirmatory factor analysis. *Journal of Educational Measurement, 24,* 17–39.

Marsh, H. W. (1992a). *Self-description questionnaire I.* Campbelltown, New South Wales, Australia: SELF Research Centre, University of Western Sydney.

Marsh, H. W. (1992b). *Self-description questionnaire II.* Campbelltown, New South Wales, Australia: SELF Research Centre, University of Western Sydney.

Martin, B., & Hoffman, J. A. (1990). Conduct disorders. In M. Lewis & S. M. Miller (Eds.), *Handbook of developmental psychopathology* (pp. 109–118). New York: Plenum.

Martin, E. (2011). The influence of diverse interaction contexts on students' sociometric status. *The Spanish Journal of Psychology, 14*(1), 88–98.

Martin, R. P. (1983). The ethical issues in the use and interpretation of the draw-a-person test and other similar projective procedures. *The School Psychologist, 38*(6), 8.

Martin, R. P. (1988). *Assessment of personality and behavior problems.* New York: Guilford.

Martin, R. P., Hooper, S., & Snow, J. (1986). Behavior rating scale approaches to personality assessment in children and adolescents. In H. Knoff (Ed.), *The assessment of child and adolescent personality* (pp. 309–351). New York: Guilford.

Martines, D. (2008). *Multicultural school psychology competencies: A practical guide.* Thousand Oaks, CA: SAGE.

Maser, J. D., & Cloninger, C. R. (1990). *Comorbidity of mood and anxiety disorders.* Washington, DC: American Psychiatric Press.

Mash, E. J., & Barkley, R. A. (1989). *Treatment of childhood disorders* (2nd ed.). New York: Guilford.

Mash, E. J., & Barkley, R. A. (Eds.). (2014). *Child psychopathology.* New York: Guilford.

Mash, E. J., & Terdal, L. G. (Eds.). (1997). *Assessment of childhood disorders* (3rd ed.). New York: Guilford.

Masten, A. S., Morrison, P., & Pelligrini, D. S. (1985). A revised class play method of peer assessment. *Developmental Psychology, 21,* 523–533.

Matarazzo, B. B., Homaifar, B. Y., & Wortzel, H. S. (2014). Therapeutic risk management of the suicidal patient. *Journal of Psychiatric Practice, 20*(3), 220–224.

Mathur, S. R., Kavale, K. A., Quinn, M. M., Forness, S. R., & Rutherford, R. B., Jr. (1998). Social skills interventions with students with emotional and behavioral problems: A quantitative synthesis of single-subject research. *Behavioral Disorders, 23,* 193–201.

Matson, J. L., & Nebel-Schwalm, M. S. (2007). Comorbid psychopathology with autism spectrum disorder in children: An overview. *Research in Developmental Disabilities, 28,* 341–352.

Mattison, R. E., Handford, H. A., Kales, H. C., & Goodman, A. L. (1990). Four-year predictive value of the children's depression inventory. *Psychological Assessment, 2,* 169–174.

Matto, H. C., Naglieri, J. A., & Clausen, C. (2005). Validity of the draw-a-person: Screening procedure for emotional disturbance (DAP:SPED) in strengths-based assessment. *Research on Social Work Practice, 15*(1), 41–46.

Mayes, T. L., Bernstein, I. H., Haley, C. L., Kennard, B. D., & Emslie, G. J. (2010). Psychometric properties of the children's depression rating scale—Revised in adolescents. *Journal of Child and Adolescent Psychopharmacology, 20*(6), 513–516.

Mayeux, L., Underwood, M. K., & Risser, S. D. (2007). *Merrill-Palmer Quarterly: Journal of Developmental Psychology, 53*(1), 53–78.

McAndless, B., & Marshall, H. (1957). A picture sociometric technique for preschool children and its relation to teacher judgments of friendship. *Child Development, 28*, 139–148.

McArthur, D. S., & Roberts, D. E. (1982). *Roberts apperception test for children.* Los Angeles, CA: Western Psychological Services.

McBurnett, K. (1996). Development of the *DSM-IV:* Validity and relevance for school psychologists. *School Psychology Review, 25*, 259–273.

McCammon, E. P. (1981). Comparison of oral and written forms of the sentence completion test for ego development. *Developmental Psychology, 17*, 233–235.

McCarney, S., & Arthaud, T. J. (2013). *Attention deficit disorders evaluation scale, 4th edition.* Columbia, MO: Hawthorne Educational Services.

McComas, J. J., & Mace, F. C. (2000). Theory and practice in conducting functional analysis. In E. S. Shapiro & T. R. Kratochwill (Eds.), *Behavioral assessment in schools: Theory, research, and clinical applications* (2nd ed., pp. 78–103). New York: Guilford.

McConaughy, S. H. (2000a). Self report: Child clinical interviews. In E. S. Shapiro & T. R. Kratochwill (Eds.), *Conducting school-based assessments of child and adolescent behavior* (pp. 170–202). New York: Guilford.

McConaughy, S. H. (2000b). Self reports: Theory and practice in interviewing children. In E. S. Shapiro & T. R. Kratochwill (Eds.), *Behavioral assessment in schools: Theory, research, and clinical foundations* (2nd ed., pp. 323–352). New York: Guilford.

McConaughy, S. H. (2005). *Clinical interviews for children and adolescents: Assessment to intervention.* New York: Guilford.

McConaughy, S. H. (2013). *Clinical interviews for children and adolescents: Assessment to intervention.* Guilford Press.

McConaughy, S. H., & Achenbach, T. M. (2001). *Manual for the semistructured clinical interview for children and adolescents* (2nd ed.). Burlington, VT: Research Center for Children, Youth, and Families.

McConaughy, S. H., Achenbach, T. M., & Gent, C. L. (1988). Multiaxial empirically based assessment: Parent, teacher, observational, cognitive, and personality correlates of child behavior profile types for 6- to 11-year-old boys. *Journal of Abnormal Child Psychology, 16*, 485–509.

McConaughy, S., & Whitcomb, S. A. (2022). *Clinical interviews for children and adolescents: Assessment to intervention* (3rd ed.). Guilford Press.

McConnell, S. R., & Odom, S. L. (1986). Sociometrics: Peer-referenced measures and the assessment of social competence. In P. Strain, M. J. Guralnick, & H. M. Walker (Eds.), *Children's social behavior: Development, assessment, and modification* (pp. 215–284). New York: Academic Press.

McDougal, J. L., Bardos, A. N., & Meier, S. T. (2009). *The behavior intervention monitoring assessment system.* New York: Multi-Health Systems.

McFall, R. M. (1982). A review and reformulation of the construct of social skills. *Behavioral Assessment, 4*, 1–33.

McIntosh, K., Campbell, A., Carter, D., & Zumbo, B. (2009). Concurrent validity of office discipline referrals and cut points used in schoolwide positive behavior support. *Behavioral Disorders, 34*(2), 100–113.

McIntosh, K., Ty, S. V., & Miller, L. D. (2014). Effects of school-wide positive behavioral interventions and supports on internalizing problems: Current evidence and future directions. *Journal of Positive Behavior Interventions, 16*(4), 209–218.

McKinney, J. D., & Feagans, L. (1984). Academic and behavioral characteristics of learning disabled children and average achievers: Longitudinal studies. *Learning Disability Quarterly, 7*, 251–264.

McKinney, J. D., McClure, S., & Feagans, L. (1982). Classroom behavior of learning disabled children. *Learning Disability Quarterly, 5*, 45–52.

McLaughlin, K. A., & King, K. (2015). Developmental trajectories of anxiety and depression in early adolescence. *Journal of Abnormal Child Psychology, 43*(3), 311–323.

McMahon, R. J., & Estes, A. M. (1997). Conduct problems. In E. J. Mash & L. G. Terdal (Eds.), *Assessment of childhood disorders* (3rd ed., pp. 130–193). New York: Guilford.

McMahon, R. J., & Forehand, R. (1984). Parent training for the noncompliant child: Treatment outcome, generalization, and adjunctive therapy procedures. In R. F. Dangel & R. A. Polster (Eds.), *Parent training: Foundations of research and practice* (pp. 298–328). New York: Guilford.

McMahon, R. J., & Forehand, R. (1988). Conduct disorders. In E. J. Mash & L. G. Terdal (Eds.), *Behavioral assessment of childhood disorders* (2nd ed., pp. 105–153). New York: Guilford.

McNamara, J. R., Holman, C., & Riegal, T. (1994). A preliminary study of the usefulness of the behavior assessment system for children in the evaluation of mental health needs in a Head Start population. *Psychological Reports, 75*(3, Pt. 1), 1195–1201.

McNamee, G. D. (1989). Language development. In J. Gabarino & F. M. Stott (Eds.), *What children can tell us* (pp. 67–391). San Francisco, CA: Jossey-Bass.

McReynolds, P. (1986). History of assessment in clinical and educational settings. In R. O. Nelson & S. C. Hayes (Eds.), *Conceptual foundations of behavioral assessment* (pp. 42–80). New York: Guilford.

Measelle, J. R., John, O. P., Ablow, J. C., Cowan, P. A., & Cowan, C. (2005). Can young children provide coherent, stable, and valid self-reports on the big five dimension? A longitudinal study from ages 5 to 7. *Journal of Personality and Social Psychology, 89*, 90–106.

Meehl, P. E. (1954). *Clinical versus statistical prediction.* Minneapolis, MN: University of Minnesota Press.

Meichenbaum, D., & Cameron, R. (1982). Cognitive-behavior therapy. In G. T. Wilson & C. M. Franks (Eds.), *Contemporary behavior therapy: Conceptual and empirical foundations* (pp. 310–338). New York: Guilford.

Meier, M. H., Slutske, W. S., Heath, A. C., & Martin, N. G. (2011). Sex differences in the genetic and environmental influences on childhood conduct disorder and adult antisocial behavior. *Journal of Abnormal Psychology, 20*(2), 377–388.

Merenda, P. F. (1996). Review of the BASC: Behavior assessment system for children. *Measurement and Evaluation in Counseling and Development, 28*, 229–232.

Merikangas, K. R., Cui, L., & Kattan, G. (2012). Mania with and without depression in a community sample of US adolescents. *Archives of General Psychiatry, 69*(9), 943–951.

Merrell, K. W. (1989). Validity issues in direct behavioral observation: Applications for behavioral assessment in the classroom. *Canadian Journal of School Psychology, 5*, 57–62.

Merrell, K. W. (1990). Teacher ratings of hyperactivity and self-control in learning disabled boys: A comparison with low achieving and average peers. *Psychology in the Schools, 27*, 289–296.

Merrell, K. W. (1993a). *School social behavior scales.* Austin, TX: Pro-Ed.

Merrell, K. W. (1993b). Using behavior rating scales to assess social skills and antisocial behavior in school settings: Development of the school social behavior scales. *School Psychology Review, 22*, 115–133.

Merrell, K. W. (1994). *Preschool and kindergarten behavior scales.* Austin, TX: Pro-Ed.

Merrell, K. W. (1995a). An investigation of the relationship between social skills and internalizing problems in early childhood: Construct validity of the preschool and kindergarten behavior scales. *Journal of Psychoeducational Assessment, 13*, 230–240.

Merrell, K. W. (1995b). Relationships among early childhood behavior rating scales: Convergent and discriminant construct validity of the Preschool and Kindergarten Behavior Scales. *Early Education & Development, 6*, 253–264.

Merrell, K. W. (1996a). Assessment of social skills and behavior problems in early childhood: The preschool and kindergarten behavior scales. *Journal of Early Intervention, 20*, 132–145.

Merrell, K. W. (1996b). Social-emotional problems in early childhood: New directions in conceptualization, assessment, and treatment. *Education and Treatment of Children, 19*, 458–473.

Merrell, K. W. (2000a). Informant report: Rating scale measures. In E. S. Shapiro & T. R. Kratochwill (Eds.), *Conducting school-based assessment of child and adolescent behaviors* (pp. 203–234). New York: Guilford.

Merrell, K. W. (2000b). Informant report: Theory and research in using child behavior rating scales in school settings. In E. S. Shapiro & T. R. Kratochwill (Eds.), *Behavioral assessment in schools* (2nd ed., pp. 233–256). New York: Guilford.

Merrell, K. W. (2001). *Helping students overcome depression and anxiety: A practical guide.* New York: Guilford.

Merrell, K. W. (2002a). *Preschool and kindergarten behavior scales* (2nd ed.). Austin, TX: PRO-ED.

Merrell, K. W. (2002b). *School social behavior scales* (2nd ed.). Eugene, OR: Assessment-Intervention Resources.

Merrell, K. W. (2002c). *Home and community social behavior scales.* Eugene, OR: Assessment-Intervention Resources.

Merrell, K. W. (2008). *Helping students overcome depression and anxiety: A practical guide* (2nd ed.). New York: Guilford.

Merrell, K. W. (2011). *Social emotional assets and resiliency scale.* Lutz, FL: Psychological Assessment Resources.

Merrell, K. W., & Boelter, E. W. (2001). An investigation of relationships between social behavior and ADHD in children and youth: Construct validity of the home and community social behavior scales. *Journal of Emotional and Behavioral Disorder, 9*, 260–269.

Merrell, K. W., & Buchanan, R. S. (2006). Intervention selection in school-based practice: Using public health models to enhance systems capacity of schools. *School Psychology Review, 35*, 167–180.

Merrell, K. W., & Caldarella, P. (1999). Social-behavioral assessment of at-risk early adolescent students: Validity of a parent report form of the School Social Behavior Scales. *Journal of Psychoeducational Assessment, 17*, 36–49.

Merrell, K. W., Caldarella, P., Streeter, A. L., Boelter, E. W., & Gentry, A. (2001). Convergent validity of the home and community social behavior scales: Comparisons with five behavior rating scales. *Psychology in the Schools, 38*, 313–325.

Merrell, K. W., Cohn, B. P., & Tom, K. M. (2011). Development and validation of a teacher report measure for assessing social-emotional strengths of children and adolescents. *School Psychology Review*. Retrieved from http://nasponline.org/publications/spr/sprmain.aspx

Merrell, K. W., Crowley, S. L., & Walters, A. S. (1997). Development and factor structure of a self-report measure for assessing internalizing symptoms of elementary-age children. *Psychology in the Schools, 34*, 197–210.

Merrell, K. W., & Dobmeyer, A. C. (1996). An evaluation of self-reported internalizing symptoms of elementary-age children. *Journal of Psychoeducational Assessment, 14*, 196–207.

Merrell, K. W., Ervin, R. A., & Gimpel, G. A. (2006). *School psychology for the 21st century: Foundations and practices.* New York: Guilford.

Merrell, K. W., Felver-Gant, J. C., & Tom, K. M (2010). Development and validation of a parent report measure for assessing social-emotional competencies in children and adolescents. *Journal of Child and Family Studies, 20*, 529–540. doi: 10.1007/s10826-010-9425-0

Merrell, K. W., & Gill, S. J. (1994). Using teacher ratings of social behavior to differentiate gifted from non-gifted students. *Roeper Review, 16*, 286–289.

Merrell, K. W., & Gimpel, G. A. (1998). *Social skills of children and adolescents: Conceptualization, assessment, treatment.* Mahwah, NJ: Lawrence Erlbaum Associates.

Merrell, K. W., & Gimpel, G. (2014). *Social skills of children and adolescents: Conceptualization, assessment, treatment.* New York: Psychology Press.

Merrell, K. W., & Gueldner, B. A. (2008). *The Guilford practical intervention in the schools series.* New York: Guilford.

Merrell, K. W., & Holland, M. L. (1997). Social-emotional behavior of preschool-age children with and without developmental delays. *Research in Developmental Disabilities, 18*, 395–405.

Merrell, K. W., Merz, J. N., Johnson, E. R., & Ring, E. N. (1992). Social competence of mildly handicapped and low-achieving students: A comparative study. *School Psychology Review, 21*, 125–137.

Merrell, K. W., Sanders, D. E., & Popinga, M. (1993). Teacher ratings of social behavior as a predictor of special education status: Discriminant validity of the School Social Behavior Scales. *Journal of Psychoeducational Assessment, 11*, 220–231.

Merrell, K. W., & Walker, H. M. (2004). Deconstructing a definition: Emotionally disturbed versus socially maladjusted, and moving the EBD field forward. *Psychology in the Schools, 41*, 899–910.

Merrell, K. W., & Walters, A. S. (1998). *Internalizing symptoms scale for children.* Austin, TX: PRO-ED.

Merrell, K. W., & Wolfe, T. M. (1998). The relationship of teacher-rated social skills deficits and ADHD characteristics among kindergarten-age children. *Psychology in the Schools, 33*, 101–109.

Mesibov, G. B., Shea, V., & Adams, L. W. (2001). *Understanding Asperger syndrome and high-functioning autism.* New York: Kluwer Academic.

Messick, S. (1965). Personality measurement and the ethics of assessment. *American Psychologist, 35*, 1012–1027.

Messick, S. (1988). *Meaning and values in test validation: The science and ethics of assessment.* Princeton, NJ: Educational Testing Service.

Mian, N. D., Carter, A. S., Pine, D. S., Wakschlag, L. S., & Briggs-Gowan, M. J. (2015). Development of a novel observational measure for anxiety in young children: The anxiety dimensional observation scale. *Journal of Child Psychology and Psychiatry, 56*(9), 1017–1025.

Michael, K. D., & Merrell, K. W. (1998). Reliability of children's self-reported internalizing symptoms over short to medium length time intervals. *Journal of the American Academy of Child and Adolescent Psychiatry, 37*, 194–201.

Mikolajewski, A. J., Allan, N. P., Hart, S. A., Lonigan, C. J., & Taylor, J. (2013). Negative affect shares genetic and environmental influences with symptoms of childhood internalizing and externalizing disorders. *Journal of Abnormal Child Psychology, 41*(3), 411–423.

Milich, R., & Landau, S. (1984). A comparison of the social status and social behavior of aggressive and aggressive/withdrawn boys. *Journal of Abnormal Child Psychology, 12*, 277–278.

Miller, D. N. (2011). *Child and adolescent suicidal behavior: School-based prevention, assessment, and intervention.* New York: Guilford.

Miller, D. N., & Nickerson, A. B. (2007). Projective techniques and the school-based assessment of childhood internalizing disorders: A critical analysis. *Journal of Projective Psychology and Mental Health, 14*(1), 48–58.

Miller, J. A., Tansy, M., & Hughes, T. L. (1998, November 18). Functional behavioral assessment: The link between problem behavior and effective intervention in schools. *Current Issues in Education* [Online], *1*(5). Retrieved November 12, 2006, from http://cie.ed.asu.edu/volume1/number5/

Miller, L. K. (1996). *Principles of everyday behavior analysis* (3rd ed.). Pacific Grove, CA: Wadsworth.

Miller, S. M., Birnbaum, A., & Durbin, D. (1990). Etiologic perspectives on depression in childhood. In M. Lewis & S. M. Miller (Eds.), *Handbook of developmental psychopathology* (pp. 311–325). New York: Plenum.

Miller, S. M., Boyer, B. A., & Rodoletz, M. (1990). Anxiety in children. In M. Lewis & S. M. Miller (Eds.), *Handbook of developmental psychopathology* (pp. 191–207). New York: Plenum.

Moreno, J. L. (1934). *Who shall survive?* Washington, DC: Nervous and Mental Disease Publishing.

Morgan, C. D., & Murray, H. A. (1935). A method for investigating phantasies. The thematic apperception test. *Archives of Neurology and Psychiatry, 34*, 289–306.

Morris, R. J., & Kratochwill, T. R. (1983). *Treating children's fears and phobias: A behavioral approach.* New York: Pergamon.

Mos, L. P. (1998). On methodological distinctions: Nomothetic psychology, or historical understanding. *Theory & Psychology Journal, 8*, 23–38.

Murray, C., & Zvoch, K. (2011). Teacher–student relationships among behaviorally at-risk African American youth from low-income backgrounds: Student perceptions, teacher perceptions, and socioemotional adjustment correlates. *Journal of Emotional and Behavioral Disorders, 19*, 1.

Murray, H. A. (1938). *Explorations in personality.* New York: Oxford University Press.

Murray, H. A. (1943). *Thematic apperception test manual.* Cambridge, MA: Harvard University Press.

Murray, T. H. (1995). Commentary on "True Wishes." *Philosophy, Psychiatry, and Psychology, 2*, 311–312.

Mustillo, S., Worthman, C., Erkanli, A., Keeler, G., Angold, A., & Costello, E. J. (2003). Obesity and psychiatric disorder: Developmental trajectories. *Pediatrics, 111*, 851–859.

Myers, K., & Winters, N. C. (2002). Ten-year review of rating scales: I. Overview of scale functioning, psychometric properties, and selection. *Journal of the American Academy of Child & Adolescent Psychiatry, 41*, 114–122.

Myles, B. S., & Simpson, R. L. (1998). *Asperger's syndrome: A guide for educators and parents.* Austin, TX: PRO-ED.

Naglieri, J. A., McNeish, T. J., & Bardos, A. N. (1991). *Draw-a-person: Screening procedure for emotional disturbance.* Austin, TX: Pro-Ed.

National Association of School Psychologists (NASP). (2016). *Integrated model of academic and behavioral supports [position statement].* Bethesda, MD: Author.

National Association of School Psychologists (NASP). (2020). *Principles for professional ethics.* Bethesda, MD: Author.

Nelson, C. M., Rutherford, R. B., Center, D. B., & Walker, H. M. (1991). Do public schools have an obligation to serve troubled children and youth? *Exceptional Children, 57*, 406–415.

Nelson, R. O., & Hayes, S. C. (Eds.). (1986). *Conceptual foundations of behavioral assessment.* New York: Guilford.

Newsom, C., & Hovanitz, C. A. (1997). Autistic disorder. In E. J. Mash & L. G. Terdal (Eds.), *Assessment of childhood disorders* (3rd ed., pp. 408–452). New York: Guilford.

Nezu, A. M. (1993). Identifying and selecting target problems for clinical interventions: A problem-solving model. *Psychological Assessment, 5,* 254–263.

Nickerson, A. B., & Fishman, C. E. (2013). Promoting mental health and resilience through strength-based assessment in US schools. *Educational and Child Psychology, 30*(4), 7–17.

Nigg, J. T., & Barkley, R. A. (2014). Attention-deficit/hyperactivity disorder. In E. J. Mash & R. A. Barkley (Eds.), *Child psychopathology* (pp. 75–144). New York: Guilford.

Nock, M. K., Kazdin, A. E., Hiripi, E., & Kessler, R. C. (2007). Lifetime prevalence, correlates, and persistence of oppositional defiant disorder: Results from the national comorbidity survey replication. *Journal of Child Psychology and Psychiatry, 48*(7), 703–713.

Norcross, J. C., Karpiak, C. P., & Santoro, S. O. (2005). Clinical psychologists across the years: The division of clinical psychology from 1960 to 2003. *Journal of Clinical Psychology, 61,* 1467–1483.

Nuttall, E. V., DeLeon, B., & Valle, M. (1990). Best practices in considering cultural factors. In A. Thomas & J. Grimes (Eds.), *Best practices in school psychology–II* (pp. 219–234). Washington, DC: National Association of School Psychologists.

Obrzut, J. E., & Boliek, C. A. (1986). Thematic approaches to personality assessment with children and adolescents. In H. M. Knoff (Ed.), *The assessment of child and adolescent personality* (pp. 173–198). New York: Guilford.

Oden, S. L., & Asher, S. R. (1977). Coaching children in social skills for friendship making. *Child Development, 48,* 496–506.

O'Gorman, G. (1970). *The nature of childhood autism* (2nd ed.). London: Butterworths.

Okazaki, S., & Sue, S. (1995). Methodological issues in assessment research with ethnic minorities. *Psychological Assessment, 7,* 367–375.

Olweus, D. (1979). Stability of aggressive reaction patterns in males: A review. *Psychological Bulletin, 86,* 852–875.

O'Neill, R. E., Albin, R. W., Storey, K., Horner, R. H., & Sprague, J. R. (2014). *Functional assessment and program development for problem behavior: A practical handbook* (3rd ed.). Stamford, CT: Cengage Learning.

Ornitz, E. M. (1989). Autism. In C. G. Last & M. Hersen (Eds.), *Handbook of child psychiatric diagnosis* (pp. 233–278). New York: Wiley.

Orvaschel, H., Puig-Antich, J., Chambers, W., Tabrizi, M. A., & Johnson, R. (1982). Retrospective assessment of prepubertal major depression with the Kiddie–SADS–E. *Journal of the American Academy of Child Psychiatry, 21,* 392–397.

Osman, A., Gutierrez, P. M., Bagge, C. L., Fang, Q., & Emmerich, A. (2010). Reynolds adolescent depression scale-second edition: A reliable and useful instrument. *Journal of Clinical Psychology, 66*(12), 1324–1345.

Ozonoff, S., Young, G. S., Carter, A., Messinger, D., Yirmiya, N., Zwaigenbaum, L., . . . & Hutman, T. (2011). Recurrence risk for autism spectrum disorders: A baby siblings research consortium study. *Pediatrics, 128*(3), 488–495.

Paget, K. D., & Reynolds, C. R. (1982, August). *Factorial invariance of the revised children's manifest anxiety scale with learning disabled children.* Paper presented at the annual meeting of the American Psychological Association, Washington, DC.

Park, C. (2011). Young children making sense of racial and ethnic differences: A sociocultural approach. *American Educational Research Journal, 48*(2), 387–420.

Park, H. S., Tappe, P., Carmeto, R., & Gaylord-Ross, R. (1990). Social support and quality of life for learning disabled and mildly retarded youth in transition. In R. Gaylord-Ross, S. Siegel, H. S. Park, S. Sacks, & L. Goetz (Eds.), *Readings in ecosocial development* (pp. 293–328). San Francisco, CA: San Francisco State University, Department of Special Education.

Parker, J. G., & Asher, S. R. (1987). Peer relations and later personal development: Are low-accepted children "at-risk"? *Psychological Bulletin, 102,* 357–389.

Partington, J. W. (2006). *The assessment of basic language and learning skills-revised.* Walnut Hill, CA: Behavior Analysts, Inc.

Paternite, C., & Loney, J. (1980). Childhood hyperkinesis: Relationships between symptomatology and home environment. In C. K. Whalen & B. Henker (Eds.), *Hyperactive children: The social ecology of identification and treatment* (pp. 105–141). New York: Academic Press.

Patterson, G. R. (1969). Behavioral techniques based upon social learning: An additional base for developing behavior modification technologies. In C. M. Franks (Ed.), *Behavior therapy: Appraisal and status* (pp. 341–374). New York: McGraw-Hill.

Patterson, G. R. (1976). The aggressive child: Victim and architect of a coercive system. In E. Mash, L. Hammerlynck, & L. Handy (Eds.), *Behavior modification in families: I. Theory and research* (pp. 267–316). New York: Bruner/Mazel.

Patterson, G. R. (1982). *Coercive family process.* Eugene, OR: Castalia.

Patterson, G. R. (1986). The contribution of siblings to training for fighting: Microsocial analysis. In J. Block, D. Olweus, & M. Radke-Yarrow (Eds.), *Development of antisocial and prosocial behavior* (pp. 235–261). New York: Academic Press.

Patterson, G. R. (2002). The early development of coercive family processes. In J. B. Reid, G. R. Patterson, & J. Snyder (Eds.), *Antisocial behavior in children and adolescents: A developmental analysis and model for intervention* (pp. 25–44). Washington, DC: American Psychological Association.

Patterson, G. R., & Bank, L. (1986). Bootstrapping your way in the nomological thicket. *Behavioral Assessment, 8*, 49–73.

Patterson, G. R., & Dishion, T. J. (1985). Contributions of families and peers to delinquency. *Criminology, 23*, 63–79.

Patterson, G. R., & Forgatch, M. S. (1995). Predicting future clinical adjustment from treatment outcome and process variables. *Psychological Assessment, 7*, 275–285.

Patterson, G. R., Ray, R. S., Shaw, D. A., & Cobb, J. A. (1969). *Manual for coding of family interactions.* New York: Microfiche Publications.

Patterson, G. R., Reid, J., & Dishion, T. (1992). *Antisocial boys.* Eugene, OR: Castalia.

Patterson, G. R., & Yoerger, K. (2002). A developmental model for early and late-onset delinquency. In J. B. Reid, G. R. Patterson, & J. Snyder (Eds.), *Antisocial behavior in children and adolescents: A developmental analysis and model for intervention* (pp. 147–172). Washington, DC: American Psychological Association.

Pattillo-McCoy, M. (1999a). *Black picket fences: Privilege and peril among the black middle class.* Chicago, IL: University of Chicago Press.

Pattillo-McCoy, M. (1999b). Hamilton Park: A planned black community in Dallas. *American Journal of Sociology, 105*, 270–272.

Pattillo-McCoy, M. (2000). The limits of out-migration for the black middle class. *Journal of Urban Affairs, 22*, 225–241.

Peach, L., & Reddick, T. L. (1991). Counselors can make a difference in preventing adolescent suicide. *The School Counselor, 39*, 107–110.

Peacock Hill Working Group. (1991). Problems and promises in special education and related services for children and youth with emotional or behavioral disorders. *Behavioral Disorders, 16*, 299–313.

Pearson Education, Inc. (2015). BOSS: Behavioral observation of students in schools (1.2.0) [Mobile Application Software]. Retrieved from https://itunes.apple.com

Peed, S., Roberts, M., & Forehand, R. (1977). Evaluation of the effectiveness of a standardized parent training program in altering the interaction of mothers and their noncompliant children. *Behavior Modification, 1*, 323–350.

Pekarik, E., Prinz, R., Liebert, D., Weintraub, S., & Neale, J. (1976). The pupil evaluation inventory: A sociometric technique for assessing children's social behavior. *Journal of Abnormal Child Psychology, 4*, 83–97.

Peterson, C. A. (1990). Administration of the thematic apperception test: Contributions of psychoanalytic psychotherapy. *Journal of Contemporary Psychology, 20*, 191–200.

Peterson, C., Warren, K. L., & Hayes, A. H. (2013). Revisiting narrative elaboration training with an ecologically relevant event. *Journal of Cognition and Development, 14*, 154–174.

Piaget, J. (1983). Piaget's theory. In P. H. Mussen (Ed.), *Carmichael's handbook of child psychology* (Vol. 1, pp. 702–732). New York: Wiley.

Piers, E., & Harris, D. (1969). *The Piers–Harris self-concept scale.* Nashville, TN: Counselor Recordings and Tests.

Pilkington, C. L., & Piersel, W. C. (1991). School phobia: A critical analysis of the separation anxiety theory and an alternative conceptualization. *Psychology in the Schools, 28*, 290–303.

Pincus, D. B., May, J. E., Whitton, S. W., Mattis, S. G., & Barlow, D. H. (2010). Cognitive-behavioral treatment of panic disorder in adolescence. *Journal of Clinical Child and Adolescent Psychology, 39*(5), 638–649.

Plomin, R., Nitz, K., & Rowe, D. C. (1990). Behavioral genetics and aggressive behavior in childhood. In M. Lewis & S. M. Miller (Eds.), *Handbook of developmental psychopathology* (pp. 119–133). New York: Plenum.

Post, R. M. (1992). Transduction of psychosocial stress into the neurobiology of recurrent affective disorder. *American Journal of Psychiatry, 149*, 999–1010.

Poteat, G. M., Ironsmith, M., & Bullock, M. J. (1986). The classification of preschool children's sociometric status. *Early Childhood Research Quarterly, 1*, 349–360.

Powell, P. M., & Vacha-Haase, T. (1994). What counseling psychologists need to know. *Counseling Psychologist, 22*, 444–453.

Power, T. J., & DuPaul, G. J. (1996). Implications of *DSM-IV* for the practice of school psychology: Introduction to the mini-series. *School Psychology Review, 25*, 255.

Powless, D. L., & Elliott, S. N. (1993). Assessment of social skills of Native American preschoolers: Teacher and parent ratings. *Journal of School Psychology, 31*, 293–307.

Poythress, N. G., Dembo, R., Wareham, J., & Greenbaum, P. E. (2006). Construct validity of the youth psychopathic traits inventory (YPI) and the antisocial process screening device (APSD) with justice-involved adolescents. *Criminal Justice and Behavior, 33*, 26–55.

Poznanski, E. O., Cook, S. C., & Carroll, B. J. (1979). A depression rating scale for children. *Pediatrics, 64*, 442–450.

Priel, B., Assor, A., & Orr, E. (1990). Self-evaluations of kindergarten children: Inaccurate and undifferentiated? *Journal of Genetic Psychology, 151*, 377–394.

Priestley, G., & Pipe, M. E. (1997). Using toys and models in interviews with young children. *Applied Cognitive Psychology, 11*, 69–87.

Prior, M., Boulton, D., Gajzago, C., & Perry, D. (1975). The classification of childhood psychosis by numerical taxonomy. *Journal of Child Psychology and Psychiatry, 16*, 321–330.

Prior, M., & Werry, J. S. (1986). Autism, schizophrenia, and allied disorders. In H. C. Quay & J. S. Werry (Eds.), *Psychopathological disorders of childhood* (3rd ed., pp. 156–210). New York: Wiley.

Pritchard, M., & Graham, P. (1966). An investigation of a group of patients who have attended both the child and adult departments of the same psychiatric hospital. *British Journal of Psychiatry, 112*, 603–612.

Prout, H. T., & Phillips, P. D. (1974). A clinical note: The kinetic school drawing. *Psychology in the Schools, 11*, 303–306.

Psimas, J. L. (2015). Social-emotional and adaptive assessment of school-age children. Retrieved from: https//:www.maspweb.com/resources/Documents/BASC-3_Psimas)2hr_MASP 2015.pdf

Puig-Antich, J., & Chambers, W. (1978). *The schedule for affective disorders and schizophrenia for school-age children.* New York: New York State Psychiatric Association.

Pullatz, M., & Dunn, S. E. (1990). The importance of peer relations. In M. Lewis & S. M. Miller (Eds.), *Handbook of developmental psychopathology* (pp. 227–236). New York: Pergamon.

Quay, H. C. (1975). Classification in the treatment of delinquency and antisocial behavior. In N. Hobbs (Ed.), *Issues in the classification of children* (Vol. 1, pp. 377–392). San Francisco, CA: Jossey-Bass.

Quay, H. C. (1977). Measuring dimensions of deviant behavior: The behavior problem checklist. *Journal of Abnormal Child Psychology, 5*, 277–289.

Quay, H. C. (1986a). Classification. In H. C. Quay & J. S. Werry (Eds.), *Psychopathological disorders of childhood* (3rd ed., pp. 1–34). New York: Wiley.

Quay, H. C. (1986b). Conduct disorders. In H. C. Quay & J. S. Werry (Eds.), *Psychopathological disorders of childhood* (3rd ed., pp. 35–72). New York: Wiley.

Quay, H. C., & Peterson, D. R. (1967). *Manual for the behavior problem checklist.* Coral Gables, FL: Author.

Quay, H. C., & Peterson, D. R. (1987). *Manual for the revised behavior problem checklist.* Coral Gables, FL: Author.

Quay, H. C., & Werry, J. S. (1986). *Psychopathological disorders of childhood* (3rd ed.). New York: Wiley.

Rabin, A. I. (1986). *Projective techniques for adolescents and children.* New York: Springer.

Range, L. M., & Cotton, C. R. (1995). Reports of assent and permission in research with children: Illustrations and suggestions. *Ethics and Behavior, 5*, 49–66.

Redden, S. C., Forness, S., Ramey, S. L., Ramey, C. T., Brezausek, C. M., & Kavale, K. A. (2001). Children at-risk: Effects of a four-year Head Start transition program on special education identification. *Journal of Child and Family Studies, 10*, 255–270.

Reep, A. (1994). Comments on functional analysis procedures for school-based behavior problems. *Journal of Applied Behavior Analysis, 27*, 409–411.

Regier, D. A., Narrow, W. E., Kuhl, E. A., & Kupfer, D. J. (2009). The conceptual development of DSM-V. *American Journal of Psychiatry, 166*, 645–650. doi: 10.1176/appi.ajp.2009.09020279

Reid, J. B. (1982). Observer training in naturalistic research. In D. P. Hartmann (Ed.), *Using observers to study behavior* (pp. 37–50). San Francisco, CA: Jossey-Bass.

Reid, J. B., Baldwin, D. B., Patterson, G. R., & Dishion, T. J. (1988). Observations in the assessment of childhood disorders. In M. Rutter, A. H. Tuma, & I. S. Lann (Eds.), *Assessment and diagnosis in child psychopathology* (pp. 156–195). New York: Guilford.

Reid, J. B., & Eddy, J. M. (2002). Interventions for antisocial behavior: An overview. In J. B. Reid, G. R. Patterson, & J. Snyder (Eds.), *Antisocial behavior in children and adolescents: A developmental analysis and model for intervention* (pp. 195–202). Washington, DC: American Psychological Association.

Reschly, D. J. (1990). Best practices in adaptive behavior. In A. Thomas & J. Grimes (Eds.), *Best practices in school psychology—II* (pp. 29–42). Washington, DC: National Association of School Psychologists.

Reschly, D. J. (1991). Mental retardation: Conceptual foundations, definitional criteria, and diagnostic operations. In S. R. Hooper, G. W. Hynd, & R. E. Mattison (Eds.), *Assessment and diagnosis of child and adolescent psychological disorders: Vol. 2. Developmental disorders* (pp. 23–67). Hillsdale, NJ: Lawrence Erlbaum Associates.

Rescorla, L., Achenbach, T., Ivanova, M. Y., Dumenci, L., Almqvist, F., Bilenberg, N., . . . & Erol, N. (2007). Behavioral and emotional problems reported by parents of children ages 6 to 16 in 31 societies. *Journal of Emotional and Behavioral Disorders, 15*(3), 130–142.

Rescorla, L. A., Achenbach, T. M., Ivanova, M. Y., Harder, V. S., Otten, L., Bilenberg, N., et al. (2011). International comparisons of behavioral and emotional problems in preschool children: Parents' reports from 24 societies. *Journal of Clinical Child and Adolescent Psychology, 40*(3), 456–467.

Reynolds, C. R. (1981). Long-term stability of scores on the revised children's manifest anxiety scale. *Perceptual and Motor Skills, 53*, 702.

Reynolds, C. R. (2007). Koppitz-2: The Koppitz developmental scoring system for the bender-gestalt test. Austin, TX: Pro-Ed Inc.

Reynolds, C. R., & Bradley, M. (1983). Emotional stability of intellectually superior children versus nongifted peers as estimated by chronic anxiety levels. *School Psychology Review, 12*, 190–193.

Reynolds, C. R., Bradley, M., & Steele, C. (1980). Preliminary norms and technical data for use of the revised children's manifest anxiety scale with kindergarten children. *Psychology in the Schools, 17*, 163–167.

Reynolds, C. R., & Kamphaus, R. W. (1992). *Behavior assessment system for children.* Circle Pines, MN: AGS.

Reynolds, C. R., & Kamphaus, R. W. (2004). *Behavior assessment system for children, second edition.* Circle Pines, MN: AGS.

Reynolds, C. R., & Kamphaus, R. W. (2015). *Behavior assessment system for children, third edition.* San Antonio, TX: PearsonClinical.

Reynolds, C. R., & Kamphaus, R. W. (2016). *Behavior assessment system for children – third edition (BASC-3): Flex monitor.* Bloomington, MN: Pearson.

Reynolds, C. R., & Paget, K. D. (1981). Factor analysis of the revised children's manifest anxiety scale for blacks, whites, males and females with a national normative sample. *Journal of Consulting and Clinical Psychology, 49*, 352–359.

Reynolds, C. R., & Paget, K. D. (1983). National normative and reliability data for the children's manifest anxiety scale. *School Psychology Review, 12*, 324–336.

Reynolds, C. R., & Richmond, B. O. (1985). *Revised children's manifest anxiety scale.* Los Angeles, CA: Western Psychological Services.

Reynolds, C. R., & Richmond, B. O. (2008). *Revised children's manifest anxiety scale, second edition.* Los Angeles, CA: Western Psychological Services.

Reynolds, W. M. (1986). *Reynolds adolescent depression scale.* Odessa, FL: Psychological Assessment Resources.

Reynolds, W. M. (1987). *Suicidal ideation questionnaire.* Odessa, FL: Psychological Assessment Resources.

Reynolds, W. M. (1989). *Reynolds child depression scale.* Odessa, FL: Psychological Assessment Resources.

Reynolds, W. M. (Ed.). (1992a). *Internalizing disorders in children and adolescents.* New York: Wiley.

Reynolds. W. M. (1992b). Internalizing disorders in children and adolescents: Issues and recommendations for further research. In W. M. Reynolds (Ed.), *Internalizing disorders in children and adolescents* (pp. 311–317). New York: Wiley.

Reynolds, W. M. (1998). *Adolescent psychopathology scale.* Odessa, FL: Psychological Assessment Resources.

Reynolds, W. M. (2000). *Adolescent psychopathology scale, short form.* Odessa, FL: Psychological Assessment Resources.

Reynolds, W. M. (2002). *Reynolds adolescent depression scale, 2nd edition.* Odessa, FL: Psychological Assessment Resources.

Rhoades, E. K. (2005). Review of the Jesness inventory–revised. In B. S. Plake, J. C. Impara, & R. A. Spies (Eds.), *The sixteenth mental measurements yearbook* (pp. 494–496). Lincoln, NE: University of Nebraska Press.

Rhodes, R. L., Ochoa, S. H., & Ortiz, S. O. (2005). *Assessing culturally and linguistically diverse students: A practical guide.* New York: Guilford.

Riccio, C. (1995). Review of the preschool and kindergarten behavior scales. *Journal of Psychoeducational Assessment, 13,* 194–196.

Riley-Tillman, T., Chafouleas, S., Briech, A., & Eckert, T. (2008). Daily behavior report cards and systematic direct observation: An investigation of the acceptability, reported training and use, and decision reliability among school psychologists. *Journal of Behavioral Education, 17,* 313–327.

Rivers, R. Y., & Morrow, C. A. (1995). Understanding and treating ethnic minority youth. In J. F. Aponte, R. Y. Rivers, & J. Wohl (Eds.), *Psychological interventions and cultural diversity* (pp. 164–180). Boston, MA: Allyn & Bacon.

Roback, H. B. (1968). Human figure drawings: Their utility in the clinical psychologists' armamentorium for personality assessment. *Psychological Bulletin, 70,* 1–19.

Robbins, R., & Merrell, K. W. (1998). Cross-informant comparisons of the home and community social behavior scales and the school social behavior scales. *Diagnostique, 23,* 204–218.

Roberts, G., Schmitz, K., Pinto, J., & Cain, S. (1990). The MMPI and Jesness inventory as measures of effectiveness on an inpatient conduct disorders treatment unit. *Adolescence, 25,* 989–996.

Roberts, G. E. (2005). *Roberts apperception test, 2nd edition.* Los Angeles, CA: Western Psychological Service.

Robins, L. N. (1966). *Deviant children grow up.* Baltimore, MD: Williams & Wilkins.

Robins, L. N. (1974). *The Vietnam drug user returns* (Special Action Monograph, Series A, No. 2). Washington, DC: U.S. Government Printing Office.

Robinson, E. A., & Eyberg, S. (1981). The dyadic parent–child interaction coding system: Standardization and validation. *Journal of Consulting and Clinical Psychology, 49,* 245–250.

Robinson-Wood, T. (2016). *The convergence of race, ethnicity, and gender: Multiple identities in counseling.* Thousand Oaks, CA: SAGE Publications.

Roff, M. (1961). Childhood social interactions and young adult bad conduct. *Journal of Abnormal Social Psychology, 63,* 333–337.

Roff, M. (1963). Childhood social interactions and young adult psychosis. *Journal of Clinical Psychology, 19,* 152–157.

Roff, M., & Sells, S. (1968). Juvenile delinquency in relation to peer acceptance-rejection and socio-metric status. *Psychology in the Schools, 5,* 3–18.

Roff, M., Sells, B., & Golden, M. (1972). *Social adjustment and personality development in children.* Minneapolis, MN: University of Minnesota Press.

Rogers, C. (1951). *Client-centered therapy.* Boston, MA: Houghton Mifflin.

Rogers, C., Gendlin, E., Kiesler, D., & Truax, C. (1967). *The therapeutic relationship and its impact: A study of psychotherapy with schizophrenics.* Madison, WI: University of Wisconsin Press.

Rogers-Warren, A. K. (1984). Ecobehavioral analysis. *Education and Treatment of Children, 7,* 283–303.

Rosell, D. R., Futterman, S. E., McMaster, A., & Siever, L. J. (2014). Schizotypal personality disorder: A current review. *Current Psychiatry Reports, 16*(7), 1–12.

Rosenblatt, R. A. (1996, March 14). Latinos, Asians to lead rise in U.S. population. *Los Angeles Times,* pp. A1, A4.

Rothbart, M. K., & Bates, J. E. (2006). Temperament. In W. Damon, R. Lerner, & N. Eisenberg (Eds.), *Handbook of child psychology. Vol. 3: Social, emotional, and personality development* (6th ed., pp. 99–166). New York: Wiley.

Rothstein, L. F. (1990). *Special education law.* New York: Longman.

Rotter, J. B., & Rafferty, J. E. (1950). *Manual for the Rotter incomplete sentences blank: College form.* New York: The Psychological Corporation.

Rutter, M., LeCouteur, A., & Lord, C. (2003). *The autism diagnostic interview-revised.* Los Angeles, CA: Western Psychological Services.

Sallee, F. R., & Spratt, E. G. (1998). Tics and Tourette's disorder. In T. H. Ollendick & M. Hersen (Eds.), *Handbook of child psychopathology* (3rd ed., pp. 337–353). New York: Plenum.

Salvia, J., & Hughes, C. (1990). *Curriculum-based assessment: Testing what is taught.* New York: Macmillan.

Salvia, J., & Ysseldyke, J. E. (2004). *Assessment* (9th ed.). Boston, MA: Houghton-Mifflin.

Sanders, D. E. (1996). *The internalizing symptoms scale for children: A validity study with urban, African-American, seriously emotionally disturbed and regular education students.* Unpublished doctoral dissertation, James Madison University, Harrisonburg, VA.

Sandoval, J. (1981). Format effects in two teacher rating scales of hyperactivity. *Journal of Abnormal Child Psychology, 9,* 203–218.

Sandoval, J., & Echandia, A. (1994). Review of the behavior assessment system for children. *Journal of School Psychology, 32,* 419–425.

Sarbaugh, M. E. (1983). Kinetic drawing-school (KS–D) technique. *Illinois School Psychologists' Association Monograph Series, 1,* 1–70.

Sater, G. M., & French, D. C. (1989). A comparison of the social competencies of learning disabled and low-achieving elementary age children. *The Journal of Special Education, 23,* 29–42.

Sattler, J. M. (1998). *Clinical and forensic interviewing of children and families.* San Diego, CA: Author.

Sattler, J. M. (2008). *Assessment of children: Cognitive foundations.* San Diego, CA: Author.

Saywitz, K. J., & Snyder, L. (1996). Narrative elaboration: Test of a new procedure for interviewing children. *Journal of Consulting and Clinical Psychology, 64,* 1347–1357.

Schatschneider, C., Lane, K. L., Oakes, W. P., & Kalberg, J. R. (2014). The student risk screening scale: Exploring dimensionality and differential item functioning. *Educational Assessment, 19*(3), 185–203.

Schilling, E. A., Aseltine, R. H. Jr., & James, A. (2016). The SOS suicide prevention program: Further evidence of efficacy and effectiveness. *Prevention Science, 17*(2), 157–166.

Schopler, E., Van Bourgondien, M. E., Wellman, G. J., & Love, S. R. (2010). *Child autism rating scale, Second Edition.* Los Angeles, CA: Western Psychological Services.

Schreibman, L., & Charlop-Christy, M. H. (1998). Autistic disorder. In T. H. Ollendick & M. Hersen (Eds.), *Handbook of child psychopathology* (3rd ed., pp. 157–179). New York: Plenum.

Schwartz, J. A., Gladstone, T. R. G., & Kaslow, N. J. (1998). Depressive disorders. In T. H. Ollendick & M. Hersen (Eds.), *Handbook of childhood psychopathology* (3rd ed., pp. 269–289). New York: Plenum.

Scotti, J. R., Morris, T. L., McNeil, C. B., & Hawkins, R. P. (1996). DSM-IV and disorders of childhood and adolescence: Can structural criteria be functional? *Journal of Consulting and Clinical Psychology, 64,* 1177–1191.

Seligman, M. (1974). Learned helplessness and depression. In R. Friedman & M. Katz (Eds.), *The psychology of depression: Contemporary theory and research* (pp. 83–113). Washington, DC: U.S. Government Printing Office.

Seligman, M. (1998, July). The American way of blame. *APA Monitor, 29*(7), 3. Washington, DC: American Psychological Association.

Seligman, M. E. P., & Csikszentmihalyi, M. (2000). Positive psychology: An introduction. *American Psychologist, 55,* 5–14.

Sentse, M., Kiuru, N., Veenstra, R., & Salmivalli, C. (2014). A social network approach to the interplay between adolescents' bullying and likeability over time. *Journal of Youth and Adolescence, 43*(9), 1409–1420.

Serbin, L. A., Lyons, J. A., Marchessault, K., Schwartzman, A. E., & Ledingham, J. E. (1987). Observational validation of a peer nomination technique for identifying aggressive, withdrawn, and aggressive/withdrawn children. *Journal of Consulting and Clinical Psychology, 55,* 109–110.

Shaffer, D., Fisher, P., Lucas, C. P., Dulcan, M., & Schwab-Stone, M. E. (2000). NIMH diagnostic interview schedule for children, version IV (NIMH DISC–IV): Description, differences from previous versions, and reliability of some common diagnoses. *Journal of the American Academy of Child and Adolescent Psychiatry, 39,* 28–38.

Shaffer, D., Garland, A., Gould, M., Fischer, P., & Trautman, P. (1988). Preventing teenage suicide: A critical review. *Journal of the American Academy of Child and Adolescent Psychiatry, 27,* 675–687.

Shapiro, E. S. (1996). *Academic skills problems: Direct assessment and intervention* (2nd ed.). New York: Guilford.

Shapiro, E. S. (2003). Behavioral observation of students in schools (BOSS). *Computer Software.* San Antonio, TX: Psychological Corporation.

Shapiro, E. S. (2011). *Academic skills problems fourth edition workbook.* New York: Guilford.

Shapiro, E. S. (2013). *Behavioral observation of students in schools.* NCS Pearson, Inc.

Shapiro, E. S., & Cole, C. L. (1994). *Behavior change in the classroom: Self-management interventions.* New York: Guilford.

Shapiro, E. S., & Heick, P. (2004). School psychologists' assessment practices in the evaluation of students referred for social/behavioral/emotional problems. *Psychology in the Schools, 41*(5), 551–561.

Shapiro, E. S., & Skinner, C. H. (1990). Best practices in observation and ecological assessment. In A. Thomas & J. Grimes (Eds.), *Best practices in school psychology—II* (pp. 507–518). Washington, DC: National Association of School Psychologists.

Shark, M. L., & Handel, P. J. (1977). Reliability and validity of the Jesness inventory: A caution. *Journal of Consulting and Clinical Psychology, 45,* 692–695.

Shattuck, P. T., Durkin, M., Maenner, M., Newschaffer, C., Mandell, D. S., Wiggins, L., ... & Cuniff, C. (2009). The timing of identification among children with an autism spectrum disorder: Findings from a population-based surveillance study. *Journal of the American Academy of Child and Adolescent Psychiatry, 48*(5), 474–483.

Sherrill, J. T., & Kovacs, M. (2000). Interview schedule for children and adolescents (ISCA). *Journal of American Academy of Child and Adolescent Psychiatry, 39*(1), 67–75.

Shields, J. M., & Johnson, A. (1992). Collision between ethics and law: Consent for treatment with adolescents. *Bulletin of the American Academy of Psychiatry and the Law, 20,* 309–323.

Shin, N., Kim, M., Goetz, S., & Vaughn, B. E. (2014). Dyadic analyses of preschool-aged children's friendships: Convergence and differences between friendship classifications from peer sociometric data and teacher's reports. *Social Development, 23,* 178–195.

Shinn, M. R., Ramsey, E., Walker, H. M., Steiber, S., & O'Neill, R. E. (1987). Antisocial behavior in school settings: Initial differences in an at-risk and normal population. *Journal of Special Education, 21,* 69–84.

Shivrattan, J. L. (1988). Social interactional training and incarcerated juvenile delinquents. *Canadian Journal of Criminology, 30,* 145–163.

Silverman, W. K., & Ginsburg, G. S. (1998). Anxiety disorders. In T. H. Ollendick & M. Hersen (Eds.), *Handbook of child psychopathology* (3rd ed., pp. 239–268). New York: Plenum.

Sinclair, E., Del'Homme, M., & Gonzalez, M. (1993). Systematic screening for preschool behavior disorders. *Behavioral Disorders, 18,* 177–188.

Singleton, L. C., & Asher, S. R. (1977). Peer preferences and social interaction among third-grade children in an integrated school district. *Journal of Educational Psychology, 69,* 330–336.

Skiba, R. (1992). Qualifications v. logic and data: Excluding conduct disorders from the SED definition. *School Psychology Review, 21,* 23–28.

Skiba, R., Grizzle, K., & Minke, K. M. (1994). Opening the floodgates? The social maladjustment exclusion and state SED prevalence rates. *Journal of School Psychology, 32,* 267–282.

Skinner, B. F. (1984). The shame of American education. *American Psychologist, 39,* 947–954.

Skinner, C. H., Dittmer, K. I., & Howell, L. A. (2000). Direct observation in school settings: Theoretical issues. In E. S. Shapiro & T. R. Kratochwill (Eds.), *Behavioral assessment in schools: Theory, research, and clinical foundations* (2nd ed., pp. 19–45). New York: Guilford.

Skinner, C. H., Rhymer, K. N., & McDaniel, E. C. (2000). Naturalistic direct observation in educational settings. In E. S. Shapiro & T. R. Kratochwill (Eds.), *Conducting school-based assessments of child and adolescent behavior* (pp. 21–54). New York: Guilford.

Slenkovitch, J. (1983). *P. L. 94–142 as applied to* DSM-II *diagnoses: An analysis of* DSM-III *diagnoses vis-a-vis special education law.* Cuppertino, CA: Kinghorn Press.

Slenkovitch, J. (1992a). Can the language "social maladjustment" in the SED definition be ignored? *School Psychology Review, 21,* 21–22.

Slenkovitch, J. (1992b). Can the language "social maladjustment" in the SED definition be ignored? The final words. *School Psychology Review, 21,* 43–44.

Sloves, R. E., Docherty, E. M., & Schneider, K. C. (1979). A scientific problem-solving model of psychological assessment. *Professional Psychology, 10,* 28–35.

Smetana, J. G. (1990). Morality and conduct disorders. In M. Lewis & S. M. Miller (Eds.), *Handbook of developmental psychopathology* (pp. 157–179). New York: Plenum.

Smith, J. D., Dishion, T. J., Moore, K. J., Shaw, D. S., & Wilson, M. N. (2013). Effects of video feedback on early coercive parent-child interactions: The intervening role of caregivers' relational schemas. *Journal of Clinical Child & Adolescent Psychology, 42*(3), 405–417.

Smith, M. D., & Belcher, R. (1985). Teaching life skills to adults disabled by autism. *Journal of Autism and Developmental Disorders, 15,* 163–175.

Snyder, C. R., & Lopez, S. (Eds.). (2001). *Handbook of positive psychology.* London: Oxford University Press.

Snyder, J., & Stoolmiller, M. (2002). Reinforcement and coercion mechanisms in the development of antisocial behavior: The family. In J. B. Reid, G. R. Patterson, & J. Snyder (Eds.), *Antisocial behavior in children and adolescents: A developmental analysis and model for intervention* (pp. 65–100). Washington, DC: American Psychological Association.

Snyder, K. V., Kymissis, P., & Kessler, K. (1999). Anger management for adolescents: Efficacy of brief group therapy. *Journal of the American Academy of Child & Adolescent Psychiatry, 38,* 1409–1416.

Snyder, S. M., Drozd, J. F., & Xenakis, S. N. (2004). Validity of ADHD rating scales. *Journal of the American Academy of Child and Adolescent Psychiatry, 43,* 1189–1190.

Soto, T., Giserman Kiss, I., & Carter, A. S. (2016). Symptom presentations and classification of autism spectrum disorder in early childhood: Application to the diagnostic classification of mental health and developmental disorders of infancy and early childhood (DC:0-5). *Infant Mental Health Journal, 37,* 486–497.

Sowislo, J. F., & Orth, U. (2013). Does low self-esteem predict depression and anxiety? A meta-analysis of longitudinal studies. *Psychological Bulletin, 139,* 213–240.

Speilberger, C. D. (1966). Theory and research on anxiety. In C. D. Speilberger (Ed.), *Anxiety and behavior* (pp. 3–22). New York: Academic Press.

Speilberger, C. D. (1972). Current trends in theory and research on anxiety. In C. D. Speilberger (Ed.), *Anxiety: Current trends in theory and research* (Vol. 1, pp. 3–19). New York: Academic Press.

Speilberger, C. D., Edwards, C. D., Montuori, J., & Lushene, R. (1973). *State–trait anxiety inventory for children.* Redwood City, CA: Mind Garden.

Speilberger, C. D., Gorsuch, R. L., & Lushene, R. E. (1970). *State–trait anxiety inventory.* Redwood City, CA: Mind Garden.

Spinrad, T. L., Eisenberg, N., Cumberland, A., Fabes, R. A., Valiente, C., Shepard, S. A., et al. (2006). Relation of emotion-related regulation to children's social competence: A longitudinal study. *Emotion, (6)*3, 498–510.

Spitzer, R. E. (1991). An outsider-insider's view about revising the DSM's. *Journal of Abnormal Psychology, 100,* 294–296.

Squire, K., Nailor, P., & Carey, J. C. (2014). *Achieving excellence: Reframing the discussion on school counseling student standards.* New York: Corwin Press.

Squires, J., & Bricker, D. (2006). *An activity-based approach to developing young children's social emotional competence.* Baltimore, MD: Brookes.

Squires, J., Bricker, D., & Twombly, E. (2004). Parent-completed screening for social emotional problems in young children: The effects of risk/disability status and gender on performance. *Infant Mental Health Journal, 25*(1), 62–73.

Squires, J., Bricker, D., & Twombly, E. (2015). *Ages and stages questionnaires: Social–emotional.* Baltimore, MD: Brookes.

Squires, J., Bricker, D., Twombly, E., Murphy, K., & Hoselton, R. (2015). *ASQ:SE-2 technical report*. Baltimore, MD: Brookes Publishing.

Squires, J. K., Waddell, M. L., Clifford, J. R., Funk, K., Hoselton, R. M., & Chen, C. I. (2013). A psychometric study of the infant and toddler intervals of the social emotional assessment measure. *Topics in Early Childhood Special Education*, *33*(2), 78.

Sroufe, L. A., & Rutter, M. (1984). The domain of developmental psychopathology. *Child Development*, *55*, 17–29.

Stark, K. D., Kaslow, N. J., & Laurent, J. (1993). The assessment of depression in children: Are we assessing depression or the broad construct of negative affectivity? *Journal of Emotional and Behavioral Disorders*, *1*, 149–154.

Steege, M., & Watson. T. S. (2003). *A practitioner's guide to conducting school-based functional assessments*. New York: Guilford.

Stickle, T. R., Kirkpatrick, N. M., & Brush L. N. (2009). Callous-unemotional traits and social information processing: Multiple risk-factor models for understanding aggressive behavior in antisocial youth. *Law and Human Behavior*, *33*, 515–529.

Stokes, T. F., & Baer, D. M. (1977). An implicit technology of generalization. *Journal of Applied Behavior Analysis*, *19*, 349–367.

Stokes, T. F., Baer, D. M., & Jackson, R. L. (1974). Programming among the generalization of a greeting response in four retarded children. *Journal of Applied Behavior Analysis*, *7*, 599–610.

Stone, L. L., Otten, R., Engels, R. C., Vermulst, A. A., & Janssens, J. M. (2010). Psychometric properties of the parent and teacher versions of the strengths and difficulties questionnaire for 4- to 12-year-olds: A review. *Clinical Child and Family Psychology Review*, *13*(3), 254–274.

Stora, B., Hagtvet, K. A., & Heyerdahl, S. (2013). Reliability of observers' subjective impressions of families: A generalizability theory approach. *Psychotherapy Research*, *23*, 448–463.

Strayer, J., & Roberts, W. (2004). Children's anger, emotional expressiveness, and empathy: Relations with parents' empathy, emotional expressiveness, and parenting practices. *Social Development*, *13*, 229–254.

Stumme, V. S., Gresham, F. M., & Scott, N. A. (1982). Validity of social behavior assessment in discriminating emotionally disabled and nonhandicapped students. *Journal of Behavioral Assessment*, *4*, 327–341.

Sue, D. W., & Sue, D. (2008). *Counseling the culturally diverse: Theory and practice* (5th ed.). Hoboken, NJ: John Wiley & Sons.

Sue, D. W., & Sue, S. (1990). *Counseling the culturally different* (2nd ed.). New York: Wiley.

Sue, D. W., & Sue, S. (1999). *Counseling the culturally different* (3rd ed.). New York: Wiley.

Sugai, G., & Horner, R. H. (2009). Responsiveness-to-intervention and school-wide positive behavior supports: Integration of multi-tiered system approaches. *Exceptionality*, *17*(4), 223–237.

Sugai, G., Sprague, J. R., Horner, R. H., & Walker, H. M. (2000). Preventing school violence: The use of office discipline referrals to assess and monitor school-wide discipline interventions. *Journal of Emotional and Behavioral Disorders*, *8*, 94–101.

Sullivan, A. L. (2010). Preventing disproportionality: A framework for culturally responsive assessment. *NASP Communique*, *39*(3).

Sullivan, A. L., & Sadeh, S. S. (2014). Differentiating social maladjustment from emotional disturbance: An analysis of case law. *School Psychology Review*, *43*(4), 450–471.

Sulzer-Azaroff, B., & Mayer, G. R. (1991). *Behavior analysis for lasting change*. Fort Worth, TX: Harcourt Brace College.

Suzuki, L. A., Ponterotto, J. G., & Meller, P. J. (Eds.). (2001). *Handbook of multicultural assessment* (2nd ed). San Francisco, CA: Jossey-Bass.

Swallow, S. R., & Segal, Z. V. (1995). Cognitive-behavioral therapy for unipolar depression. In K. D. Craig & K. S. Dobson (Eds.), *Anxiety and depression in adults and children* (pp. 209–229). Thousand Oaks, CA: Sage.

Swann, W. B., & Seyle, C. (2005). Personality psychology's comeback and its emerging symbiosis with social psychology. *Personality and Social Psychology Bulletin*, *31*, 155–165.

Swanson, S. A., Crow, S. J., LeGrange, D., Swendsen, J., & Merikangas, K. (2011). Prevalence and correlates of eating disorders in adolescents: Results from the national comorbidity survey replication adolescent supplement. *Archives of General Psychiatry*, *68*(7), 714–723.

Taba, H., Brady, E. H., Robinson, J. T., & Vickery, W. E. (1951). *Diagnosing human relations needs.* Washington, DC: American Council on Education.

Tartakovsky, E. (2012). Factors affecting immigrants' acculturation intentions: A theoretical model and its assessment among adolescent immigrants from Russia and Ukraine in Israel. *International Journal of Intercultural Relations, 36*(1), 83–89.

Teglasi, H. (1993). *Clinical use of story telling: Emphasizing the T.A.T. with children and adolescents.* Boston, MA: Allyn & Bacon.

Teglasi, H. (2001). *Essentials of TAT and other storytelling assessment techniques.* New York: Wiley.

Teglasi, H. (2010). *Essentials of TAT and other storytelling assessments* (2nd ed.). Hoboken, NJ: John Wiley & Sons.

Tellegen, A. (1986). Structures of mood and personality and their relevance to assessing anxiety, with an emphasis on self-report. In A. H. Tuma & J. Maser (Eds.), *Anxiety and the anxiety disorders* (pp. 681–706). Hillsdale, NJ: Lawrence Erlbaum Associates.

Tesiny, E. P., & Lefkowitz, M. M. (1982). Childhood depression: A 6-month follow-up study. *Journal of Consulting and Clinical Psychology, 50,* 778–780.

Tharinger, D., & Stark, K. (1990). A qualitative versus quantitative approach to evaluating the draw-a-person and kinetic family drawings: A study of mood and anxiety-disorder children. *Psychological Assessment, 2,* 365–375.

Thompson, C. L., & Rudolph, L. B. (1992). *Counseling children* (3rd ed.). Pacific Grove, CA: Brooks-Cole.

Thurber, S., & Snow, M. (1990). Assessment of adolescent psychopathology: Comparison of mother and daughter perspectives. *Journal of Clinical Child Psychology, 19,* 249–253.

Tobin, T., & Sugai, G. (1999). Predicting violence at school, chronic discipline problems, and high school outcomes from sixth graders' school records. *Journal of Emotional and Behavioral Disorders, 7,* 40–53.

Tobin, T., Sugai, G., & Colvin, G. (1996). Patterns in middle school discipline records. *Journal of Emotional and Behavioral Disorders, 4,* 82–94.

Todis, B., Severson, H., & Walker, H. M. (1990). The critical events scale: Behavioral profiles of students with externalizing and internalizing behavior disorders. *Behavioral Disorders, 15,* 75–86.

Tolbert, H. A. (1996). Psychoses in children and adolescents: A review. *Journal of Clinical Psychiatry, 57*(Suppl. 3), 4–8.

Travis, L. L., & Sigman, M. D. (2000). A developmental approach to autism. In A. J. Sameroff., M. Lewis, & S. M. Miller (Eds.), *Handbook of developmental psychopathology* (2nd ed., pp. 641–656). New York: Kluwer Academic/Plenum.

Trentacosta, C. J., Izard C. E., Mostow, A. J., & Fine, S. E. (2006). Children's emotional competence and attentional competence in early elementary school. *School Psychology Quarterly, 21,* 148–170.

Turner, S. M., Beidel, D. C., Hersen, M., & Bellack, A. S. (1984). Effects of race on ratings of social skill. *Journal of Consulting and Clinical Psychology, 52,* 474–475.

Twenge, J. M., & Nolen-Hoeksema, S. (2002). Age, gender, race, socioeconomic status, and birth cohort differences on the children's depression inventory: A meta-analysis. *Journal of Abnormal Psychology, 111,* 578–588.

Uher, R., & McGuffin, P. (2010). The moderation by the serotonin transporter gene of environmental adversity in the etiology of depression. *Molecular Psychiatry, 15,* 18–22.

Ullman, C. A. (1957). Teachers, peers, and tests as predictors of adjustment. *Journal of Educational Psychology, 48,* 257–267.

U.S. Bureau of the Census. (1993). *We the . . . first Americans.* Washington, DC: U.S. Department of Commerce.

U.S. Bureau of the Census. (2010). *The white population: 2010* (Census brief, August 2001, Document No. C2010BR-05). Washington, DC: Author.

U.S. Census Bureau. (2011a). *The Hispanic population: 2010.* (Census brief, May 2011, Document No. C2010BR-04). Washington, DC: Author.

U.S. Census Bureau. (2011b). *The black population: 2010.* (Census brief, September 2011, Document No. C2010BR-06). Washington, DC: Author.

U.S. Census Bureau. (2013). *The 2013 U.S. census bureau American community survey.* Retrieved from: https://census.gov

U.S. Census Bureau. (2021). *Race and ethnicity in the united states: 2010 census and 2020 census.* https://www.census.gov/library/visualizations/interactive/race-and-ethnicity-in-the-united-state-2010-and-2020-census.html

van den Oord, E. J. C. G., Koot, H. M., Boosma, D. I., & Verhulst, F. C. (1995). A twin-singleton comparison of problem behavior in 2–3 year olds. *Journal of Child Psychology and Psychiatry and Allied Disciplines, 36,* 449–458.

Vannest, K., Reynolds, C. R., & Kamphaus, R. (2015). *BASC-3 intervention guide and materials.* Upper Saddle River, NJ: Pearson Education, Inc.

Vasquez-Nuttall, E., Li, C., Sanchez, W., Nuttall, R. L., & Mathisen, L. (2003). Assessing culturally and linguistically different children with emotional and behavioral problems. In M. J. Breen & C. Fiedler (Eds.), *Behavioral approach to assessment of youth with emotional/behavioral disorders* (2nd ed., pp. 463–496). Austin, TX: Pro-Ed.

Vaughan, C. A. (2011). Test review: E. Schopler, M. E. Van Bourgondien, G. J. Wellman, & S. R. Love Childhood Autism Rating Scale (2nd edition). *Journal of Psychoeducational Assessment, 29*(5), 489.

Vaughn, S. (1987). TLC—Teaching, learning, and caring: Teaching interpersonal problem-solving skills to behaviorally disordered adolescents. *The Pointer, 31,* 25–30.

Veldman, D. J., & Sheffield, J. R. (1979). The scaling of sociometric nominations. *Educational and Psychological Measurement, 39,* 99–106.

Verhulst, F. C., Koot, H. M., & van der Ende, J. (1994). Differential predictive value of parents' and teachers' reports of children's problem behaviors: A longitudinal study. *Journal of Abnormal Child Psychology, 22,* 531–546.

Victor, J. B., & Halverson, C. F. (1976). Behavior problems in elementary school children: A follow-up study. *Journal of Abnormal Child Psychology, 4,* 17–29.

Vollmer, T. R., & Northrup, J. (1996). Some implications of functional analysis for school psychology. *School Psychology Quarterly, 11,* 76–92.

Volpe, R. J., DiPerna, J. C., Hintze, J. M., & Shapiro, E. S. (2005). Observing students in classroom settings: A review of seven coding schemes. *School Psychology Review, 34,* 454–474.

Volpe, R. J., & Gadow, K. D. (2010). Creating abbreviated rating scales to monitor classroom inattention-overactivity, aggression, and peer conflict: Reliability, validity, and treatment sensitivity. *School Psychology Review, 39*(3), 350–363.

Volpe, R., Gadow, K., Blom-Hoffman, J., & Feinberg, A. (2009). Factor-analytic and individualized approaches to constructing brief measures of ADHD behaviors. *Journal of Emotional and Behavioral Disorders, 17*(2), 118–128.

Volpe, R. J., & McConaughy, S. H. (2005). Systematic direct observational assessment of student behavior: Its use and interpretation in multiple settings: An introduction to the mini-series. *School Psychology Review, 34,* 451–453.

Von Ranson, K. M., & Wallace, L. M. (2014). Eating Disorders. In E. J. Mash & R. A. Barkley (Eds.), *Child psychopathology* (3rd ed.). New York: Guilford.

Wahler, R. G. (1975). Some structural aspects of deviant child behavior. *Journal of Applied Behavior Analysis, 8,* 27–42.

Wahler, R. G. (1994). Child conduct problems: Disorders in conduct or social continuity? *Journal of Child and Family Studies, 3,* 143–156.

Wahler, R. G., & Cormier, W. H. (1970). The ecological interview: A first step in out-patient child behavior therapy. *Journal of Behavior Therapy and Experimental Psychiatry, 1,* 279–289.

Wahler, R. G., & Dumas, J. E. (1986). "A chip off the old block": Some interpersonal characteristics of coercive children across generations. In P. S. Strain, M. J. Guralnick, & H. M. Walker (Eds.), *Children's social behavior: Development, assessment, and modification* (pp. 49–91). New York: Academic Press.

Wainwright, A., & MHS Staff. (1996). *Conners' Rating Scales: Over 25 years of research—an annotated bibliography.* Toronto, Ontario, Canada: Multi-Health Systems.

Waldman, I. D., & Lilienfeld, S. O. (1995). Diagnosis and classification. In M. Hersen & R. T. Ammerman (Eds.), *Advanced abnormal child psychology* (pp. 21–36). Hillsdale, NJ: Lawrence Erlbaum Associates.

Walker, B., Cheney, D., Stage, S. A., & Blum, C. (2005). Schoolwide screening and positive behavior supports: Identifying and supporting students at risk for school failure. *Journal of Positive Behavior Interventions, 7,* 194–204.

Walker, H. M. (1982). Assessment of behavior disorders in school settings: Outcomes, issues, and recommendations. In M. M. Noel & N. G. Haring (Eds.), *Progress or change: Issues in educating the emotionally disturbed: Vol. 1. Identification and program planning* (pp. 11–42). Seattle, WA: University of Washington Press.

Walker, H. M., Block-Pedego, A., Todis, B., & Severson, H. (1991). *School archival records search.* Longmont, CO: Sopris West.

Walker, H. M., Colvin, G. R., & Ramsey, E. R. (1995). *Antisocial behavior in school settings.* Pacific Grove, CA: Brooks/Cole.

Walker, H. M., & Hops, H. (1976). Increasing academic achievement by reinforcing direct academic performance and/or facilitating nonacademic responses. *Journal of Educational Psychology, 68,* 218–225.

Walker, H. M., Horner, R. H., Sugai, G., Bullis, M., Sprague, J. R., Bricker, D., & Kaufman, M. J. (1996). Integrated approaches to preventing antisocial behavior patterns among school-aged children and youth. *Journal of Emotional and Behavioral Disorders, 4,* 193–256.

Walker, H. M., Nishioka, V., Zeller, R., Severson, H., & Feil, E. (2000). Causal factors and potential solutions for the persistent under-identification of students having emotional or behavioral disorders in the context of schooling. *Assessment for Effective Intervention, 26,* 29–40.

Walker, H. M., Ramsey, E. R., & Gresham, F. M. (2004). *Antisocial behavior in school settings* (2nd ed.). Pacific Grove, CA: Brooks/Cole.

Walker, H. M., & Severson, H. (1992). *Systematic screening for behavior disorders.* Longmont, CO: Sopris West.

Walker, H. M., Severson, H. H., & Feil, E. G. (1995). *The early screening project: A proven child find process.* Longmont, CO: Sopris West.

Walker, H. M., Severson, H. H., & Feil, E. G. (2014). *Systematic screening for behavior disorders (SSBD) technical manual: Universal screening for preK–9* (2nd ed.). Eugene, OR: Pacific Northwest Publishing.

Walker, H. M., Severson, H. H., Nicholson, F., Kehle, T., Jenson, W. R., & Clark, E. (1994). Replication of the systematic screening for behavior disorders (SSBD) procedure for the identification of at-risk children. *Journal of Emotional and Behavioral Disorders, 2*(2), 66–77.

Walker, H. M., Severson, H., Stiller, B., Williams, G., Haring, N., Shinn, M., et al. (1988). Systematic screening of pupils in the elementary age range at risk for behavior disorders: Development and trial testing of a multiple gating model. *Remedial and Special Education, 9,* 8–14.

Walker, H. M., Severson, H., Todis, B., Block-Pedego, A. Williams, G., Haring, N., & Barckley, M. (1990). Systematic screening for behavior disorders (SSBD): Further validation, replication, and normative data. *Remedial and Special Education, 11,* 32–46.

Walker, H. M., Shinn, M. R., O'Neill, R. E., & Ramsey, E. (1987). A longitudinal assessment of the development of antisocial behavior in boys: Rationale, methodology, and first year results. *Remedial and Special Education, 8,* 7–16.

Walker, H. M., Steiber, S., & O'Neill, R. E. (1990). Middle school behavioral profiles of antisocial and at-risk control boys: Descriptive and predictive outcomes. *Exceptionality, 1,* 61–77.

Walker, H. M., Steiber, S., Ramsey, E., & O'Neill, R. (1993). Fifth grade school adjustment and later arrest rate: A longitudinal study of middle school antisocial boys. *Journal of Child and Family Studies, 2,* 295–315.

Walker, H. M., Zeller, R. W., Close, D. W., Webber, J., & Gresham, F. M. (1999). The present unwrapped: Change and challenge in the field of behavioral disorders. *Behavioral Disorders, 24,* 293–304.

Wallace, L. M., Masson, P. C., Safer, D. L., & von Ranson, K. M. (2014). Change in emotion regulation during the course of treatment predicts binge abstinence in guided self-help dialectical behavior therapy for binge eating disorder. *Journal of Eating Disorders, 2*(1), 35.

Walser, T. M. (2009). Systemic data-based decision making: A systems approach for using data in schools. *Articles on Best Practice,* 28.

Watkins, C. E., Campbell, V., & McGregor, P. (1988). Counseling psychologists' uses of the opinions about psychological tests: A contemporary perspective. *The Counseling Psychologist, 16,* 476–486.

Watkins, C. E., Campbell, V. L., Nieberding, R., & Hallmark, R. (1995). Contemporary practice of psychological assessment by clinical psychologists. *Professional Psychology Research and Practice, 26,* 54–60.

Watson, D. (1988). Intraindividual and interindividual analyses of positive and negative affect: Their relation to health complaints and perceived stress, and daily activities. *Journal of Personality and Social Psychology, 54,* 1020–1030.

Watson, D., & Clark, L. A. (1984). Negative affectivity: The disposition to experience aversive emotional states. *Psychological Bulletin, 96*, 465–490.

Watson, D., & Tellegen, A. (1985). Toward a consensual structure of mood. *Psychological Bulletin, 98*, 219–235.

Watson, T. S. (1998). Review of the preschool and kindergarten behavior scales. In J. C. Impara & B. S. Plake (Eds.), *The thirteenth mental measurements yearbook* (pp. 771–773). Lincoln, NE: Buros Institute of Mental Measurements.

Watson, T. S., & Steege, M. W. (2003). *Conducting functional behavior assessments: A practitioner's guide.* New York: Guilford.

Watt, S., & Norton, D. (2004). Culture, ethnicity, race: What's the difference? *Pediatric Nursing, 16*(8), 37–42.

Webster-Stratton, C. (1984). Randomized trial of two parent-training programs for families with conduct disordered children. *Journal of Consulting and Clinical Psychology, 52*, 666–678.

Wehmeyer, M. L., & Agran, M. (Eds.). (2005). *Mental retardation and intellectual disabilities: Teaching students using innovative and research-based strategies.* Washington, DC: American Association on Mental Retardation.

Weinrott, M. R., & Jones, R. R. (1984). Overt versus covert assessment of observer reliability. *Child Development, 55*, 1125–1137.

Weiss, G. (1983). Long-term outcome: Findings, concepts, and practical implications. In M. Rutter (Ed.), *Developmental neuropsychiatry.* New York: Guilford.

Weiss, G., Hechtman, L., Perlman, T., Hopkins, J., & Wener, A. (1979). Hyperactive children as young adults: A controlled prospective 10-year follow-up of the psychiatric status of 75 hyperactive children. *Archives of General Psychiatry, 36*, 675–681.

Weiten, W. (2000). *Psychology: Themes and variations* (5th ed.). Pacific Grove, CA: Wadsworth.

Weitz, S. E. (1981). A code for assessing teaching skills of parents of developmentally disabled children. *Journal of Autism and Developmental Disorders, 12*, 13–24.

Weller, E. B., Weller, R. A., Rooney, M. T., & Fristad, M. A. (1999). *Children's interview for psychiatric syndromes (ChIPS).* Arlington, VA: American Psychiatric Press, Inc.

Werry, J. S. (1986). Biological factors. In H. C. Quay & J. S. Werry (Eds.), *Psychopathological disorders of childhood* (Vol. 3, pp. 294–331). New York: Wiley.

West, D. J., & Farrington, D. P. (1973). *Who becomes delinquent?* London: Heinemann.

Whalen, C. K., & Henker, B. (1998). Attention-deficit/hyperactivity disorders. In T. H. Ollendick & M. Hersen (Eds.), *Handbook of child psychopathology* (3rd ed., pp. 181–211). New York: Plenum.

Whitesell, N. R., Beals, J., Big Crow, C., Mitchell, C. M., & Novins, D. K. (2012). Epidemiology and etiology of substance use among american indians and alaska natives: Risk, protection, and implications for prevention. *American Journal of Drug and Alcohol Abuse, 38*, 376–382.

Whitley, B. E., Kite, M. E., & Adams, H. L. (2012). *Principles of research in behavioral science.* New York: Routledge.

Wiggins, J. S. (1981). Clinical and statistical prediction: Where are we and where do we go from here? *Clinical Psychology Review, 1*, 3–18.

Wilczynski, S. M. (2009). *The national autism center's national standards project: Findings and conclusions.* Randolph, MA: National Autism Center.

Wilgenbusch, T., & Merrell, K. W. (1999). Gender differences in self-concept among children and adolescents: A meta-analysis of multidimensional studies. *School Psychology Quarterly, 14*, 101–120.

Williams, J. G., Barlow, D. H., & Agras, W. S. (1972). Behavioral assessment of severe depression. *Archives of General Psychiatry, 39*, 1283–1289.

Williams, M. S. (1997). *An investigation of internalizing social–emotional characteristics in a sample of Lakota Sioux children.* Unpublished doctoral dissertation, Utah State University, Logan.

Williamson, D. A., Bentz, B. G., & Rabalais, J. Y. (1998). Eating disorders. In T. H. Ollendick & M. Hersen (Eds.), *Handbook of child psychopathology* (3rd ed., pp. 291–305). New York: Plenum.

Wilson, M. S., & Reschly, D. J. (1996). Assessment in school psychology training and practice. *School Psychology Review, 25*, 9–23.

Wing, L. (1969). The handicap of autistic children: A comparative study. *Journal of Child Psychology and Psychiatry, 10*, 1–40.

Wisniewski, J. J., Mulick, J. A., Genshaft, J. L., & Coury, D. L. (1987). Test–retest reliability of the revised children's manifest anxiety scale. *Perceptual and Motor Skills, 65*, 67–70.

Witt, J. C., Cavell, T. A., Heffer, R. W., Carey, M. P., & Martens, B. K. (1988). Child self-report: Interviewing techniques and rating scales. In E. S. Shapiro & T. R. Kratochwill (Eds.), *Behavioral assessment in schools* (pp. 384–454). New York: Guilford.

Wittmer, D. S., & Honig, A. S. (1994). Play, story/song, and eating times in child care: Caregiver responses to toddlers and threes. In H. Goelman (Ed.), *Children's play in child care settings* (pp. 119–147). Albany, NY: State University of New York Press.

Wolf, S. (1989). Schizoid disorders of childhood and adolescence. In C. G. Last & M. Hersen (Eds.), *Handbook of clinical childhood psychiatric diagnosis* (pp. 209–232). New York: Wiley.

Wolf, S., & Chick, J. (1980). Schizoid personality disorder in childhood: A controlled follow-up study. *Psychological Medicine, 10*, 85–100.

Wolfson, J., Fields, J. H., & Rose, S. A. (1987). Symptoms, temperament, resiliency, and control in anxiety-disordered preschool children. *American Academy of Child and Adolescent Psychiatry, 26*, 16–22.

Wonderlich, S. A., Gordon, K. H., Mitchell, J. E., Crosby, R. D., & Engel, S. G. (2009). The validity and clinical utility of binge eating disorder. *International Journal of Eating Disorders, 42*(8), 687–705.

Worchel, F. F. (1990). Personality assessment. In T. B. Gutkin & C. R. Reynolds (Eds.), *The handbook of school psychology* (2nd ed., pp. 416–430). New York: Wiley.

Worthen, B. R., Borg, W. R, & White, K. R. (1993). *Measurement and evaluation in the schools: A practical guide.* White Plains, NY: Longman.

Wright, J. (2002). *Reinforcer assessment grid.* Retrieved from http:interventioncentral.org.

Yetter, G. (2005). Review of the Jesness inventory–revised. In B. S. Plake, J. C. Impara, & R. A. Spies (Eds.), *The sixteenth mental measurements yearbook* (pp. 496–498). Lincoln, NE: University of Nebraska Press.

Young, L. L., & Cooper, D. H. (1944). Some factors associated with popularity. *Journal of Educational Psychology, 35*, 513–535.

Zaback, T. P., & Waehler, C. A. (1994). Sex of human figure drawings and sex-role orientation. *Journal of Personality Assessment, 62*, 552–558.

Zahn-Waxler, C., & Radke-Yarrow, M. (1982). The development of altruism: Alternative research strategies. In N. Eisenberg (Ed.), *The development of prosocial behavior* (pp. 109–137). New York: Academic Press.

Zahn-Waxler, C., Radke-Yarrow, M., Wagner, E., & Chapman, M. (1992). Development of concern for others. *Developmental Psychology, 28*, 126–136.

Zahn-Waxler, C., Shirtcliff, E. A., & Marceau, K. (2008). Disorders of childhood and adolescence: Gender and psychopathology. *Annual Review of Clinical Psychology, 4*, 275–303.

Zangwill, W. M., & Kniskern, J. R. (1982). Comparison of problem families in the clinic and at home. *Behavior Therapy, 13*, 145–152.

Zeanah, C. H., Carter, A. S., Cohen, J., Egger, H., Gleason, M. M., Keren, M., Lieberman, A., Mulrooney, K., & Oser, C. (2016). Diagnostic classification of mental health and developmental disorders of infancy and early childhood DC:0–5: Selective reviews from a new nosology for early childhood psychopathology. *Infant Mental Health Journal, 37*, 471–475.

ZERO TO THREE. (1994). *Diagnostic classification: 0–3. Diagnostic classification of mental health and developmental disorders of infancy and early childhood* (DC: 0–3). Washington, DC: ZERO TO THREE/ National Center for Clinical Infant Programs.

ZERO TO THREE. (2005). *Diagnostic classification of mental health and developmental disorders of infancy and early childhood, revised* (DC: 0–3R). Washington, DC: ZERO TO THREE/National Center for Clinical Infant Programs.

INDEX